T0376592

The Routledge Handbook of Transport Economics

The Routledge Handbook of Transport Economics offers the first state of the art overview of the discipline of transport economics as it stands today, reflective of key research and policy. Transport is an important area of study and one which is problem rich, stimulating a great deal of debate in areas which impact on everyday lives. Much of this focuses on the practicalities of the modern-day phenomenon of mass movement and all of the issues which surround it. The discipline of economics is central to this debate, and consequently the study and application of transport economics has a chief role to play in seeking to address subjects relating to major transport issues. It can be argued that at the very heart of any transport issue or problem lies the underlying economics of the situation – understand that and you alleviate the problem.

Featuring contributions from world-leading scholars and practitioners from across the globe, all of the chapters within this book are written from a practical perspective; theory is applied and developed using real-world examples. The book examines concepts, issues, ideas and practicalities of transport provision in five key topic areas:

- public transport
- public transport reform
- economic development and transport modelling
- transport and the environment
- freight transport.

A real strength of the book is in linking theory to practice, and hence the 'economics' that are examined in this text are not the economics of the abstract, but rather the economics of everyday living. Practical and insightful, this volume is an essential reference for any student or researcher working in all areas of transport provision, ranging from planning, appraisal, regulation and freight; and for all practitioners looking to develop their professional knowledge and who are seeking professional accreditation.

Jonathan Cowie is Lecturer in Transport Economics at Edinburgh Napier University, UK, and previously held lecturing posts at University College Scarborough and Glasgow Caledonian University. He is the author of *The Economics of Transport* published by Routledge in 2010, as well as the author of many conference and journal papers in his areas of research interest. Jonathan is a Fellow of the Higher Education Academy and a long-time member of the Scottish Economic Society.

Stephen Ison is Professor of Transport Policy within the School of Civil and Building Engineering at Loughborough University, UK. He has published widely in the area of transport policy and economics and has edited, authored or co-authored eight books. He is a member of the Scientific Committee of the World Conference on Transport Research, editor of the *Journal of Research in Transportation Business and Management* and book series editor of *Transport and Sustainability*.

The Routledge Handbook of Transport Economics

Edited by Jonathan Cowie and Stephen Ison

LONDON AND NEW YORK

First edition published 2018
by Routledge
2 Park Square, Milton Park, Abingdon, Oxon, OX14 4RN

and by Routledge
711 Third Avenue, New York, NY 10017

Routledge is an imprint of the Taylor & Francis Group, an informa business

British Library Cataloguing in Publication Data
A catalogue record for this book is available from the British Library

Library of Congress Cataloging in Publication Data
Names: Cowie, Jonathan, editor. | Ison, Stephen editor.
Title: The Routledge handbook of transport economics / edited by Jonathan Cowie and Stephen Ison.
Other titles: Handbook of transport economics
Description: 1 Edition. | New York : Routledge, 2017. | Includes index.
Identifiers: LCCN 2017004355| ISBN 9781138847491 (hardback) | ISBN 9781315726786 (ebook)
Subjects: LCSH: Transportation.
Classification: LCC HE151 .R67 2017 | DDC 388--dc23
LC record available at https://lccn.loc.gov/2017004355

ISBN: 978-1-138-84749-1 (hbk)
ISBN: 978-1-315-72678-6 (ebk)

Typeset in Bembo
by Integra Software Services Pvt Ltd, India

Printed in the United Kingdom
by Henry Ling Limited

Contents

Figures

Tables

Contributors

Maria Attard is Head of Geography and Director of the Institute for Climate Change and Sustainable Development at the University of Malta. She specialises in urban transport, policy and project implementation. She has also coordinated the Geographic Information Systems (GIS) Laboratory at the University of Malta for over 14 years, published in the field of GIS education and more recently published work on voluntary geographic information and transport. Between 2002 and 2009 she served as a consultant to the Maltese government on transport strategy and policy. She was involved in major transport projects and implemented road pricing, park and ride and pedestrianisation projects in the island's capital city Valletta. She studied at the University of Malta and completed her PhD in 2006 at University College London and has published over 20 journal articles and book chapters in the areas of urban transport policy, GIS and human geography. She has contributed over 55 presentations in conferences and proceedings and has recently co-edited a book on *Sustainable Urban Transport*. Maria is currently the co-chair of Cluster 2 Transport and Environment within NECTAR, co-chair of SIG G3 and member of the Steering Committee of the World Conference for Transport Research Society.

Marco Batarce is Assistant Professor at the Universidad Diego Portales, Chile. His research fields include transportation economics, empirical industrial organisation and valuation of benefits of transport policies. He holds PhD and master's degrees in economics from the Université de Toulouse, France, and a civil engineering degree from the Universidad de Chile. In more than 15 years of professional experience, he has participated in projects of urban and interurban transport planning, demand modelling and evaluation of transport projects for Chilean public institutions and international organisations such as the Inter-American Development Bank.

John Bates is a mathematical economist, with over 40 years' experience in transportation modelling, with particular focus on travel demand. He has a detailed understanding of the principles which bind the various modelling components and has contributed substantially to the modelling guidance sections of the Department for Transport's WebTAG. He has been a leading figure in the development of stated preference techniques within the transport field and has international expertise in evaluation methodology, in particular the valuation of time savings and reliability. John works as an independent consultant, based in Abingdon. He has considerable experience as a peer reviewer/auditor and has a proven ability to get through the details of complex (and often poorly documented) models with a view to assessing their strengths and weaknesses. Based on his experience of working with many other consultants, his collaborative but demanding approach has earned considerable respect.

Valerio Benedetto has completed a PhD in transport economics and regulation awarded by the Institute for Transport Studies (ITS), University of Leeds, under the supervision of Andrew Smith and Chris Nash. His research examines the role played by economic regulation and regulatory bodies within the European railway systems. Particular focus is given to the impacts on rail efficiency and the interrelationships between structure, competition and regulation in railways. During his research, fruitful collaborations have been built with important European railway organisations, such as the Independent Regulators' Group – Rail and the Community of European Railway and Infrastructure Companies. His work has been presented and well received at meetings with these organisations and at various national and international conferences. Valerio has completed his doctoral thesis and has papers submitted to important journals in transport and economics. Before joining ITS, he completed master's degrees in economics at the universities of York (2012) and Ferrara (2010). Valerio now works as Research Associate at the University of Central Lancashire, where he designs and performs economic and statistical analysis for health-related projects.

Simon Blainey is Lecturer in Transportation at the University of Southampton's Transportation Research Group. During his career he has been involved in a range of railway-related research, with extensive experience in passenger demand forecasting and appraisal including the development of an integrated appraisal framework for new local railway stations. He has carried out rail demand forecasting work for a range of government and industry bodies, as well as providing peer review and guidance. He has contributed to the production of the Infrastructure Transitions Research Consortium's (ITRC) long-term national model of interdependent infrastructure systems (including railways) in the UK. This work is being developed further as part of the MISTRAL project, with ITRC's modelling tools being used to inform national infrastructure decision making in the UK. Simon has also worked on whole-life economic and environmental cost modelling for railway track systems as part of the EPSRC-funded 'Track to the Future' and 'Track 21' projects, and is involved in ongoing research looking at data privacy and the rail customer experience. He is Programme Lead for the University's MSc in Transportation Planning and Engineering, and teaches subjects including transport planning, transport economics, rail transport and geographical information systems for transport.

Mary R. Brooks is Vice Chair of the Marine Board of the Transportation Research Board, Washington, DC. She has been working in the shipping and ports field since the late 1970s. She has authored and published more than 25 books and technical reports, over 25 book chapters and more than 75 articles in peer-reviewed scholarly journals. She serves on seven journal boards, including the Publications Board of *Transportation Research Record*, *Maritime Policy and Management* and *Ocean Yearbook*. She is well known for her work on ports and short sea shipping in Canada, the US, South America and Australia. In 2010, Mary was Visiting Scholar at the Institute of Transport and Logistics Studies at the University of Sydney where she completed research on Australian coastal shipping and maritime reform. She is the founder and chair of the Port Performance Research Network, a network of more than 50 scholars interested in port governance and port performance issues. She is also a founding member of the International Association of Maritime Economists, served as its membership secretary and treasurer 1994–8 and on its council at three different times in its history. She retired from teaching in June 2013.

Lucy Budd is Senior Lecturer in Air Transport and Programme Director of the MSc in Air Transport Management in the School of Civil and Building Engineering at Loughborough University. Lucy has published widely in the areas of aviation planning and operations and she has a particular interest in the history of airline regulation and the geographies of airspace. Her most recent books include *The Geographies of Air Transport* (with Andrew Goetz, 2014) and *Air Transport Management: An International Perspective* (with Stephen Ison, 2016).

Thomas Budd is Lecturer in Airport Planning and Management in the Centre for Air Transport Management at Cranfield University. His main areas of expertise include airport strategic management, environmental planning and policy, and airport surface access, where he is establishing a growing international reputation and has had his work widely published. Thomas joined Cranfield in August 2014 having previously conducted his PhD research at Loughborough University, and held a research fellowship in the Centre for Transport Research at the University of Aberdeen.

Jonathan Cowie is Lecturer in Transport Economics at Edinburgh Napier University and previously held lecturing posts at University College Scarborough and Glasgow Caledonian University. He is author of *The Economics of Transport* (2010) as well as author of many conference and journal papers in his areas of research interest. These consist of the application of production theory to transport modes, transport regulation, factors affecting public transport usage, research methodologies and freight transport, particularly road and rail. Over the years, Jonathan has been involved in many different transport research projects, ranging from the economic evaluation of train protection systems to transport appraisal assessments. He lectures on transport economics, public transport, transport policy and freight transport, as well as having an active interest in undergraduate student research. Jonathan is a Fellow of the Higher Education Academy and a long-time member of the Scottish Economic Society.

Jonas Eliasson is Professor of Transport Systems Analysis at the Royal Institute of Technology. He is currently on part-time leave to be Head of the Stockholm City Transportation Department. His research interests include cost-benefit analysis of transport projects and policies, decision making in the transport sector, transport pricing in general and congestion pricing in particular, transport modelling, public and political acceptability of transport policies, valuation of travel time and reliability, and railway capacity allocation. Jonas has worked extensively with analysing, developing and applying transport policies and appraisal methodologies, often acting as expert adviser on strategic transportation issues to cities and regional and national governments. He directed the design and evaluation of the Stockholm congestion pricing system, in operation since 2006, and has worked extensively with the evaluation and redesign of it since then. He was also involved in designing and evaluating the Gothenburg congestion pricing system, in operation since 2013, and has been employed as adviser on congestion pricing to a large number of other cities worldwide. He has chaired the National Committee for Analysis of the National Transport Investment Plan and has been a member of the standing expert advisory board to the National Appraisal Guidelines Committee.

Peter Forsyth was Professor of Economics at Monash University, Australia, from 1997 to 2013, and since then he has been Adjunct Professor at Monash and Southern Cross University. Most of his research has been on applied microeconomics, with particular reference to transport economics and especially the economics of air transport, tourism economics and the economics of regulation. He has recently published a jointly edited book on liberalisation (*Liberalization in Aviation: Competition, Cooperation and Public Policy*, 2013) and a co-authored book on *Tourism Economics and Policy* (2010). He has been particularly interested in the relationship between the economics of tourism and the economics of aviation. He has been awarded research grants by the Australian Research Council and the Sustainable Tourism Cooperative Research Centre in these areas. Peter has, since 2000, been a frequent speaker at the Hamburg Aviation Conference, and in 2005 he delivered the Martin Kunz Memorial Lecture. Since then he has been an organiser of, and speaker at, the European Aviation Conference. Since 2008 he has contributed to several OECD/International Transport Forum Roundtables. Recent work has involved using computable general equilibrium models to assess the economic impacts of tourism, including special events, and in analysing tourism and aviation policy issues, such as the evaluation of airport investments and of the costs and benefits of tourism promotion. In 2015 he was elected Fellow of the Air Transport Research Society.

James (Jim) D. Frost is one of Canada's leading experts in short sea shipping and the ferry industry. He is a marketing and business development specialist, experienced in port marketing, short sea shipping and the ferry industry. He has managed a container feeder/transhipment service operating between the traditional trading links of Halifax and Boston, and was marketing manager for Marine Atlantic, a large crown corporation which operates ferry services in Atlantic Canada. Jim owns and operates MariNova Consulting Ltd., which was established in 1995, and specialises in multimodal transportation studies. He recently completed an analysis of short sea shipping on the St Lawrence Seaway for the Canadian Transportation Act Review Secretariat, as well as recent projects for a Canadian ship owner and a large Canadian energy company. Jim has a BA from McGill University, an MA from Queen's University at Kingston, an MBA from St Mary's University and is the author of three books and many articles on maritime business and economic history.

David A. Hensher is Professor of Management and Founding Director of the Institute of Transport and Logistics Studies: Australian Key Centre of Teaching and Research in Transport Management at the University of Sydney. David is Fellow of the Academy of Social Sciences in Australia, recipient of the 2009 International Association of Travel Behaviour Research (IATBR) Lifetime Achievement Award in recognition for his long-standing and exceptional contribution to IATBR as well as to the wider travel behaviour community, recipient of the 2006 Engineers Australia Transport Medal for lifelong contribution to transportation, recipient of the 2009 Bus New South Wales (NSW) (Bus and Coach Association) Outstanding Contribution to Industry Award and recipient of the 2012 best paper released by the International Association of Maritime Economists. David is also the recipient of the Smart 2013 Premier Award for Excellence in Supply Chain Management and of the 2014 Institute of Transportation Engineers (Australia and New Zealand) Transport Profession Award. He is a member of Singapore Land Transport Authority International Advisory Panel (chaired by the Minister of Transport) and past president of the International Association of Travel Behaviour Research. David is the co-founder of the International Conference in Competition and Ownership of Land Passenger Transport, now in its 23rd year. David is on the editorial boards of ten of the leading transport journals and area editor of *Transport Reviews*. He is also series and volume editor of the handbook series 'Handbooks in Transport'. He has published extensively (over 570 papers) in the leading international transport journals and key journals in economics as well as 12 books. He has over 33,800 citations of his contributions in Google Scholar. David has advised numerous government industry agencies, with a recent appointment to Infrastructure Australia's reference panel on public transport, and is called upon regularly by the media for commentary. Most recent roles include expert adviser to WestConnex (a 33km toll road in planning in Sydney), expert adviser to the Singapore update of economic parameters (with Aecom), and adviser to Deloitte on congestion intervention strategies (for AustRoads).

Robin Hickman is Reader at the Bartlett School of Planning, University College London, and Director of the MSc in Transport and City Planning. He has been a research fellow and visiting research associate at the Transport Studies Unit, University of Oxford; a visiting lecturer at the University of Malta; and previously worked in consultancy as an associate director at Halcrow, leading on transport research. He has research interests in transport and climate change, urban structure and travel, integrated transport and urban planning strategies, the affective dimensions of travel, discourses in travel, multicriteria appraisal and sustainable transport strategies in the UK, Europe and Asia. His most recent books are *Handbook on Transport and Development* (2015) and *Transport, Climate Change and the City* (2014).

Stephen Ison is Professor of Transport Policy within the School of Civil and Building Engineering at Loughborough University. He has published widely in the areas of transport policy and economics and has edited, authored or co-authored eight books. He is a member of the Scientific Committee of the World Conference on Transport Research, editor of the *Journal of Research on Transportation Business and Management* and book series editor of *Transport and Sustainability*.

Rebecca Johnson is a research fellow in the School of Geography, Earth and Environmental Sciences at Plymouth University. She has a BSc (hons) in Geography from the University of Hull and a PhD from the School of Civil and Building Engineering at Loughborough University. Her PhD adopted a realistic evaluation approach to garner a deeper understanding of publicly funded demand-responsive transport services in England and Wales. After completing her PhD she worked for a sustainable transport consultancy for five years, undertaking projects for a range of clients including local and national government and private-sector organisations. Whilst in this role she specialised in transport research projects, evaluation of sustainable and active travel measures and transport policy. Since she began working at Plymouth University in 2012 she has been involved in a European project that assessed transport policy for an ageing society across Europe; explored the use of mobility scooters in the UK; reviewed evidence relating to the social, economic and commercial benefits and costs of accessible transport; and explored the transport barriers encountered by female entrepreneurs in rural Nigeria. She specialises in the application of qualitative research methods and enjoys using these to understand transport behaviour, travel patterns and the effectiveness of transport policy measures. She is on the editorial panel of the *Institute of Civil Engineers Transport Journal* and regularly reviews papers for the *Journal of Transport and Health, Ageing and Society* and the *Journal of Research in Transportation Business and Management.*

Robert Mayer is Lecturer in Air Transport Management and Course Director for the MSc in Air Transport Management at Cranfield University. Prior to taking up his current post, Robert lectured for nine years at the University of Huddersfield where he was responsible for the BSc in Air Transport and Logistics Management. Before joining academia, Robert worked in customer relations for Austrian Airlines and in ground handling at Vienna Airport. His main areas of expertise are airline marketing and economics as well as air cargo. He also lectures on airport ground operations and airline finance. Robert holds a degree in European Economics and Business Management (UAS bfi Vienna), an MSc in Air Transport Management (Cranfield), a PgCert in Higher Education Practice (Huddersfield) and a PhD in Airline Marketing

(Loughborough). Robert is a chartered member of the Chartered Institute of Logistics and Transport, an associate member of the Royal Aeronautical Society and sits on the Education and Research Committee of the International Air Cargo Association.

Rico Merkert is Chair in Transport and Supply Chain Management and Deputy Director of the Institute of Transport and Logistics Studies at the University of Sydney, Australia. He has various leadership roles at ITLS, was Deputy Chair of the ITLS Graduate Program from 2012 to 2014 and is now Director of the ITLS Higher Degree by Research Program. Rico is Editor-in-Chief of the *Journal of Air Transport Management*, Fellow of the Higher Education Academy, Deputy Chair of the Thredbo international conference series and an appointed member of three US Transportation Research Board standing committees. Whilst being a Marie Curie Research Fellow at the Institute for Transport Studies at the University of Leeds he undertook and received a PhD in Transport Economics. His PhD and also more recent studies were heavily influenced by a research visit at Haas Business School, University of California Berkeley. He has been involved in a number of projects on transport economics and management (including strategy, organisation, forecasting, finance and mergers and acquisitions) for a range of clients such as the European Commission, UK Department for Transport, Transport for NSW and a number of major airlines. Most of his recent projects focused on the efficient management of various elements of the transport supply chain, as well as benchmarking and cost-efficiency analysis of airlines, airports, freight forwarders and bus/train operators both in the global and regional context.

Jason Monios is Associate Professor in Transport Planning and Geography and Head of the Freight Transport and Logistics group at the Transport Research Institute, Edinburgh Napier University. His primary research areas are intermodal transport planning and the geography of port systems, with a specific interest in how these two subjects intersect in the port hinterland. Jason has over 50 peer-reviewed academic publications in addition to numerous research and consultancy reports, covering Europe, North and South America, Asia, the Middle East and Africa. He has co-authored technical reports with UNCTAD and UN-ECLAC and been adviser to the Scottish parliament. Recent book publications include *Institutional Challenges to Intermodal Transport and Logistics* (2014) and *Intermodal Freight Terminals: A Life Cycle Governance Framework* (2016). He is currently co-editing a textbook on intermodal transport for publication in 2017.

Corinne Mulley is the Founding Chair in Public Transport at the Institute of Transport and Logistics Studies at the University of Sydney. Corinne is a transport economist and has been active in transport research at the interface of transport policy and economics. More recently Corinne has concentrated on specific issues relating to public transport. She led a high-profile European and UK consortia undertaking benchmarking in urban public transport and has provided both practical and strategic advice to local and national governments on transport evaluation, including economic impact analysis, benchmarking, rural transport issues and public transport management. Corinne's research is motivated by a need to provide evidence for policy initiatives and she has been involved in such research at local, regional, national and European levels. Since coming to Sydney, Corinne has created links with the federal government, serving as an expert on the Public Transport Committee and National Infrastructure Audit for Infrastructure Australia and with the NSW state and local governments where she has offered advice as an expert on, for example, the Long-Term Master Plan for NSW. Corinne continues to research in the public transport area to provide the evidence base in NSW for public transport initiatives, whether these be in the infrastructure appraisal area, the links between physical activity, public transport use and health, benchmarking, travel planning, network planning and community transport.

Chris Nash is Research Professor in the Institute for Transport Studies, University of Leeds, where he is a former director, a visiting professor in Masaryka University in the Czech Republic and a research fellow in the Centre on Regulation in Europe in Brussels. He has led many research projects in the fields of rail transport and infrastructure charging for bodies including the European Commission, Community of European Railways, Office of Rail Regulation and the World Bank. He is an associate editor of the *Journal of Rail Planning and Management* and a former editor (and still board member) of the *Journal of Transport Economics and Policy*. He has acted as specialist adviser to many bodies including the Transport Committee of the House of Commons and the European Union Committee of the House of Lords.

John Nellthorp is Senior Research Fellow in the Institute for Transport Studies at the University of Leeds, where he leads courses on Transport Investment Appraisal. He has contributed to the appraisal methods of the UK Department for Transport, the World Bank, the European Union, Transport for London and numerous other governments and transport authorities. John is an economist with over 20 years' research, consultancy and teaching experience in the transport sector. He has hands-on experience of appraisals for a wide range of interventions: his first applied work was 20 years ago for the Berneray Causeway linking Berneray and North Uist in the Western Isles; and his most recent is for eco-driving systems in cars and commercial vehicles in Europe. The main focus of his work, however, has been on the methods underlying transport appraisal. Twenty years ago, appraisals were mostly unimodal, with too little attention paid to the wider impacts on accessibility, economy, environment and quality of life. Some of these impacts are complex and without practical methods it was difficult to include them in appraisal in a meaningful way. John has contributed to bringing these impacts clearly and succinctly into appraisal and extending the reach of valuation so that they can be included in the benefit:cost ratio on a regular basis. More widely, he has challenged the limitations of conventional cost-benefit analysis and argued for more ambitious use of economic analysis in transport policy.

John D. Nelson holds the Sixth Century Chair of Transport Studies at the University of Aberdeen and is Director of the Centre for Transport Research. He also directs the Aberdeen/Heriot-Watt node of the Transport Systems Catapult University Partner Programme. He is an honorary professor at the Institute of Transport and Logistics Studies, University of Sydney. John was previously Professor of Public Transport Systems at Newcastle University and moved to Aberdeen in 2007 to take up his current post. At Aberdeen University he has also served as Director of Research and Commercialisation for the College of Physical Sciences and as Co-Director of the Research Councils UK dot.rural Digital Economy Research Hub (an 80-strong research centre). John is particularly interested in the application and evaluation of new technologies to improve transport systems as well as the policy frameworks and regulatory regimes necessary to achieve sustainable mobility. He has a long-standing research interest in flexible and demand-responsive forms of transport. John is the immediate past chairman of the Universities' Transport Study Group, which promotes transport teaching and research across the UK and Ireland.

John Preston is Professor of Rail Transport and Head of the Transportation Research Group at the University of Southampton. He holds a BA in Geography from Nottingham and a PhD in Economics from Leeds. He has over 30 years of experience in transport research and education, having previously held posts at the universities of Leeds and Oxford. His research in transport covers demand and cost modelling, regulatory studies, land use and environment interactions and economic appraisal and evaluation. This work covers all modes but with a particular emphasis on bus and rail. He has held over 130 research grants and contracts, worth over £10 million, and has published over 300 articles, book chapters, conference and working papers. His work on regulatory reform has been funded by the Economic and Social Research Council, as well as by central and local governmental bodies and by consultancies and think tanks. He is an elected fellow of the Transport Research Foundation and a fellow of the Chartered Institution of Highways and Transportation. He is a member of the International Steering Committee of the International Conference on Competition and Ownership in Land Passenger Transport that originated in Thredbo in 1989 and organised the conferences in Leeds (1997) and Oxford (2013).

Tom Rye rejoined Edinburgh Napier University as Professor in Transport and Director of its Transport Research Institute (www.tri.napier.ac.uk) in January 2015. Before this, he worked for over two years as Professor at the Division of Transport and Roads, Lund University in Sweden; whilst there he also successfully started up Sweden's new National Knowledge Centre for Public Transport, as its director. He has degrees in Geography and Spatial Planning and a PhD in Mobility Management. He also worked at Edinburgh Napier University from 1996 to 2012 but alongside academia; he spent much time seconded to consultants and local government, as well as on projects for Scottish and UK governments and the European Union. His specialisms are transport training, mobility management, transport policy evaluation and implementation, parking policy and planning for public and slow modes of transport. In his spare time, Tom enjoys ski touring, vegetable gardening, mountain biking, his six-year-old twins, real ale, playing saxophone and ukulele, learning other languages and topiary.

Andrew Smith is Professor of Transport Performance and Economics and Research Group Leader for the Economics and Discrete Choice Research Group at the Institute for Transport Studies, University of Leeds. He is a leading academic in the field of rail cost and efficiency modelling, infrastructure access pricing and marginal cost research, rail regulation and the impact of rail reforms on economic efficiency. He has published important work in these areas and has led or is leading a wide range of rail modelling projects, funded by, for example, the European Commission, EPSRC, the British Office of Rail Regulation and the UK Department for Transport. Andrew has a visiting research position at the Centre for Transport Studies (Royal Institute of Technology and VTI) in Stockholm. Andrew's current and recent PhD students are/have been in the areas of efficiency analysis in rail, health and airlines.

Kathryn Stewart is a mathematician who has worked in the field of traffic and transportation since 1999; she is currently a lecturer at Edinburgh Napier University working within the Transport Research Institute. Her main expertise falls within traffic demand management, particularly congestion charging in network systems and sustainable transport solutions. Kathryn is the branch treasurer for the Institute of Mathematics and its Applications in Scotland, Programme Chair for the Scottish Transport Research and Applications conference series, a member of the scientific committee for the International Symposium Series on Traffic Demand Management and represents the Transport Research Institute on the Edinburgh City Council Transport Forum.

Peter White is Emeritus Professor of Public Transport Systems at the University of Westminster. He retired from his teaching role at the end of August 2015 but continues to be active in public transport research in bus, coach and rail systems. He is the author of the textbook *Public Transport: Its Planning, Management and Operation* (sixth edition, 2016) and many published papers. Research interests in recent years have focused on longer-term impacts of privatisation and deregulation in the express coach and local bus markets. Other research interests include energy consumption by buses, rural public transport, the impacts of service quality and marketing on demand, and improving data collection on public transport usage. He has acted as a specialist adviser to five House of Commons Select Committee enquiries.

Allan Woodburn is Principal Lecturer in Freight and Logistics in the Planning and Transport Department at the University of Westminster, London. He is responsible for the MSc Logistics and Supply Chain Management course and is involved in a wide range of teaching, research and consultancy activities in the field of freight transport, both within the UK and internationally. In 2000, Allan completed his doctorate examining the role for rail freight within the supply chain. Since then, his main research focus has been on rail freight policy, planning and operations, particularly examining issues related to efficiency and sustainability. He has also analysed factors that influence freight mode choice decision making and carried out assessments of various rail freight markets, notably those involving the use of intermodal technologies. Since 1997, Allan has compiled an annual database of British rail freight services, which provides an invaluable source of information for trend analysis. Allan has published widely on the subject of rail freight, including 12 peer-reviewed journal papers, several book chapters and a number of research/consultancy reports. Clients that he has worked for include the Department for Transport, Transport for London, the United Nations Economic Commission for Europe and the Centre on Regulation in Europe.

1 Introduction

Jonathan Cowie and Stephen Ison

One should hardly have to tell academicians that information is a valuable resource: knowledge is power. And yet this occupies a slum dwelling in the town of economics. Mostly it is ignored.
(Stigler, 1961, p. 213)

1.1 Introduction

Transport is an important area of academic study and one which is problem rich, stimulating a great deal of debate in areas which impact on everyday lives. Such debates, however, have a very real focus on the practicalities of the modern-day phenomena of mass movement and all of the issues associated with it. It is also an area which is developing at a rapid pace, not least given new and innovative developments in technology. The discipline of economics is central to this debate, and consequently the study and application of transport economics has a major role to play in seeking to address subjects relating to major transport issues. Some would even argue that at the very heart of any transport issue/problem, lies the underlying economics of the situation – solve that and you alleviate the problem. In practical terms, this translates into matters surrounding urban and interurban traffic congestion, the public cost of the environmental impact of transport, the structure of transport markets and associated models of transport production/delivery, private versus public ownership and/or control of transport services, and the financing of infrastructure and other significant transport-related projects. In many respects, all of these fit with one interpretation[1] of Carlyle's often quoted description of economics as 'the dismal science', 'dismal' in the sense that it deals with the nuts and bolts/realities of daily life, rather than more 'enlightening' aspects.

Central to all of this is the economic problem of moving people and freight from one location to another. Transport is seldom demanded for its own sake and by its very nature is a *derived demand*. This means that both individuals and freight relocate, not for the sake of travelling, but in order to realise their maximum value, whether that be in monetary or non-monetary terms. Transport as such is a key component of any economic 'system'; the problem, however, is that it is unique in both time and space, which means that it cannot be stored or transferred. This results in the peak/off-peak nature of demand creating significant issues of congestion with the associated environmental degradation.

Congestion in many respects is the classic 'economic' problem of scarcity, either caused by too many people attempting to access a set space or too little 'space' for the level of people attempting to access it. Contemporary times have seen the introduction of pricing into the sector as part of a hard-option approach to demand management. The role of pricing, however, has a long history in the academic literature stretching back to the work of Dupuit (1844) and Pigou (1920). In addition, there have been key official government reports, most notably the Smeed Report on the *Economics of Road Pricing* (Ministry of Transport, 1964). The environmental impact of transport, be it locally in terms of health implications or more globally in relation to climate change, is a more recent area of study. Again the role of the price mechanism in terms of dealing with externalities, whether that be through direct taxation or other schemes such as creating a market in emission trading permits, highlights the significant place of transport economics in addressing the issue.

As regards organisation and governance, since the 1970s the public transport sector has been subjected to significant deregulation, most notably in terms of the bus, coach and aviation sectors. Major issues arise out of such reforms, whether it be in dealing with the relative welfare benefits of such a course of action through direct competition or through the underlying principles of contestability (Baumol, 1982). Deregulation has tended to go alongside privatisation, which in the British context has consisted of privatising airline operators, airports, the rail sector, road haulage and bus operators. The planning, provision and financing of infrastructure can also be seen as an important facet of transport economics, in particular in deciding which projects should be progressed and which should not.

With regards to freight and the whole logistics/supply chain management, von Mises (1949), in development of the theorem of consumer sovereignty in *Human Action*, made a key reference to the efficiency of what today is commonly known as supply chain management and the wider area of logistics. He also stressed the importance of innovative solutions in the delivery of goods and services at the lowest possible cost. The rapidly changing economics of these sectors has led to major reforms and innovations in distribution networks and arguably in far-reaching structural change and more general industrial organisation. These developments have all been market led and not as a result of policy, and have had such a profound impact that, along with higher-level institutional changes brought about by the General Agreement on Tariffs and Trade,[2] have led to what is more commonly known as 'globalisation', a phenomenon that continues to unfold today.

In compiling this collected volume of invited chapters, the editors recognise that there are many texts available on the subject of transport economics, ranging from a selection of introductory texts through to edited collections of intermediate and high-level chapters. All of these have had and continue to have an important role in developing the discipline of economics to the study of transport. The current volume has been compiled to complement these texts with a more practically oriented focus, which in many cases consists of the simple application of economic principles to transport issues. In some respects, therefore, the 'oddities' of reality are not assumed away and thus, contrary to the esteemed view of George Stigler given at the start of this chapter, it should hopefully not be ignored and prove to be a valuable resource. This is particularly important given that the economics of transport drives everything in the transport subject area, whether that be patronage levels, subsidy levels, policy development, traffic congestion, freight modal splits, public transport reform or ecological degradation.

1.2 Book sections and key topic areas

In putting together this handbook, the editors have identified five key subject areas to be examined:

(1) public transport;
(2) public transport reform;

(3) forecasting, public choice and transport modelling;
(4) transport and the environment;
(5) freight transport.

Public transport comprises the first two parts of the book and hence the first two of the 'five' key areas into which the book is divided. Mass movement is a key symptom of modern life, and the only way this can be achieved 'efficiently', whether that refers to economic or any other kind of efficiency, is through mass public transit. This therefore is a key area of study. In contemporary times, however, public transport has been under reform, in particular with regard to the extent provision and finance is state provided or privately provided, or indeed some balance between the two. As stated later, this is probably the second biggest issue confronting the application of economics to transport, and therefore is the second key area of study. Part III is a combination of a number of issues, ranging from economic development, public choice and transport modelling. In many respects this is the more technically orientated part of the book and examines how economic principles are directly applied to transport situations, and furthermore how these principles have crossed over into other aspects of transport research. Part IV relates to transport and the environment, and the impact of mass movement on the natural resources and natural habitat is one that has been a growing area of concern since the 1980s and one that will continue to be high on the political agenda, hence this is the fourth key area. Finally, Part V concentrates on freight transport. Much academic research surrounds passenger transport, however, comparatively little exists on freight. In many respects the reason for this is that there is considerably less policy, i.e. state intervention, in these modes, the assumption being that these can be left to the market to provide. Consequently, its importance is understated. Nevertheless, freight drives the economy and arguably wider society. This text therefore presents the opportunity to give the study of freight transport its rightful place as a fifth key area.

Part I: Public transport

One of the major issues in transport economics, if not in the wider area of the study of transport, is the organisation of public transport services so that they deliver high-quality services and represent value for money to the public purse. Given the importance of this subject, Part I covers this topic and begins with a look at mainline railways. The rail industry, however, and the economics of how it all 'works', is a vast area and is a sector which features a high number of key economic issues, such as private-versus public-sector provision, regulation, high levels of subsidy, questions over productive inefficiencies and value for (public) money, competition/contestability and a seemingly endless stream of reforms in search of some kind of 'solution' to these issues. Simon Blainey's chapter gives an important insight into a number of these underlying areas, particularly with regard to reform and the involvement of the private sector. As Simon highlights, introducing the private sector into the industry is a far from straightforward process. In contrast to the bus industry, the process, in principle, is very simple: rather than have buses owned and operated by a public-sector body, buses are owned and operated by a private-sector company. The whole issue of contracting and aligning the private-sector profit motive with public-sector aims is a whole further topic (see Chapter 7), however, the principle is relatively straightforward. With railways, introducing the private sector involves far more structural change and is more complex than a simple change of ownership. Simon's chapter outlines the various structural forms this can take, and the advantages and disadvantages of each. What Simon tends to suggest is that the rail industry, and the structure associated with delivering productively efficient and user-friendly services, is not a case of 'one hat fits all', and therefore in part explains why rail reforms have tended to be problematic and, from an academic perspective, a very interesting area to study.

As highlighted, buses, in terms of reform, should be more straightforward, however, it could be argued that although bus economics has long been studied, bus economics has equally long been misunderstood, certainly in light of the British experience with bus deregulation. Peter White's chapter attempts to go some way to addressing this lack of knowledge, and gives a good insight into the large influence that different operational conditions and practical considerations have upon operating costs. These are often overlooked in theoretical economics and in any evaluation of the impact of reforms, but they are key to understanding the underlying economic issues. A second consideration is the extent to which the market can regulate competition in order that it results in an economically efficient market outcome, or certainly something close to it. Peter uses examples from the British experience with the deregulated market, the London regulated market and the contracted socially necessary market, and shows that while there appears to be strong evidence of only limited scale economies in bus operation, large companies nevertheless tend to dominate in all three of these markets. Furthermore, profit levels appear to be well above what would be considered 'normal'. This perhaps suggests that there are still issues within bus economics that remain little understood and hence areas for further research, particularly the extent to which there exist economies in carriage (as opposed to economies in operation) and the extent to which network effects offer a competitive advantage.

Vital in the operation of any market, whether that be deregulated, regulated or subsidised, is the role of price. In most markets, price represents how much the consumer pays for the good and the amount the producer receives for it. In mainstream economic theory, the price of course represents far more than that, and ultimately represents market efficiency. In other words, the 'right' price means that we end up with the 'right' amount of production of a particular good or service, consumed by the 'right' people (i.e. those willing to pay the market price). This in turn results in the benefits from production and consumption being shared equitably between utility-maximising consumers and producers. Within public transport services the issue is clouded further by the (positive) externalities associated with the modes and hence the tendency for it to be heavily publicly funded. The price then also determines the extent to which the service is paid for by the government and the extent to which it is paid for by the user. Corinne Mulley and Marco Batarce's chapter on the pricing of public transport provides an excellent insight into the factors and influences that go into the pricing of public transport services. What they successfully do is strike a balance between theory and practicalities, and in doing so give a real insight into what goes into the pricing decisions surrounding public transport services. What we get is both a view of what public transport 'should' be doing with regard to the pricing of services, and how this is transmitted to a practical context. Highlighted particularly well is the fact that, with the one notable exception of a deregulated market, there are many factors that sit behind the pricing of public transport services, all of which are directly related to the more general economics of transport services. What Corinne and Marco outline is that there is no general approach to the pricing of transport services, with the diversity and range of influences this will depend upon policy objectives that are found under different situations and how this interacts with the underlying cost of provision.

A second component in the operation of the market is the provision of public transport information, and this has become a major topic in itself, both from an operational perspective and an academic one. In terms of basic economics the provision of perfect information forms one of the important assumptions in markets such as perfect competition. As with the provision of any service the flow of information is all important and public transport is no exception. The user needs the appropriate information at the appropriate time in order to make an informed choice as to whether to travel or not, and in the case of the former, what mode should be used. John Nelson's chapter explores the importance of market information to consumers and assesses the role of high-quality information as a key enabler of successful transport service provision. A recurring theme throughout the chapter is the critical role of smart technology. The simple question as to why the user/consumer of local public transport requires specific information is examined along with the various approaches which are taken in terms of providing that information, whether it be through the use of traditional media or the role played by smart technology. With respect to information flows, then, cost and capacity are important, while information availability, such as real-time passenger information, and accuracy tend to be impacted by levels of disruption. While this is the case, social media can aid in terms of mitigating the impact of disruption. As such, over time the provision of timely, accurate and personalised real-time information has become the priority of those charged with the development of journey planners and other channels for the delivery of information. Mobile applications have already eclipsed the limited deployment opportunities of real-time displays at bus stops and (traditional) journey planners must also be available for use on mobile devices.

The use of technology leads into Peter Forsyth's chapter on air passenger traffic. The chapter outlines the different types and forms of passenger air operator, before examining the airline cost function and the main factors of production used in the production of passenger air services. The chapter goes on to examine the key issues impacting on the use of these factors, such as the unionisation and internationalisation of labour and returns to scale, or more exactly, returns to density associated with capital equipment. Interestingly, Peter highlights that price is only used on rare occasions to manage or apportion the use of runways, which in many areas remain the constraining factor. The chapter then highlights that air fares have been steadily falling in real terms. This is put down to two main reasons. Firstly, the improvement in the efficiency of aircraft, and secondly, the use of information technology and the internet. Interestingly, Peter does not highlight competition or wider deregulation of the sector as a contributory factor. Nevertheless, what this leads to is an industry that at the general level conforms with anti-competitive market structures, but one characterised by relatively low levels of profitability. This of course is contradictory to economic theory and provides an interesting paradox and one that Peter highlights as an ongoing puzzle and as such a real gap in the research.

Part II: Public transport reform

Reform in the provision of transport services is not new. Richard Beeching was given the task in 1963 of making the then state-owned British Railways break even by 1980, which led to a high number of controversial line closures. Come the 1980s, rising subsidy levels and macro-economic pressures on government finances led many governments to seek other solutions to obtain better value for the levels of public finance being provided. In most cases this has involved introducing the private sector in one form or another in order to resolve many of these issues.

The most common approach adopted is the privately owned/publicly regulated market, which generally takes the form of services run by private-sector companies under contract to a public authority. Much research surrounds the general use of contracts in the procurement and provision of public transport services by such authorities. Most of this focuses on the practicalities of the operation of these contracts and the types of outcome (both desirable and undesirable) that result. David Hensher's chapter outlines the key components of principal-agent theory and by doing so clearly identifies the key issues that lie behind such contracts and in very clear and straightforward terms illustrates why such contracts can be difficult to draft, implement and 'get right'. The chapter also illustrates why such practices are not generalisable, hence what may 'work' in one context may not work in another. What tends to be overlooked in terms of economics in general and the provision of transport services in particular, is that at the end of the day it is about people (both in the consumer and producer roles), and whilst there may be instances where we can use theory to hypothesise how the 'average' person may behave, there remain situations where we cannot. In other words, we transgress between positivistic and social constructivist worlds. Both are relevant to the study of transport economics, and David's chapter illustrates very clearly how theory can be used to give a better understanding of the key issues in both instances. He highlights that one of the problems with operator comparisons are that qualitative differences tend to be ignored, hence the importance of normalisation or delimitation when benchmarking public transport operations. David's chapter also illustrates very well that the study of transport economics does not, or certainly should not, exist in an academic vacuum, but that there is much to be learned from studying other areas and other situations outside of the transport field. It comes therefore as a timely reminder that transport economics is a sub-discipline of economics, in much the same vein as agricultural economics, labour economics, environmental economics, industrial economics and so on.

Whilst public transport reform has tended to switch from public to private ownership, as highlighted above, in most sectors control has remained a public-sector function. The switch from public ownership therefore has introduced the need for economic regulation. This is a vast subject area, and one closely associated with the extensive work of the above quoted George Stigler. Within the transport field, public-sector bodies to a greater or lesser extent set and control the basic tools of economic competition, namely the price, frequency, market entry and in some cases even the quality (i.e. those above the legal minimum) of the service provided. Chris Nash, Valerio Benedetto and Andrew Smith detail rail regulation and highlight that while the trend over the last 40 years in the transport sector has been towards deregulation, with regards to the rail industry within Europe in the last 20 years most countries have created a new rail regulatory body. This reform has centred around seeking to achieve a separation between infrastructure and operations in addition to fostering competition between passenger and freight operators over the same infrastructure. In overseeing this process, rail regulators need to ensure there is no discrimination with competition being fair. In addition, it is important that the body responsible for rail infrastructure does not take advantage of its monopoly power. This monopoly power may manifest itself in terms of higher prices, restricted output, lower efficiency or level of service. The chapter seeks to identify which type of regulatory body is likely to succeed in terms of regulating the rail sector.

How successful these previous two areas have been, i.e. public-service contract specification and regulatory control, is the subject of the evaluation of public transport reforms, which leads into John Preston's chapter on the assessment of reformist measures. In general, this has been a major area of study for policy makers, practitioners and academics for a considerable period. This gained added momentum with the British deregulation and privatisation of the bus industry in the 1980s, followed by the privatisation of the rail sector in the 1990s. As an area of study, the issue of what really is the best supply-side organisation of public transport to meet policy aims at an acceptable public financial cost is one of the biggest challenges facing the discipline. John's chapter considers this issue from the perspective of the welfare impacts. As such, it provides an interesting read and some interesting if unexpected findings. Through deriving a counterfactual, what John finds is that in terms of bus transport, the British reforms of the mid-1980s had a fairly substantial and long-lasting negative effect on patronage, actually increasing the rate of decline that the reformed structure was implemented to reverse. Interestingly, the counterfactual suggests that bus patronage would have actually risen without the reforms. For rail, the counterfactual shows that privatisation slowed the rate of increase, suggesting that the substantial increase in rail patronage since privatisation would have occurred anyway, and in fact, may have been significantly higher. In light of these findings, it comes as no surprise that regulatory reform still remains a key subject of research, as many issues still need to be understood as to why in both cases the reforms implemented had the exact opposite effect (in terms of patronage levels) from that which was planned.

As with the rail sector outlined above, airlines have also been heavily regulated. In fact, this was the case from the outset of regular commercial flights in the early 1900s based on the premise that operators required protection from competition. In saying this, regulation provided no incentive for the control of costs or service innovation. As a result, the sector was characterised by economic inefficiency, oversupply and high prices, meaning that this was a service outside the reach of most citizens. Lucy Budd's chapter details the changes that have taken place since the late 1970s, first as a result of the US Airline Deregulation Act in October 1978 and then in other countries, starting in Europe in the 1990s with its progressive packages of reform. These have included the removal of regulations governing airline capacity, service frequency, route entitlements and control over fares on both domestic and international routes. The aim has been to increase efficiency, stimulate competition and encourage service innovation. The chapter deals with the factors that motivated the reform and the implications. Importantly, it outlines what the future may hold in a global environment where there are concerns over energy consumption and passenger security.

Part III: Forecasting, public choice and transport modelling

This section in some respects presents the nuts of bolts of economic evaluation to a number of transport-related issues, and as such presents examples of the box of tools available to economic evaluation. One of the issues that filters through from all of these chapters is the importance of economic theory and principles in the application of assessment. Within a subject area such as transport, however, there is a very real danger that these are often overlooked, and indeed in some cases never even considered. Understanding the theoretical foundation of the practical application is crucial in understanding the implications and the real 'meaning' of the results that emerge from the whole exercise.

The section begins with John Bates' chapter, in which John seeks to outline an important component of transport economics, namely the main concepts and methods used to forecast the demand for transport. The chapter specifically focuses on the movement of individuals, rather than freight, and examines the issues that are considered in the forecasting of transport services and the extent to which these relate to the basic law of demand. The chapter starts with a discussion relating to aggregate trends and the global influences, namely population, income, level of urbanisation, as well as the speed and cost as it relates to specific aspects of transport supply. The chapter details forecasting in terms of both general levels of transport and for individual modes or specific infrastructure projects, the main drivers behind the demand for transport, forecasting demand for private and public transport and the demand for new developments, and the practicalities in transport demand forecasting. The main practical considerations in the estimation of future demand and an overview of the various approaches ranging from simple trend analysis to more complex econometric models are also covered.

The chapter by John Nellthorp addresses the important aspect of 'transport appraisal', which is underpinned by economic principles and widely used in transport decision making by government and public bodies. The chapter seeks to detail what is called the common 'tool box' for transport appraisal, and as such fits very well with the main theme of this section. The tools are invariably incorporated into national and international guidance for appraisal and, as well as relating to individual investment projects, also include regional transport strategies, national infrastructure plans and potential schemes such as road pricing (a topic which is covered in the following chapter). Transport appraisal is no respecter of scale since any scheme large or small, local or international can be appraised. The chapter details how appraisal methods are developed incorporating values of travel time savings, safety, environmental and health impacts, and the wider economic impacts beyond the transport sector. Appraisal for appraisals' sake is futile and as such John details the use that is made of the output from such activity, as well as the limitations an approach such as this will clearly possess.

One area where transport appraisal has a role to play is in assessing the relative merits of schemes such as congestion pricing. The chapter by Jonas Eliasson, while not focusing specifically on appraisal, seeks to assess the role congestion pricing can play when addressing the issue of congestion, specifically in urban areas. Congestion is a facet of major cities worldwide and is the result of the overutilization of a capacity-constrained location. This is an example of market failure, where transport consumption will be higher than what could be seen as the efficient level if left unchecked. Urban transport planning must therefore be characterised by two principles: first, space must be used efficiently (space-efficient transport modes, compact land-use planning); second, policies must be introduced that strike a balance between positive and negative effects of mobility. This is where congestion pricing, as a market-based instrument, has a role to play seeking to find a better balance between the positive and negative effects of mobility. When designing congestion-charging regimes, the basic idea is one of balancing benefits against losses, benefits in the form of time savings for those who remain on the road after the introduction of the charge, and losses in the form of adaptation costs for those priced off the road. The optimal congestion charge is seen as equal to the difference between the marginal private cost and marginal social cost. This is somewhat difficult, if not impossible, to achieve in practice, thus congestion-charging design is all about finding an implementable system where the time gains for the remaining traffic is higher than the loss for the 'disappearing' ('tolled-off') trips, and high enough to cover investment and operating costs. The aim of the chapter is to discuss how the theoretical idea can be applied in practice and discuss how different cities have tackled this challenge.

With Kathryn Stewart's chapter on transport modelling and economic theory, the focus of the section switches to more theoretical considerations. Writing this book allowed the opportunity for some cross-over between subject disciplines, and the link-up between modelling and economics seemed obvious for several reasons. Firstly, transport modelling employs many basic economic concepts in order to generate models of transport systems. In many ways, incorporating more of the behavioural aspects of economics and even combining these with psychology, in other words how individuals perceive the world and thereby how they rate 'utility' in order to make a 'rational' (to them) choice, is something that from a general perspective is one area where far more research is required. Certainly within transport modelling, considerable research exists on incorporating perception biases into transport models, but perhaps there remains the difficulty of successful calibration or managing to use the results from 'big-data' type sources in an efficient manner. Secondly, transport modelling uses many of the methods and techniques found in economics, or more precisely, econometrics, with clear examples being issues surrounding discrete choice modelling and the use of logits and probits as estimation models. It therefore seems timely to include a chapter on transport modelling in a transport economics book. One criticism of transport modelling, although debatable depending from which perspective it is viewed, is that there exists a mismatch of theory and practical implementation. This particularly relates to one crucial and expanding area which is the impact of road tolling, in whatever guise that comes. To some extent, the issue has been of limited significance in the days of zero-user direct charging, however, these will become of increased importance as road tolling becomes a more common practice, i.e. as pricing decisions are introduced into route choice. It should be stated that the two disciplines, economics and transport modelling, remain separate, hence this is clear cross-disciplinary research, although perhaps more needs to be done with regard to inter-disciplinary research, and therefore Kathryn's chapter offers an important insight into how economic principles are currently used in transport modelling.

The last chapter in this section is by Rico Merkert and Jonathan Cowie, and covers the concept of productive efficiency and its measurement. 'Efficiency' is an often used term, and means many things to different people. Within an economics framework, however, it should have, or rather does have, a very specific meaning. Overlooking these clear definitions can result in unrealistic propositions with regard to the impact of regulatory reforms or completely unrealistic claims with regard to potential 'efficiency' improvements. In other words, we need to clearly define/delimit the specific issue being examined. In the chapter, Rico and Jonathan outline the main measures of efficiency, clearly distinguishing this from the concept of productivity, and illustrate the main concepts and methods used in its assessment and how this relates to economic theory. What comes through very clearly from the chapter is something very similar to John Nellthorp's thoughts with regard to appraisal for appraisal's sake, in that assessing efficiency for efficiency's sake is an often pointless exercise; there needs to be a clear reason for examining the issue. This will generally be with regard to the impact of policy, the effect of competition, the effectiveness of industrial organisation or the impact of wider macro-economic policies. Whilst sounding obvious, what this highlights is that production-efficiency levels are generally an indicator of wider economic performance and are not something that as an idea or concept sit in complete isolation.

Part IV: Transport and the environment

The natural environment is an often overlooked key resource in transport economics, not from the perspective of the negative effects the provision of transport has on it, but rather as a valuable economic resource. As such it is the factor of production that is never considered in any assessment of transport efficiency. Due to relatively free access, it is one area in which the market will never provide an efficient solution, as even under perfect competition as an externality it is assumed not to exist. Informed policy is therefore vital in this area, and the role of economics is to incorporate and evaluate in meaningful terms the effects of environmental depravation and the value of measures designed to counter such effects. That said, final decisions rest with politicians and this can lead to conflicts of interest. The chapters in this section provide examples of all of these issues and the outcomes that these produce in terms of policy initiatives.

Maria Attard's chapter deals with the environment in the provision of transport and in particular the implications of incomplete appraisals which do not take into consideration the value of nature lost in the development of transport projects. It draws on the Millennium Ecosystems Assessment (2005), which was conducted with a view to identify some of the more pressing concerns around the use of natural capital and the impact on ecosystems. It deals with the need for transport growth to be managed in a more sustainable manner, not least by the more balanced use of all transport modes. In the chapter, Maria discusses the transport impacts and some of the challenges with appraisal methodologies that integrate the value of nature and the environment in transport projects. What is clear is that we are still far from the optimum decision-making processes that will ensure there is protection of the environment, alongside economic and social considerations. A do-nothing approach has major implications, not only in terms of the environment and climate change but also in terms of natural disasters, migration and public health. As such governments and transport decision makers have to focus on their transport agendas and rethink transport projects in terms of their environmental gains.

Policy is a very important area in the operation of transport markets, as in most cases policy is required to correct for market failure, i.e. a breach in at least one of the assumptions of the perfect competition model. One of the 'problems' with policy is in its implementation, and the fact that within democratic states public acceptability is a necessary, though not sufficient, condition for success. The chapters by Tom Rye and Rebecca Johnson highlight some of the key issues in these areas. The focus of Tom's chapter is to provide an overview of the effectiveness and relative ease by which economic policy instruments can be implemented in order to address the natural environmental issues involved in the provision of transport. The chapter first considers the transport-related environmental degradation that governments need to tackle, before detailing the justification for state intervention so as to reduce environmental impacts. Following this the chapter looks at the range of policy tools at governments' disposal for reducing the environmental impacts and the theory underpinning each of these approaches, before describing the practical experience of implementing these tools via the use of case studies. These involve a range of measures including voluntary agreements, the imposition of a Pigouvian tax, the implementation of an emissions trading system and the direct regulation of transport activities. It is clear that there are various challenges with the implementation of such policy instruments, not least in transforming a theoretical concept such as 'the polluter pays' into a workable system. In the conclusion to the chapter there is a brief evaluation of the different policy options, focusing on their impact on environmental problems and the practicalities of implementation. It includes reference to the level of cooperation between agencies that is required for them to work.

Rebecca Johnson's chapter highlights many of the aforementioned issues with particular reference to the implementation of green transport policies. What Rebecca suggests is that in many high-profile cases, schemes are introduced to fulfil a political function other than the purpose for which they are put forward. In other words, they serve the need for the government to be seen to be acting upon a certain issue, even though the effectiveness of the policy may at best be highly questionable. More successful policies are either watered-down versions of the original proposal or compromises that trade what really needs to be done for public acceptability. Rebecca in some ways argues that this may just be the way of the world, certainly the way of the democratic one. What she suggests in the case of congestion charging is that ultimately the implementation of a charge will be dependent upon public acceptance, but there lies the problem, as this will only ever occur at a point of congestion considerably beyond the level that any economist would determine as optimal.

In the final chapter in this section, Robin Hickman provides a very succinct insight into the issues of transport supporting economic development, and relates this to sustainability and transport appraisal. He draws a timely reference to one of the key arguments developed in J. K. Galbraith's *The Affluent Society*, in which Galbraith developed his earlier observations over the concern with the quantity of goods produced and the rate of increase in gross national product, in which these aims would have to give way to the larger question of the quality of life that it provided. In many respects it could be argued that historically the private sector has been obsessed by growth, far more so than its concerns over profitability. This approach to business was none better exemplified than in the privatised Railtrack, where the daily share price was posted on the walls of the company's main offices. What Robin draws very clear attention to is that this obsession with economic growth is not restricted to the private sector, but is found to be highly prevalent in the public sector, particularly with regard to transport policy. The old adage that if we are rich then we must be happy seems to dominate, and whilst not directly stating it, Robin puts forward a very strong argument for a return to old-fashioned values of what actually the public sector should be doing with regard to its transport policies, and that these should take on a far wider societal and environmental viewpoint and act on the basis of the current and future public interest.

Part V: Freight transport

Freight transport underpins all aspects of material living and many if not most aspects of life beyond economic consumption, and this selection of chapters reinforces the importance of economic factors in driving the wider freight market forward. The part begins with short sea shipping, which in many parts of the world is viewed as vital to economic sustainability and future development. To underline the importance of the mode, the European Union quotes figures of 32 percent[3] for maritime for all freight carried within the European Union in 2014 (EU, 2016), which places it second behind road freight and almost three times the size of the rail sector. In the European context, all of this relates to short sea shipping. The chapter by James Frost and Mary Brooks on the subject begins by defining what is meant by short sea shipping and identifying the main features of the vessels that provide this type of transport service. It goes on to outline the main external drivers that determine the economics of short sea shipping and ferries both in the passenger and freight sectors. The chapter considers the importance and difficulties of addressing the balance between demand and supply, such that the service's economic viability is ensured. Around that the authors outline the whole area of direct and indirect competition and the underpinning area of regulation. Case studies are provided dealing with financial success and the role of subsidies.

The section then moves on to road freight, which has become the dominant mode of freight transport in the modern era. Jonathan Cowie's chapter on the subject ties in well with Robin Hickman's chapter on transport and sustainability and Allan Woodburn's following chapter on rail freight. What Jonathan argues is that modern society is largely supported by road freight, and this situation has come about simply due to the economics of the mode, and in many respects, the very simple economics of the mode. Two aspects in particular are drawn attention to: the competitive nature of the industry and the underlying cost structure. Along with wider industrial developments such as logistics principles and supply chain management practices, it is argued that these have led to the dominance of the mode in freight markets. Jonathan puts the view forward that policy to reduce the environmental impact of the mode has been largely ineffective and is an area that remains considerably underdeveloped, partly as a consequence of the practical difficulties of actually instigating meaningful policy initiatives, and partly due to a political reluctance to do so due to the high society costs that would result from such measures. The chapter's closing paragraphs highlight the ultimate importance of underlying economic principles by stressing that in this particular case, 'the market' as such has come to dominate all things materialistic and political.

Rail freight, certainly within the European context, is often viewed as 'underperforming', or certainly not achieving its full potential. Reasons for this view are difficult to perceive but are almost certainly related to the steady and consistent long-term decline in market share.[4] This has been a result of wider economic structural change, particularly the decline of heavy industry, a radical change in production methods from Fordism to post-Fordism (i.e. from fixed to flexible production) and finally perceptions of inefficient management, or certainly perceptions of a management unable or unwilling to adapt to new market conditions. All of these issues can be related to the economics of the mode, and Allan Woodburn's chapter on rail freight touches on most if not all of them. Allan makes very clear the sensitivity, in terms of economic viability, of the sector to external influences in terms of government (non-transport-related) policies, changing market conditions and the whole development of logistics and supply chain management. In particular, the chapter outlines the general structural form facing the rail freight operator, and then highlights the conditions under which rail becomes more competitive. This then leads into the types of rail freight traffic that exist, which in many ways, are similar but different to those outlined previously for road freight. One of the real factors that comes through from Allan's chapter is the issue of capacity, and the almost contradictory forces of high capacity enabling lower unit costs, but then the same issue of high capacity severely restricting the markets that can be served and/or leading to problems in filling that capacity to ensure unit costs are minimised. The chapter then outlines the public funding that is available, or has recently been made available, and what becomes very clear is that certainly within the British context, rail freight is still viewed as an economic good, i.e. one that should in principle cover its own costs. Furthermore, given the level of subsidy available to passenger transport, subsidy levels to freight represent small change, and highlight a reluctance on the part of government to fully incorporate the effect of externalities in the wider freight market. Allan also highlights the indirect effect of policies such as the phasing out of coal electricity production by 2025 and the effect this has on rail freight, before going on to consider the wider European dimension, and in particular the European Union's attempts to harmonise rail freight operations in its member states. Rail freight was once described as the most 'unique' form of transport (Cowie, 2010), and Allan's chapter simply reinforces this point.

Air freight is a well-used mode in freight markets, yet academically it is a topic that is very much understudied and considerably understated. Nevertheless, it is a subject that presents a multitude of issues with regards to how it actually 'works', or put in more basic terms, how do we end up with those goods going by air that we do and how does this whole process come about? Even the basic issue of how companies make profits out of operating air freight services is not one that can be easily answered. Whilst the subject is deserving of a whole book in itself, Thomas Budd and Robert Mayer's chapter on the air freight industry goes some way to addressing many of these points, certainly in terms of highlighting the key aspects to be considered. It will come as no surprise that while operational elements are key, they are key with respect to being key cost drivers, and what drives most other issues is related to the economics of the mode. This covers aspects such as revenue management, passenger aircraft belly holds as goods in joint supply, competition from other modes, cost drivers in other elements of the supply chain and the wider implications of global trade and global economics. What Tom and Robert's chapter highlights particularly well is the role of air freight in the whole competitive process and its strong position in the logistical chain. To that can be added the almost latent demand nature of the mode, where very quick delivery times enable logistic chains to operate at close to maximum capacity, as any problems that may arise, such as the breakdown of machinery used in the production process, can be quickly corrected through fast (air cargo) supply. One final point on this chapter is that it further highlights and stresses the diversity that exists in the wider freight market, and this is a common theme that has emerged through all of the chapters in this section of the book.

The final chapter in the section is on intermodal freight transport, which is an area that certainly within a European context has been and continues to be relatively high on the political/policy agenda. In reality, however, it is considerably underdeveloped as a mode of freight transport. This clearly begs the question as to why this should be the case. In terms of the former, it is a relatively 'attractive' area for policy development, and fills the requirement that politicians be seen to be doing something regarding the problem of the dominance of road haulage in the freight sector with its associated problems of environmental pollution and traffic congestion. In that context, intermodal transport appears to be relatively progressive and thus offers great potential. The reality is very different, and Jason Monios' chapter outlines the underlying economic principles that operate within the sector, in particular focusing on costs and how these accumulate as output (i.e. the provision of intermodal services) increases. A particular strength within this chapter is a practically orientated insight into the workings of the sector, the main actors involved, and through this Jason identifies the key factors in the successful operation of intermodal terminals. This is then related to mainstream economic theory, and the issue of the provision of overcapacity is highlighted. Interestingly, Jason highlights a lack of knowledge as to what would constitute an appropriate intermodal market structure/form that would be consistent with delivering desirable market outcomes, and this is added to the failure to spend the limited government budgets that are available. Both factors suggest a massive gap between policy perceptions and the realities of the economics of intermodal transport.

1.3 Closing remarks

In bringing together this edited collection of chapters, the editors hope that the reader gains a real insight into the practical economics behind the workings of five key areas in transport economics. The list of chosen topics and chapters is not exhaustive – transport economics is far too large a subject area to be included in one single volume – however, what has been outlined is intended to provide a high-level starting point for anyone interested in these subjects. In bringing these chapters together we have also attempted to strike a balance between theoretical underpinnings, academic discipline and practical application, which sometimes is a very hard line to tread, but what should be apparent is that the study of transport as a subject can considerably benefit from the application of economics as a discipline.

Notes

1 There are many others not so complimentary!
2 This specifically relates to trade agreements and the breaking down of trade restrictions in terms of quotas and tariffs. Such change, however, has been driven by the knowledge that trade is good for everyone, in other words, the General Agreement on Tariffs and Trade was brought about and has been driven by the underlying economics relating to economic prosperity and trade.
3 This is for tonne kilometres, which will give a higher share than either tonnes lifted or value, hence as a market share figure, this may be considered to slightly overstate the case. It does nevertheless underline the significance of maritime transport in the wider freight market.
4 Even in the US context, where rail freight market share (when expressed as tonne kilometres) remains at a relatively high level, this has seen consistent long-term decline, albeit not on the same scale as in Europe.

References

Baumol, W. (1982). Contestable Markets: An Uprising in the Theory of Industry Structure. *American Economic Review*, 72(1), pp. 1–15.
Cowie, J. (2010). *The Economics of Transport*. London: Routledge.
Dupuit, A. J. E. (1844). De *la mesure de l'utilité des travaux publics*, Annales des ponts et chaussées, Second series, Vol 8. Translated by Barback, R. (1952). On the Measurement of the Utility of Public Works. *International Economic Papers*, 2, pp. 83–110.
EU (2016). *Statistical Pocketbook 2016, EU Transport in Figures*. Luxembourg: Publications Office of the European Union.
Ministry of Transport (1964). *Road Pricing: The Economic and Technical Possibilities* (Smeed Report). London: Stationery Office.
Pigou, A. C. (1920). *The Economics of Welfare*. London: Macmillan.
Stigler, G. J. (1961). The Economics of Information. *Journal of Political Economy*, 69, pp. 213–25.
Von Mises, L. (1949). *Human Action*. New Haven, CT: Yale University Press.

Part I
Public transport

2

Passenger rail structure and reform

Simon Blainey

2.1 Introduction

This chapter examines the economics of passenger railways, the features of different structures of passenger railway operations, how these structures have changed over time and how they are continuing to change. It begins by examining the drivers of passenger rail economics, to provide an overview of the factors which affect the success (or otherwise) of particular structures. It then considers four main categories of operational structure, focusing on the extent to which they are integrated both vertically and horizontally, and providing examples of their application in practice. Issues relating to regulation and ownership are then discussed, and the chapter concludes by assessing recent changes to the structure of passenger rail markets around the world and the lessons which can be learned from these changes.

There is a commonly held 'Eurocentric' view that, in recent years, the majority of passenger rail markets have undergone a transition from a 'traditional' model of a state-owned monopoly railway operator to a 'revisionist' model comprising a single infrastructure provider with competitive tendering for the right to operate passenger services, supplemented by additional 'open access' operators. In reality, the situation is much more complex, with a high degree of variation both in operational structures between and within countries and in how these have changed over time. This chapter aims to illustrate both the diversity of operational structures and the most common variants which exist or have existed around the world.

While this chapter focuses specifically on passenger traffic, with freight traffic considered later in the book, it is also important to note that for much of railway history such a divide between passenger and freight operations would have been seen as artificial and unrepresentative of reality. Until the second half of the 20th century, the majority of railway operators dealt with both passenger and freight traffic, although there has been an increasing trend in recent years towards operators specialising in only one traffic type. This has been driven partly by a decline in one or other of the markets, and partly by changing regulatory ideologies. Despite this, on many railway networks passenger and freight traffic still operate alongside one another, and this means that it is not realistic when assessing the merits of different organisational structures to treat passenger traffic in isolation.

2.2 Drivers of passenger rail economic performance

Before considering possible organisational structures for passenger railways, it is helpful to briefly outline the key drivers of economic performance for such operations. A simplistic viewpoint might be to assume that the profitability (or otherwise) of a passenger rail operation is dependent on whether the revenue generated from fares is sufficient to cover the costs incurred in operating the services. In practice, things are a little more complicated than this since the costs of operating passenger railways are made up of a number of different components, with key elements briefly summarised as follows:

- Construction and maintenance of infrastructure: construction costs are usually incurred before services commence, and are predominantly made up of sunk costs. Maintenance costs will be incurred at intervals throughout the life of the infrastructure, and will be partly determined by the volume of traffic which operates. The extent to which passenger services are expected to cover these costs will vary from railway to railway, but on historic networks the initial construction costs have now been written off in most cases. On mixed traffic railways the share of infrastructure costs attributed to passenger and freight services can be a matter of some contention.
- Provision of signalling and safety systems: these systems are essential for the operation of railway systems, and are almost always common across all services operating on a particular route. They are usually managed and operated by the same company as the fixed infrastructure, even in vertically separated operations, although most modern signalling systems include an on-train component.
- Purchase, maintenance and operation of rolling stock: while the characteristics of rolling stock can vary hugely between operators and services, the cost of providing sufficient trains forms a significant proportion of the marginal costs of providing additional services on passenger railways.
- Staffing: this also forms a substantial proportion of the marginal costs of providing additional services, both in terms of customer-facing staff such as drivers, guards, revenue protection and (in some circumstances) station staff, and back office staff responsible for everything from management to infrastructure maintenance.
- Ticketing and information systems: while these will form a relatively small component of total costs, passenger expectations in this area have increased in recent years with developments in ICT.
- Ancillary services: passenger railway systems may decide to offer services to their passengers which go beyond simply running a train from A to B. For example, they might provide an on-board catering service, or Wi-Fi access on trains and stations. While charging for such services should in theory cover their costs, in practice it can be extremely difficult to make money from on-board catering (Briginshaw, 2013), and there is an increasing expectation that Wi-Fi services should be provided on a complimentary basis.
- Energy: the costs of the energy required both to operate trains and to provide power for railway-related systems can be substantial and are usually outside the control of the railway operator. However, because rail is usually a relatively energy-efficient mode (Pritchard et al., 2015), rising energy prices can actually have a positive impact on the economic performance of railway operators which are subject to competition from other modes.
- Managerial, regulatory, legal and transaction costs: the structure of a passenger railway operation will in itself have an impact on economic performance, depending on the level and cost of the interfaces which are required with other companies and with government.

Set against these costs there are also a number of potential sources of revenue for passenger rail operators:

- Fares: revenue from ticket sales is the most obvious source of income for passenger railways, but may be limited by factors such as government regulation.

- Ancillary services: rail operators will often also generate revenue by providing services which are complementary to their primary business of moving people from one place to another. These include things such as providing car parking at stations and selling refreshments on trains or stations.
- Subsidy: it is neither possible nor desirable to capture all the benefits generated by passenger rail operations through the fare box. For example, rail services may help to relieve road congestion, increase social inclusion and generate wider economic benefits. There can therefore be sound economic arguments for local or national governments to subsidise both the construction and the operation of passenger rail services.
- Land grants: it has not always been politically acceptable to subsidise railway operators, and therefore in lieu of subsidy there have been occasions in the past where governments have given railway companies land grants to encourage them to construct routes which would not otherwise have been economically viable. An example is provided by the US Transcontinental Railroads constructed in the 19th century, where such grants generated substantial fortunes for the promoters of the railroads (Wolmar, 2013).
- Property: a more common source of revenue for railway companies has been to carry out property developments on or around their stations. This has the dual effect of generating revenue through rent or sales and generating additional patronage as a result of the increased levels of population and economic activity around the station.
- Non-rail businesses: some rail companies may be involved in providing other forms of transport, such as bus services, or in unrelated areas of economic activity. Revenue from these businesses may in some circumstances be used to subsidise less profitable rail operations.

It is therefore clear that the drivers of passenger rail economic performance are many and varied, depending on the balance between the different factors which generate revenue and incur costs. While the level of traffic which is generated and the costs of operating services will almost always be crucial, the relative importance of different factors will vary between railway systems and over time, meaning that an organisational structure which works in one context may not necessarily be directly transferable to a different situation.

2.3 Organisational structures of passenger rail operations

Railway organisational structures are commonly differentiated by the extent to which operations are integrated 'vertically' and 'horizontally'. Vertical integration describes the extent to which the different elements of railway operations are owned and operated by the same business, focusing particularly here on whether the operation of train services and infrastructure construction and maintenance are controlled by the same firm. Horizontal integration describes the extent to which all railway operations within a given area (usually a nation state) are controlled by the same firm, considering either the relationship between passenger and freight services (Cantos et al., 2010) or the relationship between different passenger services in the area of interest. Because this chapter is concerned with passenger railways, it will focus primarily on the latter type of horizontal integration.

This section describes the four main options for railway organisational structure based on these two types of integration (or separation). While this classification provides a convenient means of differentiating between structures, it should be noted that each option contains a number of possible variants (particularly with regard to regulation and ownership, which are discussed in Section 2.4), and that there is not always a clear distinction between the options in practice, meaning that certain railway operations may not fit neatly into one of the categories. As stated above, the discussion focuses primarily on the extent to which infrastructure and operations are integrated, but it is important to remember that there are also other elements of railway operations which may or may not be integrated, such as the ownership and maintenance of rolling stock.

2.3.1 Vertical integration, horizontal integration (a)

This describes a situation where a single company controls all aspects of railway operations from track maintenance to train operations within all geographic areas of a state or region. This monopoly provision can be enforced through legislation, or may alternatively be the result of a competitive process where one railway provider has purchased, merged with or driven to bankruptcy all other providers. In practice, it is relatively rare for absolutely every railway within a region to be controlled by the national operator, and there will often be a number of other small independent (and usually vertically integrated) operations which serve small local markets whose needs are not met by the national railway system.

This structure is sometimes (rather misleadingly) known as the 'traditional' mode of railway operation, perhaps because it was the predominant structure in Europe for much of the 20th century. Examples of this structure include state railway operators such as British Railways (1948–94) and Indian Railways (1951–date).

Because network industries like railways have high fixed (and sunk) costs and very low marginal costs (Mulder et al., 2005) they tend to generate significant economies of scale, hence under such a structure the potential to fully achieve these economies may be realised. There may also be direct production efficiencies which can be obtained by the same company producing both rail infrastructure and rail operations, and Ivaldi and McCullough's (2004) study of US freight railroads found that such economies meant that the separation of infrastructure from operations would lead to a 20–40 percent loss in technical efficiency, and that horizontal separation of on-rail operations would lead to an additional 70 percent loss in operational efficiency. While these findings may not be directly transferable to passenger railways, Ivaldi and McCullough speculated that the relative complexity and inflexibility of passenger operations might lead to even stronger vertical economies between infrastructure and operations. A vertically and horizontally integrated structure allows economies of scale and density to be exploited to the full.

This structure also reflects the natural monopoly characteristics of at least some elements of railway provision, particularly infrastructure provision (Preston, 2009). It is not necessarily clear that all elements of passenger railways are natural monopolies, with for example train operations potentially being contestable (Pollitt and Smith, 2002).

Full integration minimises transaction costs which are incurred when dealing with the interfaces between different companies, and can help reduce the level and complexity of regulation which is required. It should provide clear accountability when things go wrong, as problems cannot simply be blamed on companies operating different parts of the railway system. Integration should also make it easier to provide a homogeneous customer experience for rail passengers, which can make rail travel more attractive by reducing their mental workload (Stanton et al., 2012).

In situations in which there is a social case for subsidising passenger services on routes where revenue will not be sufficient to cover costs, a fully integrated operation allows the whole system to be viewed and funded as a single integrated entity. In the case of finance, the relative levels of public and private (passenger) funding can be determined and set at rates which are deemed to be 'equitable' across the whole network, so that all potential users have approximately equal access in terms of cost. Under a fragmented system, there is a danger that the surplus revenue raised from the more popular routes/areas gets drained off in the form of private sector profits, i.e. a form of cherry picking, with a higher level of public subsidy then being required to finance loss-making but societally important services. Finally, integration simplifies the allocation of contributory revenue, where passengers use quieter services as 'feeders' for trips made mainly on busier routes (Jackson et al., 2012), and which may therefore help justify subsidising the quieter services.

As regards disadvantages, it is often suggested that the absence of competition inherent with a fully integrated structure will lead to x-inefficiencies and cost inflation in large national railway operators. This is because, in theory, a competitive market in the long run will increase the productive efficiency of the firms within it, as only the efficient firms are able to survive and keep pace with technical change. However, this only applies where markets are perfectly competitive, which is not the case for the passenger rail market, due to factors including capacity limitations and the presence of significant barriers to entry. It is incorrect to suggest that fully integrated national railway systems in the 21st century do not face competition, as in fact they are subject to high levels of competition from both road and air transport, which led to a significant contraction in passenger railway service provision in many countries in the second half of the 20th century. This, together with limits on government spending, has meant that in fact integrated railways have been forced to improve their efficiency in order to remain in operation, and where passenger railways have been unable to make sufficient efficiency savings, or to justify their need for government subsidy, they have tended to simply disappear (as occurred in Mexico in 1997, for example).

An example of inefficiencies associated with fully integrated railways is the leakage of profits (or subsidy) to provide higher wages to staff, particularly in situations where powerful trade unions can 'hold operators to ransom' by threatening to bring services to a halt. However, if operators require highly skilled workers who are in limited supply and are expensive to train (which in many countries includes train drivers, for example), separated railways may in fact be more vulnerable to wage inflation. This is because it may be more cost effective for an operator to offer staff working for a neighbouring operator a small pay rise to move companies than to train their own staff from scratch (particularly if additional staff are required at short notice), which can then initiate a cycle of pay increases as operators strive in turn to 'poach' staff from their competitors.

Finally, it is sometimes suggested that integrated railways will have less incentive for innovation. This again is due to a supposed absence of direct competition and is another component of Leibenstein's x-inefficiency. As a consequence, such operators may be less agile in serving new markets and/or in seeking and responding to new marketing opportunities than companies in separated structures.

2.3.2 Vertical integration, horizontal separation (b)

This structure has two key variants. The first variant involves having a number of different vertically integrated railway companies serving different parts of a country, with little or no spatial overlap and therefore little or no competition between operators. This is the predominant structure for passenger railways in Japan (since 1987) and Switzerland; two systems which are often held up as being exemplars of good practice in rail operations.

The second variant of this structure involves having multiple vertically integrated railway companies competing for traffic in the same part of a country, with different companies potentially having separate infrastructure serving the same corridor. Such a structure is likely to arise when there is a lack of both regulation and intermodal competition for railways in regions where there is a significant volume of traffic available. It is unlikely to persist if the level of competition from road and air transport increases, when the volume of traffic available may fall to a level where it is insufficient to sustain multiple railway routes. This increased competition for traffic, together with the economies of scale which are inherent to railway operations, means that in such circumstances companies are likely to progressively merge or be taken over, with rationalisation of infrastructure on corridors where multiple routes exist. Such a structure existed in the UK until 1923 (and to a lesser extent until 1948), and was also the model for passenger services in the US until the formation of Amtrak in 1971.

It should be noted that a horizontally separated structure does not preclude operators from accessing infrastructure owned by other operators, meaning that cross-boundary services are still possible, but such access will usually be on the basis of negotiation and not of right (Mizutani et al., 2014).

With regionally separated operations, the advantages and disadvantages are likely to be similar to those of fully integrated operations, although potentially with some loss of economies of scale depending on the size of the networks. Preston (1994) stated that the optimal network length for railway systems was around 5,500 km, and that there might therefore be economic arguments for horizontally splitting operators which were significantly larger than this. There are relatively few advantages which are unique to a structure where vertically integrated operators compete for traffic in the same region, as while it could be argued that competition might increase efficiency, any efficiency gains would almost certainly be insignificant compared to the cost involved in providing multiple independent sets of infrastructure.

As stated above, the most obvious disadvantage of this structure is the wasteful and inefficient overprovision of rail infrastructure, particularly on corridors with high traffic density. This is because two competing double-track routes provide significantly less capacity than a single integrated four-track route, as the latter arrangement allows higher and lower speed trains to operate on separate tracks.

Depending on the level of regulation there may also be a lack of integration between operators, which can cause problems for through passengers if, for example, there are no through fares, or if different operators use stations on opposite sides of a town. A lack of integration also means that passengers might perceive that there is a lower level of service than if the same number of services was provided by a single integrated operator. There may also be technical problems associated with a lack of integration between networks. For example, different companies may use different signalling systems, requiring through trains to have multiple system capability installed (as is the case for many international services in Europe), which adds extra cost.

2.3.3 Vertical separation, horizontal separation (c)

With this structure, different companies are responsible for different elements of railway operations, and for particular elements (for example train operations) in different parts of a country. In such a vertically separated structure at least some level of regulation is essential in order to manage relationships between the different businesses involved in providing railway services. Structures of this type tend to be introduced by governments with the aim of encouraging competition, improving efficiency and providing a more 'open' market for rail service provision.

There are a number of different variants of this structure, as for example vertical separation of train operations from infrastructure can be achieved in several different ways. There may be complete institutional separation (the current model in Sweden and the UK), separation of infrastructure and operations into separate subsidiaries within a holding company (the current model in Germany) or separation of key functions, such as train slot allocation and infrastructure charging, into a separate body (the model in France from 1997 to 2014) (Mizutani et al., 2014).

In practice, it is unusual for there to be horizontal separation of infrastructure operations into regional companies within a single country, although a shift towards this model has been proposed recently for the UK as one of the options being considered in a review of the national infrastructure provider Network Rail's structure is devolution of control over assets to separate 'divisions' (Shaw, 2015). Such a model is actually little different to the current situation facing international passenger service operators in Europe, who have to deal with multiple infrastructure providers when services cross international borders. It is also in some ways similar to the structure used for long-distance passenger services in the US, where Amtrak's trains run across the networks of multiple vertically integrated but horizontally separated private freight railways (Thompson, 2003).

However, it is much more common to have a mixed model with horizontal integration for infrastructure provision but horizontal separation for passenger train operations, and this is the current structure in many European countries. Within this structure there are then two possible means of introducing competition to the market. The first structure involves having off-rail competition (competition *for* the market) for franchises or concessions, with different companies bidding for the right to operate train services. This structure was pioneered by Sweden (with separation of infrastructure and operations in 1988) and then applied with a greater level of disaggregation in Great Britain from 1994. It is broadly equivalent to a system of 'quality contracts' for bus operations, as used in London. Franchising is also used for regional services in Germany, but is subtly different in that firstly, the state-owned national operator still exists and, secondly, the holding company model means there has not been full institutional separation (Nash, 2008). There is a similar situation in the Netherlands, where a state-owned firm (Nederlandse Spoorwegen) provides intercity services and a separate state-owned firm (ProRail) manages infrastructure, with concessions for regional passenger services allocated by competitive tendering.

The alternative is to have on-rail competition (competition *in* the market) for passengers, with operators bidding for individual train paths on the infrastructure network. This is the so-called 'open-access' solution, which is broadly equivalent to the deregulated bus market in the UK and is rare in practice for passenger railways, although intercity passenger services in some parts of Europe are moving towards this model. On-rail competition is much more common for freight traffic and has been introduced almost universally across Europe.

The main argument for introducing a fully separated structure is that competition should in theory drive down costs, increase industry competitiveness and improve services for passengers. However, there is only limited evidence to support this claim in practice.

Asmild et al. (2009) observed that accounting separation of railway functions led to a significant improvement in technical efficiency. However, Mizutani et al. (2014) could not find any strong evidence that the introduction of competition had any cost-reducing effects on railways in Europe and East Asia. They found that the holding company model reduced costs compared to vertical integration, but only by a small amount, and this result was of marginal statistical significance. Similarly, Cantos et al. (2010) found that the tendering and franchising process for regional passenger services in Europe did not seem to have contributed to improving efficiency and productivity, probably because of the difficulty of designing a franchising process which could assure efficient and competitive results. Smith and Nash (2014) concluded that structural reforms in Britain did not achieve lasting improvements in cost efficiency, while Preston and Robins (2013) found that in fact the shift from public vertically integrated operators to private vertically separated operators in the UK was welfare negative, probably as a result of the complex and fragmented supply-side organisational structure. They suggested that the cost impact on government was particularly negative as a result of higher costs translating into higher subsidy levels.

Again, while competition should in theory provide operators with incentives to innovate, in some circumstances it may in fact hinder innovation. The profits from innovation may not be sustainable if their presence attracts new entrants (Mulder et al., 2005), so where innovations have a long pay-back period firms may be reluctant to invest in them. In a well-regulated system competition should allow benchmarking of best practice between operators, although in practice companies may be reluctant to share information that could result in them losing competitive advantage.

One argument for adopting a structure where there is competition in the market is that open-access operators will be more agile in seeking out and serving new markets. However, the limited infrastructure capacity, which is an inherent feature of railway networks, can restrict the scope for on-rail competition, and such competition can result in the loss of economies of density, which are found in most integrated railway systems. This is particularly the case where competing operators use rolling stock with different characteristics (Mulder et al., 2005). By abstracting demand and therefore profits from services on busier routes, open-access competition can also increase the cost to government of providing unprofitable but socially necessary services elsewhere on the network.

With regard to disadvantages, the overall impact of separation on costs is rather mixed, and one reason for this is that separation can lead to an increase in transaction costs. Merkert et al.'s (2012) study of the UK, German and Swedish railway systems found that vertical separation only raised 'pure' transaction costs (those associated with negotiating and implementing contracts) by around 2–3 percent of total costs, meaning that only relatively modest savings would need to be made elsewhere to cancel out this increase. However, other transaction costs related to misaligned incentives, meaning that infrastructure and operations are poorly integrated, can potentially be much more substantial, particularly where traffic densities are high (Smith and Nash, 2014). The holding company model is likely to generate lower transaction costs than the institutionally separated model, but potentially only as long as the state railway company continues to operate most services, and Mizutani et al. (2014) note that it loses some of this advantage if new entrants take a significant market share, as envisaged by European Union (EU) legislation (see Section 2.5). The increase in transaction costs may also be exacerbated by a change in industry culture from, as Wolmar (2001) puts it, one of cooperation to one of conflict.

The need for complex regulation to manage the separated structure and ensure that the market operates satisfactorily can also add substantially to costs, as can the expense involved in the franchise competition process, which in Britain has been estimated at around £45 million per franchise process (TUC, 2015). This process may also be subject to a 'winner's curse', where because the franchising processes can incentivise bidders with imperfect information to make as low a tender as possible in order to win a contract, the successful bidder may then find that they are unable to achieve the cost savings and efficiency improvements they had promised (Cowie, 2009). Separation will also tend to reduce economies of scale and scope, reduce the potential for the rail sector to be developed and funded as a single integrated system and potentially increase staffing costs if there is a shortage of people with key skills.

Depending on the effectiveness of regulation there may be a lack of coordination between infrastructure providers and operators. Providing a 'level playing field' for passenger and freight traffic can also be a major challenge for vertically separated railway structures, with the continued risk that operators of one or both types of traffic will claim that they are being unfairly discriminated against.

Finally, it is worth noting that Nash et al. (2014) found no evidence that complete vertical separation leads to more competition. They suggest that in fact where cost savings have accompanied separation, this has arisen from increased transparency and a greater focus on where spending occurs, rather than from the introduction of competition.

2.3.4 Vertical separation, horizontal integration (d)

With this structure different companies are responsible for different elements of railway operations (for example infrastructure provision), but each of the companies is responsible for their 'element' across the whole country. This is not a situation that would tend to develop organically, and where it occurs it is usually either as an intermediate stage between full integration and full separation or as the result of market failure, where politicians and regulators have enforced vertical separation to try to encourage competition, but horizontal separation has failed to occur and the old national train operator has retained a monopoly position. This is similar to the current situation in France, where virtually all trains are still operated by SNCF. A structure of this kind might also be imposed to try to provide a 'level playing field' between passenger and freight operations by separating them into different national companies which can then bid against each other for train paths, although where this has occurred in practice open-access competition has usually been introduced for the freight market (as in several Eastern European countries).

The main potential advantages of this structure over full separation are that it simplifies the retention of common standards across a national rail network and potentially allows some economies of scale and density to be retained.

As regards drawbacks, this structure could be seen as offering the worst of both worlds, by combining the bad features of an integrated structure with the bad features of a separated structure. Cantos et al. (2010) found that where there was not a credible threat of competition, vertical separation was unlikely to have a significant impact on efficiency and productivity. Similarly, Mulder et al. (2005) suggested that because vertical separation will only generate a positive net benefit if there is a strong possibility of competition, in circumstances where this is not the case (for example due to low traffic densities or horizontal integration), the benefits of vertical separation will be negligible compared to the lost economies of scope. Vertical separation will increase costs due to the requirement for interface between different companies and the need for additional regulation, but horizontal integration will mean that any inefficiencies linked to the monopoly provision of services and infrastructure will be retained.

2.4 Regulation and ownership in the passenger rail sector

It is possible for most of the operational structures discussed in Section 2.3 to operate under a range of different regulatory regimes and ownership models, although some structures offer more flexibility in this respect than others.

Ownership models used for passenger railways range from full public ownership through to full private ownership, with various interim models in between these. Full public ownership is most common with operational structure (a) and the spatially separated variant of structure (b). There have been a few occasions where structure (d) has been implemented with full public ownership, with separate public-sector businesses responsible for infrastructure provision and train operations, as is currently the case in France. Full public ownership is not practical with structure (c), although in situations where state railway operations from different countries form a high proportion of the bidders for operating franchises (as is currently the case in the UK) it is possible to come close to a model of this kind.

Full private ownership could be implemented with any of the four structures, at least in theory, although situations where a single private company has a monopoly on passenger railway operations in a state (structure (a)) are rare. A range of mixed ownership models have existed over time, for example the current UK model of public ownership of infrastructure and private operation (at least in theory) of train services. In contrast, the current US model for long-distance passenger services involves publicly operated train services running on predominantly privately owned infrastructure. There have also been situations where publicly and privately owned vertically integrated railways have competed with each other, notably in Canada for much of the 20th century.

It can be difficult to disentangle the advantages and disadvantages of different ownership models from the debate over organisational structures, as changes in ownership have tended to occur at the same time as changes in structure. As with competition, private ownership is in theory supposed to drive down costs (both in terms of public subsidy and fares), increase efficiency and make railways more responsive to the needs of passengers. However, private companies may be overly focused on making profits for shareholders, rather than in providing the best service for passengers. Furthermore, (as noted in Section 2.2) there are good arguments for subsidising passenger railway operations in many circumstances. The franchising authority therefore needs to ensure that the specification of any contract ensures that the benefits of private provision over direct public provision result in an 'equitable' share of such benefits and hence avoid the possibility of excessive private sector profits. For more details, see David Hensher's chapter (Chapter 7) in this book on this whole subject area.

Public ownership theoretically allows any profits to be reinvested in services, although in practice they may sometimes be used to fund other areas of government spending. It arguably results in railways having clearer aims, because they should only be focused on providing a good service for passengers at a reasonable cost, rather than also making profits for shareholders. However, public operators have been criticised for being wasteful and inefficient, particularly if management decision making is 'captured' by particular interest groups.

While Boardman et al. (2009) show that privatisation of the Canadian National Railway led to overall welfare gains, this is a freight operator, and they acknowledge that their findings may not be directly transferable to passenger railways. Pollitt and Smith (2002) found that the privatisation and restructuring of Britain's railways generated substantial efficiency savings in the pre-Hatfield period, but subsequent major increases in costs (Smith, 2006) suggest that these savings were not sustainable, and a later study found that both costs per train kilometre and government subsidy had increased significantly since privatisation and restructuring (Preston and Robins, 2013). Cowie's (1999) study of small Swiss passenger railways concluded that privatisation would not in itself lead to higher efficiency, and Crompton and Jupe (2003) report that there were significant cost leakages in the form of dividends and interest payments following the privatisation of Britain's railways in the 1990s. Such payments appear to be related more to the change in ownership than the change in structure, and overall there is certainly not conclusive evidence that privatisation will reduce the costs of passenger railway operations.

The issue of economic regulation is discussed in more detail in Chapter 9, but it needs to be recognised that adequate and effective regulation is crucial if operational structures (c) and (d) are to operate satisfactorily. Regulation is also very important for structure (b) if interoperator traffic is expected to be significant, and has a role to play for structure (a) if there is private ownership to prevent monopoly operators generating excess profits. Independent regulation is perhaps less important with a fully publicly owned and integrated railway system, although it could still have an important role to play in preventing the inefficiencies which are sometimes associated with such systems.

There is a risk that the extensive regulation required for highly separated structures may have the unwanted consequence of significantly increasing costs. Even with comprehensive regulation it can be very difficult for regulators to determine appropriate usage charges for rail infrastructure, for example, because the marginal costs of using infrastructure are usually lower than average costs because they do not cover expenditure on infrastructure construction or upgrades (Mulder et al., 2005). It is also worth emphasising that, as Crompton and Jupe (2003) put it, 'regulation can do little to remedy a fundamentally flawed design'.

As well as economic regulation, regulation for safety is crucial for passenger railways under all operation and ownership models. While railway operators have often resisted such regulation on cost grounds in the past (see for example Aldrich, 2006), the high media profile given to railway accidents means that low safety standards on railways would not be politically acceptable today.

2.5 Historical trends, current status and future developments

In the early days of rail transport, most countries adopted structure (b) for their passenger rail operations, either as a conscious decision or by default due to a lack of regulation. However, some countries, for example Belgium, decided to take state control of their railways from the outset (adopting structure (a)), and in others arguments for 'reform' (i.e. state ownership) were put forward from a very early date (Galt, 1865). Fully integrated publicly owned railway companies became progressively more common over time, so that by the mid-20th century this was the dominant structure for passenger rail operations around the world. Structure (b) with private ownership did persist in some countries, for example the US (where railways have never been fully nationalised), although as competition from other modes increased, the financial viability of this structure tended to decrease.

From the 1970s onwards changes in prevailing economic philosophies led many governments to begin considering alternative structures for railway operations which better reflected neoliberal economic theories. These often included the privatisation of state-owned operators, but in a break with the past this was increasingly accompanied by a separation of functions which had relatively little precedent in railway history up to that point.

This process has been particularly apparent in Europe, and it is therefore worth considering the European example in more detail. The first move towards vertical separation in Europe came with European Directive 91/440 (passed in 1991) which required separate accounting systems for railway infrastructure and operations within all member countries of the European Commission. This separation has subsequently been progressed further through several packages of reform. The First Railway Package, which was in force from 2003, provided for open-access competition for international freight traffic across Europe's railways. The Second Railway Package, effective from 2005, included a range of directives standardising certification, safety and interoperability, and established the European Railway Agency which sets mandatory requirements for railways in Europe. The Third Railway Package, effective from 2007, focused on the 'liberalisation' (i.e. opening to competition) of international passenger services, which was supposed to be completed by 2010.

The three main intentions of this reform process can be summarised as to: 1) separate infrastructure and train operations into separate businesses (at least in terms of their accounting); 2) establish independent regulation of rail systems; and 3) provide open access to the rail operations market in the EU for any firm which wished to introduce services (Friebel et al., 2010). Some countries (for example the UK and Sweden) have introduced a much greater degree of separation than the reforms require, whereas others have only made the minimum level of changes required for compliance. However, the Third Railway Package is not seen as an end point, and there is a progressive move towards further deregulation and privatisation as part of the Fourth Railway Package. As of January 2016 this was still to be approved by the European Parliament, but once enacted it will make it compulsory to introduce competitive tendering for passenger services run under public service contracts and to allow open access for commercial services throughout Europe. While the EU favours the Swedish/British model of vertical separation, the Fourth Railway Package does not make this compulsory, instead proposing strict safeguards to ensure fair access to all operators.

The reforms being undertaken in Europe are seen as a way of helping meet the European Commission's goal of making rail the preferred transport mode for 'medium-distance' passenger travel. However, as set out above, the evidence supporting this restructuring is rather inconclusive, and it has proved difficult to establish any association beyond coincidence of timing between growth in rail use in Europe since the 1990s and the reforms which have been implemented over the same period (Preston, 2009). There appears some merit in the argument put forward by Crompton and Jupe (2003) that the restructuring and separation of passenger rail systems in order to introduce competition is driven as much by ideology as by firm evidence that such restructuring is in the best interests of passengers or taxpayers.

The situation beyond Europe is (unsurprisingly) varied, with a few countries gradually moving towards a separated model (for example Australia, particularly for interstate services), but with many others retaining a more traditional vertically integrated structure.

When considering the potential for restructuring railways, it should be noted that any change in the structure of passenger rail operations will almost certainly incur substantial transitional costs (Preston and Robins, 2013). For example, Pollitt and Smith (2002) estimated that restructuring costs associated with the privatisation of British Rail were around £1.4 billion. This clearly means that such changes should not be undertaken lightly. Friebel et al. (2010) found that 'reforms' tended to lead to a greater improvement in efficiency if they were introduced sequentially rather than if a number of measures were introduced simultaneously, and this is broadly the approach which has been followed in Europe in recent years (Preston, 2009). Such a gradual approach also has the advantage that it allows the effectiveness (or not) of individual components of the reform to be assessed, and makes it easier for ineffective measures to be reversed.

The available evidence suggests that the 'best' structure may potentially be different for railways with different characteristics. Mizutani et al.'s (2014) study of railways in Europe and East Asia found that vertical separation increased costs (relative to vertical integration) on intensively used networks and reduced them on lightly used networks, perhaps because coordination problems associated with vertical separation are more severe with high traffic densities. Similarly, Smith and Nash (2014) concluded that while vertical separation could be effective for lightly used networks (perhaps because in such circumstances there is more scope for competition to drive an increase in service levels), it will perform less well on intensively used networks, where misaligned incentives often lead companies to attempt to optimise their own costs rather than those of the system as a whole (Nash et al., 2014). If this is true then it has significant implications for policy in the EU. The European Commission's 2011 Transport White Paper contains various aspirations for rail transport which would, if achieved, greatly increase the density of traffic operating on Europe's railways. However, as traffic densities increase, this would mean that the costs associated with the vertical separation advocated in the Fourth Railway Package as a means of making rail travel more attractive would themselves increase, thereby undermining the justification for introducing the reforms in the first place. If European policy makers are serious about achieving the mode shift objectives contained in the 2011 white paper they should therefore ensure they consider the full impacts of the proposed reforms, as it may be that a more integrated passenger railway structure could be more effective in delivering cost-efficient railway operations which are capable of achieving wider transport policy goals.

References

Aldrich, M. (2006). *Death Rode the Rails: American Railroad Accidents and Safety 1828–1965*. Baltimore, MD: Johns Hopkins University Press.

Asmild, M., Holvad, T., Hougaard, J. L. and Kronborg, D. (2009). Railway Reforms: Do They Influence Operating Efficiency? *Transportation*, 36, pp. 617–38.

Boardman, A. E., Laurin, C., Moore, M. A. and Vining, A. R. (2009). A Cost-Benefit Analysis of the Privatization of Canadian National Railway. *Canadian Public Policy/Analyse de Politiques*, 35(1), pp. 59–83.

Briginshaw, D. (2013). Train Catering: Achilles' Heel or Unique Selling Point? *International Railway Journal*, www.railjournal.com/index.php/rolling-stock/train-catering-achilles-heel-or-unique-selling-point.html

Cantos, P., Pastor, J. M. and Serrano, L. (2010). Vertical and Horizontal Separation in the European Railway Sector and Its Effects on Productivity. *Journal of Transport Economics and Policy*, 44(2), pp. 139–60.

Cowie, J. (1999). The Technical Efficiency of Public and Private Ownership in the Rail Industry: The Case of Swiss Private Railways. *Journal of Transport Economics and Policy*, 33(3), pp. 241–52.

Cowie, J. (2009). The British Passenger Rail Privatisation: Conclusions on Subsidy and Efficiency from the First Round of Franchises. *Journal of Transport Economics and Policy*, 43(1), pp. 85–104.

Crompton, G. and Jupe, R. (2003). 'Such a Silly Scheme': The Privatisation of Britain's Railways 1992–2002. *Critical Perspectives on Accounting*, 14, pp. 617–45.

European Commission (2011). *Roadmap to a Single European Transport Area: Towards a Competitive and Resource Efficient Transport System*. Brussels: European Commission.

Friebel, G., Ivaldi, M. and Vibes, C. (2010). Railway (De)Regulation: A European Efficiency Comparison. *Economica*, 77, pp. 77–91.

Galt, W. (1865). *Railway Reform: Its Importance and Practicability*. London: Longman.

Ivaldi, M. and McCullough, G. J. (2004). Subadditivity Tests for Network Separation with an Application to US Railroads. *Social Science Research Network*, http://dx.doi.org/10.2139/ssrn.528542

Jackson, J., Johnson, D. and Nash, C. (2012). On the Willingness to Pay for Rural Rail Service Level Changes. *Research in Transportation Business Management*, 4, pp. 104–13.

Merkert, R., Smith, A. S. J. and Nash, C. A. (2012). The Measurement of Transaction Costs: Evidence from European Railways. *Journal of Transport Economics and Policy*, 46(3), pp. 349–65.

Mizutani, F., Smith, A. S. J., Nash, C. A. and Uranishi, S. (2014). Comparing the Costs of Vertical Separation, Integration and Intermediate Organisational Structures in European and East Asian Railways. *Journal of Transport Economics and Policy*, 49(3), pp. 496–515.

Mulder, M., Lijesen, M. and Driessen, G. (2005). Vertical Separation and Competition in the Dutch Railway Industry: A Cost-Benefit Analysis. *Third Conference on Railroad Industry Structure, Competition and Investments, Stockholm*, 21–2 October.

Nash, C. (2008). Passenger Railway Reform in the Last 20 Years: European Experience Reconsidered. *Research in Transportation Economics*, 22, pp. 61–70.

Nash, C. A., Smith, A. S. J., van de Velde, D., Mizutani, F. and Uranishi, S. (2014). Structural Reforms in the Railways: Incentive Misalignment and Cost Implications. *Research in Transportation Economics*, 48, pp. 16–23.

Pollitt, M. G. and Smith, A. S. J. (2002). The Restructuring and Privatisation of British Rail: Was It Really That Bad? *Fiscal Studies*, 23(4), pp. 463–502.

Preston, J. (1994). Does Size Matter? A Case Study of Western European Railways. *Universities Transport Study Group Conference, Leeds, January*.

Preston, J. (2009). Railways in Europe: A New Era? *Built Environment*, 35(1), pp. 5–17.

Preston, J. and Robins, D. (2013). Evaluating the Long-Term Impacts of Transport Policy: The Case of Passenger Rail Privatisation. *Research in Transportation Economics*, 39, pp. 14–20.

Pritchard, J., Preston, J. M. and Armstrong, J. (2015). Making Meaningful Comparisons Between Road and Rail: Substituting Average Energy Consumption Data for Rail with Empirical Analysis. *Transportation Planning and Technology*, 38(1), pp. 111–230.

Shaw, N. (2015). *The Future Shape and Financing of Network Rail: The Scope*. London: Stationery Office.

Smith, A. S. J. (2006). Are Britain's Railways Costing Too Much? Perspectives Based on TFP Comparisons with British Rail 1963–2002. *Journal of Transport Economics and Policy*, 40(1), pp. 1–44.

Smith, A. S. J. and Nash, C. (2014). Rail Efficiency: Cost Research and Its Implications for Policy. Discussion paper 2014–22, International Transport Forum, Roundtable Efficiency in Railway Operations and Infrastructure Management, Paris, 18–19 November.

Stanton, N., McIlroy, R., Harvey, C., Blainey, S. P., Hickford, A. J., Preston, J. M. and Ryan, B. (2012). Following the Cognitive Work Analysis Train of Thought: Exploring the Constraints of Mode Shift to Rail Transport. *Ergonomics*, 56(3), pp. 522–640.

Thompson, L. (2003). Changing Railway Structure and Ownership: Is Anything Working? *Transport Reviews*, 23(3), pp. 311–55.

TUC (2015). *Towards Public Ownership*. London: Trades Union Congress.

Wolmar, C. (2001). *Broken Rails: How Privatisation Wrecked Britain's Railways*. London: Aurum Press.

Wolmar, C. (2013). *The Great Railway Revolution: The Epic Story of the American Railroad*. London: Atlantic Books.

3
Bus economics

Peter White

3.1 Introduction

This chapter sets out the basic principles of the economics of bus operations, examining costing and pricing concepts. Other factors affecting demand and market share vis-à-vis other modes are considered. The impacts of different regulatory systems are then examined. The main emphasis is on evidence from Britain, given the extensive experience of different regulatory systems and the research literature available, but international aspects are also examined, notably through cases with sharp variations in regulatory practice (especially Chile) and the growing internationalisation of the contract market. The main focus throughout is on 'local' bus services (i.e. those stopping at frequent intervals, mainly kerbside, handling short passenger trips), but reference is also made to the experience of express coach deregulation which has produced somewhat different outcomes to that of local buses.

3.2 The structure of operating costs

3.2.1 The typical pattern in Britain

Table 3.1 shows a recent estimate of the percentage composition of local bus operating costs in Britain, based on work by the TAS consultancy. It can be seen that the largest element in those costs related directly to staff, at 60% of total costs (of which drivers comprise about 40%). Components related to distance run (fuel and spare parts) are approximately 20%, and costs associated with vehicle provision, i.e. depreciation and leasing, form about 10%. Overheads comprise about 9%. Staff-related costs tend to form a larger proportion in the case of operators in London and the south east, reflecting higher staff earnings, and the other elements by definition form a smaller proportion (but are not lower in absolute terms).

A broadly equivalent pattern may be assumed in other countries of similar real income per head levels, although the fuel cost component will vary according to taxation policy (see further discussion below). The fuel element also varies more sharply within a given country in the short term, due to fluctuations in world oil prices. In lower-income countries (such as India), labour forms a smaller proportion of the total, and fuel a relatively larger one.

It follows from this structure that most costs vary by time, rather than distance as such. The purely distance-based element (fuel, tyres and spares) is relatively small, in the order of 20 percent. Nonetheless, unit costs continue to be expressed usually in terms of distance, both in operators' own data and those published by government. However, the value of time-based costs as a better

Table 3.1 Local bus cost structure in Britain, 2011–12

Labour	58.4%
(of which, drivers)	(40.1%)
Costs varying with distance run (fuel, parts)	19.9%
Overheads	8.6%
Depreciation and leasing	10.0%
Claims	3.0%

Source: TAS Partnership, 'Bus Industry Performance 2013', as published in 'Passenger Transport', 30 August 2013

indicator was pointed out over 60 years ago (Buckpitt, 1949). The other important component is that associated with vehicle provision, normally expressed as a charge per vehicle per annum. Where a fleet is directly owned, this will comprise the depreciation charge due, or where leased, the leasing charge. Overhead costs, and those for administrative staff, are also generally allocated on a vehicle numbers basis, since the scale of depots and administrative structure are largely determined by this. A distinction may also be drawn between 'peak vehicle requirement' (PVR), i.e. the number of vehicles in service at the busiest period (typically the morning or afternoon peak, Monday to Friday), and total fleet size (which also includes vehicles undergoing maintenance). Typically, a well-maintained fleet renewed at regular intervals will have an availability of about 90 percent – i.e. a PVR of 90 would correspond to a fleet operated of 100 – but may be lower where older fleets are operated.

As a simple measure of unit operating costs, total bus kilometres run may be divided into total costs to give an operating cost per bus kilometre run. While useful in assessing trends over time (as in British data discussed further below) and making cross-sectional comparisons (subject to broadly similar operating conditions being applicable), this is a poor guide to the allocation of costs within an operation. It also measures an intermediate output (bus kilometres), rather than the ultimate output being produced (passenger trips or passenger kilometres), which is affected by average load carried. Government data published in Britain also cover cost per passenger trip (which do not distinguish trip length effects). In London, a more comprehensive approach is found, with Transport for London publishing estimates of total resource cost (including capital) per passenger kilometre by all public transport modes averaging about 23 pence in 2014–15 (Transport for London, 2015, table 5.1).

3.2.2 Allocating costs within a network

In allocating costs to specific parts of an operation (such as a particular route or time period), the following factors will also apply:

(1) The PVR for the service, determining both vehicle capital costs and overhead allocation. Labour costs for peak-only operations may also be higher per hour worked, due to difficulties in scheduling efficiently for this purpose (even where 'split shift' working is followed, average labour cost per hour is normally higher than for 'straight shift' work). Hence, operations carried out mainly at peak periods tend to have much higher unit costs per bus kilometres than those running for most of the day.

(2) Average speed attained, since the higher the speed the lower the time-based costs per kilometre run.

(3) Vehicle size: capital costs, fuel consumption and maintenance clearly rise with vehicle size, although not necessarily pro rata. Labour costs may also vary, although this will depend on the pattern of local working agreements – for example, in the immediate post-deregulation phase in Britain (from 1986) much lower rates were often negotiated for 'minibus' drivers (locally defined), encouraging widespread adoption of this vehicle type. However, in the longer term, a market-based wage will tend to reflect the local labour market rather than vehicle size as such, and in Britain this regional variation is now much more noticeable than the vehicle size component, removing an artificial incentive to the use of smaller vehicles. While total operating costs rise with vehicle size, unit costs per passenger place kilometre generally fall sharply.

(4) Unit costs at periods of low demand (typically early mornings, evenings and Sundays; and all night where such operations are run) will often be lower in bus kilometre terms, especially if a marginal or escapable costing approach is adopted, since costs of overheads and vehicle provision have already been incurred in meeting peak demand. However, wage agreements may vary (e.g. higher rates for Sunday work), affecting the degree to which marginal operating costs per hour run are lower or higher than weekday work. In many cases, although costs per bus kilometre are lower than the overall average at such times, cost per passenger trip may be high due to poor loadings, often resulting in such services being provided only on a tendered basis even where 'commercial' services operate over the same route during Monday–Saturday daytime periods.

Growing congestion, and the need to ensure service reliability, may thus increase costs even where no increase in service frequency takes place. For example, a route with a round trip time of 60 minutes and headway of 6 minutes would require ten buses and drivers. Even a very small increase in round trip time (up to 6 minutes) would thus increase this to 11 buses (i.e. by 10%), so that total cost will rise by about 8% (if 20% of costs are distance-related), and unit cost per bus kilometre likewise. The most effective means of reducing costs, irrespective of ownership or regulatory pattern, may simply be to increase speeds, through bus priorities and reducing dwell time at stops (for example, by minimising cash fare payment, now completely eliminated in London). Increased congestion also tends to worsen fuel consumption and increase emissions. Recent work by Begg (2016) has shown dramatic increases in scheduled bus journey times over the long term in a number of urban areas, with direct effects on passenger demand (due to greater in-vehicle journey time) and operating costs, plus large secondary impacts where fares are then raised to reflect higher costs.

In contrast to evening and Sunday work, the 'interpeak' period (that between approximately 0900 and 1600) often attracts reasonably good loadings (notably due to free concessionary travel for older people), and the avoidable cost of cutting services substantially below the peak levels at such times may be small, especially if shift-working agreements involve commitments to minimum shift time and pay. Coupled with the high marginal costs of peak-only operation, this has resulted in most operators in Britain offering a similar service level throughout the period between around 0800 and 1800 with only small enhancements at the peaks, often to meet school travel demand, rather than adult journeys to/from work. Recent aggregate data indicate little variation in the number of journeys operated within this period, but a sharp drop in the evenings, especially outside London (Department for Transport, 2014).

3.2.3 Economies of scale

A further consequence of this cost structure is that few economies of scale in direct operating costs may be expected, since the main components (drivers, other staff, fuel and spares) simply rise in proportion to service output. One might expect some economies of scale by depot size, as overheads are split between more vehicles, but the enquiry by the then Competition Commission (2011) only found some limited evidence for economies of scale by depot size (for 'small' depots).[1] In the light of this, the consolidation of the industry post-deregulation into five major operating groups may seem surprising. It should be borne in mind, however, that large organisations may have bargaining power with suppliers in purchase of fuel, spares and vehicles not available to smaller operators. They may also be able to raise capital more easily (either by being seen as lower risk by lenders, or being able to raise equity capital on the stock market) and find insurance easier to obtain (or cover some risks such as vehicle fire and theft internally).

3.3 Operator income and profitability

The principal source of operator income in Britain is revenue from passengers, whether through cash transactions on the vehicle, or off-vehicle ticketing. In addition, compensation is received from local authorities for the net cost (mainly in lost revenue) of offering concessionary fares to certain passenger categories (principally those aged over about 60). The 'fuel duty rebate' introduced in the 1970s offset much of the duty payable on fuel, at a level of 80 percent until recently – the effect of this was to greatly reduce net fuel costs incurred, affecting in particular marginal costs of services. The grant is now known as 'Bus Services Operator Grant' (BSOG), and is based on a more complex formula, incentivising fuel-efficient vehicles and smartcard tickets, but to a large extent remains as a rebate on fuel duty. In defining a 'commercial' service, an operator thus includes all three sources of income. Likewise, where contract payments are received for particular services, this forms part of an operator's business income. Practice in other countries varies, often with compensation paid for low fare levels offered to many categories of passenger.[2]

A return on capital invested will be expected. Where capital has been raised by loan finance, this will appear as a 'cost', but where equity capital is employed it will be in the form of dividend paid out of profits.

A simple measure of profitability is the return on sales margin, usually defined as earnings before interest and taxation as a percentage of total revenue. This provides a quick measure for comparing profit margins over time and between operators. However, a more appropriate measure may be the return on capital employed. This raises somewhat more complex questions of placing a value on the assets of the business, examined in some detail in the then Competition Commission report on the industry (2011).[3]

3.4 The demand for bus services, and elasticity values

3.4.1 Major trip purposes and other market features

The demand for local bus services is characterised by a wide mix of journey purposes, and not dominated by the adult journey to work to the extent that may be assumed. Table 3.2 shows data from the National Travel Survey (Department for Transport, 2015) indicating the composition of local bus demand by trip purpose, and the share which bus holds of travel by all modes for that purpose.

It can be seen that shopping forms the largest single element of bus journeys (25.4%), and also a purpose within which bus holds its second highest market share (8.6%). As a proxy for peak demand, the work and education trip purposes may be taken together (37.2% of all bus trips). The trips for all other purposes, which, broadly speaking, occur at other times, form a majority of total bus trips (62.8%). This mix produces a fairly good balance of peak and interpeak demand, albeit

Table 3.2 Bus journeys by purpose, 2014

Trip purpose	*Percentage of all bus trips [and bus market share of all modes' trips]*
Commuting	18.6 [7.5]
Education	18.6 [9.7]
Shopping	25.4 [8.6]
Personal business	11.8 [7.5]
Leisure	20.3 [5.0]
Other purposes	5.1 [2.6]
All purposes	99.8 [6.4]
Total trips per person per year	59.0 [921]

Source: National Travel Survey England, 2014, table 0409, 'Average number of trips (trip rates) by purpose and main mode: England 2014'. Note that data in the table are shown with trips per person rounded as whole numbers, from which above percentages have been derived. 921 is the total trips by all modes

with the risk that dependence on shopping as a trip purpose may be affected by the shift of activity away from traditional urban centres and growth in internet shopping. It should be noted that work trips are somewhat longer than those for other purposes, and thus form a greater share of bus travel when total passenger kilometre are used as the base.

The National Travel Survey also indicates the relatively higher share of demand taken by local bus among the youngest and oldest age groups, namely those still in education and younger adults, and those who are retired. Market penetration in the working-age adult group is more limited.

A correlation may be found between car ownership, income level and bus use. Typically, bus use is concentrated in lower income groups and inversely correlated with car ownership. Hence, rising car ownership will, *ceteris paribus*, cause a reduction in bus use. It should be borne in mind, however, that a considerable scatter is seen around the broad trend, with certain areas, such as Poole, Oxfordshire, and Brighton and Hove, having higher bus use (trips per head per annum) than would be expected from a linear regression of bus trip rates against car ownership (KPMG, 2016, figure 22). Furthermore, even for a given pattern of income and car ownership, bus operators may be able to substantially influence demand by action to improve service quality.

3.4.2 Elasticities of demand

A consequence of the relatively local nature of demand, and limited modal alternatives available, is that short-run demand elasticities for bus travel are relatively low. Typically, for price an average short-run elasticity of about –0.4 may be assumed (a 10% real fares rise would cause a drop in demand of about 4% over about one year), and for service level (expressed as bus kilometres run) a value of about +0.4 (i.e. a 10% increase in service level would cause a 4% increase in demand). For this purpose, changes in bus kilometres run largely correspond to changes in service frequency, although they will also reflect changes in network size and periods of time services are operated. There is some evidence of variations around these averages associated with trip purpose (Balcombe et al., 2004) and peak/off-peak periods, although not always conclusive (Molnar and Nesheim, 2010). Very short trips (below 2km) may be more price sensitive due to the ease of modal substitution by foot or cycle. Evidence from recent service improvements in Australia and New Zealand (Wallis, 2013) indicates much higher service-level elasticities with respect to vehicle kilometres run for periods such as evenings and weekends, of up to 1.1. A wider review of pricing issues is provided in the chapter by Mulley and Batarce (Chapter 4).

Over a longer period, elasticities tend to be of greater magnitude since greater scope exists for substitution by travellers – for example, bringing forward a car purchase decision, or changing travel patterns to reduce frequency of non-work trips.

A further consequence of these elasticities is that, at least in the short run, operators may be able to increase fares in real terms yet nonetheless obtain a net increase in revenue (for example, if 100 trips are made at £1 per trip, revenue is £100. A price increase of 10 percent, to £1.10, would cause a demand reduction to 96 trips, but the new revenue level would be 96 x 1.10 = £105.60). Likewise, a reduction in service, if producing a *pro rata* reduction in costs, would reduce total cost by 10 percent but with a lesser reduction in revenue. However, given the evidence of much higher price elasticities in the long term, such an increase could come close to being self-defeating. For example, if the long-run elasticity were about -0.80, the net increase in revenue would be reduced to about £1.20.

3.5 Developments prior to deregulation

The effects of external changes and the industry's response may be traced from the 1960s, as bus demand declined from high levels in the 1950s due to the impact of growing car ownership. The initial effect was a reduction in demand, to which operators responded by increases in real fares and cutting service levels. These in turn caused further decline (a 'vicious circle' effect), but nonetheless restored a revenue:cost balance. Further impacts were caused by real cost increases, especially as labour costs rose, stimulating further service reductions and/or fare increases. Furthermore, reductions in service levels at off-peak periods did not necessarily produce *pro rata* cost savings (for reasons connected with cost structure, as noted above). The clearest attempt to reduce cost per bus kilometre was by replacing on-board conductors by one-person-operation (OPO), although this saving was to some extent offset by increased running time due to extra dwell time at stops, and service quality was worsened due to slower in-vehicle journeys.

Innovation may also have been deterred by the regulatory system which protected existing operators, and made competition (either through bidding for service contracts or 'on the road') very difficult. Having said this, some useful innovation had occurred during the 1960s and 1970s, notably through the adoption of 'Travelcard' ticketing, in which cards giving unlimited travel within designated zones and periods to the holder avoided the need for cash transactions on-vehicle, and also stimulated additional travel through convenience and the zero marginal cost of extra trips. This was most noteworthy in the West Midlands, which introduced this policy at the same time as a marked shift to OPO from the early 1970s (thus avoiding substantial increases in dwell time), soon followed by other Passenger Transport Executive areas. London did not follow suit until the 1980s (White, 2016).

Powers to finance bus services enabled public authorities, especially those in the then metropolitan counties, to reduce fare levels and increase service levels, thus offsetting the negative effects of car ownership (using the elasticity effects described above), most notably in South Yorkshire, but this incurred high levels of public expenditure, and there were concerns about 'leakage' occurring in payments to inefficient incumbent operators. A further consequence of the regulatory system had been the deliberate encouragement of 'cross-subsidy' in which profitable operations offset losses elsewhere within the same operator's network when applied on a large scale, for example between low car-owning housing estates and more affluent suburbs. This was clearly regressive, in that the lower-income areas tended to be those in which bus operation was profitable. However, the shift under deregulation may have been taken too far, treating daytime and evening markets as separate, whereas over the same route these often comprise different legs of trip chains made by the same individuals.

3.6 Deregulation in Britain

3.6.1 The outcome of express coach deregulation

The first major change in Britain came about through the deregulation of the express coach system in October 1980 under the Transport Act of that year. Both local buses and the coach sector had been regulated under the Road Traffic Act of 1930, but its effects may have been more marked in the latter sector, which began to develop somewhat later than local buses. By 1930 an intensive local bus network already existed in most areas, the main effect of the act being to enable consolidation of such operators into larger regional companies without fear of further competition. Concurrently, express coach development may have been limited at a critical early stage (nonetheless express coaches competing with rail were able to continue, in contrast to the virtual prohibition of such services in most mainland European countries).

In addition to factors affecting costs described for local bus services above, seasonality had major effects on vehicle utilisation, and thus on unit costs. Direct operating costs per vehicle kilometre were typically lower than those for local buses, due to much higher average speeds. Price elasticity is generally higher in the express coach sector, in the order of -1.0 in the short run (White, 2001), due to the greater degree of modal competition (at least on trunk routes) and mix of trip purposes, with a high proportion of discretionary travel (such as visiting friends and relatives).

The 'deregulation' was extensive, removing previous controls on routes operated, timetabling and fares charged. However, quality regulation of safety-related aspects was strengthened through the operator licensing system.

The outcomes of express coach deregulation included a large growth in ridership, of about 50 percent by 1986, with strong price competition on the trunk routes and an overall reduction in price levels. Frequencies, network coverage and service quality were improved. Although there were some cases of service cuts in low-density regions due to loss of cross-subsidy, the overall effect may be judged as generally beneficial. In particular, lower-income users gained, both through the coach service offer itself and effects in stimulating lower prices competition for the off-peak discretionary market by rail. However, the impacts of smaller operators were limited. While many entered the market on deregulation, these were often short-lived. The principal operator, National Express, remained dominant. A major factor may have been the importance of network effects, offering interconnecting services at major hubs, and the marketing strength of large operators. Access to terminals was also a factor. A fuller review is provided by White and Robbins (2012).

The decision to deregulate local bus services under the Transport Act 1985 may have been influenced by the success of the coach deregulation. Its outcome also suggested that simplistic views on the scope for smaller operators to compete may not have been valid, but this lesson did not appear to have been drawn. Furthermore, the different context (notably the mix of trip purposes and resultant price elasticity) may have made extrapolation of the express coach outcome to local buses questionable.

3.6.2 The main components of local bus deregulation in Britain

One difficulty in analysing the impacts of local bus deregulation is the near simultaneous abolition of the metropolitan counties from 1 April 1986. This removed the powers of such authorities to provide high levels of comprehensive financial support, resulting in large fare increases and some service cuts, notably in South Yorkshire. Deregulation of local bus services as such followed from 26 October 1986. As in the case of express coaches, it removed controls over routes and timetables. Fares regulation had been largely removed under the 1980 act, but with limited effect in operator behaviour. In contrast to express coach, a route registration process has remained in place, hence an inventory of routes and timetables can be compiled. A period of notice was stipulated (42 days) for operators to register a new service or amend the route or timetable of an existing service.

It thus became easier for new operators to enter the market, simply by obtaining an operator licence, and then registering the service(s) they planned to run. While an operator licence specified the number of vehicles an operator was allowed to run at any one time, this was based primarily on the adequacy of maintenance facilities (and, later, financial resources) rather than forming a quantity limit on the industry as a whole.

Although often associated with deregulation, privatisation was not coincident with it (indeed, in the express coach case, the intensive competition between National Express and British Rail in the early 1980s took place when both were in public ownership). However, central government took the initiative to privatise those operators directly under its ownership (the National Bus Company in England and Wales and Scottish Bus Group within Scotland). Municipal operators (those owned by local authorities, mainly in larger urban areas) were permitted to continue in public ownership, but as 'arm's length' businesses, hence taken out of direct political control, and separately managed from the local authority as such. They were not permitted to receive general subsidies and had to bid for contracted services on the same basis as other operators. In practice, their owning authorities were often willing to accept lower profit margins than required in privatised companies. Over time, most of the municipal operators have been privatised, including all of those in the former metropolitan counties. However, those remaining have often provided high-quality services – for example, both Reading Buses and Lothian Buses (Edinburgh) have won several awards at the annual UK Bus Awards in recent years.

London was not subject to deregulation and a comprehensive public authority was retained. Bus operations were shifted from the monopolist London Regional Transport (LRT) to a mix of local subsidiaries of that body (all later privatised), and operators new to the London market, gaining service contracts through competitive tendering, creating incentives to control costs and raise service quality – LRT specifying the service level to be provided. A common fare scale was retained and a 'gross cost' contract system adopted, in which revenue was retained by LRT. Each route formed a separate contract, thus making it easier for smaller operators to enter the market (in contrast to network-wide contracts in French cities, for example). The London system thus formed an experimental (albeit unintentional) 'control' case against which the fully deregulated system elsewhere could be compared. However, London is also subject to many specific features which make direct comparisons, even with the larger conurbations, difficult. A preferable approach would have been a genuine experiment in which some of the other conurbations had been subject to a system of control similar to that in London. This would also have avoided the issue of potentially compensating private operators where a form of re-regulation is now proposed through quality contracts (discussed further below).

Under the deregulation of 1986 it was assumed that most services would be operated commercially, i.e. user fares, fuel duty rebate (now BSOG) and concessionary fare compensation would cover all costs (including a profit margin for the operator). It was accepted, however, that a number of services could not be provided on this basis, especially in low-density rural areas. Provisions were therefore introduced for contracted services to be provided in such cases. The local authority specifies the service(s) to be provided, fares typically following commercial services in the same area. These generally fill gaps in the commercial network, both in low-density areas and also during times of day (typically evenings and Sundays) when a commercial service is not registered. The commercial and tendered services thus display considerable intermixing rather than forming separate networks. Most provision is through competitive bidding, but powers also exist for 'de minimus' negotiated contracts when smaller sums are involved. Unlike provision of statutory school transport and compensation for concessionary travel, powers for tendered services are purely discretionary, not mandatory, and there is no general obligation on local authorities to ensure a particular level of service – indeed, several now make no provision for tendered services whatsoever. In practice, about 80 percent of local bus kilometres outside London have been operated commercially, the balance tendered, with some fluctuation from year to year.

3.6.3 Outcomes of local bus deregulation

These may be divided into two main periods:

(1) 1986 to about 2000, characterised by a phase of intensive (but generally not sustained) interoperator competition, an increase in bus kilometres run, and a very sharp reduction in real unit cost per bus kilometres (both in London and the deregulated region). However, ridership losses continued, which combined with an increased bus kilometres run resulted in a marked drop in average load outside London, and an approximately stable cost per passenger trip made. In London loadings were retained, resulting in a similar drop in cost per passenger trip to that in cost per bus kilometre. Total public expenditure fell sharply.

(2) About 2000 to the present. The rate of passenger decline outside London slowed, with a more stable network and greater focus on service quality, together with the effect of universal free travel for older people. In London, marked growth in service levels and other factors resulted in a very large growth in ridership. However, cost per bus kilometre has risen substantially (both within and outside London) and public expenditure has grown rapidly – outside London mainly due to concessionary compensation and within London due to a shift from a break-even position to one involving very high levels of support.

Tables 3.3 to 3.5 provide fuller details of trends in service output, fares, ridership and unit costs; operator income composition; and public expenditure. Limitations are imposed by some discontinuities in data available, notably for unit costs in London after 2007. However, some recent data published by Transport for London (2015) does enable an estimate of trends in real cost per

Table 3.3a Main indicators for local buses in England 1985/6 to 2007/8, inclusive

Variable	*London*	*Met areas*	*Rest of England*
Pax trips	+89%	–42%	–16%
Bus km run	+74%	+5%	+42%
Real fare index	+53%	+94%	+30%
Real cost per bus km*	–30%	–39%	–34%
Real cost per pax trip*	–33%	+10%	+6%

Note: * to 2006/7 only; 'real' at 2007/8 prices
Source: derived from Department for Transport, Public Transport Statistics Bulletins to 2008, inclusive

Table 3.3b Main indicators for local buses in England trends 2004/5 to 2014/15, inclusive

Variable	*London*	*Met areas*	*Rest of England*
Pax trips	+31%	–7%	+9%
Bus km run	+3%	–9%	–1%
Real cost per bus km	n/a	+16%	+19%

Source: Department for Transport, 2015, tables BUS0203b and BUS0406

Table 3.4 Local bus business income in England

Gross income percentage composition in 2009/10				
Region	*Passenger revenue*	*Gross support**	*Concessionary comp*	*BSOG*
London	47	34	12	6
Met areas	56	10	23	10
Rest of England	52	20	20	9

Note: * includes local authority associated expenditure
Source: Department for Transport, 2015, table BUS0501a

Table 3.5 Trends in bus financial support in England

	1999/2000	*2013/14*
BSOG	391	303
Concessionary compensation	592	1049
Local net support	323	885

Note: £m at 2014–15 prices
Source: Department for Transport, 2015, table BUS 0502b

bus kilometre between 2010 and 2011 and between 2013 and 2014, suggesting a reduction of about 3 percent in real terms, albeit from a fairly high absolute level.[4] Note that 1985/6 is taken as a 'base year', i.e. prior to the effects of both metropolitan counties' abolition and introduction of deregulation.

The sharp drop in real unit costs per bus kilometre, of about 45 percent by 1999/2000, both in London and the deregulated areas (White, 2014), may be explained by several factors:

- large staff reductions, especially in engineering and administrative functions;
- increased productivity of drivers, partly through 'flattening out' of peak:off-peak service ratios and producing better driver and vehicle utilisation during the working day;
- use of smaller vehicles, notably minibuses;
- changes in working conditions and pay, with marked regional variations.

Whereas before 1986, operators had made incremental service cuts in response to lost ridership and cut out conductors, deregulation and the threat of competition had a marked effect in forcing a rethink on the whole pattern of working. As services had been cut back, central engineering workshops and administrative structures had not necessarily experienced proportionate reductions. Increased service levels, especially between peaks, reversed a long-term trend of decline in provision. One may thus consider the effects of deregulation (outside London) and competitive tendering (within London) in respect of cost per bus kilometre and increased service levels to be beneficial. However, poorer wages and working conditions represented a loss to workers in the industry. Furthermore, insofar as some of them became eligible for forms of family public assistance due to low incomes, some of the cost savings in the transport budget may have been offset by increased public spending elsewhere.

The substantial increases in costs since 2000 may be attributed to:

- A need to improve wages and working conditions, in order to recruit sufficient staff, especially up to the recession in 2008. The recent KPMG study (2016, page 26) indicates a 21 percent rise in bus driver weekly real earnings between 2000 and 2013. Very marked regional differences exist, with some areas displaying high living costs (such as London and Oxford) needing to offer substantially better conditions than elsewhere.
- A need to insert additional vehicles and drivers into running schedules as congestion worsened, simply to maintain the same frequency (as illustrated earlier), and also ensure adequate reliability. Whereas in the earlier phases of deregulation the traffic commissioners were largely concerned with safety matters, increased emphasis has been placed on running reliable services in accordance with the timetable registered, and applying penalties where this has not been done. In the London case, explicit incentives are built into contracts (using the excess waiting time indicator). This has been particularly noteworthy in the last three years. The KPMG study (2016, figure 9) indicates a broadly stable productivity in terms of bus miles per member of staff between 2004/5 and 2013/14, in contrast to the improvement shown during the earlier phase of deregulation.
- Increases in some other costs, such as insurance.

Despite these increases, real unit costs per bus kilometre remain substantially below those in 1985/6.

In terms of ridership and passenger benefits, a much more mixed picture emerges. As Table 3.3 shows, while aggregate service levels improved, fare levels rose substantially in all sectors. The especially large increase in the metropolitan areas was partly due to the abolition of met counties, but nonetheless real increases continued in that sector, and also elsewhere. Whereas competition succeeded in bringing down costs, and increasing total service output, it did not produce aggregate fare reductions, even where operations had been fairly close to break-even prior to deregulation and some of the reduction in costs might have been passed on in lower fares. Where competition developed, it appeared to be based largely on service frequency, rather than fare levels as such (van der Veer, 2002), hence approximating to classic oligopolistic behaviour. A probable factor is the low short-run price elasticity, meaning that lower fares would produce an aggregate reduction in industry revenue despite ridership growth (compared with the higher elasticity in the express coach service, which produced an approximately stable real total revenue where fare changes occurred). Furthermore, given the disutility of waiting time, passengers tend to board the first bus to arrive rather than wait a possibly uncertain period for one with lower fares.

Underlying these changes were negative factors affecting bus ridership, notably rising car ownership, which has an effect irrespective of bus industry regulation or ownership. One means of looking at this effect is to consider the NTS evidence on bus trip rates by car ownership. In the case of non-car households, bus trip rates were little changed in the period to 1992-94 (White 1997), consistent with the effects of rising real fares and increased service levels offsetting each other (as one might expect, given the similar percentage changes, and magnitude of elasticities). However, in car-owning households, the bus trip rate declined.

The contrast with London is very clear. Within the first phase, broadly stable ridership was retained. In the second phase, analysis is made somewhat more complex by the effects of major improvements in service level. Briefly, the growth appears to be greater than applying existing elasticity values for fare and service changes would suggest, also affected by factors such as the more comprehensive nature of the service (growth has been fastest for evening and Sunday use), reduction in the share of trips made on cash fares and their subsequent complete elimination (improving speed and reliability), extensive bus priorities, etc. External factors have also been favourable in the London case, notably a broadly stable car ownership per head from the mid-1990s, compared with strong growth (from a low base) in some of the older conurbations elsewhere. Population growth and a high level of economic activity have also assisted bus use.

3.7 Evaluating the outcomes of deregulation and competition

The effects on producers, workers, consumers and public spending can be brought together by using cost-benefit analysis, or by modelling of changes. These may necessitate a 'counterfactual' case being proposed against which the outcomes are assessed. An early approach by the author (White 1990) indicated that a net benefit might be estimated from the London outcome, but negative in areas outwith London and the former Metropolitan Counties ('mets'). In the case of the mets, a benefit emerged from deregulation as such, due to a reduction in costs, treating separately the effects of large fare increases following met counties' abolition. A much more recent analysis by Preston and Almutairi (2014) indicates a similar outcome (dependent on modelling frameworks employed). Cowie (2014) uses disaggregate data at the level of individual operators to identify five clusters of performance, suggesting that only two of the clusters (representing about 30% of the cases) was a net user benefit observed.

A major issue arising is the role of competition, which has greatly diminished since the early phase of deregulation. The Competition Commission found that only 2.5% of services experienced effective head-to-head competition over their whole length[5] Given the aggregate nature of data available, it is not always possible to examine localised evidence where competition has occurred to see whether better outcomes were provided, as this would entail analysis at a route or corridor, rather than area, level: for example, the attitude surveys by Transport Focus cover somewhat larger areas than individual corridors, and it would be impracticable to increase sample size on the scale required (House of Commons Transport Committee, 2012). While individual examples can be found of competition inducing improvements in service levels and/or lower fares (Colson, 1996), the overall effects appear limited. In many cases, a commercially-viable service may be sustainable for one operator, but demand is not sufficient to support two or more operators in the long run. Hence at the local level a monopoly often exists, irrespective of whether the operator is locally-owned or part of a larger group.

These issues were examined in the extensive study carried out by the then Competition Commission (2011). Factors inhibiting competition included the problems of setting up an operating base in the 'territory' of another operator, and the tendency of users to board the first bus to arrive. Despite limited evidence for economies of scale, consolidation in the industry has produced an outcome in which about 70% of the turnover is represented by five large groups (Stagecoach, First, Arriva, Go Ahead, National Express). The Commission found that these groups collectively produced a rate of return on capital employed of 13.5%, 3.8 percentage points above the 'normal' cost of capital of 9.7%.

A number of 'remedies' were examined by the Commission (albeit not including the option of London-style contracting in its final report, despite considering this as an option at an earlier stage of its enquiry). These included scope for more extensive inter-operator ticketing (dominance by a major operator of products such as travelcards may make market entry by small operators more difficult), easier access to bus stations, and a more open process for net cost bidding. Changes introduced to date have been more limited, primarily relating to station access. It also planned to extend the 'block exemption' to competition rules which otherwise inhibit inter-operator ticketing, and to make operation of pay as you go smartcards within this framework easier.

A particular issue arising from the monopolistic nature of local operations and the low demand elasticities is that an operator can substantially increase real fares and/or cut services, while facing little threat of competition, even though the operator is not pursuing 'anti-competitive' actions as such. It would therefore be possible for an operator to transfer a substantial consumer surplus into a producer surplus. In the long run, however, higher elasticities may make this course of action less attractive, as the underlying core market is diminished. Conversely, an innovative operator could also achieve a similarly high profit margin (at the level causing concern to the Competition Commission) by offering an attractive service, increasing revenue and profit margin by increasing passenger volume at a given fare level. These issues are examined in more detail elsewhere by the author (White, 2014).

A particularly noteworthy case has been that of First Group, which followed a policy similar to the first hypothetical example described above. Current management has adopted a very different approach, candidly describing the previous image of the company as 'starved of investment, with a culture of cuts and price hikes' (Fearnley, 2015). In some cases, First has faced direct competition from other operators within the same area, whose market share has grown as a result, notably Stagecoach in Sheffield. In other areas, there has been relatively limited direct 'on-the-road' competition, but nonetheless a marked change in management approach has been evident. This has been assisted by the regular attitude surveys carried out by Transport Focus, which have measured indicators such as 'value for money' by the named operator as well as area. Particularly poor results were observed for First in the Greater Manchester area (where it is dominant in the northern half of the conurbation) and in Bristol. These have stimulated substantial fare reductions by First, resulting in a marked change in value for money 'satisfaction' – for example, in the Bristol area from 33 percent in 2012 to 61 percent in 2014 (Transport Focus, 2016). This has been associated with substantial ridership growth. One can thus argue that explicit comparisons with performance elsewhere may cause management action, even in the absence of direct competition. In effect, a self-correcting mechanism may exist, albeit applying on a very long timescale.

The extent to which a larger number of operators serving a given area will stimulate higher bus use can be tested by comparing bus trip rate per head with the degree of market concentration. Government data in Britain now show market shares within each local authority area in England (albeit measured by numbers of registered bus (vehicular) trips, rather than passenger volumes). Expressing this in the form of a Herfindahl index indicates no systematic correlation between low concentration and high bus use – if anything, the opposite can be seen in cases such as Brighton and Hove (KPMG, 2016, figure 24). It should be noted, however, that a low degree of concentration may merely imply a large number of operators running within a given area – they may simply serve different parts of that area (as in Surrey, for example) rather than running in direct on-the-road competition (but greater competition for tendered services in such cases would be beneficial to local authorities in controlling costs).

A further aspect of competitive behaviour is whether competition will necessarily arise to restore conditions where an incumbent had caused the local market to diminish through high fares and/or low service levels. An argument can be made that 'success' rather than 'failure' may attract competition, since a growing market can be more attractive to a new entrant (if one expects a market share of 10 percent, then in absolute terms this will be greater in a growing market than a declining one, and hence more likely to justify commercial operation). One can see in the case of Nottingham, which has an exceptionally high rate of bus use per head, not only competition between two local incumbents who have stressed marketing and service innovations (Nottingham City Transport and Trentbarton) but have also seen entry by local independents, notably 'Yourbus'.

3.8 Experience in other countries

In many respects the closest equivalent to the almost complete deregulation in Britain was that in Chile, especially the capital Santiago, from the late 1970s. The conditions this produced resulted in a very marked shift to a regulated system under public contracts. However, severe problems arose when the whole network was recast in one step as 'TransSantiago' in 2007 (Munoz and de Grange, 2010). In contrast, the approach in the regulated London market has been one of incremental change in the network.

There are a few other cases of attempting to follow the deregulation of local bus services as such in countries of similar income per head to Britain. A deregulation of local bus services in Sweden in 2012 enabling the introduction of additional services produced very little effect (Rye and Wreststrand, 2014), perhaps not surprising given the comprehensive public network already offered, and low population density outside major cities. However, the positive outcome of the express coach case in Britain has been followed by deregulation or extensive liberalisation in several other European countries, notably Sweden and Norway, followed more recently by Germany (in 2013) and France (in 2015). Germany in particular has displayed very rapid growth (Augustin et al., 2014), an initial phase of very strong interoperator competition being followed by some consolidation and emergence of dominant operators. Stagecoach-owned Megabus expanded strongly, both in international services as such and in the operation of wholly domestic express coach services within other European Union states, although many of these services have now been taken over by the dominant German operator, Flixbus.

While on-the-road local bus deregulation on the British model has not been followed elsewhere in Europe, there is concern regarding the value for money in supporting services of incumbent operators, and a shift to competitive bidding. In Scandinavia in particular, this has followed the London model of route-by-route contracts. The growth of a contracting market has also stimulated greater internationalisation of an industry which was previously dominated by publicly owned domestic operators. For example, Arriva (formerly in British ownership, now a subsidiary of DB) expanded into several other European Union member states. Within London's very large market, substantial shares are held by non-UK operators (RATP of France, Abellio of the Netherlands, Comfort Delgro of Singapore and Tower Transit of Australia). A recent shift to competitive tendering in Singapore has resulted in Go Ahead securing gross cost contracts, and the Israeli cooperative Egged has gained contracts in the Netherlands.

3.9 Future policy implications

Reverting to the British case, a strong debate continues as to whether the London model could be adopted elsewhere, especially the other major conurbations. Powers to introduce 'quality contracts' set out under the Transport Act 2000 and Local Transport Act 2008 have had no effect in practice to date. A proposal to introduce such a scheme in Tyne and Wear was reviewed by a three-person panel, which indicated a negative outcome was likely overall. In particular, the loss of future profits by incumbent commercial operators was considered a major factor (Local Transport Today, 2015), and if such compensation were to be paid, this would impose very high costs on the public sector.

3.10 The Bus Services Act 2017

In May 2016 the British government introduced a Bus Services Bill (House of Lords). It received Royal Assent, becoming an Act, in April 2017. Amendments were largely rejected by the government.

The tone of the Act is noteworthy for its marked contrast with the focus on competition per se in the 2011 report of the Competition Commission, and statements by its successor body, the Competition and Markets Authority. The emphasis is on greater coordination of services, with mechanisms set out both for franchise-style operation and more extensive partnerships between operators and local authorities. In brief, the main components are:

(1) 'Advanced quality partnership schemes': in contrast to existing statutory partnerships these would not depend on new infrastructure provision. Specified service standards may include frequency and/or timing. Maximum fare controls are also proposed. These powers would enable a greater degree of coordination than under previous competition policy, although common fare scales cannot be set.
(2) 'Franchising schemes': these can be adopted by Combined Authorities with elected mayors, and by other types of authority (but in the latter cases the Secretary of State's consent would be required). The requirements for consultation and audit are much less onerous than those arising in the Tyne and Wear case. There would be no explicit compensation to existing operators for loss of profits, but no powers to take assets such as vehicles or land. However, a scheme could be revoked with six months' notice on criteria including 'financial difficulties' for the authority (this could create substantial uncertainty for operators). The franchising authority would have the power to obtain information from operators for a period of up to five years before a proposed franchise, including trips, fares, revenue and bus kilometres run, thus removing some of the problems found in the Tyne and Wear case.
(3) 'Enhanced partnership plans and schemes': these create scope for greater coordination, but without full franchising. They would be area rather than corridor based. A scheme may specify requirements on frequency and/or timing and some other aspects (but not control of fares, except prices of multioperator tickets). Registration of services to be with local authority.
(4) Registration of bus services: where an operator seeks to vary or cancel a registration, details are to be supplied of passenger trips, fare paid and revenue to the local authority (this removes an incumbent advantage which has existed for many years, enabling an operator which has deregistered a service on which it knows the revenue to make a net cost bid on this basis).
(5) A new power prohibits local authorities from setting up new bus companies in England (despite evidence of good performance from some companies in this category, as noted above).

Responses from the operating industry generally favour the partnership approach rather than franchising, although a number of operators which have focused on the latter approach (such as RATP Dev and Tower Transit) have favoured its expansion.

3.11 Conclusions

The cost structure of local bus operation indicates little potential for direct operational economies of scale. However, where fairly complete deregulation has been attempted, as in the British case, consolidation into large groups has been observed. The extent of direct competition has been patchy, and in most cases the market appears insufficient to support more than one operator on a specific route in the long term. This in turn creates a danger of exploitation by increasing fares and/or cutting services, which on-the-road competition does not necessarily emerge to correct (but management attitudes may be influenced by evidence from other areas). It must be emphasised, however, that the aggregate nature of data available in Britain inhibits the examination of competition effects on demand at a very local level.

Much clearer evidence exists for the potential to improve efficiency and reduce costs within a comprehensive framework through a system of competitive tendering (as in the London case), as is being increasingly adopted elsewhere.

Notes

1 See paragraph 9.181 of the Competition Commission's report (2011). A 'small' depot was defined as one handing fewer than 3.8 million passengers per annum – at 100,000 passengers per vehicle per annum, this would correspond to 38 vehicles.
2 A review of definitions is currently being conducted by the International Union of Public Transport.
3 See part 10 of the Commission's report (2011).
4 Author's calculations are from data in Transport for London, 2015, pp. 81 and 103, adjusted to real terms by RPI.
5 Competition Commission report, 2011, para 11.11(b).

References

Augustin, K., Gerike, R., Sanchez, M. J. M. and Ayala, C. (2014). Analysis of Intercity Bus Markets on Long Distances in an Established and a Young Market: The Example of the U.S. and Germany. *Research in Transportation Economics*, 48, December, pp. 245–54.

Balcombe, R., Mackett, R., Paulley, N., Preston, J., Shires, J., Titheridge, H., Wardman, M. and White, P. (2004). The Demand for Public Transport: A Practical Guide. Transport Research Laboratory report TRL593.

Begg, D. (2016). The Impact of Congestion on Bus Passengers. Greener Journeys, London, June.

Buckpitt, G. E. (1949). Fallacies of Transport Economics. *Transport World*, 1 August, p. 94.

Colson, B. (1996). UK Bus Deregulation: A Qualified Success with Much Still to Offer Customers and Society at Large. *Transport Reviews*, 16, pp. 301–11.

Competition Commission (2011). Local Bus Services Market Investigation: A Report on the Supply of Local Bus Services in the UK (Excluding Northern Ireland and London). London, 20 December.

Cowie, J. (2014). Performance, Profit and Consumer Sovereignty in the English Deregulated Bus Market. *Research in Transportation Economics*, 48, pp. 255–62.

Department for Transport (2014). Annual Bus Statistics: England 2013–14. London: Department for Transport.

Department for Transport (2015). National Travel Survey: England 2014. London: Department for Transport, September.

Fearnley, G. (2015). First UK Bus Moves Forward in the Right Direction. *Eurotransport*, 2, pp. 13–15.

House of Commons Transport Committee (2012). Competition in the Local Bus Market. Third Report of Session 2012–13, HC10, September.

House of Lords (2016). *HL Bill 58, Bus Services Bill*, 20 July.

KPMG (2016). Local Bus Market Study: Report to Department for Transport. London, January.

Local Transport Today (2015). Report of Quality Contract Scheme Board in Tyne and Wear. 13 November, pp. 4–7.

Molnar, J. and Nesheim, L. (2010). A Disaggregate Analysis of Demand for Local Bus Services in Great Britain (Excluding London) Using the National Travel Survey. December.

Munoz, J. C. and de Grange, L. (2010). On the Development of Public Transit in Large Cities. *Research in Transportation Economics*, 29, pp. 379–86.
Preston, J. and Almutairi, T. (2014). Evaluating the Long Term Impacts of Transport Policy: The Case of Bus Deregulation Revisited. *Research in Transportation Economics*, 48, December, pp. 263–9.
Rye, T. and Wreststrand, A. (2014). Converging Structures? Recent Regulatory Change in Bus-Based Local Public Transport in Sweden and England. *Research in Transportation Economics*, 48, December, pp. 24–32.
Transport Focus (2016). Data from Annual Bus Passenger Survey, made available to the author.
Transport for London (2015). Travel in London, report no. 8.
Van der Veer, J. P. (2002). Entry Deterrence and Quality Provision in the Local Bus Market. *Transport Reviews*, 22(3), July–September, pp. 247–65.
Wallis, I. P. (2013). Experience with the Development of Off-Peak Bus Services. Report by Ian Wallis Associates, Wellington, New Zealand, September, published as New Zealand Transport Agency research report 487.
White, P. (1990). Bus Deregulation: A Welfare Balance Sheet. *Journal of Transport Economics and Policy*, pp. 311–32.
White, P. (1997). What Conclusions Can Be Drawn about Bus Deregulation in Britain? *Transport Reviews*, 17, pp. 1–16.
White, P. (2001). Regular Interurban Coach Services in Europe. Paper in report for the ECMT Round Table 114 (of the same title), Paris, pp. 77–109.
White, P. (2016). *Public Transport: Its Planning, Management and Operation*. London: Routledge.
White, P. (2014). An Assessment of the Competition Commission Report and Subsequent Outcomes. *Research in Transportation Economics*, 48, pp. 277–85.
White, P. and Robbins, D. (2012). Long-Term Development of Express Coach Services in Britain. *Research in Transportation Economics*, 36, 30–8.

4

The pricing of public transport services

Corinne Mulley and Marco Batarce

4.1 Introduction

Fares are money exchange between the passenger and the public transport operator. This simple exchange underpins a complex set of decisions in every urban area which have far-reaching impacts beyond the operation and use of the public transport system. It affects the accessibility of citizens and ultimately impacts urban form.

A fare to the user may be a simple money sum but it is actually part of a system determined by three components: the fare structure, the fare collection and the fare level. The responsible body for setting objectives for public transport will guide how these three elements are combined to provide the fare system in use. This is typically the government that will normally use transport policy to meet not only accessibility outcomes but also to promote social (for example to enhance social inclusion) and environmental (to encourage mode switch to public transport and reduce emissions or to reduce congestion) outcomes. Alternatively, governments may encourage transport authorities to use fares to meet demand management objectives or, if public transport is provided by private operators in a commercial, no subsidy setting, fares will reflect market and probably profit-maximising outcomes. Different objectives clearly lead to different fare levels with different implications.

This chapter develops an understanding of the framework underpinning the setting of fares. It begins with discussing the components of a fare system by looking at fare structures, fare collection systems and fare levels before turning to the micro-economic foundations of fare computation.

The penultimate section looks at how this might be put in practice using, as a case study, the bus system in Santiago, Chile. The conclusions summarise the issues and highlight some policy implications of common fare structures.

4.2 Components of a fare system

4.2.1 The fare structure

Basic mainstream economic theory would theorise that the only efficient price was where the price equalled the marginal cost. This would suggest, therefore, that all fares should be related to the distance travelled. The reality, however, is very different. For example, distance-based fares can lead to complicated fare structures, whilst passengers seek simplicity. Furthermore, interchange becomes difficult, complicated and potentially time consuming, all of which reduce the utility of the consumer, i.e. reduce economic efficiency. In reality, therefore, in the most simple of frameworks, fare structures fall broadly into three categories: flat fares, zonal fares and distance-based fares. The choice of fare structure depends on how different evaluation criteria are valued for the public transport system under consideration. There are a number of criteria for the evaluation of the fare structure including the ease of understanding for passengers, the simplicity of collection, the ability of the fare structure to generate the required revenue, how easy it is to control fares (particularly from evasion by passengers), how equitable it is and its attractiveness to passengers.

Valuing ease of understanding for passengers, simplicity of fare collection and passenger attraction mean that a system using flat fares does well where a flat fare is a fare applied to all journeys, whether long or short. However, flat fares suffer from the way in which payment does not relate to the 'quantity' of travel that is purchased, i.e. it is technically economically inefficient, since it treats long and short journeys equally, and so it is often also contended to be inequitable. Perhaps more seriously, a flat fare set at a level to recoup operating costs can mean that very short rides are too highly priced and are therefore not taken by public transport but are substituted by walking. This can significantly reduce revenue (and why in some cases a 'short hop' fare is additionally in place). In cities which are geographically constrained and where the average distance travelled has a small standard deviation, a flat fare can be a good fare structure. Cities falling into this category are often concentric around the city centre with radial routes emanating from this centre.

Exact distance-based fares are rare with some European long-distance railway systems charging by the kilometre with the implication that different routes between the same origin and destination may attract different fares. But for urban public transport systems, distance-based fares are usually characterised by broad distance-based bands, often called 'fare stages' or 'fare sections', with passengers paying for the number of stages that are traversed. Distance-based fares are normally related to the line of travel rather than geography, so that the further the distance travelled the greater is the fare. Distance-based fare structures are often 'capped' with a maximum fare thus sharing at this point some of the characteristics of the flat fare discussed above. As noted, distance-based fares are more difficult for passengers to understand, especially passengers new to a public transport system and typically passengers do not like fares being dependent on the route travelled (the public transport route may, for example be circuitous between an origin and destination for which the passenger has to pay an effective surcharge). Policing distance-based fares can be difficult as there is a requirement to know the origin and destination of the traveller. However, many of the disadvantages of distance-based fares can be overcome with more technologically based fare-collection systems based on smartcard collection where a distance-based fare can be seen as providing an equitable payment system. In practical terms, the need to raise revenues to pay for the public transport system requires cities to have distance-based fares because of their enhanced revenue-raising ability.

Zonal-based fares are more crudely graduated distance-based fares with typically a single fare applying to all intrazonal journeys with higher fares becoming payable by passengers travelling over multiple zones. The best zonal fare structures are those which have natural boundaries between zones, such as rivers, but boundaries need to be sensitive to the typical journeys of the city in question so that travellers of short trips do not end up crossing zone boundaries. Indeed, many cities with zonal systems have overlapping zones for this reason with certain stations or stops being located in more than one zone. As compared to flat fares, zonal fares introduce the complications discussed above under distance-based fares and some understanding of the geography of the area is required to ensure that passengers pay the correct fare. Whilst zonal fares will typically be higher for longer journeys, in contrast to distance-based fares, zonal fares are based on the geographical relationship between origin and destination rather than the line distance travelled on the public transport system. This tends to make zonal fares more attractive to passengers.

Within these basic fare structures there are often additional types of fare which are provided. For example, most cities offer time periodic fares: a daily, weekly or monthly pass. The pricing of these tickets is normally related to the umbrella fare structure in place so that a distance-based fare structure might give rise to unlimited daily/monthly/annual travel between a specific origin and destination. However, with the movement to smartcard technology, many of these periodic passes are being less geographically specific and will typically now provide access to specific parts (inner city, for example on the London underground) or to the whole network. In some fare systems, whether flat, distance based or zonal, there is also time of day pricing where a discount is provided to travellers in the off-peak (or a surcharge to peak travellers). As will be seen below, this difference in pricing within a fare system can be justified in relation to the different costs of operation in these time periods.

More recently a number of new types of fare structures have emerged. Of particular note are the frequent user discounts which are made possible by the use of smartcard technology which can monitor the individual's travel over the required period of time.

4.2.2 Fare collection

Fare collection has a number of components: the form of payment, the control of payment (in terms of method, the time relative to the travel time and the location) and the time and location of payment in relation to the passenger's trip time.

At the outset of mass transit, cash payment was the standard. However, in many cities this has been replaced by pre-payment schemes of different kinds for many reasons, including the operational simplifications it brings to bus operation (drivers not having to handle cash), which in turn speeds up loading times and reduces dwell times thus reducing vehicle times for passengers. Payment methods are increasingly made by passengers on a self-service basis with very many cities moving towards or having already achieved payment using smartcards or some other automated system.

Fare collection can be on-vehicle or pre-journey. Pre-paid tickets come in multiple formats, e. g. ten for the price of nine (as previously in Sydney, Australia) or in 'strips' of constant length where a different number of segments can be used for different lengths of journey (as previously in the Netherlands). Periodic tickets, as discussed above, also come into this pre-pay category. Smartcards – or their less smart predecessors with magnetic strips – offer a way of sophisticated fare collection off vehicle.

Whilst commonplace for metro and rail-based systems, payment off-vehicle has been much less common for bus travel. In recognition of this, many new bus systems, particularly bus rapid transit systems, are making provision for off-vehicle payments in 'stations' prior to boarding, motivated by the reduction in journey time with the consequential impact on the generalised cost (time and money costs of travelling) for passengers that this brings.

Monitoring whether passengers pay the correct fare is influenced by the means of fare collection. Systems can be fully gated which is more capital intensive than a system that relies more on the inspection of traveller's tickets but can lead to a lower incidence of fare evasion. Systems based on inspection are trading capital expenditure for labour expenditure: some cities have found the presence of inspectors in an ever increasing 'do it yourself' environment useful in limiting fare evasion on road-based transport where avoiding fare payment or underpaying the correct fare is easier with driver-only vehicles.

4.2.3 The fare level

Fare levels are inevitably influenced by objectives set by governments for the public transport sector, the way in which the public transport is procured and how much of the public transport system cost needs to be covered by fare revenue. For example, in Britain, the long-term objective of rail fare regulation is to shift more of the cost of providing the service onto the consumer, hence fares are regulated as Retail Price Index as the measure of inflation +1 percent. These factors need to be tempered by the impact of the elasticity of demand for public transport, which will typically vary by mode, time of day and by different urban contexts.

The setting of fare levels is influenced by the extent to which revenues from fares need to cover the costs of provision and whether it is simply the operating costs or the full cost of service provision (i.e. covering the capital cost components). This in turn is influenced by the procurement method for public transport service with private operators being more likely to require a full cost recovery. The fare level, as shown below, will be influenced by the degree of subsidy that is available as well as the objective. This chapter concentrates on first best, second best and price discrimination as possible means of fare determination with an objective of social welfare maximisation, but fare levels could also be driven by a mark-up over marginal costs, by market pricing or by some sort of yield-management approach to maximise income, and these are likely to deviate from the objective of social welfare maximisation and give different outcomes (Nash, 1978; Glaister and Collings, 1978).

Operationally, public transport costs are driven by the costs in the peak. To the extent that peak costs are higher than off-peak costs, this justifies a different fare level. However, quite how much of the peak cost is transferred to operations is not straightforward – is it just the additional costs of the peak or the full peak cost? To a certain extent this depends on the motivation for the service: for example, if the service is primarily for peak operation, such as taking children to school, then it is appropriate to allocate all peak costs to the peak. In other circumstances it is more appropriate just to allocate the marginal peak costs as additional peak costs. This is discussed in White (2009, chapter 7).

Users of public transport systems will be aware of a number of discounted fares or lower fare levels which are typically available. This suggests the relationship between costs and fare levels is not as straightforward as so far discussed. Many public transport systems offer discounts to different groups of people with students, unemployed and older people typically being targeted: how these are interpreted requires a bit more care. Most societies recognise that low or free fares improve the accessibility of older people and make it more likely that they are included in society. As a result, the government or funding body makes up the difference between the fare older people pay and the normal adult fare. When operators effectively receive the full fare for a passenger (albeit part from the passenger and part from an external body) this is called a concession fare and forms part of a society's social policy. Lower fares for children come into this same concession category. However, cheaper fares for students and the unemployed are market-based decisions based on extracting more consumer surplus (and hence revenue) through price discrimination: the fare level being lower follows from a recognition that these low-income categories of travellers travel more when the fare is low because they have a more elastic demand, and also that most tend to travel off-peak, hence fill the spare capacity during such periods. Thus, these latter discounts add to revenue in the longer term and only marginally to costs and are discussed below in the theory under price discrimination.

Fare levels do not typically differentiate between different levels of service quality in an urban public transport context, although distinguishing between first- and second-class travel with different levels of service quality is common on longer-distance rail travel. There are opportunities for differentiating in the urban context between different market segments, for example different types of service (express versus stopping services) might be charged at a different fare level because the quality of service is different. An area of contemporary concern is whether or not it is appropriate to charge a premium for special public transport services: flexible transport services (often called demand-responsive transport or paratransit) could be argued to provide a superior level of public transport which is door to door for which a premium could be applied.

4.2.4 The role of objectives

Elected governments should set the policy in which the objectives for public transport are identified. This will influence the choice of fare structure, fare collection and fare level, although frequently trade-offs are required between conflicting aspirations or objectives which are subject to constraint. In many jurisdictions it is the government that sets the objectives but the operator who is left with the requirement to meet the objectives by determining an appropriate network and fare system.

Governments need to recognise that different objectives will, even if the fare system and fare collection is held constant, have different implications for fare levels. Maximising the number of passengers or maximising cost recovery will not be possible at the same time as devising a fare system that maximises the benefit to some sector of the community such as the socially excluded. Objectives are linked to the institutional setting of the country of location with revenue-based objectives being more likely in a deregulated market and passenger-based objectives being more likely in a public transport system aimed at delivering accessibility.

Fare systems are often a compromise but can nevertheless have significant implications. A city which has a history of low fare levels will encourage lower-income individuals to trade more space for low rents on the fringes of the urban area. This type of fares policy can encourage and then reinforce undesirable land-use patterns of urban sprawl which are difficult to address effectively without creating significant low-income losers through changes in the fare system.

4.3 Pricing theory

4.3.1 First- and second-best pricing with welfare-maximising objective

First-best pricing, proposed originally by Pigou (1920) and Knight (1924), consists of charging the full marginal private and social cost to users (consumers) for the goods they consume. The cost here would include the operating cost, users' costs such as travel, waiting and access time, and externalities such as congestion, pollution and noise. The fundamental idea is to make individuals pay all the costs they impose on society. This standard micro-economics theory thus identifies that the price obtained under conditions of perfect competition corresponds to the marginal cost of production or marginal operating costs. This price maximises social welfare because the maxima of users' and firms' surpluses are reached. In the transportation industry, this perfect-competition condition is in the vast majority of cases not met. For example, in the case of private transport, road congestion is an externality that distorts the market equilibrium and the marginal cost does not match the price paid for car users. In the case of public transport, market distortions also exist, for instance Gómez-Lobo (2007) shows that the competitive equilibrium price is above marginal cost because users experience search cost when they wait for the bus with a lower fare, which induces price dispersion. Also, users of mass transit systems with high levels of overcrowding experience increases in travel time because of the impossibility of boarding over-crowded buses and the increased dwell times at bus stops. This is an externality similar to road congestion, because increased demand increases travel time for all users. The goal of public transport pricing is to maximise social welfare eliminating market distortions.

The total cost of public transportation includes operation cost plus users' cost (travel, waiting and access time). Mohring (1972) shows that the average (total) cost of public transportation decreases as more individuals use public transport, and therefore public transportation production exhibits economies of scale and, specifically in this context, in the carriage of passengers rather than in the production of services. However, when making transport decisions, users do not consider how they contribute to the decreased waiting cost of other users suggesting that the appropriate fare to charge must be lower than the operation (production) marginal cost. Typically, the average operating cost is lower than marginal cost so that if first-best pricing is used (where price = marginal cost) there will be a gap between total fare revenue and operating cost, making it necessary to provide subsidies to attain economic efficiency. So with this marginal-cost pricing scheme, although social welfare is maximised, subsidies will be necessary, as demonstrated below.

Consider that total social welfare (W) equals the aggregate users' benefit (B) minus users' cost (UC) and operating cost (OC). Total user cost is $c(Q)Q$, where $c(Q)$ is the average user cost (travel, waiting and access time). The marginal operating cost function is $m(Q)$, which is a function of the travel demand Q. If $gp(Q)$ is the inverse demand function, in equilibrium the individual willingness to pay is equal to generalised transport price (fare and monetary value of average travel, waiting and access time), and the sum over all users is the aggregate users' benefit. Then, the welfare function to maximise is:

$$W = B - UC - OC = \int_0^Q gp(q)dq - Qc(Q) - \int_0^Q m(q)dq. \tag{4.1}$$

The first order condition to maximise the total social welfare is:

$$gp(Q) - c(Q) - Q\frac{\partial c}{\partial Q} - m(Q) = 0. \tag{4.2}$$

As the inverse demand includes the cost experienced by user $c(Q)$ (i.e. average travel, waiting and access time) and the fare charged is $p(Q)$, we get the condition:

$$p(Q) = Q\frac{\partial c}{\partial Q} + m(Q). \tag{4.3}$$

As the 'Mohring effect' shows that average user cost decreases with total demand, the first term on the right-hand side is negative, and the fare is thus lower than the operating marginal cost.

In transport systems with high demand, the benefits of increasing demand may be reduced because of congestion on buses and stops (or stations). For instance, in the metro system of Santiago, waiting time has increased because the crowding in both trains and stations impedes the passenger's ability to board the first train that arrives. In Bogotá, the bus rapid transit system experiences 'bus on bus' congestion in the stations because of the high frequency of buses required for the demand. In these scenarios, the economies of scale vanish for high levels of demand in the short term. Indeed, if the congestion effect is high enough to increase average travel time, the optimal fare will be higher than the short-run operating marginal cost.

Sustainable pricing policy, however, must be based on long-term marginal costs, which include the cost changes to routes and the additional fleet required to provide for the higher demand, typically in peak periods. Therefore, the congestion effect of public transport demand will be present only in peak periods, and fares higher than marginal cost are consistent with peak load pricing.

So far, we do not consider the effect of the public transport fare on demand for alternative transport modes. If the authority's object is to maximise social welfare taking into account the cross-price elasticity of demand, the resulting public transport fares will include a correction term proportional to the difference between marginal cost and price charged in all transport alternatives (Jara-Díaz, 2007). For instance, consider the case of two alternatives for transportation: bus and car. The planner fixes the fare level of bus by maximising the social welfare of all transport users (car and bus). Therefore, the optimal fare is:

$$p(Q_b) = m(Q_b) + Q_b \frac{\partial c}{\partial Q_b} + \frac{Q_a}{Q_b} \frac{\varepsilon_{a,b}}{|\varepsilon_{b,b}|} (p_a - m_a), \tag{4.4}$$

where Q_b and Q_a are the demand for bus and car, respectively, $\varepsilon_{a,\ b}$ is the cross-price elasticity of car demand to bus price, $\varepsilon_{b,b}$ is the price elasticity of bus demand, p_a is the generalised price paid for car users (including operation cost of car and travel time in money units) and m_a is the total marginal cost of car travel.

As private transport is often underpriced, because car users do not internalise congestion effects nor take into account any fixed costs of car use, the optimal bus fare is below operating marginal cost. Again, subsidies for public transport are justified on grounds of social welfare maximisation.

Unless the marginal cost is higher than average cost, bus operators need subsidies to cover total operating costs. When the available subsidies are limited or non-existent then this first-best price is unfeasible and the transport authority needs to use another pricing strategy. A theoretical solution is to maximise the total welfare subject to a budget constraint to obtain a second-best price. Second-best price was first promoted in a general way by Lipsey and Lancaster (1956) and Baumol and Bradford (1970).

When there is a limited budget for subsidies, welfare-maximising fares include a term related to the cost of public funds. If λ is the shadow cost of public funds, government needs to collect \$(1 +λ) in taxes to give \$1 of subsidy to the firms. The ratio $\lambda\,/(1+\lambda)$ is the Ramsey index. Then, the public transport fare without competing modes becomes:

$$\begin{aligned} p(Q) &= Q\frac{\partial c}{\partial Q} + m(Q) + \frac{\lambda}{1+\lambda} \frac{Q}{\dfrac{\partial Q}{\partial p}}, \\ &= Q\frac{\partial c}{\partial Q} + m(Q) + \frac{\lambda}{1+\lambda} \frac{p(Q)}{\varepsilon(Q)} \end{aligned} \tag{4.5}$$

where $\varepsilon(Q)$ is price elasticity of bus demand. The optimal fare keeps the same structure as the first-best prices, internalising the positive externality of public transport demand. If there is no subsidy from the government and a balanced budget constraint is imposed, λ is not the shadow cost of public funds, but becomes the Lagrange multiplier in the welfare-maximising problem. If the user cost is constant or not affected by the changes in the demand level, the expression for the second-best price is:

$$p(Q) = m(Q) + \frac{\lambda}{1+\lambda} \frac{p(Q)}{\varepsilon(Q)}. \tag{4.6}$$

The second-best price for bus with competing modes is more complex; but it is also composed of the operating marginal cost, the demand externality and the distortion in markets of transport alternatives (see Jara-Díaz, 2007, chapter 4 for details).

Alternatively, when marginal operating cost is smaller than the average operating cost, the optimal pricing strategy is a two-part tariff (Coase, 1946). Assuming there is no Mohring effect for simplicity, a two-part tariff is composed by a fixed (entry or 'flagfall') fee that allows passengers to use the bus system, and a per-unit price that corresponds to the bus fare paid for each trip. As the objective is to maximise social welfare subject to a break-even constraint, the per-unit price is given by the marginal cost and the remaining fraction of total cost is covered by revenues from the fixed fee. Therefore, if C is the total operation cost, the two-part tariff comprises a fixed fee f and a per unit price p given by the following equations:

$$\begin{aligned} p(Q) &= m(Q) \\ f(Q) &= C(Q) - p(Q)Q \end{aligned} \tag{4.7}$$

However, one problem with this type of pricing schedule is that the fixed fee excludes some users from travelling by public transport. This happens when the net benefit of undertaking a number of trips (paying the per-unit price) is less than the total cost of travelling (fixed fee plus trips by per unit price). If all users are assumed to be identical, such that the demand function is the sum of their individual demands, then the individual is excluded from the market if:

$$\int_0^Q p(q)dq - f(Q) - p(Q)Q \leq 0, \tag{4.8}$$

where $p(q)$ is the inverse demand function and the first term is the gross consumer surplus. As all individuals are identical, (4.8) is an all-or-nothing condition.

Typically, users have heterogeneous preferences. For instance, when travel utility depends on a parameter θ, which is distributed across the population. In this case, the exclusion condition depends on the distribution of preferences and will affect only that fraction of users that obtain lower utility from travelling. To compute the fixed fee with heterogeneous users, the marginal user who is indifferent between travelling paying the fixed fee and not travelling must be identified (for details see Wilson, 1993; Laffont and Tirole, 1993).

Another problem of the two-part tariff is the demand income effect. When an income effect is present, the total demand depends on the fixed fee and (4.7) is not valid to find the tariff components. Moreover, the fixed fee may exclude a significant part of the population with low income. Such an effect is particularly relevant in developing countries with low salaries and low car ownership, where users usually have no alternative transport mode. Nevertheless, with subsidies from the government it is possible to implement two-part tariffs, with the poorest people or special groups of users (e.g. unemployed, elderly) receiving discounted fixed fees, provided there is a way of identifying the members of the group.

4.3.2 Price discrimination with profit-maximising objective

As discussed above, fare levels are sometimes computed using price discrimination between different segments of the market. This presumes that public transport operators exert their market power and act as monopolists in setting fare levels. This is independent of the fare structure and fare-collection method.

If the public transport firm can provide $Q(p)$ units when it charges a fare of p, then the firm's profits when the cost function is C are:

$$\pi(p) = pQ(p) - C(Q(p)). \tag{4.9}$$

Under a uniform (non-discriminatory) price strategy, maximising profits gives the first order condition (rearranged) of:

$$\frac{p - C'(Q(p))}{p} = \frac{1}{\varepsilon}, \tag{4.10}$$

where ε is the elasticity of demand. This formulation, often referred to as the price-cost margin or 'Lerner index' (Lerner, 1934), shows that the optimum fare for first-degree discrimination is inversely proportionate to the elasticity of demand. Discriminatory prices are variations on this general formula.

There are three types of price discrimination, all based in theory on a profit-maximising objective (a departure from the social-maximising objective of the first- and second-best pricing discussed above).

First-degree price discrimination is sometimes called personalised pricing. This occurs where price, and in this case the fare level, is set to precisely match the consumer's willingness to pay. This allows the operator to capture the full consumer surplus for themselves and in this sense profit maximisation is tantamount to maximising welfare, assuming equal marginal utilities of money between shareholders/producers and consumers. In the mass transit market, it is not possible to practise this degree of discrimination.

Second-degree price discrimination is also known as non-linear pricing, in which the price per unit depends on the quantity bought by the consumer. In public transport, this type of discrimination is present in systems with travel passes, for instance, weekly or monthly passes. The objective of second-degree price discrimination is the same as the first-degree one, but it recognises the impossibility of identifying every user's willingness to pay. For instance, airlines attempt to discriminate between business and leisure travellers because the former have higher willingness to pay, but at the moment of the ticket purchase there is no way to distinguish them. Therefore, airlines define prices according to more favourable conditions for each type of user, such that each self-selects into the right price segment. For instance, to target a leisure traveller, the cheaper price ticket might be valid only if the time away includes a Saturday.

In general, the problem of second-degree price discrimination is to construct price-quantity packages that give the users incentives to self-select. This means every user selects the package constructed for them and they do not have the incentive to pretend to be a different type of user. The way to determine the optimal second-degree price strategy is by maximising monopoly profits subject to an incentive-compatibility constraint and a participation constraint (see details in Wilson, 1993; or Laffont and Tirole, 1993). The resulting price-quantity packages are such that users with high demand get lower price per unit than users with low demand. This non-linear price is usually presented as a menu of two-part tariffs, in which high-demand users pay a high fixed fee and low (or zero) per-unit price, and low-demand users pay low (or zero) fixed fee and high per-unit price. For the interested reader, Carbajo (1988) presents a rigorous analysis of travel passes as a non-linear pricing strategy.

Third-degree price discrimination is much more applicable to the public transport market. Third-degree price discrimination is sometimes called 'group pricing'. If different segments of the market can be identified, then applying the inverse elasticity rule can generate additional revenues for the operator. This is the basis of giving discounts to students and unemployed persons with lower incomes and typically more elastic demand: the lower fares encourage these members of the community to travel more thus providing higher revenue in total for the operator. Provided the segment of the market can be identified through age, status or geography so that arbitrage is prevented (reselling a lower price of the good for a higher price), then third-degree price discrimination will work. Clearly, public transport operators need to have information about their target markets for this to be implemented. The welfare implications of third-degree price discrimination are not straightforward, in some cases enhancing welfare and in other cases decreasing it.

4.4 Case study: welfare-maximising bus fares in Santiago, Chile

The case study illustrates alternative fares that maximise the total welfare for financing the bus system in Santiago, Chile. In the first case, we have a budget-balanced fare assuming no subsidy. In the second case, the amount of available subsidy is assumed fixed by the Chilean government and the corresponding budget-balanced fare is calculated. In the third case, a two-part tariff with and without subsidy is computed. However, whilst these fares are computed by maximising total welfare, the welfare measure used does not include externalities, either positive or negative, of bus operation. Hence the effects of bus fares on car demand and the computed fares do not maximise total social welfare but serve to illustrate how setting bus fares might be achieved practically in a number of scenarios. It should also be noted that the public transport system of Santiago also includes a subway network, but in this case study there is a single focus on buses.

The bus system of Santiago has an integrated payment system, where users pay only once for a trip with up to two transfers. The only payment method is a prepaid electronic card. Therefore, the fare needs to finance the cost of the complete trip even if the users travel on more than one bus line. To estimate the fare by trip, the average number of legs per trip in the system is used, which was 1.605 in 2011. Therefore, the fare will be 1.605 times the optimal payment per leg. In determining the fare, the price is attached to a leg because the cost of provision depends on the number of users that board the buses.

The demand model estimated by Batarce and Galilea (2013) is used for analysing different fare systems in this case study. They define an aggregate demand model where the only variable is the bus fare, but they take into account the trend of potential demand growth and the monthly seasonality, and estimate the model with aggregate demand data from June 2007 to December 2011. We adopt the model and fix the growth trend and monthly seasonality on December 2011. Finally, the demand model we use is a linear-elasticity model given by:

$$q = M\exp(\theta - \eta p), \tag{4.11}$$

where $M = 4.181$, $\theta = 4.766$ and $\eta = 0.001$. These parameters mean the potential demand is 4.181 million passengers, the reservation utility for travelling is 4.766, which is the logarithm of the maximum number of trips that the average user will travel in a month if the bus fare is zero. This functional form implies that demand price elasticity (ε) is proportional to the fare.

$$\varepsilon = \frac{dq}{dp}\frac{p}{q} = -\eta p. \tag{4.12}$$

The cost function is estimated for this case study with a panel data from Santiago collected by Batarce and Galilea (2013). The cost function is specified using two measures of transport output: total passenger flow and driven kilometres. The first measure is a demand-related output and the second is a supply-related output (Small and Verhoef, 2007). This definition of transport output allows the marginal cost to be separated between the cost of transporting an additional passenger and the cost of driving an additional kilometre. In addition, the degree of scale economies is equal to the inverse of the cost elasticity to aggregated output (Jara-Díaz and Cortés, 1996). To control for the level of capital in use, the cost function includes average fleet size as a variable. In turn this implies short-run costs are modelled.

The cost structure is modelled using the following function:

$$C_i = K_i \exp(\alpha_1 q_i + \alpha_2 q_i^{\beta} + \gamma d_i + \delta b_i), \tag{4.13}$$

where C_i is the firm i's total cost, q_i is the number of passengers, d_i is driven kilometres during the period, and b_i is the number of buses operated by the firm i. The technology is represented by K_i and is specific for each firm as it includes differences related to the geographical area where each firm operates. For this case study, we include in K_i the effect of input prices, as this case is not considering the effect of these on fare determination. Estimated parameters K_i, α_1, α_2, β, γ and δ are presented in the appendix. This cost function allows us to obtain the fixed cost of operating bus services keeping frequencies but without passengers on board. The fixed cost represents the cost of providing bus services.

Bus fares are computed using (4.6). With price elasticity of demand given by (4.12), the optimal fare is the solution of the following equation:

$$p(Q) = m(Q) + \frac{\lambda}{1+\lambda}\eta. \tag{4.14}$$

The fare is the result of an equilibrium problem, since marginal costs depend on the demand, which in turn depends on the fare. In the first case presented, the budget-balanced fare without subsidy equals the average cost of the bus system. The value of λ (Lagrange multiplier) is such that the fare equals the average cost (see Table 4.1).

The second case (budget-balanced fare with fixed subsidy) assumes the transport authority gives an annual subsidy for the operation of the Santiago bus system. The available annual subsidy for the group firms is 232 million USD, which is the amount of subsidy for the operation of the bus system approved by the Chilean government in April 2012. It is used to pay a fraction of the fixed costs. In this case, λ is fixed a priori since it represents the shadow cost of public funds. We assume λ to be equal to 0.5 and this gives a new equilibrium for a budget-balanced fare of 1.08 USD (Table 4.1), which is equal to the current fare of the bus system. The closeness of these fares suggests the assumptions made for fare computation are sensible, since the authority's objective function to determine bus fare is to maximise social welfare (i.e. minimum fare) subject to covering the system costs.

Table 4.1 Fare and monthly demand for the studied cases

Case	*Fare (USD)*	*Monthly demand (million trips)*
Current fare (December 2011)	1.08	60.0
Budget-balance fare without subsidy	1.70	44.2
Budget-balance fare with fixed subsidy	1.08	60.0
Two-part tariff without subsidy	$f = 19.6$, $p = 0.45$	81.7
Two-part tariff with subsidy	$f = 15.3$, $p = 0.45$	81.7
Pareto-improving menu with subsidy	Option 1: $f_1 = 0$, $p_1 = 1.08$ Option 2: $f_2 = 15.3$, $p_2 = 0.45$	–

In the next two cases, two-part tariffs are computed with and without subsidy (see Table 4.1). If all users are assumed to be identical, such that the demand function is the sum of their individual demands, then the exclusion condition is:

$$\frac{1}{\eta}q(\theta + 1 - \ln q) - Nf - pq \leq 0, \tag{4.15}$$

where N is the number of users (or the number of payment-card holders). The first term of (4.15) is the gross consumer surplus. The net benefit of travelling under the two-part tariff is 49.1 USD in the case with subsidy and 44.8 USD without subsidy. We assume N to be equal to the 4.5 million passengers using a payment card.

The two-part tariffs are calculated assuming both exclusion and income effects are not present, and therefore the demand depends only on the per-unit price level (see Table 4.1). The only difference between the two cases is the amount of the fixed fee, which is reduced by 22 percent through subsidy. In this case, demand increases by a large amount, which implies in turn that frequency and fleet need to increase to transport the new demand. Assuming the ratios of demand to buses and demand to driven kilometres in 2011 remain constant, the fleet and the driven kilometres are increased to match such ratios given the new demand. Then, cost increases not only because of the demand but also because of the additional buses and kilometres.

Implementation of a two-part tariff benefits users with large demand for bus trips, but prevents other users from travelling at all, as discussed above in the theory and, of course, it is desirable to implement pricing schedules that do not worsen any user's welfare. Pricing schedules that have this property and that do not reduce the firm's revenue are said to be Pareto-improving (Wilson, 1993). When the bus fare is a uniform price for all trips, a Pareto-improving change can be made by introducing a two-part tariff as an option available to travellers. The new pricing schedule is a menu with two options: the existing uniform price p_1 or the new two-part tariff composed by a fixed fee f and a per-unit price p_2. An informed traveller is better off under the new pricing schedule because they retain the option to travel under the uniform price. In fact, travellers making less than $q^{\star} = f / (p_1 - p_2)$ trips prefer to remain with the old fare. Table 4.1 shows the Pareto-improving menu of prices resulting from the budget-balanced fare with subsidy and the two-part tariff with subsidy too.

The results in Table 4.1 show that the Santiago transport authority seems to fix the fare level to maximise welfare, given the available amount of subsidy, even though this objective function is not overtly stated. Without a subsidy, the fare level required to cover the cost of the system is 57 percent higher than the fare with a subsidy and the demand is reduced to 74 percent of the current demand. This decline in demand will have a significant impact on citizen mobility as a large proportion of households have no car and bus is the only transport alternative. In terms of demand increases, the two-part tariff is the most effective pricing schedule, either with or without a subsidy, since this leads to a demand level 36 percent higher than the current level. However, the assumption behind the computation of the two-part tariff implies no exclusion through the implementation of a fixed fee, which seems to be questionable for Santiago where spending on public transport reaches 15 percent of the average household income. To overcome the problem of exclusion, the Pareto-improving pricing schedule is proposed as the best compromise. It is not possible to determine the final demand level of the Pareto-improving schedule because of the assumptions on demand modelling, but users making less than 24 trips per month should prefer the uniform price ($1.08), and the rest of the users, the two-part tariff.

4.5 Final comments

A fare system for public transport is a unique combination of the fare structure, fare-collection method and the fare level. Whilst decisions on the first two components may appear more straightforward, this chapter shows the way in which all three interact – led by the objectives for public transport policy (and transport policy more generally) by the political governance of the jurisdiction. As discussed above, the ultimate choice of fare system can have wide-ranging implications for urban areas: it influences the quantity of travel undertaken by citizens, the time of day of travel and can impact on the ultimate shape of the city.

In terms of economic theory, this can give the greatest guidance to the determination of the level and structure of fares. There are nevertheless several aspects to consider when setting fares on public transport systems. For instance, fares determined by reference to economic criteria rely on a good understanding of costs and if the authority determining the fares has limited information on cost, they are clearly impeded from charging fares close to the theoretical ones. And it is typically the case that the authority fixing the fares may have little information on public transport costs. Using approximate criterion, however, can lead to a welfare-maximising fare level, as the case study of this chapter shows. Indeed, Santiago transport authority fixes the fare level so as to keep it as low as possible to cover costs with the available annual subsidy and yet this comes close to a theoretically derived fare.

Understanding the cost structure of public transport operations suggests that fares should vary according to travel distance and time of day to reflect the differing marginal costs of producing the provided service. Even though in theory this distinction is a direct extension of the basic first-best formulation, limited information on demand and costs can prevent its direct application.

A lack of information on costs gives rise to practical problems of implementation. However, in order to meet social policy objectives for public transport, it is also important to consider the equity of a fare system, usually to meet social inclusion goals. When equity is a consideration, and especially when there are limited alternatives, urban segregation or inadequate income distribution a different approach that uses a flat fare structure may be needed, as shown in the case study. This response to ensure that all citizens can travel is particularly important in cities where a significant portion of the population have public transport as their only motorised option.

Another practical problem comes from the way in which costs of provision are higher in the peak and applying a maximum welfare criterion leads to high fares for peak periods. However, for all users, the demand for travel in the peak hour is more inelastic because of the need to travel to work and this is particularly relevant for low-income workers who do not have any alternative. Meeting the needs of low income but reflecting the welfare-driven economic rules can lead to a theoretically consistent way of introducing an equity (political) criteria into the welfare-maximisation framework by weighting differently the groups of users in the objective function. This, however, needs additional information on demand and costs for every type of user identified in the objective function which is unlikely to be available.

These factors serve to show that creating a fare system is a complex task that can be guided by theoretical economic pricing rules. In practice, implementing the guidance requires much more information than is usually available and the fare system is typically the outcome of sometimes conflicting objectives with significant implications for the urban area and its citizens.

Appendix

The parameters of the cost model used for the case study are presented in Table 4A.1. The model assumes there are 13 firms operating in Santiago, and the total cost of the system is the weighted sum of these costs according to the demand of each firm in December 2011.

Table 4A.1 Parameters of the cost function

Parameter	*Parameter value*	*Demand in December 2011*
K_1	2.7888	14.644
K_2	2.6997	12.575
K_3	3.3220	11.654
K_4	2.4185	10.342
K_5	3.3220	16.406
K_6	2.7888	8.745
K_7	2.7888	17.757
K_8	2.7888	12.021
K_9	3.2228	31.688
K_{10}	2.3071	42.092
K_{11}	2.6098	18.400
K_{12}	2.3089	45.262
K_{13}	2.7024	31.180
α_1	0.19394	
α_2	-0.07317	
β	1.20000	
γ	0.00006	
δ	0.00084	

References

Batarce, M. and Galilea, P. (2013). Cost and Fare Estimation for the Urban Bus Transit System of Santiago. Paper presented at Transport Research Board Meeting, Washington, DC.

Baumol, W. J. and Bradford, D. F. (1970). Optimal Departures from Marginal Cost Pricing. *American Economic Review, Papers and Proceedings*, 60(3), pp. 265–83.

Carbajo, J. C. (1988). The Economics of Travel Passes: Non-Uniform Pricing in Transport. *Journal of Transport Economics and Policy*, pp. 153–73.

Coase, R. H. (1946). The Marginal Cost Controversy. *Economica*, 13(51), pp. 169–82.

Glaister, S. and Collings, J. J. (1978). Maximisation of Passenger Miles in Theory and Practice. *Journal of Transport Economics and Policy*, 12(3), 304–21.

Gómez-Lobo, A. (2007). Why Competition Does Not Work in Urban Bus Markets: Some New Wheels for Some Old Ideas. *Journal of Transport Economics and Policy*, 41(2), pp. 283–308.

Jara-Díaz, S. (2007). *Transport Economic Theory*. Oxford: Elsevier.

Jara-Díaz, S. and Cortés, C. (1996). On the Calculation of Scale Economies from Transport Cost Functions. *Journal of Transport Economics and Policy*, 30, pp. 157–70.

Knight, F. H. (1924). Some Fallacies in the Interpretation of Social Cost. *Quarterly Journal of Economics*, 38, pp. 582–606.

Laffont, J. and Tirole J. (1993). *A Theory of Incentives in Procurement and Regulation*. Cambridge, MA: MIT Press.

Lerner, A. P. (1934). The Concept of Monopoly and the Measurement of Monopoly Power. *Review of Economic Studies*, 1(3), pp. 157–75.

Lipsey, R. G. and Lancaster, K. J. (1956). The General Theory of Second Best. *Review of Economic Studies, 24*(1), pp. 11–32.

Mohring, H. (1972). Optimization and Scale Economies in Urban Bus Transportation. *American Economic Review*, 591–604.

Nash, C. A. (1978). Management Objectives, Fares and Service Levels in Bus Transport. *Journal of Transport Economics and Policy*, 12(1), 870–5.

Pigou, A. C. (1920). *The Economics of Welfare*. London: Macmillan.

Small, K. A. and Verhoef, E. T. (2007). *The Economics of Urban Transportation*. New York: Routledge.

White, P. (2009). *Public Transport: Its Planning Management and Operation*, 5th edition. London: Routledge.

Wilson, R. A. (1993). *Nonlinear Pricing*. New York: Oxford University Press.

5

Perfect information and intelligent transport systems

John D. Nelson

5.1 Introduction

For a public transport service to be used, the public must know where and when the service is provided. This simple maxim has often proved to be a non-trivial consideration for operators and customers alike. This chapter explores the importance of market information to consumers and assesses the role of high-quality information as a key enabler of successful transport service provision. A recurring theme is the critical role of smart technology.

The chapter is organised as follows. The first section considers why consumers (i.e. passengers) need information and explores the role of 'perfect information' in the context of the market for local public transport and the specific information requirements of public transport users, taking account of the challenges posed by the deregulation and privatisation of bus services in Great Britain. The following sections contrast approaches to the provision of public transport information via traditional media and the possibilities offered by the use of smart technology in public transport markets. Detailed attention is given to the development of journey planners and the emerging role of social media and its contribution towards smarter journey planning. The particular case of transport disruption is considered.

5.2 Why do consumers need information?

The information requirements of travellers are well known and have been documented extensively (see for example Papangelis et al., 2016a). At its most basic, for a public transport system to be used, the public must know *where* and *when* the service is provided (Suen and Geehan, 1987).

Traditionally, the information requirements of public transport users have been summarised as relating to: *pre-trip* (what opportunities are available for the journey that I would like to make and (ideally) how much will it cost?); '*at-stop*' (I'm committed to this journey so is the service I plan to use operating as expected and will I be able to get a seat?); and *en route* (is the journey progressing as planned and in the case of disruption, how will I recover my trip?). The information available to passengers, and indeed operators, has often been found lacking in situations of disruption; it will be argued below that the advent of social media to some extent offers a potential remedy in this respect.

5.2.1 What do we mean by perfect information?

In a situation of perfect information (in a market), consumers (in this case, public transport passengers) and producers (in this case, transport service providers) are assumed to have perfect knowledge of relevant factors such as price, utility, quality and means of production. In game theory perfect information pertains when all players are fully aware of all events or moves that have occurred previously and can use this to inform their decisions.

High-quality information is a key enabler of successful transport service provision. It is not unreasonable from the passenger's perspective to expect that an operator or authority will endeavour to provide information about travel possibilities and to reduce uncertainty, especially in response to disruption. Since public transport services are run for the benefit of the travelling public it is important that they are aware of the available services, both pre-trip and en route. From the passenger perspective there is considerable evidence that easily understandable journey planning information fosters confidence and positive attitudes towards the public transport service (Papangelis et al., 2016b). From the operator perspective, transport as with any other good or service will not sell itself and good-quality information offers the potential to unlock latent travel demand.

Applications of real-time passenger information (RTPI) were introduced from the mid-1980s, initially in the context of passenger information at bus stops (PIBS), and helped to reinforce the idea of passenger information as an important determinant of travel by public transport. Since then Intelligent Transport Systems (ITS) have become widespread and Nelson and Mulley (2013), reflecting on the emergence of ITS, note that a number of applications (including seamless real-time travel and traffic information) have become key elements, contributing to the efficient coordination of the overall transport chain. But a key question remains: to what extent is the public transport sector able to exploit the wider benefits of ITS?

A relevant case is that of ITS presence on project evaluation. In an early contribution, Mulley and Nelson (2000) noted that any project (e.g. the provision of PIBS) requires the generation of streams of benefits and costs, and that where these rely on estimates of the numbers of people involved, the presence of ITS will make the evaluation procedure more accurate. Similarly, the presence of ITS should provide positive benefits to the consumer seeking to evaluate the potential travel choices available to them; we will return to this argument when considering the particular case of passengers facing disruption.

According to Papangelis et al. (2016b), the principal benefits arising from RTPI may be summarised as: reduced perceived waiting time, increased willingness to pay, adjusted travel behaviour, positive psychological effects, enhanced mode choice, and higher customer satisfaction and image; all of which have the potential to contribute to a more efficient market outcome. Several studies have reported reduced perceived waiting time as a positive effect of RTPI and this is discussed further below. The effect of RTPI on increased willingness to pay after the deployment of RTPI systems is less clear cut. Vermeulen and Dziekan (2005) illustrate that not all systems are valued equally and not all travellers are willing to pay for such a service. The main argument here is that the traveller expects that the public transport provider should supply this information free of charge, although there has been a gradual acceptance of the charge associated with SMS-based information services. Nevertheless, an increased willingness to pay is a possible effect of RTPI. In terms of adjusted behaviour, the following strategies are found to be the most prevalent: reduction of disutilisation of waiting time, decisions leading to more efficient travelling (e.g. taking an alternative bus from a different stop that arrives close to a destination) and other adjusting strategies (e.g. letting a crowded bus pass by, adjusting walking speed) (Dziekan and Sedin, 2005).

Positive psychological effects arising from the provision of RTPI relate mainly to perceived control, feelings of security, reduced uncertainty and increased ease of use (e.g. Schweiger, 2003). Mishalani et al. (2006) found that only a very limited number of passengers thought that RTPI would significantly change their way of travelling. Overall, higher customer satisfaction and improved image of the transport operator have been observed to result from the provision of RTPI.

5.2.2 The local public transport context

The deregulated bus market in Great Britain outside of London enabled by the Transport Act of 1985 has been extensively documented. In Great Britain, bus services are operated on a commercial basis with competitive tendering used to support services not provided by the market but which are deemed socially necessary. In London, a franchise approach is taken where route-based bus contracts are given subject to competitive tendering. The immediate aftermath of the introduction of deregulation in October 1986 was characterised by confusion for passengers as one of the outcomes of the (so-called) 'bus wars' between operators was the disappearance of printed bus timetables at bus stops as bus operators sought to cut costs. Although options for real-time passenger information were already technically feasible by this time (see discussion below), development was hampered by issues of ownership and cost of equipment and a suspicion developed between operators over the perceived need to avoid advertising the late arrival of one's own bus.

Mulley and Nelson (2000), commenting on the case of the UK bus industry, noted that the sharper competitive environment created by deregulation and privatisation had generated a need for more and better passenger information. This remains true to the present day where with the advent of the concept of Mobility as a Service (MaaS)[1] it remains crucially important to understand the role that regulation and standardisation may play in the provision of information about available travel choices.

Considering the approach to the evaluation of the specific case of real-time passenger information at bus stops Mulley and Nelson (2000) demonstrated that the inclusion of actors in the evaluation process (on a spectrum between business case and social cost benefit analysis) will depend on who provides the ITS system. Based on the UK case the following scenarios emerged: public provision of the ITS infrastructure; public authority requires installation and pays only for roadside installation; private investment; and public–private partnerships and quality. Whilst the social case for RTPI has been largely made, bus deregulation, particularly in the early years, has strongly hindered the economic case for RTPI.

5.3 Traditional media in public transport information

Traditionally, there have been a wide variety of information sources available to public transport users. These have included visual (e.g. via signs), printed (timetables and leaflets), spoken or automated (interactive) means. Other typologies have concentrated on the 'how' (verbal or visual), 'what' (personal or general) and 'where' (public or private) nature of passenger information. These typologies are essentially complementary whether one is talking about traditional or contemporary means of providing passenger information. This is illustrated by a bus user using conventional leaflets to plan a journey in advance and real-time information to reinforce travel options in the course of a journey.

Suen and Geehan (1987), in an early analysis of new technology applied to passenger information systems, developed a typology which drew a distinction between content (real-time versus schedule), type of media (passive, active or interactive), access to media (e.g. telephone, display, keyboard) and form of presentation (digital display, VDU, television, automated voice). To this day, traditional media remains important and often complementary to that available via smart technologies, although increasingly printed media (e.g. comprehensive bus timetable books) has become less available.

White (2017) confirms the importance of information to public transport users and stresses the need for information about the services, such as exact timetable, frequency and likely in-vehicle time as requirements which allow the user to judge the door-to-door duration of a journey. Although traditional methods of information have been available to address the travellers' requirements for certainty around connecting and return journeys, as well as fares information, there have been obvious limitations, particularly with respect to accuracy and timeliness. The importance of the additional information challenges posed by the British regulatory context is highlighted by Howes and Rye (2005), who note that information provision is a matter of significant concern amongst both users and non-users of public transport in the UK; they attribute this to the much greater frequency of service changes following deregulation and privatisation. By contrast, in other European countries information is not generally seen as a significant issue.

The key, argues White (2017), is to reduce the information needs of the bus user and therefore their uncertainty (e.g. by improving frequency and reliability) and to couple this with the use of real-time solutions to provide assistance and reassurance. Attention is now turned to the impact of the significant advances made over the last 30 years with respect to the deployment of smart technology to improve public transport information.

5.4 The uses of smart technology in public transport markets

5.4.1 Real-time passenger information for journey planning

As noted above, applications of RTPI at bus stops became more widespread from the mid-1980s. This was partly as a by-product of longer-term developments in automatic vehicle locationing (AVL) systems. As early as 1958, London Transport had experimented with the bus electronic scanning indicator system in which bus location was achieved by means of roadside scanning units which projected a beam of light reflected back by a code plate (fixed to the side of the bus) to the scanner unit as a coded light pattern. The scanner translated this to an electronic code which was passed to a control centre. With the introduction of radio channels in the early 1970s buses could be polled on a data channel which allowed them to supply information on the distance travelled which was determined in terms of total counts of wheel revolutions from a known origin. In this way the early principles of AVL were established. Since then the use of some form of AVL has become almost ubiquitous and as of December 2013, 94 percent of the 358,000 buses in England were fitted with AVL (DfT, 2015).

Today, bus management systems allow operators to track and monitor their buses against the timetable or scheduled headway. Information from the systems can be provided to the public in the form of real-time passenger information through various means: bus stop displays; SMS messages to individual subscribers; and websites. Contemporary applications of AVL equipment use a GPS receiver fitted to each bus together with a radio transmitter, a central server and at stop signs. The bus communicates its position either on a regular (every 30 seconds) basis or by exception (when it reaches a certain point or does not reach a certain point within a time-limited period). The central server then interprets the information from the bus and communicates the information using another radio transmitter, to the bus stop signs or to websites and mobile devices on request.

Today, more than 2,500 bus stops in London are equipped with 'countdown' RTPI displays. Corsar et al. (2016) cite other successful examples of RTPI deployed in urban locations ranging from Chicago to Stockholm and beyond. Experience to date demonstrates that the public have an appetite for timely, accurate and reliable information; a conclusion supported by numerous studies (e.g. Mishalani et al., 2006).

Although the provision of real-time passenger information to bus stop displays has been shown to reduce perceived wait time by between 20–30 percent (see Caulfield and O'Mahony, 2009), this does not result in an actual reduction in wait time. If passengers were to be informed of real-time bus information (e.g. via their mobile device) before they arrive at the bus stop then actual savings in wait time could be experienced as passengers have the opportunity of optimising (i.e. delaying) their bus stop arrival time and thus reducing time spent waiting at a stop. Since the value of time for passengers waiting for a bus has been widely documented to be approximately twice the value of time for passengers after they have boarded the vehicle the benefits of this are reinforced.

5.4.2 Internet-based journey planners

Whilst much attention has been given to the delivery of RTPI at bus stops the provision of real-time information for journey planning via the internet became possible from the late 1990s and an early evaluation is given by Lyons and Macdonald (1998). In the UK, Transport Direct was a multimodal journey planner developed by the government which covered road, rail, walking, cycling and ferry options. The origins of Transport Direct lie in the Integrated Transport White Paper of 1998, which made a commitment to the creation of a nationwide multimodal journey planner, which was reaffirmed by the government in the Ten-Year Plan (2000). Lyons et al. (2007) provide the historical context for the setting up of Transport Direct from the initial scoping of a multimodal travel information service in 2000 through to the formal launch in December 2004 and the recording of over 10 million user sessions in the first two years. Although widely considered to be a successful initiative Transport Direct closed in September 2014 after almost ten years of operation when the government concluded that there were plenty of other journey-planning services provided by the private sector; the result, some might argue, of the open data agenda.

Another example of a multimodal journey planner is Sydney's 131500[2] (now www.transportnsw.info), which has been operated by Serco since July 2010 on behalf of Transport for New South Wales (TfNSW), the statutory authority of the New South Wales (NSW) government. Transportnsw can be used to illustrate how journey planners are responding to changes in technology and customer demand, and gradually moving closer towards an environment of perfect information, whereby the journey planner is implemented as part of a multichannel communication strategy. Nelson and Mulley (2013) report on the evaluation of the 131500 journey planner using a survey which covered four principal aspects: journey-planner content; institutional and legal issues; organisational issues; and technical issues.

In terms of *content*, the modes incorporated are bus and coach, rail and ferry; light rail has been added following the purchase of Metro Transport Sydney by the NSW Government in 2012 after which the light rail network has expanded. Information provided to the user includes routes and schedules, whilst fares information is approximated to the cost of travel via an Opal smartcard (users are also provided with information to encourage them to purchase an Opal smartcard as well as information about paper ticket options). Users can customise walking times (+/-2km/h from a default of 4km/h) via a 'plan your trip' function. The itinerary can be modified to reflect user preference for fastest trip, fewest changes and least walking. Geographical coverage is local and regional. Users can view 'transport status' via the website and since 2014 a variety of apps for real-time information have been made available which allow users to track services and receive service update 'alerts'. Previously users only had access to a (still existing) link to the Roads and Traffic Authority's 'traffic live' site, a graphical representation of general traffic-flow conditions for selected modes which requires interpretation by the user.

Information is displayed to users in tabular form using icons to indicate modes involved and there are clickable links to an interactive map database. The language of the journey planner is English and background information about how to use the journey planner is available in a further six languages. As noted, itineraries can be calculated by shortest travel time, trips with the least service changes and trips with the least walking, but these are not storable by users. An earlier SMS real-time bus information service has been withdrawn. The possibility of booking travel tickets is limited to Country Link rail services (via a link to the TrainLink pages). Social networking media (principally Twitter and Facebook) are used to communicate with users of transportnsw and links are provided to social media accounts for TfNSW train, bus, rail, ferry and traffic updates. YouTube and Instagram accounts are also provided.

In terms of *institutional* and *legal issues* the source of funding for transportnsw is the NSW government that is also the owner of the journey planner (Department of Transport) and intellectual property rests with the developer (MDV). There are no private sources of funding. In terms of *organisational issues*, the maintenance of transportnsw is contracted to consultants (Serco). Data are updated daily from transport operators who provide data directly to the Department of Transport. The Department of Transport has responsibility for overall data management and an open data policy is promoted. There are no particular issues of data management other than the need to maintain a standard format. Apart from personal internet access, journey-planning information may also be obtained via telephone and at dedicated offices located at Circular Quay and Central Station as well as several transport shops in the central business district.

Technical issues relating to transportnsw include an average response time to the most frequent journey-planner questions of 5 seconds and a maximum response time of 8 seconds to a complex journey involving six changes. The journey planner has the capability to interface to other systems to receive queries from external systems. There is also a mobile website version of transportnsw (established in 2012) which is part of the multichannel delivery model with a key focus on mobile applications. TfNSW is also promoting an open data policy based on recent UK experience piloted by the Department for the Environment, Food and Rural Affairs. Dedicated pages provide access to the NSW Public Transport Data Exchange Program and access to data is provided under license agreements.

5.5 Towards perfect information?

The example of the transportnsw journey planner shows how over time, and with the evolution of personal mobile devices such as smartphones, provision of RTPI has become more targeted to the individual and available at more stages of the journey. Real-time information provided via apps or websites may be checked in advance of or during a journey and allow travellers to amend their journeys as required (Watkins et al., 2011). Corsar et al. (2016) note that although there are clear benefits to travellers, such systems increase complexity for the service provider, as they require a comprehensive, system-wide network for gathering data on vehicle locations. Apps providing RTPI have been steadily entering the market, particularly for urban areas, with options such as OneBusAway, Citymapper, Transit App, NextThere and Moovit providing RTPI platforms for multiple cities. Other service providers such as the Chicago CTA provide bespoke apps that are reflective of traveller needs in their particular cities.

In terms of benefits to users, evidence from a study reported by the US Department of Transportation (2006) revealed that 95 percent of Transit Tracker users accessing the real-time bus arrival information system via either phone or the internet agreed the system reduced their wait time. However, there are at present, no solid measures of what the average reduction in wait time actually is. Further evidence from the OneBusAway system implemented in Seattle, US, found that 91 percent of users reported spending less time waiting while 8 percent reported no change (Ferris et al., 2010). The actual wait time savings will vary according to the frequency of the bus services in place. For instance, passengers using a frequent service with a 10-minute headway would not benefit from real-time passenger information as much as those using a service with a 30-minute headway.

A growing number of apps rely on crowdsourcing data from users to provide timely updates on traffic and travel. This type of application can be participatory, where the user actively provides information, or opportunistic, in which applications run in the background of a smartphone and collect sensor information from ongoing activities (Corsar et al., 2016). In systems such as Waze, drivers can actively share pertinent information such as delays due to traffic accidents, road hazards and fuel prices with others using the system. Traffic-congestion data available on GoogleMaps, on the other hand, is created from data collected while running GoogleMaps with location sharing enabled on a user's smartphone or other connected mobile device (NCTA, 2013).

5.5.1 There's an app for that!

The experience of designing and evaluating an RTPI system is described by Corsar et al. (2016). A smartphone application was developed for use in rural locations (GetThereBus) as part of the Informed Rural Passenger project. The app crowdsources real-time public transport data from passengers, along with providing access to real-time updates and timetable information. Crowdsourcing involves outsourcing tasks to a (typically large) group of people (the *crowd*). In GetThereBus, the crowd consists of passengers on relevant bus services that are given the task of tracking (and sharing) the location of a bus via the app; this information is then used as part of an RTPI system.

The main findings of an evaluation study with the GetThereBus app are discussed in Papangelis et al. (2016b); in summary, the participants reported that the RTPI affected their perceived control over the journey, reduced their waiting time, increased their willingness to pay for services like the GetThereBus app and the information it provides, made the bus service easier to use, improved their perceptions towards the bus service and affected their decision making.

5.5.2 The emerging contribution of social media

The use of social media platforms such as Twitter is rapidly emerging as a medium to allow for real-time sharing of information between public transport operators and their passengers as well as other key information providers such as agencies and broadcasters. With social media the information is shared in both *formal* (i.e. via updates sent directly from public transport operators and agencies to their followers) and in more *informal* (such as through passenger reports of delays or disruptions) ways (Gault et al., 2014).

As evidence of the move towards social media, Accenture (2013) noted that passengers desire more frequent communication from, and greater access to, transport providers via this medium. Properly used, social media offers operators valuable insight into the passenger experience, including their attitudes and behaviour. Furthermore, travellers can alert others to delays and disruption at an early stage – often before the operator even becomes aware of a problem, thus contributing to the objective of perfect information. A study exploring the use of social media with rail passengers showed how Twitter is increasingly important as an additional channel of information during disruption (Passenger Focus and Abellio, 2012); a finding supported by Pender et al. (2014). Analysis of usage of social media by public transport operators appears to indicate a preference for Twitter rather than Facebook, as Facebook is often considered too personal and social (Passenger Focus and Abellio, 2012).

A study by Gault et al. (2014), completed as part of the Social Journeys project, investigated the use of Twitter amongst three subsidiaries of a major UK bus operator. Findings revealed a number of emerging strategies in the use of social media, namely: persistent conversation, provision of real-time information and identity management.

- The persistent conversation is the communication occurring between passengers and a set of *personas* through Twitter. This means that a relationship can be built up between the bus company and their customers over a more extended period of time than is otherwise possible when the bus drivers are the main communication interface. This relationship construction reflects an important role that social media can play as it helps reintroduce a social element of customer engagement that is otherwise lacking.
- The provision of real-time information relates to the ways in which information on an unplanned disruption is communicated through this channel. The alternative strategies for doing this were described in terms of being proactive or reactive when disseminating such information to passengers. The scale of the bus network and proximity of the social media operators to the bus network managers are major influences on deciding which approach is adopted.
- The identity management relates to the ways in which personas are used to communicate with passengers, and their configurations (e.g. the ownership and management of aliases) are largely dependent on the resources available within the organisation. The ability for a transport operator to build a meaningful relationship with their customers can be influenced by the ownership the Twitter operators hold of these identities.

Further evidence of the importance of social media to the transport operator perspective is given by Collins et al. (2013), who found that evaluation of short social media messages to determine rider satisfaction could be beneficial to public transport agencies insofar as: the cost of data collection is minimal; data can be collected in real-time; user-specific needs can be assessed; and data can provide meaningful insight as to why a particular sentiment is felt.

A further current interest relates to how social media may be linked with journey planners or otherwise to provide dynamic transport information (rather than a journey planner just using social media as an alternative communication channel, as in the examples put forward by Gault et al., 2014). The integration of data crowdsourced from social media with transport information primarily reliant upon structured data from transport agencies has been explored in contexts as diverse as campus transport, traffic prediction and via crowdsourced transport information systems such as Waze. Results from the development of the experimental TravelBot system are discussed below.

5.5.3 The special case of disruption

The critical role that real-time information can play at times of disruption has been a common thread in this chapter. Working in a rural context Papangelis et al. (2016a) investigated the strategies employed by bus travellers when they encounter disruption. The most common coping strategy is 'time buffering' (where individuals usually make an assumption that they will be late, or that something will go wrong, and therefore build in time). Not surprisingly, access to accurate real-time information is probably the best way to insulate against disruption. Papangelis et al. (2016a) identify that kinship networks are also utilised as a way to protect against disruptions. Kinship networks are composed of weak ties and strong ties. An individual's strong ties generally consist of family members and close friends, work colleagues and school peers that are considered to be as close as familial links. The weak ties are usually friends of people from the strong ties network, or other passengers, where they have a strong dependence on the connectivity to the individuals' travel patterns. The information the passengers are seeking from these networks is usually to increase their situational awareness and information on how to mitigate the effects of disruptions. Individuals exchange information through kinship networks via various technologies, including smartphone applications, social media, emails, phone calls and text messages.

A series of studies has enabled greater understanding of the role of social media in managing disruption and its use by both operators and passengers. This has helped define the requirements for the TravelBot system (Corsar et al., 2015), described below. The first study explored the transport-operator perspective of social media usage (Gault et al., 2014) which was discussed earlier, a follow-up study examined the passenger perspective of social media and a third explored how a technology solution may facilitate a dialogue between the operator, passengers and between fellow passengers.

An awareness of their social media habits and usage patterns was helpful to identify particular times of day where commuters using public transport are likely to engage with information made available through social media channels. In the context of their social media usage, passengers confirmed that it was relaxing to have time for other activities such as reading; however, there was frustration from being subjected to delays and not receiving any explanation for them or not having the ability to do anything about it. In response to this a further study (the *Tweeting Travel* project) sought to demonstrate a range of dialogues between passengers and an automated travel assistant via social media. The purpose of this was to gain insights into the information and technology requirements to support such dialogues. However, the automated system in this instance was actually two people who were acting in the role of the system using the Wizard of Oz methodology (Dow et al., 2005).

From the above studies the TravelBot system was developed to support a user study aimed at exploring the use of social media as a source of information and the user experience of a system that automates RTPI via social media. The TravelBot system monitors Twitter for messages describing events and, when such a message is identified, TravelBot attempts to determine if the event may adversely affect the transport network. If so, details of the event are compared with the planned and ongoing journeys of each TravelBot user to identify if their journey(s) may be disrupted by that event. If a potential disruption is identified, then a personalised message is created using natural language generation techniques and sent to the user alerting them of the potential issue. Before each planned journey commences users are also provided with a message providing expected departure times for bus services they use based on real-time information provided by NextBus API. The TravelBot system is designed to facilitate sharing of information about disruptions among the users who may be travelling on the same or intersecting bus routes. The underlying information ecosystem is described by Corsar et al. (2015).

In evaluation users indicated a clear shift in confidence in allowing the real-time information provided to affect their advance travel plans – a clear demonstration of the effects of providing better-quality (closer to perfect) information. Participants also confirmed that they were reading the information that was being pushed in the form of direct messages; this indicates that personalisation of travel alerts in the form of Twitter direct messages was found to be valuable for those making use of the system.

5.6 Conclusions: future possibilities and changes

As shown in this chapter there is a long history of providing passenger information to public transport passengers. A key factor in influencing customer satisfaction is through empowering customers with a sense of certainty about their journey, particularly where disruption occurs. Real-time information is critical to the elimination of uncertainty and is now a basic expectation of customers. Moreover, the journey-planning experience needs to be supported by access to information that is user friendly, user empowered, reliable and efficient (Nelson and Mulley, 2013).

Over time the provision of timely, accurate and personalised real-time information has become the priority of those charged with the development of journey planners and other channels for the delivery of information. Mobile applications have already eclipsed the limited deployment opportunities of real-time displays at bus stops and (traditional) journey planners must also be available for use on mobile devices, and are at the heart of current developments in MaaS.

Common to all applications is the tension between awareness of what passengers want and the cost and reliability of providing it. Although some transport operators are using Twitter to communicate with passengers (and better still, to engage in dialogue) it must be recognised that embracing and exploiting this requires investment both in time and effort.

The move along the pathway towards perfect information is shown by the experience of developing apps (such as GetThereBus) whereby passengers can now be seen as producers of passenger information as well as consumers. To recognise the benefits of enhanced data sharing between the parties involved, a clear pathway to delivery by the key stakeholders is essential. Nevertheless, so long as issues of quality, provenance and trust can be adequately dealt with a truly rich resource has become available to the transport operator and passenger alike.

Acknowledgements

The Informed Rural Passenger and Social Journeys projects were supported by the award made by the RCUK Digital Economy programme to the dot.rural Digital Economy Research Hub at the University of Aberdeen; award reference: EP/G066051/1.

Notes

1 MaaS is variously defined but the essential idea is to see transport or mobility not as a physical asset to purchase (e.g. a car) but as a single service available on demand and incorporating all transport services from cars to buses to rail.

2 Details of the weblink for this site and for all other transport planner tools outlined in this chapter are given below in alphabetical order: Chicago CTA (www.ctabustracker.com); Citymapper (www.citymapper.com); Moovit (http://moovitapp.com); NextBus API (www.travelinedata.org.uk/traveline-open-data/nextbuses-api/); Next There (www.nextthere.com); OneBusAway (http://onebusaway.org); Transit (http://transitapp.com); Transportnsw.info (www.transportnsw.info); TravelBot (https://github.com/SocialJourneys); Waze (www.waze.com).

References

Accenture (2013). Public Transportation Users Predict Big Increases in the Use of Smartphones, Paperless Travel and Social Media, New Accenture Survey Reveals. https://newsroom.accenture.com/news/public-transportation-users-predict-big-increases-in-the-use-of-smartphones-paperless-travel-and-social-media-new-accenture-survey-reveals.htm (accessed 5 March 2016).

Caulfield, B. and O'Mahony, M. (2009). A Stated Preference Analysis of Real-Time Public Transit Stop Information. *Journal of Public Transportation*, 12(3), 1–20, http://131.247.19.1/jpt/pdf/JPT12-3Caulfield.pdf (accessed 4 March 2016).

Collins, C., Hasan, S. and Ukkusuri, S. V. (2013). A Novel Transit Rider Satisfaction Metric: Rider Sentiments Measured from Online Social Media Data. *Journal of Public Transportation*, 16(2), pp. 21–45.

Corsar, D., Markovic, M., Gault, P., Mehdi, M., Edwards, P., Nelson, J. D., Cottrill, C. and Sripada, S. (2015). *TravelBot: Journey Disruption Alerts Utilising Social Media and Linked Data?* 14th International Semantic Web Conference (ISWC2015, Bethlehem), PA, 11–15 October.

Corsar, D., Beecroft, M. and Cottrill, C., Nelson, J. D., Edwards, P., Velaga, N. and Sripada, S. (2016). Build an App and They Will Come? Lessons Learnt from Trialling the GetThereBus App in Rural Communities. Proc. 48th Annual UTSG Conference, 6–8 January.

DfT (2015). *Annual Bus Statistics: England 2014/15*. London: Department for Transport.

Dow, S., MacIntyre, B., Lee, J., Oezbek, C., Bolter, J. D. and Gandy, M. (2005). Wizard of Oz Support throughout an Iterative Design Process. *Pervasive Computing, IEEE*, 4(4), pp. 18–26.

Dziekan, K. and Sedin, S. (2005). Customer Reactions to the Implementation of a Trunk Bus Network in Stockholm. Paper presented at the 56th UITP World Congress, 5–9 June, Rome, urn:nbn:se:kth:diva-8226 (accessed 8 March, 2016).

Ferris, B., Watkins, K. and Borning, A. (2010). OneBusAway: Results from Providing Real-Time Arrival Information for Public Transit. *CHI 2010, 10–15 April, Atlanta, GA*, http://dl.acm.org/citation.cfm?id=1753597 (accessed 4 March 2016).

Gault, P., Corsar, D., Edwards, P., Nelson, J. D. and Cottrill, C. (2014). *You'll Never Ride Alone: The Role of Social Media in Supporting the Bus Passenger Experience*. EPIC 2014: Ethnographic Praxis in Industry Conference Proceedings, pp. 199–212.

Howes, A. and Rye, T. (2005). *Public Transport: Citizens' Requirements. HiTrans Best Practice Guide 5*. Skytta: HiTrans.

Lyons, G. D. and Macdonald, M. (1998). Traveller Information and the Internet. *Traffic Engineering and Control*, 39(1), pp. 24–32.

Lyons, G., Avineri, E., Farag, S. and Harman, R. (2007). Strategic Review of Travel Information Research. *Final report to the DfT*. http://webarchive.nationalarchives.gov.uk/+/http:/www.dft.gov.uk/adobepdf/245385/249577/Strategic_Review_of_Travel_1.pdf (accessed 12 March 2016).

Mishalani, R. G., McCord, M. M. and Wirtz, J. (2006). Passenger Wait Time Perceptions at Bus Stops: Empirical Results and Impact on Evaluating Real-Time Bus Arrival Information. *Journal of Public Transportation*, 9(2), pp. 89–106.

Mulley, C. and Nelson, J. D. (2000). The Presence of ITS: The Implications for the Business Case versus the Social CBA Evaluation for Investment. *ITS Journal*, 6, pp. 69–82.

NCTA (2013). How Google Tracks Traffic. 3 July, www.ncta.com/platform/broadband-internet/how-google-tracks-traffic/ (accessed 11 March 2016).

Nelson, J. D. and Mulley, C. (2013). The Impact of the Application of New Technology on Public Transport Service Provision and the Passenger Experience: A Focus on Implementation in Australia. *Research in Transportation Economics*, 39, pp. 300–308.

Papangelis, K., Velaga, N. R., Ashmore, F., Sripada, S., Nelson J. D. and Beecroft, M. (2016a). Exploring the Rural Passenger Experience, Information Needs and Decision Making during Public Transport Disruption. *Research in Transportation Business and Management*, 18(1), pp. 57–69, doi: 10.1016/j.rtbm.2016.01.002

Papangelis, K., Nelson, J. D., Sripada, S. and Beecroft, M. (2016b). The Effects of Mobile Real Time Information on Rural Passengers. *Transportation Planning and Technology*, 39(1), pp. 97–114.

Passenger Focus and Abellio (2012). Short and Tweet: How Passengers Want Social Media during Disruption. www.transportfocus.org.uk/research/publications/short-and-tweet-how-passengers-want-social-media-during-disruption (accessed 5 March 2016).

Pender, B., Currie, G., Delbosc, A., Shiwakoti, N. (2014). Social Media Use during Unplanned Transit Network Disruptions: A Review of Literature. *Transport Reviews*, 34(4), pp. 501–521.

Schweiger, C. (2003). Real-Time Bus Arrival Information Systems. TCRP Synthesis 48. Transportation Research Board, http://onlinepubs.trb.org/onlinepubs/tcrp/tcrp_syn_48.pdf (accessed 8 March 2016).

Suen, L. and Geehan, T. (1987). Information for Public Transport Users. In Bonsall, P. and Bell, M. (eds), *Information Technology Applications in Transport*. Utrecht: VNU Science Press, pp. 287–318.

US Department of Transportation (2006). Real-Time Bus Arrival Information Systems, Return-on-Investment Study, www.fta.dot.gov/documents/Final_Report_-_Real-Time_Systems_ ROI_Study.doc (accessed 4 March 2016).

Vermeulen, A. and Dziekan, K. (2005). *The Added Value of Real-Time Information and Effects to Customer Behaviour.* Paper presented at the Inform Norden International Conference, Reykjavik.

Watkins, K. E. Ferris, B., Borning, A., Scott Rutherford, G. and Layton, D. (2011). Where Is My Bus? Impact of Mobile Real-Time Information on the Perceived and Actual Wait Time of Transit Riders. *Transportation Research Part A: Policy and Practice*, 45(8), pp. 839–48.

White, P. (2017). *Public Transport: Its Planning, Management and Operation.* London: Routledge.

6
Passenger air traffic

Peter Forsyth

6.1 Introduction

In this context, 'air transport' is taken to refer to public transport (primarily by airlines) using fixed-wing aircraft and helicopters. In the main, the emphasis here is on passenger transport, though it needs to be noted that the freight role of aviation is important, albeit considerably smaller in revenue terms than the passenger role (see Chapter 23). Much of this task is handled by medium to large passenger jet aircraft. Business jets have a role also.

Many of the older established airlines, such as British Airways, Delta and Lufthansa, are nowadays called full services carriers (FSCs) or 'legacy' airlines. In the years since airline deregulation (see Chapter 10) a new type of airline has emerged, namely the low-cost carrier (LCC) – these include Ryanair, easyJet and Southwest. In the past, charter airlines had a major role to play, especially in Europe, but their role has been taken over by the LCCs, though they still exist to fill specific functions. Regional airlines, which use smaller jets and turboprop aircraft, are regarded as a separate type, as are commuter airlines, which operate even smaller aircraft to small cities. Most airfreight is carried in the bellies of passenger aircraft, though some dedicated freight aircraft are used, including those operated by freight-only airlines.

This chapter starts by outlining airline costs and demand. This leads on to a discussion of issues which make use of basic cost and demand analysis, including the role of LCCs, networks and alliances, market structures and profitability and cost competitiveness. There have been some externalities which have been a particular concern with aviation – these include noise and greenhouse gas emissions. Finally, a new topic in the study of aviation is briefly introduced, the suggestion that aviation, like surface transport, might have some 'wider economic benefits' (WEBs) which need to be taken into account.

6.2 The basics: costs and demand

6.2.1 The airline cost function

The airline cost function was a subject which attracted considerable attention until about 20 years ago; to a degree the main questions, such as whether there are economies of scale and density, have been resolved, though there are still some queries. Most analyses of costs start by looking at the different factors and their pricing, and then the output characteristics which affect costs, such as stage lengths, are examined, and this can lead into the measurement of efficiency (see Gillen et al., 1990). In addition, there are other aspects, such as delays and networks, which have an impact on costs, which need to be considered.

Factors of production

Cost analyses of airlines typically recognise four factors: labour, fuel, capital and other purchased inputs, such as airport or IT services. Labour is always a significant cost element. Airlines tend to spend 20–30 percent of their costs on labour (Oum et al., 2000, 2008; Doganis, 2006). Often labour costs are divided into flight labour costs (pilots and cabin crew) and other labour – maintenance, ground support, marketing and the like. Airlines differ widely in terms of the use they make of sub-contracting; a large FSC, such as Lufthansa, will tend to do things such as aircraft maintenance in-house, while a small LCC will contract it out, and thus it will spend a smaller proportion of its costs on labour.

There are two aspects of labour which are attracting interest of late. The first is unionisation of the workforce, which has a direct effect on wage levels and working conditions. In years gone by, airlines were usually heavily unionised, however, this has been changing. One of the main reasons why LCCs have been able to offer lower fares is they often have non-union workforces. Furthermore, those which have union workforces usually have much simpler union structures (e.g. one union for the whole airline) – both of these aspects the FSCs are trying to copy.

The second aspect is the question of which country the labour is hired in. In the past, most employees of an airline came from its home country, save for some labour hired in destination countries (e.g. British Airways would hire staff in the US to service its US flights). There were some exceptions to this – Cathay Pacific from Hong Kong hired staff from the destinations it flew to. This has been changing, as airlines have been seeking to take advantage of international labour markets, and even FSCs such as Qantas have been hiring more of their staff internationally. The Gulf carriers have hired extensively in low-wage countries such as India. This trend is controversial and unions have been concerned about the practice.

Fuel is also a substantial cost item, accounting for between 15 and 40 percent of costs, depending on oil prices, and the type of airline (e.g. whether the airline is an LCC or not). Most airlines pay about the same price for their fuel (claims that Gulf airlines obtain cheap fuel are unsubstantiated). Some airlines hedge fuel prices, which gives them a temporary advantage at a cost. Some domestic airlines pay a little more as a result of state-based taxes, for example in the US. Older aircraft do use more fuel than newer aircraft, and thus airlines which have newer aircraft spend a smaller proportion of their costs on fuel.

Capital and equipment costs tend to be around 10 percent of costs, and aircraft costs are a major part of these. Airlines may own or lease their aircraft. Some airlines tend to use new aircraft (Gulf airlines, LCCs such as Ryanair) while others use older aircraft (US FSCs). Newer aircraft are more costly to acquire but they use less fuel.

Other purchased inputs is a broad category, and in some cases can be nearly 50 percent of costs (if an airline makes extensive use of sub-contracting), though normally it is rather less than this. It includes IT services, marketing and the rent of premises. It also includes airport services. These can be high or low, depending on the type of airline. They will be high for FSCs using expensive (but convenient) city airports such as London's Heathrow, or low for LCCs using smaller regional airports (Doganis, 2006).

A distinction which is sometimes made is between direct operating costs (including flight crew salaries, fuel, airport charges, maintenance and aircraft depreciation) and indirect operating costs (including ticketing, passenger services, promotion and general administrative costs) (Doganis, 1986). Total costs are split roughly half and half between the two of these.

Service and output characteristics

There are several aspects which will influence costs, which, for want of a better term, may be called service and output characteristics. These lead to the question of whether there are economies of scale in airline services, and more to the point, economies of density.

Airline costs depend upon stage lengths flown. In most cases, a flight of 2,000km will cost less than two flights of 1,000km. This is partly due to the time spent at airports, taxiing and increased fuel burn on take-off and landing (Gillen et al., 1990). There are some exceptions to this rule. In particular, very long flights incur extra costs. Flights of 14 or 16 hours' duration require more crew per passenger, to give crew rest breaks. This is highly relevant at the moment, where there currently exists a race between the long-haul carriers such as Qantas, Singapore Airlines and Emirates as to who has the longest flight. Currently (April 2016) it is Emirates with its Dubai–Auckland flight, though Qatar Airways is planning to introduce a longer Doha–Auckland flight in 2017. Longer flights also have an advantage in that they require less time stopping at airports for refuelling – passengers mainly prefer a direct London–Singapore flight to a flight which stops at Dubai.

Another important aspect is aircraft size. An aircraft which has 300 seats will be less costly to operate than one with 150 seats on a per seat basis. Thus, until recently, most long-haul routes were dominated by large aircraft, such as the Boeing 747 and Airbus A340. However, as ever, there is a trade-off to be made. Passengers value frequency as well as lower fares, and increased frequency is possible if airlines use smaller aircraft. As a result, short-haul airlines, including the LCCs, operate medium-sized aircraft, such as the Airbus A320 or Boeing 737, which have about 150–80 seats, rather than the largest aircraft, the Airbus A380, which can seat 550 passengers.

Airline costs depend on the load factor of the flight – costs per passenger will be higher if the aircraft is 70 percent full than if it is 80 percent full. In the days before deregulation, many flights were relatively empty, with load factors of 60 percent or less, though it depended very much on the market. At the same time, charter flights were achieving load factors of 90 percent or more. Since then, LCCs have been able to achieve high load factors, but this has also been the case with many FSCs – essentially, airlines, no matter what their type, have been able to use yield management (see below) to increase load factors.

Service quality is another major determinant of cost. Service quality has many dimensions. Some are obvious – it costs more to provide services to a first or business class passenger than an economy class passenger. The size of the seats, the legroom, whether or not showers are provided, whether the passenger is provided with meals, all have an impact on costs. Airlines often claim that it is in the premium classes that they make their money, but it is also the case that they incur costs here.

However, there are other aspects of quality which are costly to provide. One of these is connecting services, an aspect which is beginning to be recognised as highly important. FSCs operate with more buffer time, in as much as they allow more time between flights to allow connections, than do LCCs. They also move passengers' baggage from flight to flight. Most LCCs operate on the basis that they are non-connecting flights – if a passenger misses a flight because their previous flight was late, that is their problem (though this is changing a little).

6.2.2 Economies of scale and density

For many years, until the 1970s, airlines were believed to be subject to increasing economies of scale. This presumption gave rise to the view that airlines were natural monopolies which should be regulated. However, empirical studies of the 1970s did not support this – several studies suggested that airlines were subject to constant returns, at least for most levels of output (there were some scale economies for very small airlines, operating three or five aircraft) (Caves et al., 1984). The situation in the airline industry seems to indicate this: small, medium and large airlines coexist side by side, and small airlines can operate efficiently and at low cost.

While airlines are not subject to economies of scale, they are subject to economies of density. Consider what happens when there is an increase in the number of passengers in a market, assuming that there is a fixed number of airlines. The additional passengers can be handled by an airline using larger aircraft. If this is the case, costs per passenger will fall. Alternatively, suppose that the additional passengers are handled by the airlines using more of the same type of aircraft. In this case, frequency will increase, and even though there is no cash cost reduction, there will be a benefit to passengers through a reduction in convenience and generalised costs (including delay costs to the passengers). Normally, when there is an increase in the number of passengers, the airlines will increase the average size of the aircraft and operate more flights. Passengers will enjoy a mix of lower fares and increased convenience.

Economies of density lie at the heart of many things, which we observe in the airline and other transport industries. These economies are critical when airlines are designing their networks. Many airlines use a hub and spoke network – while flights may be less direct, the airline is able to fly more and bigger aircraft, thus reducing costs (Oum and Tretheway, 1990).

6.2.3 Delays

One unavoidable consequence of aviation is that flights are often delayed, which imposes a cost on passengers and the airlines which fly them. There are many sources of delays, one being adverse weather. Flights can be delayed when aircraft cannot take off or land due to fog or storms. To a degree, better and more advanced equipment, e.g. ILS CAT III, mitigate delays, but such investments are only worthwhile for larger airports.

A very important source of delays comes about because the capacity of equipment or facilities is fixed and demand exceeds capacity. A major source of delay is the limits on capacity at airports, particularly in terms of runways, but also taxiways, gates and aprons. Taxiways can be congested and gates and aprons may be full. However, the most important constraint is normally that on runways (De Neufville and Odoni, 2003). A runway can normally handle about 40 movements (take-offs and landings) in an hour, depending upon the type of aircraft, the mix of aircraft and their speed. If demand exceeds this, delays will mount. There are several ways in which these delays can be moderated. (Note Heathrow has two runways and handles a little over 80 movements per hour.)

The most common of these, except in the US, is the slot system (Czerny et al., 2008). Airport runways which are subject to excess demand can be rationed by slots – essentially, airlines are required to have a 'slot' to use the runway at a particular time. Without a slot, the airline is not permitted to use the airport. Most slots are held by existing users of the airport (grandfathering), and if the airline wished to use the airport and it does not have a slot for that hour, it will have to choose a less busy period, fly to an alternative airport, or not fly at all. In some cases, there is an active market for slots. The best example of this is in the UK, where slots to use London Heathrow, and to a lesser extent Gatwick, can be purchased in an active market. A pair of slots (landing and take-off) in Heathrow was recently (early 2016) sold for US $75 million. In other countries airlines exchange slots, though the market is rather less transparent.

In other markets, prices are used to ration capacity. However, with airport runways this is very rare, though it does occasionally happen. With London Heathrow, at different times there has been an element of peak pricing, but the main burden of rationing the scarce runway capacity falls on slots. Sydney airport has tried explicit peak pricing, and currently there is some peak pricing at Brisbane.

The US is an outlier in that, except for a very few airports, runways are not rationed by any explicit rationing device. It is a matter of first come, first served. As a result, with popular airports which have demand exceeding capacity demand is rationed by delays. Queues develop and delays are the result – delays can be several hours for a flight. All in all, the costs of these delays can be very large (Morrison and Winston, 2008); the problem is recognised, but there has been little willingness on the part of the authorities to address it.

While runways and airside constraints are the main cause of delays and high costs, passenger constraints can also be important. Terminals can become congested and this results in delays in moving about the terminals and falling passenger comfort and convenience. In addition, increased security measures are now a cause of delay. Investment to expand terminals can be the solution to this problem, though this is not always easy, especially in constrained sites such as many in the US, Europe and parts of Asia, for example Japan.

Another system which is liable to get congested is the air traffic control (ATC) system. ATC covers a number of aspects, including the handling of aircraft moving on the ground, take-offs and landings and en-route air navigation. National and regional (e.g. EuroControl handling European Union (EU) flights) bodies control the various stages of flights. The sky is not unlimited and in particular areas, such as northeast USA and parts of Europe, skies are congested. As a result, flights may be required to take indirect routings, resulting in delays and higher operating costs. In addition, in some locations, such as around South Korea's main hub airport, flight paths are constrained by geographical and political factors – Incheon is close to North Korea. While there are many documented inefficiencies in ATC, reform has been difficult to achieve. This is partly because of the multinational nature of aircraft routes – in Europe, a flight from London to Greece will pass through airspace controlled by many different national authorities. There are proposals to achieve a 'single European sky', but progress in achieving this has been slow.

6.2.4 *Technical change and its growth*

The most obvious indicator of technical progress in aviation lies in the path of air fares over the decades (see Doganis, 2006, p. 16). They have been steadily falling in real terms and seem to be set to continue to do so for some time to come. There are several reasons for this, but two of them stand out. Firstly, there is the improvement in the efficiency of aircraft, and secondly, is the use of information technology and the internet.

Commercial aircraft have become steadily more productive over time. There are further advances in aircraft technology expected for the next few years and beyond. A critical aspect of this is fuel efficiency, but there are also improvements in the efficiency of maintenance. There have been improvements across the range of aircraft types, from small turboprops to large jets. The Boeing 737 of today is more fuel efficient than that of 1967, and future versions of it will be improved still further. Airlines of today travel at much the same speed as those of 1975, and the maximum range of the aircraft has increased slightly over time.

There are some second-order questions which are yet to be resolved. One of these concerns the role of very large aircraft, such as the Boeing 747 and Airbus A380. For decades, the former dominated long-distance routes, though it has been losing ground to the slightly smaller, newer Boeing 777 and Airbus A330. Airbus thought that it would dominate the long-haul market with its A380, which entered service ten years ago. In fact, sales are now tapering off, and only Emirates has bought many of them. On the other hand, the smaller, newer and for their size, very fuel efficient Boeing 787 and Airbus 350 have been selling very well. A significant change has been the use of IT. The extensive use of IT and the internet has become very obvious to the passenger and there has been a revolution in how tickets are sold, flights are managed and how airlines are handling passengers at the airport (Doganis, 2006). Some of the advances were pioneered by LCCs in their quest for more efficient ways of providing their product – an example of this comes with internet booking. Labour-intensive tasks are now done by computers or by the passenger, leading to significant cost savings.

6.2.5 Demand and yield management

Demand elasticities

As with other industries, the demand for aviation is conventionally measured by econometrically estimated elasticities. A useful summary of elasticities is that contained in Gillen and Morrison (2007) and their results are summarised in Table 6.1.

Overall demand is elastic, though some market segments are inelastic. Long-haul elasticities are lower than short-haul elasticities – this is what can be expected, given that travellers typically have more options for short-haul travel than they do for long haul. Elasticities for business travel are normally much lower than for leisure travel (except for long-haul domestic flights, where the two elasticities are much the same).

Yield management

As with other services such as hotel services and telecommunications, the output of airlines ceases to exist once the flight has taken off. There may be plenty of capacity on a flight, but it is of no value if the flight has taken off. In addition, the marginal cost of an additional passenger is low. As a result, airlines have always been concerned to make the best use of their non-storable inventory, thus they have become experts in yield management (Kraft et al., 1986). There are two significant aspects of yield management: one is that the airlines attempted to practise price discrimination, and the other is that they were attempting to fill empty seats on the plane. Either one or both of these aspects may be present with specific devices to manage yields.

In the early years, airlines had a very simple price structure: a basic (economy) and a premium (business) fare. In the 1960s charter airlines became a major force in leisure travel; these airlines had high load factors and low prices and only served markets if they were sure that they could fill the aircraft (Doganis, 1986). By the late 1970s, airlines were experimenting with standby fares – the most famous of these was the Laker 'Skytrain' between London and New York: passengers

Table 6.1 Own price elasticities of demand

Market segment	*No. of estimates*	*Mean elasticity*
Long-haul international business	16	–0.265
Long-haul international leisure	49	–1.04
Long-haul domestic business	26	–1.15
Long-haul domestic leisure	6	–1.104
Short-haul business	16	–0.7
Short-haul leisure	4	–1.52

Source: Gillen and Morrison, 2007

would queue for low-priced tickets and those who missed out, missed out (Doganis, 1986). As with charters, the objective was to fill the aircraft. About the same time, legacy airlines began instituting cheaper tickets to those passengers who were prepared to stay at their destination over a Saturday night. This was an example of price discrimination, since these passengers did not impose lower costs on the airline than other passengers – rather the attempt was to segregate inelastic business travellers from elastic leisure travellers. This said, price discrimination can have some positive aspects. Cheaper tickets to leisure travellers mean that the demand for services is increased, and this means that frequencies will be higher. Business travellers who put a high value on frequency will gain (Frank, 1983).

The devices which airlines use to implement yield management have changed over the years, and the emergence of LCCs and internet booking has again changed the favoured devices (Doganis, 2006). Airlines now offer lower fares several weeks before the flight and increase them over time, such that the fare offered two hours before the flight (when business travellers dominate) may be several times the lowest price of weeks ago. This may not always happen – if the flight is poorly booked, fares may stay low. Both aspects of yield management are present. Airlines have also made good use of 'unbundling' – charging separate prices for different aspects of the service, such as providing food and carrying baggage. Some of this results in lower costs to the airline, but there is also an element of price discrimination – putting a bag on a flight may cost $20 when the flight is booked, $40 three days later and $80 at check-in at the airport.

6.3 Applying the theory to policy and strategic issues

6.3.1 The growth and significance of low-cost carriers

One of the most significant developments of the past 20 or 30 years has been the development of LCCs. Indeed, it is notable that LCCs have formed a distinct type of market segment.

LCCs emerged after the deregulation of the airline industry (Lawton, 2002; Calder 2002). This came about in the late 1970s to early 1980s in the US. Other countries, such as Canada, Australia and Brazil, followed, and in the 1990s Europe as a whole deregulated (Gross and Luck, 2013; Budd and Ison, 2014; Budd et al., 2014). The response of the market to the removal of regulation was not so much greater competition between established airlines (though this did happen) as the creation of a new market segment, the LCC. Initially new airlines were slow to establish themselves in a sustained manner, but some airlines, such as Southwest in the US and Ryanair in Europe, did succeed.

Several factors underlay their success (see Lawton, 2002). The LCCs were able to gain a foothold in markets, not by being slightly cheaper than the old carriers, the FSCs, but by being a lot cheaper. As a result, individual airlines grew rapidly and consequently the LCC market segment also grew steadily, though many entrants did fail (see Budd et al., 2014). The LCCs provided a different product (fewer frills, more dense seating, little provision for connections), they paid lower prices for their inputs (cheaper, more distant airports, lower wages) and they were more efficient with high aircraft and other factor input utilisation rates. FSCs have realised that their markets have been under threat and to a degree they have responded. They have increased seating densities, provided less by way of in-flight food, changed their pricing structures and in some cases they have simplified their timetables. However, they are constrained from replicating the LCC model exactly – they still wish to serve the premium end of the market, and this means that they need to have longer turn-arounds to facilitate connections, they still need to operate from the more expensive central city airports and they are locked into higher union wages. As a result, in more mature markets, some FSCs are surviving, but most are not prospering.

6.3.2 Networks and alliances

Airlines try to build networks which are profitable. In doing so, they need to take note of the various aspects of airline economics – the advantages and limitations of larger aircraft, the benefits from high frequencies, regulatory constraints (whether the airline is permitted to operate in a specific route), the availability of aircraft and the degree of competition on routes on which they would like to fly.

FSCs typically choose to operate on a hub and spoke basis, as noted before this is a structure which enables good frequencies, good connections and relatively low costs (Oum and Tretheway, 1990). In the US before deregulation, airlines were constrained in terms of the routes they were permitted to fly on. After deregulation, they gravitated to the hub and spoke network. In Europe, airlines already had hub and spoke networks, based on the main cities in the country, such as Paris for Air France and Frankfurt for Lufthansa, and after liberalisation they preserved their networks, though sometimes with adjustments (for example, Lufthansa added a Munich hub).

While LCCs are using hub airports (for example, easyJet uses some major hubs, e.g. London Gatwick), they make much less use of this type of network. Their emphasis is on point to point services, and they have been more opportunistic in the routes they fly to. Until recently they have not been interested in connecting traffic – passengers may connect from flight to flight, though many airlines do not make it easy for them to do so. Things are changing, however, and some airports, such as Malpensa in Italy, are making it easier for passengers of LCCs to connect their own flights. As they have become larger they have been developing 'bases' – airports from which they are flying several services and at which they are basing a number of aircraft. Some LCCs (especially the 'hybrid' carriers, which are partly low cost but which offer a higher standard of service, such as Air Berlin) are seeking connecting traffic.

Airline alliances have become an important way in which airlines develop their networks. Airlines often wish to provide a wide range of destinations, and one effective way in which they can do this is to form alliances. Airline alliances go back a long way (in the 1930s Imperial Airways had an alliance with Qantas to serve the London–Sydney route), but they did not have a major presence until around the mid-1990s (Doganis, 2006). Initially alliances were quite unstable and airlines would change partners regularly. Eventually, the alliance structure became more settled, with most larger (non-LCC) airlines joining one of three alliances – the largest 'Star' (including Lufthansa, United and Singapore Airlines), 'Sky Team' (including Air France-KLM and Delta) and 'One World' (including British Airways, American and Japan Airlines). Some airlines have been reluctant to join alliances and Emirates was one of these, though recently it has joined Qantas in a close alliance. In addition, there are a range of smaller and rather ad hoc alliances which gain and lose members regularly, such as that between Qantas and Air New Zealand (now ended).

Alliances provide network and other advantages. There are many ways in which alliances can reduce costs in providing spares, maintenance facilities and joint marketing. They can be positive on the passenger and shipper side, in particular, they can improve connectivity by coordinating services, and frequent flier programmes can be linked, providing benefits for passengers. Alliances can be useful in circumventing regulatory restrictions, for example, when an airline flies to another country, an alliance partner can connect to provide services which the first airline is not permitted to operate. A common way in which alliances operate is through code shares, whereby an airline which does not operate a service on its own equipment can code share with another and attach its own code to it. This may be a minor convenience to passengers but it may be accompanied by financial arrangements between the two airlines. In many cases, the alliance arrangements will extend as far as the two airlines operating joint-venture services.

Alliances can be complementary or anti-competitive. Most alliance arrangements are complementary, in the sense that several airlines can provide a better or lower-cost service than each of the individual airlines would be able to provide. However, alliances can be anti-competitive. If two airlines which currently dominate a route and which are currently competing form an alliance, competition is reduced. This will be of concern to competition authorities who may block it – many alliance arrangements will thus be subject to the scrutiny of these authorities (Oum and Park, 1997). International alliances require the approval of competition authorities of all countries involved. Airlines propose alliances and argue for them, citing the convenience and cost advantages they bring. The competition authority will evaluate the proposed alliance, setting the claimed benefits against the costs of less competition. If the alliance is on a route on which there is already strong competition they will most likely approve it (for example, Emirates and Qantas were permitted to operate a joint venture between London and Sydney because there was already a lot of competition on this route). On the other hand, if the authorities judge that the alliance would lead to a substantial reduction in competition, it may not approve the alliance.

6.3.3 Market structures and profitability

For the period since deregulation, airlines have been unable to sustain profitability. The industry is cyclical, and there are times when the industry is very profitable, but these are followed by long periods of loss making and poor profitability. In the days before deregulation and open skies, industry returns were protected by regulation. In domestic markets fares were set such that the airlines were able to achieve profitability, and in international markets capacity controls were set such that profits were the result.

At the time of deregulation, the expectation was that the airlines would not have any problems in operating profitably, taking one year with another. Several expected that markets, such as city pair markets, would be very competitive, with many airlines serving all but small, low-density markets. At the same time as deregulation, the theory of contestability of markets was developed. Several writers on contestability also wrote on airlines and saw the airline industry as an excellent test bed for the contestability theory (Baumol et al., 1982; Bailey et al., 1985). According to this theory, if there were only a small number of airlines in a market fares would be disciplined by potential competition, and actual competition would not be necessary. If fares were high, new entrants would emerge and force down fares.

The upshot of the contestability debate was that empirical studies showed that actual competition did matter, and that potential competition was not sufficient to keep airfares no higher than cost (Morrison and Winston, 1987). This would suggest that one of the key elements of contestability theory, namely low entry barriers, is not present in the airline market. However, there are some elements of contestability in airline markets. The best example of this is the 'Southwest effect'. Empirical studies have suggested that when Southwest operates on a route, fares on other adjacent routes that Southwest does not operate on also tend to be low as other airlines are wary of possible competition from Southwest (Bennett and Craun, 1993). Apart from this effect, when there is limited competition, fares tend to be higher, if anything suggesting that airlines should not have problems in sustaining profitability.

While there are many airlines operating from most medium to large airports, the market structure could not be described as 'competitive'. There are only a small proportion of routes with three, four or more airlines flying directly from one airport to another. With longer-distance routes, such as London to Singapore, there can be rather more (and also, there can be several airlines which take indirect routes involving stops). However, such routes are in a minority. The typical airline route is thus one which can be described as oligopolistic. There can be collusion amongst airlines (in earlier days, airlines serving international routes were actually encouraged to collude). However, while there have been some instances of collusion (for example, there was a cargo cartel which many of the major airlines around the world participated in), most airline markets are regarded as fairly free of collusion. Where small numbers of airlines serve a route there may be tacit collusion. This is very difficult to prove – if Qantas and Virgin Australia decide to cease a loss-making struggle for market share, does this amount to tacit collusion (O'Sullivan, 2015)?

There are, of course, some routes on which only one airline operates. These tend to be low-density routes to smaller centres and can be regarded as monopolies. Airlines can charge high fares on these routes, and quite often they do. The situation is complicated by the fact that, in spite of being a monopoly, airlines cannot achieve cost recovery on routes to smaller or remote centres. Often, to ensure that services are maintained, governments subsidise these routes. Thus, Australia subsidises routes to remote communities and the EU subsidises routes to remote destinations, such as the Azores, the Canary Islands and the Scottish islands.

The typical airline route is one which has two, three or maybe four airlines offering a direct service, sometimes along with other airlines offering an indirect service. This may seem to be quite oligopolistic and suggest that airlines have considerable market power. Simple oligopoly models would suggest this is the case. The reality is rather different. It is the case that the number of airlines on a route makes a difference – fares will be higher on a route served by two airlines than on a route served by three.

In spite of this, if airlines do have market power, they seem to be singularly unsuccessful in taking advantage of it. As noted before, most airlines struggle to achieve sustained profitability. There have been some possible reasons for this (see e.g. Button, 1996 for a discussion of the 'empty core' theory). There are some exceptions, notably amongst the LCCs. The leading LCCs, such as Southwest, Ryanair and easyJet, have been consistently profitable. They have been growing rapidly and accessing new markets where air fares have been higher in the past – perhaps when the markets stabilise, the profitability of the FSCs may come closer to the norm. Apart from the LCCs, the lack of profitability of the airline industry is an ongoing puzzle.

6.3.4 Cost competitiveness

A good way of analysing what is going on in the airline industry is to assess the cost competitiveness of individual airlines. Cost competitiveness is a measure of the cost of providing the product – this will depend on the prices of the factors which the airline employs and its efficiency in using them (see above). In the airline context, it makes allowance of other aspects which also affect costs, such as stage length. It determines how profitable the airline is when competing with other airlines (Oum et al., 2000, 2008).

In years gone by in domestic markets such as that of the US, the factor prices faced by airlines were much the same for all airlines – for example, Delta did not have an advantage over United (see Table 6.2). After deregulation this changed – LCCs paid lower wages and sometimes paid less for airports (especially in Europe). Often, the LCCs were more efficient as well. This has put considerable pressure on the FSCs. To some extent they have been leaving markets, but they are also attempting to lower costs by concluding industrial agreements which have the effect of lowering wages. They are also attempting to increase their efficiency, and in some cases (e.g. Aer Lingus) becoming more like LCCs. As they are only part way through this transformation, many are achieving profitability only in very good years.

Cost competitiveness is also very much an issue with international airlines. In early years, international routes were highly regulated, and only two airlines, from each of the countries at

Table 6.2 Cost competitiveness: US Airlines, 1998, relative to Air Canada unit cost

Airline	*Observed unit cost difference*	*Due to stage length*	*Due to output mix*	*Input prices*	*Efficiency*	*Cost competitiveness*
Alaska	8.2	5.6	–0.2	–1.4	4.5	3.1
American	–16.8	0.4	–0.8	–1.7	–12.4	–14.1
America West	–26.8	6.5	1.0	–14.7	–22.8	–37.5
Continental	–23.3	1.5	–1.2	–4.9	–20.3	–25.2
Delta	–6.0	4.2	3.0	5.8	–16.4	–10.6
Northwest	–16.3	1.6	1.6	11.5	–29.6	–18.0
United	–17.9	–0.2	–1.0	3.5	–18.7	–15.1
US Air	13.6	9.2	1.5	3.8	0.4	4.1

Source: Oum et al., 2008

each end of the route, were permitted to serve it. While their cost competitiveness could differ, regulation ensured that the higher-cost airline was able to be profitable by charging high fares, and the lower-cost airline reaped high profits. Cost competitiveness becomes important when airlines are liberalised, which they have been since about 1980. Airlines which are not cost competitive are at a disadvantage when competing against those which are. A good example of this was with the Europe to Asia markets (see Table 6.3).

Asian airlines were originally not very cost competitive – they paid lower wages, but their efficiency was not high. However, several of them, such as Singapore Airlines and Korean Air, were able to increase their efficiency and thus their cost competitiveness. These airlines are now encountering high wages and thus they are not as competitive as they were, but other airlines are now setting the competitive benchmark.

Cost-competitiveness issues are at the heart of the Gulf airline issue. The Gulf airlines, specifically Emirates, Etihad and Qatar Airways, have grown very rapidly, and they are a considerable force in the market. Some European and US carriers have been arguing that they are being forced to compete on a non-level playing field as Gulf airlines' governments are subsidising them. Whether or not this is so, a much more important aspect of the issue is that

Table 6.3 Cost competitiveness: World Airlines, 1993, relative to American unit cost

Airline	*Observed unit cost difference*	*Due to stage length*	*Due to output mix*	*Input prices*	*Efficiency*	*Cost competitiveness*
American	0.0	0.0	0.0	0.0	0.0	0.0
United	–1.7	–1.2	0.2	3.7	–3.8	–0.1
Delta	13.5	7.7	3.1	7.4	–5.6	1.8
Japan Air Lines	50.1	–13.0	3.0	38.4	14.3	52.7
Singapore	–30.6	–20.0	6.8	–20.3	3.9	–16.3
Korean Air	–25.2	–0.8	0.1	–23.8	0.8	–22.9
Air France	19.3	–1.2	–0.8	8.8	12.4	21.2
Lufthansa	29.2	11.2	–2.0	16.8	3.8	20.6
British Airways	21.9	–2.4	11.0	–2.9	10.2	7.3
KLM	3.3	–6.2	1.7	16.0	–5.3	10.7

Source: Oum et al., 2000

the Gulf airlines are very cost competitive compared to European and US carriers. In particular, the Gulf carriers have low labour costs, partly because of tax arrangements in the Gulf (airline employees in the Gulf do not pay income tax), and also because the airlines make extensive use of low-cost sources of labour. This is a source of advantage which is not likely to be short lived.

6.4 Externalities: noise and emissions

6.4.1 Noise

Of the several externalities of aviation, the ones which have attracted the most attention are noise and emissions, especially greenhouse gas emissions. Noise is a very obvious externality and it has been a problem with aviation since the early days, but it became a particular problem when jet aircraft was introduced in the 1950s. In fact, aircraft have become steadily quieter since then, though the fact that there are more aircraft generating noise means that the problem is still a major one. Noise is a real problem when airports are planned or extended, and when new airports are planned, designers normally take a lot of care to site them such that noise is minimised. Often there are limits on building houses and community facilities close to the airport. Measuring aircraft noise has become a detailed science.

There have been several ways in which the cost of noise has been evaluated, but the most popular is that of measuring house price depreciation in properties close to the airport relative to those which are equally close but are free of noise. This approach has been used since the (Roskill) Commission on the Third London Airport (1970), and since then techniques have been refined considerably (Nelson, 1980; Daley, 2010).

While the technique is straightforward there is something of a conundrum in what the noise cost estimates say. Almost always, the noise as measured is quite small relative to other cost elements, such as infrastructure or delay costs. In spite of this, noise costs have a very high public profile. New airports or runways can be guaranteed to produce a public outcry, demonstrations and sometimes civil disobedience, which may last for years. Political decision makers are aware of this, and they are at pains to hose down the issue. There are several ways in which noise emissions can be reduced (Daley, 2010). The most popular of these is the curfew of flights at night, which are operative for many city airports. Several airports ban the use of noisy aircraft. Attempting to use the price mechanism has been less successful. A number of airports impose higher landing fees on noisier aircraft, but the problem is that the higher fees are not set at such a level as to make much of a difference to airlines' behaviour (though they do raise additional revenue for the airport). Some airports have sought to impose 'noise budgets', but again, the shadow price of noise as set is not sufficient to make a large difference in noise.

6.4.2 Emissions

Aviation generates several emissions, especially around airports. In general, these are not regarded as particularly large though some can be harmful, such as carcinogens, and others can cause cardio-respiratory complaints. However, there is one type of emission which is of particular concern and these are greenhouse gas emissions, which are regarded as contributing to global warming. There are several gas emissions and they have different effects; these effects can be short or very long lived. Of particular concern are CO_2 emissions, which are both prevalent and long lasting, but others, such as methane, nitrous oxide and particulates, are also damaging. To make things more complicated, different parts of the cycle – taxiing, take-off, cruise and landing – have different impacts on emissions (Daley, 2010).

Aviation poses special problems. It accounts for about 2 percent of total global emissions of CO_2, which would suggest that it should not be much of a worry. However, it is suggested that the damaging effect on aviation's emission could be up to three times more than this, because of the effects of other gasses and contrails, though the research in this is not settled. Furthermore, aviation is a fast-growing industry and its percentage share of total emissions is likely to grow steadily, so projections are that aviation will account for a growing percentage of total gas emissions in the future.

A further problem is that aviation is locked into a single technology, with aircraft requiring jet fuel, and there are no practical substitutes. Over time, aircraft are becoming more fuel efficient, by about 1 percent per annum. Substituting possibilities are greater for other modes, for example, electric cars and high-speed rail can be powered by nuclear and solar-generated electricity in time. There is some scope for aircraft to be powered by biofuels, but these are not likely to be able to make a big impact for many years to come.

Assuming that aviation will generate an increasing share of the world's emissions of greenhouse gas emissions, there is considerable debate as to whether this creates a problem or not. The economist's view is that it will not – the important thing is that efficient policies are adapted in all industries, so that the costs of emissions are minimised over time. This is the view of the Stern Report (Stern, 2007). It may be that aviation will account for a growing percentage of emissions, but if other industries with more scope to change their technique of production do so, the cost of adapting will be met at minimum cost. The issue then is to design efficient ways of reducing aviation emissions.

There have been several ways suggested in which aviation's emissions can be reduced. A popular one is voluntary action, whereby passengers or airlines take actions which have the effect of reducing emissions. Many airlines are now experimenting with biofuels. Another is through offsets – most airlines offer their passengers the option of paying more and offsetting the emissions by contributing to a recognised offsetting arrangement. Eight percent of Qantas passengers are purchasing offsets and this number is growing (Freed, 2016).

Governments can implement emissions trading schemes (ETS) and impose taxes to reduce emissions. The most important of these is the EU ETS, which has included aviation since 2012. This has worked as planned, though it has yet to have a large impact on emissions because aviation has not been generating as many emissions as expected (because of the lower growth in aviation) and the fact that carbon prices are lower than expected (because of the slower growth in the EU economy). There have been disputes with non-European countries as to whether their airlines should be part of the scheme – for the time being they are not included. Other countries have instituted ETS which apply to aviation – for example, New Zealand. For a time Australia imposed an emissions tax which included aviation.

Given that emissions are a global problem, the ideal solution might be a global mechanism. For some time, the International Civil Aviation Organization (ICAO) has been working towards designing a 'market-based mechanism' to reduce emissions. It may come up with a good design, however, ICAO does not have any authority to compel governments to implement it.

6.5 An emerging issue

The existence (or otherwise) of WEBs, or wider economic impacts as they are now known in the UK, is becoming a controversial issue in aviation policy analysis. When the UK's Airports Commission published its recommendations for additional airport capacity (including additional runways at Heathrow or Gatwick airports) it paid considerable attention to possible WEBs (Airports Commission, 2015).

WEBs is a new idea for aviation. They have been discussed for almost 20 years in the context of surface transport (Venables, 2007; Vickerman, 2013) and studies of motorways, urban rail lines and high-speed trains regularly include estimates of them. The concept is now being used in aviation policy studies, such as whether to build a new airport or what the costs and benefits of Airline Passenger Duties are. The concept of WEBs in surface transport is now common in the UK and has spread to Europe, Australia and New Zealand. It is likely that WEBs in aviation will become a controversial issue in aviation.

The idea of WEBs is that there are some benefits from transport which have not been captured in evaluations (such as cost-benefit evaluations) in the past. There are several forms of these. Better transport can lead to more efficient location of industries, which can lead to gains in productivity. When employees produce more, some of the gains are taxed and thus they do not benefit from the whole of the output increase. Thus there are some benefits from the better transport which are not taken account of in conventional evaluations. There are differences between surface transport and aviation, and thus the concept of WEBs cannot be used in exactly the same way as it is in surface transport. Nonetheless, the idea that there may be external effects and tax effects in aviation which have not been counted before can have some currency.

In the case of aviation, many have suggested that increased connectivity is an important effect which has been either ignored or undervalued in policy evaluation (Airports Commission, 2015). In fact, the interest in connectivity predates the recognition that it may be a source of wider economic benefits. For a number of years, researchers in aviation (and especially those from a geographical background) have developed measures of connectivity (Burghouwt and Redondi, 2013). Connectivity is a broad term and it can be used in several ways. It can be used to measure how well a city or an airport is connected to the rest of the world, especially with direct flights. The idea can be used in the context of airlines – some airline networks (such as those which have a hub at their centre, such as Emirates) are more connected than others (such as Ryanair, which does not have a central hub).

Originally, researchers made estimates of connectivity without intending to use them in further analysis; sometimes airports or cities would highlight their connectivity as a selling point, but no more. More recently, there has been analysis of the consequences of greater connectivity. Analyses were carried out of the implications of connectivity for variables of interest, such as productivity of cities, or regional or national income or of trade. There have been several econometric analyses in the US, Canada and Europe, and these have suggested a positive link between connectivity and productivity and output (InterVISTAS, 2006; Smyth and Pearce, 2007). In many cases, these links are quite strong. There are still, however, some questions to be answered, the most important of which is the causality question – are more connected cities more productive, or does greater productivity give rise to a city being more connected?

6.6 Concluding comments

Aviation is a topic area which has been analysed quite extensively over the past 40 or so years. As a result, lines of inquiry have been relatively well settled, at least in terms of the theory. A good example of this is the analysis of costs and demand, which is a building block needed to understand a range of issues. What is lagging behind is the application of this theory – we know how to measure the efficiency of airlines and airports, but there are few recent empirical studies of airlines, even though there are now many of airport efficiency. This lack of empirical work carries through to other areas, for example, there is much debate about the Gulf carriers and the advantages they might have relative to European and US carriers. There is little by way of assessments of the cost competitiveness of the different groups of carriers, however; just how cost competitive is Emirates compared to Lufthansa or United?

While some markets have matured, others are still changing. The legacy carriers are still coming to terms with the challenge posed by the LCCs – to what extent will they be able to compete effectively if they are still locked into higher wage contracts? European airline markets have had to take the EU emissions trading scheme into account, though its impact so far has been small, mainly due to the low carbon price. How well will they cope with a higher carbon price? There are many unanswered questions in the aviation market.

References

Airports Commission (2015). Airports Commission Final Report. Airports Commission, London, July.

Bailey, B., Graham, D. and Kaplan, D. (1985). *Deregulating the Airlines*. Cambridge, MA: MIT Press.

Baumol, W., Panzar, J. and Willig R. (1982).*Contestable Markets and the Theory of Industry Structure*. New York: Harcourt Brace Jovanovitch.

Bennett, R. and Craun, J. (1993). The Airline Deregulation Evolution Continues: The Southwest Effect. Office of Aviation Analysis, US Department of Transportation.

Budd, L. and Ison, S. (eds) (2014). *Low Cost Carriers: Emergence, Expansion and Evolution*. Farnham: Ashgate.

Budd, L., Francis, G., Humphreys, I. and Ison, S. (2014). Grounded: Characterising the Exit of European Low Cost Airlines. *Journal of Air Transport Management*, 34, pp. 78–85.

Burghouwt, G. and Redondi, R. (2013). Connectivity in Air Transport Networks: An Assessment of Models and Applications. *Journal of Transport Economics and Policy*, 47(1), pp. 35–53.

Button, K. (1996). Liberalising European Aviation: Is There an Empty Core Problem? *Journal of Transport Economics and Policy*, 30(3), pp. 275–91.

Calder, S. (2002). *No Frills: The Truth behind the Low Cost Revolution in the Skies*. London: Virgin Books.

Caves, D., Christensen, L. and Tretheway, M. (1984). Economies of Density versus Economies of Scale: Why Trunk and Local Service Airlines Differ. *Rand Journal of Economics*, 15, Winter, pp. 471–89.

Commission on the Third London Airport (Roskill Commission) (1970). *Papers and Proceedings: Stage III Research and Investigation–Assessment of Short-Listed Sites, Vol. 7, Parts 1 and 2*. London: HMSO.

Czerny, A., Forsyth, P., Gillen, D. and Niemeier, H.-M. (eds) (2008). *Airport Slots: International Experiences and Options for Reform*. Farnham: Ashgate.

Daley, B. (2010). *Air Transport and the Environment*. Farnham: Ashgate.

De Neufville, R. and Odoni, A. (2003). *Airport Systems Planning, Design and Management*. New York: McGraw Hill.

Doganis, R. (1986). *Flying off Course*. London: Allen and Unwin.

Doganis, R. (2006). *The Airline Business*, Second Edition. London: Routledge.

Frank, R. (1983). When Are Price Differentials Discriminatory? Journal of Policy Analysis and Management, 2(2), pp. 238–55. Reprinted in Forsyth, P., Button, K. and Nijkamp, P. (2002). *Air Transport: Classics in Transport Analysis*. Cheltenham: Edward Elgar.

Freed, J. (2016). Rising Number of Qantas Passengers Paying Premium for Carbon Offsets. *Sydney Morning Herald*, 6 June.

Gillen, D. and Morrison, W. (2007). Air Travel Demand Elasticities: Concepts, Issues and Measurement. In Lee, D. (ed.), *Advances in Airline Management: The Economics of Airline Institutions, Operations and Marketing*. Amsterdam: Elsevier.

Gillen, D., Oum, T. and Tretheway, M. (1990). Airline Cost Structure and Policy Implications: A Multiproduct Approach for Canadian Airlines. *Journal of Transport Economics and Policy, XXIV*, January, pp. 9–34.

Gross, S. and Luck, M. (eds) (2013). *The Low Cost Carrier Worldwide*. Farnham: Ashgate.

InterVISTAS (2006). *Measuring the Economic Rate of Return on Investment in Aviation*. Vancouver: InterVISTAS.

Kraft, D., Oum, T. and Tretheway, M. (1986). Airline Seat Management. *Logistics and Transportation Review*, 22, June, pp. 115–30.

Lawton, T. (2002). *Cleared for Take-Off: Structure and Strategy in the Low Fare Airline Business*. Farnham: Ashgate.

Morrison, S. and Winston, C. (1987). Empirical Implications and Tests of the Contestability Hypothesis. *Journal of Law and Economics*, 30(1), pp. 53–66.

Morrison, S. and Winston, C. (2008). Delayed! US Aviation Policy at a Crossroads. In Winston, C. and de Rus, G., *Aviation Infrastructure Performance: A Study in Comparative Political Economy*. Washington, DC: Brookings Institution Press, pp. 7–35.

Nelson, J. (1980). Airports and Property Values: A Survey of Recent Evidence. *Journal of Transport Economics and Policy*, XIV, January, pp. 37–52.

O'Sullivan, M. (2015). *Mayday: How Warring Egos Forced Qantas Off Course*. Sydney: Viking Books.

Oum, T. and Park, J.-H. (1997). Airline Alliances: Current Status, Policy Issues and Future Directions. *Journal of Air Transport Management*, 3(3), pp. 133–44.

Oum, T. and Tretheway, M. (1990). Airline Hub-and-Spoke System. *US Transportation Research Forum*, 30.

Oum, T. H, Yu, C. and Li, M. (2000). Modelling Performance: Measuring and Comparing Unit Cost Competitiveness in Airlines. In Hensher, D. and Button, K. (eds), *Handbook of Transport Modelling*. London: Pergamon, pp. 609–24.

Oum, T. H, Yu, C. and Li, M. (2008). Modelling Cost Competitiveness: An Application to the Major North American Airlines. In Hensher, D. and Button, K. (eds), *Handbook of Transport Modelling*, Second Edition. London: Elsevier, pp. 729–42.

Smyth, M. and Pearce, B. (2007). Aviation Economic Benefits. IATA Economics Briefing.

Stern, N. (2007). *The Economics of Climate Change: The Stern Review*. Cambridge: Cambridge University Press.

Venables, A. (2007). Evaluating Urban Transport Investments. *Journal of Transport Economics and Policy*, 41(2), pp. 169–88.

Vickerman, R. (2013). The Wider Economic Impacts of Mega Projects in Transport. In Priemus, H. and van Wee, B. (eds), *International Handbook on Mega-Projects*. Cheltenham: Edward Elgar, pp. 381–98.

Part II

Public transport reform

7

Public service contracts

The economics of reform with special reference to the bus sector

David A. Hensher

7.1 Introduction and background

The provision of route bus services in many developed economies has changed considerably over the years. Following an initial situation that typically involved private-sector provision up until the 1970s, as is still common among most developing economies, public-sector monopolies became the norm. A substantial swing to private-sector service provision then began in the 1980s, largely driven by a desire to reduce the growing call of services on the public purse and to provide scope for private-sector innovation, which was thought likely to improve customer services and reduce costs (Hensher and Wallis, 2005).

In the developed world, there has been a growing interest in creating a competitive environment in which to deliver improved passenger transport services that not only grows patronage but also reduces the amount of subsidy payment from government to operators, be they public or private. With the exception of the UK outside London and in New Zealand where economic deregulation was the prevailing environment in which the private sector was involved in the bus sector, in most other locations where competition was deemed suitable, the rights to provide service have been increasingly achieved through competitive tender (CT). The enthusiasm for private delivery of route bus services through CT has varied between countries, with negotiated contracts still popular in mainland Europe, with a few exceptions such as Norway, Sweden and the Netherlands; however, the winds of change have begun to revise the agenda as a result of European Union competition policy. Australia has always had a significant private-sector presence in bus service provision (for example, in Melbourne and parts of Sydney), and the role of the private sector was increased through the tendering out of services in Adelaide and Perth in the 1990s (Wallis and Hensher, 2007). Sydney has since moved (in 2013) from negotiated contracts to CT but only for private operators, protecting the less efficient public operator (see Hensher, 2015a for full details). Singapore in early 2015 put all of its bus services out to tender with 11 bidders. The US mainly sees management contracts that involve another party running services under contracts that are owned by the state.

Changes in ownership, and their impacts, have been of such interest to various stakeholders that a biennial international conference (known as the Competition and Ownership in Land Passenger Transport Conference or the Thredbo Conference series) has been established to review progress, problems and achievements and suggest directions for improvement. This series, held every second year for the past two decades (www.thredbo-conference-series.org/), is now in its 27th year, having held 14 very influential meetings throughout the world (see Hensher, 2015b).

Interest in public-sector contracts has clearly been growing among those involved with public passenger transport. As governments move towards separation of regulation from operations, explicit contracts are becoming more common. The incentive implications of different contracts (including cost-plus, gross-cost, gross-cost with incentives, and net-cost) have been explored in numerous case studies. Classical agency theory describes the way in which principals (i.e. regulatory authorities) and agents (operators) trade-off risk sharing and effort incentives when forming a contract. Typically, operators are assumed to be risk averse and authorities risk neutral. Risk can be efficiently allocated to the regulatory authority, but this gives the operator no incentive for effort. As a result, we would expect to find operators bearing at least some risk, the optimal amount depending on the preferences of both parties as well as other factors such as the cost of monitoring effort.

The current chapter draws on the wider literature in economics that explores the role of contracting in the delivery of efficient and effective services, which is very relevant to the passenger transport sector. There is an increasing interest in the type of contracts that govern transactions between regulators and public transport operators amongst transport researchers. The use of performance-based contracts (PBCs) is designed to enhance operator performance via incentives (such as patronage growth and service enhancements). PBCs have been suggested as a contract form more likely to deliver an efficient outcome than the prevalent fixed-fee or cost-plus approaches (Hensher and Stanley, 2003; Carlquist, 2001; Johansen et al., 2001). Such contracts therefore are partly designed to replicate the rewards that would be found in a free market. However, the use of PBCs in public transport has been limited to a few countries such as Norway (Fearnley et al., 2005), New Zealand (Wallis, 2003) and Australia (Hensher and Stanley, 2003). Are these the only public transit environments where the use of incentive contracts is efficient, or is there simply a lag in diffusion of this more efficient contracting technology? The transport literature is strangely silent on this issue.

When looking for answers outside the transport literature, it is immediately apparent that an extraordinary amount of theoretical and empirical research has been undertaken relating to the use of different contract forms. Literally thousands of studies have been conducted which seek to explain and optimise contract use (for an overview of the literature see Boerner and Macher, 2002; Shelanski and Klein, 1995; Lyons, 1996; and Masten and Saussier, 2000). For example, empirical research has been applied to defence (e.g. Crocker and Reynolds, 1993; Adler et al., 1999), agriculture, health (Gaynor and Gertler, 1995), mineral exploration, information technology (Banerjee and Duflo, 2000), education, construction (Bajari and Tadelis, 2001), fund management, electricity and much more. In their survey of the literature on transaction cost economics, much of which is directly relevant to contract choice, Boerner and Macher (2002) incorporated over 600 studies. Inclusion of relevant studies using principal-agent theory, and from related fields such as psychology and law, would be expected to add to this number exponentially. Contracts are everywhere and ongoing questions about the foundations of contract theory make this an open and fertile area of research. This chapter draws on the broader literature as a way of revealing the potential strengths and weaknesses of alternative ways to garner greater performance from the delivery of bus services that are primarily under the control of the public sector but which are increasingly delivered by the private sector on behalf of the public sector.

7.2 Contract theory and risk

The cost of contracting, both within and between firms, is central to the 'make or buy' question introduced in Coase's famous 1937 article that founded the modern theory of the firm. Informed by both transaction cost economics and the neoclassical paradigm, a branch of enquiry emerged relating to incentive systems (Holmstrom and Milgrom, 1991, 1994). This line of research focuses on the incentive problem between a principal and an agent. Gibbons (2005) shows the relationship between incentive theory and other branches of the theory of the firm: rent-seeking theory (e.g. Williamson, 1979, 1985; Klein et al., 1978); property-rights theory (e.g. Grossman and Hart, 1983; Hart and Moore, 1990) and adaptation theory (e.g. Simon, 1951; Williamson, 1991). Cheung (1969) and Stiglitz (1974) were among the first to apply what we now recognise as the classical principal-agent framework with risk aversion attitude, in an attempt to explain the existence of sharecropping. Interest in the moral hazard induced by sharecropping can be traced to Adam Smith's *The Wealth of Nations*.

Using the sharecropping example, we briefly describe the model in general form, as presented by Gibbons (1998), to illustrate the central role of risk allocation and incentives on contract choice. Consider an agent who takes an unobservable action a to produce output y. For example, the production function might be linear $y = a + \varepsilon$, where ε is a random variable with mean 0 and variance σ^2. The principal owns the output but contracts to share it with the agent by paying a wage w contingent on output. For example, the wage contract might be linear, $w = s + by$, where the intercept s is the salary and the slope b is the bonus rate. The agent's payoff is $w - c(a)$, the realised wage minus the disutility of action, $c(a)$. The principal's payoff is $y^{\star} - w$, the realised output net of wages where $y^{\star}$ is the dollar value of the output.

The farmer's objective is to maximise their expected utility by choosing their optimum effort level given the terms of the land contract. Because effort is unobservable and because there is uncertainty in farm production, there is moral hazard for any contract where the farmer does not receive 100 percent of y. The principal maximises expected profits by choosing the optimal contract parameters, usually some combination of salary s and bonus b (a share of y).

The key idea in this model is that the agent is risk averse (the principal may be too). The equilibrium contract that solves this model trades off the incentive effects of paying a greater bonus to the agent against the agent's risk aversion. The extreme case $b = 0$ offers the agent complete insurance against uncertainty in the weather, σ^2, but no incentives to increase output y. The other extreme, $b = 1$, gives the agent 100 percent of the output risk y, removing moral hazard, but offers no insurance. The efficient bonus rate is between 0 and 1, and it depends on σ^2 and the risk preferences of the two parties. For a risk-neutral farmer, $b = 1$ is a first-best solution, but a risk-averse farmer prefers a contract where income is insured to some extent. For a risk-averse farmer, the size of σ^2 will determine both the likelihood of observing a bonus contract and the size of the bonus.

While sharecropping is the traditional application, it is easy to apply the agency model to the public transport context. From this perspective the cost of offering a PBC to a (risk-averse) operator is that it imposes risk on their compensation, which causes higher contract costs. The risk imposed on contractors is increasing in the uncertainty of the environment so that the standard test of the trade-off is to show that incentive pay is lower in more certain environments.

Agent risk aversion is a necessary condition in the principal-agent model because the farmer's margin relates only to the farmer's (unobservable) effort. In this classical paradigm, which dominates the literature relating to optimum contract form, the need to share risk efficiently is traded off against the need to provide efficient incentives. Surprisingly, of the few studies that have examined risk sharing and contract choice, most have failed to find evidence to support the view that risk preferences are important (see Prendergast, 2002 for an overview of the empirical work in this area).

In addition to agent risk-aversion attitude, agent risk-neutrality attitude has been explored in what is known as a pure incentives framework. There is an extensive literature relating to contracts under conditions that complicate agent incentives. These include double-sided moral hazard (Lafontaine, 1992; Eswaren and Kotwal, 1985; Lafontaine and Bhattacharyya, 1995), multitask agency (Holmstrom and Milgrom, 1991; Baker, 1992, 2002), monitoring costs (Alston et al.,1984; Prendergast, 2002; Lafontaine and Slade, 2001), measurement costs (Allen and Lueck, 1992a, 1993) and delegation (Prendergast, 2002; Foss and Laursen, 2005).

Transaction cost economists have examined incentives in the lens of incomplete contracting and the resulting moral hazard, showing that asset specificity, uncertainty, complexity and transaction frequency influence contract choice (Williamson, 1979; Goldberg, 1990). This empirical work shows that optimal contract choice depends on specific knowledge of production processes to capture accurately complex incentive trade-offs. In general, incentive contracts will be attractive where the costs of measuring performance are low and the opportunities for moral hazard are large and many.

Before moving on, it is worth noting that the role of risk preferences in determining optimal contract form is an open area of research. Despite the lack of empirical evidence, risk aversion may be an important driver; and if this were the case, the implications of ignoring the risk-sharing/incentives trade-off are profound. See Kim and Wang (2004) for a discussion of how important risk preferences are in shaping contract choice even if the agent is almost neutral.

7.3 Efficient contracting

Contract theorists have analysed different types of contracts and contract clauses and the factors that lead to their use in a variety of settings. Studies of contract choice typically analyse the choice among various types of contracts, usually cost-plus contracts and fixed-fee contracts (e.g. Eswaren and Kotwal, 1985; Allen and Lueck, 1992a, 1992b), and examine attributes of the current transaction to determine the optimal contract. Results are specific to the situation being investigated; however, clues emerge about the type of environments that are conducive to performance-based contracting.

7.3.1 The output that the principal cares about can be easily described

Output is not always easy to measure and validate. In a famous article 'on the folly of rewarding A, while hoping for B', Kerr (1975) provided numerous examples of the unwelcome consequences of PBCs that distort rather than enhance an agent's effort to produce what the principal wants. Incentive payments tend to overemphasise tasks that are highly visible, objective and easily quantified and measured. Gibbons (1998) provides an overview of the role of subjective assessments in incentive contracts. Holmstrom and Milgrom (1991) formalised this 'multitask' problem. In their model, the seller engages in two tasks: effort in cost reduction, ec, and effort in quality enhancement, eq. Their model employed two extreme assumptions: (1) the tasks are perfect substitutes in the seller's private cost function, g(ec + eq), and (2) costs are verifiable but quality is not. The model shows that giving the seller incentives to reduce costs will cause him to ignore quality considerations completely and engage only in cost reductions. If quality is important to the principal, this is not a good outcome. In a different context, Manelli and Vincent (1995) show that if the buyer cares a lot about quality, using an auction mechanism (which is associated with a fixed price) is not efficient.

The case study provided by Stanley and Hensher (2004), describing the use of incentive contracts in the train and tram industry in Melbourne, Australia, indicates that it may be relatively easy to describe public transport output in an incentive contract. In the public transport context, 'the best single measure of the success of a specific contracting regime is the growth in patronage' (Hensher and Wallis, 2005, p. 312) which, depending on technology, can be relatively easy to measure.

7.3.2 The agent has considerable discretion in their actions

Bajari and Tadelis (2001) show that cost-plus contracts are preferred to a fixed-price contract for complex projects which are expensive to design and associated with a low level of completeness or a high probability that adaptations will be needed. Conversely, more simple projects, with lower uncertainty, greater completeness and low probability of adaptations, will be procured using fixed-price contracts. The intuition for this result stems from the trade-off between providing ex ante incentives and avoiding ex post transaction costs due to costly renegotiation. In fixed-price contracts, risk is allocated mainly on the contractor ($b = 1$), while in cost-plus contracts the contractor bears very little risk ($b = 0$). High incentives of fixed-price contracts reduce costs but also dissipate ex post surplus due to renegotiation. Low incentives of cost-plus contracts do not erode ex post surplus but provide no incentive for cost-saving effort. Thus, the introduction of PBCs would be most effective in more complex situations.

Another way to look at this is to consider that output-based incentive pay is more likely to be observed in cases where contractors have considerable discretion. There is little need to base pay on output when inputs are monitored. Thus, uncertain environments result in the delegation of responsibilities, which in turn generates incentive pay based on outputs (Prendergast, 2002).

7.3.3 The agent owns assets

Grossman and Hart (1983) and Hart and Moore (1990) formalised a model of incomplete contracting consistent with earlier transaction cost theory – contracts are incomplete (bounded rationality), contracts are not self-enforcing (opportunism), court ordering is limited (non-verifiability) and the parties are bilaterally dependent (transaction-specific investments) – but they further assumed that there is no costly ex post renegotiation (they assume common knowledge of pay-offs and costless bargaining). Their focus is instead on how different configurations of physical asset ownership, to which residual rights of control accrue, are responsible for efficiency differences at the ex ante stage of the contract.

In the same spirit, Holmstrom and Milgrim's (1991) model shows that the optimal contract is different for an asset owner (called a contractor in the model) and a non-owner (employee). Measured performance p reflects one action a1, but another action a2 changes the value v of an asset used in the production process. These two actions compete for the agent's attention. As before, the employee is paid only on measured performance ($w = s + bp$) but the contractor receives both wages and any change in the asset's value ($w + v$). Thus, the contractor has great incentive to invest in a2, and it will require a larger bonus rate, b, to focus the contractor's attention on a1 than is the case for an employee who is not distracted by v.

7.3.4 Why are performance-based contracts so rare?

McAfee and McMillan (1986) analyse a model in which risk-averse contractors bid and the buyer is faced with both adverse selection and moral hazard. The model shows that the trade-off between risk sharing, incentives and information cause incentive contracts ($0 < b < 1$) to be generally desirable and that cost-plus contracts ($b = 0$) are never optimal. However, they acknowledge that most government contracts are fixed-fee or cost-plus, and this is confirmed overwhelmingly in the literature. How can we explain this?

Hart and Holmstrom (1987) suggest that optimal contracts (incentive contracts) are often extremely complicated. In the presence of moral hazard, optimality means inclusion of all relevant information and detailed specification of multiple contingencies. That contracts are usually simple in practice is a result of incomplete information, leading to what Bajari and Tadelis (2001) describe as a 'non-convex' procurement problem resulting in extreme contracts. They argue that there is a fundamental difference between a fixed-price contract and an incentive contract, where a fixed-price contract requires no cost measurement. This leads to a clear discontinuity in the cost of measuring and monitoring costs, and implies that fixed-price contracts will dominate contracts that are 'close' to fixed-price, and as it becomes costlier to measure costs, fixed-price contracts will dominate a larger set of incentive contracts. Similarly, they suggest a fundamental difference between a cost-plus contract and incentive contracts, as there is a risk of costly distortion where incentives are introduced. Therefore, solutions close to cost-plus will be dominated by cost-plus contracts.

Schwartz and Watson (2004) use a legal framework to help explain the popularity of simple contracts. There is a trade-off between the costs of contract complexity with gains from efficient investment incentives: higher contracting costs result in simpler contracts. Agents have preferences for high or low renegotiation costs depending on contract complexity (a complex contract requires high renegotiation costs to retain the incentive scheme). They argue that contract law (for example, the prohibition of contract-renegotiation bans) discourages complex contractual forms by making renegotiation relatively cheap.

So should incentive contracts be used more often? Dye and Sridhar (2005) use moral hazard severity to help explain that simple contracts can be optimal, despite the potentially vast array of performance measures that are 'marginally informative' (see Holmstrom, 1979). Paul and Gutierrez (2005), looking from a practitioner angle, disagree. This is an open research question.

7.4 An overview of contract regimes in passenger transport

7.4.1 Competitive tendering

Competition is important to ensure that privatisation improves efficiency. Many cities have introduced competition for the market through competitive tendering of licences to operate public transport services for a specified duration, for example, 15 years to operate a rail line or 5 years to operate a package of bus services. Cherry picking of profitable routes could be prevented by packaging unprofitable routes with profitable ones or by provision of government subsidies. Licences could be awarded based on a number of criteria, e.g. track record, proposed fares and services, or required amount of government subsidies.

Interested operators would submit competitive bids proposing high levels of service, low fares and low level of government subsidies in order to win the tenders. If there is intense competition for the tender, the winning bid would be close to the outcome with market competition. The transport regulator would enter into a contract with the winning operator based on the proposed terms. The operator has the incentive to be as efficient as possible to maximise profits for the limited duration of the licence. Extension of the licence could be contingent on the incumbent operator's performance. The threat of replacement after expiry of the licence incentivises the incumbent to maintain good performance.

Due to the durable, immobile nature of transport investments, and the essential service nature of public transport, both parties – the operator and the regulator acting on behalf of passengers – are vulnerable to opportunistic behaviour of the other party. A long-term contract could protect both parties from opportunism by establishing clear commitments. The level of commitment depends on the completeness of the contract; a more complete contract is able to cover more contingencies (Hensher, 2010). However, it is undesirable and impossible to write a complete contract with a long duration if the environment is changing rapidly. A contract that is overly prescriptive may be inflexible to changing circumstances. Drafting a relatively complete contract may be too difficult and the transaction costs too high (Gomez-Ibanez, 2003).

London's bus system is the oft-cited example of how one of the world's largest urban bus systems has benefited from CT at the route level. London began privatising its government-run bus operator and tendering bus services in 1985 and the conversion was completed by 1999. Cox (2004) compared the situation in London before and after the conversion, and found significant productivity improvement and cost reductions. Prior to privatisation and CT, bus costs per vehicle kilometre had risen 79 percent between 1970 and 1985. This trend was reversed with costs per vehicle kilometre falling by 48 percent from 1985 and 2001. Annual capital and operating expenditures dropped 26 percent, despite service expansion of a similar magnitude in the same period. Unit costs fell 48 percent and productivity measured by level of service per unit of currency increased 91 percent. Government subsidies were reduced substantially and reached a low of zero subsidies in 1997/8. Similar benefits were observed for Copenhagen, Stockholm, San Diego, Denver and Las Vegas after CT was introduced (Cox, 2004).

These cost savings, however, were often one-offs – a windfall gain. Many of the cities which experienced cost savings after introducing CT saw unit costs rising in subsequent tenders, for example, in London, Copenhagen and Stockholm (Hensher and Wallis, 2005), despite the primary focus of CT being to lower costs, subject to prescribed service levels. This has stimulated discussion on alternatives to CT, such as negotiated performance-based contracts (NPBCs) between regulators and operators, where there is greater emphasis on service improvement.

7.4.2 Negotiated performance-based contracts

The evidence that savings from competitive tendering (CT) diminish beyond first-round tenders, together with dissatisfaction with what competitive tendering has delivered for service improvements in some jurisdictions, has encouraged the search for alternative awarding mechanisms that can sustain performance pressure (Hensher and Wallis, 2005). An important development has been the focus on the theory and practice of NPBCs, particularly as an alternative to competitive tendering, as a means to award the right to provide service (see, for example, Hensher and Stanley, 2003; Stanley et al., 2007; Yvrande-Billon, 2007b; Hensher and Stanley, 2008).

A common rationale for NPBCs is to deal with the inevitable uncertainty that creates difficulty for ex ante contract specification and tender bidding, by adopting an awarding mechanism that can be adaptive and sustain performance pressure during the course of the contract. These areas of uncertainty relate, in particular, to questions that relate to service quality, which have proven to be much more difficult to specify in tender requirements than price but are increasingly recognised as the key to desired policy outcomes. By focusing on performance pressure during the contract, NPBCs reflect alliance contracting as used in such areas as building and construction and in infrastructure public-private partnerships more broadly. CT remains a fall-back mechanism in the event that service providers operating under NPBCs do not measure up adequately against their key performance indicators.

A further important rationale seen by some proponents of NPBCs is the belief that this contract form is most likely to support a trusting partnership between purchaser and provider, particularly for system planning, and that, given scarce skills on both sides, such a relationship is more likely to maximise goal achievement through service provision than an awarding mechanism based on CT (Stanley et al., 2007). Australian bus contracts have been pioneers in the development of NPBCs, founded on trusting partnerships, whereby contracts are renegotiated with existing operators, subject to meeting certain conditions. Melbourne and more recently Sydney are examples of this approach (Hensher and Stanley, 2010).

Wallis et al. (2010) review the Adelaide experience with three rounds of tendering bus services and conclude that there is little to gain in terms of cost efficiency and quality enhancement by going to a fourth round of tendering. They argue that a move to NPBCs can not only reduce the considerable transactions costs (associated with tendering) but also offers the opportunity to work closely with efficient incumbents to grow trust and build patronage (mindful of the realities of the market for public transport services). It also reduces the uncertainty associated with renewal through tendering, where a very efficient incumbent operator can still lose the right to provide services. Under tendering, there is a real and observed risk of incumbents tending to not commit to longer-term investment in the industry (both physical and human resources) where contract continuity is uncertain, even when all the boxes are ticked on performance. Similar experiences have arisen elsewhere, such as in the Netherlands. Wallis et al. (2010, pp. 89–98) state:

> A key attribute of competitive tendering for the periodic selection of operators of subsidised public transport services is to secure the provision of specified services at efficient cost levels. This has proved particularly effective where services were previously provided by an inefficient monopoly operator. The arguments for the adoption of competitive tendering in preference to negotiation with the incumbent operator may be less clear-cut in other cases…
>
> The conclusions drawn from the assessment against relevant South Australian Government objectives are that the [negotiated contract] NC strategy is clearly preferred against the group of 'quality' criteria, and also on balance preferred against the group of 'supplier market and cost' criteria. These conclusions are essentially supported by the assessment against international differentiating factors, which concludes that the current Adelaide situation has a number of features which indicate that an NC strategy is likely to be more appropriate in this case. These two assessments together lead to the conclusion that, given the Adelaide situation at the time of the assessment, there was a strong case for adopting an NC-based strategy (with CT as the fallback) rather than CT as the primary strategy.
>
> *(2010, p. 96)*

In very general terms, negotiation is the process through which parties perceive one or more incompatibilities between them, and work to find a mutually acceptable solution. In contrast to competitive tendering, which is framed to determine the value of a product or service, negotiation is designed to create the value of the product or service.

Provisions to guard against regulatory capture are critical in a negotiated performance-based contractual process. Australian experience suggests that, under NPBCs, transparency and accountability can be achieved if the following four conditions are in place (Hensher and Stanley, 2010):

(1) Performance benchmarking to ensure that operator performance is efficient and effective. This benchmarking needs to be subjected to independent verification. Key performance indicators and the threat of competition (through tendering), in the event of inadequate performance, assist the maintenance of competitive pressure and efficient performance.

(2) An open-book approach to costs, achieved through an independent auditor. Operators whose costs appear to be high through this analysis must justify their numbers or face a cut in remuneration. Those whose costs appear low have the opportunity to argue for an increase. Under competitive tendering, it is less likely that operators see any obligations to reveal their cost structures, since government has awarded them a contract based on the offered price under competition. Thus the benchmarking and open-book auditing under NPBCs provides a much better way to obtain detailed data on operator performance that can be used to benchmark in a very meaningful way, controlling for differences that are not under the control of the operator.
(3) The appointment of a probity auditor to oversee the negotiation process.
(4) Public disclosure of the contract.

Australian experience across jurisdictions that tender and those that negotiate is that there is a tendency for cost convergence. A number of operators who provide service under each regime have noted this trend. This result underlines the importance of negotiation as an alternative approach.

Under a negotiated approach, benchmarking plays an important role, designed to monitor and ensure efficiency and effectiveness through the life of a contract, and not just at the point of contract completion. We discuss benchmarking in detail in a later section. Incentives built into a negotiated contract conditioned on market-linked benchmarks, and the ultimate sanction of tendering if non-compliant, enable the incumbent operator to at least prove their worth initially and then, provided the regulator does their job, would deliver true value for money at minimum transaction cost, even after allowing for the regulatory costs that should be common to all regimes, be they competitive tendering or negotiation.

There is a growing body of theoretical and empirical evidence to support the promotion of awarding mechanisms with formal and informal devices, aimed at economic efficiency and effectiveness through the life of the contract, i.e. ex ante and ex post coordination. Building on growing arguments to support NPBCs instead of CT, Bajari et al. (2002) suggest that CT performs poorly when 'projects' are complex and contractual design is incomplete. Area-wide metropolitan bus contracts fit this circumstance. This literature argues that competitive tendering can stifle communication between buyers (i.e. the regulator) and sellers (i.e. the service provider), preventing the buyer from utilising the contractor's expertise when designing the project (which could be a network in the public transport setting).

Authors such as Yvrande-Billon (2007a), drawing on the French experience, promote the case for greater emphasis on establishing a credible regulatory scheme able to govern the procurement of public services ex post, arguing that focusing on introducing market mechanisms via competitive tendering per se ex ante does not guarantee better value for money. Implicit in her arguments is the need to develop trusting partnerships and (incomplete) commercial contracts with unambiguous incentive and penalty structures throughout the life of a contract, with market mechanisms such as competitive tendering always present as a way forward when operators fail to comply under reasonable notice.

This focus may well enable a greater emphasis on achieving social objectives in contrast to commercial objectives; some might say the tendering 'paranoia' may have taken governments away from the real objectives of social obligation and maximising net social benefit per dollar of subsidy, as recognised by Preston (2007), to a disproportionate and overzealous focus on cost containment and reduction. We would argue that the key issue is not 'applying the wrong kind of competitive tender to the wrong market' (Preston, 2007), but the inappropriateness of any form of competitive tender where the transaction costs are so high as to nullify any financial gains at the expense of the relative neglect of broader social obligations, which place as much emphasis on benefits as on costs. The exception is typically a first-round tender when moving from a historically entrenched publicly provided public transport service. The latter usually delivers huge windfall financial gains (Hensher and Wallis, 2005; Wallis and Hensher, 2007).

Through negotiations and performance incentives, NPBCs may better enable the regulator to tap an operator's expertise to facilitate innovation, patronage growth and service improvement. In addition, transaction costs of NPBCs are likely to be lower than CT as operators do not have to spend significant sums of money to prepare tender proposals. Efficient incumbent operators also face less uncertainty associated with renewal of licences, thus encouraging them to make long-term investments. Importantly, negotiation increases trust between the regulators and the operators which enables better communication and quicker resolution of issues arising from the inevitable incompleteness and lack of clarity in contracts, thus saving time and money (Hensher and Stanley, 2010). Critics point out that there are risks of regulatory capture and collusion by operators with NPBCs. However, these risks are also present in CT. NPBCs could complement CT, with CT as a last resort when incumbent operators fail to meet their contractual obligations.

Analysis of a survey of bus contracts throughout the world confirmed the effects of increased trust in improving operators' perceived clarity and completeness of contract obligations, which in turn improves the effectiveness of NPBCs and reduces the uncertainty with negotiations (Hensher, 2010).

Hensher (2015a) investigated CT and NPBCs in five cities in Australia. Using data to link CT prices of successful bids to NPBC outcomes, the evidence suggests that the gains from CT are generally illusory or overstated (outside of the situation of an incumbent public operator). It appears from the evidence presented by Hensher (2015a), in the Australian setting, that testing the market for value for money through competitive tendering, in situations where incumbent contract holders are from the private sector, is not consistent with the well-held view that such a procurement plan is looking after the interests of society, compared to benchmarked actioned NPBCs.

7.5 Establishing a setting in which to compare the performance of operators

When there is an interest in comparing the performance of bus contracts (or operators), it is essential that this is undertaken in such a way that clear and valid statements can be made about how one contract performs relative to one or more other contracts. It is often the case that individuals, be they operators, associations or the government regulator, make comments on how efficient one operator is compared to another operator. I am often asked how such individuals can make such comments! A common concern is that 'surely they are not comparing like with like?'

While one can never be sure what a specific person actually does to form a view (factual or otherwise) as to how well one operator compares with another operator (or indeed an entire sector), there are nevertheless some good practical and meaningful principles to adhere to so that sensible debate can occur. The great majority of commentary appears to be based on a simple comparison of the gross cost per in-service kilometre (which excludes the margin and removes dead running kilometres). While the exclusion of the operator's margin and dead running time is permissible, as long as the margin is eventually revealed and included as a cost to those who pay for the contract services (notably the government and through them the taxpayers), the failure to recognise sources of influence on cost efficiency that are not under the control of the operator and which vary by contract location is very poor analysis, resulting in nothing more than a comparison of 'apples with oranges'.

So what should we do? As a start we need to identify those features of service provision that incur a disproportionate cost impact across contract areas, that the operator has effectively no control over, and are a recognition of the reality of operating in a specific jurisdiction. To make a valid comparison these differences must be recognised and accounted for. We call this 'normalisation', although some people often talk of 'standardisation'.

In the context of metropolitan bus operations in Australia, the main influences that are outside of the control of an operator are (Hensher, 2015a) (i) the speed on the road (the result often of traffic congestion, but also road alignments including traffic lights), (ii) the amount of in-service kilometres out of each bus each year (called bus utilisation), which impacts on the amount of capital and hence capital cost, and (iii) the spread of service hours, which can be defined to describe the proportion of service hours on evenings and weekends when higher labour costs associated with penalty rates typically are incurred.

These three main sources of systematic variations for which normalisation adjustments should be made to the raw or 'gross' cost efficiency indicator can be explained as follows:

Average peak speed. Slower average peak speed, due to traffic congestion for instance, will typically increase driving time and operating costs. The effect of normalisation will be to improve the Cost Efficiency indicator cost for a Contract Region with low average peak speed relative to the industry median, and vice versa, to account for the impact of differences in average peak speed.

Spread of operating hours. A higher ratio of timetabled operating hours during evenings and weekends when penalty rates of pay apply will typically increase operating costs. The effect of normalisation will be to improve the Cost Efficiency indicator for a Contract Region with a higher ratio of operating hours during evenings and weekends relative to the industry median, and vice versa, to account for the impact of differences in spread of hours.

Average vehicle utilisation. A higher number of annual service kilometres per peak vehicle because of higher timetabled route frequencies will have the effect of diluting fixed costs and improving the Cost Efficiency indicator. The effect of normalisation will be to improve the Cost Efficiency indicator for a Contract Region with lower service kilometres per peak vehicle relative to the industry median, and vice versa, to account for the impact of differences in vehicle utilisation.

If there is a desire to compare any combination of contract situations, one must control through normalisation those influences that explain differences that are due to the local situation and which cannot and should not be the basis of making comments on whether one operator (or contract) is more or less cost efficient than another operator (or contract).

How does normalisation work? The most popular method involves replacing the impact of a specific influence not under the control of the operator (but essentially under the control of the operating environment), such as average or median speed of a specific location, with the average speed associated with all locations in a comparison. The median is a preferred measure if the distribution of the variable deviates from a normal distribution across a sample. The same rule would apply to all selected influences that need to be 'normalised' as a way of removing the influence of these factors on the comparison of operator performance. However, the story does not stop there. Before we can normalise the gross cost per in-service kilometre (GC/INSKm), we need to find out what role these normalisation criteria play in explaining differences in GC/INSKm, so that we can then ensure that this role is used as a weight to allow for the replacement of the contract-specific level of say speed with the average or median speed of the sample of all contracts being compared. These weights are obtained using a regression model that assures that all influences on differences in GC/INSKm are accounted for (which includes those influences under the control of the operator).

Intuitively, the formula for net cost per in-service kilometre (NC/INSKm) can be illustrated as follows using only two influences, one being under the control of the operator (call it influence X) and one not under the control of the operator, call it influence Y. w is the weight attached to the influence of variables X and Y. The formula for two operators, 1 and 2, is:

NC/INSKm for operator 1= $w_x{\star}X_1 + w_y{\star}$ (average or median of Y across all contracts)
NC/INSKm for operator 2= $w_x{\star}X_2 + w_y{\star}$ (average or median of Y across all contracts).

We now have two very useful measures of cost efficiency: the initial GC/INSKm and NC/INSKm. What do we do with this extra information? The most meaningful role for NC/INSKm is in assisting in deciding how cost efficient an operator is relative to other operators after controlling, through normalisation, for the influences that they have no control of, which are effectively what comes with the territory when you operate there.

A comparison of an operator's GC/INSKm with their NC/INSKm is not really very informative, since it only tells us whether the real costs of service provision are higher or lower than the normalised cost; however, this does not help in understanding whether an operator is relatively cost efficient or not. That requires a comparison of NC/INSKm with an agreed benchmark level. The focus should thus be on NC/INSKm. As interesting as direct comparisons of NC/INSKm are between any pair of operators or across the entire set of contracts (possibly ranking operators on NC/INSKm), a more useful exercise is to benchmark each operator relative to an agreed benchmark. Using this information to benchmark operators against some reasonable level that most operators are able to achieve provides a very positive way forward in providing the right incentives to ensure improvements in cost efficiency over time.

For example, we might obtain the average or median level of NC/INSKm from the entire set of contracts being assessed and then see which contracts have an NC/INSKm which is lower than this average or median. A contract or operator who has a lower NC/INSKm will be deemed to have satisfied the performance benchmark. An operator with a higher NC/INSKm will be deemed to have not satisfied the performance benchmark, and may be required to explain their current situation prior to the imposition (if deemed appropriate) of a target adjustment in cost efficiency gain over an agreed period. This is the basis of effective benchmarking[1] and should be used in any procurement regime that involves negotiation or in monitoring the performance of operators who were initially awarded a contract through competitive tendering.

A final comment is a question for all analysts – are you using valid methods to undertake a comparative assessment of performance? You cannot and never should simply take, for example, the gross cost per in-service kilometre and use it to make statements about whether one operator is more or less cost efficient than another operator (in situations that are potentially so different). Our real fear and concern is that this is exactly what is happening in many sectors, including the bus transport sector.

7.6 Conclusions

This chapter provides an overview of various economic theories that are relevant in informing an inquiry into the pros and cons of alternative public-sector contracting regimes. Given the various theoretical perspectives, we then consider the case for competitive tendering versus negotiated contracts, highlighting some of the broader social welfare obligations of government in the delivery of passenger transport services.

The role of effective actionable benchmarking under both competitive tendering and negotiated contracts is presented with a suggested practical way to undertake such benchmarking in order to ensure that operators are being compared in a meaningful way.

By working through the suite of theoretical frameworks and the experience to date in implementing a number of service reforms through a contracting strategy, the reader should be in a better-informed position to assess the value to society of future proposals.

Note

1 This explanation is relevant to any benchmarking exercise or performance assessment regime and can be applied to other key performance indicators such as network effectiveness (defined as passengers per in-service kilometre) or customer satisfaction. Once we have controlled through normalisation for influences not under the control of the operator, meaningful comparisons can be made and benchmarks can be defined. Benchmarks based on gross (i.e. unadjusted) cost or gross network effectiveness and gross customer satisfaction are not only misleading, they can easily result in penalising (or rewarding) operators in circumstances that have been incorrectly assessed.

References

Adler, T. R., Scherer, R. F., Barton, S. L. and Katerberg, R. (1999). An Empirical Test of Transaction Cost Theory Validating Contract Typology. *Journal of Applied Management Studies*, 7, pp. 185–90.

Allen, D. W. and Lueck, D. (1992a). The Back-Forty on a Handshake Specific Assets, Reputation and the Structure of Farmland Contracts. *Journal of Law Economics and Organisation*, 8, pp. 366–76.

Allen, D. W. and Lueck, D. (1992b). Contract Choice in Modern Agriculture Cash Rent versus Cropshare. *Journal of Law and Economics*, 35, pp. 397–426.

Allen, D. W. and Lueck, D. (1993). Transaction Costs and the Design of Cropshare Contracts. *RAND Journal of Economics*, 24, pp. 78–100.

Alston, L., Dutta, S. and Nugent, J. (1984). Tenancy Choice in a Competitive Framework with Transaction Costs. *Journal of Political Economy*, 92, pp. 1121–133.

Bajari, P. and Tadelis, S. (2001). Incentives versus Transaction Costs: A Theory of Procurement Contracts. *RAND Journal of Economics*, 32(3), pp. 387–407.

Bajari, P., McMillan, R. and Tadelis, S. (2002). *Auctions versus Negotiations in Procurement: An Empirical Analysis*, Department of Economics, Stanford University, CA, October.

Baker, G. (1992). Incentive Contracts and Performance Measurement. *Journal of Political Economy*, 100, pp. 598–614.

Baker, G. (2002). Distortion and Risk in Optimal Incentive Contracts. *Journal of Human Resources*, 37, pp. 728–51.

Banerjee, A. and Duflo, E. (2000). Reputation Effects and the Limits of Contracting: A Case Study of the Indian Software Industry. *Quarterly Journal of Economics*, 115, pp. 989–1017.

Boerner, C. and Macher, J. (2002). *Transaction Cost Economics: An Assessment of Empirical Research in the Social Sciences*. Working Paper, Georgetown University.

Carlquist, E. (2001). Incentive Contracts in Norwegian Local Public Transport: The Hordaland Model. Paper presented at the 7th International Conference on Competition and Ownership of Land Passenger Transport, Molde, Norway, June.

Cheung, S. (1969). Transaction Costs, Risk Aversion, and the Choice of Contractual Arrangements. *Journal of Law and Economics*, 12, pp. 23–45.

Coase, R. (1937). The Nature of the Firm. *Economica*, 4, pp. 386–405.

Cox, W. (2004). *Competitive Tendering of Public Transport*. Presentation to the Urban Road and Public Transit Symposium, Montreal.

Crocker, K. and Reynolds, K. (1993). The Efficiency of Incomplete Contracts: An Empirical Analysis of Air Force Engine Procurement. *RAND Journal of Economics*, 24, pp. 126–46.

Dye, R. A. and Sridhar, S. S. (2005). Moral Hazard Severity and Contract Design. *RAND Journal of Economics*, 36, pp. 78–93.

Eswaren, M. and Kotwal, A. (1985). A Theory of Contractual Structure in Agriculture. *American Economic Review*, 75, pp. 352–67.

Fearnley, N., Bekken, J. and Norheim, B. (2005). Optimal Performance-Based Subsidies in Norwegian Intercity Rail Transport. *International Journal of Transport Management*, 2, pp. 29–38.

Foss, N. J. and Laursen, K. (2005). Performance-Pay, Delegation and Multitasking under Uncertainty and Innovativeness: An Empirical Investigation. *Journal of Economic Behaviour and Organization*, 58, pp. 246–76.

Gaynor, M. and Gertler, P. (1995). Moral Hazard and Risk Spreading in Partnerships. *RAND Journal of Economics*, 26, pp. 591–613.

Gibbons, R. (1998). Incentives in Organizations. *Journal of Economic Perspectives*, 12, pp. 115–232.

Gibbons, R. (2005). Four Formal(izable) Theories of the Firm? *Journal of Economic Behaviour and Organization*, 58, pp. 190–245.
Goldberg, V. P. (1990). Aversion to Risk Aversion in the New Institutional Economics. *Journal of Institutional and Theoretical Economics*, 146, pp. 216–22.
Gomez-Ibanez, Jose A. (2003). *Regulating Infrastructure: Monopoly, Contracts, and Discretion*. Cambridge, MA: Harvard University Press.
Grossman, S. J. and Hart, O. D. (1983). An Analysis of the Principal-Agent Problem. *Econometrica*, 51, pp. 7–45.
Hart, O. and Holmstrom, B. (1987). Theory of Contracts. In Bewley, T. (ed.), *Advances in Economic Theory*. New York: Cambridge University Press.
Hart, O. and Moore, J. (1990). Property Rights and the Nature of the Firm. *Journal of Political Economy*, 98 (11), pp. 1119–58.
Hensher, D. A. (2010). Incompleteness and Clarity in Bus Contracts: Identifying the Nature of the *ex ante* and *ex post* Perceptual Divide. *Research in Transportation Economics*, 29(1), pp. 106–17.
Hensher, D. A. (2015a). Cost Efficiency under Negotiated Performance-Based Contracts and Benchmarking for Urban Bus Contracts: Are There Any Gains through Competitive Tendering in the Absence of an Incumbent Public Monopolist? Paper presented at the 13th International Conference on Competition and Ownership of Land Passenger Transport (Thredbo 13), Oxford, 15–19 September, 2013, *Journal of Transport Economics and Policy*, 49(1), pp. 133–48.
Hensher, D. A. (2015b). Keeping the Debate Informed on Reforms in Land Passenger Transport: The Influence of the Thredbo Series. *Transport Reviews*, 34(6), pp. 671–3, http://dx.doi.org/10.1080/01441647.2014
Hensher, D. A. and Stanley, J. (2003). Performance-Based Quality Contracts in Bus Service Provision. *Transportation Research Part A*, 37(5), pp. 19–38.
Hensher, D. A. and Stanley, J. K. (2008). Transacting under a Performance-Based Contract: The Role of Negotiation and Competitive Tendering. *Transportation Research Part A*, 42(10), pp. 1295–301.
Hensher, D. A. and Stanley, J. K. (2010). Contracting Regimes for Bus Services: What Have We Learnt after 20 Years? *Research in Transportation Economics*, 29, pp. 140–4.
Hensher, D. A. and Wallis, I. (2005). Competitive Tendering as a Contracting Mechanism for Subsidising Transportation: The Bus Experience. *Journal of Transport Economics and Policy*, 39(3), pp. 295–321.
Holmstrom, B. (1979). Moral Hazard and Observability. *Bell Journal of Economics*, 10, pp. 74–91.
Holmstrom, B. and Milgrom, P. R. (1991). Multitask Principal-Agent Analyses Incentive Contracts, Asset Ownership and Job Design. *Journal of Law Economics and Organisation*, 7, pp. 24–52.
Holmstrom, B. and Milgrom, P. R. (1994). The Firm as an Incentive System. *American Economic Review*, 84, pp. 972–91.
Johansen, K. W., Larsen, O. and Norheim, B. (2001). Towards Economic Efficiency in Public Transport. *Journal of Transport Economics and Policy*, 35, pp. 491–511.
Kerr, S. (1975). On the Folly of Rewarding A, While Hoping for B. *Academy of Management Journal*, 18, pp. 769–83.
Kim, S. K. and Wang, S. (2004). Robustness of a Fixed-Rent Contract in a Standard Agency Model. *Economic Theory*, 24, pp. 111–28.
Klein, B., Crawford, R. A. and Alchian, A. A. (1978). Vertical Integration, Appropriable Rents, and the Competitive Contracting Process. *Journal of Law and Economics*, 21, pp. 297–326.
Lafontaine, F. (1992). Agency Theory and Franchising Some Empirical Results. *RAND Journal of Economics*, 23, pp. 263–383.
Lafontaine, F. and Bhattacharyya, S. (1995). Double-Sided Moral Hazard and the Nature of Share Contracts. *RAND Journal of Economics*, 26, pp. 761–81.
Lafontaine, F. and Slade, M. (2001). Incentive Contracting and the Franchise Design. In Chatterjee, K. and Samuelson, W. (eds), *Game Theory and Business Applications*. Boston, MA: Kluwer.
Lyons, B. R. (1996). Empirical Relevance of Efficient Contract Theory Inter-Firm Contracts. *Oxford Review of Economic Policy*, 12, pp. 27–52.
Manelli, A. M. and Vincent, D. R. (1995). Optimal Procurement Mechanism. *Econometrica*, 63(3), pp. 591–620.
Masten, S. E. and Saussier, S. (2000). Econometrics of Contracts: An Assessment of Developments in the Empirical Literature on Contracting. *Revue d Economie Industrielle* 0(92), pp. 215–36.
McAfee, P. and McMillan, J. (1986). Bidding for Contracts: A Principal-Agent Analysis. *RAND Journal of Economics*, 17, pp. 326–38.

Paul, A. and Gutierrez, G. (2005). Simple Probability Models for Project Contracting. *European Journal of Operational Research*, 165, pp. 329–38.
Prendergast, C. (2002). The Tenuous Trade-Off between Risk and Incentives. *Journal of Political Economy*, 110, pp. 1071–102.
Preston, J. (2007). Comments on Hensher. *Transport Reviews*, 27(4), pp. 427–31.
Schwartz, A. and Watson, J. (2004). The Law and Economics of Costly Contracting. *Journal of Law Economics and Organization*, 19, pp. 2–31.
Shelanski, H. and Klein, P. (1995). Empirical Research in Transaction Cost Economics: A Review and Assessment. *Journal of Law Economics and Organization*, 11, pp. 335–61.
Simon, H. (1951). A Formal Theory of the Employment Relationship. *Econometrica*, 19, pp. 293–305.
Stanley, J. and Hensher, D. A. (2004). Melbourne's Public Transport Franchising: Lessons for PPPs. *Australian Accounting Review*, 33(14), pp. 42–50.
Stanley, J., Betts, J. and Lucas, S. (2007). Tactical Level Partnerships: A Context of Trust for Successful Operation. In Macario, R., Viegas, J. and Hensher, D. A. (eds), *Competition and Ownership in Land Passenger Transport*. Amsterdam: Elsevier, pp. 437–52.
Stiglitz, J. E. (1974). Incentives and Risk-Sharing in Sharecropping. *Review of Economic Studies*, 41(2), pp. 19–55.
Wallis, I. (2003). Incentives Contracts in Urban Public Transport. Paper presented at the 8th International Conference on Competition and Ownership of Land Passenger Transport, Rio de Janeiro.
Wallis, I. and Hensher, D. A. (2007). Competitive Tendering for Urban Bus Services: Cost Impacts: International Experience and Issues. In Macário, R., Viegas, J. M. and Hensher, D. A. (eds), *Competition and Ownership in Land Passenger Transport*. Oxford: Elsevier, pp. 453–88.
Wallis, I., Bray, D. and Webster, H. (2010). To Competitively Tender or Negotiate: Weighing Up the Choices in a Mature Market. *Research in Transportation Economics*, 29(1), pp. 89–98.
Williamson, O. (1979). Transaction-Cost Economics: The Governance of Contractual Relations. *Journal of Law and Economics*, 22, pp. 233–61.
Williamson, O. (1985). *The Economic Institutions of Capitalism Firms, Markets, Relational Contracting*. New York: Free Press.
Williamson, O. (1991). Comparative Economic Organization: The Analysis of Discrete Structural Alternatives. *Administrative Science Quarterly*, 36, pp. 269–96.
Yvrande-Billon, A. (2007a). The Attribution Process of Delegation Contracts in the French Urban Public Transport Sector: Why Is Competitive Tendering a Myth? In Macário, R., Viegas, J. M. and Hensher, D. (eds), *Competition and Ownership in Land Passenger Transport*. Oxford: Elsevier, chapter 27.
Yvrande-Billon, A. (2007b). Comments on Hensher. *Transport Reviews*, 27(4), pp. 421–6.

8
Rail regulation

Chris Nash, Valerio Benedetto and Andrew Smith

8.1 Introduction

The trend of the last 40 years in the transport sector has been towards deregulation, and in the US that has also been true of the rail sector, where in 1980 the Staggers Act largely removed regulation. Yet in Europe in the last 20 years almost every country has created a new rail regulatory body. How has this come about?

Essentially it has been a part of the reform of European railways designed to achieve at least a degree of separation of infrastructure from operations and to introduce competition between different freight and passenger operators over the same infrastructure. The first and foremost task of the new regulators is to ensure that the terms of that competition are fair; that there is no discrimination favouring one operator over another.

But there is a second task that may be given to the regulator and that is to ensure that the infrastructure manager performs efficiently in terms of prices, output, investment and quality of service. The main reason why such regulation may be needed is that the infrastructure manager is a natural monopoly; rarely in Europe is there an alternative infrastructure manager to whom a train operator might turn. But there are other reasons also for concern, such as the prevalence of externalities in the transport sector and inefficient pricing on other modes.

The next section expands on the reasons for rail regulation in the European context. We then turn to the literature for guidance on the nature of the regulatory body most likely to succeed in regulating the rail sector. We conclude that Britain comes close to having such a rail regulator and examine the experience of Britain and the degree to which its rail regulatory body has succeeded in its objectives. Finally, conclusions are offered.

8.2 Why regulate transport?

As noted in the introduction and also highlighted in several other chapters throughout the book, the general trend in transport of the last 40 years has been towards deregulation, not regulation. The common view has been that in the provision of transport services the most efficient approach is to leave competing operators to determine what services should be provided and at what price. Where a continued role for government in specifying services and fares is necessary, for instance where a specified standard of services requires subsidy or where a degree of integration that is not provided by the market is desired, then the predominant view favours competition for the market by means of competitive tendering. The natural monopoly element of the transport system has been seen as largely resting with the infrastructure and even here, in some modes (mainly sea and air), the fact that the basic infrastructure is free for all to use and that there is competition between alternative terminals has been seen as leaving less need for regulation.

It is in road and rail transport that the natural monopoly argument for a single infrastructure manager is strongest. In general, the argument for regulation of a natural monopoly rests on its potential to exploit its market power to raise prices by restricting output below the socially efficient level. Yet for these modes in most countries (rail in North America being the principal exception) the infrastructure is provided by the state on a not-for-profit basis; pricing, capacity and quality of service decisions are taken by the state and until recently there has been seen to be no need for a separate regulator. What is different about rail now? In the rail sector in Europe, the big change has been the desire of the European Commission to introduce competition between different train operators either in the market (in the case of commercial operations) or for the market through a competitive franchising system where public service obligations and subsidies are involved. When all rail services as well as infrastructure were provided by a single state-owned company, there was not seen to be a need for independent regulation; prices, services, investment and efficiency were simply dealt with by negotiation between the relevant ministry and the railway. But there was widespread discontent at the resulting combination of declining market share and increasing subsidies. Hence the desire for market opening.

In terms of providing fair terms of competition for new entrants, the problem is that the state does not only provide the infrastructure but is also the main operator. In all European countries except Britain this remains the case for the passenger sector. But in almost all of the larger countries, with again Britain being the main exception, it is also true of freight (Nash, 2013).

Simply this fact of common ownership, with the infrastructure manager and the main train operator usually being controlled by the same ministry, would be enough to raise suspicions of discrimination. But, in fact, European legislation still permits the infrastructure manager and train operator to be part of the same holding company (although if such an infrastructure manager is responsible for pricing and allocation of capacity then its management must be independent of that of any train operator). It is clear that the Commission would prefer to see infrastructure and train operations in totally separate companies (and did propose this as part of the fourth railway package). But a number of member states, led by Germany, have successfully opposed this measure. Similar debates have occurred in the other network industries (energy, telecoms) with differing solutions adopted at different times and in different countries. But within the transport sector, no other mode has the same issue of the relationship between a monopoly infrastructure manager and the main operator, so the requirement for stronger regulation to make competition work is unique to rail.

Thus, the Commission sees regulation as crucial to the success of its policy of introducing competition within the rail sector, and has recently strengthened the regulatory requirements as part of the recast of the first railway package (European Commission, 2012). The recast reaffirms the key role of the regulatory authority in ensuring non-discrimination in terms of access to the infrastructure and charging for its use (Article 56). The recast also increases the independence of these bodies, requiring their autonomy from public entities which may influence their decisions (Article 55). Thus regulators through this legislation are now required to be independent of both government bodies and railway undertakings. Previously in many countries the regulatory role was played by the ministry or by a body under direct ministerial control. That is no longer permitted. In addition, the activities of sanctioning, audit, investigation and appeals procedures were strengthened, and greater cross-border collaboration is required (Article 57).

Furthermore, supplementary actions highlighted the width of powers that these regulatory authorities were accorded. Article 30 allows them a role within the management of contracts between these governments and network managers, allowing regulatory authorities to evaluate the adequacy of the amount of funds provided for the required capacity and capability of the infrastructure for the period of the contract. To do this would require them to consider the efficiency of the infrastructure manager. A state-owned, not-for-profit monopoly may not have an incentive to exploit its monopoly power to make excessive profits, but it may still lack incentives to optimise efficiency (as Hicks said, the best of all monopoly profits is a quiet life – Crozet et al., 2012). Moreover, Article 56 introduced stronger powers for regulators in respect of monitoring of accounts. This confers on the regulators the possibility of requiring financial accounts of infrastructure managers and railway undertakings, and data on track access charges and the financial performance of infrastructure managers.

8.3 What makes for an effective regulator?

There is a considerable literature on the issue of what makes for an effective regulator, considering the role and operations of regulatory bodies, as well as its interrelationships with the government and the various types of stakeholders (such as regulated companies, trade unions, local public administrations and incumbent). A word of warning is in order at the outset, however. Circumstances vary greatly between European countries in terms of the nature of traffic, the amount of competition and the organisation of the infrastructure manager (whether completely separate from all train operators or integrated in the same government-owned holding company as the operator(s)). This diversity may help to explain why regulatory activities are more developed in some countries than in others. This importance of the context in regulation is emphasised by Gassner and Pushak (2014), who highlight how the same regulatory arrangements may not be optimal for all countries. Specifically relating to railways, an important study in this area was produced following an OECD (Organisation for Economic Co-operation and Development) round table discussion of experts on the role of economic regulators (OECD/ITF, 2011). Central in these references is the focus on the significance of independence, not just from the infrastructure manager and train operators, but also from government which, as noted above, may often have a vested interest in discrimination in favour of the operators it owns. One of the primary objectives of the regulator should be the pursuit of non-discrimination, connected with situations in which particular operators enjoy advantageous conditions for the access to relevant infrastructure. To achieve this, the regulator needs to be provided with appropriate human and financial resources and be accountable for its decisions, thanks to a clear distinction between its responsibilities and those of the government (or other relevant agencies). The way the regulator reaches its goals is ideally transparent, displaying publicly the process and the results that substantiate specific decisions. Moreover, the avoidance of bowing to short-term political aims confers stability and predictability. Lastly, an effective regulator would be able to intervene on issues on its own initiative (and not only when requested by regulated businesses).

Two of the most common problems faced by regulators are information asymmetries and the danger of regulatory capture. We have already noted the powers given to rail regulators under European legislation to require infrastructure managers to provide them with the necessary information for them to undertake their role. Regarding regulatory capture, this is usually explained as being the result of the intense pressure regulators come under from the industry they are regulating compared with the relatively weak position of consumers. But in the rail sector, the regulator is essentially protecting one set of companies (train operators) from the monopoly power of another company – the infrastructure manager. Thus there is no such acute imbalance between the powers of the different interested parties, except – as already noted – for the likely interest of the government in the outcomes of the regulatory process. In this context,

Fremeth and Holburn (2010) point out that the minimisation of information asymmetries and the possibility of regulatory capture could depend on three factors: the regulator's experience, the size, skills and experience of its staff and the existence of similar policies previously implemented by other agencies. In some countries, the rail regulator is part of a multisector regulatory body (e.g. energy, telecommunications), thus offering opportunities to cross-fertilise skills and ideas across sectors; in any case, the ability to interact with and learn from other regulatory bodies with a longer history may be an important factor.

Besides these points, and observing other network industries like telecommunications (OECD, 2000), it is argued that regulatory oversight is better achieved by a collegiate body rather than by a single person, and the related members should maintain their roles only for fixed staggered terms. Moreover, an external body should report on the activity carried out by the regulator, in order to evaluate its performance.

On this last topic, Niemeier (2011) also signals the importance of the cost effectiveness of a regulator, the objectives and procedures of which should be monitored by a third party through a cost-benefit analysis. The significance of the cost-effectiveness analysis is highlighted by Ponti (2011) as well, especially in terms of the presence of transaction costs attributable to the regulatory activity.

A particularly important source of information for rail regulators is represented by the powers of demanding data which may be used to study the efficiency of the infrastructure manager and the multiannual financial equilibrium of the infrastructure managers (European Commission, Directive 2012/34/EC). Since only in a few countries does the regulator seem to play an active role in efficiency control, the European experience of this in the rail sector turns out to be limited. Lessons could be learnt from practices employed in comparable network industries: in the energy sector, for instance, the related extensive literature (Haney and Pollitt, 2009, 2011, 2013) notes the international diffusion of benchmarking methods, such as frontier-based and average benchmarking, as well as reporting on the challenges raised when conducting such studies.

An important source of information on the state of rail regulation within the European Union is the Rail Liberalisation Index reports produced by IBM and Kirchner (2002, 2004, 2007, 2011). These studies provide an overview on the state of the liberalisation processes in the European Union countries, calculating indices and formulating rankings in order to evaluate which countries are denoted by 'advanced', 'scheduled' and 'delayed' progress. Even if the aim of these reports is not only centred on the regulatory state of each country in the sample, some of the drivers selected by those authors reflect and confirm the findings of this chapter. These include drivers covering the general aspects of the authority (including elements like independence, accountability and transparency), the objectives of the regulation (for instance, the responsibilities of the regulatory authority) and its powers (involving the possibility of imposing coercive means, or the nature of the investigations that are allowed to be performed). Another important IBM study on rail regulation was produced in 2006 (IBM Business Consulting Services, 2006), where a survey was conducted in order to assess the regulatory conditions of rail network access in Europe. It identified three forms of rail regulation – regulation by a specific economic regulator; regulation by a rail authority whose main function related to safety and standards; and regulation by the relevant ministry. Generally, regulation appeared to be more effective when undertaken by a specific economic regulator.

The most recent evidence on the characteristics of rail regulators comes from a survey reported in Benedetto (2016). This collected information from a sample of European regulators, infrastructure managers and railway undertakings in order to verify how the regulatory structures of European railways conform to this ideal benchmark. It found that most regulators do now have adequate experienced staff and resources and are independent from day-to-day political interference. Regulators usually have the necessary powers to make legally binding decisions and to impose penalties, and appear to meet the necessary standards of transparency and accountability. However, the role of regulators in promoting competition levels is generally restricted to the preservation of non-discrimination, while having little involvement in designing tenders, which in any case are still only used to allocate public-service contracts in a minority of cases around Europe. Few regulators have regulatory powers on monitoring the efficiency and quality of the railway system, particularly in relation to the approval of access charges and control of infrastructure managers' efficiency and performance; generally this role rests with government.

Therefore, a number of formal requirements appear to have been met, but powers directly to influence costs and performance of infrastructure managers are rare. In general, the only way the regulator can influence costs is by promoting competition, but whilst this may impact on the costs of train operators, it will have little impact on the costs of infrastructure managers.

To what extent do empirical studies find evidence of rail regulators successfully influencing costs? The treatment of regulation in studies of rail costs remains very limited and the results varied. For instance, while Wetzel (2008) recommends the introduction of an independent regulator because of its benefits in terms of reducing costs, Friebel et al. (2010) find similar benefits but only when this reform is accompanied by supplementary actions involving vertical and horizontal unbundling and open access to market. A key issue, however, in these previous studies is the relatively simple approach to measuring regulation, which is achieved by including dummy variables for the presence of an independent regulator; rather than reflecting in more depth the powers and responsibilities of regulators in different countries and at different times.

In general, a number of data and method limitations affecting studies of railway reforms have been overcome in recent studies (Mizutani et al., 2014 and van de Velde et al., 2012). The samples, for instance, include Britain (Britain being the country in which rail reform has been carried furthest), whereas most previous studies excluded it because of the difficulty of obtaining data. Further, a key contribution of these papers (drawing also on Mizutani and Uranishi, 2013), is that the effects of vertical separation compared to more integrated structures will depend on how intensely the network is used. A high proportion of freight traffic may also remove the benefits of vertical separation, presumably because freight traffic tends to vary much more on a day-to-day basis than passenger, requiring much closer cooperation between train operator and infrastructure manager than is the case for passenger traffic.

Benedetto (2016) and Smith et al. (2015) present the latest empirical evidence on the effects of rail regulation. This study aims to determine the impact of regulation on the efficiency levels of a sample of European railway systems for the period 2002–10 by employing a purposely developed regulation index based on those inputs to the IBM index that are relevant for regulation, rather than dummy variables, as widely utilised by previous literature. The findings differ depending on the way outputs are measured, with regulation producing cost reductions either when combined with vertical separation or when accompanied by competition. Whilst the combined impact of vertical separation and 'average' levels of regulation (i.e. regulation at the mean level of the regulation index) only reduces costs when train density is below the sample mean, the combination of vertical separation and 'strong regulation' (i.e. regulation at the maximum level of the regulation index) may reduce costs for all but the densest railways.

8.4 British experience

Britain is a country that comes close to the theoretically ideal regulatory arrangements both in terms of the nature of the regulatory body and its powers and responsibilities. It has an independent regulatory board with a substantial skilled staff and more than 20 years' experience of rail regulation, which itself built on earlier experience of other regulatory bodies. Moreover, as well as approving track access charges and access agreements and investigating allegations of discrimination, it has the powers to investigate the efficiency and performance of the infrastructure manager, to set targets and to impose penalties if these are not reached. It also has some powers regarding maintenance of competition in other parts of the rail industry, although these are delegated by the Competition and Markets Authority to whom it refers significant issues, as well as being the safety regulator. But in this section we concentrate on the experience of the British rail regulator in economic regulation of the infrastructure manager.

The Office of the Rail Regulator was created in 1994 under the 1993 Railways Act as an independent regulatory body; except during a transition phase, it has no obligation to take directions from the minister, but it does have to take into account the implications of its decisions for government finance. At that time it was headed by a single rail regulator, but in 2004 it was revised to constitute a regulatory board (the Office of Rail Regulation); at the same time it also became the safety regulator. More recently, in 2015 it has added the duty to monitor the performance and efficiency of the provider of the national road system, Highways England, when that became a government-owned company instead of a government agency. So although still known by the abbreviation ORR, this now stands for the Office of Rail and Road.

ORR is responsible for licensing both infrastructure managers and train operators, for regulating track access charges and conditions and for monitoring the performance and efficiency of infrastructure managers (not just Network Rail but also HS1, the owner of the high-speed line from London to the Channel Tunnel).

When the national rail company, British Rail, was split into a separate infrastructure manager and train-operating companies in 1994 (Nash and Smith, 2011), the infrastructure manager – Railtrack – was established as a totally separate commercial organisation and it was privatised by the public sale of shares in 1997, becoming the only privately owned national rail infrastructure manager in Europe. As it was not permitted to participate in train operations it had no obvious reason to behave in a discriminatory manner. Nevertheless, issues arose, for instance regarding the negotiation of a two-part tariff with the largest freight operator, EWS, which gave it an advantage in competition with other freight operators, as well as regarding access to freight terminals (which were privatised as part of individual freight operators, who obviously had an incentive to prevent other operators from using them, rather than being owned by Railtrack).

But the prime concern of ORR in its early days was with Railtrack's performance and charges. Track access charges were initially regulated on the basis of the usual (in Britain) 5-year periodic review (known officially as control periods), with charges in-between reviews regulated on the usual RPI-X basis, with settlements designed to enable Railtrack to finance its activities including its cost of capital but to prevent long-term monopoly profits.

It is a well-recognised consequence of price regulation that it may reduce incentives to improve capacity and quality. In the case of Railtrack it was intended to give the company incentives in this respect through a performance regime, which would offer bonuses where they were responsible for performance in excess of set benchmarks in terms of punctuality and reliability, and penalties for shortfalls. Railtrack itself was responsible for determining whether it or the train operator caused delays, but where the cause was external factors such as weather or was undetermined, responsibility was attached to Railtrack. There was also an appeals committee to deal with disputes regarding causation. However, ORR soon concluded that these incentives were inadequate to deal with the long-run state of the infrastructure and became concerned at the perceived low level of Railtrack investment and at various indicators of a deterioration in the state of the track – in particular the level of broken rails (see Figure 8.1 and Smith, 2006). It thus became more active in directly regulating investment and performance.

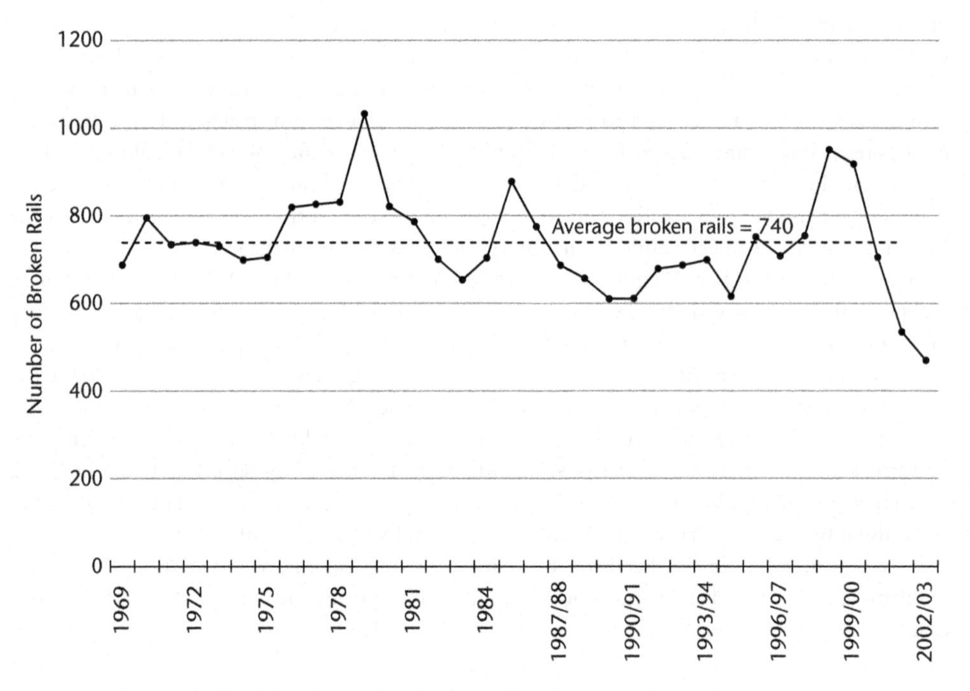

Figure 8.1 The number of broken rails on the British rail network
Source: adapted from Smith, 2006

It was indeed a broken rail which caused the fatal accident at Hatfield, UK, in October 2000 which set in motion the course of events which led to the bankruptcy of Railtrack. Railtrack was already in some difficulty because of a large increase in the cost of the major West Coast main line renewal and upgrade project to which it had committed itself. But after Hatfield, it imposed severe speed restrictions, for which it had to compensate train operators, and greatly increased spending on maintenance and renewals. As a result of this it became bankrupt and, following a period in administration, was transformed into a not-for-dividend company limited by guarantee, with no shareholders but overseen by members appointed to represent government, the rail industry and the general public. Initially it was argued that this structure maintained its role as a private company although all its debts were guaranteed by the state, but in 2014 it was ruled to be legally owned by the state and as a result the role of the public members has been abolished.

Whilst the prime responsibility for the demise of Railtrack must rest with its management, as usual in such cases the question arises as to whether some responsibility should be attached to ORR. Whilst ORR had correctly identified the problem of deterioration of the state of the infrastructure, and taken action on it, arguably it did not act quickly and decisively enough.

These events posed ORR with severe problems. Firstly, in dealing with the crisis, the government largely bypassed ORR, and indeed threatened legislation to bring it under government control if it intervened (this in turn provoked a strong response from the privatised rail operators who saw the independence of ORR as crucial to their confidence in the future costs and performance of the infrastructure manager). But secondly, how should it react to the massive increase in the infrastructure manager's costs? In fact in the next periodic review[1] it allowed Network Rail a very large increase in income which had to be met largely from government grants. This led to a further review of the structure of the rail industry to see how to prevent such an unexpected imposition on government funds by an independent body from occurring again. The result was the structure which more or less survives to this day.

Currently the rail industry in Britain comprises the following principal stakeholders:

(1) Government, which through the Department for Transport specifies the services to be delivered under franchise agreements, awards the franchises to train operators by means of competitive tenders, regulates some fares and also sets out its objectives regarding the capacity and capability of the infrastructure and the money it is prepared to contribute to achieving these targets. Increasingly these functions are being devolved, most completely in the case of Scotland but also for franchising in the case of Wales, Greater London and Merseyside, whilst a coalition of local authorities (Rail North) shares with the Department for Transport the management of the northern franchise.
(2) Privately owned passenger train operators, most of whom run services under government franchises, although there is a small amount of purely commercial open access operation.
(3) Privately owned freight train operators.
(4) Network Rail, which is responsible for maintenance, renewal after operation and enhancement of the infrastructure.
(5) Rolling stock leasing companies from whom most train operators lease their rolling stock (there has been debate as to whether these should be brought under the regulatory umbrella, but so far that has not happened).
(6) The regulator, ORR.

The setting of financial and performance targets, investment levels and track access charges is driven by the following process. At the start of the periodic review, the Department for Transport sets out its targets for the infrastructure in the form of its High Level Output Specification and also sets out its willingness and ability to fund achievement of these in its Statement of Funds Available.

Meanwhile, the regulator considers what finance the infrastructure manager will need to achieve these targets if it operates efficiently. As part of this process, it undertakes benchmarking studies to determine how efficient Network Rail is relative to other rail infrastructure managers and utilities, and from this determines the extent to which future cost reductions should contribute towards the achievement of these targets (Smith et al., 2010). Finally, in the light of the level of grant provided by the government directly towards Network Rail, it determines the level of track access charges. These are set at the estimated level of short-run marginal wear and tear costs in terms of additional maintenance and renewal costs plus congestion costs, reflecting the increased unreliability when routes operate at high levels of capacity utilisation. There is also a mark-up on freight charges for those commodities deemed able to bear such a charge without undue loss of traffic to cover the fixed costs of providing for freight traffic such as freight-only lines.

To the extent that government grants do not cover the remaining costs of the network, there is also a fixed charge levied only on franchised passenger operators. This charge simply shares out these costs on the basis of metrics such as train kilometres and revenue. Since franchises are awarded on the basis of competitive tendering, it may reasonably be assumed that these fixed charges simply reduce the premium or increase the subsidy paid for the franchise in question. Moreover, any changes in fixed or variable charges during the period of a franchise are passed through to the government in the form of changes in premiums or subsidies. Thus it is in effect the government that bears these costs one way or another.

ORR again recognised that the performance regime was not an adequate incentive to invest and – as well as maintaining its own supervision of investment plans and performance of Network

Rail – introduced a small volume incentive payment, so that Network Rail would get something beyond recovery of its own marginal costs from an expansion in traffic.

8.5 How well has rail regulation in Britain performed?

It has already been noted that ORR may have to bear some of the blame for the bankruptcy of Railtrack and the subsequent increase in costs. By 2005, the total cost of the passenger railway had risen by 35 percent in real terms compared with costs at the completion of privatisation in 1997 (Table 8.1); see also Smith and Nash (2014). Whilst most of the increase relates to infrastructure, it is also the case that passenger train operating costs increased and at a faster rate than train kilometres. Since then Network Rail has succeeded both in reducing costs and improving performance, having been set stringent targets by ORR in its 2008 periodic review of the company's finances. Based on the benchmarking studies noted above, Network Rail was required to achieve efficiency targets of 23.5 percent over the period 2009–14. In the event, Network Rail achieved savings of 15.5 percent – substantial, but well below the 23.5 percent target (ORR, 2014). After this good progress the situation deteriorated markedly, with Network Rail's efficiency performance declining by 8 percent over the two years 2015 to 2016 against a target of a 10 percent improvement (see ORR, 2016).

Overall, McNulty's work (2011) – which benchmarked the British rail system (infrastructure manager and train operators) against other European systems – concluded that British costs were some 30 percent higher than best practice. To a considerable extent he saw this as the result of a misalignment of incentives between infrastructure managers and train operators. This was despite Britain having the most sophisticated systems of track access charges (differentiated by hundreds of different types of vehicle to reflect differential wear and tear and also by location and time to reflect congestion) and the most sophisticated performance regimes in Europe. Essentially, the problem he saw was a lack of incentive for the train operator to assist the infrastructure manager in providing infrastructure of the appropriate capacity and quality in the most cost-effective way, for instance in the planning of maintenance, renewals and enhancements to optimise system costs.

McNulty saw two possible routes to overcoming this problem. The first was to expose train operators to infrastructure cost risk. If they bore the total cost of the infrastructure they used and were not shielded from changes in this cost by government guarantees then they would have the

Table 8.1 Passenger rail costs, Great Britain (2011/12 prices)

Rail costs (£bn, 2011/12 prices)	*1996/7*	*2005/6*	*2011/12*
Infrastructure expenditure			
Maintenance	1.1	1.4	1.0
Renewal and enhancements	1.5	3.7	4.6
Other operating costs	1.0	1.4	1.5
Subtotal	3.6	6.5	7.1
TOC costs net of access charge	4.2	5.8	5.9
Total passenger rail costs	7.8	12.3	13.0
Unit cost measures (£)			
Total passenger rail costs per passenger train km	20.2	27.0	25.4
Infrastructure costs per passenger train km	9.2	14.4	13.9
TOC costs (net of access) per passenger train km	11.0	12.6	11.5

Source: Smith and Nash, 2014

appropriate incentive to press for and cooperate in actions to reduce it. For this to be effective it would be necessary to reformulate the fixed charges on franchisees to ensure that they were responsive to franchisees' actions, by basing them on incremental or avoidable costs as well as removing the passing through of any changes in these costs to government. ORR is consulting on such changes as part of the current periodic review (ORR, 2015). To the extent that bidders add an additional risk premium as a result of such changes, there could be an offsetting cost to government.

The second was to reintroduce a degree of vertical integration by leasing the relevant infrastructure to the franchisees, or by the formation of alliances in which staff are placed under common management and revenues and costs shared between franchisees and the infrastructure manager. The first such alliance, between Stagecoach and Network Rail for the delivery of the services of South West Trains, ended in 2016, but a second started in 2015 in the case of Scotrail services in Scotland. Debate on the effectiveness of alliances continues; it seems agreed that this first one did not succeed in reducing costs but its proponents claim that it did make considerable progress in improving the state of the infrastructure in a cost-effective way.

Both approaches have their shortcomings. In the first case, fixed costs cannot all be uniquely attributed to a specific operator; there are some costs (for instance that of a single track line) that need to be incurred for a train service to be provided at all, and other costs may be joint between operators (for instance, if provision of the desired level of intercity and regional services requires double track for either of them even if the other were not there). In its latter days, British Rail overcame this problem by designating a prime user amongst the different service sectors for each asset, with other users simply paying avoidable or incremental cost. Whilst this has an element of arbitrariness when two or more sectors are making extensive use of the same assets, it does have the advantage of placing clear responsibility for all assets on a specific sector or operator.

In the case of alliances, such an arrangement clearly reintroduces incentives for discriminatory action in favour of the passenger franchisee above other train operators over the route in question. For this reason freight operators are clearly nervous of this development, and it makes the job of the regulator regarding avoiding discrimination more difficult, although charging and capacity allocation remain the responsibility of Network Rail centrally and do not form part of the alliance.

In either case, another problem is the limited life of the franchise, which gives the franchisee a very short time horizon compared with the life of infrastructure assets. As a partial solution to this, McNulty (2011) recommended longer franchises, although following difficulties with the letting of the first such franchise, the government appears to have rejected this recommendation. Longer franchises may (in the right circumstances) encourage train operators to take increased risk with respect to infrastructure costs through alliances.

Thus there is no simple solution to the problem of misalignment of incentives; all approaches require trade-offs between advantages and disadvantages.

In 2015, the future of both Network Rail and ORR again came under scrutiny. In the case of Network Rail, the issues were delays and cost increases in major projects, and particularly electrification of the Great Western mainline. As noted earlier, Network Rail's efficiency performance has thus taken a significant step backwards since 2015.

Breaking it up into regional bodies and outright privatisation were again considered, but the conclusion of the Shaw report, which was commissioned to advise on the way forward, was that neither of these should be pursued outright (Shaw, 2016). Rather, a form of yardstick competition should be introduced. Network Rail should be separated into a systems operator role which needed to be performed centrally, and operations, maintenance and renewal of the infrastructure should be decentralised to bodies with their own accounts, which could be regulated individually and benchmarked against each other. Some might be concessioned to the private sector. At the same time the Department for Transport consulted on the role of ORR given the changed status of Network Rail as a government body, and considered taking over some of ORR's functions itself, but again protests from the private sector largely deterred it from doing so.

8.6 Conclusion

The growth of independent rail regulatory bodies in Europe arises mainly from the desire to ensure that new entrants into the rail markets are not hampered by discrimination by infrastructure managers. Such discrimination is most likely when infrastructure managers and train operators are both part of the same holding company, but may occur in any event when infrastructure managers and the main train operators are both owned by government. It may also occur in terms of access to other facilities, including depots and marshalling yards, when these are owned by specific train operators rather than infrastructure managers.

However, there is another important role played by some rail regulators and that is in regulating the efficiency and performance of infrastructure managers. Separation of infrastructure from operations creates a monopoly infrastructure manager, in practice under government ownership and one step removed from the final customer.

A review of the literature suggests that the characteristics of an effective regulator include being run by a regulatory board independent from day-to-day political interference, adequate experience and staffing, appropriate responsibilities and powers to carry them out and transparency and accountability in their operations. It appears that the regulatory authority in Britain has all these characteristics and is one of the few regulators in Europe to play an important part in seeking high performance and efficiency from the infrastructure manager. Moreover, the current structure for the periodic review has provided clarity in the relative roles of government and regulator, with the government setting the budget constraint and the regulator determining what can be done within it. Thus Britain is used as a case study to see how successful the regulatory authority has been in practice.

The evidence from Britain suggests that reliance on incentives such as sophisticated track access charges and performance regime is inadequate to ensure that the infrastructure manager performs efficiently. Nor is the fact that the British rail regulator has most of the characteristics of an ideal rail regulator as identified from literature adequate to ensure a fully successful outcome; although it does appear that ORR has had some success in improving the efficiency and performance of Network Rail, it has fallen well short of targets based on benchmarking studies and the cost falls come from a very high base. However, it should be noted that, from a system-efficiency perspective, anecdotal evidence suggests that vehicle designs in Britain have been impacted by the variable track access charging regime, indicating that accurate pricing can and does have a beneficial effect.

In most European countries, the regulator plays no part in this aspect of controlling the infrastructure manager; instead it is performed by government as part of the negotiation of multiannual contracts between government and infrastructure manager. However, government bodies are not best placed to undertake an objective and independent review of efficiency using the latest benchmarking techniques. Nevertheless, benchmarking has its limitations, as most countries have a single large infrastructure manager, and benchmarking studies therefore have all the difficulties of international comparisons. The possibility (recommended for Britain by the Shaw report) of breaking up the infrastructure manager into a number of regional bodies with only those activities that must be performed at the national level remaining at headquarters would have the advantage of making possible yardstick competition, in which such bodies are benchmarked against each other. This would put rail on a similar footing to utilities such as water and energy distribution networks where different companies in different parts of Britain are benchmarked against each other.

But again, whilst the approach of placing the regulator in charge of ensuring the performance and efficiency of the infrastructure manager has had some success in Britain in recent years, it has not been totally successful. McNulty (2011) concluded that this was largely due to the misalignment of incentives between infrastructure managers and train operators. This leads us back to fundamental issues about the structure of the railway. In the British circumstances and approach to the introduction of competition into the rail industry, where passenger trains dominate and most are provided under franchises, possible solutions exist in terms of making the franchisee responsible for operating the majority of trains in a particular area responsible for fixed as well as variable infrastructure costs, or implementing vertically integrated franchises or alliances. Even so, such a move requires careful implementation and significantly increases the risks to train operators. But where there is a more even balance of passenger and freight traffic and a variety of operators making similar use of the same infrastructure, it is more difficult to achieve such an alignment of incentives without a return to vertically integrated monopoly railways.

Note

1 This was an interim review (that is, within the standard 5-year review period), conducted in 2002/3 as a result of the very large cost increases that had occurred and Railtrack's replacement by Network Rail.

References

Benedetto, V. (2016). The Impacts of Regulatory Structures on the Efficiency of European Railway Systems. PhD thesis, University of Leeds.

Crozet, Y., Nash, C. A. and Preston, J. (2012). Beyond the Quiet Life of a Natural Monopoly: Regulatory Challenges Ahead for Europe's Rail Sector. Policy paper for Centre on Rail Regulation in Europe.

European Commission (2012). Directive 2012/34/EU of the European Parliament and of the Council of 21 November 2012 Establishing a Single European Railway Area (recast). Brussels: European Commission.

Fremeth, A. R. and Holburn, G. L. F. (2010). Information Asymmetries and Regulatory Decision Costs: An Analysis of U.S. Electric Utility Rate Changes 1980–2000. *Journal of Law, Economics and Organization*, 28 (1), pp. 127–62.

Friebel, G., Ivaldi, M. and Vibes, C. (2010). Railway (De)Regulation: A European Efficiency Comparison. *Economica*, 77(305), pp. 77–99.

Gassner, K. and Pushak, N. (2014). 30 Years of British Utility Regulation: Developing Country Experience and Outlook. *Utilities Policy*, 31, pp. 44–51.

Haney, A. B. and Pollitt, M. G. (2009). Efficiency Analysis of Energy Networks: An International Survey of Regulators. *Energy Policy*, 37(12), pp. 5814–930.

Haney, A. B. and Pollitt, M. G. (2011). Exploring the Determinants of 'Best Practice' Benchmarking in Electricity Network Regulation. *Energy Policy*, 39(12), pp. 7739–846.

Haney, A. B. and Pollitt, M. G. (2013). International Benchmarking of Electricity Transmission by Regulators: A Contrast between Theory and Practice? *Energy Policy*, 62, pp. 267–81.

IBM and Kirchner, C. (2002, 2004, 2007, 2011). *Rail Liberalisation Index: Comparison of the Status of Market Opening in the Rail Markets of the Member States of the European Union, Switzerland and Norway*. Berlin: IBM.

IBM Business Consulting Services (2006). *Rail Regulation in Europe: Comparison of the Status Quo of the Regulation of Rail Network Access in the EU-25 Countries, Switzerland, and Norway*. Zurich: IBM.

McNulty, Sir R. (2011). Realising the Potential of GB Rail: Final Independent Report of the Rail Value for Money Study. London: Department for Transport and Office of Rail Regulation.

Mizutani, F. and Uranishi, S. (2013). Does vertical separation reduce cost? An empirical analysis of the rail industry in European and East Asian OECD Countries. *Journal of Regulatory Economics*, 43(1), pp. 31–59.

Mizutani, F., Smith, A. S. J., Nash, C. A. and Uranishi, S. (2014). Comparing the Costs of Vertical Separation, Integration, and Intermediate Organisational Structures in European and East Asian Railways. *Journal of Transport Economics and Policy*.
Nash, C. A. (2013). Rail Transport. In Finger, M. and Holvad, T. (eds), *Regulating Transport in Europe*. Cheltenham: Edward Elgar.
Nash, C. A. and Smith, A. S. J. (2011). Britain. In Drew, J. and Ludewig, J. (eds), *Reforming Railways: Lessons from Experience*. Hamburg: Eurail Press, pp. 89–102.
Niemeier, H. (2011). Effective Regulatory Institutions for Air Transport: A European Perspective. In OECD, *Better Economic Regulation: The Role of The Regulator*. ITF Round Tables, No. 150. Paris: OECD Publishing, pp. 35–69.
OECD (2000). *Telecommunication Regulations: Institutional Structures and Responsibilities*. OECD Digital Economy Papers, 48. Paris: OECD Publishing.
OECD/ITF (2011). *Better Economic Regulation: The Role of the Regulator*. ITF Round Tables, No. 150. Paris: OECD Publishing.
ORR (2014). Network Rail's Efficiency and Financial Performance from 2009–2014 Control Period 4, CP4. London.
ORR (2015). Network Charges: A Consultation on How Charges Can Improve Efficiency. London.
ORR (2016). Annual Efficiency and Finance Assessment of Network Rail 2015–16. London.
Ponti, M. (2011). Transport Regulation from Theory to Practice: General Observations and a Case Study. In OECD, *Better Economic Regulation: The Role of the Regulator*. ITF Round Tables, No. 150. Paris: OECD Publishing, pp. 93–112.
Shaw, N. (2016). The Future Shape and Financing of Network Rail: Final Report and Recommendations. London: Department for Transport.
Smith, A. S. J. (2006). Are Britain's Railways Costing too Much? Perspectives Based on TFP Comparisons with British Rail 1963–2002. *Journal of Transport Economics and Policy*, 40, pp. 1–44.
Smith, A. S. J. and Nash, C. A. (2014). Rail Efficiency: Cost Research and Its Implications for Policy. *International Transport Forum Discussion Paper*, 22. Paris: OECD.
Smith. A. S. J., Wheat, P. and Smith, G. (2010). The Role of International Benchmarking in Developing Rail Infrastructure Efficiency Estimates. *Utilities Policy*, 18, pp. 86–93, doi: 10.1016/j.jup.2009.06.003
Smith, A. S. J., Benedetto, V. and Nash, C. A. (2015). The Impacts of Economic Regulation on the Efficiency of European Railway Systems. Thredbo 14 Conference: International Conference Series on Competition and Ownership in Land Passenger Transport, Santiago, Chile, 20 August–3 September.
van de Velde, D., Nash, C. A., Smith, A. S. J., Mizutani, F., Uranishi, S., Lijesen, M. and Zschoche, F. (2012). *EVES-Rail: Economic Effects of Vertical Separation in the Railway Sector*. Brussels: CER.
Wetzel, H. (2008). European Railway Deregulation. Working paper 86, Institute of Economics, Leuphana, University of Lüneburg.

9

The impact of regulatory reform on public transport markets

John Preston

9.1 Introduction

Throughout the world, the traditional operation of public transport markets (defined here as bus and rail) evolved to become based on public ownership and control (Gomez-Ibanez and Meyer, 1993) as a result of concerns regarding various forms of market failure and concerns that public transport was a quasi-public good, or more strictly a merit good, which provides the public with a basic level of mobility (Gwilliam, 1987). For example, in the UK, the bus industry grew rapidly and somewhat chaotically in the 1920s, leading to concerns about public safety and the 'curious old practices' that emerged from what was seen by some to be wasteful competition (Foster and Golay, 1986). As a result, the Road Traffic Act of 1930 regulated the bus industry in terms of quantity (operators required road service licenses), fares and safety in a system controlled by government-appointed traffic commissioners.

Rail too attracted public interest right from the outset, given the death of the politician William Huskisson following the opening ceremony of the Liverpool to Manchester railway in 1830 (Wolmar, 2007). Regulation followed, originating with William Gladstone's 1844 Railways Act, in part motivated by concerns relating to the natural monopoly features of the industry and with an emphasis on price regulation, originating with workmen's tickets.

For both industries, public control was followed by public ownership. In local transport, municipalities started playing a role with the development of tramways, such as those of Huddersfield Corporation in the UK that began operation in 1883 – the first in the UK. Over time, such municipalities developed motorbus services, with Huddersfield Corporation beginning operations in 1921 (Mulley and Higginson, 2013, pp. 270–1). Further impetus was given by the creation of the London Passenger Transport Board in 1933 by Herbert Morrison, which brought most of London's public transport system into public ownership. Public ownership of the bus industry was completed as a result of the 1947 and 1968 Transport Acts, which brought the Thomas Tilling Group and British Electric Traction Group respectively into state control. The mainline railways in the UK were more resistant to nationalisation, despite difficulties in raising the necessary capital to renew assets following the First World War. A temporary solution was the 1923 Groupings that established the Big Four, who it was believed would have the necessary scale to invest at the level required. However, the Second World War led to a further investment crisis, resulting in the nationalisation of the industry as a result of the 1947 Transport Act and the creation of the British Transport Commission. Similar trends towards public control and ownership could be observed throughout the world, albeit that railways systems in Europe came under public ownership earlier (or in some cases from the outset), in the main due to strategic defence reasons (Wolmar, 2009).

However, over time, the benign public interest explanations of regulation came to be criticised, particularly from academics in the US (Stigler, 1971; Posner, 1975). This viewpoint stressed the role of vested interest groups in the emergence of regulation. According to this stance, the main reason for the 1930 Road Traffic Act in the UK was to provide protection for the mainline railways and the municipal tramways from competition from buses. Moreover, regulatory capture was seen as being endemic due to information asymmetries between the regulator and the regulated firms. Even if the Road Traffic Act was introduced for the right reasons, the regime was quickly captured by the large bus operators who ensured it operated in their best interests. Moreover, the regime may have exhibited regulatory creep, with justified intervention with regards to the quantity and quality of service being provided extending into less justifiable interventions in terms of fares. In addition, a variant of Goodhart's Law may have operated, with activity switching from the regulated stage-carriage services to unregulated private hire and excursions and tours services.

The result was seen to be regulatory failure that exceeded the initial market failure. Features were thought to include high costs and low productivity, with productive inefficiencies arising from the X-inefficiencies identified by Liebenstein (1966), allocative inefficiencies arising from inappropriate mixes of fares and services and dynamic inefficiencies arising from a lack of innovation. This view was related to a more general critique of nationalised industries and a move towards privatisation (Vickers and Yarrow, 1988). Privatisation was believed to introduce the disciplines of the capital market, such as bankruptcy and takeover constraints, that were absent for state-owned enterprises. It was thought to lead to a better definition of property rights and principal–agent relationships and less government interference, but where the industry has some natural monopoly characteristics there would be a need for an independent regulator. Privatisation would also provide greater managerial incentives (and emoluments) and reduce the power of organised labour, which has been important in public transport industries.

Consistent with the ascendancy of neoliberalism, at least in the Anglo-Saxon world, public transport entered into an era of deregulation. The first moves were made in the US, starting with the airline (1978), trucking (1980) and interstate bus (1982) industries and the lifting of rail regulations (principally with respect to freight rates) as a result of the Staggers Act 1980. However, the UK was an early and enthusiastic adopter and it is these experiments in industrial organisation that will provide the focus for this chapter. In the next section, we will outline the legislation that reformed the local bus industry in the UK in the mid-1980s and the national rail industry in the mid-1990s. The following sections will review the key trends in these two markets/industries following the reforms and will attempt to develop quantitative assessments of the success of these reforms. In doing so, the chapter draws heavily on doctoral research undertaken at the University of Southampton (Robins, 2012; Almutairi, 2013; Preston and Almutairi, 2013, 2014; Preston and Robins, 2013). We will then conclude by examining the policy implications of this work.

9.2 The reforms of the local bus and national rail industries in the UK

The starting point for buses is the 1980 Transport Act which deregulated express coach services in Great Britain, leading to substantial on-the-road competition (competition-in-the-market) between National Express (the incumbent), British Coachways (the entrant – formed by a consortium of independent coach operators) and numerous independents. Reviews of the early stages are provided by Barton and Everest (1984), Kilvington and Cross (1986) and Douglas (1987), with a later assessment provided by Thompson and Whitfield (1995). A key feature of coach competition was its impact on rival rail services (competition-between-markets), with an early study being that of Bleasdale (1983). This is a phenomenon that more recently has been repeated in France (2015) and Germany (2013) (Guihery, 2015; Knorr and Lueg-Arndt, 2014).

The 1980 Transport Act also removed fares regulation from local ('stage carriage') bus services and changed the burden of proof for new services from the entrant to the incumbent. The few cases of competition that this provoked were reviewed by Savage (1985). More importantly, the 1980 Act deregulated local bus services in three trial areas. This mainly highlighted the need for continued subsidy of rural services which could be administered by tendering, a form of competition-for-the-market or off-road competition (Fairhead and Balcombe, 1984). However, there was considerable competition on-the-road in one urban centre in the three trial areas, namely Hereford, which was reviewed by Evans (1988).

Buoyed by the perceived success of the 1980 Transport Act and driven forward by an enthusiastic minister (Nicholas Ridley), the Buses White Paper was published in 1984 and stimulated considerable academic debate between the proponents of the reforms, such as Beesley and Glaister (1985), and those who were more critical (Gwilliam et al., 1985). The ensuing 1985 Transport Act deregulated local bus services in Great Britain outside London. It also introduced a raft of other measures including the privatisation of the National Bus Company, the commercialisation (and, in most cases, subsequent privatisation) of municipal public transport companies, the tightening of residual regulation, particularly with respect to safety and competition policy, and the introduction of tendering for socially necessary services. Early reviews included those of Pickup et al. (1991) and Balcombe et al. (1992). Later reviews included those of Mackie and Preston (1996) and a series of articles in the journal *Transport Reviews* initiated and concluded by White (1995, 1997). Subsequent legislation has left the regulatory regime broadly the same. The 2000 Transport Act and the 2008 Local Transport Act tried to give some impetus to statutory quality partnership and quality contracts respectively but have not changed things substantially (see, for example, Rye and Wretstrand, 2014). A bigger change has been the introduction of nationwide concessionary fare schemes, starting in Wales in 2002, Scotland in 2003 and England in 2008.

London was excluded from the remit of the 1985 Transport Act because bus and underground services had been transferred from local authority control to central government control as a result of the 1984 London Regional Transport Act, a rare case of nationalisation during the Thatcher era. London Regional Transport embarked on a gradual introduction of comprehensive tendering. Between 1984 and 1994, 40 percent of the bus network was put out to tender, with tendering subsequently introduced quickly for the remainder, following the privatisation of London Buses Limited's operating companies. A useful description of this process is given in Kennedy et al. (1995). Almost by accident, the government had created a controlled experiment in which competition-in-the-market and competition-for-the-market in the local bus industry could be compared. The sense in which London is apart from the rest of the UK (or more specifically the rest of England) has been exacerbated by devolution. The 1999 Greater London Authority Act created an elected Mayor of London (Ken Livingstone 2000–8, Boris Johnson 2008–16, Sadiq Khan 2016–) who, through Transport for London, has considerable power over transport policy.

The reforms to the railway industry came later than those of the bus and coach industry, in part due to the adverse reaction to the Serpell Report which contemplated large reductions of the rail network (Serpell, 1983) but also due to the success of the commercialisation of British Rail in the 1980s (Gourvish, 2002). However, by the late 1980s radical voices were calling for privatisation (for example, Redwood, 1988) and this was fuelled by deteriorating performance in the late 1980s and early 1990s, partly due to the economic downturn but also due to increasing costs. The response was the 1992 New Opportunities for Railways White Paper which was followed by the 1993 Railways Act. This divided the state-owned enterprise into profitable and non-profitable entities through a process of horizontal and vertical separation which saw the creation of some 100 new businesses. Some 25 passenger train operating companies were created and franchised in 1996 and 1997. A form of competition-for-the-market (competition for the tracks) was therefore introduced, but with plans for open-access competition-in-the-market to be introduced in 2002, with a limited amount of competition (up to 20 percent of a train operating company's revenue) permitted from 1999 onwards. In the event, this open access was regulated to ensure that it was 'not primarily abstractive' and, to date, has been limited to niche markets. Rail freight was also horizontally separated (initially into seven operating companies) but here open-access competition was permitted from the start. As well as being horizontally separated, the industry was also vertically separated, with the infrastructure authority, Railtrack, floated on the London Stock Exchange in 1996, three rolling stock leasing companies sold in 1996 (and sold on by the following year) and some 60 other businesses privatised raising some £4.4 billion for the Exchequer. By contrast, the receipts from bus companies' sales had been relatively modest. The sale of 70 National Bus Company, 9 Scottish Bus Group and 11 London Buses Limited subsidiaries only raised around £650 million (all figures out-turn prices). Two new regulatory bodies were created, namely the Office of the Rail Regulator (ORR), with responsibility for regulating Railtrack and promoting competition within the industry as a whole, and the Office of Passenger Rail Franchising (OPRAF), with responsibilities for administering the franchising process. It should be noted that although the railways were privatised, in many respects regulation of fares and services was increased. Early reviews of the privatisation of British Rail included Harris and Godward (1997), Freeman and Shaw (2000) and Shaw (2000).

Unlike the bus industry, the initial rail industry reorganisation was relatively short-lived. In the move from a command and control system to a more market-based system of contracts, a lacuna was apparent in terms of strategy. The 2000 Transport Act attempted to rectify this by replacing OPRAF with the Strategic Rail Authority (SRA), but then events took over. In October 2000 a major accident occurred at Hatfield which revealed serious flaws in the way that Railtrack procured infrastructure maintenance. Network wide temporary speed restrictions were put in place and remedial works quickly commissioned. However, this led to Railtrack being placed in receivership in October 2001 and being eventually replaced by Network Rail, initially set up as a company limited by guarantee,[1] in October 2002. It was perceived that SRA had not provided the strategic leadership required and had overcommitted the government financially. This led to the 2004 Future of Rail White Paper and the 2005 Railways Act, which abolished the ill-fated SRA, with its functions being taken over by the Department for Transport (DfT). A procedure was developed by which the DfT would detail what it required from Network Rail (high-level output specification) and the money it had available (statement of funds available) and a negotiation would ensue moderated by the ORR. Despite the 2007 Delivering a Sustainable Railway White Paper and 2012 Reforming Our Railways Command Paper, this is broadly the situation as it stands at the time of writing, although the Shaw Report has proposed some internal restructuring of Network Rail (DfT, 2016).

Our focus on the UK might be seen as idiographic but the deregulation and privatisation of public transport has been a global phenomenon (Gomez-Ibanez and Meyer, 1993). Bus deregulation has occurred, with varying degrees of success (and permanence), in Algeria, Chile, Morocco, New Zealand and Sri Lanka. Similarly, experiments with bus tendering/franchising can be found in Australia, Denmark, France, Jamaica, Malaysia, the Netherlands, Sweden, the

United States and Uzbekistan (Preston, 2001). Railway privatisation has occurred in Japan, New Zealand (where it has since been reversed), several countries in Latin America (Argentina, Brazil, Chile, Mexico) and some countries in Africa (Ivory Coast, Nigeria) (Campos and Cantos, 2000). Within Europe, a number of states have experimented with rail franchising, including Germany, Sweden and Switzerland (Van de Velde, 1999).[2]

9.3 Trends in deregulated and/or privatised public transport markets in Great Britain

In this section is a brief review of some of the trends in the bus and rail markets, with the key baseline year being 1985/6 for bus deregulation (bus deregulation's D-day took place on 26 October 1985) and 1994/5 for rail (the first private franchise began operating in February 1996).

9.3.1 Local bus

For buses, Figure 9.1 shows that the secular decline in bus demand in Great Britain outside London[3] continued and indeed seemed to have a marked one-off decline around the time of D-day. Demand subsequently stabilised around the year 2000, although this is most likely due to the impact of concessionary fares. By contrast, bus demand in London appeared fairly stable up to the mid-1990s, fluctuating in line with the economy. However, from the mid-1990s onwards there has been strong growth. In part, this may be related to external economic factors but is also linked with internal factors related to travelcards, concessionary fares, the congestion charge and the Oyster card (both of which were introduced in 2003).

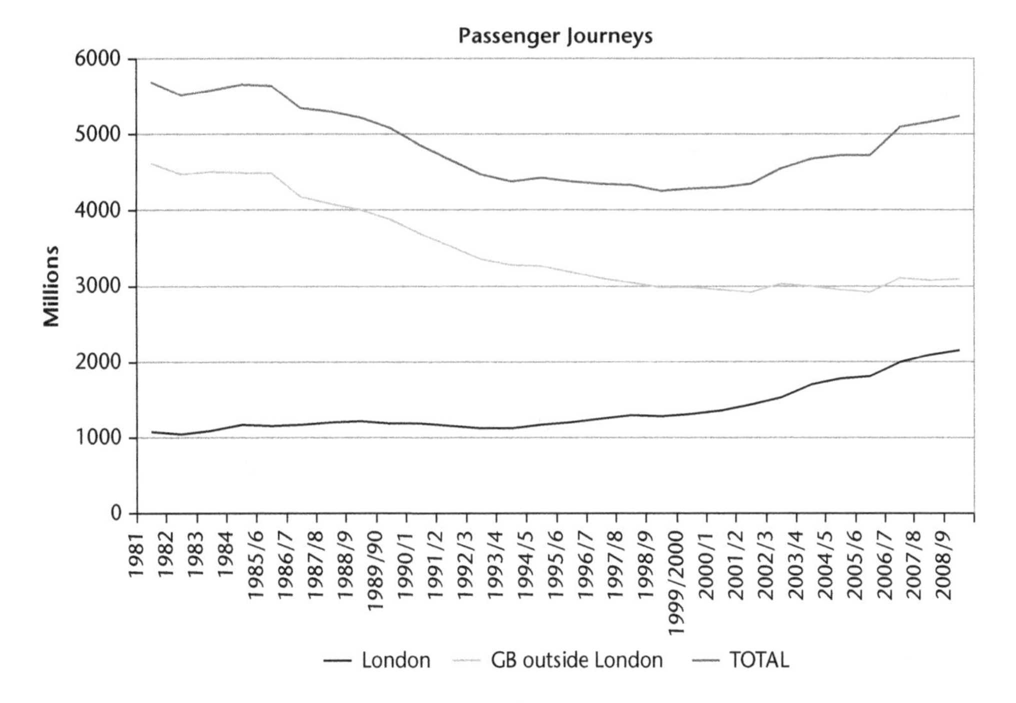

Figure 9.1 Bus trips in Great Britain 2001–2008/9
Source: Almutairi, 2013, based on statistics provided by the DfT

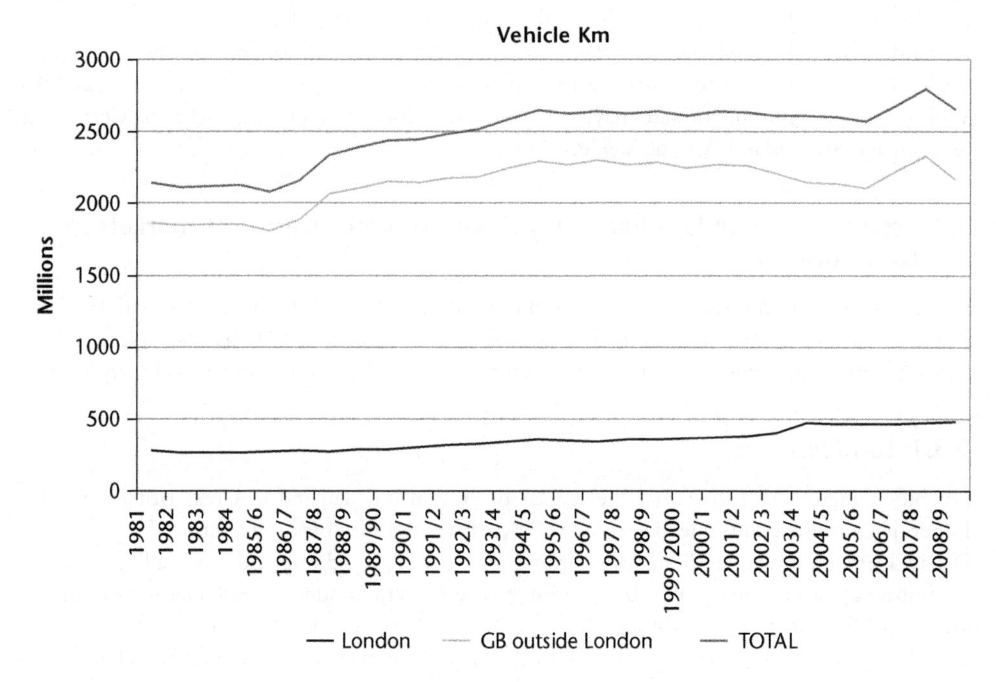

Figure 9.2 Bus vehicle kilometres in Great Britain 1981–2008/9
Source: Almutairi, 2013

In contrast to demand, for supply Figure 9.2 shows there was a break in the trend around 1985/6, with a large increase in the service supplied in Great Britain outside London. Service levels stabilised in the mid-1990s but with another, temporary increase around 2008, probably associated with concessionary fares. London again provided a contrast, with a more steady increase in vehicle kilometres, with the exception of 2003 when there was a bigger increase related to the introduction of the congestion charge.

Figure 9.3 shows that fares (measured in terms of receipts per passenger kilometre) have tended to increase in real terms in both Great Britain outside London and in London. The main exception seems to be in London during Ken Livingstone's first term of office (2000–04). It should be noted that the lower fares in London are likely to be associated with shorter trip lengths.

Figure 9.4 shows that real operating costs per vehicle kilometre show a similar pattern in Great Britain outside London and in London with steep declines from 1985/6, stabilising around the year 2000 and subsequently increasing gradually. The higher unit costs in London may be explained by higher wage rates, lower vehicle speeds (in part due to higher boarding and alighting rates) and lower vehicle utilisation.

Figure 9.5 also shows similar trends with respect to the amount of real subsidy the bus industry received in Great Britain outside of London and in London, excluding fuel duty rebate (later re-branded bus service operators grant). A decline in subsidy followed 1985/6, reaching a minimum in the year 2000 (and buses in London getting close to a zero subsidy system). However, there have been subsequent increases, with these increases being particularly steep in London.

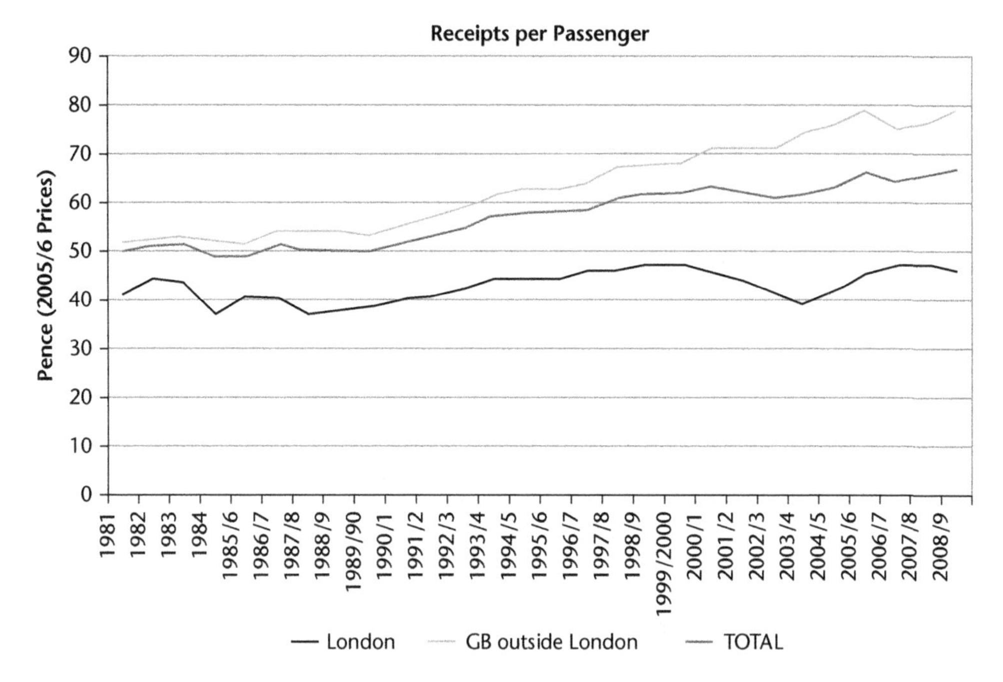

Figure 9.3 Receipts per bus passenger in Great Britain 1981–2008/9
Source: Almutairi, 2013

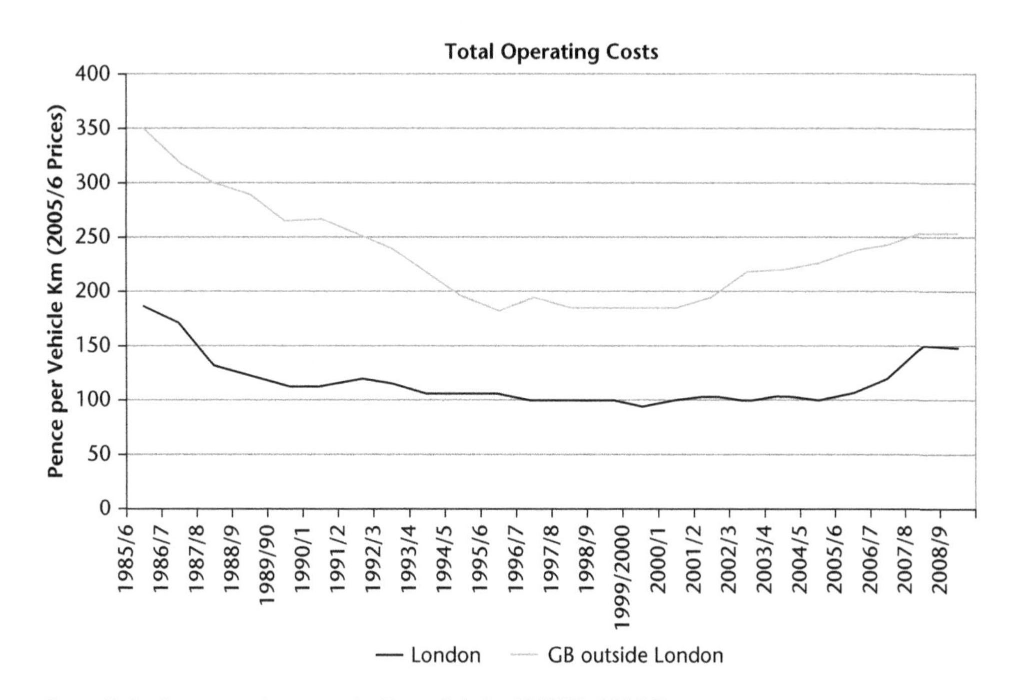

Figure 9.4 Bus operating costs in Great Britain 1985/6–2008/9
Source: Almutairi, 2013

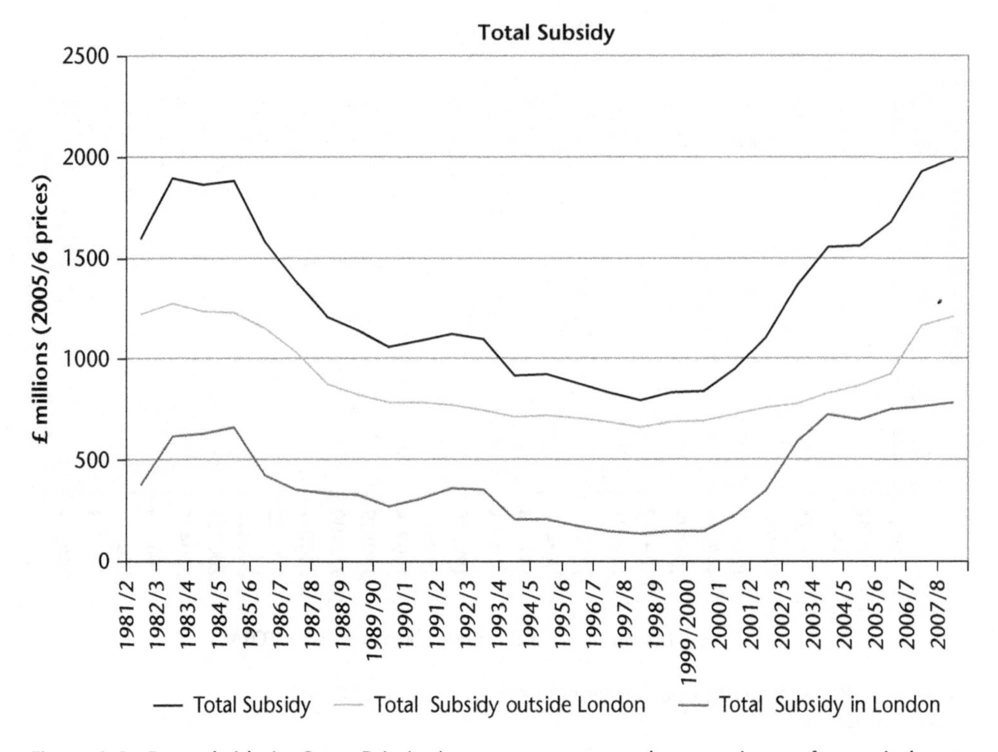

Figure 9.5 Bus subsidy in Great Britain (revenue support and concessionary fares reimbursement) 1981/2–2007/8
Source: Almutairi, 2013

9.3.2 National Rail

Figure 9.6 shows the trends in passenger rail demand, with 1994/5, appearing to represent a turning point from demand that fluctuated with the economic cycles to demand that was sharply increasing. This trend is evident across all three passenger sectors: London and the South East; Long-Distance Inter City; and Regional.

Figure 9.7 shows the impact of fares regulation, in terms of real revenue per passenger kilometre. The trend for real fare increases prior to 1994/5, particularly for the London and South East business sector, ceased, although increases became apparent for long-distance operators from 2000 onwards.

The situation with respect to operating costs is difficult to ascertain, but extending the analysis of Smith (2006), there is an apparent increase in operating costs per train kilometre in the period preceding the reforms, but then there are steep rises from 2001 onwards that are related to the ramifications of the Hatfield accident (Figure 9.8).

The implications of these trends for subsidy are shown by Figure 9.9. A pattern of fluctuation related to economic cycles is apparent and there are some reductions associated with privatisation receipts around 1995/6, but there is a sharp increase from 2001, again associated with the Hatfield accident. A summary of these trends over the study period (starting from 1985/6 for bus and 1994/5 for rail) is given by Table 9.1.

What are noticeable are the very different trends in the different markets/industries. For buses outside London, the combination of increased fares and service levels and reduced demand is

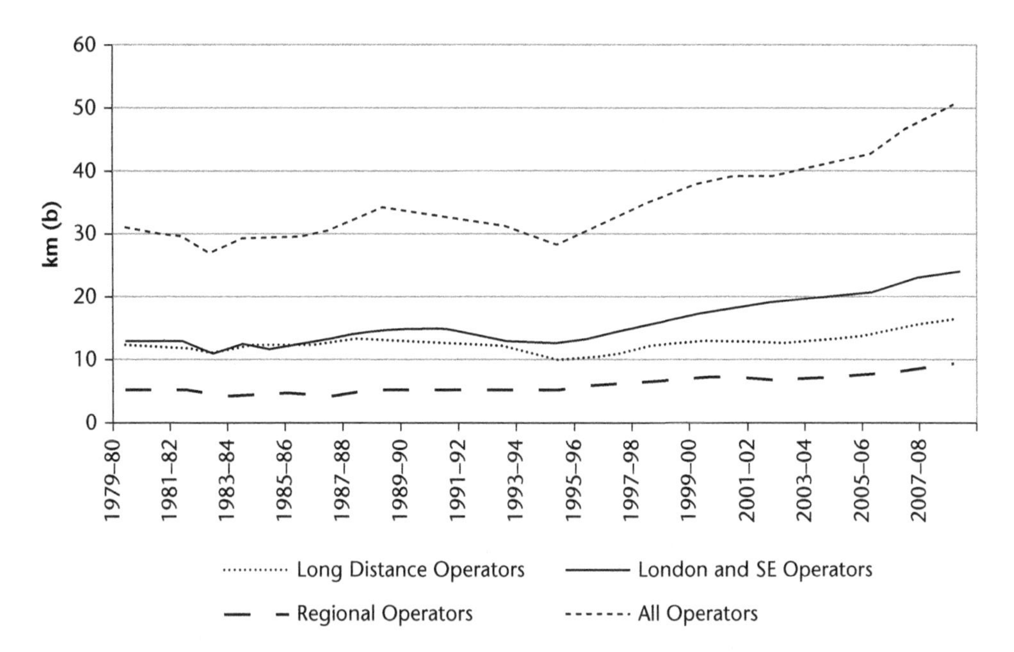

Figure 9.6 Rail passenger kilometres 1979/80–2008/9
Source: Robins, 2012, based on data provided by the Office of Rail Regulation. Data series truncated to 2008/9 to be consistent with subsequent welfare analysis. Some updates are provided in Table 9.1

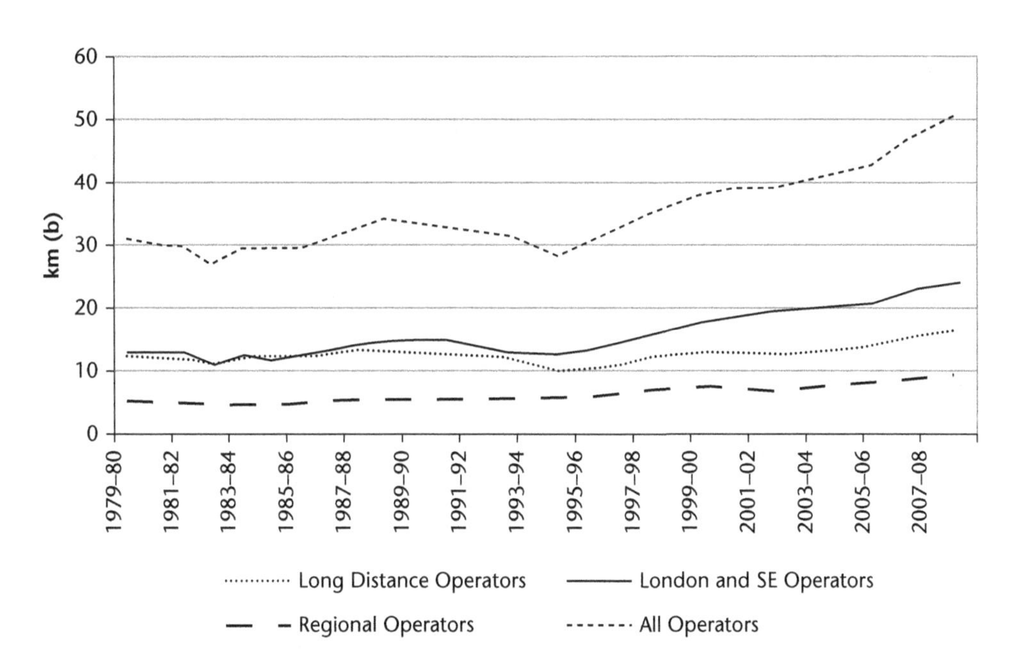

Figure 9.7 Rail revenue per passenger kilometres 1979/80–2008/9 (2008 prices)
Source: Robins, 2012

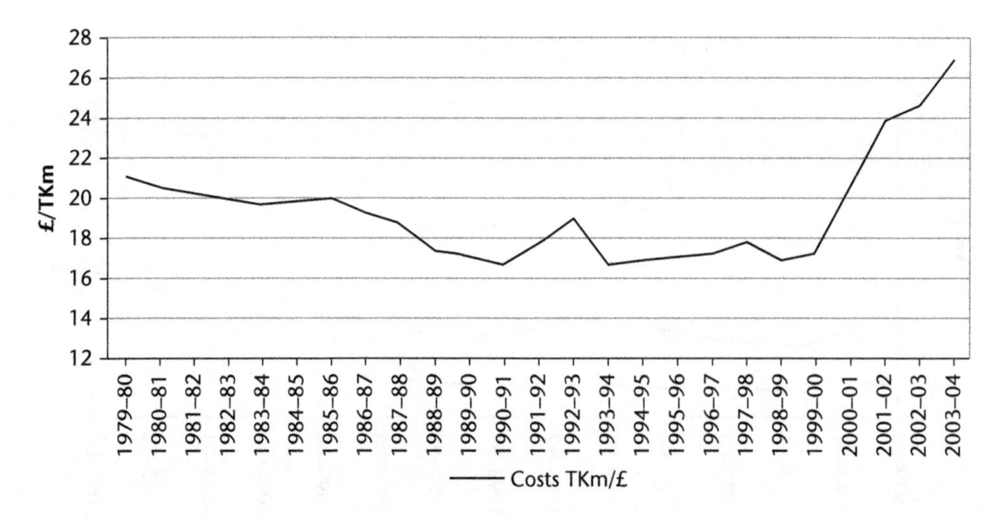

Figure 9.8 Total costs per train kilometres (2008 prices)
Source: Robins, 2012, based on Smith, 2006

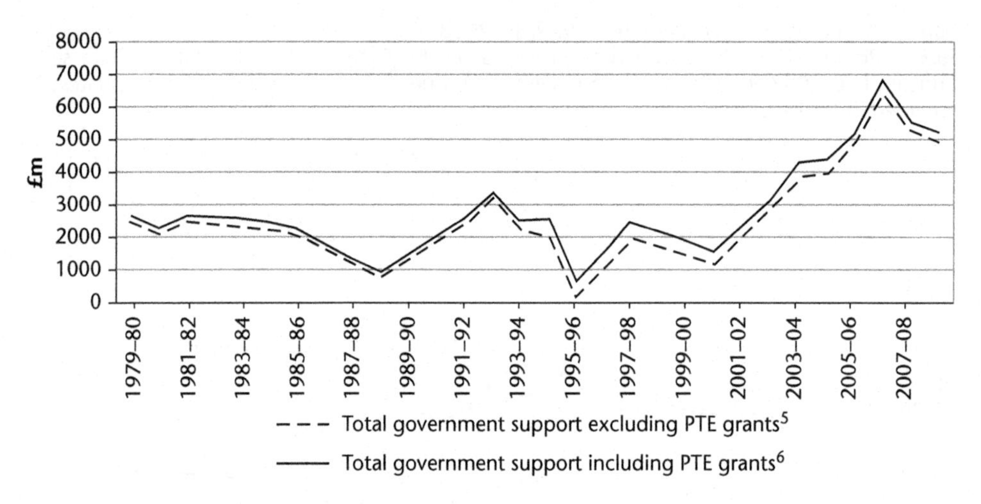

Figure 9.9 Net government support to rail 1979/80–2008/9 (2008 prices)
Source: Robins, 2012

suggestive of wasteful oligopolistic competition (Evans, 1987). For London, the increasing demand whilst fares and service levels are also increasing might indicate a more coordinated policy of welfare maximisation (or as a proxy passenger miles maximisation) (Glaister, 1987). For national rail, the successes on the demand side seem to be negated by failures in terms of costs. The reasons for this are not clear but could be related to transitional and transaction costs, but also to losses of economies of scope and to emerging diseconomies of density.

The figures in parentheses indicate that the broad trends are continuing. Outside London, bus demand is continuing to fall and fares are continuing to increase, albeit at reduced rates. However, services are now being cut back and unit costs are increasing. In London, bus demand has

Table 9.1 Changes in main indicators in the local bus and the national rail markets following bus deregulation (1985/6) and rail privatisation (1994/5) up to 2008/9. Figures for 2014/15 given in parentheses

	Buses outside London	*Buses London*	*National Rail*
Demand	-31% (-38%)	+87% (+105%)	+69% (+125%)
Real fares	+55% (+61%)	+15% (+33%)	+4% (+6%)
Service levels	+20% (+12%)	+78% (+77%)	+34% (+52%)
Real unit costs	-20% (-15%)	-28% (N/A)	+54% (+57%)
Real subsidy	+5% (N/A)	+84% (+42%[1])	+109% (+79%)

Source: Almutairi, 2013; DfT, 2015; TAS, 2016; Robins, 2012

Note: [1]Data for 2013/14; N/A not available; bus cost data for London and bus subsidy data for Scotland and Wales not available on a comparable basis

continued to increase (although there are signs that it is beginning to stall) and fares are also continuing to increase. Service levels have stabilised and subsidy is being reduced. For national rail, demand and service levels have continued to increase strongly, whilst fares have been broadly stable. Unit costs have stabilised and government support is beginning to come down in real terms.

9.4 An assessment

In providing a long-term assessment of bus deregulation we need to recognise that 'evaluation research is tortured by time constraints' (Pawson, 2002). In particular, such assessments are plagued by the problem of determining the counterfactual – what would have happened in the absence of the policy interventions? This requires the analyst to disentangle the impacts of external factors and of other policy interventions and was addressed by the development of econometric models of demand (and costs and prices in a recursive system for bus) and extrapolation of key explanatory variables. In terms of the Maryland Scientific Methods Scale of Evaluation Robustness, the approach here might be characterised as level 2 (where level 5 is the gold standard), being based on before and after comparisons using control variables. For reasons of brevity a quick outline of the econometric methods used is provided.

It should be noted that this work is updating other studies that have attempted to quantify the effects of public transport reforms in Great Britain. For bus deregulation studies include those of White (1990), Mackie et al. (1995) and Romilly (2001), whilst for rail privatisation studies include those of Harris and Godward (1997), White (1998) and Pollitt and Smith (2002).

The kernel of the assessment of the bus modelling work was a partial adjustment model, shown by (9.1), in which bus trips per capita for area i in time period t (Q_{it}) were estimated as a function of real fares (F), vehicle kilometre (VK), income (Y), the lagged dependent variable (Q_{it-1}) time (t) and dummy variables to represent deregulation (DD) and different regions (RDV). The results are given by Table 9.2.

$$LnQ_{it} = \alpha - 0.114\, LnF_{it} + 0.179\, LnVKM_{it} - 0.343\, LnY_{it} + 0.842\, LnQ_{it-1} - 0.071DD + 0.009t + \sum_{i}^{i-1} \beta_i RDV_i. \quad (9.1)$$

Table 9.2 Bus demand model used to determine the counterfactual

	Coefficient	*Standard error*	*z*	*p>|z|*
Constant (α)	3.067	1.081	2.84	0.005
Fare (βF)	-0.114	0.037	-3.08	0.002
Service (βv)	0.180	0.059	3.06	0.002
Income (βY)	-0.343	0.126	-2.73	0.006
Lag (βQ-1)	0.842	0.024	24.93	0.000
Dereg DV (βDD)	-0.071	0.014	-4.93	0.000
Time trend (βt)	0.009	0.003	3.34	0.001
London DV	0.054	0.026	2.09	0.037
Mets DV	0.004	0.021	0.20	0.839
Scotland DV	-0.016	0.028	-0.55	0.582
Wales DV	-0.037	0.013	-2.84	0.005

Note: R2 0.997, Rho 0.142, Wooldridge test 9.162 (p 0.039), Modified Wald test 6.13 (p 0.294), BP LM test 10.057 (p 0.4335)
Source: Almutairi, 2013

This model gave an excellent goodness of fit. Alternative functional forms and lag structures were tested but statistical tests supported the fixed effects partial adjustment model. The model indicated a fares elasticity of -0.11 in the short run and -0.72 in the long run. For vehicle kilometre, the elasticity was 0.18 in the short run and 1.14 in the long run, whilst the corresponding figures for income were -0.34 and -2.18, respectively. The deregulation dummy variable indicated a one-off reduction in demand of 7 percent in the short run, rising to 36 percent. The impacts took a relatively long way to work their way through, with 90 percent of adjustment taking 14 years to occur. This is consistent with the analysis of trends that showed that the impacts of deregulation were waning by around 2000. Subsequent work on the bus econometrics involved developing separate models for London and Great Britain outside of London, in terms of demand, costs and prices. This allowed changes in subsidy to be analysed as an external effect.

The most appropriate (and best fitting) model for rail was found to be an unlagged semi-log model, as shown by (9.2).

$$LnPKM_t = \alpha + \beta RPKM_t + \gamma TKM_t + \delta GDP_t + \theta PRIV + \mu HAT + \rho STRIKE. \quad (9.2)$$

This modelled the natural log of passenger kilometre (PKM) in year t as function of real receipts per passenger kilometre (RPKM), train kilometre (TKM), gross domestic product (GDP) and a series of dummy variables related to privatisation (PRIV), the Hatfield accident (HAT) and industrial disputes (STRIKE). The results are shown by Table 9.3.

Again, the model has a very good fit, with the implied elasticities, evaluated at the mean values, being -0.62 for fares, 0.90 for train kilometres and 0.39 for income.[4] The dummy variables indicated that the disruptions associated with the privatisation process resulted in a 9 percent decline in demand between 1992/3 and 2005/6, whilst the Hatfield accident led to a 5 percent decline between 2000/1 to 2006/7 and strikes led to 6 percent reductions in 1982/3 and 1991/2.

For both bus and rail, the change in welfare (W) was estimated as the sum of the change in consumer surplus (CS) and change in producer surplus, with the latter estimated as the difference between the change in total revenue (TR) and total cost (TC) – see (9.3).

Table 9.3 Rail demand model used to determine the counterfactual

Coefficient	*Value*	*t-statistic*
α	2.923	17.106
β	-5.690	-2.817
γ	0.0024	7.093
δ	3.68762E–07	3.614
θ	–0.092	-8.575
μ	–0.051	-3.117
ρ	–0.063	-3.283
Adjusted R2	0.983	
Durbin-Watson	1.453	

$$\Delta W = \Delta CS + \Delta TR - \Delta TC. \tag{9.3}$$

For bus, the change in consumer surplus was estimated using the rule of half where F1(2) is the fare in the before (after) situation and Q1(2) is the demand in the before (after) situation, as shown in (9.4).

$$\Delta CS = \frac{1}{2}(F_1 - F_2)(Q_1 + Q_2). \tag{9.4}$$

For rail, given the demand function used, the change in consumer surplus can be estimated by direct integration, as shown by (9.5).

$$CS = \int_{RPKM}^{Max} PKM\ dRPKM = -\frac{1}{\beta}PKM. \tag{9.5}$$

Table 9.4 shows that of the 87 percent increase in bus usage in London between 1985/6 and 2008/9, 54 percentage points can be explained by the counterfactual. In other words, only around 38 percent of the demand increase could be ascribed to policies related to the comprehensive tendering system. By contrast, outside London, the counterfactual would have anticipated a modest increase in demand (of 9 percent – much of it driven by population increases[5]), whereas the outcome was a 31 percent decline. In this instance all of the decline (and more) might be attributed to deregulation. This finding is broadly consistent with the estimate provided by the deregulation dummy variable.

For rail, the model forecasts a 70 percent increase in demand, of which 22 percentage points could be explained by the counterfactual. In this case, around 69 percent of the demand increase might be attributed to the reforms related to privatisation.

Table 9.4 Comparison of actual bus demand and that modelled as the counterfactual

	London		*Outside London*	
	Actual	*Counterfactual*	*Actual*	*Counterfactual*
1985/6	1152	1223	4489	4462
2008/9	2149	1885	3084	4884
Change	+87%	+54%	–31%	+9%

Source: Preston and Almutairi, 2013

Table 9.5 Welfare impacts of bus reforms 1985/6 to 2008/9: initial analysis (present values, £ million, 2005/6 prices)

	London	*Outside London*
ΔCS	+ 1,505	−7,320
ΔTR	+46	−4,038
ΔTC	−1,763	−15,751
ΔW	+3,314	+4,393

Source: Preston and Almutairi, 2013

Table 9.6 Welfare impacts of bus reforms 1985/6 to 2009/10: updated analysis (present values, £ million, 2008/9 prices)

	London				*Outside London*			
	Subsidy included		*Subsidy excluded*		*Subsidy included*		*Subsidy excluded*	
	Constant	*Trend*	*Constant*	*Trend*	*Constant*	*Trend*	*Constant*	*Trend*
ΔCS	+399	+451	+2,363	+4,348	−24,044	−16,299	−15,560	+7,358
ΔPS	+3,516	+2,676	+3,416	+2,458	+11,778	+12,630	+8,536	+5,573
ΔW	+3,915	+3,127	+5,779	+6,806	−12,266	−3,669	−7,024	+12,931

Source: Preston and Almutairi, 2014

The initial assessment with respect to bus deregulation is given by Table 9.5. This indicates that for London there are increases in both consumer and producer surplus, whilst by contrast for the market outside London there are large reductions in consumer surplus, but these are more than offset by even larger increases in producer surplus, arising from increases in cost efficiency. This assumes there are not material externalities, for example from bus demand switching to car.

A more detailed assessment is given by Table 9.6, which is based on separate demand models for the bus market in London and outside of London. Whereas in Table 9.5 some internal variables (such as vehicle kilometre, prices and operating costs) were held constant at 1985/6 values, in Table 9.6, past trends are also extrapolated. For example, some of the reductions in vehicle operating costs are due to favourable trends in labour and fuel prices. Moreover, a recursive model is developed that permits the assessment of the impact of subsidy changes. This makes relatively little difference to the results for London, although excluding the impact of subsidy changes strengthens the case for the regulatory reforms. Outside London, the changes do make a big difference, with the welfare effect being negative for three of the four modelled scenarios.

Table 9.7 shows the corresponding assessment for the national rail system. Although there are welfare positive changes in years 1, 4 and 5, overall the changes are strongly welfare negative, with the increases in consumer surplus and in total revenues being more than offset by the large increases in total industry costs.

Neither of the two assessments are comprehensive. For the case of national rail, there was an attempt to evaluate some other items. The net benefit from sales was estimated at £1.22 billion, but this was offset by transitional costs of £0.65 billion. External benefits as a result of the transfer of road traffic to rail was estimated at £0.16 billion, whilst assuming a shadow price of public

Table 9.7 Welfare impacts of rail reforms 1994/5 to 2008/9 (2008 prices)

	Change in revenue	*Change in total industry costs*	*Change in consumer surplus*	*Welfare change*
1995/6	0.036	–0.059	0.132	0.227
1996/7	0.061	0.705	0.270	–0.373
1997/8	0.111	0.845	0.684	–0.051
1998/9	0.185	1.099	0.940	0.027
1999/2000	0.257	1.407	1.163	0.014
2000/1	0.210	3.244	0.999	–2.035
2001/2	0.231	5.058	1.083	–3.744
2002/3	0.247	5.699	1.117	–4.335
2003/4	0.268	7.132	1.195	–5.669
2004/5	0.319	6.594	1.371	–4.911
2005/6	0.354	5.788	1.298	–4.136
2006/7	0.482	5.037	1.906	–2.649
2007/8	0.572	5.593	2.257	–2.764
2008/9	0.630	7.461	2.579	–4.252
Totals	3.957	55.077	16.993	–34.652
Present values	£2.84	£39.84	£12.34	–£24.65

Source: Preston and Robins, 2013

Table 9.8 Summary of welfare changes in the bus and rail markets

	Buses outside London	*Buses in London*	*Rail*
Welfare change per capita	+£110	+£569	–£297
Ratio of CS to PS	–0.63	+0.83	–0.33

funds of 1.2 leads to an estimated deadweight welfare loss of £7.6 billion, resulting from additional grants and subsidies.

Table 9.8 draws on Tables 9.5 and 9.7 to summarise. With respect to buses, even if we take the optimistic viewpoint of deregulation given by Table 9.5, the comprehensive tendering regime in London appears greatly superior in terms of welfare gain per capita and this viewpoint is reinforced by the findings of Table 9.6. Competition-for-the-market appears superior to competition-in-the-market in the case of buses – it has eradicated productive inefficiencies without a simultaneous reduction in patronage. However, rail privatisation, which has a substantial element of competition-for-the-market in terms of franchising, is welfare negative and substantially inferior in its impacts to either of the bus reforms in Table 9.8. A feature of all three reforms is that the changes in producer surplus are greater than the changes in consumer surplus.

9.5 Conclusions

Given the above analysis, the following conclusions can be drawn. In the regulatory reforms examined in Great Britain, supply side effects have tended to dominate demand side effects. For the bus industry this suggests that 50 years of public control and/or ownership did indeed lead to considerable X-inefficiencies. However, competition-for-the-market appears to be as effective as competition-in-the-market in reducing these inefficiencies, at least if accompanied by privatisation and horizontal separation of the large operators (such as London Buses Limited and the National Bus Company). One note of caution is that costs do seem to have been increasing again since around 2000 and this is a pattern that is repeated for contracting-out regimes elsewhere in the world (Hensher and Stanley, 2010).

Contrary to the expectations from other liberalisations, including local bus, rail privatisation led to substantial cost increases, although some of these excesses are now being scaled back. Commercialisation in the 1980s had arguably captured much of the efficiency gains, whilst the rail industry is more complex technologically and organisationally than the bus industry. The fragmentation of the bus industry seemed to enhance the efficiency gains but in rail it might be argued that it enhanced the efficiency losses. Future rail reforms might focus on standardising the technology and simplifying the organisation. Transaction costs have often been argued to be the main source of the cost increases but empirical studies find these have only made a modest contribution, although there are severe difficulties with measurement (Merkert et al., 2012). An alternative explanation is that vertical separation can lead to higher costs, particularly for high-density, mixed traffic railways, in part due to misaligned incentives (van de Velde et al., 2012), whilst excessive horizontal separation may have also played a role (Smith and Wheat, 2007).

Liberalised public transport markets will tend to provide more service at higher fares. This was the outcome for the deregulated bus market outside London, which has exhibited forms of oligopolistic competition. In some areas the dominant firm may have established monopoly powers and is able to cut back services whilst increasing fares (Glaister, 2001; Competition Commission, 2011). The liberalised rail market also exhibits some tendency to lead to higher service levels and fares, although the latter are constrained by price regulation.

For bus deregulation, our use of a dynamic model suggests that the policy had a life of around 14 years and hence was fundamentally completed around the year 2000. The next phase involved moves towards quality partnerships and a national concessionary fares system. However, quality partnerships have only taken off in a relatively limited number of locations, most notably Brighton and Oxford. The key barrier is probably related to the role of local authorities who are unable to provide the necessary infrastructure, particularly for bus priority, and are unwilling to do so if the benefits are largely captured by private profit. The most likely way forward is therefore London-style quality contracts – the Buses Bill that is currently going through Parliament is permissive in that respect. However, local authorities may remain the constraint, as very few will have the necessary expertise or finance to set up comprehensive tendering at a whole-network level. Indeed, in 2016 many authorities are contemplating withdrawing from the tendering of socially necessary services due to budget cuts (for example Derbyshire and Oxfordshire).

For rail it is more difficult to determine when the policies around rail privatisation ended. Some might argue that the liberalised policies were never really given a chance (Glaister, 2004). For example, Foster (1994) had expected passenger services to evolve into something akin to the local bus market outside London, with the vast majority of services provided by open-access, commercial services. Our modelling suggests that the disruptive phase of the reforms lasted until 2006/7, if the Hatfield accident is viewed as a result of the reforms – a period of over ten years. The next phase of the process is not yet clear. The McNulty Review clearly diagnosed the industry's problems in terms of excessive costs (DfT and ORR, 2011), but was unable to provide a suitable treatment – with the subsequent creation of the Rail Delivery Group being arguably a symptom more than a cure. The Shaw Report fell short of recommending some form of privatisation of Network Rail's activities, instead favouring devolution at the route level (DfT, 2016). The Competition and Markets Authority (2016) is calling for more on-track and off-track competition, but there must be concern that this will lead to more vertical and horizontal separation, when arguably what the industry needs is more centralised control.

In conclusion, long-term policy evaluation is a worthwhile exercise but we need to beware of the 'ruthless arithmetic extraction of net success' (Pawson, 2002). Nonetheless, the results of the British experiments do seem to illustrate the success of the comprehensive tendering of bus services in London, the relative failure of bus deregulation outside London and the absolute failure of the rail reforms, even if some elements (such as franchising) may have had successes (Preston, 2015). Given this, it is likely that the next turn of the regulatory cycle will be back towards public ownership and control (Gwilliam, 2008) and indeed there is some evidence of this already happening in the local bus market in France (TfQL, 2015). The fact that so few countries in the world have copied the British experiments or continued with them (Chile, New Zealand) may be the biggest indictment of all.

Acknowledgements

An earlier version of this chapter was presented to the Institute of Transport and Logistics Studies, University of Sydney, 3 July 2012, as part of an exchange funded by the World Universities Network. I am grateful for the comments of the editors on an earlier draft but any errors that remain are, of course, my own. Dawn Robins' doctoral research was jointly funded by the Economic and Social Research Council and consultants Oxera. Talal Almutairi's doctoral research was funded by the Kuwaiti Government.

Notes

1 Network Rail was reclassified as a nationalised industry in 2014.
2 Useful international reviews are provided by the International Conference on Competition and Ownership in Land Passenger Transport – see www.thredbo-conference-series.org/
3 Public transport in Northern Ireland remained under public ownership and control.
4 With this functional form, elasticities are determined by the coefficient values times the value of the variable of interest. For example, the mean receipt of £0.109 per passenger kilometre is multiplied by -5.69 to give a fares elasticity of -0.62. The impact of the dummy variables is computed by the exponent of the parameter value. For example, exp(-0.092) is 0.912, which indicates a 9 percent reduction.
5 Population outside London grew by 8 percent over this period. Note that this counterfactual assumes that fares and service levels are held constant. Alternate (and arguably more realistic) trend assumptions would assume falls in service levels and increases in fares which will lead to falls in demand. Although income grew by 72 percent outside London over this period, the effect of the negative income elasticity was offset by the positive time trend.

References

Almutairi, T. (2013). Evaluating the Long Term Impact of Transport Policy: The Case of Bus Deregulation. PhD Thesis, Faculty of Engineering and the Environment, University of Southampton, May.

Balcombe, R. J., Astrop, A. J. and Fairhead, R. D. (1992). Bus Competition in Great Britain since 1986: A National Review. Research Report 353. Crowthorne: TRRL.

Barton, A. J. and Everest, J. T. (1984). Express Coach Services in the Three Years Following the 1980 Transport Act. Transport and Road Research Laboratory Report 1127. Crowthorne: TRRL.

Beesley, M. E. and Glaister, S. (1985). Deregulating the Bus Industry in Britain – (C) Response. *Transport Reviews*, 5, pp. 133–42.

Bleasdale, C. (1983). The Effects of Deregulation on Inter City Rail Services. *PTRC Summer Annual Meeting*, Seminar L.

Campos, J. and Cantos, P. (2000). Railways. In Estache, A. and de Rus, G. (eds), *Privatization and Regulation of Transport Infrastructure: Guidelines for Policymakers and Regulators*. Washington, DC: World Bank.

Competition Commission (2011). *Local Bus Services Market Investigation. Provisional Findings Report*. London: Competition Commission.

Competition and Markets Authority (2016). *Competition in Passenger Rail Services in Great Britain – A Policy Document*. CMA, London.

DfT (2015). *Transport Statistics Great Britain 2015*. London: DfT.

DfT (2016). *The Shaw Report: The Future Shape and Financing of Network Rail*. London: DfT.

DfT and ORR (2011). Realising the Potential of GB Rail. Final Independent Report of the Rail Value for Money Study, May.

Douglas, N. J. (1987). *A Welfare Assessment of Transport Deregulation: The Case of the Express Coach Market in 1980*. Aldershot: Gower.

Evans, A. (1987). Competition and Other Economic Regimes for Bus Services. *Journal of Transport Economics and Policy*, 21, pp. 7–36.

Evans, A. (1988). Hereford: A Case Study of Bus Deregulation. *Journal of Transport Economics and Policy*, 22, pp. 283–306.

Fairhead, R. D. and Balcombe, R. S. (1984). Deregulation of Bus Services in Trial Areas 1981–84. Transport and Road Research Laboratory Report 1131. Crowthorne: TRRL.

Foster, C. (1994). *The Economics of Rail Privatisation. Discussion Paper 7*. London: CIPFA.

Foster, C. and Golay, J. (1986). Some Curious Old Practices and Their Relevance to Equilibrium in Bus Competition. *Journal of Transport Economics and Policy*, 20, 2, pp. 191–216.

Freeman, R. and Shaw, J. (2000). *All Change: British Railway Privatisation*. Maidenhead: McGraw-Hill.

Glaister, S. (1987). *Allocation of Urban Public Transport Subsidy*. In Glaister, S. (ed.), *Transport Subsidy*. Newbury: Policy Journals.

Glaister, S. (2001). The Economic Assessment of Local Transport Subsidies in Large Cities. In Grayling, T. (ed.), *Any More Fares?* London: IPPR.

Glaister, S. (2004). British Rail Privatisation: Competition Destroyed by Politics. Competencia en el Transporte Ferroviario. Madrid: Fundación Rafael del Pino.

Gomez-Ibanez, J. A. and Meyer, J. R. (1993). *Going Private: The International Experience with Transport Privatisation*. Washington, DC: Brookings Institution.

Gourvish, T. (2002). *British Rail 1974–97: From Integration to Privatisation*. Oxford: Oxford University Press.

Guihery, L. (2015). New Development of the Intercity Bus Market in France: Is It the Comeback of the Road? 14th International Conference on Competition and Ownership in Land Passenger Transport. Santiago, Chile.

Gwilliam, K. (1987). Market Failure, Subsidy and Welfare Maximisation. In Glaister, S. (ed.), *Transport Subsidy*. Newbury: Policy Journals, pp. 6–25.

Gwilliam, K. M (2008). Bus Transport. Is There a Regulatory Cycle? Transportation Research A, 42(9), pp. 1183–94.

Gwilliam, K. M., Nash, C. A. and Mackie, P. J. (1985). Deregulating the Bus Industry in Britain: (B) The Case Against. *Transport Reviews*, 5, pp. 105–32.

Harris, N. G. and Godward, E. W. (1997). *The Privatisation of British Rail*. London: Railway Consultancy Press.

Hensher, D. and Stanley, J. (2010). Contracting Regimes for Bus Services: What Have We Learnt after 20 Years? *Research in Transportation Economics*, 29, pp. 140–4.

Kennedy, D., Glaister, S. and Travers, T. (1995). *London Bus Tendering*. London: London School of Economics.

Kilvington, R. P. and Cross, A. S. (1986). *Deregulation of Express Coach Services in Great Britain*. Aldershot: Gower.

Knorr, A. and Lueg-Arndt, A. (2014). Intercity Bus Deregulation in Germany: Intramodal and Intermodal Effects after Two Years. 14th International Conference on Competition and Ownership in Land Passenger Transport. Santiago, Chile.

Liebenstein, H. (1966). Allocative Efficiency vs. X-Efficiency. *American Economic Review*, 56(3), pp. 392–415.

Mackie, P. and Preston, J. (1996). *The Local Bus Market: A Case Study of Regulatory Change*. Aldershot: Avebury.
Mackie, P., Preston, J. and Nash, C. (1995). Bus Deregulation: Ten Years On. *Transport Reviews*, 15(3), pp. 229–51.
Merkert, R., Smith, A. and Nash, C. (2012). The Measurement of Transaction Costs: Evidence from European Railways. *Journal of Transport Economics and Policy*, 46(3), pp. 349–65.
Mulley, C. and Higginson, M. (eds) (2013). *Companion to Road Passenger Transport History*. Walsall: Roads and Roads Transport History Association.
Pawson, R. (2002). Evidence-Based Policy: The Promise of 'Realist Synthesis'. *Evaluation*, 8(3), pp. 340–58.
Pickup, L., Stokes, G., Meadowcroft, S., Goodwin, P., Tyson, B. and Kenny, F. (1991). *Bus Deregulation in the Metropolitan Areas*. Aldershot: Avebury.
Pollitt, M. and Smith, A. (2002). The Restructuring and Privatisation of British Rail: Was It Really That Bad? *Fiscal Studies*, 23(4), pp. 463–502.
Posner, R. A. (1975). The Social Cost of Monopoly and Regulation. *Journal of Political Economy*, 83(4), pp. 807–27.
Preston, J. M. (2001). Bus Service Regulation and Competition: International Comparisons. In Grayling, T. (ed.), *Any More Fares? Delivering Better Bus Services*. London: Institute for Public Policy Research.
Preston, J. (2015). Deja Vu All over Again? Rail Franchising in Britain. International Conference on Competition and Ownership in Land Passenger Transport. Santiago, Chile.
Preston, J. M. and Almutairi, T. (2013). Evaluating the Long Term Impacts of Transport Policy: An Initial Assessment of Bus Deregulation. *Research in Transportation Economics*, 39, pp. 208–14.
Preston, J. M. and Almutairi, T. (2014). Evaluating the Long Term Impacts of Transport Policy: The Case of Bus Deregulation Revisited. *Research in Transportation Economics*, 48, pp. 263–9.
Preston, J. M. and Robins, D. (2013). Evaluating the Long Term Impacts of Transport Policy: An Assessment of Rail Privatisation. *Research in Transportation Economics*, 39, pp. 134–244.
Redwood, J. (1988). *Signals from a Railway Conference*. London: Centre for Policy Studies.
Robins, D. (2012). *Evaluating the Long Term Impacts of Transport Policy: The Case of Passenger Rail Privatisation in Great Britain*. PhD thesis, Faculty of Social and Human Sciences, University of Southampton.
Romilly, P. (2001). Subsidy and Local Bus Service Deregulation in Britain: A Re-Evaluation. *Journal of Transport Economics and Policy*, 35(2), pp. 161–94.
Rye, T. and Wretstrand, A. (2014). Converging Structures? Recent Regulatory Change in Bus-Based Public Transport in Sweden and England. *Research in Transportation Economics*, 48, pp. 24–32.
Savage, I. P. (1985). *The Deregulation of Bus Services*. Aldershot: Gower.
Serpell, D. (1983). *The Review of Railway Finances*. London: HMSO.
Shaw, J. (2000). *Competition, Regulation and the Privatisation of British Rail*. Aldershot: Ashgate.
Smith, A. (2006). Are Britain's Railways Costing Too Much? Perspectives Based on TFP Comparisons with British Rail 1963–2002. *Journal of Transport Economics and Policy*, 40(1), pp. 1–44.
Smith, A. and Wheat, P. (2007). A Quantitative Study of Train Operating Companies Cost and Efficiency Trends 1996 to 2006: Lessons for Future Franchising Policy. *European Transport Conference*.
Stigler, G. (1971). The Theory of Economic Regulation. *Bell Journal of Economics*, 2, pp. 3–21.
TAS (2016). *Rail Industry Performance 2016*. Long Preston: TAS Publications and Events.
TfQL (2015). Building a World-Class Bus System for Britain, www.transportforqualityoflife.com
Thompson, D. and Whitfield, A. (1995). Express Coaching: Privatisation, Incumbent Advantage and the Competitive Process. In Bishop, M., Kay, J. and Mayer, C. (eds), *The Regulatory Challenge*. Oxford: Oxford University Press.
Van de Velde, D. (ed.) (1999). *Railway Reform and the Role of Competition: The Experience of Six Countries*. Aldershot: Ashgate.
Van de Velde, D., Nash, C., Smith, A., Mizutani, F., Uranishi, S., Lijesen, M. and Zschoche, F. (2012). *EVES-Rail: Economic Effects of Vertical Separation in the Railway Sector*. Brussels: Community of European Railways.
Vickers, J. and Yarrow, G. (1988). *Privatization: An Economic Analysis*. Cambridge, MA: MIT Press.
White, P. R. (1990). Bus Deregulation: A Welfare Balance Sheet. *Journal of Transport Economics and Policy*, 24(3), pp. 311–32.
White, P. R. (1995). Deregulation of Local Bus Services in Great Britain: An Introductory Review. *Transport Reviews*, 15, pp. 185–209.

White, P. R. (1997). What Conclusions Can Be Drawn about Bus Deregulation in Britain? *Transport Reviews*, 17, pp. 1–16.
White, P. (1998). Financial Outcomes of Rail Privatisation in Britain. *European Transport Conference.*
Wolmar, C. (2007). *Fire and Steam: A New History of the Railways in Britain.* London: Atlantic Press.
Wolmar, C. (2009). *Blood, Iron and Gold: How the Railways Transformed the World.* London: Atlantic Books.

10
Airline deregulation

Lucy Budd

Aircraft are just marginal costs with wings.

(Alfred E. Kahn, US airline economist and former chairman of the US Civil Aeronautics Board, Washington Post, 12 April 1978)

10.1 Introduction

For reasons of national security, defence and economic protection, airlines have historically been heavily regulated, both nationally and internationally. The strict economic regulatory environment that emerged during the early–mid-20th century was designed to promote the development of national civil air transport industries by protecting pioneering airlines from competition and preventing new operators from entering the market. However, economic protection provided no incentive for cost control or service innovation. With competition all but eliminated and with national governments dictating airfares, capacity, service frequency and route licences, the post-1945 global airline industry was, until the late 1970s, characterised by economic inefficiency and high prices which ensured flying, whether domestically or internationally, remained beyond the financial means of most citizens.

The passing of the US Airline Deregulation Act (ADA) in October 1978, which occurred alongside other interstate transport reforms, marked the beginning of a new phase in airline economic history. Following the US's lead, other countries, starting with European nations in the 1990s, have sought to progressively remove regulations governing airline capacity, service frequency, route entitlements and fares on both domestic and international services to increase efficiency, stimulate competition and encourage service innovation. This regulatory reform has resulted in a number of both anticipated and unintended consequences, and similar policies of deregulation have now been applied, with varying degrees of enthusiasm and success, in sectors as diverse as domestic energy tariffs, telecommunications and the provision of local authority services. The aim of this chapter is to explore the factors which motivated regulatory reform in the global airline industry and examine the short-, medium- and long-term implications for demand and supply, and the provision of commercial air transport services. The chapter will investigate the extent to which other countries have sought to replicate the US experience of airline deregulation and discuss the possible future trajectory of regulatory reform in the commercial air transport industry.

The chapter is structured into four principal sections. Sections 10.2 and 10.3 provide the context to deregulation of the domestic US airline industry. They detail the historical regulation of the industry from its origins in the early 20th century to the late 1970s. Section 10.4 discusses the economic motivation for the ADA, describes the Act's content and examines the short-, medium- and long-term demand and supply side implications of its implementation. Section 10.5 explores deregulation in the rest of the world, with a particular focus on Europe, Asia and Africa. Section 10.6 discusses the future for airline (de)regulation in an era of global economic uncertainty and increasing concerns about long-term energy security, new challenges to international geopolitical relations and a changing global climate.

10.2 From Wrights to regulation, the early years of commercial flight in the US

According to the conventional history of flight, humankind first took to the air in a heavier-than-air powered machine on the morning of 17 December 1903 on the sand dunes of Kill Devil Hills, near Kitty Hawk, North Carolina. At 10.35am, Orville Wright opened the throttle and successfully coaxed the Wright Flyer into the air, where he sustained it in forward flight for 12 seconds before landing 120ft (36.6 metres) away on a site equal in elevation to that which he had departed. Despite photographic evidence, US politicians and the public remained sceptical of the achievement, but, undeterred, the Wright brothers continued their experiments into lift, flight control and propulsion. Recognising the potential military and commercial applications of their invention, the Wright brothers sought to protect their intellectual property to safeguard any future sales. In 1907, they unveiled their first production aeroplane and, in 1909, sold their first machine to the US Army. Ten years after the first flight, the St Petersburg-Tampa Airboat Line signed a contract with the St Petersburg Board of Trade to operate commercial passenger flights across Tampa Bay in Florida. Despite only performing 172 flights and carrying 1,200 passengers before services ceased in May 1914, the airline proved the utility of using aircraft for the scheduled aerial conveyance of passengers and freight.

Between 1911 and 1918, the US government sponsored a series of experimental airmail flights. These culminated, in 1918, with the commencement of regular airmail services between Washington, Philadelphia and New York. Airmail was flown on government-operated aircraft until February 1926 when the Contract Air Mail Act of 1925 (commonly known as the Kelly Act) obliged the US Post Office to contract commercial carriers to operate the flights. The Kelly Act was instrumental in creating a private domestic US airline industry. Successful bidders for the airmail contracts included Varney Air Lines (which later became part of United Airlines), the Robertson Aircraft Corporation (which would become part of American Airlines), Juan Trippe (the founder of Pan American Airways), National Air Transport (which would later become National Airlines), Western Air Express (which would merge to form TWA) and the Ford Air Transport Service. Each company was remunerated commensurate with the weight of mail they transported.

In the late 1920s, Western Airlines inaugurated an experimental passenger service between Los Angeles and San Francisco. Despite carrying over 5,000 passengers, the services generated insufficient revenue to cover the seat mile operating costs and the services had to be cross-subsidised by the carrier's airmail services. As a consequence, it was decided that some form of domestic (and later international) economic regulation would be required to support the orderly development of US passenger air transport. The economic argument favouring regulation was that the high cost of entry meant that in most markets only one carrier could profit from providing a service and so strict regulation would prevent damaging competition from occurring between service providers.

In recognition of the anticipated future economic importance of aviation to the national economy, the US government passed the Air Commerce Act in 1926. This Act charged the US

Secretary of Commerce with encouraging air commerce by granting him the authority to issue traffic rights, licence pilots, issue airworthiness certificates, establish domestic airways, invest in en route navigation aids and investigate accidents. The need for the latter, in particular, was acute. Despite rapid innovation in aircraft design and propulsion during the First World War, flying in the mid-1920s remained a relatively dangerous proposition characterised by frequent forced landings and accidents (see Bilstein, 1984). Following a number of fatal crashes a new Civil Aeronautics Act was passed in 1938. This established a new independent Civil Aeronautics Authority (CAA) which was given the responsibility of investigating aircraft accidents and ensuring that adequate, efficient and economic air services were provided in the US at 'reasonable rates' without unfair competition.

The 1938 Act established the basis of public control over US air services (Stratford, 1967). It preserved all existing airmail contracts, effectively making the carriers de facto public utilities, and gave the CAA the power to regulate airfares and determine which carriers could serve which routes and the extent to which these services would be subsidised. As a result, every new domestic route, cargo rate and passenger airfare had to be approved through a complex bureaucratic process. It was argued that this level of regulation would not only ensure the orderly development of air services in the national interest (thus fulfilling the need to act as a social good) but it would also guarantee that air services would be provided to remote and rural areas below cost price to promote regional economic development (TRB, 1991).

The CAA was replaced in 1940 by a new Civil Aeronautics Board (CAB). The CAB, which existed between 1940 and 1984, was given the responsibility of regulating domestic fares, awarding routes, issuing operating licences and ensuring public safety. In an effort to prevent 'destructive competition' the CAB prohibited any form of interstate air service competition. Charter operations were restricted, local flights were only permitted under strict conditions and price competition was eradicated. One of the primary aims of this economic regulation was to restrict the number of airlines that could operate point-to-point US interstate trunk and international scheduled passenger services. As a result of the 1938 Act, 16 incumbent airlines were authorised to fly the interstate trunk services between major cities (TRB, 1991). Significantly, no new certificates were awarded for the next 40 years, despite 79 applications being submitted to the CAB between 1950 and 1974 alone (Jordan, 2005). By 1978, these same carriers (now reduced to 11 through mergers) accounted for 94 percent of US scheduled airline traffic (TRB, 1991). The 11 carriers were: American, Braniff, Continental, Delta, Eastern, National, Trans World, Northwest, Pan American, United and Western.

The regulated market conditions protected the 11 trunk carriers from competition and gave the CAB authority to set fares. Fares were regulated through direct CAB (dis)approval of proposed increases and by the creation of a single fare (or a narrow range of fares) for flights on a particular route, irrespective of passenger demand (TRB, 1991). Interstate airfares thus remained expensive and beyond the financial reach of most US citizens. Although the highly regulated environment prevented the trunk airlines from making any more than a modest profit, it protected them from competition, guarded them against financial loss regardless of economic conditions and eliminated the possibility of failure.

In addition to controlling routes and fares, the CAB also held authority over market entry and exit and the provision of subsidies. To prevent service duplication and protect the incumbent carriers from potentially disruptive competition, the CAB rarely granted approval for new airlines to enter the market and insisted that applications for new routes were accompanied by evidence of public need and an assurance that existing operators would not be financially disadvantaged as a result of its introduction. Profitable routes were often awarded to airlines experiencing financial difficulty or to cross-subsidise a loss-making service that the CAB required them to perform (TRB, 1991; Cook, 1996).

As well as fostering inefficiency and preventing price competition, the regulated system was also highly bureaucratic and labour intensive. Any proposed change to airfares, route entitlements or market entry required complex administrative and judicial approval. For example, it was reported that the volume of paperwork involved in deciding which new Midwestern towns should receive an air service stood over 9ft (2.7 metres) high while another widely cited example of the system's inefficiencies was that it reportedly took the CAB eight years to approve Continental Airlines' request for permission to fly between San Diego and Denver (Petzinger, 1995). Although the CAB controlled airfares, routes, market entry and subsidies, it had no authority to dictate the types of aircraft that were flown or the levels of in-flight service that were offered and this provided an opportunity for the airlines to differentiate their products using service attributes rather than price. In economic terms this constituted classic oligopolistic behaviour.

The introduction of larger, faster, more comfortable and more fuel-efficient passenger aircraft into airline service in the 1950s not only encouraged more people to fly but also reduced airlines' operating costs. This had a profound effect on demand for domestic flights in the US as aircraft progressively replaced trains as the preferred mode of long-distance intercity transport. In August 1958, six years after the British airline BOAC had introduced the world's first jet-powered aircraft into revenue passenger service and a year before Pan Am would inaugurate Boeing 707s on routes across the North Atlantic, President Eisenhower signed a new Federal Aviation Act into law. The 1958 Act transferred some of the CAB's functions to a new independent Federal Aviation Agency (which subsequently became the Federal Aviation Administration in 1967 when the CAB's accident investigation functions were transferred to the new National Transportation Safety Board).

By the early 1960s, one of the most pressing aviation issues facing the federal government concerned the setting and validity of domestic airfares. Following a series of congressional complaints about high fares and the process of tariff setting during the decade, a formal investigation was launched in 1969. This uncovered evidence of pricing and service anomalies that were disadvantaging consumers and hindering economic growth. Jordan (1970), for example, discovered that costs and fares on regulated interstate trunk routes were twice as expensive as those of unregulated intrastate carriers on comparable routes. For example, unregulated airfares between San Francisco and Los Angeles (a distance of 390 miles) were about half those charged on the comparable (but regulated) 430-mile interstate Boston–Washington route.

Moreover, as Douglas and Miller (1974) reported, under conditions of price regulation, non-price competition occurred in the form of increased flight frequencies. This soon led to an oversupply of seats and costs which rose to meet fares rather than fares which fell to meet costs. In response to congressional and consumer concerns, the CAB conducted a domestic passenger fare investigation (DPFI) between 1970 and 1974. The DPFI sought to determine the rate of return all airlines were entitled to and establish a 'just and reasonable' rate that would ensure carriers could satisfy the responsibility of providing the social good of a reliable public transport service while simultaneously generating a profit for their stockholders (Rosenfield, 1972). As an interim measure, the CAB imposed a new industry-wide mileage-based domestic fare formula. Under this cost-based pricing regime, airfares in all domestic US origin-destination (O/D) markets were set according to an average system-wide operating cost per flight. This approach ignored cost differences in providing services in different O/D markets but allowed smaller markets and shorter sectors (which were proportionally more expensive to operate) to benefit from artificially low prices at the expense of longer higher-density sectors. This system formally pegged airfares to the distance flown through the application of a standard mileage-based formula called the Standard Industry Fare Level.

The acquisition of new high-capacity wide-bodied jet aircraft during the 1960s and 1970s presented new challenges for US carriers. Seating over three times as many passengers as the narrow-bodied aircraft they replaced, the new DC-10s, L1011s and B747s exacerbated existing oversupply issues. Domestic load factors (a measure of the proportion of seats sold on a flight) fell from 70 percent in 1950 to 50 percent by 1970 (Cook, 1996). In order to stimulate demand, the airlines sought CAB approval to lower their fares, initially without success.

To the extent that the regulations permitted, airlines began to employ a primitive form of yield management by offering last-minute discount fares and promotional rates to try and encourage passengers who otherwise wouldn't fly. In common with other transport modes, aircraft seats are a perishable commodity and once a flight departs those potential revenue streams are lost. Consequently, airlines were keen to maximise the revenue-generating potential of each and every service by heavily discounting unsold inventory close to departure.

The CAB maintained that rather than discounting seats, the airlines should raise their fares to cover their losses, a proposition the carriers claimed would drive passengers away and further exacerbate their increasingly precarious financial predicament. Unable to price differentiate, the airlines were forced to respond using the only strategy that was left available to them – product differentiation. American Airlines installed piano bars in their half-empty B747s and, in common with other carriers, introduced more comfortable and lavish in-flight services. Food, drink, seat comfort, cabin ambience, cabin crew and in-flight service levels thus became important strategic tools but even minor changes in cabin amenities, such as the provision of pay-per-use headphones for the in-flight entertainment system, required CAB approval.

10.3 Moves towards deregulation

Although domestic airline regulation had allowed a limited number of trunk carriers to prosper it had also kept ticket prices artificially high and created a situation in which most airfares bore little relation to the actual cost of providing the service. The economic and political arguments favouring deregulation began to gain considerable support during the early 1970s. Proponents of deregulation believed that regulations governing market access, frequency, capacity and fares were outdated, were stifling competition and preventing consumers from enjoying the benefits of a more liberalised competitive market. They argued that regulation, far from stifling competition, had merely forced airlines to engage in destructive non-price competition which had led to structural inefficiencies, oversupply and low load factors.

Deregulation's advocates anticipated that removing the CAB's authority to set fares and grant route licences and allowing airline operators greater freedom of market entry and exit would improve consumer welfare as carriers could adjust to price changes in their input and output markets. This would, it was claimed, reduce losses resulting from a suboptimal balance of service level and price and lessen the incentive for airlines to pass on the high costs of inefficiency to their consumers. It was also believed that the potential for monopolistic behaviour would be mitigated by the introduction of a more contestable market. Critics countered that deregulation and unrestricted competition would lead to a 'race to the bottom' in which service quality and safety standards would decline, non-profitable but socially essential air services would be abandoned in favour of more lucrative routes, airfares would rise and the welfare of airline employees would fall.

Despite these concerns, the tide was turning in favour of deregulation. By the mid-1970s, considerable structural changes were already occurring in the domestic US airline industry. In 1975 the CAB started to liberalise charter airline requirements, granted more new route applications and allowed airlines to offer an increased number of super discounted tickets on off-peak services. In April 1976 the CAB announced its formal support for deregulation, a statement which ultimately triggered its own abolition. The Cornell University economist Alfred E. Kahn was subsequently appointed chairman of the CAB by President Carter with the remit of leading the US airline industry into deregulation.

In 1977 the US domestic air freight market was liberalised and approval of discount and promotional fares became the norm (Sickles et al., 1986). This had two immediate effects. In the freight sector, operators could, for the first time, charge a premium for express delivery and passenger airlines could market a greater range of fare products. In response, American Airlines introduced Super Saver discounts (which were as much as 45 percent cheaper than standard coach (economy) class fares) on selected routes, while Texas Air launched its 'Peanuts' fares (TRB, 1991). American's Super Saver fares were very popular and increased the airline's traffic by 60 percent, proving cheaper airfares stimulated consumer demand. These moves towards deregulation culminated in October 1978 with the signing of the ADA. Although it was just one of a number of reforms passed by the Carter Administration in the late 1970s and early 1980s that sought to liberalise US interstate transport (others included the 1980 Motor Carrier Act and the 1982 Bus Regulation Reform Act), it was to have profound implications both for the US and for the global air transport industry.

10.4 The 1978 Airline Deregulation Act

On 24 October 1978 US Congress passed a law that enabled airlines to set their own fares and routes. The ADA amended the Federal Aviation Act of 1958 so as to 'encourage, develop, and attain an air transportation system which relies on competitive market forces to determine the quality, variety and price of air services' (US Congress, 1978, p. 1). This involved 'the encouragement, development and maintenance of an air transport system [which relied] on actual and potential competition to provide efficiency, innovation and low prices and to determine the variety, quality and price of air transportation services' (p. 2). The ADA also sought to remove restrictions on market entry and exit through 'the encouragement of entry into air transportation markets by new carriers, the encouragement of entry into additional markets by existing carriers and the continued strengthening of small air carriers' (p. 2).

The ADA immediately replaced the system of absolute government control with competitive market forces. The Act increased market access, granted fifth freedom flying rights (the right to pick up and set down commercial passengers and freight on a route between two foreign states that starts or terminates in the home state) to all US carriers, removed capacity constraints, lifted restrictions on where airlines could fly and revoked the CAB's authority to regulate fares. The removal of price controls meant that airlines could, for the first time, price fares according to route-specific operating conditions rather than averaging them out over the system as a whole.

10.4.1 Deregulation's impact

Deregulation created a number of immediate spatial, economic and operational effects. In a bid to increase revenues, reduce costs and protect their market share at major airports, incumbent carriers moved away from the railroad-inspired point-to-point network to a hub and spoke operation. Consolidating regional flights at key hub airports conferred a number of important strategic benefits for the airlines. They increased operational efficiency, improved flight frequencies (which provided an important marketing advantage), lowered costs and created 'fortress hubs' that effectively prevented the market entry of new carriers (Button et al., 1998; Adler, 2001). They also enabled the airlines to service a greater number of city pairs without the commensurate increase in costs associated with flying point-to-point routes. The creation of hub and spoke systems also improved consumer welfare for the majority of travellers as it offered them a greater number of connection possibilities and lower fares. However, scheduling flights in waves to optimise connection times also led to congestion and delays at key hubs, increased the airline's vulnerability to the effects of adverse weather at its main operating base(s), eliminated convenient non-stop services and obliged some passengers to spend many hours in transit.

The spatial reorganisation and concentration of flights at key hubs combined with the new freedom of market entry and exit created an opportunity for new carriers to operate the vacated point-to-point services and inaugurate new flights on un(der)served routes. Between 1978 and 1985, 24 new jet-operating carriers were formed in the US (Cook, 1996) and the incumbent carriers' share of traffic on trunk routes fell from 94 to 77 percent (TRB, 1991). Many of the new operators adhered to the 'low-cost' approach to doing business which had been pioneered by Texas-based Southwest Airlines. This low-cost philosophy enabled them to minimise their operating costs and pass the savings onto consumers in the form of lower fares which in turn stimulated further demand.

The introduction of new competition into a price-sensitive market caused airfares to fall in real terms and passenger numbers to rise. In the four years after deregulation, passenger embarkations had increased by 55 percent while airfares on major routes had fallen by 17 percent (Encaoua, 1991). According to Morrison and Winston (1986), deregulation led to a $6 billion (in 1977 dollars) annual improvement in traveller welfare. Business travellers, in particular, benefitted from the increased flight frequency, improved connectivity and the growth in regional flights to major hubs that the regulatory reform stimulated.

However, despite some notable consumer benefits, the airline industry in the 1980s was volatile. Oil embargoes, a national US air traffic controllers' strike and nationwide recession combined to create a challenging operating environment. Many of the new entrant airlines were not able to sustain operations and either failed or were quickly taken over by existing carriers. Major failures included Air Florida (1979–84), Pacific Southwest (1979–87), New York Air (1980–6) and People Express (1981–6, see Case study below). Tellingly, 57 percent of the 129 new airlines that commenced operations between 1979 and 2003 operated for four years or less (Jordan, 2005). By 1988, competition, consolidation and bankruptcy had led to the once major trunk carriers Pan Am, Braniff and Eastern exiting the market.

10.4.2 Case study: the rise and fall of People Express

People Express was founded in 1981 in the immediate aftermath of deregulation. Marketing itself as the 'smart' way to fly, the carrier pioneered many low-cost innovations. It competed on price, not service, and established operations at cheaper and less congested secondary airports (its New York flights operated from Newark, not La Guardia or JFK). The airline only provided what was necessary for safe and cheap flights and introduced charges for checking in hold baggage and purchasing in-flight refreshments. As a consequence, People Express was able to undercut the airfares charged by many of its full-service rivals. Passenger numbers increased and the carrier expanded rapidly. By 1984, it had transformed Newark Airport into the country's eighth busiest passenger facility and was accepting a new aircraft into the fleet every three weeks (Petzinger, 1995). Later that year it introduced B747 flights to London for $149 one way. By 1985, the carrier was serving 50 destinations across North America and Europe.

People Express had not invested in a computerised reservation system (CRS). As passenger numbers increased, telesales could not cope with the volume of incoming calls and it was estimated that as many as 6,000 potential customers a day could not get through to the reservations centre. The airline was also encountering a new phenomenon of no shows. Inexpensive airfares meant passengers often booked a ticket but then did not turn up for the flight. People Express responded by overbooking flights (i.e. selling more tickets than there were actual seats on the aircraft). This maximised the airline's revenue but created considerable challenges when the majority of passengers who held a valid ticket wished to fly.

More problematically, the lack of CRS meant People Express couldn't practise revenue management. As a result, the airline had to sell all the seats on a flight at a fixed price (e.g. $99 or $149 one way). Major carriers, including American Airlines, who did have access to a CRS and could practise revenue management, were able to match or even undercut People Express' fares on a limited number of seats. This meant that they could dramatically discount a small proportion of seats on certain services and advertise very attractive headline fares while recouping the shortfall by selling other seats at a higher price. CRS-equipped airlines soon devised a fare structure that contributed to People Express' failure. They discounted fares on routes on which they directly competed with People Express by as much as 70 percent. Unable to sustain its losses, People Express was wound up in 1986 and its assets were acquired by Continental.

One explicit aim of deregulation was to allow airlines to move towards a more market-oriented pricing and route system. This led to concerns that the removal of subsidies for air services to smaller communities would mean that such routes would be abandoned and the communities isolated. Although the growth in smaller commuter airlines after deregulation compensated for some of the subsidy loss, a new programme, called the EAS (Essential Air Service) scheme, was introduced to support socially necessary yet financially unviable air services to remote and rural US communities. The EAS programme guarantees small communities access to a regular commercial air service by providing a direct subsidy to airline operators. As of 2016 over 160 communities (the majority of which were in Alaska) were supported. The EAS subsidises two to four return trips a day with 19-seat aircraft to a major hub. Carriers are selected on the basis of service reliability, marketing and interlining arrangements with a larger carrier at a major hub.

As well as transforming the spatial characteristics of airline networks, deregulation also transformed airline labour relations, airline management activities and airline financial performance. Encumbered by expensive legacy labour contracts and institutional inertia, some incumbent carriers found the transition to a highly competitive market challenging. Deregulation forced airline managers to actively control their inventory to maximise yields and revenues and price services according to consumer demand. Freed from CAB control, airlines were able to determine the fare levels, with associated services, amenities and restrictions, for a set of products in individual origin-destination markets and this led to the emergence of a much wider range of fare and service combinations. A range of fare categories for travel on a particular route were developed, with fares varying according to time and class of travel (peak/off-peak, first/business/economy), length of trip (including any minimum stay restrictions), the age of the travellers (children, infants, babies) and relevant demand factors (such as a major sporting, religious or cultural event). This range of fare products enabled consumers to maximise their utility by trading off price, schedules, ticket flexibility and service levels.

US airline deregulation undoubtedly produced significant and long-term benefits to US travellers by increasing competition and lowering fares. However, these benefits were only available to domestic passengers as international services remained regulated by a series of complex bilateral and multilateral air service agreements (ASAs). ASAs were introduced as a consequence of the 1944 Chicago Convention to ensure the orderly peacetime development of international commercial air services and to ensure that each nation state had an equal opportunity to develop its own air transport system. ASAs were reciprocally negotiated between two governments. They determined which routes could be flown, which airports/destinations could be served, which carriers could operate the services, the frequency and capacity of the flights and the airfares that could be charged. This historical exchange of international air traffic rights based on an anticipated balance of benefits and costs led to the development of over 3,000 ASAs worldwide and a market that is often characterised by little competition (ITF, 2015). Consequently, the deregulation of international air services has proved to be a more time-consuming and politically problematic process.

10.5 Towards international open skies

The plethora of international ASAs meant that international air service liberalisation could not be accomplished as easily as domestic deregulation. Moves towards liberalisation have taken the form of individual open skies agreements (OSAs) between specific countries. One of the first was signed between the US and the Netherlands in 1992 and this led to the trans-Atlantic alliance between KLM and Northwest Airlines. Further OSAs were agreed between the US and Canada (1995 and 2006) and the US and European Union (2007, amended in 2010). To date, the US has signed 116 OSAs, and Winston and Yan (2015) estimate that OSAs have saved travellers at least US$4 billion since 1992. An additional $4 billion in savings could, Winston and Yan suggest, be realised if the US negotiated similar open skies agreements with other countries that have large volumes of international traffic. However, despite the apparent benefits, concerns about OSAs have been articulated with some US carriers alleging that state-owned airlines in the Middle East, in particular, are gaining an unfair competitive advantage.

10.5.1 Airline deregulation in Europe

The idea of deregulating Europe's air transport market to emulate the apparent public policy success of the US experience was first tentatively discussed in the late 1970s. As had been the case in the regulated era in the US, Europe's air transport system was highly oligopolistic and rising public dissatisfaction with high airfares combined with the rise of free-market neoliberal philosophies and increased pressures on public spending pushed the issue of airline deregulation further up the political agenda. However, the European situation differed from the US one in two important respects. Firstly, unlike the US, Europe comprised a large number of autonomous sovereign states, each with its own laws, currency, language and administrative procedures. Secondly, the European airline sector was, at the time, dominated by a small number of state-owned national flag carriers who held bilateral traffic rights on key routes. These factors conspired to make the formation of a unified European policy on air transport deregulation highly problematic.

The United Kingdom, under the Conservative leadership of Prime Minister Margaret Thatcher, was one of the most enthusiastic advocates of reform. The UK signed an open-market bilateral air service agreement with the Netherlands in 1984 to stimulate competition on the route between London and Amsterdam. This agreement removed the existing capacity regulations, dissolved the duopoly formerly enjoyed by British Airways and KLM, and led to the UK signing similar agreements with other countries for other routes. Concerned that national self-interest would lead to an irrevocable politically and economically damaging fragmentation of the European air transport market, European governments sought to liberalise the continent's airline market through three coherent packages of measures.

The first, ratified in 1987, allowed European airlines to increase capacity and sell a greater range of discounted and promotional fares. The second, passed in 1990, removed market constraints and granted fifth freedom flying rights to all European carriers, while the third (passed in 1997) created a single regulatory structure, introduced a free pricing regime and granted

Table 10.1 The low-cost subsidiaries of selected European airlines

Parent company	*Country of origin*	*Type of operation*	*Low-cost subsidiary*
bmi	UK	Full service	Bmibaby
British Airways	UK	Full service	Go Fly
Hapag-Lloyd	Germany	Charter	Hapag-Lloyd Express
KLM UK	UK/Netherlands	Regional	Buzz
MyTravel	UK	Charter	MyTravelLite
SAS	Scandinavia	Full service	Snowflake
Thomson	UK	Charter	ThomsonFly
Transavia	Netherlands	Charter	Basiq Air

cabotage which gave European airlines the freedom to treat all European markets as domestic territory for the purpose of providing air services. According to Kassim (1997, p. 212), the third package represented 'one of the most important developments in aviation' as it ended the use of restrictive bilateral air service agreements and deprived national governments of the economic and regulatory instruments that they had previously used to control air services.

The newly liberalised operating environment was suddenly made conducive to competition. New carriers formed to take advantage and existing ones expanded to maximise the opportunities afforded through cabotage. As in the US, the incumbent full-service operators adapted to the changing environment with varying degrees of enthusiasm and success. New-found freedom of market entry and exit prompted a wave of new entrant low-cost airlines to emerge and compete on price with the incumbent operators. These low-cost airlines pursued the business model pioneered by Southwest Airlines that only provided what was necessary for safe and efficient flight. These included using a single type of aircraft in an all-economy class configuration, operating from secondary airports, incentivising internet reservations and focusing on ancillary revenue generation.

In the 20-year period between 1992 and 2012, 43 low-cost carriers were established in Europe (Budd et al., 2014). Many established European full-service carriers (and even some charter operators) set up low-cost subsidiaries to counter the new threat and protect their market share (Table 10.1). Despite some success, the parent airlines were not able to operate two distinct business models and the low-cost subsidiaries were either sold off or reabsorbed into the parent company. Overall, 77 percent of the new low-cost European start-ups identified by Budd et al. failed. There have, however, been some notable successes. Low-cost airlines EasyJet and Ryanair have grown into two of the biggest passenger airlines in the continent and their business approach has been adopted by other transport providers, including long-distance coach and rail operators.

Liberalisation has undoubtedly resulted in a much more contestable European airline market and consumers have benefited from a greater range of services, fare products and flight frequencies. However, in order to protect consumer interests in the event of airline failure, delay or mishandled luggage and prevent non-transparent pricing and marketing, it has proved necessary to maintain a degree of pan-European regulatory control and intervention.

10.5.2 Airline deregulation in the rest of the world

Following the US and Europe's lead, countries in Australasia, Africa, Latin America and the Middle and Far East initiated policies of airline deregulation and liberalisation from the mid-1990s onwards. These interventions, which have variously occurred at the bilateral, regional and international levels, had similar effects in that they opened up the market to new competition, enabled new carriers to emerge who competed on price, stimulated passenger demand and lowered airfares. In the case of Chile, for example, airline deregulation enabled the market entry of new low-cost operators, including Sky Airlines, who competed on price with the incumbent full-service flag carrier LAN Chile. The effect of increased post-deregulation competition was a 24 percent rise in passenger numbers and an 18 percent reduction in average airfares (InterVISTAS, 2009).

The progressive liberalisation of individual air transport markets has also, over time, led to the emergence of regional aviation blocks who seek to achieve regulatory convergence and agreement in the field of international air services and who negotiate on behalf of their members. The 1996 Mercosur sub-regional agreement on air transport services (involving Argentina, Bolivia, Brazil, Chile, Paraguay and Uruguay) and Members of the Andean Community Pact (Bolivia, Colombia, Ecuador and Peru) have both taken steps to deregulate air services within certain Latin American nations by removing ownership and control restrictions on member state carriers. Further north, the Association of Caribbean States is pursuing a 'community of interest' with the aim of deregulating air services in the region (ITF, 2015). On the other side of the Atlantic, the 1999 Yamoussoukro Decision created the conditions necessary for the gradual liberalisation of intra-African air services, while in the Far East ten members of the Association of South East Asian Nations set a target of establishing a single aviation market within their territories by 2015 (ITF, 2015). However, despite such moves, barriers to entry still exist and the global regulatory framework remains complex.

10.5.3 Barriers to further airline deregulation

At the international level, ASAs are still used on many international routes, particularly where there is a mismatch in the balance of demand between the two contracting nations. Other exogenous barriers to entry take the form of airport slot restrictions and airport operating curfews, which limit the availability of desired departure and arrival times, political decisions regarding airport development, expansion and charging regimes and restrictions on the foreign ownership of airlines. The European Union, for example, limits foreign ownership to 49 percent of total shares while the US imposes a cap of 25 percent. Furthermore, although many states have deregulated their airline markets and opened up airport operators and ground handling agents to the forces of commercialisation and privatisation (albeit to varying extents), the infrastructure on which air transport depends, namely the provision of air traffic services, remains fully or majority state owned. Indeed, the majority of the world's air navigation service providers (ANSP) remain state-owned entities and even of those that have been partially privatised (such as the UK's NATS) the government maintains majority ownership for reasons of defence and national security. There is some evidence that a market for air traffic control services at individual airports is emerging in Europe. For example, in 2014 Germany's ANSP DFS won the contract to provide air traffic control services at London Gatwick airport.

In addition to these external factors, a number of endogenous barriers can also be identified. These include the widespread use of frequent flyer programmes, customer relationship marketing strategies, corporate discount schemes and travel agent commission overrides which direct customers and repeat revenue to certain airlines and in so doing distort the market and disadvantage those carriers who do not have access to them.

10.6 The future of airline deregulation

Airline deregulation is widely considered to have improved consumer welfare by increasing efficiency and lowering airfares, yet the processes and implications are far from uniform or complete. Many world regions and countries, particularly in emerging economies, still maintain relatively high levels of both domestic and international regulation and so significant potential for future welfare gains remain. The cycle of deregulation leading to increased competition, new airlines, lower airfares, more passengers and greater price discrimination and production differentiation is now well established and its effects confirmed by almost 40 years of economic appraisal, analysis and debate.

Although considerable potential still exists for airline deregulation at the bilateral, domestic, regional and international levels, there is also considerable potential for business and service innovation among both the passenger and freight side of the airline business which will be driven by changes in technology. For example, low-cost long-haul services, although dismissed as being unviable following the collapse of Freddie Laker's SkyTrain in 1982, are now being successfully operated by companies including Air Asia X (Malaysia), Scoot (Singapore), JetStar (Australia), WestJet (Canada), Wow Air (Iceland) and Norwegian (Norway). Unlike their predecessors, these carriers are employing new high-capacity and fuel-efficient twin-engine aircraft, including the B737/787 and A330/350, to lower their operating costs and carve out an operating niche in an otherwise crowded marketplace. At the other end of the passenger market, new business jets, operating models and leasing arrangements are making flying possible for a growing number of high net worth individuals who eschew the perceived or real inconveniences and stresses of flying in the post-deregulation era.

Other changes, while not as immediately obvious, are nevertheless likely to have a profound effect on the airline industry in the future. Deregulation and liberalisation of computer reservation systems and the increased use of digital and social media by consumers are creating new opportunities for airlines to develop and market new products to appeal to increasingly price-sensitive consumers while simultaneously helping them to lower their costs. Whatever the future holds for airline (de)regulation will undoubtedly be driven by changes in the global economic and competitive landscape.

10.7 Conclusion

Airline deregulation is generally considered to be a public policy success story. In the near 40 years since the US domestic airline market was deregulated, the global airline market has become more contestable. Effective price and non-price competition between carriers has lowered airfares, increased connectivity, facilitated product innovation and enabled more people to travel to more places, more cheaply, than ever before. It has changed the nature of airline marketing practice and prompted some innovative, imaginative and occasionally controversial marketing campaigns and it has transformed both public expectations and experiences of flying. It has also led to job creation, supported indirect employment in travel and tourism, and enabled people to take advantage of a greater range of personal, educational and professional opportunities overseas.

Yet, in addition to increasing consumer welfare and promoting regional economic development, airline deregulation has had some unintended and undesirable social, economic and environmental consequences. The growth of low-cost flights has inflicted aircraft noise and pollution on a greater number of airport communities and the growing number of flights is offsetting the incremental improvements in aircrafts' environmental performance. Rapid expansion of routes and services has also led to concerns about public safety. In parts of Asia, in particular, insufficient regulatory oversight has contributed to a number of fatal crashes and serious accidents to aircraft operated by start-up carriers.

There have also been a range of social costs. Some carriers have been accused of 'social dumping' on account of their policies of allegedly employing foreign staff on inferior terms and conditions of employment. The ability of carriers to withdraw underperforming routes at short notice also has economic consequences for staff and regional economies which have become dependent on the inward investment and passenger flows delivered by low-cost operators. A further final unanticipated social cost concerns antisocial behaviour that is perpetrated by groups of travellers who reportedly access low-cost flights with the sole purpose of accessing entertainment and cheap alcohol.

Almost 40 years have now passed since the US domestic airline market was deregulated. Having developed under a 40-year period of strict economic regulation from 1938 to 1978 the US industry now has greater flexibility to respond to market forces. The subsequent adoption of deregulation policies by other nations and in international markets has enabled each country to develop an aviation system that both reflects and responds to its own air transport needs. However, this process remains both incomplete and uneven, and the worldwide air transport system is still influenced by the effects of historical regulations that were used as tools of (inter)national geopolitical negotiation and influence. In order for a truly competitive airline market to emerge, countries will have to deregulate not only their airlines but also their airports, air navigation service providers and all the other elements of the air service delivery chain. It is only then that the full welfare gains, anticipated by the first proponents of deregulation in the 1970s, will be realised.

References

Adler, N. (2001). Competition in a Deregulated Air Transportation Market. *European Journal of Operational Research*, 129, pp. 337–45.

Bilstein, R. E. (1984). *Flight in America: From the Wrights to the Astronauts*. Baltimore, MD: Johns Hopkins University Press.

Budd, L., Francis, G., Humphreys, I. and Ison, S. (2014). Grounded: Characterising the Market Failure of European Low Cost Airlines. *Journal of Air Transport Management*, 34, pp. 78–85.

Button, K., Haynes, K. and Stough, R. (1998). *Flying into the Future: Air Transport Policy in the European Union*. Cheltenham: Edward Elgar.

Cook, G. N. (1996). A Review of History, Structure and Competition in the U.S. Airline. *Industry Journal of Aviation/Aerospace Education and Research*, 7(1), pp. 33–42.

Douglas, G. and Miller, J. C. (1974). *Economic Regulation of Domestic Air Transport*. Washington, DC: Brookings Institute.

Encaoua, D. (1991). Liberalizing European Airlines, Cost and Factor Productivity Evidence. *International Journal of Industrial Organisation*, 9, pp. 109–24.

InterVISTAS (2009). *The Impact of Air Service Liberalisation on Chile*. London: InterVISTAS-EU Consultancy.

ITF (2015). *Liberalisation of Air Transport: Policy Insights and Recommendations*. Paris: ITF with the OECD.

Jordan, W. A. (1970). *Airline Regulation in America: Effects and Imperfections*. Baltimore, MD: Johns Hopkins University Press.

Jordan, W. A. (2005). Airline Entry Following U.S. Deregulation: The Definitive List of Start-Up Passenger Airlines, 1979–2003. Paper presented at the annual meeting of the Transportation Research Forum, George Washington University, Washington, DC, www.trforum.org/forum/downloads/1005_deregulation_paper.pdf (accessed 9 February 2016).

Kassim, H. (1997). Air Transport and Globalisation: A Sceptical View. In Scott, A. (ed.), *The Limits of Globalization: Cases and Arguments*. London: Routledge, pp. 202–22.

Morrison, S. and Winston, C. (1986). *The Economic Effects of Airline Deregulation*. Washington, DC: Brookings Institute.

Petzinger, T. (1995). *Hard Landing: How the Epic Contest for Power and Profits Plunged the Airlines into Chaos*. London: Aurum Press.

Rosenfield, S. B. (1972). Factors in Determination of the Validity of Domestic Airline Fares. *Missouri Law Review*, 37(2), pp. 246–66.

Sickles, R. C., Good, D. and Johnston, R. L. (1986). Allocative Distortions and the Regulatory Transition of the U.S. Airline Industry. *Journal of Econometrics*, 33, pp. 143–6.

Stratford, A. H. (1967). *Air Transport Economics in the Supersonic Era.* London: Macmillan Press.
TRB (1991). *Winds of Change: Domestic Air Transport since Deregulation.* Washington, DC: Transportation Research Board National Research Council.
Winston, C. and Yan, J. (2015). Open Skies: Estimating Travelers' Benefits from Free Trade in Airline Services. *American Economic Journal: Economic Policy*, 7(2), pp. 370–414.

Part III

Forecasting, public choice and transport modelling

11

Forecasting the demand for transport

John Bates

11.1 Introduction

Transport involves the movement of either persons or goods between one place and another. This chapter focuses on the movement of persons; the movement of goods is dealt with in Chapters 20 to 24.

The chapter begins with a discussion of aggregate trends, typically at the national level. Here it is possible to identify some of the global influences – population, income, level of urbanisation and the speed and cost of different parts of the transport supply. However, while some analysis is possible at this level, the spatial concentration of transport means that aggregate forecasting is rarely of great importance – what is typically required are forecasts within corridors, possibly differentiated by mode and time of travel. Thus it is necessary to move quite quickly to a greater level of detail.

Much of the variation in travel patterns can be explained by variations in types of person, and the more advanced conventional models have made substantial use of this kind of information. The major sections of this chapter will provide a brief and critical account of these approaches.

11.2 Aggregate analysis of transport

While the railways, and their ability to convey large numbers at high speeds, revolutionised long-distance travel (until the aviation market opened up even longer distances), it is the car which has become the most important aspect of personal transport throughout the developed world, and increasingly in developing countries. Thus an analysis of both car ownership and car travel shows the trends and suggests some of the influencing factors. Whereas formerly most people would have to rely on some form of public transport to get over distances which could not be comfortably walked, the role of public transport has been substantially reduced by the growth of car ownership. And while the railways have generally preserved the gathering of common information, despite recent tendencies to greater fragmentation, reliable statistics on bus travel are harder to come by. In this section, the discussion will concentrate on car and rail.

Travel by air and sea is also of importance, primarily to those who supply the services. However, with a view to the main picture, these will be ignored here, since they constitute a very small proportion of total travel. For an example of air travel forecasting procedures, the reader is referred to Gillen et al. (2004) and DfT (2013).

The number of cars registered in Great Britain (GB) in 1950 was 1.98 million: by 2014 it had risen to 28.2 million, over 14 times as many. In that same period, the GB population has grown by about 28 percent (from 48.8 million to 62.7 million). A similar pattern has been seen in most developed countries, though the relative growth in the US has been substantially less, starting from a higher base in 1950. Internationally, the level of motorisation is defined as the number of cars in relation to population (though a better measurement would be to relate it to the adult population).

In a list of 191 countries compiled by Wikipedia (https://en.wikipedia.org/wiki/List_of_countries_by_vehicles_per_capita) from various sources, about one-third had levels below 50 vehicles per 1,000 population, one-third were in the range 50–200 and the remainder had levels ranging from 200 to 900. Of the larger countries, the US is certainly the highest with over 800 vehicles per 1,000 population. In recent years the growth rate has declined, with decreases seen in some years. In GB, the average annual rate of increase in the number of cars from 1950 to 2010 was 4.5 percent, but in the last 20 years this has fallen to only 1.6 percent. This is a typical pattern, as shown in Figure 11.1. Note that the graph is more or less linear (implying a gradually declining rate of growth) between 1950 and 2005, but since then overall growth has been more or less zero.

Although part of the explanation is probably related to the world economic depression, it can be seen that the period of zero growth pre-dates this. This has led to the 'peak car' theory (see e.g. Goodwin, 2012). It remains highly controversial – while most analysts would accept the notion of 'saturation' for the level of motorisation, the idea that it should fall requires a major change in behaviour. In support of this, some interesting analysis relating to the behaviour of young people has been carried out by Le Vine and Jones (2012).

The growth of car ownership is fundamental, since, as Figure 11.2 shows, based on data for GB and using a log scale, the growth of car traffic (measured in billion car kilometres) closely matches the growth in cars. The ratio of the two gives the approximate average kilometres travelled per

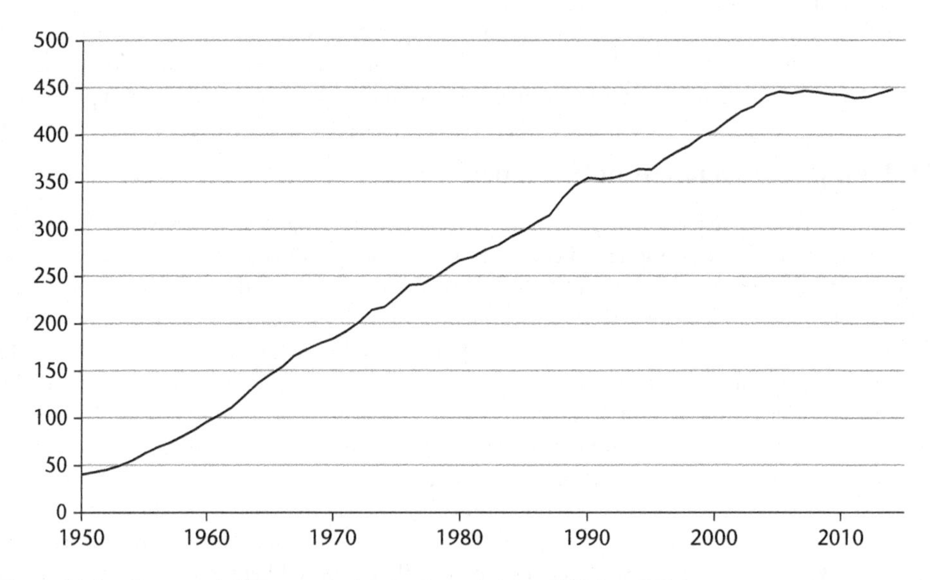

Figure 11.1 Cars per 1,000 population in Great Britain, 1950 to 2014
Source: drawn from DfT, 2015 and UK population statistics, adjusted for Northern Ireland

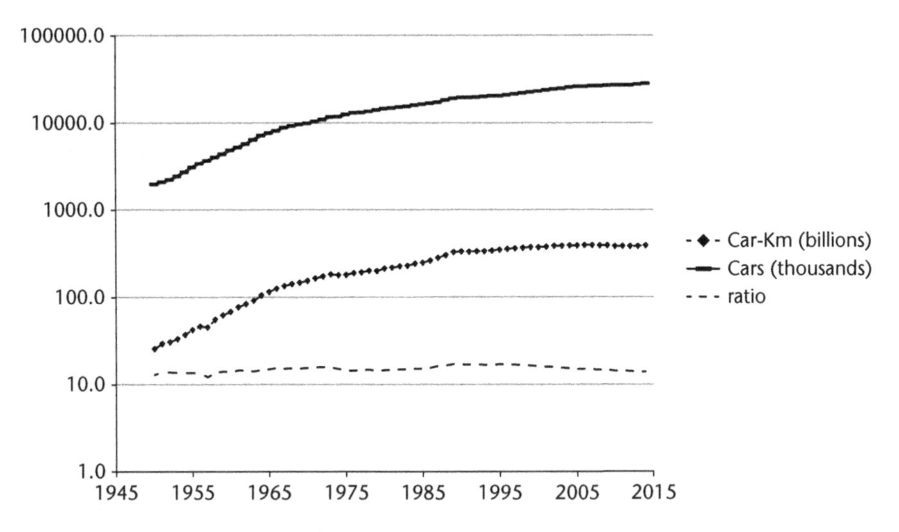

Figure 11.2 Car traffic and car ownership, Great Britain, 1947 to 2014
Source: drawn from DfT, 2015

year (in thousands), and it can be seen that apart from minor fluctuations, which can largely be associated with fuel prices, there has been little change over a period of 60 years.

By normalising for the increase in cars, it can be seen that the trend in average miles per car has been consistently downwards since 1989. Plotting the pattern over a longer period and comparing this with an index of fuel costs, as in Figure 11.3, suggests that rising costs may have played a

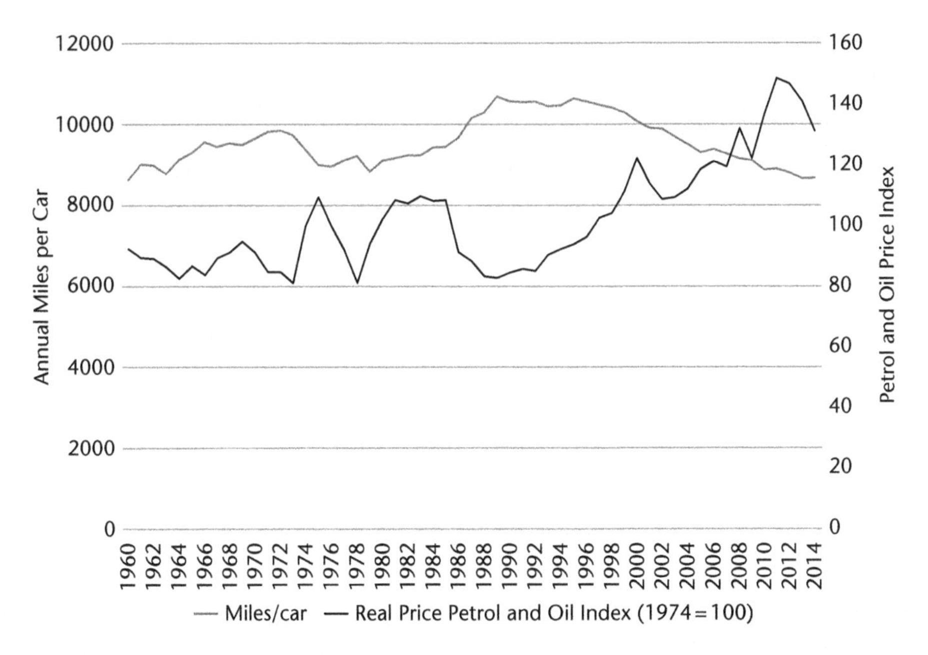

Figure 11.3 Annual average car mileage and real fuel prices, Great Britain, 1960 to 2014
Source: drawn from DfT, 2015

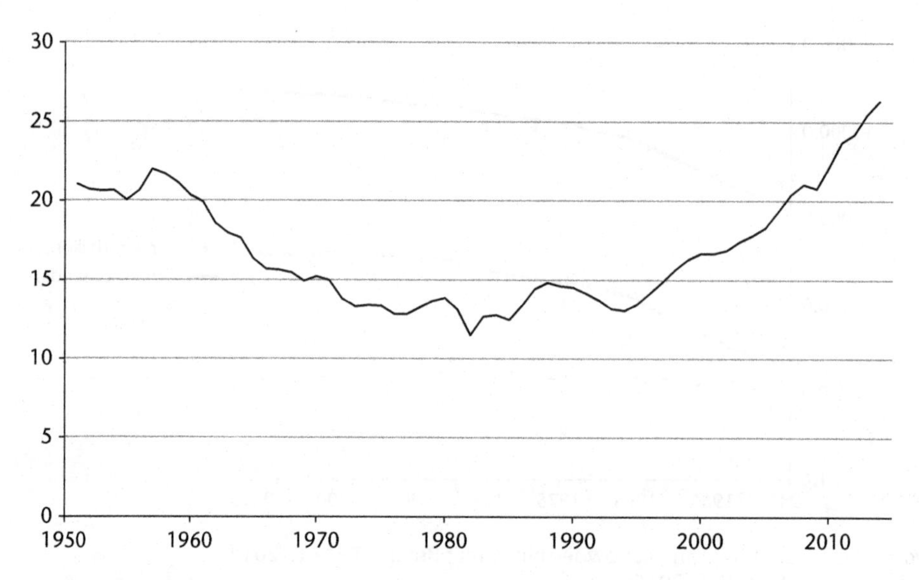

Figure 11.4 Annual rail journeys per head, Great Britain, 1950 to 2014
Source: drawn from DfT, 2015

part. Indeed, this is confirmed by a substantial piece of analysis from Graham and Glaister (2005). There is general agreement on a fuel price elasticity in the range -0.1 to -0.5 (see Dunkerley et al., 2014) with a central estimate of –0.3.

A rather different kind of aggregate analysis is indicated by Figure 11.4, which shows the pattern of rail journeys per head in GB over the last 60 years. From the mid-1950s, there was a steady decline from about 22 trips per year down to a low point of 11.5 in 1982, partly because of the reduced services available but also concomitant with the strong growth in car ownership described above. But since 1994 (interestingly, the year in which the system began to be privatised, though it took three years to complete), there has been a steady growth. Part of this can be attributed to rising income (though this was of course a feature of the whole period), while road congestion and rising fuel prices have also been suggested, as well as changes in the pattern of services.

Although much analysis of these figures has been carried out, it has generally been necessary to investigate at a more detailed spatial level, particularly because of the range of possible fares on offer at different times. The income elasticity of rail demand is generally considered to be around or in excess of 1, depending on the market being investigated. Current elasticities to fares are also generally close to -1 (indicating that fares are set so as to maximise revenue), though they tend to be lower for the commuting market and in urban areas. However, this result can be considered highly dependent on the structure of the industry, which varies considerably between countries. Speed and frequency of service are also known to affect rail demand.

Overall, it can be said that the aggregate demand for travel will be affected by income (especially via its influence on car ownership), the price of travel (by different modes) and the speed of travel, including, for public services, the frequency with which they are scheduled. However, to understand more about how travel is distributed, both in space and time, it is necessary to carry out the analysis at a more detailed level.

11.3 A more detailed analysis

Since most people will have a permanent residence, the underlying reason for movement is essentially to take part in activities which either cannot be performed in the home or which can be more advantageously performed outside the home. A common piece of terminology is the '(home-based) tour', which involves a series of movements beginning and ending at the home. The majority of these tours have a single destination, so that they are uniquely associated with an activity, but a significant minority have multiple destinations, leading to 'non-home-based' trips (NHB), where neither end is the home. Based on analysis of the GB National Travel Survey, NHB trips are about 15 percent of all trips.

Different activities are associated with different types of person (for example, employed people go to work, children go to school), and also are performed with different frequencies (shopping might be a weekly activity, while work is daily). Hence, it makes sense to categorise travel by the different 'purposes' of the motivating activities. While the definitions are a matter of convention, it is standard to recognise at least journeys to work, journeys to education, journeys associated with work ('employers' business'), and 'other' purposes. The extent to which this last category is further sub-divided will vary according to the requirements of the forecasts: for example, the National Transport Model of GB further recognises (a) shopping and personal business, (b) recreation, and visiting friends and relatives, and (c) holidays and day trips.

Thus the starting point for forecasting the demand for transport is to recognise the set of activities/purposes which are of interest, and to classify the resident population in terms of the characteristics most relevant for taking part in those activities.

11.3.1 Household travel surveys

The primary source of travel information is the household survey, which for transport purposes is usually associated with a travel diary. In a number of developed countries, national travel surveys are carried out on a regular or occasional basis. For example, the US Department of Transportation Federal Highway Administration has conducted surveys (the National Household Travel Survey) in 1969, 1977, 1983, 1990, 1995, 2001 and 2009, and the latest survey began in April 2016. By contrast in GB, the National Travel Survey has been annual since 1988, though since 2013 Scotland and Wales have withdrawn from the survey. Similarly, in the Netherlands there has been an annual survey since 1985, though some changes in both the method and the name of the survey have taken place over that period. Interviewing techniques vary, in some cases face to face and in other cases by phone or the internet.

The majority of household travel surveys are on a daily basis. In this respect, the GB survey is unusual, since it involves a seven-day diary and thus gives a record of weekly travel for all persons interviewed.

Of course, travel propensity will vary with local customs and lifestyles, but the main sources of variation are very well understood from analysis of these national surveys. Given the author's experience, the description here largely follows the GB analysis, but very similar conclusions can be drawn from corresponding analysis of other datasets (see e.g. descriptions of the Dutch National Model (LMS): although not all the information is in the public domain, a reasonable description is given in Willigers and de Bok, 2009).

In passing, it should be noted that there has been ongoing debate as to whether the appropriate unit of analysis is the 'trip' (i.e. a movement between two locations) or the 'tour', which is a series of movements starting and ending at the same place (usually the home, but in some cases other locations such as the workplace). Of practical importance is that most travel data is collected as trips – it is really only the travel diary which permits the analysis of tours, by linking successive trips. The Dutch National Model is a good example of a model based on tours: in practice, the distinctions are of detail rather than substance.

The UK Department for Transport (DfT) has commissioned two major investigations in order to forecast national patterns of trip generation. The first made use of the NTS data from 1988 to 1996 (WSP, 2000) while the second used data from 1995 to 2006 (WSP, 2009). The DfT's National Trip End Model (NTEM) currently only uses results from the first study, though the model is currently under review. In combination with official estimates of changes in population and employment, etc., the DfT produces forecasts of trip ends for various future years, known as TEMPRO.

The NTEM models trip rates considering eight home-based (HB) and seven NHB trip purposes. It considers variables such as gender, person type (child (0–15), senior (65+) and four categories for adults of working age – full-time employed, part-time employed, student and unemployed/inactive), household structure (based on the number of adults), car ownership and area type (eight levels of urbanisation). Essentially, therefore, this is a category model, where the number of trips by purpose is estimated for each combination. Of course, not all the combinations generate statistically different trip rates for each purpose, but the general level of explanation is high and consistent. In addition, these rates demonstrate considerable stability over time.

Using these NTEM classifications, recent work by Lucas et al. (2013) has shown that a simple linear model for trips per person (Y) of the type:

$$Y = \alpha_{\text{person-type}} + \beta_{\text{fem}}.\delta_{\text{fem}} + \Sigma_{\text{area-type}}\beta_{\text{area-type}}.\delta_{\text{area-type}} + \beta_{\text{adults}}.(N_{\text{adults}}-1) + \beta_{\text{cars}}.\ N_{\text{cars}} \qquad (11.1)$$

(where the δ variables are 'dummies' (0,1) indicating the presence of a particular characteristic, and the N variables denote the number of adults and cars in the household, α is a constant associated with each person-type, and β is the set of estimated parameters) can explain 78 percent of the observed variation in the number of trips made, based on NTS data for the period 2002–10. Of course, further variables will account for some of the variation, but for the purposes of forecasting travel these become increasingly impractical for forecasting, since they themselves need to be predicted in the first place.

It can be seen that even the relatively modest model described above places some demands on the availability of underlying data. In addition to forecasts of population by age and gender, further classification is required by household structure, car ownership and working status. While population forecasts are typically available using standard demographic techniques, the further classifications are less readily available, particularly at the level of spatial detail which is so essential for transport demand. However, government agencies typically require forecasts of households, since this is the natural unit for the planning of dwellings, and forecasts of employed persons are also commonly made for economic planning, using participation rates.

Because the travel demand forecasts require a multivariate classification of the population, a common approach is that of 'prototypical sampling' (see e.g. Daly, 1998). Essentially, this starts off with a reasonable size representative sample of the population, and then applies a series of weights so that the marginal totals along various dimensions agree with external forecasts, while maintaining the internal structure of the sample as far as possible.

The importance of car ownership for the forecasting of travel (the work by Lucas et al. (2013) suggests that the average number of trips made per person per week rises by about 2.5 for each car in the household) and its dependence on income were noted above. Car ownership can be modelled using the same approach of prototypical sampling, to take account of its further dependence on household structure and the level of urbanisation, though it may be possible to develop appropriate marginal totals without an explicit requirement for income data at the personal or household level. There is a large literature on car ownership forecasting (for an informative review, see De Jong et al., 2004). Further discussion, with particular reference to the European context, is given in Bates (2015).

Of course, merely having a prediction of the number of trips 'generated' by households for different purposes in different areas is only a preliminary: there is a need to predict where the persons will travel to, and what means of transport they will use. There will also be interest in the network implications of such travel, at different times of day, and this is where the sensitivity to time and cost plays an important role. These are the subjects of the next section.

11.4 The 'four step' model

As the author noted in an earlier article (Bates, 2007), the four-stage model has been extensively used and extensively criticised, but the reason for its survival lies essentially in its logical appeal. The four stages relate to:

(1) trip generation (and attraction),
(2) trip distribution,
(3) modal split, and
(4) assignment,

and each stage addresses an intuitively reasonable question: how many travel movements will be made, where will they go, by what mode will the travel be carried out, and what route will be taken?

The first step (trip generation) is essentially the topic of the previous section, and concerns the basic reasons for travel. Given appropriate zonal variables, the total number of movements T_i can be calculated for each zone i. But where people travel to, and by what means, is, as noted, much more to do with the time and cost associated with different kinds of journey.

11.4.1 Distribution and modal split

Although traditionally the steps of trip distribution and modal split have been distinguished, with considerable early debate about the order in which they should be carried out, it is probably wiser to see them as two aspects of the same problem (sometimes referred to as the 'DMS' model – distribution and modal split). Clearly, a first requirement is to have an appropriate location for the activity to be carried out at the destination. If there is no difference between locations in terms of the ability to carry out the activity (for example, a newspaper is the same whether purchased from a local store or a major shopping centre), one would expect the 'nearest' destination to be chosen, though even here – given that transport typically involves an outlay of both time and money – there might be differences in the definition of 'nearest' according to the relative 'weight' placed on these two aspects. The trade-off between time and money, usually referred to as the value of travel time savings, is of major importance for transport modelling and appraisal, and there is a large literature on this within transport economics.

In fact, however, destinations are likely to differ to a considerable extent in terms of the 'quality' with which a given travel purpose can be accomplished. Partly, of course, this is a question of the detail with which travel purposes are defined. For example, 'shopping' can vary from the purchase of a single newspaper to the weekly food shop or the search for substantial consumer durables. And the quality can depend not only on whether a particular item can be bought, but also the range of choice and the price of the items. Similarly, for the journey to work, there is a vast array of possible types of employment, with different pay and conditions, not all of which are within the scope of any one person.

As far as the mode of travel is concerned, most destinations will be theoretically accessible on foot or by cycle, but the effort involved in traversing long distances quickly renders these modes impractical. Using surveys such as the GB National Travel Survey shows that:

(1) the trip length distribution falls away rapidly (62% of all trips are less than 5 miles, a further 32% are in the range of 5–25 miles, with only 6% being longer than 25 miles), and
(2) the proportion of walk trips longer than 2 miles is tiny. This is illustrated in Figure 11.5, where the modes are added 'cumulatively', so that the space between the top two curves represents the car modes.

So the majority of trips are 'local'. Nonetheless, the contribution to total distance travelled by the longer-distance trips is substantial: the 6% of trips longer than 25 miles account for 42% of total distance travelled. The shape of the distributions also varies by trip purpose, with the mean distance for trips to work and, in particular, on employers' business being longer. This is a further reason for distinguishing different trip purposes, though this needs to be viewed realistically: based on the 2014 NTS (Table NTS0409) for England, 16% of trips are commuting, 12% education (including escort trips), 19% shopping and 10% personal business – only 3.5% are employers' business. The remaining 35% are for leisure and 'other escort' purposes.

The conclusion is that the choice of destination and mode needs to be based on:

(1) the (relative) attractiveness of the destination for the travel purpose;
(2) the cost of reaching the destination by various modes; and
(3) the time and effort of reaching the destination by various modes.

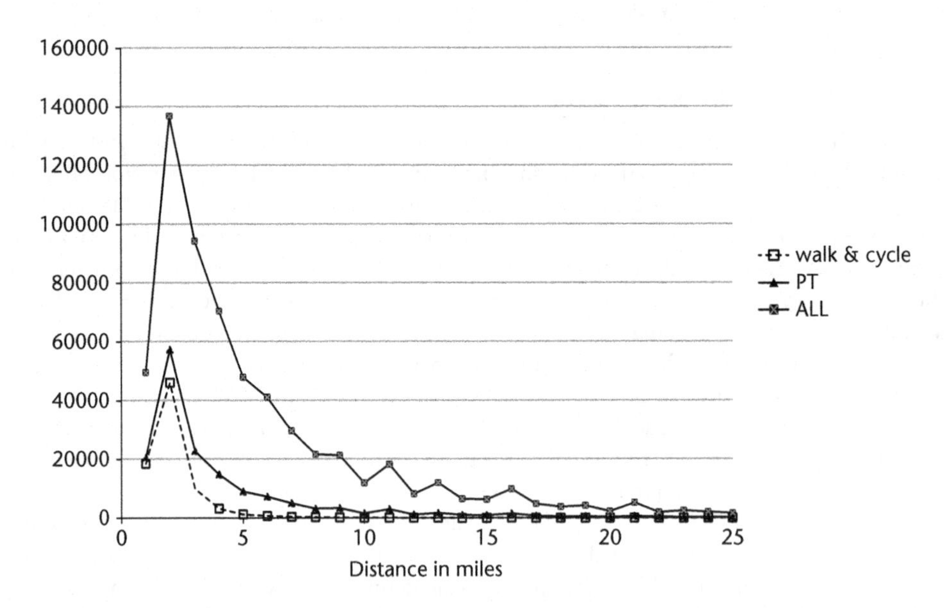

Figure 11.5 Trip length distribution by cumulative modes, Great Britain, 2009/10
Source: National Travel Survey, 2009–10, author's analysis (the scale on the vertical axis denotes the sample)

While the first item can be derived from available information at the zonal level, the last two items typically require access to a network or 'supply' model: this is the primary role of the assignment step, as is discussed later.

It is now more or less axiomatic within the transport modelling community that the DMS model be treated as a discrete choice model using the principles of random utility (see for example Train, 2002). Hence, with this approach in mind, a conditional indirect utility specification of the type:

$$U_{jm|i} = f\left(U_j^{dest},\ C_{ijm},\ U\left(t_{ijm}\right)\right) \tag{11.2}$$

is suggested, where i denotes the residence, j is a possible destination for the activity, m is a possible transport mode for accessing the destination and C, t are respectively the money cost and time to reach the destination. Conventionally, the total travel time is broken down into different components k such as in-vehicle, walking and waiting, potentially with different weights reflecting the comfort and effort involved.

There is an extensive literature on these types of models (see, for example, Ben-Akiva and Lerman, 1985, chapter 10; Daly, 1987). The standard approach is to postulate a function along the following lines:

$$U_{jm|i} = \ln\left(A_j\right) + \alpha_m + \beta_c\ C_{ijm} + \beta^m t\left(t^1{}_{ijm} + \sum_{2}^{K} w_k\ t^k{}_{ijm}\right) + \varepsilon_{ijm} \tag{11.3}$$

where A is a measure of attraction for the destination zone ('size variable'), α is the modal constant for mode m, C is the monetary cost for mode m, t^1 is the time travelling in the main mode m, and t^k are other travel time components (walking, waiting, etc.) associated with the journey, with appropriate weights w^k, with k ranging from 2 to K. Traditionally, the (linear) combination of cost and time components is referred to as 'generalised cost', though this term predates the development of the discrete choice theory. In line with the basic law of demand, a negative coefficient β on the cost and time components is expected.

Appropriate assumptions about the distribution and partition of the random term ε_{ijm} will result in the nested logit model, in which one of the two choices (either mode or destination) is postulated to be conditional on the other (alternatively, when no partition is assumed and ε_{ijm} is distributed as Type 1 extreme value (Gumbel), the multinomial logit model is obtained). This type of structure is the mainstay of contemporary transport models. While these models may often include a large number of constant terms, partly relating to the characteristics of the choices and partly to the persons making the choices, their main forecasting power relates to the cost and time variables, since these are the items directly affected by transport policy.

The nested logit model provides an appropriate way of combining the two choice processes, thus resolving an early controversy about the correct 'ordering' of the mode choice and distribution models (for a discussion of the key contributions, see Ortúzar, 2001 and Carrasco and Ortúzar, 2002). The higher-level (less sensitive) component uses a formula for utility which is in some way an 'average' of the lower-level utility (the so-called 'composite cost' or 'inclusive value' (logsum) formula, as shown in, for example, Ben-Akiva and Lerman, 1985).

The ordering of the two components is essentially a matter for empirical determination, with a test based on the relative values of the scaling parameters (inversely proportional to the error term) for rejecting an inappropriate hierarchy. The overwhelming empirical evidence from European studies has been that mode choice should be either above or at the same level as destination choice (though there is some contrary evidence from northern America): the official UK guidance from the DfT ('WebTAG') advocates such a structure.

In practice, it is probably the case that for most models used in developed countries, mode choice is of relatively low importance: the car mode dominates to such an extent that possible switches between car and public transport (PT) can be considered a secondary issue, and even where there is a reasonable supply of public transport, it is probably largely used by those who do not have access to a car.

By contrast, in major urban areas with substantial public transport infrastructure, mode choice may be much more important – at least for trips to and from the central area. Viewed in this light, tests of the DMS model demonstrate that the pattern of sensitivities implied by the structure is not very intuitive. This is not a refutation of the evidence on the relative sensitivity of mode and destination choice, but relates more to the restrictions of the standard nested logit approach.

The general effects can be summarised in the tabular presentation for a single production zone shown in Figure 11.6 which illustrates the effect of a change (increase) in the PT generalised costs to zone J.

Given the increase in the PT generalised cost, the dark grey indicates a significant decrease in demand, while the light grey shows a small uniform increase, and the patterned shading an even smaller uniform increase. A particular feature of the (nested) logit model is that for any given cost change for movement 'i-J' by mode m, the (relative) impact on the mode m whose cost has changed will be the same for all destinations $j \neq J'$, and cross-modally, for destination J as well.

In principle, one might expect in this case a larger (relative) PT response to 'nearby' destinations, and a larger (relative) highway response to the destination zone J. In other words, having accepted the large reduction in PT demand for zone J as being broadly reasonable, most of the remaining 'lost' demand would be expected to switch to nearby PT destinations, thereafter to highway for destination J, then to other further PT destinations. It is not obvious why there should be any (first-round) demand effect on any other slow and highway destinations. This would change the tabular presentation shown in Figure 11.6 to Figure 11.7, with the unshaded cells implying no change.

However, this 'intuitive' response is not feasible, since the standard nested logit imposes severe restrictions on the model sensitivity, essentially due to the error structure – specifically the size and correlation between the error terms associated with each choice alternative.

Destination zone → ↓ Mode	1	2	...	J	...	N
Highway						
Public transport						

Figure 11.6 Destination zone/mode choice, example 1

Destination zone → ↓ Mode	1	2	...	J	...	N
Highway						
Public transport						

Figure 11.7 Destination zone/mode choice, example 2

For the multinomial logit, all alternatives have the same error variance, and there is no correlation between alternatives. The nested logit allows for correlation ρ between the error terms relating to some of the choices. The correlation ρ is associated with the logsum scaling coefficient θ.

There would therefore seem to be some basis for considering an alternative structure, which could allow the desired 'intuitive' effects. Two possibilities within the logit family are the cross-nested logit (CNL) and the heteroscedastic extreme value model: for a useful summary of these and other models see Bhat and Koppelman (2012). The advantage about the CNL is that, like the standard nested logit, it is possible to obtain the model results without using numerical integration methods (typically these are done by means of simulation).

For the purposes of this discussion, the essential features of the nested logit model can be illustrated by considering a two-mode three-destination example. Writing m to denote mode (car and public transport (pt)) and j for destination, there are thus six possible choice alternatives mj. The implied error structure for the six alternatives is as follows:

$$\begin{array}{ll} hwy & 1 \\ & 2 \\ & 3 \\ pt & 1 \\ & 2 \\ & 3 \end{array} \begin{pmatrix} 1 & \rho_H & \rho_H & 0 & 0 & 0 \\ \rho_H & 1 & \rho_H & 0 & 0 & 0 \\ \rho_H & \rho_H & 1 & 0 & 0 & 0 \\ 0 & 0 & 0 & 1 & \rho_P & \rho_P \\ 0 & 0 & 0 & \rho_P & 1 & \rho_P \\ 0 & 0 & 0 & \rho_P & \rho_P & 1 \end{pmatrix} .\sigma^2 \tag{11.4}$$

The characteristic is that there is correlation within the two 'nests' (destinations within highway, and destinations within pt), which indicates that these options have a level of 'similarity' which is governed by the 'logsum' or structural parameters. If the correlation values ρ are all set to zero, then the model collapses to the (single-level) MNL model, as is found when the structural parameters θ are equal to 1.

In this model, there is no correlation between any of the highway alternatives and any of the pt alternatives.

The outcome of such an error structure is that a change in the cost for any given public transport alternative J will have the same proportionate effect on all highway alternatives j (and vice versa). However, as noted earlier, it would be reasonable to expect it to have a greater impact on highway alternative J than for other $j \neq J$. In principle, this can be achieved by allowing some correlation between the highway alternative J and the pt alternative J. While the actual details are not precise, an impression can be gained by considering the following error matrix:

$$\begin{array}{ll} hwy & 1 \\ & 2 \\ & 3 \\ pt & 1 \\ & 2 \\ & 3 \end{array} \begin{pmatrix} 1 & \rho_H & \rho_H & \rho_Z & 0 & 0 \\ \rho_H & 1 & \rho_H & 0 & \rho_Z & 0 \\ \rho_H & \rho_H & 1 & 0 & 0 & \rho_Z \\ \rho_Z & 0 & 0 & 1 & \rho_P & \rho_P \\ 0 & \rho_Z & 0 & \rho_P & 1 & \rho_P \\ 0 & 0 & \rho_Z & \rho_P & \rho_P & 1 \end{pmatrix} .\sigma^2 \tag{11.5}$$

where the elements ρ_Z allow for correlation for the same destination across modes (NB the level of correlation could be allowed to vary by destination zone). It turns out that this can be achieved by the CNL model, which is a generalisation of the nested logit model allowing individual alternatives to belong to more than one nest.

The CNL model can be specified in line with Hess et al. (2012, footnote 5) with some tidying of notation. Let i represent the possible combinations mj. Making use of the 'availability parameter' α_{in}, the conditional probability pr[i | n] over all elements i in the choice set for nest n can be written as:

$$pr[i|n] = \frac{\alpha_{in}.\exp(V_i/\theta_n)}{\sum_k \alpha_{kn}.\exp(V_k/\theta_n)} \tag{11.6}$$

where θ_n is the structural parameter associated with nest n, with $\alpha_{in} \geq 0$ and $\sum_n \alpha_{in} = 1$ for all i and n. Note that this formulation gives the possibility that any alternative can be included in any nest, with $\alpha_{in} = 0$ when i is not included in n.

Each nest n obtains a composite utility $V{*}_n$ given by the usual logsum term:

$$V{*}_n = \theta_n.\ln\sum_k \alpha_{kn}.\exp(V_k/\theta_n) \tag{11.7}$$

and the probability of the nest n is then given as:

$$pr[n] = \frac{\exp(V{*}_n)}{\sum_{n'=1}^{N} \exp(V{*}_{n'})}. \tag{11.8}$$

It is straightforward to show that this can be rewritten as:

$$pr[n] = \frac{\left(\sum_k \alpha_{kn}.\exp(V_k/\theta_n)\right)^{\theta_n}}{\sum_{n'=1}^{N}\left(\sum_k \alpha_{kn'}.\exp(V_k/\theta_{n'})\right)^{\theta_{n'}}}. \tag{11.9}$$

Hence, the probability of choosing alternative i is given by the product of the two probabilities, summed over all the possible nests n, so that:

$$pr[i] = \sum_n \frac{\left(\sum_k \alpha_{kn}.\exp(V_k/\theta_n)\right)^{\theta_n}}{\sum_{n'=1}^{N}\left(\sum_k \alpha_{kn'}.\exp(V_k/\theta_{n'})\right)^{\theta_{n'}}} \cdot \frac{\alpha_{in}.\exp(V_i/\theta_n)}{\sum_k \alpha_{kn}.\exp(V_k/\theta_n)}. \tag{11.10}$$

This formula applies equally to the current (nested logit) model and the CNL, though in the standard nested logit model, the outer summation over n is not strictly necessary, since each i can only be in one nest n, and the values of α_{in} are either 0 or 1.

Only three further steps are required to convert the nested logit model to CNL:

- more nests must be defined
- the appropriate allocation parameters α_{in} must be defined for each additional nest
- further structural parameters θ_n are needed for each additional nest.

For straightforward illustrative purposes a further nest can be defined for each destination zone. For the 2 mode 3 destination example given, the allocation parameters become:

$$\begin{array}{llccccc} & & n=1 & n=2 & n=3 & n=4 & n=5 \\ hwy & 1 & \alpha_{[h1],1} & 0 & 1-\alpha_{[h1],1} & 0 & 0 \\ & 2 & \alpha_{[h2],1} & 0 & 0 & 1-\alpha_{[h2],1} & 0 \\ & 3 & \alpha_{[h3],1} & 0 & 0 & 0 & 1-\alpha_{[h3],1} \\ pt & 1 & 0 & \alpha_{[p1],1} & 1-\alpha_{[p1],1} & 0 & 0 \\ & 2 & 0 & \alpha_{[p2],1} & 0 & 1-\alpha_{[p2],1} & 0 \\ & 3 & 0 & \alpha_{[p3],1} & 0 & 0 & 1-\alpha_{[p3],1} \end{array} \qquad [11.11]$$

where nest 1 is the highway nest, nest 2 is the public transport nest and nests 3, 4 and 5 correspond to zones 1, 2 and 3, respectively. As noted above, it is a requirement of the CNL that for any alternative i $\Sigma_n \alpha_{in} = 1$ (see Bierlaire, 2006).

Using the formula for pr[i], it can be seen that each probability will consist of the sum of two terms, one associated with the mode (as in the standard model) and one (additional term) associated with the zone.

To the author's knowledge, this kind of structure has not been used in any major forecasting model process, and it represents something of a challenge. However, some initial testing in the London context suggests that it might have substantially more reasonable properties, and current plans are to develop the approach further.

In whatever way the DMS model is formulated, there is a further possibility of taking the logsum or composite utility from the highest level and using this as an index of accessibility. In this way, the underlying trip rates can be modified as a response to changes in the transport level of service. While such effects, insofar as they can be ascertained, are typically small, they have been included in some models (for example, the Dutch National Model).

11.4.2 Assignment

Regardless of the details of the specification, the outcome of the DMS model allows the total trips T_i for a given purpose to be allocated to mode and destination combinations [mj], giving modal matrices T_{ijm}. These can then be assigned to appropriate modal networks.

The distinction between the P/A (production/attraction) matrix form that is required for demand models and the O-D (origin-destination) form for assignment models is worth emphasising. For matrices to be sensitive to land-use changes, including sociodemographic change, they need to recognise the home end of trips (the most important source of the production of trip making). But it is the O-D matrices used for assignment that form, to a large part, the basis of model validation, typically comparing with traffic or passenger counts, and for network analysis it is irrelevant for any particular movement which zone is the production and which the attraction.

To convert to O-D format, the all-day P/A matrix needs to be allocated between outward and return movements and transposed for the return movement. In most cases, the assignment is on a period-specific basis (usually an hour) rather than for the whole day. This means that further factoring by time period (t) is required. Hence the process of P/A to O-D conversion can be described as follows. Introduce a further argument (d) to indicate direction: d = 1 for outward and d = 2 for return. Apply direction and time of day factors – these will certainly vary by purpose h and might also vary to some extent by sub-area zones. Then the corresponding period-specific O-D matrices are:

$$A^h_{ijmt} = T^h_{ijm} \cdot \pi^{h,d=1}_t + T^h_{jim} \cdot \pi^{h,d=2}_t \qquad (11.12)$$

(note the transpose in the second term).

For non-home-based purposes (n), a simpler approach is commonly used.

Given the O-D matrices, the next stage is to consider assignment. Although assignment is treated as a single model stage, it in fact relates to a number of separate processes, which may be described as:

(1) choice of route (or path) for each i–j combination;
(2) aggregating i–j flows on the links of the chosen paths (loading);
(3) dealing with supply-side effects (capacity restraint or public transport overcrowding) as a result of the volume of link flows relative to capacity; and
(4) obtaining the resulting cost for each i–j combination.

In practice iteration of the above steps is required to achieve convergence.

Item (4) produces the required cost matrices C for further iterations of the demand model (note that these may need to be converted back appropriately to P/A form). However, item (2) also permits comparisons to be made with vehicle counts on the highway network and with corresponding counts on public transport networks. This is discussed further below.

11.4.3 *'Incremental' approaches*

A central problem for the DMS model is that, when using a standard zoning system, the majority of the destination alternatives will be far away whereas, as noted earlier, the majority of the actual trips are local. The result is that the fit of these models to the surveyed or observed base year data can often be quite poor, or particularly challenging and time consuming to calibrate satisfactorily. General experience is that, even when considerable effort has been expended in constructing the DMS model, the resulting 'synthetic' (by which is meant a matrix which has been derived using a mathematical function of the network generalised cost C) matrices of travel that are assigned to a network do not give acceptable levels of link flows, compared with external evidence. For this reason, it has become normal practice in application to make much more explicit use of so-called 'observed' matrices (more correctly, matrices which are built by making substantial use of sample intercept surveys collecting the origins and destinations of trips). The application of common types of incremental models is discussed below.

Of course, it is always possible to improve the fit of the model to surveyed data by introducing arbitrary additional parameters. The aim is, however, to find a principled way of doing this that satisfies statistical rigour while still involving appropriate levels of detail.

The outcome flows V_a on any link a can be compared with observed counts. However, even if the observed counts were considered 100 percent accurate, any disagreement will not only be due to problems with the DMS model, but could also stem from problems with the assignment model. Given all this, it would be unwise to expect too high a degree of consistency between the outcome flows and the observed counts.

What is ultimately required is a reconciliation between the direct observations of trips – largely from household and other surveys – and the traffic statistics. This is problematic for a number of reasons. Firstly, some of the travel that might be picked up in (national) travel surveys is excluded: for example, the UK NTS specifically excludes the following types of motorised trips as they are commercial rather than personal travel:

- trips made specifically to deliver/collect goods in the course of work;
- trips made by professional drivers or crew in the course of their work;
- trips made by taxi drivers if they are paid or charge a fare for making a trip; and
- trips made by professional driving instructors whilst teaching or driving their vehicles in the course of their work.

In addition, any household-based survey will exclude trips made by foreign residents. The impact of this will depend strongly on the size of the country and its geographical location: given its island geography, this is of lower significance for the UK, but small and centrally located countries like Austria may have a substantial component of 'transit' traffic. The Dutch LMS has a special module to deal with through traffic originating outside the Netherlands.

Finally, on the traffic measurement side, there are major issues relating to vehicle type recognition, and vans (light commercial vehicles) in particular. As detailed in Wigan and Rockliffe (1998), vans occupy an intermediate position between personal and freight transport. They can be used as quasi-cars, they can be used for certain types of business trips which are on the margin of being excluded from national travel surveys, and they can be used to transport freight – particularly in the context of urban distribution. Moreover, traffic counts employing solely axle detectors will have difficulty distinguishing vans from cars.

In any case, problems occur when, after reasonable adjustments to the network, it is concluded that significant differences remain which are essentially attributable to the matrix. Ideally, further data should be introduced to the whole modelling procedure in such a way that the DMS model is modified to be consistent with the observed data, including counts. Unfortunately, there is very little documented experience of how to do this.

An alternative approach, widely used, is to modify the assignment (O-D) matrix, using various techniques that can be referred to as 'matrix estimation from counts' (for a straightforward introduction, see chapter 12 of Ortúzar and Willumsen, 2011). At its most general, this consists of a model form for the (estimated) matrix $\widetilde{A}_{ij}$, the parameters of which are estimated under a selection of constraints, which may relate to row and column totals, totals within different sub-matrices or total traffic flows across defined screenlines (thus introducing network elements relating to paths). Furthermore, they may range from 'hard' equality constraints, which must be satisfied, to 'soft' inequality constraints, which may be downgraded by assigning them lower weights or bounds (taken to reflect the modeller's estimate of confidence in them).

With the current state of practice, if this position is encountered, the most common approach to forecasting is to use a 'pivot' version of the assignment model. Essentially, after converting the forecast output of the demand model from P/A to O-D, the resulting matrix is not directly assigned, but is compared with a base case matrix from the demand model also converted to O-D, and the implied changes are used to adjust the independently validated assignment matrix.

There are thus two types of incremental modelling, (a) on the demand side, on a P/A basis, and (b) on the assignment side, on an O-D basis. These two incremental variants are entirely independent of each other, so that there are four possible combinations, which can be described according to Figure 11.8.

In these types, the number (1 or 2) refers to whether the demand model is absolute (1) or incremental (pivot) (2), while the letter (A or B) refers to whether the assignment matrix is taken

Assignment →	Matrix converted direct from demand P/A matrix	Independent matrix adjusted for predicted O-D change
Demand ↓		
Absolute	**1-A**	**1-B**
Pivot	**2-A**	**2-B**

Figure 11.8 Incremental model types

directly from the demand model (A) or merely uses the demand model to adjust an independent base assignment matrix (B).

Type 1-A is the traditional approach already described, with an absolute demand model and direct assignment (after conversion to O-D format), although this is now seldom used since, while it might represent a valid model of behaviour, it does not usually give a satisfactory level of base-year validation.

Type 1-B takes the traditional (absolute) approach to the demand model, but uses the predicted changes (resulting from a scheme or policy) to modify an independently derived (and validated) O-D assignment matrix, as briefly discussed at the end of the last section. This adjustment could be done in a number of ways, proportionally, additively, or by a mixture of the two – discussed further below. This is used by a number of models (for example, the London Transport Studies model).

Type 2-A (the generally preferred method) replaces the demand model by an incremental or pivot form, relative to a P/A base matrix, in a way which is described below. The resulting P/A matrix, after conversion to O-D, is directly assigned to the network.

Type 2-B is a combination of Types 1-B and 2-A, where, even after pivoting from a base matrix in the demand model, it is still considered necessary to make further modifications to the resulting O-D matrices for assignment (for example, because the base pivot matrix fails to provide satisfactory network flows).

There has been some confusion about the terms incremental, pivot, etc. A useful paper by Daly, Fox and Patruni (2012) describes various approaches, noting at the outset that 'The methods used for pivoting are diverse, sometimes giving substantially different results for the same inputs'. They note that the UK DfT's WebTAG distinguishes the following kinds of models (M2, paragraph 4.3.1):

- absolute models, that use a direct estimate of the number of trips in each category;
- absolute models applied incrementally, that use absolute model estimates to apply changes to a base matrix; and
- pivot-point models, that use only the cost changes to estimate the changes in the number of trips from a base matrix.

Unfortunately, this does not distinguish between whether the pivoting relates to the demand (P/A) matrix or the assignment (O-D) matrix. As Daly et al. note, the third method 'pivot-point' can only be applied validly on a P/A basis.

On the demand side, for Types 2-A and 2-B, there are two main possible options: method (i) adjusts the demand model so that it produces the base matrix T^0 given an associated base cost matrix C^0, while method (ii) continues to use an absolute model, but applies the predicted change to the independently derived base matrix T^0. Method (i) thus falls into the pivot-point category, while method (ii) is an 'absolute model applied incrementally'.

Method (ii) is used extensively in the models built by RAND Europe and described by Daly et al. (2012). The basic idea is to run the unadjusted (absolute) demand models to give synthetic estimates $S^0 = f(C^0)$ and $S = f(C)$. For each element of the matrix (ij, say), the ratio of the estimates S_{ij}/S^0_{ij} is then multiplied by the corresponding base matrix element T^0_{ij}. Hence the outcome result can be written as:

$$T_{ij} = T^0_{ij}.\left(S_{ij}/S^0_{ij}\right) \text{ or equivalently } T_{ij} = S_{ij}.\left(T^0_{ij}/S^0_{ij}\right). \qquad (11.13)$$

Under specified conditions this method can be shown to give the same result as method (i).

On the assignment side (Types 1-B and 2-B), there is currently no guidance on how to implement the adjustment to the assignment matrices. While the best approach would be to incorporate the adjustments in the demand model so that there is no need to adjust the assignment model, a method for achieving this is currently lacking.

The need for this assignment adjustment will arise when the base P/A matrix T^0, after converting to O-D form and making any other required corrections (e.g. for time period, car occupancy) to obtain the corresponding A^0, is found not to be compatible with some trusted assignment base matrix (B^0, say). If there is no way of further adjusting T^0, how should a shift from the base matrix to B (with corresponding assignment matrix A) be treated?

As Daly et al. note, the RAND method can be used in this case as well. As with the demand-side variant, the unadjusted (absolute) demand models are run to give synthetic estimates $S^0 = f(C^0)$ and $S = f(C)$. However, before applying the ratio to the O-D matrix, these matrices are converted to O-D form A^0 and A, so that the actual matrix B which is assigned has the default value:

$$B_{ij} = B^0{}_{ij}.\left(A_{ij}/A^0{}_{ij}\right) \text{or equivalently } B_{ij} = A_{ij}.\left(B^0{}_{ij}/A^0{}_{ij}\right). \tag{11.14}$$

This can be expected to produce (a) more credible estimates of flows and (b) more credible estimates of generalised cost for the next round of the demand model. However, because multiple adjustment ratios (by direction and by time period) are being applied to the same underlying demand element, there is no obvious way in which the adjustments can be conveyed to the demand model. This in turn means that the adjustment will not have any effect on model elements which are not subject to pivoting. In other words, while the RAND method has apparently the significant advantage that it has more general applicability (and in particular can be applied to the assignment matrices), it is not currently clear whether it can have any impact on the wider outcomes from the demand model.

How much of a disadvantage this is depends on the use to which the model will be put. If the overwhelming use is to investigate highway schemes and other highway-related policies, then it will be no disadvantage at all, and indeed constitutes a significant advantage over the pivot-point method in this case. But for other modes the problem is that the forecast matrices remain at the synthetic level (unless pivot matrices can be independently developed for them). Unless it turns out that the pivoting adjustments are generally small (in other words, that the synthetic highway matrices produce reasonably realistic assignments without pivoting), it seems unlikely that the synthetic matrices for the other modes can be considered very useful. At the very least, they will require substantial validation.

As is well known, the sensitivity of discrete choice models is strongly affected by the shares of the various alternatives (modes, destinations). Hence, in principle, there is virtue in bringing the demand model as close as possible to the best estimate of the base position, and this is the philosophy behind the recommended 2-A type model.

11.4.4 Criteria for model acceptance

Given that the aim is to forecast changes in demand, there are key criteria which the model needs to meet. While these have not generally been codified, good practice would indicate that in the base year the model should be corroborated by reliable sources relating to the total number of trips, distance travelled, average trip length and mode split, separately by trip purpose, and more specifically for the trip length distribution.

In addition, with regard to its forecasting use, it should deliver as far as possible plausible elasticities with respect to travel time and cost, separately by mode and purpose, and make use of values of time that can be supported by other research.

These criteria suggest a combination of providing assurance that in the base year the model reasonably represents the observed pattern of travel, and that it has the right sensitivities to the key cost and time variables. For example, the UK DfT's guidance (WebTAG) requires the model to have an overall elasticity of car kilometres to fuel cost in the range -0.25 to -0.35, and an elasticity of public transport trips with respect to public transport fares in the range –0.2 to -0.9.

11.4.5 Forecasting

Given such a model, the process of forecasting can be essentially considered in two stages. It is useful to make a conceptual distinction between changes resulting from exogenous developments (broadly, land-use and sociodemographic changes) and those associated with changes in generalised cost. The UK DfT's guidance recommends the establishment of a 'reference case' in which adjustments are made to the trip ends, usually on the basis of official 'TEMPRO' forecasts (unless a local trip end model is available): these take account of expected land-use changes, including new developments. On the assumption that generalised costs do not change, these changes can be implemented on the base-year matrices by the method of bi-proportional fitting.

The change in the matrix is likely to have consequences on generalised cost via the supply model (e.g. additional congestion). In addition, there will be other changes (e.g. to the network, or because of changes to the components of generalised cost such as fares, parking and fuel prices) which will need to be reflected in modelling the Do-Minimum (DM) situation. Once a stable DM forecast has been obtained, further policies involving changes in generalised cost can be tested.

11.5 Concluding remarks

While an overall summary of key variables at the aggregate level has been provided, this chapter has concentrated on setting out a general procedure for analysis and forecasting which follows the line of the four-stage model: beginning with car ownership, then dealing with trip generation by all modes, allocating trips to destinations and modes, and after reconciliation with other data sources, assigning trips to networks. This can be done separately for different periods.

Most trips are short and predominantly home-based. This provides a challenge for the development of reliable travel matrices for longer distances, because of the low frequency of longer-distance interurban trips (leading to sampling issues) and the level of spatial definition. While the advent of 'big data' is likely to lead to improvements, there is much to be done before data sources such as mobile phone records can be reliably reconciled with genuine travel movements. In particular, the need to impute travel purpose for such data is currently a major obstacle, given the important travel variations associated with different purposes.

The chapter has discussed the approach followed by best practice and identified some of the key difficulties in producing reliable matrices of travel. More research is needed in the general area of 'Matrix Estimation' in order to bring together disparate sources of data with different statistical properties, with the intention of establishing both national traffic levels and local variations. Data remain a problem, and there is significant variation in sources and availability between countries, despite efforts at 'harmonisation' at the European level.

Acknowledgements

Figure 11.5 is based on the author's own analysis of NTS data for 2002–10, kindly provided by the UK Data Archive at the University of Essex. I would also like to thank Jonathan Cowie for his assistance in the preparation of this chapter for publication.

References

Bates J. J. (2007). History of Demand Modelling. In Hensher, D. A. and K. J. Button (eds), *Handbook of Transport Modelling*. Oxford: Pergamon.

Bates J. J. (2015). Demand for Road Transport. In Nash, C. (ed.), *Handbook of Research Methods and Applications in Transport Economics and Policy*. Cheltenham: Edward Elgar, chapter 9.

Ben-Akiva, M. and Lerman, S. R. (1985). *Discrete Choice Analysis: Theory and Application to Travel Demand*. Cambridge, MA: MIT Press.

Bhat, C. and Koppelman, F. S. (2012). Activity-Based Models of Travel Demand. In Hall, R. W. (ed.), *Handbook of Transportation Science*. London: Springer Science and Business Media.

Bierlaire, M. (2006). A Theoretical Analysis of the Cross-Nested Logit Model. *Annals of Operations Research*, 144, pp. 287–300.

Carrasco, J. A. and Ortúzar, J. de D. (2002). Review and Assessment of the Nested Logit Model. *Transport Reviews*, 22(2), pp. 197–218.

Daly, A. J. (1987). Estimating 'Tree' Logit Models. *Transportation Research Part B: Methodological*, 21, pp. 251–67.

Daly, A. J. (1998). Prototypical Sample Enumeration as a Basis for Forecasting with Disaggregate Models Transportation Planning Methods. Proceedings of Seminar D, AET European Transport Conference, Loughborough University, 14–18 September.

Daly, A., Fox, J., Patruni, B. and Milthorpe, F. (2012). Pivoting in Travel Demand Models, presented at ATRF, Perth, Western Australia.

De Jong, G., Fox, J., Pieters, M., Daly, A. and Smit, R. (2004). Comparison of Car Ownership Models. *Transport Reviews*, 24, pp. 379–408.

DfT (2013). *UK Aviation Forecasts*. London: DfT.

DfT (2015). *Transport Statistics Great Britain*. London: HMSO.

Dunkerley, F., Rohr, C. and Daly, A. J. (2014). Road Traffic Demand Elasticities: A Rapid Evidence Assessment. RAND Europe RR-888-DFT, December, prepared for Department for Transport.

Gillen, D. W., Morrison, W. G. and Stewart, C. (2004). Air Travel Demand Elasticities: Concepts, Issues and Measurement. Department of Finance, Government of Canada, www.fin. gc. ca/consultresp/ Airtravel/airtravStdy_e. html (accessed 15 September 2016).

Goodwin, P. (2012). Peak Travel, Peak Car and the Future of Mobility: Evidence, Unresolved Issues, Policy Implications, and a Research Agenda. Discussion paper no. 2012–13. Prepared for the Roundtable on Long-Run Trends in Travel Demand 29–30 November, OECD International Transport Forum.

Graham, D. J. and Glaister, S. (2005). Decomposing the Determinants of Road Traffic Demand. *Applied Economics*, 37(1), pp. 19–28.

Hess, S., Fowler, M. Adler, T. and Bahreinian, A. (2012). A Joint Model for Vehicle Type and Fuel Type Choice: Evidence from a Cross-Nested Logit Study. *Transportmetrica*, 39(3), pp. 593–625.

Le Vine, S. and Jones, P. (2012). On the Move: Making Sense of Car and Train Travel Trends in Britain. Report for the RAC Foundation, www.racfoundation.org/assets/rac_foundation/content/download ables/on_the_move-le_vine_&_jones-dec2012.pdf

Lucas, K., Bates, J., Moore, J. and Carrasco, J. (2013). Modelling the Links between Travel Behaviours and Social Disadvantage. Paper presented at the Universities' Transport Studies Group 45th Annual Conference, Oxford, January.

Ortúzar, J. de D. (2001). On the Development of the Nested Logit Model. *Transportation Research*, 35(2), pp. 213–16.

Ortúzar, J. de D. and Willumsen, L. G. (2011). *Modelling Transport*. Chichester: Wiley.

Train, K. E. (2002). *Discrete Choice Methods with Simulation*. Cambridge: Cambridge University Press.

Wigan, M. and Rockliffe, N. (1998). Freight Survey Requirements for Urban Areas. Proceedings of the 19th ARRB Conference, Sydney, 7-11 December, Volume 1, pp. 109–31.

Willigers, J. and de Bok, M. (2009). Updating and Extending the Disaggregate Choice Models in the Dutch National Model. Paper presented at the European Transport Conference, Glasgow.

WSP (2000). Land-Use Indicators and Trip-End Models. Final report for HETA Division of the Department of the Environment, Transport and the Regions.

WSP (2009). Research into Changing Trip Rates over Time and Implications for the National Trip End Mode. Draft final report for Department for Transport, May 2009.

12

The principles behind transport appraisal

John Nellthorp

12.1 Introduction

'Transport appraisal' refers to a set of methods that are underpinned by economics and are widely used by governments and public bodies to support transport sector decision making. Many countries share what can be seen as a common 'toolkit' for transport appraisal,[1] although the scope of the appraisal and key components, such as the parameters, vary considerably. These tools can be found incorporated into national guidance on appraisal methods (e.g. Department for Transport (DfT), 2016); in international guidance, for example at the European Union (EU) level or the methods of the World Bank and other international financial institutions (Bickel et al., 2006; World Bank, 2005; European Investment Bank, 2005; Asian Development Bank, 2013); and crucially in appraisal practice across a large number of projects every year. Moreover, the applications of appraisal extend beyond investment projects to include regional transport strategies, national infrastructure plans and even road pricing and technological innovations. The scale of the initiatives being appraised ranges from the largest to the very small, and from international to local.

The main purpose of this chapter is to show how appraisal methods are built up from a set of economic principles, and to provide a broad introduction to the tools of economic appraisal used in the transport sector. Reflecting the range of methods used in practice, the chapter focuses on cost-benefit analysis, but will also touch on financial appraisal and multiple attribute-based methods, each of which plays a distinct role. Attention will be given to ways in which the methods can be used intelligently to play to their strengths and minimise their weaknesses, and the chapter will highlight areas where research is helping to address some of the known limitations and improve appraisal methods for the future.

The structure of the chapter will be as follows:

- *Section 12.2* introduces the basic problem of resource allocation in the transport sector;
- *Section 12.3* describes the underlying economic principles, and how appraisal has evolved to this point through research, debate and application – this includes the need for valuation of impacts as part of an economic appraisal;
- *Section 12.4* outlines how the valuation of impacts is undertaken, including values of travel time savings, safety, environmental impacts, health impacts and wider economic impacts beyond the transport sector;

- *Section 12.5* shows how this feeds through into the appraisal results and how they are used; and
- *Section 12.6* addresses some remaining limitations and widens the scope to discuss multiple attribute-based methods and their role in the transport decision maker's toolkit.

12.2 The basic problem to be resolved

The basic problem being addressed by all appraisal methods is the problem of resource allocation, one of the fundamental issues in economics. In a public choice setting the core question is: how, in a situation of finite resources and a wide range of possible uses, should we decide which initiatives should go ahead, and which not? Related questions concern timing – what is the optimal timing and phasing of various initiatives – and also funding and governance choices. In transport, specific questions include, for example: 'Is this high speed rail line good value for money?'; 'Which of these options for the airport rail link is preferred?'; 'Among this long list of road improvement projects, which should be prioritised?'; 'Are these walking and cycling measures worthwhile?'; 'What is the best package of urban transport measures we can recommend for this city?'; and so on. Governments and transport authorities face a plethora of such questions. Some are politically controversial, others are more easily resolved. It is this wide set of public choices which transport appraisal aims to support, by providing suitable evidence and a rationale for decision making.

What makes these resource allocation questions particularly difficult is their multidimensional nature. First of all, there are many alternatives (and they may not be independent of each other). For example, there may be a few clear alternatives at the project level, but standing back there may also be alternative ways of delivering mobility and accessibility improvements to the same population, e.g. using different combinations of modes, or different combinations of capital versus revenue spending. Figure 12.1 shows how capital spending on transport has been favoured relative to revenue spending in the UK, during the period of public spending restraint following the global financial crisis of 2008. More widely there are choices to be made about funding urban versus interurban transport, and lagging versus leading regions. Of course the resources could also

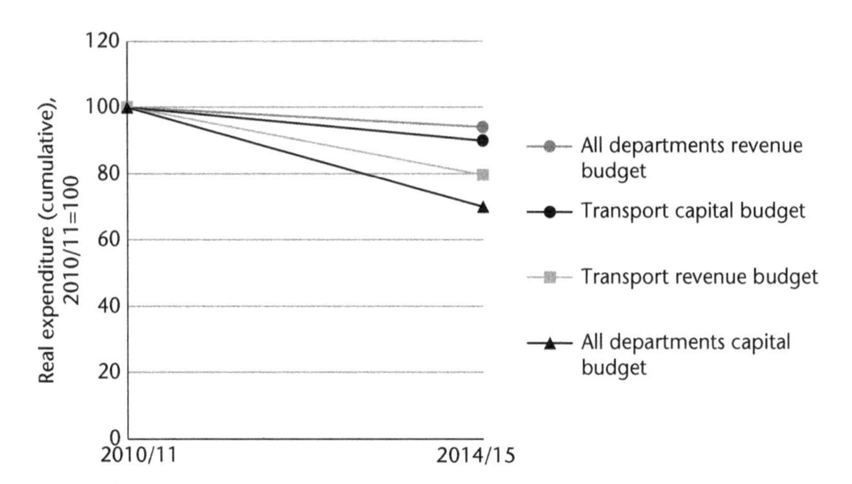

Figure 12.1 Recent trends in capital versus revenue spending on transport versus other sectors, UK 2010/11–2014/15
Source: HM Treasury (2010)

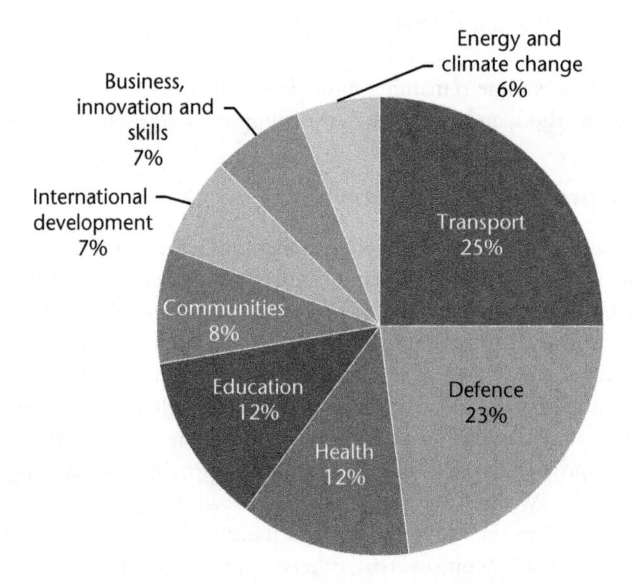

Figure 12.2 Shares of public capital spending by sector in the UK, 2015/16
Source: HM Treasury (2013)

be used in other sectors, such as housing, education or health. Figure 12.2 shows the allocation of public capital spending during a challenging economic period in the UK: transport was allocated the largest share of public capital, and the government attributed this partly to the availability of appraisal results making a strong case for the transport department's proposals (House of Commons Transport Committee, 2011, p. 33).

Sometimes proposals are multisectoral or multimodal, adding to the complexity of the problem. A classic case is the development of new housing and improved transport services as part of a coordinated land-use and transport plan (Geurs et al., 2012). There are many other cases where interdependencies arise just within the transport network, such as provision of pedestrian or cycle access to stations for the 'last mile' of the trip, or integration of bus and rail services.

Secondly, modern governance arrangements mean that projects typically involve one or more private-sector partners as well as a public authority, e.g. a passenger or freight train-operating company and a rolling stock-leasing company, and perhaps a separate infrastructure owner. This means that there is not a unitary 'decision maker', but a set of decision makers to be satisfied – probably with differing objectives.

Thirdly, the impacts of transport interventions are potentially extremely wide-ranging, including health effects, impacts on the environment and social impacts as well as economic impacts on households and businesses in the transport sector and elsewhere. An evidence-based transport appraisal could potentially be concerned with all of these.

Moreover, these decisions invoke some of the major debates about the motives for public action: is it to stimulate economic growth; to maximise wellbeing; to limit climate change and decarbonise the economy for the sake of future generations; and/or to reduce inequality? It is very difficult to abstract key transport investment decisions from this wider set of debates about public policy.

Faced with this complex, multi-layered and sometimes politically charged set of issues raised by resource allocation problems in the transport sector, economic appraisal tries to offer a systematic and rational approach – no small challenge. The approach offered is one in which people and their preferences feature prominently; to the surprise of many newcomers to the topic, it is neither mechanistic nor focused mainly on the financial flows – they are an important part of a much wider picture. It can, however, be time consuming and expensive to undertake an appraisal consistent with the guidelines in various countries, and for this reason there has been a movement towards 'proportionate' appraisal, and a more tailored approach for smaller interventions or early-stage sifting of options.

12.3 Basic principles underlying transport appraisal

The principles underlying modern transport appraisal have evolved over the last 250 years into a formal framework which is widely shared. Today's principles reflect the concerns of modern economics and politics, but retain important elements from the early formulations. In this section, the main principles will be covered under the following broad headings:

- appraisal as part of the public choice process;
- the basis for valuation;
- the treatment of time and the future; and
- aggregation – across networks and people.

12.3.1 Appraisal as part of the public choice process

Appraisal is a comparative form of analysis, focused on revealing and comparing the consequences of different courses of public action. Pearman et al. (2003) summarised the range of applications in the transport sector as 'projects, programmes and policies', which widens the scope to include both pricing and regulatory changes, and regional or national transport plans, as well as the classic application – investment appraisal. It is also possible to apply these methods to technology initiatives, such as intelligent speed adaptation or electric vehicles (e.g. Carsten and Tate, 2005; Massiani, 2015), which are another common use of public resources in the transport sector.

At both the project level and the policy level, it is conventional to think of a 'cycle' of decision making (Figure 12.3) starting with objective setting, and then proceeding through:

- identification of options, i.e. alternative means of achieving the objectives;
- *ex ante appraisal* of the options – this typically takes the form of a 'sifting' or 'screening' process applied to a long list of options, followed by a more detailed appraisal of the resulting shortlist;
- selection of the option(s) to take forward;
- implementation, accompanied by a *monitoring* exercise to gather data on this critical stage and help ensure delivery is in line with plans;
- *ex post evaluation*, in which the actual rather than predicted outcomes of the intervention are measured and compared with the prior predictions; and
- feedback from the ex post evaluation to future project/policy development.

Potentially the most useful timing for an analysis of the costs and benefits of a project is *before* implementation: if there are better alternatives, it is important to discover this in time to change the selection of options. Hence in the transport sector, *ex ante appraisal* is widely used. Alongside this, a great deal of effort is spent on the modelling and forecasting of future outcomes that are necessary for this kind of analysis (Ortúzar and Willumsen, 2011; Hensher and Button, 2008).

Meanwhile, there is an increasing awareness of the value of *ex post evaluation*, and the real outcome data it produces. For example, Flyvbjerg et al. (2004) compared the *ex post* construction costs for a

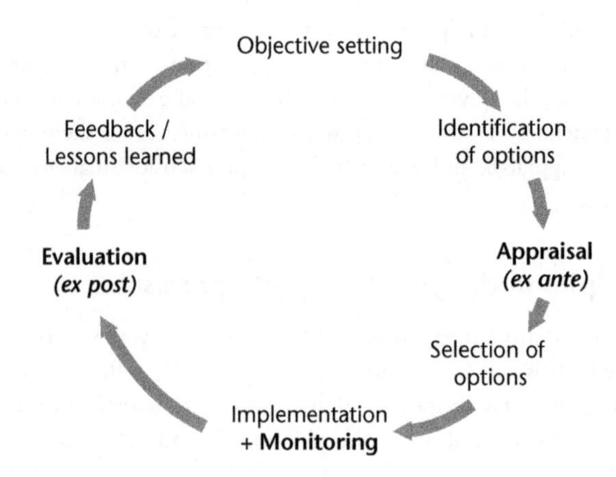

Figure 12.3 The project (or policy) cycle

sample of 258 transport projects worldwide with the *ex ante* appraisals and found evidence of systematic bias, with an average cost overrun of 28 percent. One consequence of this has been a direct feedback into project development, in the form of an *optimism bias adjustment* in ex ante appraisal, which tapers away as the project proceeds through the project cycle and is subject to greater scrutiny (DfT, 2014a). The optimism bias adjustment is added to the risk-adjusted cost at each stage (Table 12.1). By the final stage, the cost will include the results of a full *quantitative risk analysis* for major projects, replacing the optimism bias adjustment to a great extent. In this way, the appraisal method provides an incentive to gain confidence in cost estimates *before* final approval is given.

Flyvbjerg et al. (2005) also identified that demand forecasts were on average overestimated by 106 percent for rail projects and underestimated by 9 percent for road projects, although the standard deviation was large in both cases. Putting the demand side and cost side together, Kelly et al. (2015, p. 90) found that the benefit:cost ratio (BCR) was overestimated for half their sample and underestimated for the other half of their sample of ten EU cohesion-funded projects, with no clear modal pattern. Their conclusion was that ten years on from Flyvbjerg's pioneering work, there is still 'a clear need to improve the quality and consistency of *ex ante* analysis – particularly in the areas of capital cost estimation, travel demand modelling and risk analysis'.

Despite its apparent usefulness, ex post evaluation has tended to be conducted only for a sample of projects, for example Kelly et al. (2015) found this to be the case in only 15 percent of European Investment Bank projects, whilst the Highways Agency (2015) highlighted that only

Table 12.1 Optimism bias adjustments in ex ante appraisal, based on ex post analysis

Mode	*Stage of project development process*		
	Stage 1 = pre-feasibility†	*Stage 2 = option selection*†	*Stage 3 = design development*†*/final approval*
Road projects	44%	15%	3%
Rail projects	66%	40%	6%
Fixed links (bridges or tunnels)	66%	23%	6%

Note: † stage descriptions based on the 'GRIP' framework for rail projects
Source: based on UK data, DfT (2014a)

37 percent of Local Network Management Schemes in England costing less than £10 million had undergone ex post evaluation. There are exceptions, however, such as the French Internal Transport Act (Loi d'Orientation des Transport Interieurs), which requires an evaluation for all major projects (>€82 million), and the Highways England 'Post-Opening Project Evaluation' for Major Schemes with the same requirement (>£10 million) (Kelly et al., 2015; Highways England, 2016). Overall, the practice of ex post evaluation appears to be growing. In this, there is a degree of convergence between transport and other sectors such as public health, where ex post evaluation of either 'randomised controlled trials' or 'natural experiments' is seen as the gold standard in evidence-based policy (Gibbons et al., 2014). There remain some barriers, though, to the wider use of ex post evaluation in transport, in particular:

- insofar as transport interventions are unique in design or otherwise geographically specific, it may be hard to transfer the impacts found from one intervention to another;
- there may be a large number of unobserved variables in the population or local economy which vary from place to place and which influence interventions' success (Gibbons et al., 2014, p. 430); and
- if the impacts really are very case-specific, then the problem of identifying a counterfactual (without the intervention) becomes more difficult, and there is a tendency to rely on using *ex ante* models to project forward using different assumptions – so the estimates still rely to some extent on models rather than 'real' data.

This progress with *ex post* evaluation has not, for the moment, reduced the widespread practice of ex ante appraisal in the transport sector. Central to most transport appraisal is a clear definition of the scenarios being compared. These typically comprise:

- a *do-something scenario* – including the intervention (labelled '1' in the formulae below);
- a realistic *do-minimum scenario* – excluding the intervention (labelled '0' in the formulae below).

The *impacts* of the intervention are the difference between the do-something and the do minimum outcome, on any indicator. The *definition of the do-minimum* is therefore both a key component of the appraisal assumptions, and also a potential source of manipulation in the hands of a biased or self-interested party, for example a project promoter facing an under-resourced government decision maker. One clear way to 'game' the appraisal system is for the promoter to choose a 'worse' do-minimum, or even a do-nothing scenario: this could include no upgrades to the transport network over the whole appraisal period, leading to levels of congestion and crowding that in reality would not be tolerated. Appraisal guidance therefore tends to recommend that the do-minimum should include essential maintenance and renewals, and all committed (and not yet implemented) interventions, and also to assume further minor interventions, for example work to relieve bottlenecks or extend trains, in order to keep the network functioning at an 'acceptable' level. Of course, it is a challenge to define a common do-minimum across all interventions, yet this would be desirable to ensure comparability across appraisals. One function of national transport models, where they exist, is to help provide this comparability of do-minimum or 'baseline' assumptions across projects and policy proposals. Since the period of interest stretches out across the next 40 years or more, and uncertainty is endemic over such long periods, a scientific approach would recognise a range of possible future scenarios (Hill et al., 2012). Indeed, it is good practice, and increasingly common, for large projects to be tested against a range of future scenarios. These could be presented as sensitivity tests, or assigned probabilities and included in the quantitative risk analysis.

12.3.2 The basis for valuation

The French engineer-economist Jules Dupuit (1844) was the initiator of what we now think of as cost-benefit analysis in the transport sector. He introduced the idea that the 'public utility' of a project can be measured in terms of individuals' *willingness-to-pay* (WTP) for the services provided. He identified *consumer surplus* as the difference between the maximum amount an individual would be willing to pay and the amount they would actually be asked to pay; he defined the overall public utility of a project as the sum of the individual consumer surpluses created, net of the costs of the project to government and business (today we would refer to the *social net present value* (NPV) instead of the 'public utility'); and he showed how pricing can impact on the demand for the project, revenues, costs and the total public utility.

In modern transport appraisal, the analysis has been deepened and extended in several important ways, but retains key elements from Dupuit. Moreover, Dupuit's analysis shows how both the financial motives of a private-sector provider and the public motives of a government or transport authority can – and should – be dealt with separately but consistently in an appraisal. We will begin by defining the source of value in a transport appraisal, and will generalise to a discussion of all the main elements of a typical appraisal in the transport sector.

Willingness-to-pay

Underpinning all economic appraisal is the idea that the fundamental source of value is individuals' own assessments of the value of the intervention, expressed by their willingness-to-pay for the services it provides. In Dupuit's words:

> The purchaser never pays more for the product than the value he places on its utility... political economy has to take as the measure of the utility of an object the maximum sacrifice which each consumer would be willing to make in order to acquire the object.
>
> *(Dupuit, 1844, p. 262)*

In this respect economic appraisal is very 'decentralised': what matters to people, matters in appraisal. People's preferences will be studied and taken into account, and the ways in which this is done form a central part of appraisal methodology.

Figure 12.4 shows the market demand for a generic service, expressed as a set of demands for individual units, each unit represented by a bar whose height equals the willingness-to-pay for

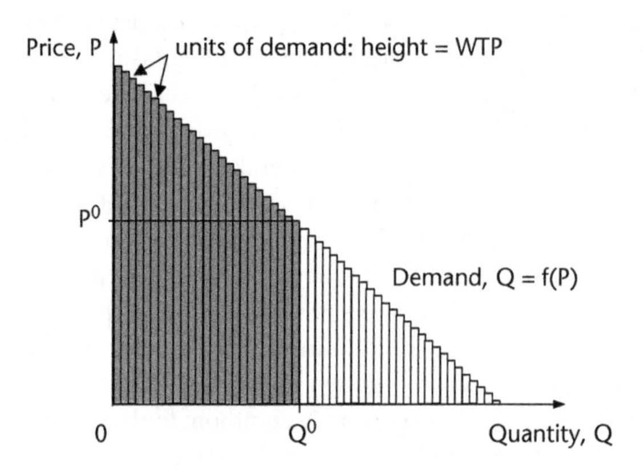

Figure 12.4 Market demand and WTP

that unit, placed in descending order. If the market price is set at P^0 (using the standard notation for the price in the do-minimum scenario), then all those units to the left of Q^0 will be bought, since WTP > price, whilst the units to the right of Q^0 will not be bought, since WTP < price.

Generalised user cost

Transport is different from other services in that users are required to input their time as well as their money to undertake a trip (Becker, 1965). This gives rise to the concept of *generalised user cost* or simply *generalised cost* (GC) which is a composite cost measure including 'time costs', money costs and any other sources of disutility from travel. The composition of generalised cost can therefore differ between passenger transport and freight – e.g. passengers may experience discomfort as part of the disutility of travel, whilst freight is not affected by comfort. Also the party paying the costs may differ between different trip purposes – typically:

- freight and business travel – the shipper or employer pays;
- commuting or other non-business travel (including leisure, visiting friends and relatives, shopping or personal business) – the individual travelling usually pays.

As well as introducing GC, it is important to note that transport is a network service. The market is spatially differentiated, and this is usually addressed by breaking the study area into zones, and denoting travel from zone i to zone j using the subscript ij. We also add the subscript m to indicate the mode of transport being used (m is usually the 'main mode', which may be supplemented by various access modes to/from the origin and final destination). In practice, there is likely to be further disaggregation, with the data being separated by trip purpose, time of day, day of week and potentially more detailed vehicle types, although we will abstract from that for clarity here. Putting the above together, we obtain:

$$GC_{ijm} = t_{ijm}v_{t,m} + c_{ijm} + w_{ijm} \tag{12.1}$$

where $v_{t,m}$ is the value of travel time corresponding to mode m; t_{ijm} is the travel time between i and j by mode m; c_{ijm} are the money costs of travel between i and j by mode m; w_{ijm} represents any other disutility of travel between i and j by mode m (discomfort, for example), expressed in money units.

Returning to the market demand function, we can now express this in a suitable way for transport appraisal, using GC_{ijm} (other subscripts suppressed) instead of the plain money price. We also add a supply function, S_{ijm}, which we show as upward-sloping due to the congestibility of the transport network – additional traffic tends to increase generalised user cost.[2] Market equilibrium is found where the marginal WTP for a trip is equal to the marginal cost of supplying it, *both expressed in units of generalised cost* (Figure 12.5).

Consumer surplus and user benefit measurement

Figure 12.5 also allows us to define the consumer surplus, CS^0. This is the excess of the consumers' WTP (in GC units) over the equilibrium GC, across all units demanded, T^0. The result is a net measure of the value offered by the service, at the market level.

It is now possible to measure the impact of the intervention on the users. Figure 12.6 shows a reduction in the generalised costs of travel due to an intervention – for example, a faster service, lower fares, better vehicle efficiency, a more direct route, reduced crowding, greater comfort,

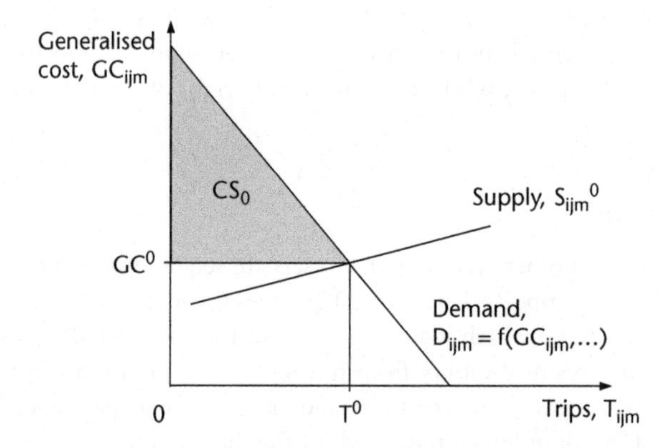

Figure 12.5 Equilibrium and consumer surplus in a transport market, *ijm*

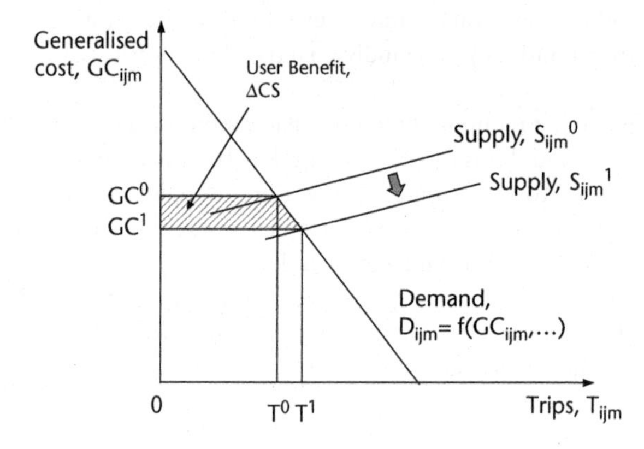

Figure 12.6 User benefit due to a transport improvement in market *ijm*

etc. The user benefit is measured by the shaded area ΔCS, which is given by the integral of the demand function with respect to GC, between the do-minimum and do-something equilibria:

$$\Delta CS_{ijm} = \int_{GC_{ijm}{}^{0}}^{GC_{ijm}{}^{1}} D_{ijm}\, dGC_{ijm}. \tag{12.2}$$

In the vast majority of transport appraisals, the demand function between GC^0 and GC^1 cannot be readily integrated, and instead the assumption is made that a simple linear approximation will give sufficient accuracy. The data points usually available from the transport model are ($T^0{}_{ijm}$, $GC^0{}_{ijm}$) and ($T^1{}_{ijm}$, $GC^1{}_{ijm}$) for all *ijm* (known as the trip and cost matrices), and the formula to estimate the user benefits based on the simplified, trapezium-shaped shaded area is known as the *rule-of-a half*:

$$\Delta CS_{ijm} \approx 0.5\left(GC_{ijm}^{0} - GC_{ijm}^{1}\right)\left(T_{ijm}^{0} + T_{ijm}^{1}\right). \tag{12.3}$$

Nellthorp and Hyman (2001) found that this assumption is reasonable for small changes in *GC* and *T*, but as the size of the change increases towards +/-33 percent, it becomes necessary to estimate between one and three additional points on the demand function between GC^0 and

GC^1 and interpolate, in order to obtain results accurate to +/−10 percent in user benefits. De Jong et al. (2005) go further and explore the use of the logsum measure of user benefits, based on the underlying discrete choice models in the Dutch National Model System. They conclude that where feasible, this approach gives a more accurate estimate of the user benefits, and is able to handle new modes (in the do-something) and new trip generators or attractors – both of which require additional steps under the rule-of-a-half approach (see Nellthorp and Hyman, 2001).

Finally, it is worth noting that when demand (not only supply) functions shift, for example when a competing mode is improved, the rule-of-a-half can still be used, subject to an assumption that the income elasticities of demand in the different markets are equal, and there is a judgement that divergences from this are not big enough to seriously bias the results (Jones, 1977, p. 99). This makes it possible to conduct multimodal appraisals in complex cases where more than one mode is improved and where modes interact.

Economic versus financial appraisal

Having discussed the role played by WTP in determining the market equilibrium and the measure of user benefits in a 'matrix-based appraisal', we can now take a wider view of the sources of value in economic and financial appraisal.

Economic appraisal is based in welfare economics, which is concerned with the impact on people's welfare, or wellbeing. Conceptually, individuals can be described as having a utility function, U_k, in which the arguments are anything that affects individual k's welfare.[3] It is an important limitation, however, that there is no commonly agreed means to directly measure utility.[4] Instead, WTP is used as a yardstick to measure people's strength of preference for changes in the transport system, which gives a *proxy* for the change in U_k. Yet willingness-to-pay is driven not only by individuals' strength of preference but by their ability to pay (or, conversely, by their *marginal utility of money*).

Research in welfare economics indicates that as income increases, the marginal utility of money falls (e.g. Layard et al., 2008). This is not surprising, since at low income levels there are basic needs still to be met, whereas at high income levels the individual already has a high material standard of living and the scope for gains in wellbeing from additional personal spending may be small. The research evidence points towards a constant value of around −1.0 in advanced economies,[5] for the *elasticity of marginal utility with respect to income*, that is:

$$\eta = \frac{dU}{U} / \frac{dm}{m} = -1. \tag{12.4}$$

This implies that the value in terms of utility from a change in money income varies according to the person's starting income level, as in Table 12.2. Here, $\overline{m}$ is the mean income in the society.

Table 12.2 Weights reflecting the marginal utility of income at different income levels

	Weights	
	elasticity, η= −1.0	*elasticity, η= −2.0*
$0.25\overline{m}$	4	16
$0.5\overline{m}$	2	4
$\overline{m}$	1	1
$2\overline{m}$	0.5	0.25
$4\overline{m}$	0.25	0.0625

The values in the table show the relative value of an additional unit of income – or measured WTP – at a particular income level, compared with its value at the mean income level. These are often referred to as 'distributional weights' in appraisal (e.g. HM Treasury, 2011) – they are the weights that would need to be applied to 'raw' WTP estimates of value to restore them to welfare-based estimates in an economic appraisal.

To apply these weights would require us to be able to identify the 'final incidence' of all the benefits in transport appraisal, in order to know the incomes of the beneficiaries. Unfortunately that is hampered by:

(1) the beneficiaries of freight and business user benefits being spread widely across the economy – the final consumers of the products and services transported being far removed from the analysis in a typical transport model;
(2) for other categories of benefits – time savings to households, accident reduction, reductions in noise and air pollution – the models used to analyse projects and policies tend not to identify individuals by their income group, although there are exceptions.

An alternative approach, which is widely used across most countries with transport appraisal methods, is to adopt *standard appraisal values* which are appropriate for the mean income level in the country concerned. Thus the non-working values of time, safety values and so on used in appraisal (see Section 12.4) do not vary with the income of the beneficiary (or the victim or sufferer). A single standard value is used, which avoids biasing investment towards regions and groups with higher money incomes – though also tends to obscure any subtle differences in welfare impact on different groups in the process.

By contrast, *financial appraisal* is focused entirely on the financial flows:

- costs – including planning, construction, operation, maintenance and renewal costs; and
- revenues – including fares, toll receipts, franchise payments, and revenues from taxes on vehicle ownership and use, and on property or business premises where these are affected by transport interventions – for example, the business rate supplement that has been used to help fund the Crossrail project (Table 12.3).

As Figure 12.7 illustrates, there is no equality between (or unique relationship between) the impact of an intervention on revenues and its impact in terms of user benefits. Intuitively this is not surprising, since the user benefits are based on a surplus over and above the amount paid.

Furthermore, the benefits *and* the revenues are dependent upon the pricing policy adopted. In the example in Table 12.4, two different perspectives on the same bridge project are given: a public authority with 'welfare-maximising' objectives and an unregulated private sector owner with commercial objectives. The optimal pricing policy depends upon the objectives driving the project, and the outcomes in terms of user benefits and revenues are correspondingly different. A toll of zero maximises welfare[6] but requires taxpayers or other sources to fund the project; a toll of $1 maximises welfare subject to a constraint that users cover the costs of the bridge; and a toll of $7 maximises revenue and profitability for a purely commercial supplier. Results such as Table 12.4 illustrate the case for publicly regulated infrastructure provision – for example, using a concession agreement[7] to combine private construction and operation, with public planning and procurement.

The above example leads us finally to a statement of the overall goal in economic appraisal, which is to maximise the gain in 'social surplus', not simply consumer surplus.

Table 12.3 Financial package to cover the capital costs of Crossrail, £billions

Funding source	*Financial contribution (£bn)*
Transport for London	
Direct contribution	1.9
Sale of land and property	0.5
Business contributions	
Business rate supplement @ 2.5%	4.1
Developer contributions	0.3
Community infrastructure levy	0.3
City of London Corporation	0.25
Heathrow Airport Limited	0.23
London businesses (various)	0.1
Network Rail funded works	2.3
Department for Transport grant contribution	4.8
Total	14.8

Source: National Audit Office (2014)

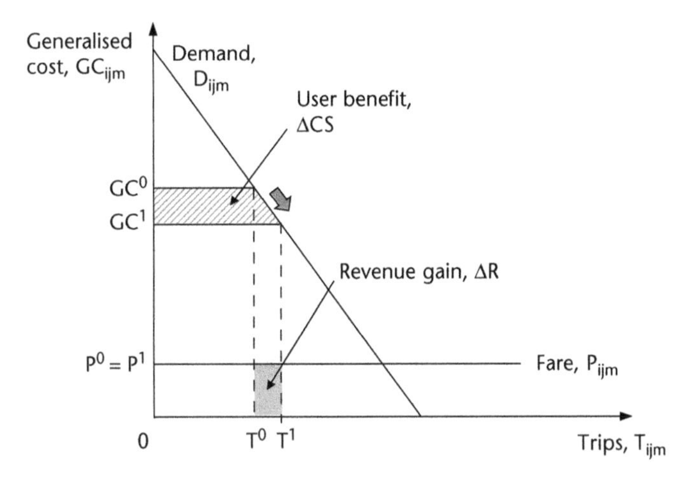

Figure 12.7 Revenue impact versus user benefit

$$Net\ Social\ Benefit, NSB = \Delta Social\ Surplus = \Delta CS + \Delta PS + \Delta GS + \Delta Externalities. \quad (12.5)$$

The justification for including *producer surplus, ΔPS,* which is given by the change in revenue net of the change in costs, is that producers' profits are distributed through various channels, e.g.dividends feeding into pension funds, not simply lost to the population.[8] *Government surplus* is clearly relevant since it can either be used to fund public services or returned to the population through lower tax rates. Lastly, defining the economic appraisal in welfare terms means that 'a benefit is defined as anything that increases human well-being' (Pearce and Hett, 1999). Similarly, early cost-benefit studies tended to cite 'comprehensiveness' as a guiding principle – the range of impacts to be quantified and valued should include any that impact on welfare. *Externalities* are impacts for which

Table 12.4 User benefits and revenues from a bridge, under different toll regimes

Toll, $	*Crossings per annum*	*Revenue per annum, $*	*User benefits per annum, $*	*Annualised costs of provision, $*	*Welfare change, $*
14	0	0	0	925,000	–925,000
13	71,429	928,571	35,714	925,000	39,286
12	142,857	1,714,286	142,857	925,000	932,143
11	214,286	2,357,143	321,429	925,000	1,753,571
10	285,714	2,857,143	571,429	925,000	2,503,571
9	357,143	3,214,286	892,857	925,000	3,182,143
8	428,571	3,428,571	1,285,714	925,000	3,789,286
7	500,000	3,500,000	1,750,000	925,000	4,325,000
6	571,429	3,428,571	2,285,714	925,000	4,789,286
5	642,857	3,214,286	2,892,857	925,000	5,182,143
4	714,286	2,857,143	3,571,429	925,000	5,503,571
3	785,714	2,357,143	4,321,429	925,000	5,753,571
2	857,143	1,714,286	5,142,857	925,000	5,932,143
1	928,571	928,571	6,035,714	925,000	6,039,286
0	1,000,000	0	7,000,000	925,000	6,075,000

Note: the analysis, although not the numbers, follow Dupuit's simple bridge example (1849)

no money compensation is paid – they usually occur where markets are absent, for example, there is no market for clean air, yet pollution by road vehicles leads to measurable damage to human health and wellbeing. This, along with many other externalities, are included in transport appraisal using valuation techniques that will be discussed in Section 12.4.

To conclude this section, it is worth reflecting that in both economic appraisal and financial appraisal, money is used as the *numeraire*. Money is used worldwide as the standard numeraire good, or measure of value, and in this sense it is natural to do so in appraisal as well. Nevertheless, its meaning is quite different in each type of appraisal:

- in economic appraisal it is used as a proxy for welfare, and is based on WTP adjusted (using distributional weights or by applying standard values) to take account of differences in the marginal utility of money across people;
- in financial appraisal it is used purely to capture the financial flows involved in the project – costs and revenues.

12.3.3 Treatment of the future

One important extension of the principle that 'individual preferences count' is the treatment of the future in transport appraisal. Appraisals typically cover the costs and benefits over several decades, reflecting the long life expectancy of some of the assets created and the long stream of impacts predicted by forecasting models. So the question arises, how should these future costs and benefits be valued?

First of all, we define 'individual preferences' to include individuals' preferences about their future welfare as well as the present day and we extend the scope to include individuals not yet born who may be impacted by the project or policy. Thus the focus of interest is not only on net social benefit for one year (as in the simplified example above), but a stream of net social benefits

Table 12.5 Expected asset lives for infrastructure components

Asset type	*Mode*			
	Roads	*Railways*	*Airports*	*Sea Ports*
Earthworks/drainage	100	100	100	Up to 50
Pavement	20 to 25		10 to 15	
Road surface	10		10 to 15	
Track		14 to 40		
Bridges/tunnels	Up to 100	Up to 100	Up to 100	
Signalling		10 to 50		
Electrification		33		
Telecomms		7 to 40		
Buildings	50	30 to 40	Up to 60	Up to 50
Equipment	12		4 to 20	2 to 30

Source: Tweddle et al. (2003)

Table 12.6 Appraisal periods and discount rates – international comparisons

Country	*Appraisal period*	*Discount rate*
UK	60 years (default for infrastructure)	3.5% (3.0% after first 30 years)
Germany	Varies	3%
Netherlands	100 years/infinite	2.5% (plus 3% risk premium)
Sweden	40–60 years	3.5% (changed from 4% recently)
USA	Varies, typically 25–30 years	7% (with sensitivity test for 3%)
Australia (NSW)	Varies (e.g. 30 years for roads; 50 for rail tracks and tunnels; 35 for rail rolling stock; 15 for buses)	7% (with sensitivity tests for 4% and 10%)
New Zealand	30 years max. for roads	8%

Source: Mackie and Worsley (2013)

running from the first year in which the project creates an impact to the last. This then raises the question, what period does the appraisal need to cover?

A principle widely cited in the literature is that the appraisal should cover the useful life of the longest-lived assets created (e.g. World Bank, 2005). This will ensure that for as long as the project is expected to deliver useful services, these will be valued. In fact transport projects – particularly infrastructure projects – can create assets with extremely long lives, for example earthworks and structures such as bridges and tunnels may have a design life of 100 years or more (Table 12.5), even if the vehicles and equipment (such as track and signalling) required to use them have much shorter lives.

Governments and transport authorities usually take a pragmatic stance on the issue of the *appraisal period*. Instead of varying this between every project or policy, some countries adopt default or standard appraisal periods, particularly for infrastructure (see Table 12.6). Variations are then made when:

(1) the life of the longest-lived asset is significantly shorter than the standard appraisal period, for example, a project to introduce new bus vehicles may assume a 15-year asset life;

(2) there is expected to be some *residual value* left in the assets at the end of the standard appraisal period – in which case this value is estimated and typically reported as a separated item within the appraisal. The calculation of residual value follows essentially the same method, but starting from the final year of the standard appraisal period.

How, then, are these future costs and benefits valued? The starting point is the valuation evidence (see Section 12.4), which indicates that the unit values of some items within the appraisal are increasing or decreasing over time, for example values of travel time savings appear to be growing approximately in line with real GDP per capita[9] (Abrantes and Wardman, 2011). These trends are reflected in the streams of future benefits and costs.

The additional step that is taken is to apply a *discount rate* to future costs and benefits. There are two different theoretical bases that can be used to set the discount rate in economic appraisal, and the first of these is the source of the lower rates seen in international practice (Table 12.6, upper rows). The *social time preference rate* is the rate at which people are willing to trade current benefits for future benefits in a public decision-making context. It is expressed as a discount rate, r, which is applied in the following way:

$$\text{Present Value, } PV = B_y \times DF_y = \frac{B_y}{(1+r)^y} \tag{12.6}$$

where the Present Value is the discounted value of a future benefit, B_y, received in year y, which is indexed to a *base year for discounting*. E.g. if the base year for discounting is 2015, and the benefit is received in 2018, then y=3; the effect of the discount rate on B_y is to multiply it by a Discount Factor, DF_y, for year y. E.g. if the discount rate is 3 percent, the Discount Factor for year 2015 would be 1/ (1.03^3) = 0.915.

The content of the social time preference rate (STPR) is usually defined as follows:

$$r = STPR = \mu g + \rho. \tag{12.7}$$

In this formula, due originally to Ramsey (1928), the term μg relates to the utility obtained from consumption at different points in time: g is the growth rate in real consumption over time due to rising productivity (say, 2 percent per annum); whilst μ is the elasticity of the marginal utility of consumption with respect to consumption – in other words the rate at which rising consumption feeds through into increasing real living standards and welfare. Estimates of μ vary, but 1 is the value adopted, for example, in the UK (HM Treasury, 2011), giving μg = 2 percent per annum. The rationale here is that if people expect rising living standards – for themselves and others – in the future, then they would prefer to trade some of their future consumption for consumption now, and this is a basis for weighting down future net benefits in the appraisal.

The term ρ contains an item called 'pure time preference', which is evident in *individual time preference* and may relate to a fundamental myopia or short-sightedness in people's preferences. These factors are more difficult to justify as part of a *social time preference rate*, and some authors argue this should be set to zero. ρ can also contain an allowance for catastrophic risk – the risk that nobody may be here to appreciate the benefits after a catastrophic event, which devalues benefits further into the future. In the UK, for example, ρ=1.5 percent, giving a total STPR of 3.5 percent.

The alternative basis for the discount rate is an *opportunity cost rate*, reflecting the return that could have been obtained on other investments. The US rate of 7 percent is a good example, and is designed to approximate 'the marginal pretax rate of return on an average investment in the private sector in recent years' (Nordhaus, 2013, p. 188). As Table 12.6 shows, this is a typical opportunity-cost-based rate for economic appraisal. In practice, most finance ministries set a rate

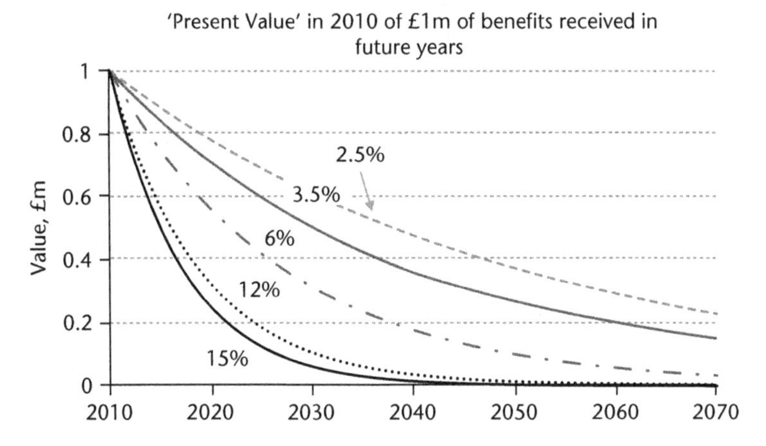

Figure 12.8 Effect of discounting on future benefit (and cost) streams

centrally, to be applied to most or all public projects, which aids comparability across transport and other sectors.

The impact of discounting on the economic case for projects and policies is substantial. Figure 12.8 shows the impact of various discount rates on future benefits (or costs). For investment projects, where the costs are mostly in the short term, and the benefits arise over the long term, the impact is clearly negative. The higher the discount rate the greater the impact, and this can have implications for the investment portfolio – e.g. the World Bank's 12 percent rate gives any benefits beyond a 30-year horizon very little weight indeed, which weakens the case for investments with a very long asset life – urban metros, for example. There is an argument that these higher rates are necessary to reflect risk in particular contexts, however the prevailing view is that wherever possible, risk and discounting should be separated, with risk treated explicitly using a *quantitative risk analysis*.

Finally, note that discounting is applied in financial appraisal as well as economic appraisal: in this case, the discount rates are usually on a financial, private-sector opportunity cost-type basis, such as the expected rate of return on capital in the sector concerned. This may reflect sector-specific risks – e.g. Peña-Torres and Pearson (2000, p. 122) found higher rates, in the region 10–15 percent, in the nuclear industry. Transport sector rates would typically be lower than this; and under recent economic conditions rates in Europe have been as low as 4–7 percent real (6–9 percent nominal).

12.3.4 Aggregation across people and networks

The last topic to cover within the basic principles is the approach to aggregation. This is a topic with a large hinterland in the literature, however it can be crystallised by the practical question: How should the appraisal results be structured and reported, so that they inform the questions that matter in decision making? Obviously this implies looking at the motivations of the public decision maker.

Textbook welfare economics begins with the concept of Pareto efficiency as a goal of public policy (for example see Varian, 2014). A Pareto-efficient allocation of resources is one where no further 'Pareto improvements' are possible – that is, it is not possible to make someone better off without also making someone else worse off. In fact, this turns out to be the usual situation in transport policy: for example, infrastructure projects usually lead to the displacement and disruption of homes and businesses; and measures to improve the urban environment for active travel tend to slow down motorised traffic. Compensation measures exist, but are difficult to target perfectly. The criterion of a *Pareto improvement*, which requires all individuals to gain or be indifferent to the intervention, is therefore often seen as being beyond practical reach. Transport appraisal does, however, take forward important principles from this:

- firstly, it is concerned with the gains to individuals from the intervention – it treats the gains to all individuals equally and provides an aggregate measure *in welfare terms* of the net benefit from the intervention;
- secondly, it is concerned with distribution[10] – it investigates and reports the impacts on specific groups (e.g. DfT, 2015a), and where losses are expected – as in the case of local communities and infrastructure construction – procedures exist to mitigate, compensate or prevent the loss (e.g. Pearce, 1999; HS2, 2016). Some of these procedures are part of the project development process and should activate before the project reaches a full appraisal. In addition to these safeguards, there is a case that much more could be done to focus transport policy on improving the transport conditions faced by socially excluded and vulnerable people, and to reflect this in the analysis done around projects and policies – see e.g. Lucas et al. (2016) for some of the latest thinking on these issues.

To address the way aggregation is done in cost-benefit analysis (CBA) generally, and in central government appraisals and evaluations, we can introduce the *Kaldor-Hicks criterion* (Kaldor, 1939; Hicks, 1939; HM Treasury, 2011). This uses the device of 'hypothetical compensation': if losses could be offset against the benefits of the project, whilst leaving a net gain overall, the project is said to be an improvement on the Kaldor-Hicks criterion. In practice, this gives an aggregate measure of the welfare change due to the intervention:

$$B_y = \sum_{k=0}^{K} B_{k,y} \tag{12.8}$$

where B_y, the social benefit in year y, is given by the sum of the individual benefits in year y, across all individuals k. All benefits are in the money numeraire (Section 12.3.2).

Putting together (12.5), (12.6) and (12.8), we have a formula for the aggregate welfare calculation in absolute terms, the NPV created by the intervention:

$$NPV = \sum_{y=0}^{Y} \left\{ \left[\left(\sum_{k=0}^{K} \Delta CS_{k,y} + \Delta Ext_{k,y} \right) + \Delta PS_y + \Delta GS_y \right] / \left[(1+r)^y \right] \right\}. \tag{12.9}$$

A project or policy with a positive NPV is one which creates a welfare improvement, seen from the highest aggregate level. It may not do so, of course, when seen from the level of one specific group or individual in society. Since the 1990s at least,[11] economic appraisal has not been strictly tied to the Kaldor-Hicks criterion. It has been made clear multiple times by governments (e.g. DfT, 2013a) and research studies (e.g. Annema et al., 2017; Odeck, 2010; Nellthorp and Mackie, 2000; Nilsson, 1991) that decisions are not based on NPV alone. The key factors in decision making which can be seen reflected in today's appraisal frameworks include:

- distributional analysis – gains and losses by group;
- financial and governance requirements for a successful intervention;

- financial appraisals for the main stakeholders and for the public accounts;
- demonstration of fit with wider policy;
- project management requirements, such as evidence of commitment, funding and management processes in place.

The inclusion of these additional factors in decision making means that in almost every country reviewed in recent comparative studies (Mackie and Worsley, 2013; Bickel et al., 2006), appraisal is undertaken using a wider framework comprising a CBA plus additional information. To give one example, the '5-Case Business Case' (DfT, 2013b) comprises: an economic case (including CBA); a strategic case; a financial case; a commercial case; and a management case. The economic case extends beyond the NPV, including disaggregated economic results and a social and distributional analysis.

The aggregate welfare calculation can also be done in relative terms, which turns out to be extremely useful in allocating a limited budget. The *BCR* is a measure of the incremental benefits of the intervention as a proportion of the incremental costs – applying discounting as in the NPV:

$$BCR = \frac{\sum_{y=0}^{Y}\{B_y/[(1+r)^y]\}}{\sum_{y=0}^{Y}\{C_y/[(1+r)^y]\}}. \tag{12.10}$$

In general, choosing interventions with the highest BCR among the options identified should ensure that the greatest possible value-for-money is obtained from the finite resources available, and should ensure the greatest total NPV from a given total resource.[12] BCR then becomes an indicator that governments can monitor and potentially compare with other sectors (Table 12.7).

An important caveat is that the definition of *C*, the costs of the intervention, is critical in making the BCR useful in decision making. Many definitions are possible, e.g.:

- all costs to all groups;
- all costs to an organisation, e.g. all costs to government, or all costs to the promoter;
- capital costs only, to one organisation – useful if the organisation's capital budget is constrained and the purpose of appraisal is to assemble the best investment programme within a given budget.

In practice, the definition of the BCR varies between and even within countries. In order to compare interventions, a consistent definition is needed, and efforts have been made recently to standardise the BCR definition within the UK. Table 12.8 shows the effect of two alternative

Table 12.7 Value for money (VfM) of transport capital spending

Year	*Percentage of spend by category*			
	BCR < 1.5	*BCR 1.5–1.9 Medium VfM*	*BCR 2.0–3.9 High VfM*	*BCR ≥ 4.0 Very High VfM*
2014	3	7	41	48
2013	0	6	80	14
2012	0	0	42	58
2011	0	0	63	37

Source: DfT (2015c)

Table 12.8 Alternative BCR formulations and their effect

Impact	*Project*		
	A	*B*	*C*
Net user benefits	120	400	400
Infrastructure cost	40	40	40
Indirect tax change	20	20	(40)
NPV	100	380	320
BCR(1)	3.5	10.5	9
BCR(2)	6	20	5

Source: DfT (2009)

definitions on the value of the BCR that were considered for use (DfT, 2009). Both BCR(1) and BCR(2) are based on all costs to the public-sector transport budget, however BCR(1) includes the indirect tax change effect (additional fuel tax, VAT and so on) in the benefits, whilst BCR(2) defines it as a negative cost, which would be justified if it fed into the transport budget, relieving the budget constraint. The difference in BCRs is potentially large. BCR(1) was chosen as the official formulation; a consequence is that public transport interventions, which tend to reduce indirect tax revenue, are relatively favoured.

Lastly, there is a need to aggregate across networks, and this raises some interesting economic issues. Having estimated user benefits at the zone-pair (or link) level (12.3), when aggregating up it is important to check for interactions within the transport network. For example, improvement of one link can create demand shifts between links or modes of transport; these in turn can create congestion/decongestion effects and trigger economies/diseconomies of scale, scope and density in transport networks. For these reasons, it is usual to run a transport network model – often a multimodal one – to generate the trip (T_{ijm}) and cost (GC_{ijm}) data needed to conduct an appraisal. There are also positive externalities from increasing connectedness which play into the network-wide demand outcomes, and appear through agglomeration effects – now increasingly being studied in transport and economy modelling (Laird et al., 2005; Venables et al., 2014).

12.4 Valuation

The topic of valuation deserves special attention: values have a strong influence over the appraisal results for different types of intervention; and this is a topic where research evidence is directly useful in public choice. The basic rationale for valuation was introduced in Section 12.3.2. Here it is outlined how this is implemented using different forms of data, and a brief summary of the evidence base is given, highlighting recent developments.

12.4.1 Measuring value

The methods used to derive the values used in transport appraisal can be grouped under three broad headings:

(1) *Market prices*. When markets are complete and perfectly competitive, market prices give a measure of both the marginal willingness-to-pay and the marginal social cost of producing a service, which leads to an efficient allocation of resources. Indeed, the first fundamental theorem of welfare economics states that any equilibrium in perfectly competitive markets

will be Pareto efficient. For example, elements of construction costs and vehicle-related costs (such as construction materials, labour, vehicles and vehicle parts – tyres, etc.) are usually treated as admissible into appraisal with relatively little adjustment, since they are derived from markets which are seen as highly competitive and well functioning.

(2) *Implicit or surrogate markets*. Sometimes the impacts of transport interventions are not in the form of traded services or commodities. A prime example is travel time reductions: travel time is a service quality attribute which lacks its own specific market. In order to value the benefits, one approach is to use real market data (*revealed preference* (RP) data) on travel choices to infer the marginal value of travel time. In the case of externalities such as noise, the housing market is used as a surrogate market. House prices are observed to vary with noise and other externalities from transport, and *hedonic pricing* methods are used to extract the marginal WTP for noise reduction (see Section 12.4.3).

(3) *Choice experiments*. Where markets give too little information, it is necessary to rely on hypothetical choice experiments to obtain marginal values. There is extensive use of *stated preference* (SP) and the *contingent valuation method* which seek to explore what individuals' WTP *would be*. A great advantage of choice experiments is that they allow an investigation of parts of the demand function which are not revealed by current or past experience, e.g. what would be the demand for a greatly improved service, or a redesigned street? Choice experiments can also provide a second source of value alongside RP data, so that appraisal values can be based on a synthesis, taking into account the potential biases in each, e.g. in valuing time savings or transport noise (see Arup et al., 2015; Nellthorp et al., 2007).

Alongside these valuation methods is a decision which each authority must make, about the *unit of account* for its economic appraisals. As Sugden (1999) pointed out, it does not matter which of these is chosen, as long as it is consistently applied across all interventions that are going to be compared. The difference in the NPV between the two units of account is in the region of 15–20 percent (higher in 'market prices'). Meanwhile there should be no impact on the BCR because all items of both costs and benefits are affected – again, provided the principles are applied consistently:

- *Market prices unit of account*. All costs and benefits are valued from the final consumer's perspective, which includes indirect taxes – VAT, etc.
- *Factor cost unit of account*. All costs and benefits are valued from a producer's perspective, which excludes indirect taxes.

Sweden, the US and the UK are three countries that use market prices-based values in transport appraisal, whilst most other countries and international institutions use factor cost (Mackie and Worsley, 2013).

12.4.2 Travel time

One of the main motivations for transport policy is to improve accessibility, and a major part (although not the whole) of this is the time taken to travel. Investments in high-speed rail are examples of the continued appeal of faster travel between major centres, even in advanced economies with an existing, dense transport network. For example, approximately 72 percent of the benefits of the planned HS2 line from London to the north of England are from time savings (DfT, 2014b) and a similar proportion was found in a proposed highway investment programme (Eddington, 2006). For highways, decongestion through increased capacity can be a source of time savings, although congestion may return in the long run with traffic growth.

Another aspect of accessibility is the disutility of time spent travelling, not simply the amount of time spent. Travel in crowded conditions, time spent waiting at bus stops and in insecure station environments, for example, are all deterrents to mobility. Conversely, on-board WiFi, real-time information and segregated cycle paths all help to reduce the disutility (or generalised cost) of travel by the respective modes. For example, in the case of HS2, 11 percent of the benefits come from reduced crowding on rail services (DfT, 2014b); other projects may be entirely focused on crowding reduction – e.g. investments in additional train carriages.

In order to estimate the reduction in generalised cost due to improvements in any of these factors, we need a set of *values of travel time savings*, $v_{t,m}$ in (12.1). Underpinning these values area theoretical model, data, analysis and an interpretation of the results. The theoretical model[13] differs between *working time* (or time 'on employer's business') and *non-working time*, which includes commuting to/from work and the full range of other non-work trip purposes (e.g. leisure, visiting friends and relatives). For *non-working time*, the individual's willingness-to-pay for reductions in travel time is understood as comprising two elements, their 'resource value of time' which reflects the overall time pressure on the individual, ρ/λ, and their marginal utility of time spent travelling, dU/dt:

$$v_{t,m} = \frac{\psi_{t,m}}{\lambda} = \frac{\rho}{\lambda} + \frac{dU/dt}{\lambda}. \tag{12.11}$$

In each term, the λ on the bottom is the marginal utility of money, introduced in Section 12.3.2. Typically, a higher-income individual would have a lower λ and a higher WTP, all else being equal. In appraisal, the equity implications of this are addressed by using a standard value of non-working time across all income groups, in most countries. The term dU/dt allows for a different marginal utility of time spent in different conditions. Table 12.9 illustrates the variation in time values arising.

The valuation of *working, or business travel time* is undergoing a reassessment: the traditional *cost saving approach* (CSA) is being questioned in the light of increased use of mobile devices while

Table 12.9 Values of non-working time in different conditions – examples

	Commuting, £/hour		*Other non-work travel, £/hour*	
Standard value	9.95		4.54	
Percentage of working time value	*52%*		*24%*	
Multipliers:				
Access time to public transport stop	2.0		2.0	
Waiting or interchange time	2.0		2.0	
Late time	2.4–3.0		2.4–3.0	
Crowding*:	Seated	Standing	Seated	Standing
75% load factor	0.95		1.14	
100% load factor	1.05	1.62	1.26	1.94
150% load factor	1.27	1.99	1.53	2.39
200% load factor	1.55	2.44	1.86	2.93

Notes: standard value applies to 'in-vehicle time' not in crowded or congested conditions, and is also used for walking and cycling time as the main mode; late time is delay at the public transport stop; values are at 2010 prices and values
Source: appraisal guidance, UK (DfT, 2016) and * Wardman and Whelan (2011)

travelling (Lyons and Urry, 2005; Fickling et al., 2009; Wardman and Lyons, 2016). The CSA posited that working time savings could be valued according to the saving to the employer from one less unit of labour employed, in other words the wage rate plus overheads. This assumed that either:

- the amount of labour employed could be reduced in line with any time savings, saving labour costs; or
- travel time saved could be fully converted to productive work time, increasing output; or
- some combination of the two.

The *Hensher approach* (Hensher, 1977; Fowkes et al., 1986) is a more sophisticated theoretical starting point. It recognises not only the saving to the employer as in the CSA, but also:

- the possibility that some travel time is used productively for work (a proportion p of the time saved), and that the productivity of this time can differ from that in the workplace (by a factor q);
- the employee's valuation of transferring time from travel to work (V_W), or from travel to leisure (V_L), bearing in mind the marginal utility of time spent in each activity x (dU/dt_x); and
- there may be a reduction in fatigue leading to increased marginal output, MPF

$$v_t = MPL(1 - r - pq) + V_W(1 - r) + V_L r + MPF \tag{12.12}$$

where MPL is the marginal product of labour, assumed equal to labour costs (wages+overheads) in a competitive equilibrium; and a proportion r of the time saved is reused as leisure rather than work.

Arup et al. (2015) have conducted new research, using both RP and SP data, which reveals a great deal of detail about the Hensher parameters. They appear to be context dependent, e.g. they vary between the outward and return leg, between modes, by trip duration and by seniority of employee. Exemplar parameters are $p \approx 0.4$, $q \approx 0.9$ and $r \approx 0.6$, but there are many instances where the parameters differ widely from this. Estimating MPF has so far proved difficult, and V_W is sometimes assumed to be zero. In general, the complexity of implementing the Hensher approach has tended to limit its applications to date: Wardman et al. (2015) found a total of 11 previous studies, across Australia, the Netherlands, New Zealand, Norway, Sweden, Switzerland and the UK.

A third, theoretically simpler approach to valuing working time is to directly investigate employers' *WTP* for travel time savings using data on their actual choices (RP) or questions about their hypothetical choices (SP). In fact, the evidence is more often taken from the travelling employees themselves, asking them to answer 'according to company guidelines'. The study by Arup et al. (2015) compared WTP results with the Hensher approach and the CSA.

The main outcomes from this recent body of research are:

- There is now plentiful evidence that some proportion of business travel time is used productively, although the proportion varies widely between contexts and between studies (0.05 to 0.65 is an indicative range).
- The Hensher equation (12.12) makes clear that there are many factors which could increase or decrease the value relative to the CSA, not only the productive use of travel time. Empirically the latest evidence suggests the CSA and the Hensher-based values are fairly close, when comparing average values across all modes (the most complete practical version of the Hensher equation produces a value 0.95 times the CSA value, according to Wardman

Table 12.10 Values of working time based on WTP versus the cost saving approach (2010 prices and values)

Mode	*Distance, km*	*CSA, £/hour*	*WTP, £/hour*
Car	0–50	Driver 27.06	10.08
	50–100	Passenger 20.52	16.30
	100+		25.12
Rail	0–50	31.96	10.08
	50–100		16.30
	100+		36.19
Bus	0–50	16.63	10.08
	50–100		16.30

Source: DfT (2015b)

et al., 2015, p. 207). Only for rail and bus does the Hensher-based value fall substantially below the CSA (0.73 and 0.83, respectively).

- The WTP-based values are interesting, as they suggest a value slightly higher than the CSA at long distances (>100km), but significantly below it at shorter distances (Table 12.10). Wardman et al. (2015) conclude that the CSA should now be replaced by the Hensher and WTP approaches, but that research is urgently needed to understand the remaining inconsistencies between these approaches and their empirical results.

Worldwide, the appraisal guidance used by each country includes appraisal values of time with some variant of the categories given above – see Mackie and Worsley (2013) for a recent review. These appraisal values are underpinned by a large number of studies: a meta-analysis found 1,749 valuations of passenger travel time across 226 studies between the years 1960–2008 (Abrantes and Wardman, 2011). Values of freight time are also important, and these are reviewed by de Jong (2008) who finds that SP methods dominate, partly due to commercial sensitivity around actual choices.

A critique of the use of time savings in appraisal by Metz (2008) highlighted evidence that in the long run, daily travel time appears to be remarkably constant at around one hour per person on average, and therefore savings in travel time per trip appear to be used by individuals to enable more travel, with potential implications for sustainability and urban sprawl. Counter to this is the evidence that travel demand is shifting towards more sustainable modes and car use is starting to decline in countries with highly developed transport systems (e.g. Millard-Ball and Schipper, 2011; Goodwin and van Dender, 2013), whilst the global trend is towards urban living (United Nations, 2014). Cities are capable of supporting sustainable mass transit systems, many of which are electrified. When making the case for more and better mass transit, and for better walking and cycling facilities, the values of time and journey quality above are applied to these modes and produce substantial benefits (e.g. see Sections 12.4.4 and 12.5). Meanwhile, the environmental and health consequences of different transport strategies are also counted in the appraisal, and the following sections examine these.

12.4.3 Safety and environmental externalities

The valuation approaches mentioned above can be applied not only to the user benefits but also to the external effects, in particular:

- *safety* – changes in the number of accidents or in the severity of accidents and injuries that occur; and
- *environment* – including the local, regional and global environmental impacts of interventions.

Table 12.11 provides a summary of the methods used and references to key sources of values, focusing on recent international review studies. In some cases, reducing these externalities can be the main focus of the intervention: for example, Elvik (2007, p. 65) found that by switching from the current road safety policy in Norway to a more optimal mix of measures, selected using cost-benefit analysis, it was possible to raise the BCR of the policy as a whole from 1.10 to 1.73. Technology is another important source of safety benefits in transport: e.g. Carsten and Tate (2005) found high BCRs, above 7, for the introduction of intelligent speed adaptation in cars. A key parameter in safety appraisal is the *value of statistical life* (VOSL) which applies to each fatality saved (or added) by the intervention, and in many countries is greater than £1.5 million ($2 million) – the average in the EU is $3.6 million (OECD, 2012). Values for serious and slight injuries are typically in the region of 1/10th and 1/100th of the VOSL, respectively.

Climate change, air pollution and noise are now widely valued in transport appraisals. This is greatly aided by the existence of tools, often spreadsheet-based, that allow the impacts to be

Table 12.11 Valuation of safety and environment – methods and sources

Category	*Impact (and composition)*	*Valuation methods*	*Sources*
Safety	Injuries (fatal, serious, slight)	WTP for risk reduction, using *choice experiments* *Hedonic pricing (HP)* in labour market for occupational risk *Lost output* using wage and life-expectancy data	RA; MW
	Costs to public services and business	*Direct estimates* of costs to health and emergency services, legal and insurance and material damage	
Environment	Climate change	Forecasts of future values in the *EU Emissions Trading Scheme* *Marginal abatement costs* *Shadow price of carbon*	RA; MW; ST
	Air pollution (local and regional) – particulates, sulphur and nitrogen oxides (SO_x, NO_x) and volatile organic compounds (VOCs)	*Impact pathway approach:* emissions-dispersion-exposure-impact modelling Health damage valued using values for *quality-adjusted life years (QALYs)* and *VOSL Abatement costs* where air quality limits would be breached	RA; MW
	Noise	*HP* in the property market *SP* choice experiments	RA; MW; NB

Note: RA=Ricardo-AEA (2014) for European values; MW=Mackie and Worsley (2013) for a sample of international values including Australia (NSW), Germany, the Netherlands, New Zealand, Sweden, the UK (England) and the US; ST=Stern (2006); NB=Nellthorp et al. (2007)

quantified and valued relatively easily given transport model outputs for future years (e.g. vehicle kilometres by vehicle type in different area types; or noise maps showing the number of properties within each contour)(e.g. DfT, 2016). Such tools can be applied, for example, to the evaluation of low-emissions zones or noise barriers. Meanwhile, the relatively small share of environmental benefits (or disbenefits) in the final appraisal of many infrastructure projects tends to hide an important bigger picture: that environmentally damaging options have often been screened out or redesigned earlier in the project cycle (e.g. see Nellthorp, 2010).

Other environmental impacts are not widely valued using these economic techniques. For example, landscape, biodiversity and heritage impacts tend not to be included in CBA despite the existence of research studies, e.g. Maddison and Mourato (2002), who used the *contingent valuation method* to establish a large net heritage benefit (£114 million) from relocating the highway into a tunnel near the Stonehenge World Heritage Site. The challenge with these impacts is their case specificity, which explains why only the largest projects (or largest impacts) tend to be subject to economic analysis.

12.4.4 Health and active travel

The last ten years have seen a breakthrough in the field of health-impact appraisal of transport initiatives. This is embodied in the World Health Organization's 'HEAT' tool (Kahlmeier et al., 2011), which is based on large sample, peer-reviewed health research: this shows that reducing inactivity through increased walking and cycling leads to a marked reduction in mortality risk. The mortality reduction can be quantified using a dose-response relationship and then valued using the same VOSL used in safety valuation. The implications are striking:

- regular cycling reduces the risk of all-cause mortality by 10 percent compared with no cycling (the 'relative risk education'), and the equivalent figure for walking is 11 percent;
- further health benefits are obtained by additional walking and cycling up to a 'cap' of 45 percent risk reduction for cycling, or 30 percent risk reduction for walking (equivalent to about 7.5 hours per week of each activity);
- when applied to an example walking and cycling infrastructure project, the health benefits could be as large as 50 percent of the other measured benefits (DfT, 2014c) – that is without including morbidity impacts which remain outside the World Health Organization method.

Moreover, many appraisal methods include WTP-based values for improved journey quality, or 'ambience' whilst walking and cycling. These feed into the user benefits, as they reduce the generalised cost (or perceived disutility) of mobility by these modes. Whether there is any double counting between these and the health benefits is an open question at this stage, however, the magnitude of the benefits is on the face of it quite substantial (29 percent of the benefits in the DfT (2014c) example). Davis (2014) provides a useful summary of the evidence on BCRs for walking and cycling investments, finding an average BCR in the range of 5–6, which supports the idea that smaller investments, focused on active travel, can produce 'very high' value for money compared with other uses of public budgets.

12.4.5 Wider economic impacts

Finally, it is important to consider how the wider economic impacts of transport provision play into economic appraisal. For many decades, the conventional view was that the benefits measured in the transport market were a satisfactory proxy for the final benefits that would be felt in the transport-using sectors of the economy. For example, the benefits to business would be fully captured by the time savings and cost savings associated with faster/more efficient transport, and any benefits to commuters would be fully captured by a careful estimation of the reductions in the generalised cost of commuting – including all the elements noted above. Where projects stimulated more economic activity, or more commuting or leisure travel, the benefits would be captured through the benefits to new users (the triangle forming the right-hand part of the user benefits in Figure 12.6).

It was recognised from the start that this required the assumption of competitive markets and no positive externalities in the transport-using sectors, but only in the last 20 years or so has a serious research effort been directed towards questioning this, and dealing with the consequences for appraisal (e.g. Standing Advisory Committee on Trunk Road Assessment, 1999; Graham, 2007; Venables et al., 2014). It is now understood that there may be:

- *agglomeration effects* when transport projects or policies increase the 'effective density' of economic activity by reducing the generalised cost of movement – this has the consequence (quantified by Graham, 2007) of increasing the productivity of businesses across the economy, most strongly in sectors such as financial services (this is analogous to the productivity effect of business clustering observed by Porter, 1990);
- additional benefits to business due to the presence of *imperfect competition in product markets*, so that price exceeds marginal cost and there is a net revenue gain; and
- benefits to taxpayers from increased *income tax revenue*, as more individuals are employed and there is a move towards higher-paid jobs.

These are additional because they are positive externalities from transport improvement, not simply reflections in transport-using markets of transport cost (or time) reductions. The magnitude of the additional benefits varies from case to case, however there is now widespread evidence of benefits increasing by 10–80 percent (e.g. Venables et al., 2014, and an example is given in the following section).

12.5 Cost-benefit analysis and financial appraisal

Having considered the principles underlying transport appraisal and discussed how values are derived and applied for the main impacts, it is possible to bring everything together in a cost-benefit analysis or financial appraisal. The key difference between these two, as noted above, is their scope: cost-benefit analysis is concerned with welfare and takes account of impacts on *all* groups; whereas financial appraisal is focused on the financial revenues and costs, usually to one organisation. A common output indicator from a financial appraisal is the Financial Internal Rate of Return, which is defined as the discount rate which sets the Financial NPV to zero. In other words, it is an equivalent constant rate of return from an initial investment. If the project or policy does not take the form of an investment, a private-sector organisation may still be interested in the year-by-year impact on its cash flow, or on accounting ratios such as its return on capital employed (i.e. earnings before interest and tax/capital employed). Meanwhile, governments are typically interested in the impact on the public accounts (NPV to the public accounts). Both the private-sector financial NPV(s) and the NPV to the public accounts will feed into the economic cost-benefit analysis, because it is comprehensive – including the impacts on those groups (12.5).

A recent example that illustrates many of the aspects covered in this chapter is the appraisal of the high-speed rail project HS2, which would connect London with the Midlands (Phase 1) and the north of England (Phase 2), with trains running on to Scotland. Table 12.12 shows how the

Table 12.12 HS2 cost-benefit analysis results

Benefits, £bn			
Impact group	*Impact*	*Phase 1*	*Full Network*
Users (rail)	Time and cost savings	20.0	51.2
	Crowding reduction	4.1	7.5
Users (road)	Decongestion	0.6	1.2
Wider economy	Agglomeration	2.4	8.7
	Imperfect competition	1.7	4.0
	Increased labour-force participation	0.2	0.5
Society (externalities)	Safety, noise (car and rail), climate change	0.4	0.8
Public accounts	Indirect tax revenue	–1.2	–2.9
Total		28.1	71.0
Costs, £bn		*Phase 1*	*Full network*
Transport budget	Capital costs	21.8	40.5
	Operating costs	8.2	22.1
	Revenues	–13.2	–31.1
Total		16.7	31.5
Summary		*Phase 1*	*Full network*
NPV, £bn		11.4	39.5
BCR		1.7	2.3

Source: based on results in DfT (2014b). Landscape impacts not shown, due to uncertainty, but would reduce both BCRs by 0.1

CBA is constructed: group by group, covering all monetised impacts. Note that the loss of indirect tax revenue due to the shift from car to rail is treated as a negative benefit (as discussed in Section 12.3.4), whilst the fare revenue is treated as a negative cost – this makes no difference to the NPV, but keeps the BCR focused on the benefits relative to the net impact on the transport budget, the particular BCR definition chosen. At 2.3, the BCR of the full network is classified as 'High value for money' whilst the BCR of Phase 1 alone is in the 'Medium' class at 1.7.

Amongst other findings, it is clear that the wider economic impacts are crucial to raise the full network BCR into the 'High value for money' category – they amount to an additional 23 percent over the other benefits. The safety and environmental externalities are small, however, many billions have been spent on mitigation and design choices to ensure this is the case.

From the provider's financial perspective (or the transport budget if the net costs are passed through to government as in other rail appraisals), revenues are more than enough to cover the operating costs, however, the capital costs will require public funding – motivated by the 'high' economic BCR obtainable. Table 12.13 gives more detail from the financial appraisal,

Table 12.13 DfT capital budget for HS2, 2015/16–2020/21

Year	*2015–16*	*2016–17*	*2017–18*	*2018–19*	*2019–20*	*2020–21*	*Total*
Cost, £m	980	1,729	1,693	3,300	4,000	4,498	16,210

Source: DfT (2014d)

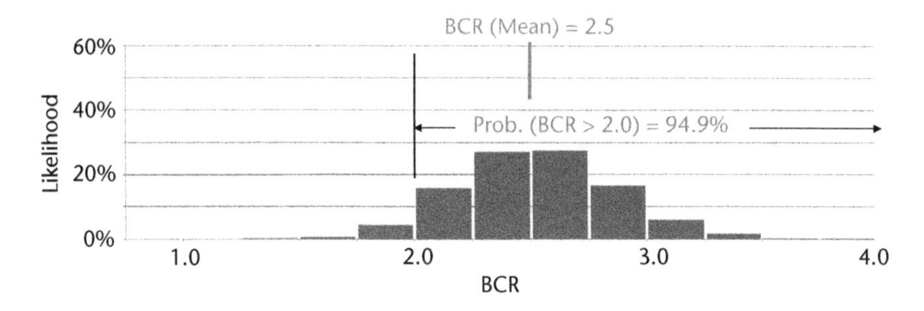

Figure 12.9 HS2 risk analysis results
Source: based on DfT (2015d)

showing annual cash flows for the immediate period 2015/16–2020/21 during construction. These are based on the median (50th percentile) cost estimates, including a 26 percent risk contingency. Once the project is open and operating in a 'steady state', the financial operating surplus to the rail industry is expected to be £300 million per annum (DfT, 2014d).

Taxpayers in areas not directly impacted by the project stand to lose financially, from the loss of indirect tax revenue plus the net costs of the project, therefore an astute policymaker would be keen to examine ways to ensure they do not feel neglected by transport policy overall.

Another useful aspect of the HS2 appraisal is a quantitative risk analysis, which communicates clearly to the decision maker how the risks around various components combine into a probability distribution on the BCR. Hence, for example, Figure 12.9 shows that it is 94.9 percent probable that the BCR will exceed the 'High' threshold of 2.0. The mean BCR is slightly higher in this updated appraisal.

Other interesting appraisals that illustrate the adaptability of these methods include the appraisal of national road pricing (Nash, 2007), as well as the safety policy and technology examples and the walking and cycling examples cited above. Any intervention which affects the generalised costs of travel or freight movement, or the wider economic impacts, or the externalities from transport, should be susceptible to an appraisal using the 'toolkit' of economic methods outlined in this chapter.

12.6. Conclusions and multiple attribute-based methods

It is important to recognise the limitations of the economic 'toolkit'. The situations where CBA is most difficult are those where:

- *resources needed to conduct an appraisal are lacking* at the project level – the classic example being 'small projects'– or at the government level when authorities do not actively maintain an appraisal system;
- *data is lacking* – the classic case being early-stage sifting and screening of options, before design, modelling and forecasting have been undertaken;
- *impacts being scrutinised have not hitherto been valued in CBA*, e.g. biodiversity or 'policy fit'-type considerations, *or are very case-specific* requiring potentially expensive research, e.g. heritage impacts;
- *impacts are too large scale or systemic* – this implies that the authority lacks a system-wide model to predict the impacts of policy changes or major projects: national transport models, land-use and transport interaction models and regional economic models all have roles to play in filling this gap.

In the first three situations, there may be a case to change the approach: *multiple attribute-based methods* can be extremely helpful in providing decision support in situations of limited resources, limited data or barriers to valuation. In broad terms, these involve assessing the performance of each option against a set of predefined criteria. They may be unweighted, leaving the decision maker to aggregate across the criteria, or they may use explicit numerical weights on the criteria. The Department for Communities and Local Government (2009) gives an extensive survey of the methods available including weighting techniques. DfT's (2011) Early Assessment and Sifting Tool is an example, implemented using a standard spreadsheet.

In fact, it is very common for transport appraisals to include a CBA nested within an unweighted multiple-attribute framework. The HS2 appraisal, for example, has descriptive 'scores' on a 7-point scale for: townscape; heritage; biodiversity; water environment; and six other impacts for which monetised assessments were lacking (DfT, 2014b). For smaller projects, a 'proportionate appraisal' typically includes monetisation of a narrower range of impacts. The framework helps provide a common appraisal structure for all interventions. One effect of setting out a fairly comprehensive appraisal framework may be to initiate a discussion about the implicit values of the non-monetised impacts in decision making (e.g. Nellthorp and Mackie, 2000). There may then be a resurgence of effort later on to monetise these items – this has certainly been the UK experience since 2004.

Comparing international practice at present, two trends are evident (e.g. see Mackie and Worsley, 2013). On the one hand there are signs of convergence, for example a remarkable commonality of approach in relation to the overall CBA principles, and values of time and safety. On the other hand, innovation is always leading CBA in different directions, for example the recent innovations in wider economic benefits or health benefits, which are having a substantial effect on BCRs of certain types of interventions in a subset of countries.

The growing interest in *ex post* evaluations (Section 12.3.1) has yielded some useful lessons for *ex ante* appraisals, particularly on optimism bias and the need for effective modelling. On a note of caution, most *ex post* evaluations come only one to five years into the benefit stream which may be as long as 60 years, so the need for forecasting is not eliminated and to some extent they are best seen as updated *ex ante* appraisals or 'work in progress'.

Despite periodic critiques of CBA, many of the 'problems with CBA' as an approach are not insurmountable. They do, however, require a certain amount of effort and resources on the part of the public authority acting as 'gatekeeper', who incurs the costs of maintaining and developing the appraisal guidance, and also the project promoter – although modelling and appraisal costs remain very small compared with the resources spent on projects themselves (usually <1 percent). Intelligent use of multiple-attribute tools and 'initial' appraisals appears to be helpful, combined with appraisal early enough to inform all the decision points we are looking to influence. One tension always seems to remain in appraisal between policy fit – a top-down perspective – and CBA, which is inherently bottom up in its approach to valuation. This may be a creative tension, in that CBA helps keep the appraisal open to the true range of effects on individual welfare, perhaps a vital complement to the 'command and control' nature of government.

Notes

1 E.g. countries in Europe, North America and Oceania (see Mackie and Worsley, 2013), in Asia (e.g. Asian Development Bank, 2013) and in Africa and South America (e.g. African Development Bank, 2016; Gómez-Lobo, 2012).

2 Mass transit systems exhibiting economies of scale, scope or density would potentially be counter-examples, when operating at low to moderate load factors.

3 Or indeed 'matters' to individual 'k' – authors such as Hausman and McPherson (2009, p. 1) are quick to point out that preferences are not always self-interested and that individuals sometimes prefer options that appear to be worse for them. There are numerous ways in which a transport intervention could potentially impact on a person's welfare – for example, by increasing their money income, reducing their money expenditure, increasing their opportunities, reducing their travel time on journeys taken, improving their health, exposing them to risks, improving their environment, or threatening their quality of life through various impacts.
4 Not only is there a lack of agreement about what is the most appropriate definition of utility and how it should be measured, there is also a long-standing disagreement over the legitimacy of interpersonal comparisons of utility at all. These factors have helped maintain the use of money as the numeraire in appraisal from Dupuit (1844) to the present day.
5 Clements et al. (2001) indicate a higher mean η value across 42 countries of approximately -2.1.
6 User benefit minus the net cost (cost-revenue) to the bridge supplier.
7 Or other forms of public-private partnership.
8 And if large profits will be made, the appraisal will help to make them transparent – leading potentially to a discussion about how they will be distributed.
9 The intertemporal elasticity of the value of time savings with respect to real GDP per capita was found to be 0.90.
10 Following the contribution of Little (1950).
11 E.g. the Common Appraisal Framework, MVA et al. (1994).
12 Interventions which generate a positive financial impact for the government, such as road pricing, are an exception, as they can produce a negative BCR and have the best economic case.
13 The model is due to Becker (1965), DeSerpa (1971), Evans (1972) and MVA et al. (1987) in particular.

References

Abrantes, P. A. L. and Wardman, M. R. (2011). Meta-Analysis of UK Values of Travel Time: An Update. *Transportation Research*, Part A, 45, pp. 1–17.

African Development Bank (2016). *Sirari Corridor Accessibility and Road Safety Improvement Project: Isebania-Kishi-Ahero (A1) Road Rehabilitation, Appraisal Report.* Abidjan: AFDB.

Annema, J.A., Frenken, K., Koopmans, C. and Kroesen, M. (2017). Relating cost-benefit analysis results with transport project decisions in the Netherlands. *Letters in Spatial and Resource Sciences*, 10(1), pp. 109–27.

Arup, Institute for Transport Studies and Accent (2015). *Provision of Market Research for Value of Travel Time Savings and Reliability. Phase 2 Report.* London: DfT.

Asian Development Bank (2013). *Cost-Benefit Analysis for Development: A Practical Guide.* Mandaluyong City, Philippines: ADB.

Becker, G. S. (1965). A Theory of the Allocation of Time. *Economic Journal*, 75(299), pp. 493–511.

Bickel, P., Friedrich, R., Burgess, A., Fagiani, P., Hunt, A., De Jong, G., Laird, J. J., Lieb, C., Lindberg, G., Mackie, P., Navrud, S., Odgaard, T., Ricci, A., Shires, J. D. and Tavasszy, L. (2006). *HEATCO Deliverable 5: Proposal for Harmonised Guidelines.* Stuttgart: University of Stuttgart.

Carsten, O. M. and Tate, F. N. (2005). Intelligent Speed Adaptation: Accident Savings and Cost-Benefit Analysis. *Accident Analysis and Prevention*, 37(3), pp. 407–16.

Clements, K. W., Yang, W. and Chen, D. (2001). The Matrix Approach to Evaluating Demand Equations. *Applied Economics*, 33, pp. 957–67.

Davis, A. (2014). *Claiming the Health Dividend: A Summary and Discussion of Value for Money Estimates from Studies of Investment in Walking and Cycling.* London: DfT.

de Jong, G. C. (2008). Value of Freight Travel-Time Savings. In Hensher, D. A. and Button, K. J. (eds), *Handbook of Transport Modelling: Volume 1.* London: Elsevier.

de Jong, G. C., Daly, A. J., Pieters, M. and van der Hoorn, A. I. J. M. (2005). The Logsum as an Evaluation Measure: Review of the Literature and New Results. *Transportation Research Part A*, 41(9), pp. 874–89.

Department for Communities and Local Government (2009). *Multi-Criteria Analysis: A Manual.* London: DCLG.

Department for Transport (DfT) (2009). *NATA Refresh: Appraisal for a Sustainable Transport System.* London: DfT.

Department for Transport (2011). *Early Assessment and Sifting Tool (EAST) Guidance.* London: DfT.

Department for Transport (2013a). *Value for Money Assessment: Advice Note for Local Transport Decision Makers.* London: DfT.

Department for Transport (2013b). *The Transport Business Cases.* London: DfT.
Department for Transport (2014a). *TAG Unit A1.2 Scheme Costs.* London: DfT.
Department for Transport (2014b). *HS2 Outline Business Case: Economic Case.* London: DfT.
Department for Transport (2014c). *TAG Unit A5.1 Active Mode Appraisal.* London: DfT.
Department for Transport (2014d). *HS2 Outline Business Case, Section 4: Financial Case.* London: DfT.
Department for Transport (2015a). *TAG Unit A4.2 Distributional Impact Appraisal.* London: DfT.
Department for Transport (2015b). *Understanding and Valuing Impacts of Transport Investment: Values of Travel Time Savings.* London: DfT.
Department for Transport (2015c). *Percentage of DfT's appraisal project spending that is assessed as high or very high value for money.* London: DfT.
Department for Transport (2015d). *HS2 West Midlands to Crewe Strategic Outline Business Case Economic Case.* London: DfT.
Department for Transport (2016). *Transport Analysis Guidance: WebTAG*, www.gov.uk/guidance/transport-analysis-guidance-webtag (accessed 1 June 2016).
DeSerpa, A. (1971). A Theory of the Economics of Time. *Economic Journal*, 81, pp. 828–46.
Dupuit, A. J. E. (1844). De la mesure de l'utilité des travaux publics. *Annales des Ponts et Chausées, Second edition, Volume 8. Translated as: On the Measurement of the Utility of Public Works. International Economic Papers*, 2, pp. 83–110.
Dupuit, A. J. E. (1849). De l'influence des péages sur l'utililité des voies de communication. *Annales des Ponts et Chausées, 2e série, 1er semestre.* Translated as: 'On tolls and transport charges', *International Economic Papers*, 11, pp. 7–31.
Eddington, R. (2006). *The Eddington Transport Study.* London: Stationery Office.
Elvik, R. (2007). *Prospects for Improving Road Safety in Norway*, TØI Report 897/2007. Oslo: TØI.
European Investment Bank (2005). *RAILPAG: Railway Project Appraisal Guidelines*, www.eib.org/attachments/pj/railpag_en.pdf
Evans, A. (1972). On the Theory of the Valuation and Allocation of Time. *Scottish Journal of Political Economy*, 19, pp. 1–17.
Fickling, R., Gunn, H., Kirby, H. R., Bradley, M. and Heywood, C. (2009). *Productive Use of Rail Travel Time and the Valuation of Travel Time Savings for Rail Business Travellers*, Final Report to the Department for Transport. London: DfT.
Flyvbjerg, B., Skamris Holm, M. K. and Buhl, S. L. (2004). What Causes Cost Overrun in Transport Infrastructure Projects? *Transport Reviews*, 24(1), pp. 3–18.
Flyvbjerg, B., Skamris Holm, M. K. and Buhl, S. L. (2005). How (In)accurate Are Demand Forecasts in Public Works Projects? The Case of Transportation. *Journal of the American Planning Association*, 71(2), pp. 131–46.
Fowkes, A. S., Marks, P. and Nash, C. A. (1986). *The Value of Business Travel Time Savings*, Working Paper 214. Leeds: Institute for Transport Studies.
Geurs, K. T., Krizek, K. J. and Reggiani, A. (2012). *Accessibility Analysis and Transport Planning.* Cheltenham: Edward Elgar.
Gibbons, S., Nathan, M. and Overman, H. G. (2014). Evaluating Spatial Policies. *Town Planning Review*, 85(4), pp. 427–32.
Gómez-Lobo, A. (2012). Institutional Safeguards for Cost Benefit Analysis: Lessons from the Chilean National Investment System. *Journal of Benefit-Cost Analysis*, 3, pp. 1–30.
Goodwin, P. and van Dender, K. (2013). Peak Car: Themes and Issues. *Transport Reviews*, 33(3), pp. 243–54.
Graham, D. J. (2007). Agglomeration, Productivity and Transport Investment. *Journal of Transport Economics and Policy*, 41, pp. 317–43.
Hausman, D. M. and McPherson, M. S. (2009). Preference Satisfaction and Welfare Economics. *Economics and Philosophy*, 25(1), pp. 1–25.
Hensher, D. A. (1977). *Value of Business Travel Time.* Oxford: Pergamon Press.
Hensher, D. A. and Button, K. J. (eds) (2008). *Handbook of Transport Modelling*, Second edition. Amsterdam: Elsevier.
Hicks, J. R. (1939). The Foundations of Welfare Economics. *Economic Journal*, 49, pp. 696–712.
Highways Agency (2015). *11th Annual Evaluation Report: Post Opening Project Evaluation of Local Network Management Schemes.* London: Highways Agency.
Highways England (2016). *Post Opening Project Evaluation (POPE) of Major Schemes Main Report, Meta-Analysis 2015.* Guildford: Highways England.

Hill, N., Brannigan, C., Smokers, R., Schroten, A., van Essen, H. and Skinner, I. (2012). *Developing a Better Understanding of the Secondary Impacts and Key Sensitivities for the Decarbonisation of the EU's Transport Sector by 2050*. London: AEA Technology.

HM Treasury (2010). *Spending Review 2010, Cm 7942*. London: TSO.

HM Treasury (2011). *The Green Book: Appraisal and Evaluation in Central Government*. London: TSO.

HM Treasury (2013). *Public Spending Round 2013, Cm 8639*. London: TSO.

House of Commons Transport Committee (2011). *Transport and the Economy*, Third Report of Session 2010–11. London: TSO.

HS2 (2016). *Guide to HS2 Property Schemes*. London: HS2.

Jones, I. S. (1977). *Urban Transport Appraisal*. London: Macmillan.

Kahlmeier, S., Kelly, P., Foster, C., Götschi, T., Cavill, N., Dinsdale, H., Woodcock, J., Schweizer, C., Rutter, H., Lieb, C., Oja, P. and Racioppi, R. (2014). *Health economic assessment tools (HEAT) for walking and for cycling. Methodology and user guide. Economic assessment of transport infrastructure and policies. 2014 Update*. Copenhagen: WHO.

Kaldor, N. (1939). Welfare Propositions of Economics and Interpersonal Comparisons of Utility. *Economic Journal*, 49(195), pp. 549–52.

Kelly, C. E., Laird, J. J., Costantini, S., Richards, P., Carbajo, J. and Nellthorp, J. (2015). Ex Post Appraisal: What Lessons Can Be Learnt from EU Cohesion Funded Transport Projects? *Transport Policy*, 37, pp. 83–91.

Laird, J. J., Nellthorp, J. and Mackie, P. J. (2005). Network Effects and Total Economic Impact in Transport Appraisal. *Transport Policy*, 12(6), pp. 537–44.

Layard, R., Mayraz, G. and Nickell, S. (2008). The Marginal Utility of Income. *Journal of Public Economics*, 92 (8–9), pp. 1846–57.

Little, I. M. D. (1950). *A Critique of Welfare Economics*. Oxford: Clarendon Press.

Lucas, K., van Wee, B. and Maat, K. (2016). A Method to Evaluate Equitable Accessibility: Combining Ethical Theories and Accessibility-Based Approaches. *Transportation*, 43, pp. 473–590.

Lyons, G. and Urry, J. (2005). Travel Time Use in the Information Age. *Transportation Research Part A Policy and Practice*, 39(2–3), pp. 257–76.

Mackie, P. J. and Worsley, T. (2013). *International Comparisons of Transport Appraisal Practice: Overview Report*. Leeds: Institute for Transport Studies.

Maddison, D. and Mourato, S. (2002). Valuing Different Road Options for Stonehenge. *Conservation and Management of Archaeological Sites*, 4(4), pp. 203–12.

Massiani, J. (2015). Cost-Benefit Analysis of Policies for the Development of Electric Vehicles in Germany: Methods and Results. *Transport Policy*, 38, pp. 19–26.

Metz, D. (2008). The Myth of Travel Time Saving. *Transport Reviews*, 28(3), pp. 321–36.

Millard-Ball, A. and Schipper, L. (2011). Are We Reaching Peak Travel? Trends in Passenger Transport in Eight Industrialized Countries. *Transport Reviews*, 31(3), pp. 357–78.

MVA Consultancy, ITS University of Leeds and TSU University of Oxford (1987). *Value of Travel Time Savings*. Newbury: Policy Journals.

MVA Consultancy, Oscar Faber TPA and Institute for Transport Studies, University of Leeds (1994). *Common Appraisal Framework for Urban Transport Projects*, Report to the PTE Group and Department of Transport. London: HMSO.

Nash, C. (2007). Developments in Transport Policy: Road Pricing in Britain. *Journal of Transport Economics and Policy*, 41, pp. 135–47.

National Audit Office (2014). *Report by the Comptroller and Auditor General: Crossrail, HC965*. London: TSO.

Nellthorp, J. (2010). UK Experience of Implementing Noise Values in Transport Appraisal, 3 Years On. *Proceedings of the Internoise 2010 Conference*, pp. 6021–30.

Nellthorp, J. and Hyman, G. (2001). *Alternatives to the Rule of a Half in Matrix Based Appraisal*. Paper presented at the European Transport Conference, Homerton College, Cambridge, 10–12 September 2001.

Nellthorp, J. and Mackie, P. J. (2000). The UK Roads Review: A Hedonic Model of Decision-Making. *Transport Policy*, 7(2), pp. 127–38.

Nellthorp, J., Bristow, A. L. and Day, B. (2007). Introducing Willingness-to-Pay for Noise Changes into Transport Appraisal: An Application of Benefit Transfer. *Transport Reviews*, 27(3), pp. 327–53.

Nilsson, J. (1991). Investment Decisions in a Public Bureaucracy: A Case Study of Swedish Road Planning Practices. *Journal of Transport Economics and Policy*, 25, pp. 163–75.

Nordhaus, W. (2013). *The Climate Casino: Risk, Uncertainty, and Economics for a Warming World*. New Haven, CT: Yale University Press.

Odeck, J. (2010). What Determines Decision-Makers' Preferences for Road Investments? Evidence from the Norwegian Road Sector. *Transport Reviews*, 30(4), pp. 473–94.

OECD (2012). *Mortality Risk Valuation in Environment, Health and Transport Policies.* Paris: OECD.

Ortúzar, J. de D. and Willumsen, L. G. (2011). *Modelling Transport*, Fourth edition. Chichester: John Wiley and Sons.

Pearce, D. W. (1999). Methodological Issues in the Economic Analysis for Involuntary Resettlement Operations. In Cernea, M. (ed.), *The Economics of Involuntary Resettlement: Questions and Challenges.* Washington, DC: World Bank.

Pearce, D. W. and Hett, T. (1999). *Review of Technical Guidance on Environmental Appraisal.* London: EFTEC.

Pearman, A. D., Mackie, P. J. and Nellthorp, J. (2003). *Transport Projects, Programmes, and Policies: Evaluation Needs and Capabilities.* Aldershot: Ashgate.

Peña-Torres, J. and Pearson, P. J. G. (2000). Carbon Abatement and New Investment in Liberalised Electricity Markets: A Nuclear Revival in the UK? *Energy Policy*, 28(2), pp. 115–35.

Porter, M. E. (1990). *The Competitive Advantage of Nations.* London: Macmillan.

Ramsey, F. P. (1928). A Mathematical Theory of Saving. *Economic Journal*, 38(152), pp. 543–59.

Ricardo AEA (2014). *Update of the Handbook on External Costs of Transport. Report for the European Commission DG MOVE.* London: Ricardo-AEA.

Standing Advisory Committee on Trunk Road Assessment (1999). *Transport and the Economy.* London: TSO.

Stern, N. (2006). *The Economics of Climate Change: The Stern Review.* Cambridge: Cambridge University Press.

Sugden, R. (1999). *Treatment of Taxation in Multi-Modal Cost Benefit Analysis.* Norwich: University of East Anglia.

Tweddle, G., Nellthorp, J., Sansom, T., Link, H., Stewart, L. and Bickel, P. (2003). *Pilot Accounts: Results for the United Kingdom*, Annex to Deliverable D8 Pilot Accounts, Results for Tranche B Countries, UNITE Project. Leeds: ITS, University of Leeds.

United Nations (2014). *World Urbanization Prospects: The 2014 Revision.* New York: United Nations, Department of Economic and Social Affairs, Population Division.

Varian, H. R. (2014). *Intermediate Microeconomics: A Modern Approach*, 9th edition. New York: W. W. Norton.

Venables, A. J., Laird, J. J. and Overman, H. G. (2014). *Transport Investment and Economic Performance: Implications for Project Appraisal.* London: DfT.

Wardman, M. R. and Lyons, G. (2016). The Digital Revolution and Worthwhile Use of Travel Time: Implications for Appraisal and Forecasting. *Transportation*, 43(3), pp. 507–30.

Wardman, M. R. and Whelan, G. R. (2011). Twenty Years of Rail Crowding Valuation Studies: Evidence and Lessons from British Experience. *Transport Reviews*, 31(3), pp. 379–98.

Wardman, M. R., Batley, R. P., Laird, J. J., Mackie, P. J. and Bates, J. (2015). How Should Business Travel Time Savings Be Valued? *Economics of Transportation*, 4, pp. 200–14.

World Bank (2005). *Toolkit for the Economic Evaluation of Transport Projects.* Notes TRN5–26. Washington, DC: World Bank, http://go.worldbank.org/09MMD2C490

13
Congestion pricing

Jonas Eliasson

13.1 Introduction

The fundamental reason for the existence of cities is that they enable high accessibility. High accessibility is associated both with economic gains such as higher wages and productivity and opportunities to satisfy specialised interests and lifestyles. The history of human civilisation is a history of urbanisation. Scientific and cultural progress rest on two cornerstones: one is the written language, enabling us to communicate innovations and experiences over distance and time; the other is cities, which have always been our engines of innovations and discovery. Since the demand for and the rewards of high accessibility have accelerated over the last two centuries, this has fuelled urbanisation at an ever higher pace.

But when firms and individuals all strive to be close to each other, congestion is inevitable. Congestion is hence a fundamental characteristic of cities: it is not due to failures of transport planners, or something that can be eliminated by improved urban planning or transport systems with higher capacity. While both of them may help, they cannot eliminate the fact that urban space is an inevitable constraint. The fundamental tension of cities is that the better accessibility they provide, the more people and firms they will attract, and the higher will the demand for transportation become – but this increases congestion, which causes accessibility to deteriorate. Since most negative effects of transportation – congestion, crowding, emissions, noise – are external, transport consumption will be higher than what would be the efficient level, if left unchecked. Urban transport planning must therefore be characterised by two principles: first, space must be used efficiently (space-efficient transport modes, compact land-use planning); second, policies must be introduced that strike a balance between positive and negative effects of mobility. This is where congestion pricing fits in.

The purpose of congestion pricing is to find a better balance between positive and negative effects of mobility. When designing congestion charges, the intuitive idea is that benefits must be balanced against losses – benefits in the form of time savings for remaining car trips, and losses in the form of adaptation costs for the disappearing car trips. In theory, the optimal congestion charge is to charge drivers exactly in proportion to the loss of time they cause other drivers, i.e. equal to the difference between marginal private cost and marginal social cost. However, this theoretical concept is infeasible to implement exactly, since it would vary by link and each minute. A more practical definition is that a congestion charge is a charge that makes driving costs better reflect the time loss a car trip causes other drivers. In practice, congestion charging design is about finding an implementable system where the time gains for the remaining traffic is higher than the loss for the 'disappearing' ('tolled-off') trips, and high enough to cover investment and operating costs.

The aim of this chapter is to discuss how the theoretical idea can be applied in practice, and discuss how different cities have tackled this challenge. Section 13.2 gives a brief overview of the major operational urban congestion pricing schemes. Section 13.3 gives a summary of the theory of congestion pricing, stressing the points that are important for applications. Section 13.4 discusses benefits and costs in practice. Section 13.5 gives a summary of the vast literature of public and political opinions of congestion charges. Finally, Section 13.6 presents some speculations about the future of congestion pricing.

13.2 Operational congestion charging systems

13.2.1 Singapore

Singapore pioneered the idea of congestion charging in practice, first by its Area Licensing Scheme (ALS) introduced in 1975, and then by its Electronic Road Pricing system (ERP) replacing the ALS in 1998. The ALS required drivers of private cars and motorcycles to buy and display a paper licence when entering the urban centre during peak hours. The ALS was replaced by the ERP in 1998, where payments are drawn from a prepaid cash card in the vehicle when it passes under a toll gantry. The number of gantries has increased over time; in 2013 there were 71 gantries (Agarwal et al., 2015). Some of the gantries form a cordon around the urban centre, while some are placed on expressways. The rates are revised four times per year by the Singapore Land and Transport Authority (LTA), based on how measured speeds deviate from 'ideal' speeds, which are set to 20–30 km/h on arterial roads and 45–65 km/h on expressways (Menon, 2000; Menon and Kian-Keong, 2004).

Since Singapore has had congestion charges in place for so long, it is rather pointless to compare the effect of the charges to a counterfactual situation without charges. However, it is clear that the charges are effective. Olszewski and Xie (2005) show that the regular revisions of the charges by the LTA have substantial effects on traffic levels and congestion. Menon (2000) showed that the change from ALS to ERP decreased traffic levels by 15 percent, since charges were then levied per trip rather than per day.

13.2.2 London

The London congestion charge was introduced in 2003. Vehicles were subject to a £5 charge per day if they drove in a centrally located area on weekdays between 07:00 and 18:00. The charged area was extended to the west in 2007–11, but then returned to the original definition. The charge has been increased several times, and is now (2016) £11.50. Emergency vehicles, disabled blue badge holders, buses and 'ultra-low emission vehicles' are exempt, while residents in the area get a discount (90 percent) and drivers signing up for automatic payment get a £1 discount.

Drivers are responsible for paying the charge (several payment channels are available), while automatic number plate recognition is used for identifying vehicles (although an automatic debit system has recently been introduced). This is different from the systems in for example Singapore, Sweden and Norway, where it is not the responsibility of drivers to calculate the charge or remember to pay (Singapore uses a cash card, while the Swedish and most Norwegian systems automatically send invoices to the vehicle owner). The main drawback of placing this responsibility on the driver is that it severely limits how charges can be designed: any differentiation in time or space has to be extremely coarse in order not to place an unreasonable cognitive burden on the driver. Moreover, the operating cost of the London system is very high compared to other systems – around £80 million in 2014 (Transport for London, 2015), which is around eight times higher than for example the Swedish and Norwegian systems which have similar numbers of passages (the London system handles around 450,000 vehicle movements per day (Dix, 2006)).

The charge has had a persistent effect on traffic volumes, although establishing its exact effect against a counterfactual situation with no charge of course becomes more difficult over time. In 2007, four years after the introduction, the number of chargeable vehicles entering the zone had decreased by 30 percent, leading to an overall traffic decrease of 16 percent (Transport for London, 2007). The corresponding changes in vehicle kilometres (VKT) were a 25 percent reduction of potentially charged vehicle kilometres and an overall VKT reduction of 12 percent (Givoni, 2012). These numbers had been broadly stable since the introduction. The immediate effect on congestion was a reduction of around 30 percent. Over time, road space has been reallocated from cars to other modes (buses, bicycles, pedestrians) and other uses, making direct comparisons difficult. In 2007, Transport for London (TfL) concluded that a direct comparison between 2002 and 2006 gave an 8 percent reduction of congestion, but if factors affecting the then-current road capacity were taken into account, TfL concluded that the charges were 'continuing to deliver congestion relief that [was] broadly in line with the 30 percent reduction achieved in the first year of operation'. In 2014, TfL concluded that congestion levels had remained stable since 2006 (Transport for London, 2014).

This highlights an interesting and non-trivial policy choice, which applies to any city introducing congestion pricing. The freed-up road capacity, which at first leads to travel time savings for drivers, does not necessarily have to be used for improving car travel times in the long run. Another option is to use it for other purposes: bus lanes, bike lanes, pedestrians or whatever is deemed to yield the best 'value per square meter'. The important thing is that choices of space allocation must be made consciously; the freed-up space must not be squandered, since it is a hard-earned, scarce and valuable resource.

13.2.3 Stockholm

Stockholm introduced its congestion pricing system in 2006, first as a seven-month trial followed by a referendum, and then permanently in 2007 (descriptions of the political story can be found in Gullberg and Isaksson, 2009 and Eliasson, 2014). Vehicles crossing a cordon around the inner city (in any direction) were charged[1] 2€ in peak hours (7:30–8:30 and 16:00–17:30), 1.50€ in the 30-minute periods before and after the peaks, and 1€ the rest of the day (6:30–18:30). Nights and weekends are free. Charge levels have remained essentially unchanged until 2016, when a new charge was introduced on the western bypass (Essingeleden), and the original charges were increased to 3.50€ in peak hours and to 1.10€ during midday, gradually increasing and decreasing before and after the peak periods.

The charges decreased traffic volumes across the cordon by around 20 percent during charged hours, leading to reductions of queuing times of around 30–50 percent on the affected arterials and to emission reductions in the inner city of around 10–15 percent (depending on type of emissions) (Eliasson et al., 2009). Traffic levels across the cordon have remained stable ever since the introduction, despite inflation, economic growth, increased population and increased car ownership all contributing to a general traffic increase in the rest of the region. This indicates that the relative effect of the charges, compared to the counterfactual, has increased over time, as people have got more time to adjust (Börjesson et al., 2012).

13.2.4 Milan

Milan introduced an environmental charge called Ecopass in 2008. The charge was levied on vehicles entering an 8 km^2 zone in the urban centre on weekdays 7:30–19:30 (only once per day). Vehicles were identified by cameras using automatic number plate recognition at 43 toll gantries at the perimeter of the zone, with drivers being responsible for paying the charge retroactively.

The charge was designed primarily to curb emissions, so it was differentiated according to emission standards: Euro3-compliant vehicles and alternative-fuel cars were exempt, while more polluting vehicles paid a charge varying from 2€ to 10€ depending on emission standards. Originally, the idea was to tighten the rules for which vehicles were exempt over time, but this never happened due to political opposition (Croci and Douvan, 2015).

In the first year, the number of charged vehicles decreased by 56 percent, leading to an overall traffic reduction of 21 percent. This reduced emissions by 14–23 percent (depending on type of emission) and decreased the number of days with pollutant levels over threshold levels (Danielis et al., 2012), which was the main purpose of the system. Congestion and accidents were also reduced substantially. Around three-quarters of total time savings occurred outside the zone (Danielis et al., 2012). Gradually, however, the congestion reduction decreased because of car substitution: before the introduction, 42 percent of the traffic was made up of vehicles that would be subject to the charge, but by 2011 this share had decreased to around 10 percent, and the overall traffic reduction had been reduced to 11 percent in 2011 (compared to 2007) since exempt vehicles had to a large extent replaced the charged vehicles.

The Ecopass system was introduced as a one-year trial, which was then extended a year at a time. In 2011, proponents of the original charge pushed through a referendum about extending the system to cover a larger area and all types of vehicles. Eighty percent of the voters were in favour, and in 2012 a redesigned system, Area C, replaced the Ecopass system (Beria, 2015; Croci and Douvan, 2015). The system was first introduced as a trial, but made permanent in April 2013. The Area C charges were designed to have a stronger effect on congestion: the baseline charge is 5€ for all vehicles to enter the zone (per day), although commercial vehicles and cars parking in private parking areas pay 3€. Heavily polluting vehicles (Euro 0 petrol and Euro 0–2 diesel) are not allowed to enter at all. Residents get 40 free entries per year, after which they pay 2€. In all, this means that only 41 percent of vehicles pay the full charge. The Area C scheme decreased traffic further: traffic volumes in 2012–13 were 38 percent lower than in 2007 (before Ecopass). Emissions (PM10) were estimated to have decreased by 18 percent compared to 2011 levels.

13.2.5 Gothenburg

Gothenburg introduced its congestion charging system in 2013. The scheme consists of a cordon with two additional tolling borders sprouting out from the cordon. Charges are levied 6:00–18:30 on weekdays and range from 8 SEK to 18 SEK depending on the time of day. Vehicles are charged when they cross a toll border in any direction, but only have to pay one charge during any one-hour period. The Gothenburg system uses the same technology and invoicing system as Stockholm.

Traffic across the toll cordon was reduced by 12 percent, and average congestion indices on the relatively small number of congested links were reduced from 160 to 80 percent (Börjesson and Kristoffersson, 2015). Most of the affected links were not congested even before the charges, however.

The Gothenburg congestion charges have two purposes: to generate revenues for an infrastructure package and to reduce road congestion. The background was that Stockholm had managed to use their toll revenues to strike a deal with the national government, where the revenues were leveraged with national funding to fund a large infrastructure package. Inspired by this, Gothenburg negotiated a similar deal. The deal prescribed that the system should generate around 1 billion SEK per year (a third more than the Stockholm revenues, despite Gothenburg being less than half the size of Stockholm), with the secondary objective to reduce congestion as efficiently as possible given the revenue constraint. However, Gothenburg did not have a lot of road congestion; it was limited to a few junctions and the morning rush hour. This led to a fierce political debate. Descriptions of the political story and the changes in public opinion can be found in Börjesson et al. (2016) and Börjesson and Kristoffersson (2015).

13.2.6 Other systems

Norway was the second pioneer of urban road pricing, after Singapore. Oslo, Bergen and Trondheim all introduced road pricing systems in the late 1980s or early 1990s and several other cities have followed. However, most of the Norwegian systems are not intended to reduce congestion, but merely to generate revenues for infrastructure investments (although there are a few examples where there have been secondary objectives as well, such as congestion reduction or environmental improvements, for example, the Trondheim system). The Norwegian systems are still interesting from a technical point of view, but since most are designed not to affect traffic, they mostly fall outside the scope of the chapter.

A few comparatively small towns have introduced some form of congestion pricing; the most well known are Durham (UK, 2002) and Valletta (Malta, 2007) (Attard and Ison, 2010; Santos, 2004). This context is obviously different, but experiences from these cities confirm many of the main conclusions from other cities, for example that drivers are indeed sensitive to pricing.

In the United States, the HOT lane concept (High-occupancy vehicles and toll) is relatively common. The idea is to charge one lane on a multilane expressway to provide a virtually congestion-free alternative. Several studies indicate that this can be a viable option to decrease average congestion levels, increase throughput and yield a net social benefit (Burris and Stockton, 2004; Janson and Levinson, 2014).

13.3 Costs and benefits of congestion pricing: theory

This section gives a brief summary of congestion pricing theory. The purpose is not to attempt to summarise the large literature in this field, but to give a quick and accessible overview, and to point out some specific conclusions which are important from an applied point of view.

Consider a road[2] with a travel time t which depends on the traffic volume D, so we have $t = t(D)$. This is called a volume-delay function, and is normally characterised by $t'(D) \geq 0$ and $t''(D) \geq 0$. Assume that drivers' generalised travel cost c is the sum of the travel time[3] and a toll $\tau : c = t(D) + \tau$. Let $p(D)$ be the inverse demand function, that is $p(D) = c$. The total social benefit B is the sum of the consumer surplus $\int_0^D p(x)dx - cD$ plus the toll revenues τD:

$$B = \int_0^D p(x)dx - cD + \tau D = \int_0^D p(x)dx - [t(D) + \tau]D + \tau D = \int_0^D p(x)dx - t(D)D. \quad (13.1)$$

The optimal toll τ^* can be obtained by solving for the optimal volume D^* (by differentiating B with respect to D and setting equal to zero):

$$\frac{dB}{dD} = p(D^*) - t'(D^*)D^* - t(D^*) = 0. \quad (13.2)$$

Using that $p(D) = t(D) + \tau$, we get the optimal toll τ^*:

$$\tau^* = t'(D)D. \quad (13.3)$$

To give this an interpretation, define the social cost SC as the sum of the aggregate generalised cost minus toll revenues: $SC = (t(D) + \tau)D - \tau D = t(D)D$. The derivative of the social cost is the marginal social cost $MSC = t(D) + t'(D)D$. The optimal toll τ^* is equal to the difference between the MSC and users' generalised travel cost (without toll).

The welfare gain B of a toll τ which changes demand from D_0 to D_1 is the change in consumer surplus plus the toll revenues, which gives

$$\begin{aligned} B(\tau) &= \int_0^{D_1} p(x)dx - (t(D_1) + \tau)D_1 + \tau D_1 - \int_0^{D_0} p(x)dx + t(D_0)D_0 \\ &= t(D_0)D_0 - t(D_1)D_1 - \int_{D_1}^{D_0} p(x)dx. \end{aligned} \tag{13.4}$$

The first two terms are the change in total travel time, and the integral is the welfare loss of adaptation costs (the welfare loss for disappearing car trips). This shows the intuitive idea explained in the beginning: congestion pricing involves balancing total travel time gains (the first two terms) against the welfare losses of adapting to the charges (the integral). The toll revenues do not appear in the social benefits; they are just a transfer. In practice, of course, they are of enormous importance. The formula is true for any toll – not just an optimal toll. Hence, congestion charges do not have to be optimal to deliver social benefits; it is enough that they generate time gains larger than the adaptation costs. This is of great practical importance. Determining the optimal toll by calculating the marginal social cost is a very difficult task in practice, while measuring aggregate travel time gains and assessing adaptation costs (using e.g. the rule-of-a-half) is relatively straightforward. This is what makes it possible to design and evaluate practically implementable congestion charges.

The formula can be rewritten in a way that allows it to be drawn in a well-known and illuminating diagram. Rewriting $t(D_0)D_0 - t(D_1)D_1 = \int_{D_1}^{D_0} MSC(D)dD$, we get $B(\tau) = \int_{D_1}^{D_0} MSC(D)dD - \int_{D_1}^{D_0} p(x)dx$. The social benefit of a toll τ can then be drawn as the shaded triangle in Figure 13.1 (the figure shows the benefits of an optimal toll); it is the difference between the integral under the MSC curve and the integral under the inverse demand curve, from the initial demand D_0 to the resulting demand D_1.

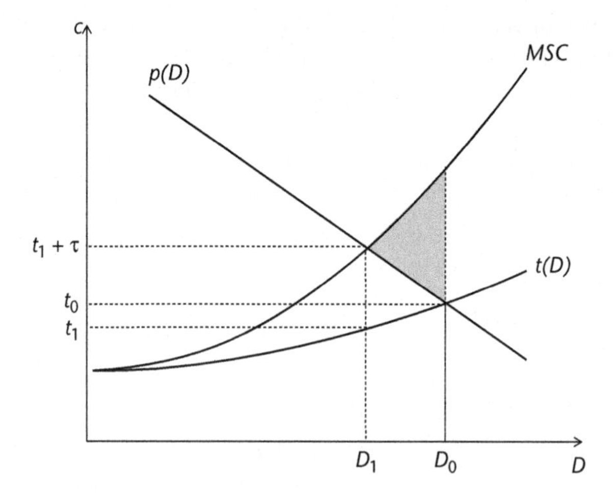

Figure 13.1 Net social benefits of an optimal congestion charge

From Figure 13.1, a number of important conclusions can be drawn. First, the magnitude of the toll benefits depends on two things: the slope of the demand curve and the difference between MSC and $t(D)$. The slope of the demand curve is a measure of how easy it is for drivers to adapt to the charges, i.e. to avoid them: the more difficult it is to adapt, the steeper is the slope, and the smaller the toll benefits will be. In order for a toll to deliver large benefits, it must be reasonably easy for drivers to find alternatives to paying the charge (other modes, destinations, routes, departure times) – at least for a subset of their trips. The difference between MSC and $t(D)$ is a measure of the congestion on the road – severe congestion means that the difference is big. Hence, tolls will only yield large benefits if congestion is severe. This is also intuitively obvious, but surprisingly enough, this point often needs to be emphasised in applied practice (see the Gothenburg case above).

Second, toll revenues (the rectangle with size $\tau * D_1$) are often large compared to the net social benefit (the shaded triangle). From a pure social cost-benefit point of view, the toll revenues are just a transfer; but in reality it is a transfer between different groups of citizens. The use of the revenues, and the political power over the revenues, is hence crucial for the political economy of congestion charges. Moreover, it may be seen as unreasonable to redistribute large sums of money in order to generate a small net benefit. A judgement must be made whether the net social benefit is large enough to justify the redistribution of money.

Third, the marginal benefit of the toll decreases quickly as the toll increases from zero towards the theoretically optimal level. In other words, a relatively low toll will deliver a substantial share of the theoretically maximal benefits. Considering the argument above, that the net benefit needs to be large enough to warrant the redistribution of money, aiming for the optimal toll level may not necessarily be seen as worthwhile or even justified – a moderate toll may be sufficient. A related point is that, intuitively speaking, it is not so important to set precisely the optimal toll and achieve the optimal demand. To see this, imagine that demand is a little higher or lower than the optimal demand D_1. The welfare loss from this deviation will be the little triangle between the $p(D)$ and MSC curves with width equal to this deviation from the optimal demand. This loss of benefit will clearly be small compared to the benefit generated by the toll. This is important from a practical point of view, since the optimal toll cannot be determined (or charged) in practice – partly because demand curves cannot be measured exactly, partly because demand and travel times vary randomly across days.

Fourth, even the optimal toll will not reduce congestion to zero; at the optimal demand level, there will still be congestion. How much depends on the slope of the demand curve: the steeper the slope, the higher the congestion level will be at optimal demand (all else equal).

13.3.1 Alternative theoretical analyses

The theoretical model above is called a static model of congestion, because the congestion function (the volume-delay function) $t(D)$ does not take into account that congestion first builds up and then dissipates, and that drivers may change their departure times to avoid the worst queues. A theoretical model that takes this into account is called dynamic. The most common dynamic model in the theoretical literature is the so-called 'bottleneck' model of congestion. Drivers are assumed to arrive at a bottleneck in a certain order, queue up and wait, and then pass through the bottleneck in first in-first out order. This causes queues to first build up and then dissipate. The optimal congestion charge in this model varies over time (an analysis can be found in Arnott et al.,1993). The conclusions from the dynamic model are different from the static in two ways: the optimal toll will eliminate queues completely, and drivers will be just as well off as before the toll even before revenue recycling (not worse off, as in the static analysis). The latter is because drivers' welfare losses from paying the toll and rescheduling their trips are exactly offset by their reduced travel times. The net social benefit is the resulting toll revenues.

The conclusions from the bottleneck model depend crucially on the assumption that the capacity of the bottleneck is constant, in other words that the flow through the bottleneck does not decrease when a queue starts to form. In reality, however, this is often unrealistic. Consider an urban area such as the downtown of a city. When there is congestion, the average flow decreases essentially everywhere; on the micro level, cars and queues hinder each other, so the more congestion there is, the lower the overall flow becomes. This phenomenon is called hypercongestion, and does not occur in the bottleneck model of congestion. An alternative theoretical model of congestion, the so-called 'bathtub' model, captures this by assuming that the average speed in an area depends on the number of vehicles in that area. Analysing congestion pricing in this model, but still accounting for the dynamic nature of congestion (drivers have different departure times and congestion builds up and then dissipates) leads to very different conclusions than in the bottleneck congestion model (Fosgerau, 2015). The conclusions are in many ways similar to the conclusions from the static analysis, but since dynamics are accounted for in the model, the analysis can also show how incentives for departure time shifts can increase the benefits of charging.

13.4 Costs and benefits of congestion pricing in practice

13.4.1 Costs and benefits for drivers

Car drivers are affected in three ways by congestion charges: they benefit from improved travel times and travel time reliability, but on the other hand they pay the congestion charge and adapt their travel patterns to the charges (which constitutes a welfare loss). Adding these effects together, the average effect for drivers is usually negative. It is therefore not surprising that most drivers are usually opposed to congestion charges. However, there are exceptions to the rule of thumb that drivers are worse off on average, and there are sub-groups of drivers who are winners. Drivers with high values of time – distribution traffic and business travellers, for example – may value the time gains more than the paid charges, and may hence be better off. Some drivers may enjoy benefits of reduced spillback congestion without actually paying the charge. 'Spillback congestion' refers to queues propagating from a bottleneck onto other roads, blocking traffic not actually going through the bottleneck. Reducing such queues by charging the bottleneck will hence also benefit traffic not going through the bottleneck. This traffic will hence get time benefits but no increase in travel cost, and are obviously net winners. Reduction of spillback congestion was an important effect both in Stockholm and in Milan. In Milan, Danielis et al. (2012) calculate that private drivers were actually on average better off from the Ecopass system, because of large time savings outside the zone (over three-quarters of time savings occurred outside the zone).

Note, though, that this describes 'objective' economic consequences. Whether car drivers in reality will feel like 'winners' or 'losers' is also influenced by several other factors, in addition to objective or rational self-interest. We will discuss public attitudes to congestion charges below; at this point, let us just stress that although economic self-interest is an important determinant of attitudes to congestion charges, it is not the only important factor by far.

Many drivers seem to overestimate monetary and adaptation costs ex ante, and underestimate the benefits the traffic reduction yields. Surveys before the introduction of the Stockholm charges indicated that private car traffic would be reduced by 5–10 percent across the cordon during charged hours. When the survey was repeated three months after charges were in place, the result was the same: the answers from respondents indicated that the private car traffic over the toll cordon had been reduced by 5–10 percent. However, traffic measurements showed that in reality, private car traffic had been reduced by around 30 percent. In other words, around three-quarters of the reduction in car trips across the cordon seemed to have gone unnoticed by the drivers themselves. This is most likely because travel patterns vary considerably across days and months, so small changes may go unnoticed by travellers themselves. In Stockholm, less than a quarter of the charged vehicles on any given day are made up of 'habitual' car drivers, who drive across the cordon daily. The remaining three-quarters of traffic only pass the cordon occasionally or rarely. Travel patterns also change because circumstances change. Some illuminating Swedish figures: during one year, 20 to 25 percent of the workforce change jobs, and 15 to 20 percent of the population move. Clearly, identifying specific 'winners', 'losers' and 'who changed' in such circumstances is difficult, and in the long run almost pointless.

13.4.2 Revenues for the government

From drivers' point of view, then, congestion pricing may not seem such a good idea. However, the revenues from the charges are of course not lost; they are transferred to the government. The whole point of congestion charges is that adding toll revenues and drivers' welfare losses together gives a positive net social benefit. In other words, the toll revenues are more than enough to compensate the drivers. Whether drivers will be net 'winners' or 'losers' therefore depends on how revenues are spent (remember, though, the caveat that attitudes in reality depend on several other factors in addition to self-interest).

From the point of view of the government, congestion pricing is thus an attractive source of tax revenue. Whereas standard taxes, such as income tax or value-added tax, have negative net effects[4] on the economy (deadweight losses), congestion pricing is a tax source which has positive net effects on the economy. However, this also means that the net benefit of congestion pricing depends on how revenues are used. For example, if a large share of revenue is needed for investment and operating costs, net benefits may become negative; or if the government uses the revenue inefficiently on, say, infrastructure with costs exceeding benefits (and which would otherwise not be built), total benefits may also turn negative.

13.4.3 Congestion pricing increases efficiency – but not necessarily accessibility

The point that net benefits are positive although drivers may lose (on average) shows that what congestion pricing really does is increase the efficiency of the road system: a scarce resource, road space, is allocated in a more efficient way. But congestion pricing does not necessarily increase accessibility; on the contrary, drivers may (on average) feel that their accessibility has in fact decreased, since their generalised travel costs increase if they value the shorter travel times less than the cost of the tolls.

Whether congestion charges will increase or decrease accessibility in a real case depends on several factors. The possibility to achieve an overall increase in accessibility is higher when drivers are heterogeneous (e.g. have different values of time) and when spillback congestion is widespread (i.e. concentrated bottlenecks cause congestion over large areas).

13.4.4 Consequences for public transport users

Public transport passengers may suffer from increased transit crowding when some drivers switch to transit. This can be remedied by increasing transit capacity, and the cost for this may at least partly be covered by increased fare revenues. If the transit capacity is limited and difficult to increase, however, and if the relative passenger increase is large, increased crowding may cause substantial social costs, and this must be taken into account when designing a congestion pricing system and when evaluating its social costs and benefits. However, this potential problem is often exaggerated. In many cities, analyses and experiences show that the increase of transit passengers is small in relative terms, simply because transit passenger volumes are often large where road congestion is severe. For example, London, Stockholm, Gothenburg and Milan all experienced an increase in transit volumes by just a few percent. Whether increased transit crowding is a problem in a specific city hence depends on local circumstances.

Transit passengers may benefit if less street congestion improves the running times and reliability of buses. There is empirical evidence that this indeed happened in London (Leape, 2006), Stockholm (Eliasson et al., 2009) and Milan (Danielis et al., 2012).

Most cities which have introduced congestion pricing have combined it with an expansion of public transport. This may have dual benefits: it can make alternatives to driving more attractive, which tends to increase the benefits of the congestion charge (the demand curve in Figure 13.1 becomes flatter), and it amends the potential problem of increased transit crowding. Perhaps the most important reason, however, may be to increase public acceptability: spending money on public transport may signal to voters that the charge is not 'just another tax' but part of a strategy to improve overall accessibility.

13.4.5 Environmental benefits

Environmental benefits of congestion charges are usually comparatively small (Eliasson, 2009), but may still be important. The reason that they are usually relatively small is that while congestion is a non-linear phenomenon, meaning that a moderate traffic reduction may lead to huge congestion reductions, environmental benefits are essentially linear in traffic volumes – a 10 percent traffic reduction reduces emissions by around 10 percent. Better traffic flow may increase the emission reduction somewhat, but on the other hand, heavy vehicles emit more per kilometre and that traffic is usually reduced less than average. However, environmental benefits exist and are usually positive, and although they may be relatively small, they may be politically significant: voters tend to care much more about environmental issues than about efficient use of scarce road space.

Environmental benefits may still be substantial, however. The Milan Ecopass system was expressly designed to curb emissions by charging the most polluting vehicles, and it also succeeded in substantially decreasing traffic with these vehicles, resulting in lower emission levels. Still, emission benefits were still smaller than other kinds of benefits (Danielis et al., 2012). The general lesson that can be learnt is that differentiating the charge with respect to vehicle type can have a considerable effect on the composition of traffic and on vehicle sales. Stockholm results confirm this: in its first years, the Stockholm system exempted alternative-fuel vehicles and this contributed to a considerable increase in sales of such vehicles (Börjesson et al., 2012; Whitehead et al., 2014, 2015).

13.4.6 Safety benefits

The sign of safety effects of congestion charges is theoretically ambiguous. Lower traffic levels tend to decrease the number of accidents, ceteris paribus, but higher speeds may counteract this effect and even lead to an increase in severe accidents. Empirical evidence, however, indicates that the net effect is positive and can in fact be substantial (Danielis et al., 2012; Green et al., 2016). Eliasson (2009) reaches similar conclusions using accident modelling based on traffic measurements for Stockholm.

13.4.7 *Investment and operations costs*

Building and operating a large-scale urban road pricing system is not cheap: investment and operating costs may be substantial compared to the benefits delivered by the charges. If the purpose of a road user charge is just to generate revenue, there are usually more cost-effective ways to do this. What increases the cost of urban congestion charges compared to common toll roads is, first, that it is easy to restrict access to toll roads to stop non-paying vehicles from entering, and second, that toll road operators do not have to care much about the time lost for drivers queuing to pay. Since the fundamental reason for congestion pricing is that space is scarce, space-consuming toll plazas are not an option, which (usually) means that physical access restrictions are infeasible; and since the main benefit of congestion pricing is time savings, having a system which wastes drivers' time in a new form of queue is not beneficial. This means that congestion pricing systems must build on automatic free-flow identification. The problem is not the added technical complexity – in fact, the technical cost of such systems is nowadays not very high; the main cost drivers are the handling of payments and setting up an enforcement system. The latter especially can be legally complicated, which can increase costs. For example, different countries may have different regulations regarding what constitutes a legally valid proof-of-passage. Is an automatic registration of a number plate enough? Does there have to be a photo of the number plate, or even of the entire car? If so, are such photos compatible with privacy legislation? These questions (and many others) can be extremely complicated and expensive to solve.

Operating costs vary widely between cities, although exact figures are seldom published. The London system is by far the most expensive, with an operating cost of around 1€/vehicle (Transport for London, 2015). The Milan Area C system now appears to have reduced its operating cost to slightly more than 0.30€/vehicle, which would be less than half the cost from the time of Ecopass. The Stockholm and Gothenburg systems have operating costs of around 0.13€/vehicle, slightly higher than most of the largest Norwegian systems, which have an average operating cost of around 0.11€/vehicle (Odeck, 2008). Investment costs also vary. In Milan, a camera identification system was already in place before the Ecopass system, so the investment cost for Ecopass was limited to 7 million € (Croci and Douvan, 2015). The Stockholm and London systems had investment and start-up costs of around 200 million € (Eliasson, 2009; Hamilton, 2011; Santos et al., 2008). In both cases, the technical systems were developed 'from scratch', which presumably increased costs compared to a situation where a system can be acquired 'off the shelf'. The extremely heated political context in the two cities also contributed to high costs, since the government, the responsible public agencies and the contractor all wanted to be certain that the technical system worked flawlessly from the start. Hamilton (2011) provides an excellent discussion of political and technical cost drivers for congestion charging systems.

13.4.8 *Wider economic effects*

Changes in accessibility have repercussions on the rest of the economy, such as the labour market, the housing market and the market for commercial floor space. If congestion charges cause a drop in overall accessibility, this may cause additional social welfare losses since there are distortions on these markets in the form of taxation and agglomeration/ spillover effects.

Parry and Bento (2001) point out that if there are distortionary taxes on labour income, and if congestion charges cause accessibility to decrease, and if this in turn leads to a decrease in labour supply, welfare losses on the labour market may outweigh the benefits in the transport system. It is crucial how the toll revenues are used, however. If they are spent on decreasing the distortionary labour taxes, then the congestion charges are guaranteed to yield a net social surplus. To this should be added (although Parry and Bento do not explicitly point this out) that in equilibrium, the marginal benefit of public spending should be equal to the marginal cost of public funds (i.e. the marginal deadweight loss of taxation); otherwise, the government should simply decrease both their spending and the taxes in the initial situation. Hence, as long as the government spends the revenues on something where the marginal benefit is at least as high as the MCPF, congestion charges are guaranteed to deliver net benefits, even considering welfare losses on the labour market. Anderstig et al. (2016) analyse the interactions between the Stockholm congestion charges and the labour market. They conclude that the effect on economic output is in fact positive, since workers with high values of time experience an increase in accessibility, and the relationship between economic output and accessibility is much higher for workers with high values of time than for workers with low values of time.

A common fear is that congestion pricing will affect retail in the charged area negatively. However, studies of such effects have not found any support for this hypothesis, except possibly for locations close to the toll border (Croci and Douvan, 2015; Daunfeldt et al., 2009, 2013; Quddus et al., 2007a, 2007b). This coincides with the conclusions of Eliasson and Mattsson (2001), who use a generic simulation model to show that location effects can be expected to be (very) small, except possibly close to a toll ring. However, there is some evidence from Singapore (Agarwal et al., 2015) that the rents retailers pay for their floor space may decrease, which may be a sign that the gross profitability of retail stores decrease. On the other hand, if this is compensated by decreased rents (which would be the theoretical expectation), then the overall supply of retail would stay more or less constant (although property owners might lose). Agarwal et al. (2015) do not find any similar effects on rents for office or residential real estate.

13.4.9 Equity effects

A common argument against congestion charges is their supposedly negative equity effects. Whether equity effects in fact are negative depends on the specific travel pattern of the city, the design of the system and also on the use of revenues. Very broadly speaking, most equity studies have concluded that rich people will pay more in tolls than the poor, since they drive more, especially in inner cities where congestion is most severe.

However, it should be stressed that equity effects are often discussed in a short-term or narrow way, simply comparing the situation before and after charges are introduced. But congestion charges are not an instrument for redistributing income: it is a way to make the price of driving more 'correct', to make it better reflect the true social cost of driving. Prices are almost always the same for everyone, regardless of income or wealth (for very good reasons). The desire for increased income equity is instead usually handled by taxation and welfare systems; not even essential goods such as food and clothes are usually subsidised (except in special cases). If the default position therefore is that prices are, generally, equal for everyone, then it is natural to argue that the distributional effects of corrective taxes – taxes which are introduced to make the prices 'right' in the sense that they reflect full social costs – are in fact essentially irrelevant. At least, one should realise that arguing against such corrective taxes with equity arguments is logically equivalent to arguing that the good in question (car travel in rush hours, in this case) should be subsidised for equity reasons – and this is often a much less persuasive or intuitively appealing argument.

13.5 Public and political support for congestion pricing

13.5.1 Public attitudes to congestion pricing

Individuals' attitudes to congestion charges depend on many factors. Rational self-interest is obviously one of them: people will tend (all else equal) to be more positive to congestion charges the less they pay, the more travel time they gain, the higher they value travel time savings and the easier they have to adjust to the charges (for example, the more satisfied they are with public transport). Individuals also become more positive if revenues are used in a way they appreciate, which can be viewed as a form of self-interest (Börjesson et al., 2016; Eliasson, 2014; Eliasson and Jonsson, 2011; Gaunt et al., 2007; Hamilton et al., 2014; Hårsman and Quigley, 2010; Jaensirisak et al., 2003; Jones, 2003). But self-interest is not the only determinant by far. Attitudes to congestion charging are also affected by a number of other factors.

Environmental concerns and engagement strongly increase support for congestion charges (Börjesson et al., 2016; Eliasson, 2014; Eliasson and Jonsson, 2011; Hamilton et al., 2014; Jaensirisak et al., 2003). In the political debate, environmental benefits often play a more important role than time savings and efficient use of space, since environmental issues usually invoke stronger positive emotions than transport efficiency.

Support for congestion charges is related to trust in the government, and support for public interventions in general (Hamilton et al., 2014). Scepticism to congestion pricing can be caused by scepticism to the government's ability to design and manage such a system, or use the revenues efficiently (Dresner et al., 2006; Kallbekken and Sælen, 2011). It can also be associated to a more fundamental dislike of public interventions in general. This finding may partly explain the apparent paradox that left-wing parties are often more in favour of congestion pricing than liberal/conservative parties, despite the latter usually being more in favour of market-based solutions.

Support for congestion pricing is correlated with viewing pricing mechanisms in general as 'fair', for example supporting general principles such as 'user pays' or 'polluter pays'.

Hamilton et al. (2014) and Börjesson et al. (2016) show that self-interest only explains 20–50 percent of the total explained variation in attitudes (using data from Stockholm, Helsinki, Lyon and Gothenburg); the rest is explained by the attitude factors above.

How attitudes to congestion pricing is linked to other attitudes, such as fairness, equity, environment and so on, most likely depends on how congestion charges are framed in the specific local discourse – in other words, what congestion charges are 'perceived' as. When people are faced with a new issue where attitudes are not well developed, attitudes to the new issue are often formed by associating it to some other issue which is perceived to be 'similar' in some sense, and where the individual already has a well-developed attitude (Heberlein, 2012). The new issue then inherits the attitude from the familiar one. (This is similar to what Kahneman (2011) calls the substitution heuristic.) Such new attitudes, which are based on limited experience, knowledge and emotions, tend to be less stable, and may change comparatively easily. In particular, they may change if they are associated with another issue, a process sometimes called reframing. For example, depending on how it is framed, congestion charges may be perceived as a tax, an environmental policy or a way to improve efficiency – and this perception may change if charges are reframed, for example due to how the local debate evolves. Eliasson (2014) argues that it was not until congestion pricing was reframed from solely a transport-efficiency policy to an environmental policy that it entered the political agenda in Stockholm. This came at the price of a more polarised debate, since arguments turned from mostly technical/rational to more moral/emotional. This might have been a necessary price to pay, since without this moral/emotional association, the policy might not have generated enough political engagement. Once the charges were in place, however, the moral/emotional dimension was gradually discharged, not least due to the earmarking of revenues for a new road, which could be interpreted as signalling that congestion pricing was not an 'anti-car' measure, but merely a technical/rational tool for traffic control, similar in nature to traffic signals or speed limits. Since then, the Stockholm congestion charges have more or less stopped making any particular political controversies.

In most cities where congestion charges have been introduced, support has increased after the introduction. The same phenomenon has been observed for the US HOT lanes (Burris et al., 2007; Finkleman et al., 2011). Part of the explanation seems to be that benefits turn out to be larger and problems smaller than expected (Eliasson, 2008; Schuitema et al., 2010). However, status quo bias (and possibly reframing) seem to be at least as important (Börjesson et al., 2016; Eliasson, 2014). Schade and Baum (2007) show that support increases when respondents think that the change is unavoidable.

13.5.2 Gaining political support

Gaining political support for congestion pricing is different from getting public support (or acceptability). Obviously, politicians' willingness to introduce congestion pricing is influenced by public attitudes – but public support is neither a necessary nor a sufficient condition for getting political support. Crucial for the analysis and understanding of political acceptability are power issues: the power over the design of the charging scheme, the power over the revenues, and how the charges and their revenue stream will affect decisions and funding of transport investments in general. Many politicians have stated that their main argument against introducing the congestion charge is the uncertainty about the political power over scheme design and revenues. Adding to these uncertainties is the uncertainty about how the existence of a new revenue stream might affect the complicated negotiations between national, regional and local levels about infrastructure financing.

13.6 The future of congestion pricing

The social benefits that congestion pricing can bring will continue to increase, as urbanisation continues and urban space becomes an ever scarcer resource. A very large number of cities around the world are exploring the possibilities and are more or less actively considering introducing congestion charges.

Congestion pricing is a mature policy measure. There is a large body of evidence and experience regarding design, effects and technology which can be used by other cities. Almost all systems now use some variant of automatic number plate recognition linked to an automatic invoicing system. This begs the question whether more advanced technology that allows even more fine-tuned pricing schemes (say, distance-based pricing differentiated in time and space) is an attractive way forward. So far there is little to support that the added benefits of such systems would be worth the higher costs. Passage-based systems seem to be flexible enough to deliver high benefits at a relatively low cost. Satellite-based technologies which require installations in the vehicle but little roadside investments are attractive alternatives when the charged area is large, the number of vehicles is small and those vehicles are already subject to public regulations and inspections; the typical case is heavy goods vehicles in an entire country. For urban congestion pricing, however, the area is usually small, the number of vehicles huge, and they are subject to limited inspections and regulations, which makes passage-based systems which require no intervention in the vehicles more attractive. Hence, I would personally not expect that satellite-based technology becomes the method of choice for urban congestion pricing any time soon.

However, despite available technology and overwhelming evidence that congestion pricing works, the political case for congestion pricing remains difficult. In my own experience, there seem to be four main political obstacles, described as follows.

Loss aversion and status quo bias are hard-wired in human nature. The potential losses of paying charges and having to adjust loom larger than the potential gains of travel time in the minds of voters and decision makers. Even those who would not be directly affected can be subject to pure status quo bias. This makes it difficult to build enough public and political support ex ante. Even if that can be done, it needs to be maintained during the several years it takes to go from idea to implementation, which can be extraordinarily difficult in an unstable political landscape.

It is easier to identify the losers from congestion pricing than the winners. The losers are here and now, and are easy to identify and organise in self-interested pressure groups. The winners are more dispersed, and perhaps only exist in the future, or may not realise that they will win ex ante. Moreover, there are often many winners who win a little and few losers that feel that they lose a lot. Perhaps surprisingly, this is not a recipe for a successful political idea, despite that there are more winners than losers. This is because winners may not care enough to let it affect how they vote, while for the losers it can be the most important issue in an election.

Congestion pricing increases the efficiency of the transport system – but not many voters care enough about efficiency that it becomes an important political issue. Congestion and the resulting long travel times can be an important issue, but increasing travel costs just because travel times are long is to most voters incredibly counterintuitive. However, voters do often seem to care about urban environmental issues – emissions, noise, more space for pedestrians – so this may sometimes be a more important selling point. For an issue to be politically interesting, it must generate enthusiasm among a sufficiently large group of voters. Since transport efficiency is not an issue that many voters feel strongly about, the issue has a very limited political upside. Even large gains in transport efficiency may not be valued enough by voters to be worth the political cost in terms of some voters feeling they will become worse off.

For many politicians, the main obstacle is not so much the lack of public support but uncertainties regarding the power over revenues, scheme design and so on, and how introducing congestion pricing (and especially the resultant toll revenue stream) may upset the delicate balance of power between national, regional and local levels, and the continuous negotiations about, e.g., financing responsibilities and allocation of funding.

The fundamental obstacle for congestion pricing is that its primary positive effect – more efficient use of scarce space – is something that only generates lukewarm enthusiasm. While most would agree that efficiency is worth striving for in principle, it does not stir up enough positive emotions to be worth substantial political risks. Congestion pricing is in many respects similar to other traffic-control measures, such as traffic signals and speed limits; most would agree that they are needed, but few are enthusiastic supporters of them. The difference is that traffic signals and speed limits are already there, while congestion pricing is still something new and unknown – and then, status quo bias decides the issue for most people.

In the cities where congestion pricing has been successfully introduced, it is often because of an alliance between three groups: traffic planners wanting the efficiency gains, environmentalists wanting the environmental benefits and politicians looking for a revenue source. When this works it can indeed be a powerful political strategy. Many lessons can be learned from the cities which have succeeded and those who have failed – both things to do and things to avoid.

However, congestion charges in the hands of politicians merely looking for revenues is a dangerous tool. One of the most insightful (albeit a little cynical) arguments against congestion pricing is that it is dangerous to open up a new source of tax revenue which may be perceived as 'free money' by politicians – especially if a large share of traffic comes from other constituencies.

There are clearly incentives for politicians to overcharge drivers from other constituencies and to overinvest in infrastructure by borrowing money against future toll revenues, spend the money today and leave the bill to future car drivers. Institutional frameworks which enforce fiscal discipline and prevent tax exporting are virtually necessary.

Still, congestion pricing deserves to be used much more than it is. It has the potential to bring huge social benefits at a comparatively low cost and can also have desirable long-term consequences on urban structure and overall travel patterns. The technology is available, there is experience and evidence of how charges should be designed, and as long as benefits are delivered and revenues are not squandered, it is possible to build public support for it. More cities should dare to make the leap.

Notes

1 Costs are converted from Swedish kronor using a conversion rate of 10 kr = 1€.
2 Instead of a single road, one can also think of an area with a dense road network, such as the downtown of a city; similar relationships hold between traffic volumes and travel times (Daganzo, 2007; Daganzo et al., 2011; Geroliminis and Daganzo, 2008).
3 We assume that the travel time has been converted to an equivalent monetary cost. Hence, this exposition tacitly assumes that drivers have the same value of travel time.
4 Of course, the social benefits generated by *spending* the tax revenue are (hopefully) larger than the social loss caused by collecting them (the deadweight loss).

References

Agarwal, S., Koo, K. M., and Sing, T. F. (2015). Impact of electronic road pricing on real estate prices in Singapore. *Journal of Urban Economics*, 90, pp. 50–9.

Anderstig, C., Berglund, S., Eliasson, J., and Andersson, M. (2016). Congestion charges and labour market imperfections. *Journal of Transport Economics and Policy*, 50(2), pp. 113–31.

Arnott, R., de Palma, A., and Lindsey, R. (1993). A Structural Model of Peak-Period Congestion: A Traffic Bottleneck with Elastic Demand. *American Economic Review*, 83(1), pp. 161–79.

Attard, M. and Ison, S. G. (2010). The Implementation of Road User Charging and the Lessons Learnt: The Case of Valletta, Malta. *Journal of Transport Geography*, 18(1), pp. 14–22.

Beria, P. (2015). Effectiveness and Monetary Impact of Milan's Road Charge, One Year after Implementation. *International Journal of Sustainable Transportation*, 10(7), pp. 657–69.

Börjesson, M. and Kristoffersson, I. (2015). The Gothenburg Congestion Charge: Effects, Design and Politics. *Transportation Research Part A: Policy and Practice*, 75, pp. 134–46.

Börjesson, M., Eliasson, J., Hugosson, M. B. and Brundell-Freij, K. (2012). The Stockholm Congestion Charges—5 Years On: Effects, Acceptability and Lessons Learnt. *Transport Policy*, 20, pp. 1–12.

Börjesson, M., Eliasson, J. and Hamilton, C. (2016). Why Experience Changes Attitudes to Congestion Pricing: The Case of Gothenburg. *Transportation Research Part A: Policy and Practice*, 85, pp. 1–16.

Burris, M. and Stockton, B. (2004). HOT Lanes in Houston-Six Years of Experience. *Journal of Public Transportation*, 7(3), pp. 1–21.

Burris, M., Sadabadi, K., Mattingly, S., Mahlawat, M., Li, J., Rasmidatta, I. and Saroosh, A. (2007). Reaction to the Managed Lane Concept by Various Groups of Travelers. *Transportation Research Record: Journal of the Transportation Research Board*, pp. 74–82.

Croci, E. and Douvan, A. R. (2015). Urban Road Pricing: The Experience of Milan. In Kreiser, L., Andersen, M. S., Olsen, B. E., Speck, S. and Milne, J. E. (eds), *Carbon Pricing: Design, Experiences and Issues*. Cheltenham: Edward Elgar.

Daganzo, C. F. (2007). Urban Gridlock: Macroscopic Modeling and Mitigation Approaches. *Transportation Research Part B: Methodological*, 41(1), pp. 49–62.

Daganzo, C. F., Gayah, V. V. and Gonzales, E. J. (2011). Macroscopic Relations of Urban Traffic Variables: Bifurcations, Multivaluedness and Instability. *Transportation Research Part B: Methodological*, 45(1), pp. 278–88.

Danielis, R., Rotaris, L., Marcucci, E. and Massiani, J. (2012). A Medium Term Evaluation of the Ecopass Road Pricing Scheme in Milan: Economic, Environmental and Transport Impacts. *Economics and Policy of Energy and the Environment*, 2, pp. 49–83.

Daunfeldt, S.-O., Rudholm, N. and Rämme, U. (2009). Congestion Charges and Retail Revenues: Results from the Stockholm Road Pricing Trial. *Transportation Research Part A: Policy and Practice*, 43(3), pp. 306–9.

Daunfeldt, S.-O., Rudholm, N. and Rämme, U. (2013). Congestion Charges in Stockholm: How Have They Affected Retail Revenues? *Transportmetrica A: Transport Science*, 9(3), pp. 259–68.

Dix, M. (2006). *How Much Does the Scheme Cost: The London Experience.* Paris: International Transport Forum.

Dresner, S., Dunne, L., Clinch, P. and Beuermann, C. (2006). Social and Political Responses to Ecological Tax Reform in Europe: An Introduction to the Special Issue. *Energy Policy*, 34(8), pp. 895–904.

Eliasson, J. (2008). Lessons from the Stockholm Congestion Charging Trial. *Transport Policy*, 15(6), pp. 395–404.

Eliasson, J. (2009). A Cost-Benefit Analysis of the Stockholm Congestion Charging System. *Transportation Research Part A: Policy and Practice*, 43(4), pp. 468–80.

Eliasson, J. (2014). The Role of Attitude Structures, Direct Experience and Framing for Successful Congestion Pricing. *Transportation Research A*, 67, pp. 81–95.

Eliasson, J. and Jonsson, L. (2011). The Unexpected 'Yes': Explanatory Factors behind the Positive Attitudes to Congestion Charges in Stockholm. *Transport Policy*, 18(4), pp. 636–47.

Eliasson, J. and Mattsson, L.-G. (2001). Transport and Location Effects of Road Pricing: A Simulation Approach. *Journal of Transport Economics and Policy*, 35(3), pp. 417–56.

Eliasson, J., Hultkrantz, L., Nerhagen, L. and Rosqvist, L. S. (2009). The Stockholm Congestion Charging Trial 2006: Overview of Effects. *Transportation Research Part A: Policy and Practice*, 43(3), pp. 240–50.

Finkleman, J., Casello, J. and Fu, L. (2011). Empirical Evidence from the Greater Toronto Area on the Acceptability and Impacts of HOT Lanes. *Transport Policy*, 18(6), pp. 814–24.

Fosgerau, M. (2015). Congestion in the Bathtub. *Economics of Transportation*, 4(4), pp. 241–55.

Gaunt, M., Rye, T. and Allen, S. (2007). Public Acceptability of Road User Charging: The Case of Edinburgh and the 2005 Referendum. *Transport Reviews*, 27(1), pp. 85–102.

Geroliminis, N. and Daganzo, C. F. (2008). Existence of Urban-Scale Macroscopic Fundamental Diagrams: Some Experimental Findings. *Transportation Research Part B: Methodological*, 42(9), pp. 759–70.

Givoni, M. (2012). Re-assessing the Results of the London Congestion Charging Scheme. *Urban Studies*, 49(5), pp. 1089–105.

Green, C. P., Heywood, J. S. and Navarro, M. (2016). Traffic Accidents and the London Congestion Charge. *Journal of Public Economics*, 133, pp. 11–22.

Gullberg, A. and Isaksson, K. (2009). The Stockholm Trial. In Gullberg, A. and Isaksson, K. (eds), *Congestion Taxes in City Traffic: Lessons Learnt from the Stockholm Trial.* Lund: Nordic Academic Press.

Hamilton, C. J. (2011). Revisiting the Cost of the Stockholm Congestion Charging System. *Transport Policy*, 18(6), pp. 836–47.

Hamilton, C. J., Eliasson, J., Brundell-Freij, K., Raux, C. and Souche, S. (2014). *Determinants of Congestion Pricing Acceptability (No. 2014:11).* CTS Working Paper. Centre for Transport Studies, KTH Royal Institute of Technology.

Hårsman, B. and Quigley, J. M. (2010). Political and Public Acceptability of Congestion Pricing: Ideology and Self-Interest. *Journal of Policy Analysis and Management*, 29(4), pp. 854–74.

Heberlein, T. (2012). *Navigating Environmental Attitudes.* New York: Oxford University Press.

Jaensirisak, S., May, A. D. and Wardman, M. (2003). Acceptability of Road User Charging: The Influence of Selfish and Social Perspectives. In Schade, J. and Schlag, B. (eds), *Acceptability of Transport Pricing Strategies*. Oxford: Elsevier.

Janson, M. and Levinson, D. (2014). HOT or Not: Driver Elasticity to Price on the MnPASS HOT Lanes. *Research in Transportation Economics*, 44, pp. 21–32.

Jones, P. (2003). Acceptability of Road User Charging: Meeting the Challenge. In Schade, J. and Schlag, B. (eds), *Acceptability of Transport Pricing Strategies*. Oxford: Elsevier.

Kahneman, D. (2011). *Thinking, Fast and Slow.* New York: Farrar, Straus and Giroux.

Kallbekken, S. and Sælen, H. (2011). Public Acceptance for Environmental Taxes: Self-Interest, Environmental and Distributional Concerns. *Energy Policy*, 39(5), pp. 2966–73.

Leape, J. (2006). The London Congestion Charge. *Journal of Economic Perspectives*, 20(4), pp. 157–76.

Menon, A. P. G. (2000). ERP in Singapore: A Perspective One Year On. *Traffic Engineering and Control*, 41(2), pp. 40–5.

Menon, A. P. G. and Kian-Keong, C. (2004). ERP in Singapore: What's Been Learnt from Five Years of Operation? *Traffic Engineering and Control*, 45(2).
Odeck, J. (2008). How Efficient and Productive Are Road Toll Companies? Evidence from Norway. *Transport Policy*, 15(4), pp. 232–41.
Olszewski, P. and Xie, L. (2005). Modelling the Effects of Road Pricing on Traffic in Singapore. *Transportation Research Part A: Policy and Practice*, 39(7–9), pp. 755–72.
Parry, I. W. H. and Bento, A. (2001). Revenue Recycling and the Welfare Effects of Road Pricing. *Scandinavian Journal of Economics*, 103(4), pp. 645–71.
Quddus, M. A., Bell, M. G. H., Schmöcker, J.-D., and Fonzone, A. (2007). The Impact of the Congestion Charge on the Retail Business in London: An Econometric Analysis. *Transport Policy*, 14(5), pp. 433–44.
Quddus, M. A., Carmel, A. and Bell, M. G. H. (2007). The Impact of the Congestion Charge on Retail: The London Experience. *Journal of Transport Economics and Policy*, 41(1), pp. 113–33.
Santos, G. (2004). Urban Road Pricing in the UK. *Research in Transportation Economics*, 9, pp. 251–82.
Santos, G., Button, K. and Noll, R. G. (2008). London Congestion Charging. *Brookings-Wharton Papers on Urban Affairs*, 1, pp. 177–234.
Schade, J. and Baum, M. (2007). Reactance or Acceptance? Reactions towards the Introduction of Road Pricing. *Transportation Research Part A: Policy and Practice*, 41(1), pp. 41–8.
Schuitema, G., Steg, L. and Forward, S. (2010). Explaining Differences in Acceptability before and Acceptance after the Implementation of a Congestion Charge in Stockholm. *Transportation Research Part A: Policy and Practice*, 44(2), pp. 99–109.
Transport for London (2007). *Impacts Monitoring: Fifth Annual Report*. London: TfL.
Transport for London (2014). *Public and Stakeholder Consultation on a Variation Order to Modify the Congestion Charging Scheme Impact Assessment*. London: TfL.
Transport for London (2015). *Annual Report and Statement of Accounts 2014/15*. London: TfL.
Whitehead, J., Franklin, J. P. and Washington, S. (2014). The Impact of a Congestion Pricing Exemption on the Demand for New Energy Efficient Vehicles in Stockholm. *Transportation Research Part A: Policy and Practice*, 70, pp. 24–40.
Whitehead, J., Franklin, J. P. and Washington, S. (2015). Transitioning to Energy Efficient Vehicles: An Analysis of the Potential Rebound Effects and Subsequent Impact upon Emissions. *Transportation Research Part A: Policy and Practice*, 74, pp. 250–67.

14

Transport modelling and economic theory

Kathryn Stewart

14.1 Theoretical behavioural underpinnings of transport modelling

Classical transport models have been refined and developed over time such that several classifications may now be presented and discussed. The main classifications start from whether the model is termed 'static' or 'dynamic', that is whether the model represents a fixed time slice or if it includes time as a model variable. Static models assume that within a modelled period, time is invariant and the model outputs relate in the aggregate across that time period, whereas dynamic models allow the passage of time within the model. The next main classification is the level of unit modelled; models are described as 'macroscopic' where traffic is modelled as a fluid (where vehicles are aggregated into traffic flow) and 'microscopic' where individual vehicles are modelled explicitly. An intermediate version of these is termed 'mesoscopic'. Finally there is a distinction between 'deterministic' models, those where model outputs are identical for each model run, and 'stochastic', which allow for random variations.

The first traffic model to understand is termed the four-stage model. This encompasses stage 1 – traffic generation, stage 2 – traffic distribution, stage 3 – modal split and stage 4 – traffic assignment. The assignment part is often described as vehicle routing and it is within the routing part that much behavioural theory to be discussed in this chapter is present.

14.1.1 Traffic generation

This element of the modelling process is concerned with traffic forecasting and is related to land-use planning and service provision. As the vast majority of travel is a derived demand in behavioural terms, every population centre is a potential trip generator and consequently every new residential development will generate potential trips. In modelling terms such trips are located at 'origins' or 'sources'. However, the demand for travel (excluding freight) is predicated upon a desire to access services, hence there must be a desire, i.e. a basic demand, to travel to a trip attractor; a facility such as a workplace, educational establishment or leisure provision. Such attractors are termed 'destinations' or 'sinks'. The scope of a traffic model exists between the origins and the destinations of the model, these are the points where traffic enters and leaves the model. Such origins/destinations often cover a significant geographical area where trips might begin or end and models do not generally exist at the microscopic level in terms of the traffic-generation points, rather the forecast traffic appears within a model zone at a point termed the

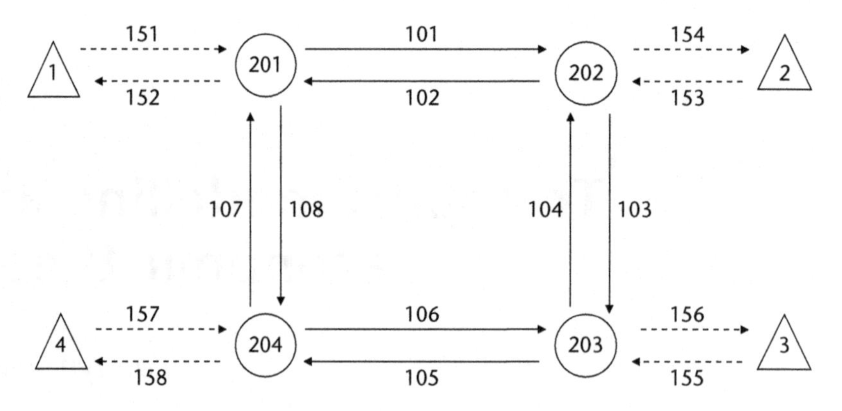

Figure 14.1 Simple network model

zone-centroid. This is the theoretical point at which all trips from a zone in which traffic is generated enter the model scope. This traffic then joins the model structure through a device termed a pseudo-link or zone-centroid connector which may be assigned a non-zero travel cost to illustrate the length of average journey undertaken to reach the modelled area – thus the zone-centroids act as entry/exit points and define the extent of the area modelled. The roads and junctions within a modelled area are termed 'links' and 'nodes' and may be represented by a network diagram – within microscopic models such a network diagram is a geographically accurate representation of roads and junctions, but within macroscopic models the links are indicative of roads and form topological representations which do not convey geographical accuracy. A popular and well-known example of a topological map is the London Underground map which conveys information regarding connectivity of links and nodes, but which does not convey geographical accuracy in terms of link length or direction. An example of a simple network model is shown in Figure 14.1 (triangles represent zones (origins/destination), circles represent junctions (nodes), lines represent roads (links) and dotted lines are zone-centroid connectors (which allow traffic entry to the 'real' network)). The detail of quantifying the amount of trips generated or attracted by services or facilities is covered in Chapter 11.

14.1.2 Traffic distribution

Once the forecasting process has provided quantification for trips generated at an origin or attracted to a destination, the modelling process requires that such trips should be distributed into a trip matrix. This process takes a number of origins which all generate trips and destinations which attract trips and distribute the trips generated at any origin between potential destinations. For each zone where trips are generated, people wish to travel to access employment, goods and services, and hence the trips will be distributed to different destinations which attract trip makers. The process of distribution may be achieved theoretically using models such as 'the gravity model' (Ortuzar and Willumsen, 1994), where closer destinations with higher populations are assumed to be more attractive and an iterative procedure based on location weightings is utilised. At a simple level, the weighting may be a distance function, but may be refined into utility function-based weightings. In practice, however, matrix estimation is further refined and calibrated using survey data, tracking data and traffic-count information at various points. The underlying principle is that of utility maximisation, in that the user will select an option from their choice set which maximises their personal utility. In terms of transport modelling utility may consist of many factors including personal preferences, comfort and safety. However, whilst these factors are undoubtedly important behavioural considerations, the most important factors in travel utility are assumed to be travel time and financial cost, such that travel cost is often used to denote journey time. In more complex models a full generalised cost function could be used that better describes realistic personal utility, but of course such models are more difficult to calibrate in practice, resulting in time being the most commonly used proxy measure for generalised cost.

14.1.3 Modal split

A transport model is taken to include all feasible transport modes for the desired context, whereas a traffic model is more typically used to describe the private car or road-based element. Hence after a trip matrix is produced, all the trips between all origin-destination pairs must be separated into travel by each mode covered by the model. At a minimum this will include private car and bus-based public transport, but may also include rail, air and ferry, as appropriate. The mechanism for separating trips may be theoretical or empirical (or a combination) and the theoretical mechanism is again based on random utility theory. The utility of each option in a discrete choice set is determined and the aggregate number of trips assigned to each mode is then calculated using these utility functions. In principle, under a paradigm of perfect information and perfectly rational decision makers, it could be argued that all travellers should be assigned to the mode which maximises their personal utility, and as the proxy for this is often travel time then all users should wish to travel by the fastest mode available. However, assuming sufficient capacity, this could result in no mode splitting, a clearly unrealistic outcome as preference and availability is critical in mode choice decisions. As a result, the mechanisms used for mode choice includes a probabilistic element where the 'cheapest' mode is obviously the most attractive and has the highest probability, but the other modes are also assigned probabilities based on relative utility such that when modal split occurs all modes are assigned travellers. Thus the principle of discrete choice modelling (when users have to select a single option from a finite set of alternatives) is utilised, and 'the probability of an individual choosing a given option is a function of their socioeconomic characteristics and the relative attractiveness of the option'.

Socioeconomic characteristics are assumed to influence attitudes and perceptions, and this in turn will determine the level of utility an individual will derive from choosing a particular option. Discrete choice models are based on random utility theory. To represent the attractiveness of the alternatives the economic concept of utility is used. A utility function measures the degree of satisfaction that people get from their choices and conversely a disutility function represents the generalised cost that is associated with each choice. Such choice models have been frequently applied to many situations to explain how choice between competing alternatives is made. Each alternative is described by a utility (or disutility) function, and the probability associated with an individual's choice of each of the competing alternatives is expressed mathematically in terms of utilities. In order to predict if an alternative will be chosen, according to the model, the value of its utility must be compared with those of alternative options such that a probability value between 0 and 1 is obtained:

$$\text{e.g. utility (car): } U_c = a_0 - a_1.T_1 - a_2.\ T_2 - a_3.C + a_4.NC \qquad (14.1)$$

where T_1 = in vehicle time, T_2 = access time, C = travel cost, NC = number of cars in household and a_i (where i = 0 to 4) are weightings.

A commonly used model is the Logit type although other formulations are also feasible. The Multinomial Logit (MNL) model is used to calculate the proportion (probability) of trips that will select a specific mode k from the set of available modes designated U_i according to the following relationship:

$$P_k = \frac{\exp U_k}{\Sigma \exp U_i}. \tag{14.2}$$

Variations of the MNL (such as hierarchical or nested logit) may be used when alternative modes are not independent, i.e. there are groups of alternatives more similar than others, such as public transport modes versus the private car.

14.1.4 Route choice

Route choice shares common elements with modal choice but with important distinctions. Firstly, route choice falls within discrete choice theory: if three routes are available then a driver may choose route A or B or C, there is no choice continuity. Thus in some circumstances, similar logistic choice functions may be appropriate for route choice. However, whilst mode choice is clearly distinct (albeit with some important hierarchical elements), the road network is formed of connected links such that routes between any OD pair may have elements of overlap. This is illustrated in Figure 14.2, which represents a simple grid network with single OD pair and no looping paths.

It may easily be seen that for the square of side 1 there are two distinct routes from top left to bottom right, but as the side of the square increases, the individual links within each complete route (or path) increase exponentially with increasing amounts of overlap (for a grid of side 10 there are approximately 185,000 paths).

Thus the fourth stage in the modelling process is concerned with the trip maker's choice of route between pairs of zones by each mode. This involves assigning each trip to the highway links or roads in the highway network or to the public transport network. In economic terms the transportation system may be expressed in terms of the demand for travel (trips) and the supply of road and public transport capacities. Trip generation, distribution and modal split models represent the demand for travel and are normally expressed within OD matrices. The supply side of the transportation system is represented by road network and public transport system with trips being assigned to the available routes/services. Traditionally, traffic assignment has been primarily concerned with the problem of determining the distribution of traffic on highway networks. Public transport assignment problems associated with the assignment of passengers using public transport services (such as bus, tram or rail) are more difficult to model than those of private cars and are beyond the scope of this chapter. For further reading see Gentile et al. (2016).

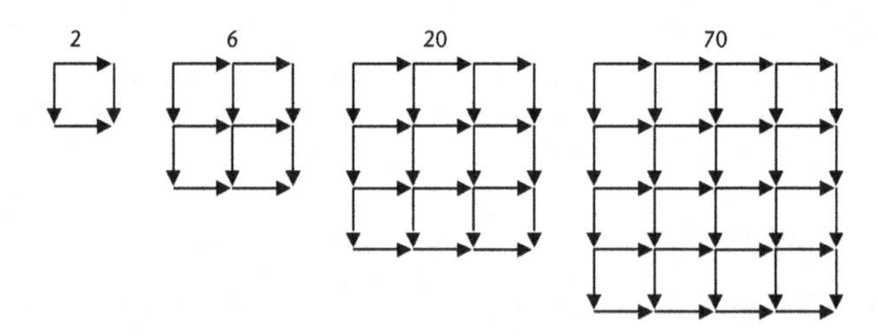

Figure 14.2 Number of paths from the north-west corner to the south-east corner of grids

The basic assumption in assignment (route choice) is that travellers choose the route which offers the least perceived individual costs. A number of factors influence the choice of highway route when driving between two points. These include journey time, distance, monetary cost, congestion, queues, types of manoeuvres required, type of road, scenery, signposting, roadworks, reliability of travel time and habit. Producing a generalised cost expression correctly calibrated to include all behavioural choice elements is difficult and impractical, therefore, simplifying assumptions are needed. The most basic models use travel time as a proxy for the full generalised costs, whereas the majority of assignment programs allow the user to allocate weights to travel time and distance (and often road tolls) in order to represent drivers' perceptions of these factors. The weighted sum of these values may then be utilised as a generalised cost in route-choice estimation.

14.2 Static models

As with economics, in any form of modelling it is necessary to make certain assumptions when formulating the model. This often results in a relatively simple initial model which may be refined and adapted to represent reality more closely. For example, it is clear that in reality traffic assignment is dynamic, and demand is constantly changing with time. Vehicles will enter a network and respond and make decisions which are based on the current conditions at that time. However, static models are generally more mathematically tractable and are widely used as the basis for modelling. Static models use a fixed set of demands, for example the average demands over a certain time period, often the morning peak.

It is also generally assumed that drivers are influenced by travel costs, in that they would wish to minimise their costs, and for simplicity of illustration in this chapter such costs are taken to be equivalent to travel time (although generalised cost may be substituted throughout). In the simplest case of traffic assignment it is assumed that all drivers wish to minimise their travel cost (or time), and that they have a perfect knowledge of the network. They all therefore identify the quickest (or shortest) route through the network for their particular journey, and choose that route. This would result (if cost were independent of flow) in what is known as an All or Nothing assignment, i.e. that all traffic chooses a particular route, and so no traffic chooses other routes. This is obviously not the case as it is clear from observation of traffic in networks that route spreading occurs, and so models are accordingly refined to take this into account (by defining cost-flow relations which increase cost with increasing congestion), resulting in the case of deterministic equilibrium assignment. Deterministic assignment models assume that drivers have perfect knowledge of network costs, and as this is not generally the case, stochastic models, where drivers act to minimise their perceived costs, may be preferred, and such stochastic elements may act as a proxy for missing (i.e. difficult to estimate) elements from the full generalised cost. The concept of the system optimal where drivers are routed to optimise system flows rather than to minimise personal costs is then introduced and elastic demand in network assignment modelling is then discussed.

14.2.1 Deterministic equilibrium assignment

Deterministic assignment is an assignment method which assumes drivers to have perfect knowledge of the network through which they travel, so that if each link has an associated cost function, then the driver is assumed to be able to determine the cheapest route for their particular journey and to act to minimise their cost (this is commonly known as Wardrop's first principle (Wardrop, 1952)). These cost functions are said to be separable, in that they can be defined for a particular link (as opposed to route) under the assumption that junction effects are negligible in comparison

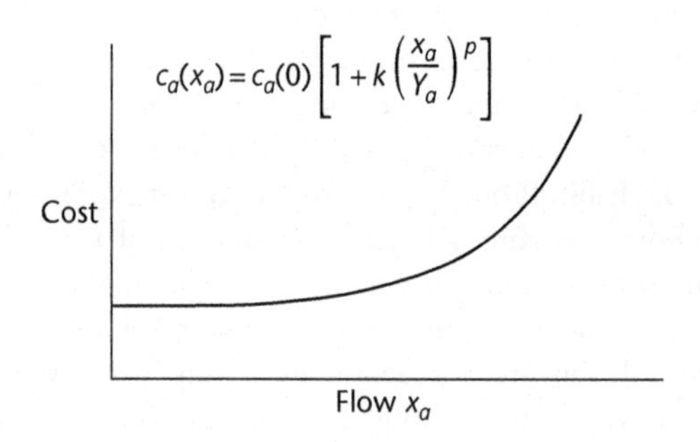

Figure 14.3 BPR cost-flow relation

with link effects and can thus be ignored. This sort of assignment is applicable to congested urban networks, where the cost functions incorporate capacity restraints. A commonly used cost function is that taken from the US Bureau of Public Roads (1964):

$$C_a(x_a) = c_a(0)[1 + k(x_a/Y_a)^p] \tag{14.3}$$

where x_a is the flow, $c_a(0)$ is the free-flow cost, Y_a is the theoretical capacity (for free-flowing traffic) and k and p are parameters which will determine the effect on travelling time as this capacity level is reached and then exceeded; as illustrated in Figure 14.3.

Thus cost can be seen to increase as flow along a link increases, and this dependence of cost upon flow means that route spreading will occur, rather than an all-or-nothing solution, as an additional driver will seek the cheapest route taking into account the increased cost on links due to increased flows, and so the cheapest route will not always be the same as the cheapest route in free-flow conditions.

The assumptions given above result in a traffic assignment known as User Equilibrium (UE) or Wardrop Equilibrium (Sheffi, 1985): 'For each OD pair, at user equilibrium, the travel time on all used paths is equal, and (also) less than or equal to the travel time that would be experienced by a single vehicle on any unused path.' UE can also be described as a selfish equilibrium, as every driver acts to minimise their personal cost.

The concept of UE can be easily illustrated by the use of a simple two-link network, such as that given in Figure 14.4 (for simplicity the value of p as in the BPR function (14.3) is taken as 1, giving a linear relationship). As before, the following notation is used: (C_i, X_i: path-costs, path-flows), (c_i, x_i: link-costs, link-flows).

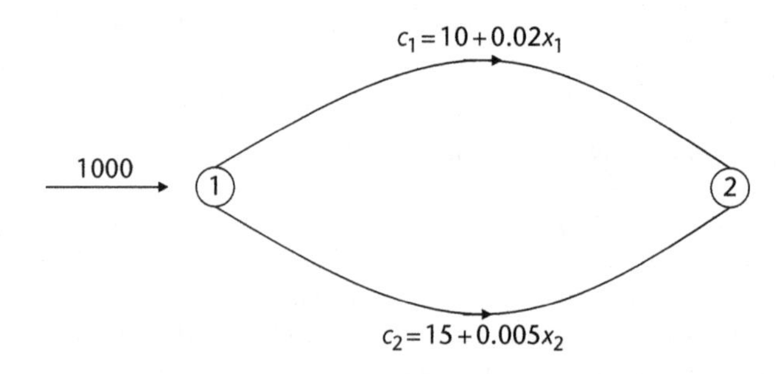

Figure 14.4 Two-link network

There is a demand of 1,000 vehicles between origin 1 and destination 2.

In this simple network therefore, the high road (C1) has a lower initial cost than the low road (C2), but this cost rises at a faster rate with increases in traffic flow. The principles of user equilibrium state that at equilibrium the travel time (or cost) should be equal for each OD pair. In this two-link example, each link is also a path, so $C_i = c_i$ and $X_i = x_i \; \forall i$. Here, therefore:

$$C_1 = C_2 = c_1 = c_2. \tag{14.4}$$

The demand of 1,000 must be split between the two paths, so:

$$x_1 + x_2 = 1000. \tag{14.5}$$

Equations (14.4) and (14.5) may then be readily solved to give the solution:

$$x_1 = 400 \qquad x_2 = 600 \qquad c_1 = c_2 = 18.$$

That is, 400 vehicles will use the upper path and 600 the lower path, resulting in a common cost of 18 for either path. The total network travel cost (TNTC) for UE would therefore be 18,000.

Clearly in the case of more complex networks the solution process to find the flow vector is non-trivial, established iterative algorithms being used (Sheffi, 1985). The premise being that for any given set of cost-flow functions, it is possible to carry out an all-or-nothing (AON) assignment, i.e. where all of the traffic between any given OD pair is assigned to the cheapest route. In assigning the traffic in such a manner, however, the traffic on each route will affect the cost on each route, so that the cheapest route (under congested conditions) will probably be different, thus under Wardrop's principle route, spreading will occur. If initially the procedure is started with a vector of flows $\boldsymbol{x}^n$ and its associated costs $\boldsymbol{c}^n$, then if an AON loading is carried out based on these costs, the flow pattern obtained $\boldsymbol{y}^n$ is referred to as the auxiliary of $\boldsymbol{x}^n$. $\boldsymbol{x}^{n+1}$ is then set to equal $\boldsymbol{y}^n$ and the procedure is repeated as in:

$$\boldsymbol{c}^0 \rightarrow \boldsymbol{x}^1 \rightarrow \boldsymbol{c}^1 \rightarrow \boldsymbol{y}^1 = \boldsymbol{x}^2 \rightarrow \boldsymbol{c}^2 \rightarrow \ldots.. \tag{14.6}$$

This is referred to as a 'hard speed change' and is unlikely to converge, but rather oscillates. To overcome this, a 'soft speed change' is used to move from the current flow pattern $\boldsymbol{x}^n$ to a weighted combination of $\boldsymbol{x}^n$ and $\boldsymbol{y}^n$ so that the new flow pattern $\boldsymbol{x}^{n+1}$ is given by:

$$\boldsymbol{x}^{n+1} = \boldsymbol{x}^n + \lambda_n(\boldsymbol{y}^n - \boldsymbol{x}^n) \tag{14.7}$$

where λ_n is the 'step length' i.e. the distance moved from $\boldsymbol{x}^n$ towards $\boldsymbol{y}^n$. The method of successive averages, where $\lambda_n = 1/n$ is equivalent to an even split among the previously calculated routes, has been proved to converge to the UE solution (albeit slowly) (Sheffi, 1985). More efficient algorithms such as the Frank-Wolfe algorithm, where an optimum step length is utilised, rely on the Beckman formulation of an objective function for UE (1985, p. 7) (Beckman et al., 1956) and its formulation as an equivalent minimisation problem.

$$Z_{UE} = \int_0^{x_a} c_a(u)du \tag{14.8}$$

subject to:

$$\sum_k f_k^{rs} = q_{rs} \forall r, s$$
$$f_k^{rs} \geq 0 \ \forall r, s \tag{14.9}$$
$$x_a = \sum_{rs} \sum_k f_k^{rs} \delta_{a,k}^{rs} \ \forall k, r, s$$

where f_k^{rs} is the flow on path k from origin r to destination s and $\delta_{a,k}^{rs}$ is an indicator variable which is set to 1 if that path passes through link a, and is otherwise zero.

14.2.2 Stochastic assignment

Route spreading, which is an observed phenomenon in traffic assignment, can be modelled by applying cost-flow relations to simulate congestion. In the deterministic case previously discussed, it was assumed that drivers have perfect knowledge of these relations and act rationally to minimise their total travel costs. Stochastic assignment methods, however, assume that instead of drivers having a 'perfect' knowledge of the varying OD costs of a network, they have a variable perception of these costs. Such methods, therefore, are more realistic but do not result in an individual user maximising their utility, but rather their *perceived* utility.

Thus route choice can be determined by applying discrete choice models, based on concepts of utility maximisation and random utility (Sheffi, 1985). Most models assume either a normal distribution for link costs (probit) or distribute traffic across a route set by use of the logistic function (logit); these methods are described below.

Traditionally, deterministic assignment has been used to model congested urban networks, however, if the same methods are applied to uncongested interurban networks they tend to result in an all-or-nothing type solution (all traffic on the fastest route), which is unrealistic in practice. Stochastic methods may be used to assign trips to different routes across interurban networks in a similar manner to mode choice in the four-stage model. However, if congestion is significant then a purely stochastic route assignment does not account for the increasing travel time as a route becomes increasingly congested and, thus, hybrid Stochastic User Equilibrium (SUE) methods have been developed, which include both a stochastic part (to account for imperfect knowledge) and an equilibrium part to account for rerouting due to congestion effects.

Stochastic methods are based on the assumption that a driver minimises their *perceived* cost, or chooses the alternative that gives the highest utility under an assumption of imperfect knowledge. Utility functions U_k are typically expressed as the sum of a deterministic component V_k and a random error component ξ_k, where k is a member of the set of alternatives:

$$U_k = V_k + \xi_k \qquad \forall k. \tag{14.10}$$

The probability that an alternative is chosen is the same as the probability that that alternative has the highest utility in the choice set. Whilst not being entirely exhaustive (Sheffi, 1985), the most commonly used stochastic method models assume either a Normal distribution (probit models) or the Gumbel distribution (logit models) for the random error component (i.e. drivers' perception error ξ_k).

The logit model is based on the use of the logistic function, which is a choice function used to choose between two or many alternatives and employs the same formulation as that discussed for mode choice.

It may be written:

$$p_i = \frac{\exp(-\theta.C_i)}{\sum_j \exp(-\theta.C_j)} \tag{14.11}$$

where p_i is the probability of choosing alternative i, C_i is the cost associated with route i and θ is a dispersion parameter; the lower the value of θ, the higher the level of uncertainty, conversely a high value of θ would correspond to drivers having an accurate view of actual route costs, i.e. the deterministic case. Thus the deterministic case (perfect knowledge) may be considered to be included in the stochastic formulation as a limiting case.

The use of such a choice model to produce a stochastic assignment requires route costs (travel times) to be known. This creates some technical difficulties regarding path enumeration; as Figure 14.2 illustrates a network with a reasonable number of roads (links) produces an unreasonable number of theoretically possible different routes (paths), and the possibility of looping paths in fact results in the number of mathematically feasible routes being infinite. Of course, as such paths would be assigned a tiny proportion of the total traffic under a discrete choice model (as a convoluted lengthy or looping path would have low utility) there is little purpose in enumerating all paths (even all non-looping paths). Hence in practice, techniques exist to extract 'reasonable' paths (e.g. Dial, 1971) onto which a stochastic choice assignment of traffic may be loaded. A further difficulty with the logit formulation is that once the reasonable paths have been determined, the basic form of the method does not account for route overlaps. For example, three completely distinct routes would have traffic assigned in the same way as a single route together with two routes including a significant overlap. Further, if each route had around equal travel time, then they would be assigned around one-third of the traffic irrespective of any overlap. Finally, the logit method assigns traffic based on an absolute difference in cost (time), for example a 5-minute difference in journey time will produce the same route choice proportions whether the difference relates to route times of 5 and 10 minutes or route times of 200 and 205 minutes. In the first case, one route takes twice as long as another, whilst in the second, the 5-minute difference may well not be perceived as 'any difference at all'. It would seem reasonable to require a model to account for the difference in journey time in relation to the total journey time when assigning traffic. Consequently, whilst the standard logit discrete choice model is appropriate for the modal choice stage within the four-stage model, its use in the routing stage has some inherent difficulties and due to this other stochastic choice, models have been derived for routing purposes, for example, probit and Monte Carlo methods.

The probit model assumes that the random error term (see (14.9)) is normally distributed, and that the joint density function of these errors is Multivariate Normal.

Thus the probability distribution of cost for each link is Normal, with mean μ usually being the value of the free-flow cost, and variance σ^2 assumed to be proportional to the mean:

$$\beta = \text{Variance/Mean} = \sigma^2/\mu \Rightarrow \sigma^2 = \mu\beta \tag{14.12}$$

$$c_a \sim \text{N}(c_a(x_a),\ \beta c_a(x_a))\ \forall a. \tag{14.13}$$

The probit model solves the problem of overlapping paths by the use of correlations between the path cost perception errors.

In the case of only two alternatives, it is reasonably straightforward to calculate the probabilities for travel on each link, but this is not the case if there are more alternatives. There are various methods of solution for the many alternative cases: one is numerical integration of a multiple integral (Rosa and Maher, 2002a). A second alternative utilises 'Clark's Method' (Clark, 1961), where a successive approximation method is used, where the maximum of two normally distributed random variables is approximated by another Normal variable. Alternatively, a Monte Carlo simulation may be used (e.g. Burrell, 1968), whereby a random value representing the perceived travel time of a link is sampled from the density function for that link, and an all-or-nothing assignment is carried out based on the set of sampled perceived travel times across all network links. The process of sampling and assignment is repeated (multiple times) and then averaged to give the final flow pattern.

In isolation a stochastic traffic assignment based on applying a discrete choice model to a set of reasonable paths will result in the distribution of traffic across a network, however, it only produces a sensible distribution when the path costs are fixed (i.e. there is negligible congestion effect). The principles of stochastic methods to allow for imperfect knowledge and a traffic equilibrium process to model congestion effects are combined to create SUE assignment. This is based on the premise that each driver will act to minimise their *perceived* route cost, which follows a distribution such as those given in the logit or probit models. Thus deterministic user equilibrium can be viewed as being a special case of the SUE problem, where the 'distribution' of costs has zero variability. In SUE modelling, the perceived costs are not modelled solely as random variables, but also have a dependency on flow, in that the *mean travel time* is taken to be a function of flow.

Sheffi and Powell (1982) formulated an unconstrained minimisation problem, for which the solution is the SUE flow pattern:

$$Z_{SUE}(\mathbf{x}) = \sum_a x_a c_a(x_a) - \sum_a \int_0^{x_a} c_a(x)dx - \sum_{rs} q_{rs} S_{rs}(\mathbf{x}) \tag{14.14}$$

where S_{rs} is the satisfaction function, i.e. the mean perceived travel cost between OD pair rs. However, the solution of this does not prove to be straightforward. The method of successive averages has also been applied by Sheffi but suffers from slow convergence in congested networks. Consequently, whilst SUE is more behaviourally realistic than UE as it accounts for imperfect knowledge, in practice, the deterministic UE model assuming perfect knowledge is more computationally attractive.

14.2.3 Elasticity of demand

> The concept of 'predict and provide' is essentially that 'solving congestion by road building is like solving obesity by buying larger trousers'.
>
> *(anon)*

The assignment models previously described have assumed a fixed demand matrix; in reality, however, if travel times increase (by perhaps monetary tolling or road narrowing) then some trips will be suppressed and demand will reduce, and conversely if costs decrease (by perhaps network improvement) suppressed trips will be released and demand will increase. Indeed, transport is similar to other goods in that if the price of a good decreases then the demand for that good increases, i.e. transport is not exempt from the basic law of demand! Thus demand should be viewed as elastic[1] rather than fixed. The SACTRA report on 'Trunk Roads and the Generation of Traffic' (Department for Transport, 1994) considered the effect of induced traffic related to network improvement and concluded that demand elasticities should be incorporated into modelling methodology. A report by MVA (1997) examined the converse effect of traffic suppression in the case of capacity reduction. Hence modelling methodology should incorporate elastic demand and this can be done in a simple way by allowing the trips between any OD pair to vary with the inverse of travel costs. If it is assumed that the demand Q is dependent on the travel cost C (between an O-D pair), then that demand is termed *elastic*. If a small percentage change $^{\Delta C}/_{C}$ in a travel cost results in a proportional change $^{\Delta Q}/_{Q}$ in the demand, then the elasticity e for travel is given by the ratio:

$$e = \frac{^{\Delta Q}/_{Q}}{^{\Delta C}/_{C}}. \tag{14.15}$$

As with price elasticity for normal goods, in this case the *elasticity* will always be negative as an increase in *cost* results in a decrease in *demand* (if e were zero, then demand is inelastic or fixed; Figure 14.5).

If D(.) is a decreasing function, this may be written:

$$q_{rs} = D_{rs}(u_{rs})\forall r, s \tag{14.16}$$

where u_{rs} is the minimum travel cost between origin r and destination s.

The inclusion of elastic demand in deterministic assignment models is well understood and incorporated into commercial assignment software. The UE problem may be readily extended to UEED (user equilibrium with elastic demand), by the inclusion of an inverse demand term in the standard objective function (Beckman et al., 1956).

$$Z_{\mathrm{UEED}} = \sum_{a} \int_{0}^{x_a} c_a(\omega)d\omega - \sum_{rs} \int_{0}^{q_{rs}} D_{rs}^{-1}(\omega)d\omega. \tag{14.17}$$

This may be reduced to solution by a standard UE algorithm by the addition of a dummy pseudo-link between each OD pair, to which suppressed traffic is assigned. The unit-cost function for such links are derived from the inverse demand function (Sheffi, 1985).

In the case of stochastic assignment the inclusion of elastic demand in stochastic assignment models is not as straightforward as in deterministic. Leurent (1994) presented a solution for logit-based SUE by use of a dual algorithm, and a more general solution by simultaneously minimising the two objective functions, (14.18) and (14.19), for SUE and ED was derived by Maher and Hughes (1998).

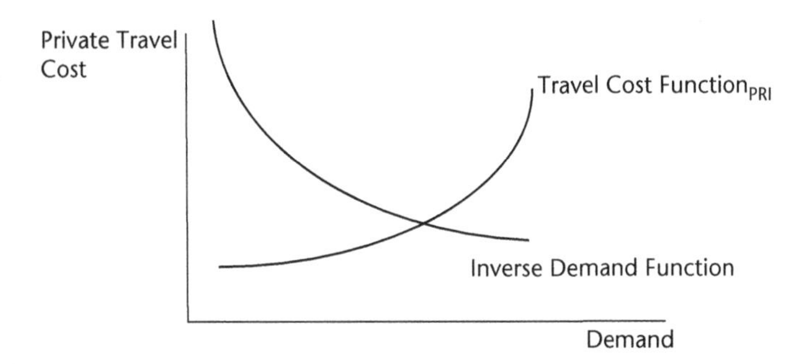

Figure 14.5 Equilibrium under elastic demand

$$Z_{SUE}(\mathbf{x}) = \sum_a x_a c_a(x_a) - \sum_a \int_0^{x_a} c_a(x)dx - \sum_{rs} q_{rs} S_{rs}(\mathbf{x}) \tag{14.18}$$

$$Z_{ED}(\mathbf{x}, q) = \sum_{rs} q_{rs} S_{rs}(\mathbf{x}) - \sum_{rs} \int_{q_0}^{q_{rs}} D_{rs}^{-1}(q)dq \tag{14.19}$$

where rs comprises the network OD pairs, q_{rs} is the flow between OD pair rs, S_{rs} is the satisfaction for users on rs and $D_{rs}^{-1}(.)$ is the inverse demand function. Maher and Hughes (1998) further proposed the Balanced Demand Algorithm, where at each iteration the demands and network costs are maintained in balance. A single objective function was subsequently derived as a modification to the Sheffi and Powell (1982) SUE objective function (Rosa and Maher, 2002b).

$$Z_{SUEED}(\mathbf{x}) = \sum_a x_a c_a(x_a) - \sum_a \int_0^{x_a} c_a(x)dx - \sum_{rs} \int_{S_{0rs}}^{S_{rs}(\mathbf{x})} D_{rs}(S_{rs}(\mathbf{c}(\mathbf{x})))dS_{rs}. \tag{14.20}$$

Thus standard modelling techniques for static traffic assignment are fully able to account for demand elasticities that occur. Clearly the calibration of such elasticities is an issue for practical considerations, but from a theoretical perspective the standard economic elasticity principles which apply within routing may be included in aforementioned equilibrium models in an appropriate manner. The alternative paradigm of micro-simulation models which are discussed in Section 14.3 do not offer similar objective-based methods to handle elastic demand.

14.2.4 System optimisation

The theory which results in UE traffic distribution is that a driver acting rationally to minimise their personal travel cost (or maximise their personal utility) will, under an assumption of perfect knowledge, choose the fastest route. The aggregate effect of many such drivers acting in their own self-interest results in Wardrop/UE, which is sometimes termed a 'selfish' equilibrium. As John Nash highlighted, it is possible to achieve a better result for the system overall if individuals could be made to act 'altruistically' and make decisions that supported a system or social optimum. Thus the aggregate effect of individual drivers acting to minimise their own travel costs does not minimise the total travel cost (or time) in the network (TNTC). This is the classic economics problem of a high level of externalities which is found in most if not all transport markets and results in a divergence of private and public costs. If the latter were taken fully into account in the individual's decision, this would theoretically be best for the system as a whole (Wardrop's second principle). A traffic distribution which does give a minimal TNTC is known as a System/Social Optimal (SO) flow pattern. This may be formalised in the non-linear program below (Sheffi, 1985).

$$\text{Minimise } Z_{SO} = \sum_a x_a c_a(x_a) \; \forall a \tag{14.21}$$

subject to:

$$\sum_k f_k^{rs} = q_{rs} \; \forall r, s$$
$$f_k^{rs} \geq 0 \; \forall k, r, s \tag{14.22}$$

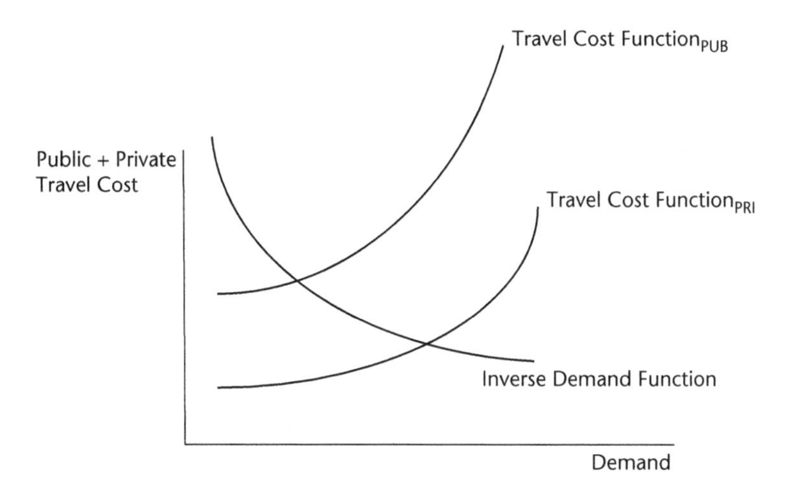

Figure 14.6 Equilibrium under elastic demand including public cost

where (14.21) states the objective function to minimise TNTC (where TNTC is simply the sum of the travel costs across each link-a of the network) and (14.22) provides flow constraints between OD pairs and a non-negativity constraint for flow.

The social optimal traffic distribution may be determined by optimisation of an objective function or by the principle of welfare maximisation, whereby instead of paying a personal cost the user is required to bear the full cost of their externalities and be charged a *marginal cost* which reflects both the private cost to the individual and the public costs imposed by the individual on the whole system (Figure 14.6).

More specifically in terms of traffic the full marginal cost includes the externality of the congestion cost which each additional driver imposes on all the other drivers, i.e. under congested conditions every additional driver will increase the travel cost (on each link) for every user of that link and marginal cost pricing implies that each driver should personally bear this total cost to maximise aggregate welfare.

In terms of static traffic assignment, the SO solution may be obtained by carrying out a UE type assignment, but by using marginal link costs rather than unit link costs in the assignment algorithm. Marginal cost functions may be obtained as below:

$$m_a = \frac{d}{dx_a}(x_a c_a(x_a)) = c_a + x_a \frac{dc_a}{dx_a} \tag{14.23}$$

where $m_a(x_a)$ is the marginal cost on a link, and is modelled as the rate of change of the product of x_a, the link flow and $c_a(x_a)$ is the link cost as per the link-cost function. If link costs are modelled using the BPR function it can be shown that the marginal cost function may be written in BPR format as:

$$m_a(x_a) = c_a(0)[1 + k(1+p)\left(\frac{x_a}{X_a}\right)^p. \tag{14.24}$$

It should be noted from both (14.23) and (14.24) that the marginal cost for travel is strictly greater than the unit cost; i.e. paying for one's full externality is always more expensive than paying only for one's private cost.

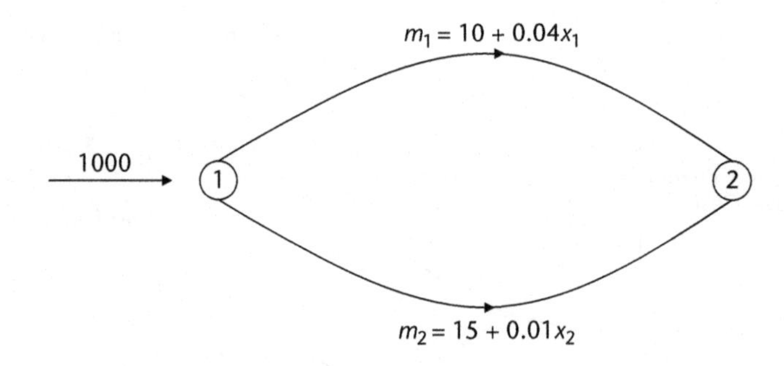

Figure 14.7 Two-link network with marginal cost-flow functions

This can be illustrated using the same two-link network as before, the marginal cost functions (i.e. the cost including the marginal public costs) being as given in Figure 14.7.

For the SO case, the system is solved so that the marginal costs between OD pairs are equal, hence in this case:

$$m_1 = m_2.$$

This produces a flow pattern of: $x_1 = 300$ $x_2 = 700$ where the marginal path costs are equal: $m_1 = m_2 = 22$.

The cost of the externality at this level of traffic, therefore, is four units per vehicle. Note also that the route with the higher variable cost, and thus the one that has greater marginal effects, now has less traffic assigned to it. The original unit cost functions are then used to calculate the actual (unequal) link costs, giving:

$$c_1 = 16 \qquad c_2 = 18.5.$$

Consequently the minimum value of the total network cost is TNTC = 17,750, which is clearly less than the UE value of TNTC = 18,000. However, as drivers do not take into account the marginal public costs of their actions, the more costly user equilibrium is the distribution that would occur in practice. Hence if traffic could be 'forced' into the distribution above, then all drivers would bear a travel cost which is equal to the full cost, i.e. one that includes externalities, and social welfare would thus be maximised. This is demonstrated by a lower 'altruistic' aggregate network cost relative to the higher 'selfish' aggregate network cost achieved when drivers act to minimise their private costs. Unfortunately, the SO traffic distribution is unstable, because if drivers have perfect knowledge of the actual travel costs, then any driver observing $c_1 = 16$ versus $c_2 = 18.5$ would select route 1 as would subsequent drivers and the traffic flow would redistribute to return to the stable UE/selfish equilibrium solution. To minimise total network travel time in practice, a mechanism to induce users to follow the SO flow distribution is required and such a mechanism is found in road tolling, whereby individuals are forced to choose between time and money, hence this comes down to how much individuals value their time. A monetary toll may be imposed upon the faster/cheaper route such that a proportion of users will redistribute to the alternative route, and the toll should reflect the value of the time saved. If this toll is levied at the correct level, i.e. that required to produce the correct amount of redistribution, then a social optimal traffic assignment should be achieved.

14.2.5 Modelling tolling

There has been much debate relating to the theory and practice of road user charging or road tolling which is further considered in Chapter 13. The modelling of tolling has likewise been much considered and methodologies are generally divided into first-best and second-best optimisation. First-best models tend to refer to link or path-based tolling schemes, which in theory should result in optimisation of the system (SO in the deterministic case), or economic benefit maximisation (marginal social cost pricing: MSCP) and second best refers to sub-optimal schemes (such as cordon schemes where not all links may be tolled). In this section, first-best methods are discussed for the deterministic case, marginal social cost pricing is illustrated, alternative feasible toll sets are presented and the minimal revenue toll problem is defined. The concept of the minimal revenue toll problem is of particular interest with respect to equity and distributional concerns inherent in tolling and the main equity considerations are highlighted. Finally, a brief comment on issues of tolling under principles of stochastic modelling is made.

First-best optimisation: deterministic case

The SO flow pattern is the flow pattern where the total network travel cost is minimised in the case of deterministic assignment, but this is not a stable flow pattern. If route costs are not equal between an OD pair and drivers have perfect knowledge, then the SO flow pattern would not be maintained as drivers would change route to seek to minimise their personal cost, and so the traffic distribution would revert to the UE flow pattern. The SO pattern is therefore the flow pattern that would be desirable, rather than the pattern which would naturally occur (Sheffi, 1985). As highlighted above, tolling is a method to make the SO flow pattern stable, by equalising the 'total' cost for travel along a path by placing additional charges (tolls) on links, so that a stable equilibrium is obtained, and thus an SO flow distribution is achieved under a UE traffic assignment model. Thus whilst it is theoretically possible to determine the minimal TNTC by SO assignment, some additional measure is required to obtain this flow pattern in practice. So if an SO assignment is required, it is necessary to modify the cost-flow functions so that the 'selfish' driver is forced to act 'altruistically'. This can be achieved by imposing additional costs (i.e. tolls) on network links.

Marginal social cost price tolls

The classic economics solution to obtaining an SO flow pattern is to impose MSCP tolls, whereby a toll equal to the difference between the marginal social cost (that is imposed upon the network by the driver) and marginal private cost (that the driver experiences) is levied on each link (e.g. Pigou, 1920; Smith, 1979; Sheffi, 1985), in other words this would be the Pigouvian tax solution, thus making the total cost for the link equal to $m_a(x_a)$ as:

$$t_a(x_a) = m_a(x_a) - c_a(x_a) \tag{14.25}$$

where $t_a(x_a)$ is the MSCP toll for the link x_a. Expanding the example two-link network would thus have the cost functions as given in Figure 14.8 where:

$$t_1 = 22 - 16 = 6$$
$$\text{and } t_2 = 22 - 18.5 = 3.5.$$

Solving for UE equating the new cost functions and maintaining the demand such that:

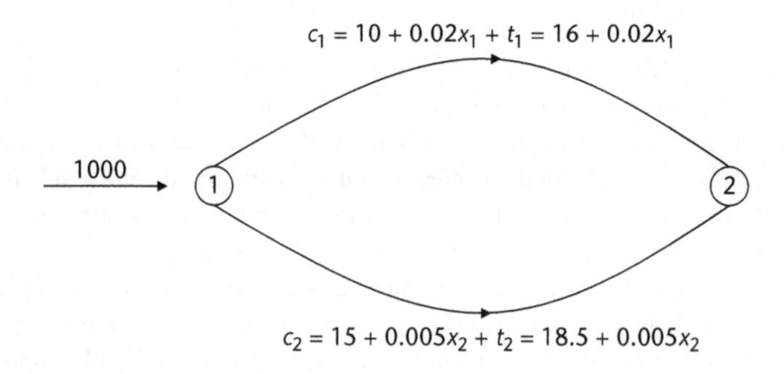

Figure 14.8 MSC P tolls

$$x_1 + x_2 = 1000,$$

gives the solution flow pattern:

$$x_1 = 300 \qquad x_2 = 700 \qquad (c_1 = c_2 = 22\ )$$

which is the same as that obtained under SO (Figure 14.5). The total network cost is 22,000, but this figure includes the toll revenue (4,250), so that TNTC = 17,750, the required minimum value (excluding the toll revenue). Note, however, that the toll imposed should equate to the value that individuals put on their time, if not then this will not produce the SO solution. One further assumption of the above is that it assumes perfectly inelastic demand, hence the demand for travel on this network is not affected by the imposition of the toll. As discussed later in this chapter, incorporation of such effects is extremely difficult, and it may be hypothecated in the above solution that if the revenue raised was used to compensate the marginal effect of those displaced from the network, through for example increased expenditure on public transport, then in effect this does reflect an optimal outcome, i.e. it is Kaldor-Hicks efficient.

MSCP tolls, however, whilst theoretically forcing the user to pay for their 'total' cost, tend to be in practice rather high, and may be problematic to implement from a political perspective (Dial, 1999; Newbery and Santos, 2003, Wong et al., 2003). There is however some evidence that efficient marginal social cost-based pricing may be more acceptable to the general public than policy makers might suppose, if such schemes are presented as part of an overall package of measures (Sikow-Magny, 2003). As highlighted above, crucial in this respect is expenditure of the revenue raised through the toll.

Other feasible toll sets

In terms of modelling, tolls which produce the SO flow pattern are non-unique, for example once a valid toll set (such as that for MSCP tolls) is obtained to give an SO flow pattern for a network, adding or subtracting a constant will still result in the toll set producing SO flows. This can be illustrated in the case of the two-link example.

The cost functions including the MSCP tolls are:

$$c_1 = 16 + 0.02x_1 \qquad c_2 = \ 18.5 + 0.005x_2.$$

The addition of a constant vector $a_i = a$ will give:

$$c_1 = 16 + 0.02x_1 + a \qquad c_2 = 18.5 + 0.005x_2 + a$$

which will clearly cancel out in the solution for UE, giving the same 'altruistic' optimal flow distribution.

Thus the possibility exists for further optimisation, i.e. additional criteria could be imposed so that a unique toll set could be obtained to satisfy certain conditions. One such possibility is to maximise the toll revenue, which might seem to be politically interesting. In the case of constant demand, there would not be a toll set which maximised revenue as there is no upper bound, however, under elastic demand a stable equilibrium should exist. In reality very high tolls would discourage more drivers from using the network, very low tolls would not, and so a toll set to maximise revenue exists at some intermediate value. However, in practical terms if MSCP tolls are calculated, they appear rather high and raise some equity concerns, hence an alternative objective is to seek minimal revenue tolls (which could be scaled by a constant value to achieve any desired toll revenue level).

'Minimal revenue' tolls assume that all tolls are strictly non-negative; if this condition were relaxed it would be possible theoretically to calculate 'zero revenue' tolls or Robin Hood tolls (Hearn and Ramana, 1998). Thus a driver could receive credits for using an 'unpopular' longer route, or would incur debits for using a 'popular' fast route. In a way this concept has similarities to those in the government's document 'Paying for Road Use' (Commission for Integrated Transport, 2002), where tolling charges are proposed within a 'fiscally neutral' scheme. This could be considered as maximising political acceptability. Of course in practice the running costs of any scheme would need to be funded by scheme revenues which would impose an additional constraint on the toll regime chosen, so that a 'Robin Hood' scheme would in practice be 'revenue neutral' rather than genuinely 'zero revenue'.

The minimal revenue toll problem may thus be formulated as:

$$Minimise \sum_a [(x_a(c_a).(t_a)] \tag{14.26}$$

where x_a are SO link flows and t_a are link tolls, subject to $t_a \geq 0 \; \forall a$, TNTC maintaining the SO value and all used paths having common costs.

For example, in the two-link case where the SO flow pattern is desired it can be seen that:

$$\text{Toll Revenue} = 300t_1 + 700t_2$$

and if the link toll is set to be equal to the MSCP toll plus a constant a then:

$$t_1 = 6 + a \qquad t_2 = 3.5 + a$$

and thus:

$$\text{Toll Revenue} = 4250 + 1000a.$$

If it is required that $t_i \geq 0 \; \forall_i$ as for minimal revenue tolls, it can be seen that the smallest possible value for a is 3.5.

$$\text{Thus } t_1 = 2.5 \quad t_2 = 0$$

and Toll Revenue = 750.

Minimal revenue tolls show a reduction from MSCP tolls of around one order of magnitude on test networks, and so in themselves may be more politically acceptable. They also have the

Table 14.1 Toll comparison

	MSCP	*Minimal revenue*	*Robin Hood*
t_1	6	2.5	1.75
t_2	3.5	0	–0.75
Toll revenue	4250	750	0

useful property of assigning zero tolls to many links (and it may be possible to maintain zero-tolled routes through the network which is beneficial from an equity viewpoint). Zero-tolled links could further be logistically beneficial depending on what technology was used for toll collection, for example, if on-street beacons were to be used, fewer beacons would be required than for MSCP tolls which tend to toll every link.

However, if non-negativity constraints are not imposed, as for 'Robin Hood' tolls, the total Toll Revenue may be made zero where, in the two-link example:

$$a = -4.25 \quad \text{and} \quad t_1 = 1.75 \quad t_2 = -0.75.$$

Such a scheme would therefore be fiscally neutral (discounting the transaction costs). Thus for the simple two-link example, tolls can be summarised as shown in Table 14.1.

Equity considerations

There are two types of equity impacts which are commonly considered: spatial (or horizontal) equity and social (or vertical) equity. It is perceived to be important that charging schemes are seen to be 'fair' in some way (Jones, 2003), and whilst economic marginal social cost price tolls might be viewed as fair from one perspective (in that they charge all road users for their externalities), the fact that such costs might be much harder to bear (i.e. a greater proportion of income) for lower-income groups might make them 'socially' unfair, and that socially marginal journeys are not equal to economically marginal journeys. Furthermore, given the derived nature of demand, marginal benefits from the journey undertaken will be unequal, but this will not be reflected in the (fixed) toll. Thus low-income groups will be less willing to pay for road use irrespective of a potentially higher marginal benefit and it is assumed that road pricing would primarily benefit the better-off (Schade, 2003). Furthermore, the better-off may often be able to be more flexible in their working arrangements and may be able to avoid a peak-hour charge entirely (Frey, 2003). The concept of link-based rather than cordon-based charging schemes might make charging more acceptable from a social equity perspective; the potential existence of untolled links and untolled routes imply that there will be a trade-off in routing based upon a person's own value of time, those of higher-income groups may choose to take the quicker, tolled links in their route, whereas the lower-income groups have the option of taking untolled links and possibly routes (depending on their journey), albeit with a greater time cost.

Issues of spatial equity arise from the differences in where people live and travel with respect to the charging points. This is a particularly problematic issue with respect to cordon or area schemes, as it is obviously possible for a person to live just outside a boundary and need to travel to just within it. This is particularly inequitable if the cordon charge is set up in such a way that a similar person who lived just within the boundary with a similar trip distance did not have to pay. Again, link-based schemes would considerably reduce the impact of spatial equity as it is primarily a cordon scheme problem. A system whereby everyone who used a particular link (at a particular time) being charged the same amount would certainly appear to be fairer.

Stochastic case

Whilst the SO in the deterministic case is well known, system optimisation in the stochastic case is rather less clear. Yang (1999), Penchina (2002, 2004) and Yildirim and Hearn (2005) have assumed a utility-maximising framework for optimisation in the stochastic case, i.e. where economic benefit is maximised under MSCP tolling. The flow pattern so achieved is termed the Stochastic Social Optimum (Maher et al., 2005). In system terms this solution corresponds to the flow pattern where the perceived total network cost is minimised (PTNTC), but this is generally not the same flow solution as where the 'actual' total network travel cost (TNTC) is minimised: a solution that could theoretically produce larger network benefit. Thus as stochastic models are 'more realistic' in terms of user behaviour, the 'desired flow pattern' in the stochastic case must be considered when designing a tolling scheme (Stewart, 2007).

14.3 Dynamic models

The preceding sections of this chapter have concentrated on providing an explanation of economic principles implicit in traffic modelling under the assumption of 'static' conditions. Clearly there is no realistic circumstance where traffic is genuinely time invariant, but for many practical purposes, stable solutions for model outputs are required (such as total flow on a road, network travel time), and modelling traffic within a fixed 'time slice' is an appropriate methodology. However, there are problems where the temporal nature of traffic needs to be understood at a more disaggregate level – for example, disruption due to incidents, propagation of queues and boundary effects when a time-related traffic-management measure commences or terminates (e.g. bus lanes, parking control, congestion charging). A dynamic model is any traffic model that explicitly includes time as a model variable, consequently, instead of a single demand matrix for a time period, a demand profile will be required and the model itself will provide a profile of outputs for any given time increment within the modelled period. Most dynamic models are either dynamic equilibrium models or are simulation models. Equilibrium models attempt to extend the static methodology as previously described and mathematically model traffic conditions such that a stable equilibrium flow profile solution is achieved. From this similar model, outputs of flow and travel time may be extracted. Simulation models on the other hand do not achieve any sort of stable equilibrium-based solution but instead simulate individual vehicles (or packets of vehicles in mesoscopic models) with a set of behavioural characteristics attached and simulate each vehicle travelling through a network.

14.3.1 Dynamic equilibrium models

In a dynamic equilibrium a user is assumed to minimise their travel time (or generalised cost function) and the equilibrium solution is found where no driver can improve their utility by either rerouting or by changing their departure time choice, i.e. we have Pareto optimality. Such models are theoretically similar to macroscopic static models, and whilst input data such as demand are required to have a time profile, they are still macroscopic, i.e. they are given as flow per unit time. In a similar manner to equilibrium models dealing with congestion, by a process of route spreading (once the shortest route is full, other longer but less congested routes become equally attractive), departure choice is also spread so that once the most favourable departure times lead to congestion, drivers will alter their departure time choice to avoid congested conditions – in the models this is formulated by the use of departure and arrival penalties so that a decrease in utility from departing at a less favourable time is balanced by a less congested journey. Whilst in conceptual terms the addition of time-profiled inputs and outputs is not difficult to understand or imagine, the mathematical tractability of the resulting formulations is such that in practical terms these models can be difficult to implement. Indeed analytical macroscopic assignment models continue to be a difficult research problem (e.g. Heydecker and Addison, 2006) and no generally accepted dominant approach exists. There are a number of complexities inherent in such formulations, but in basic terms the algorithms needed to achieve stable equilibriums require a very large number of iterations to reach convergence. Consequently, even with a high capability of modern processors realistic network sizes require impractical CPU time and do not necessarily provide a commensurate improvement in output data when compared to static models. There is substantial academic effort ongoing within the field of dynamic equilibrium traffic modelling (see Tampere et al., 2010), however, most commercial models either utilise the static methodologies with fairly course time slices (such as am peak, off-peak, pm peak) with output data from a time period used as input data for the next time period or apply commercial micro-simulation packages as illustrated in Figure 14.9.

14.3.2 Micro-simulation models

Micro-simulation models offer an alternative theoretical approach to equilibrium models but are not so readily aligned to mainstream economic principles of utility maximisation. In micro simulation a vehicle is the fundamental unit modelled and each vehicle is given behavioural characteristics as individual mathematical models. Thus each vehicle requires a *car-following* model whereby a vehicle will accelerate to a desired distance behind a leading vehicle and will then match the preceding vehicle's speed and respond to any deceleration. In addition to this *overtaking* models allow a vehicle with a higher desired speed to pass slower vehicles where traffic conditions allow. *Gap-acceptance* models apply at junctions and within the overtaking models and traffic signals, and junction features provide a stimulus to which a modelled vehicle will respond. Every micro-simulation model requires a geographically accurate road network model with accurate representation of lane widths and junction features, and demand matrices (which may be time-profiled) are used in conjunction with a stochastic *release model* to generate vehicles at the edges of the network. To allow for variation between drivers, most of the individual behavioural models have a stochastic variation such that some drivers will accept smaller gaps or have higher desired speeds. The individual elements given above are related to traffic dynamics rather than to economic principles, however, as in the case of static models the issue of routing remains a utility-maximisation problem. Micro-simulation models increased in feasibility and popularity due to improvement in computing power in relatively recent years, and when a model runs it applies all of the constituent model elements on a small time increment (e.g. 0.5 seconds) basis and then updates each vehicle in terms of location and speed for each time step. Consequently, such models can provide graphical output such as moving traffic simulation which appears to be continuous. The routing element is harder to simulate in real time than other model components as the behavioural response of rerouting due to congestion is stimulated by traffic delay, which is experienced at a longer time interval than the increment used for *car following*. In uncongested conditions, a vehicle will select the fastest route based on road lengths, expected junction delay and permitted speed, but under congestion the delay caused by other vehicles is required. Thus micro-simulation models generally either utilise a routing pattern based on a static equilibrium solution or they use a dynamic feedback process where fastest routes are recalculated every one or two minutes in response to the travel time of modelled traffic.

Many commercial micro-simulation models exist, for example VISSIM (www.ptv.de) and S-paramics (www.sias.co.uk); functionality will generally include an ability to impose road tolls on

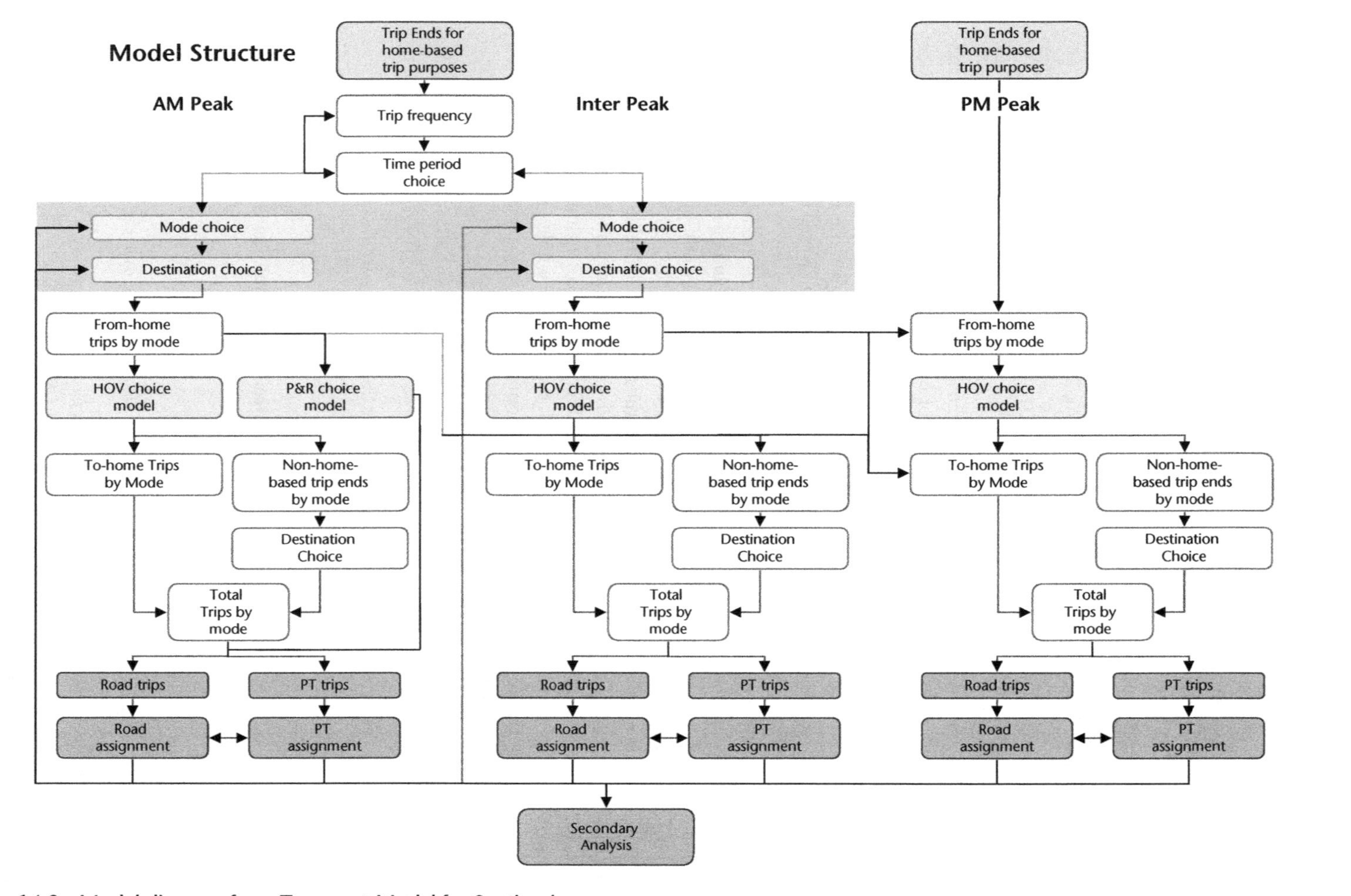

Figure 14.9 Model diagram from Transport Model for Scotland
Source: Lumsden (2009), reproduced courtesy of Transport Scotland

links for which a generalised cost function is required which normally comprises a weighted sum of travel time, travel distance and monetary cost (toll). A realistic value of time is then required (time valuation is discussed in detail in Chapter 12). Outputs from micro-simulation models are generated for each time increment, but these may be aggregated to provide output data which are similar to that from other models if required. A complication inherent in micro simulation is that the stochastic nature of the vehicle-release element results in every micro simulation run being slightly different. When two schemes are compared, therefore, a slight preference to one scheme may be due to a preferable scheme or may be due to statistical differences from the model runs themselves. It is therefore necessary to average several runs for each individual scheme to ensure statistical confidence when comparing schemes (Seaman, 2006).

14.4 Summary

This chapter has presented the constituent parts of the classical four-stage traffic model and explained the importance of the economic principle of utility maximisation within the mode choice and routing elements of such models. The economics of traffic generation and distribution are discussed in more detail in earlier chapters. The economics of demand elasticity as related to traffic models is presented and the theory of road tolling/congestion charging as marginal pricing theory is illustrated in modelling terms. The use of utility maximisation is well illustrated by static traffic models but for completeness a discussion of dynamic models is also included. The four-stage model has been extended significantly in practice and commercial models whether macroscopic or microscopic in nature will include numerous extensions and additional features; an integration of land-use models with transportation models assist long-term planning (e.g. Land Use and Transport Integration in Scotland, www.transport.gov.scot/latis). Most transport/traffic models will include emissions modelling capability and the integration of public transport services and cycles/motorbikes within full transportation models rather than being traffic (private vehicle)-focused models are under continual development. Recent advances include nano simulation where an individual person is modelled including walk stages of the whole (potentially) multimodal trip. However, the fundamental principles of economics within transportation modelling remain well understood within the four-stage model as described here.

Acknowledgement

The author would like to thank Transport Scotland for the use of Figure 14.9.

Note

1 In modelling terms there is no particular significance between large or small changes in demand, hence demand is either 'elastic' (changing) or 'inelastic' (fixed).

References

Beckman, M., McGuire, C. B. and Winston, C. B. (1956). *Studies in the Economics of Transportation.* New Haven, CT: Yale University Press.

Burrell, J. E. (1968). Multipath Route Assignment and Its Application to Capacity Restraint. *Proceedings of the 4th International Symposium on the Theory of Road Traffic Flow*, Karlsruhe, West Germany.

Clark, C. E. (1961). The Greatest of a Finite Set of Random Variables. *Operations Research*, 9, pp. 145–62.

Commission for Integrated Transport (2002).*Paying for Road Use*, www.cfit.gov.uk

Department for Transport Standing Advisory Committee on Trunk Road Appraisal (1994). *Trunk Roads and the Generation of Traffic.* London: HMSO.

Dial, R. B. (1971). A Probabilistic Multipath Traffic Assignment Modal which Obviates Path Enumeration. *Transportation Research*, 5, pp. 83–111.
Dial, R. B. (1999). Minimal-Revenue Congestion Pricing Part I: A Fast Algorithm for the Single Origin Case. *Transportation Research*, 33B(3), pp. 189–202.
Frey, B. S. (2003). Why Are Efficient Transport Policy Instruments So Seldom Used? In Schade, J. and Schlag, B. (eds), *Acceptability of Transport Pricing Strategies*. London: Elsevier, pp. 27–62.
Gentile, G., Florian, M., Hamdouch, Y., Cats, O. and Nuzzolo, A. (2016). The Theory of Transit Assignment: Basic Modelling Frameworks. In Gentile, G. and Noekel, K. (eds), *Modelling Public Transport Passenger Flows in the Era of Intelligent Transport Systems*. London: Springer, pp. 287–384.
Hearn, D. W. and Ramana, M. V. (1998). Solving Congestion Toll Pricing Models. In Marcotte, P. and Nguyen, S. (eds), *Equilibrium and Advanced Transportation Modeling*. Alphen aan den Rijn: Kluwer Academic Publishers, pp. 109–24.
Heydecker, B. G. and Addison, J. D. (2006). Analysis of Dynamic Traffic Assignment. *Proceedings of the 1st International Symposium on Dynamic Traffic Assignment*, Leeds, June.
Jones P. (2003). Acceptability of Road User Charging: Meeting the Challenge. In Schade, J. and Schlag, B. (eds), *Acceptability of Transport Pricing Strategies*. London: Elsevier, pp. 27–62.
Leurent, F. (1994). Elastic Demand, Logit-Based Equilibrium Traffic Assignment with Efficient Dual Solution Algorithm. Unpublished preprint, INRETS, Paris France.
Lumsden, K. (2009). Presentation to LATIS User Group, Roxburgh Hotel, Edinburgh, 14 May.
Maher, M. J. and Hughes, P. C. (1998). New Algorithms for the Solution of the Stochastic User Equilibrium Problem with Elastic Demand. *Proceedings of the 8th World Conference on Transport Research*, Antwerp.
Maher, M., Stewart, K. and Rosa, A. (2005). Stochastic social optimum traffic assignment. *Transportation Research Part B: Methodological*, 39, pp. 753–767.
MVA (1997). *Impact of Highway Capacity Reductions*. Report on Modelling. Woking: MVA.
Newbery, D. and Santos, G. (2003). Cordon Tolls in Eight English Towns: Theory Simulations and Impacts. *Proceedings of the Theory and Practice of Congestion Charging: An International Symposium*, Imperial College London.
Ortuzar, J. and Willumsen, L. (1994). *Modelling Transport*. Chichester: Wiley.
Penchina, C. (2002). Flexibility of Tolls for Optimal Flows in Networks with Fixed and Elastic Demands. *Proceedings of the 2002 Annual Meeting, Transportation Research Board*, Washington, DC.
Penchina, C. (2004). Minimal-Revenue Congestion Pricing: Some More Good News and Bad News. *Transportation Research*. 38B, pp. 559–70.
Pigou, A. C. (1920) *The Economics of Welfare*. New York: Macmillan.
Rosa, A. and Maher, M. J. (2002a). Algorithms for Solving the Probit Path-Based Stochastic User Equilibrium Traffic Assignment Problem with One or More User Classes. In Taylor, M. A. P. (ed.), *Transportation and Traffic Theory in the 21st Century. Proceedings of the 15th International Symposium on Transportation and Traffic Theory*. London: Pergamon Press, pp. 371–92.
Rosa, A. and Maher, M. J. (2002b). Stochastic User Equilibrium Traffic Assignment with Multiple User Classes and Elastic Demand. *Proceedings of the 9th Meeting of the Euro Working Group on Transportation*, Bari, Italy, pp. 392–7.
Schade, J. (2003). European Research Results on Transport Pricing Acceptability. In Schade, J. and Schlag, B. (eds), *Acceptability of Transport Pricing Strategies*. London: Elsevier, pp. 109–36.
Seaman, E. (2006). How to Reduce the Gambling Element of Some Transport Planning Decisions. *Traffic Engineering and Control*, 47(6), pp. 220–3.
Sheffi, Y. (1985). *Urban Transportation Networks: Equilibrium Analysis with Mathematical Programming Methods*. Upper Saddle River, NJ: Prentice Hall.
Sheffi, Y. and Powell, W. (1982). An Algorithm for the Equilibrium Assignment Problem with Random Link Times. *Networks*, 12, pp. 191–207.
Sikow-Magny, C. (2003). Efficient Pricing in Transport: Overview of European Commission's Transport Research Programme. In Schade, J. and Schlag, B. (eds), *Acceptability of Transport Pricing Strategies*. London: Elsevier, pp. 13–26.
Smith, M. J. (1979). The Marginal Cost Taxation of a Transportation Network. *Transportation Research*, 13B, pp. 237–42.
Stewart, K. (2007). Tolling Traffic Links under Stochastic Assignment: Modelling the Relationship between the Number and Price Level of Tolled Links and Optimal Traffic Flows. *Transportation Research A*, 41, pp. 644–54.

Tampere, C. M. J., Viti, F. and Immers, L. H. (eds) (2010). *New Developments in Transport Planning: Advances in Dynamic Traffic Assignment.* Cheltenham: Edward Elgar.

US Bureau of Public Roads (1964). *Traffic Assignment Manual.* Washington, DC: US Department of Commerce.

Wardrop, J. G. (1952). Some Theoretical Aspects on Road Traffic Research. *Proceedings of the Institute of Civil Engineers,* 11(1), pp. 325–78.

Wong, S. C, Ho, H. W, Yang, H. and Loo, B. (2003). The First-Best and Cordon-Based Second-Best Congestion Pricing in a Continuum Traffic Equilibrium System. *Proceedings of the Theory and Practice of Congestion Charging: An International Symposium,* Imperial College London.

Yang, H. (1999). System Optimum, Stochastic User Equilibrium, and Optimal Link Tolls. *Transportation Science,* 33(4), pp. 354–60.

Yildirim, M. B. and Hearn, D. W. (2005). A First Best Toll Pricing Framework for Variable Demand Traffic Assignment Problems. *Transportation Research,* 39B, pp. 659–78.

15

Efficiency assessment in transport service provision

Rico Merkert and Jonathan Cowie

15.1 Introduction

The idea of 'efficiency' and its measurement has become a key evaluation method within transport studies, and most research questions have related to one form or other of the organisation of the supply side of the industry or the more general operating environment. Given the high level of public funds allocated to the provision of transport services, most issues have centred on the notion of providing value for money and hence reducing the levels of subsidy required to support such services. While focus has also been devoted to growing patronage (and hence the need for subsidies), a key aspect in this policy objective is that of reducing the cost of providing transport services, and hence the reason that efficiency assessment has become all-important and the main tool in assessing the effectiveness of such policies.

'Efficiency' is a word commonly used in the English language and relates essentially to avoiding 'waste'. Therefore, writing this book chapter 'efficiently' would be where the authors avoid waste, which would mean spending as little time as possible writing it. Even that simple example highlights some major issues in efficiency assessment, as there is clearly a problem and the statement needs to be amended to 'spending as little time as possible writing a chapter that fully meets the requirements of the editors of the book'. Consequently, we need to avoid waste in the production of something that is fit for purpose. Therefore, when examining efficiency, we need some idea of the objective to be achieved. In an alternative scenario, it is possible that the authors would be given a limited period to write something that is as good as it can be for the given time frame, perhaps under the condition that both quality and quantity of the product or service have to fulfil certain minimum service-level requirements.

Within a free-market system, and one which adheres to the assumptions of perfect competition, market efficiency occurs where the price equals the marginal cost. What this means is that for 'full' efficiency to be achieved (we will return to this idea more formally in due course), then for each and every product/service, the minimum level of resources should be employed in its production, the 'right' combination of those resources should be used and it should be consumed by the 'right' people, i.e. those that value it most and hence are willing to pay the market price.

Relating this basic principle to the study of transport economic 'efficiency' raises a number of issues, however, most of these are related to the fact that the operational structure of most transport modes does not conform to the assumptions of perfect competition. As a consequence, there has been a long tradition of a very high level of government intervention in transport markets, both in operational terms (either directly through direct provision or through regulatory controls) and in financial terms in the form of subsidy and public procurement. Inevitably, therefore, the price charged to the user will, in many cases, be less than the marginal (private) cost of the service provided, and thus we have lost the measure of 'efficiency'. As a consequence, if 'performance' is to be assessed, then some other metric is required. If all that matters is whether passengers have been transported from A to B, then in this respect things would be fairly straightforward. However, as indicated in the paragraphs above, performance measurement of transport services is usually much more complex than that.

The main themes of this chapter surround the ideas and concepts behind the other performance metrics that are used, and the chapter itself is written as an introduction with respect to efficiency and productivity assessment. It is primarily aimed at those that have knowledge of the underlying theoretical principles of production. We begin by highlighting those elements of theory relevant to the study of efficiency measurement, then develop the ideas of efficiency and productivity, before examining some of the commonly used methods of assessment. The chapter ends with an examination of the limitations of such approaches. Throughout the chapter, the focus is on the conceptual ideas and issues rather than the technical elements involved in undertaking efficiency assessments. Where possible, we have attempted to simplify the problem without losing the theoretical and technical underpinnings. Those that want to take the subject further are recommended to consult other texts, which we provide a reference to at the end of the chapter. One example of this 'simplification' is that in this chapter we only examine long-run efficiency, not efficiency in the short run, i.e. the case where all input factors can be varied.

15.2 Economic theory underpinning efficiency assessment

Surprisingly often overlooked, the assessment of efficiency is ultimately an evaluation of some form of production process, which will consist of one or more desirable and undesirable outputs as well as a number of factor inputs. The actual specification of the outputs and inputs will be considered later in the chapter; at this point the choice of the output measure to be used has a direct link with theory, and specifically to that concerning the aim of the producer. This is normally assumed to be one of a profit maximiser. A naive implication would be that such firms will therefore seek to maximise revenue and minimise costs, as this results in the 'maximum' profit. Those with a rudimentary understanding of economic theory will realise that the first assumption implies neither of the second two. The monopolist, for example, will always produce below the minimum efficient scale (MES) point on the long-run average cost curve, hence will profit maximise but not cost minimise. The first theoretical consideration therefore is the aim of the firm; is it to profit maximise, sales maximise, cost minimise at the MES point, cost minimise elsewhere on the average cost curve or some (consistent) combination of two or more of these aspects?

Generally speaking, for simplification, profit and sales maximisation are assumed to minimise average cost, certainly for a given level of output. The assumption of profit maximisation is generally more consistent with a free market, hence the firm attempts to sell as much produce/ service that will maximise profit, in an efficiency assessment therefore the output chosen will generally be a demand-based measure. For transport operators, however, there exist many situations where profit maximisation is achieved through sales (revenue box plus potential subsidy) or patronage maximisation, hence 'the problem' to be solved by the operator is of a very different nature. British franchise passenger train operators, for example, in effect have a contract with the transport authority, the Department for Transport Rail Group, to provide set services in the franchised area under a regulated price. For this many receive a pre-negotiated payment which will represent the difference between the revenue raised and the operator's profit/cost of providing the service. In order to maximise profit, the operator needs to ensure that trains carry as many passengers as possible, and furthermore, that the maximum possible revenue/yield is 'extracted' from each passenger, hence revenue maximise rather than sales maximise. Given that each additional passenger carried will have a relatively small effect on running costs, then along with cost minimisation this will maximise profits. The 'efficiency' question therefore simplifies (in a productive sense) to running trains as efficiently as possible, hence the appropriate output measure to use is a supply-side measure, such as train kilometres. Whilst the general guide would be that where the aim of the firm is consistent with passengers carried, such as is the case with profit maximisation, a demand-side measure should be used (such as passenger kilometres) and where it is consistent with the provision of a service a supply-side one (such as vehicle kilometres) should be used, it is not always straightforward and knowledge of the industry being studied is important. For example, for London bus operators, the 'problem' would appear to be relatively straightforward, as the nature of the contract is that the operator receives the full cost of running the service (plus profit), with all revenue going to the authority. Cost minimisation in this case directly equates with profit maximisation, and the 'problem' for the operator is to run buses as efficiently as possible, rather than carry passengers as efficiently as possible. In this case, the output to be used would appear to be a supply-side one, such as vehicle kilometres. Such considerations, however, are important but not straightforward, as in this case due to the nature of bus services and particularly the issue of heavy usage, passengers carried would almost certainly be a more appropriate measure to use as it is those factors which will have a significant effect on costs (or factor input utilisation to be more exact).

Moving on directly to production theory, the first issue is to consider the extent to which output changes with regard to varying levels of the inputs. This relationship between output and input is known as the production function, and is key in efficiency assessment. Three examples of long-run production functions are shown in Figure 15.1. Beginning with production function A, this is the theoretical long-run production function. Hence at first, as the inputs capital (K) and labour (L) are increased, the output rises at an increasing rate, and the firm is therefore said to experience increasing returns to scale. As the process of adding inputs continues, then production reaches a point where it begins to tail off, in other words, increases at a decreasing rate, over which range the firm is said to experience decreasing returns to scale. In order to avoid 'waste' therefore, the firm, given a free choice, i.e. one that is solely aiming to maximise total factor productivity, should produce at the point where all the gains to be achieved from increasing returns have been exhausted before further input additions encounter decreasing returns. There is therefore such a

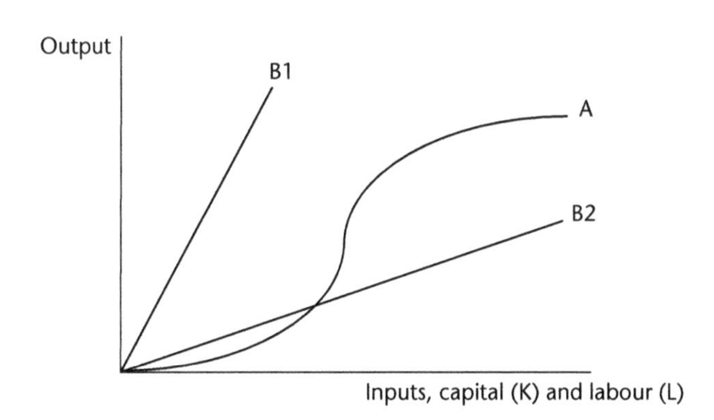

Figure 15.1 CRS and VRS production functions

thing as the optimal firm size, in theory at least, and if maximising total factor productivity is the only concern of the firm then all firms should 'aspire' to be of that size. A second consideration for efficiency assessment arising out of variable returns to scale is that failure to take these into account can result in considerable over or underestimations of the efficiency of the firm.

This begs the question as to what is the alternative to the theoretical position of variable returns to scale? Returning to Figure 15.1, the production function labelled B1 indicates a linear relationship between the output and the inputs. Examining this further, it shows that over the whole range of the production function the same rate of change of the output is achieved for a given rate of change of the inputs, irrespective of whether this is at the low or high end of the function. In other words, returns in terms of the output from adding inputs does not vary, it is fixed, or 'constant'. Hence production function B1 has the underlying assumption of constant returns to scale. Note that this does not eradicate the possibility of scale gains, in other words the output increases at a faster rate than the change in inputs, as is the case with B1. Production function B2 on the other hand is an example of constant returns to scale where there are scale losses, hence larger firms are less productive. In practice, however, no discrimination is made between these divisions, hence all scale gains are referred to as increasing returns and vice versa, the only discrimination is with reference to the underlying assumptions of variable and constant returns.

Space and potential loss of focus prevent a full consideration of costs and how these vary with changes in firm size, however, to outline very briefly, the S shape of the long-run production function leads to the U shape of the long-run average cost curve (as well as an S shape total cost function), and the general assumption is that the MES point is located at the point of inflection on the long-run production function, as in the long run all factors are in effect 'variable'. As a consequence, increasing returns equate with economies of scale and decreasing returns equate with diseconomies of scale. The two terms therefore tend to be used interchangeably.

15.2.1 Isoquant curves and isocost lines

A second aspect of underlying theory with reference to efficiency assessment is the issue of the relationship between the factor inputs themselves. These are obviously the factors of production, but from a practical perspective (and as implied in Figure 15.2) will generally only include

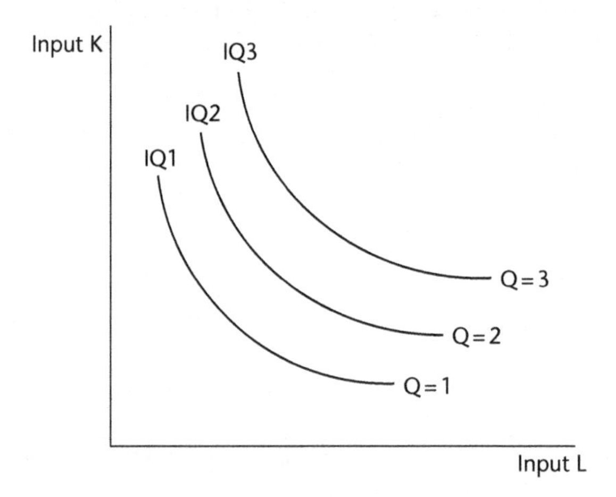

Figure 15.2 Isoquant curves

measures of capital (K) and labour (L). Both are required to produce the output and to that extent they are complementary. Furthermore, if output is to be increased, then (generally) more capital and more labour will be required. This is what was illustrated in Figure 15.1. However, around that issue of complementarity there will be a degree, or varying degrees, of substitutability between the inputs. Hence we could 'replace' labour with capital, or likewise, replace capital with labour. For example, 'transport services' could be produced by rickshaws (high labour, low capital) or light rapid transit (low labour, high capital), or there can be variation within a far more specific definition of the output, such as the provision of bus services, or finally even in how some functions are performed – maintenance for example can be either provided in-house or contracted out.

This relationship between the inputs is illustrated graphically in the form of isoquant curves ('iso' meaning 'same', hence same quantity), of which hypothetical examples are given in Figure 15.2. This shows the combination of the two inputs, in this case capital and labour, required to produce three different levels of output, which are labelled Q1 to Q3 and for simplicity represent quantities one, two and three or any multiple thereof. Taking the lowest level of output (IQ1), what it shows is that as we move along the curve from left to right, then at first larger quantities of capital are being substituted by relatively smaller quantities of labour, however, as this effect continues then capital becomes harder to substitute, until we end up at the right of the isoquant where small quantities of capital are being substituted by relatively large quantities of labour. This changing relationship between the factor inputs is known as elasticities of substitution, and as illustrated will vary over the levels of inputs that are employed. For example, if we had constant elasticities then the isoquant would be of a linear form. The implication and/or importance of elasticities of substitution in efficiency assessment should be clear – the underlying production function that is specified should 'allow for' this changing relationship across the whole length of the function, in other words, it 'should' exhibit varying elasticities of substitution. This is not unreasonable, as we may expect in any production or transport service provision process that proportionately larger elements of capital are required at higher levels of production. If they are not incorporated, then as with varying returns to scale, this is likely to lead to inaccurate estimation of efficiencies, or to be more precise, 'inefficiency' wrongly attributed to the firm where the problem is in the actual specification of the underlying production function. In practice, although all may not agree, in transport services the effect of varying elasticities of substitution tends to be less critical than, for example, the effect of variable returns to scale, as most firms will tend to employ similar levels of the inputs. This is something we return to in Section 15.3.

So far, all this discussion has considered is the productivity of the firm, or to be precise, the total factor productivity of the firm. It still leaves an important question unanswered, which is basically, if we can produce the output using different combinations of the factor inputs, then which is 'the best', for example, the lowest total cost, combination of the inputs to use? For this we need to consider the costs and the relative productivities of the inputs that are being considered. We can augment this information into Figure 15.2 with the addition of isocost lines, as in Figure 15.3.

Isocost lines are linear as the price of the factors will not vary over the level of the factor being employed, hence each subsequent unit will cost the same as the previous. The slope of the isocost line represents the relative cost of the two inputs, labour and capital. Focusing on IQ1 in Figure 15.3, then what this shows is that at production points B1 (more capital) and B2 (more labour) the production cost will be the same, hence in a certain sense the firm would be indifferent to these two positions. Neither of these points minimise the cost of production; this occurs at point A, which is tangential to IQ1. As this is the production point with the lowest cost, then this is the one

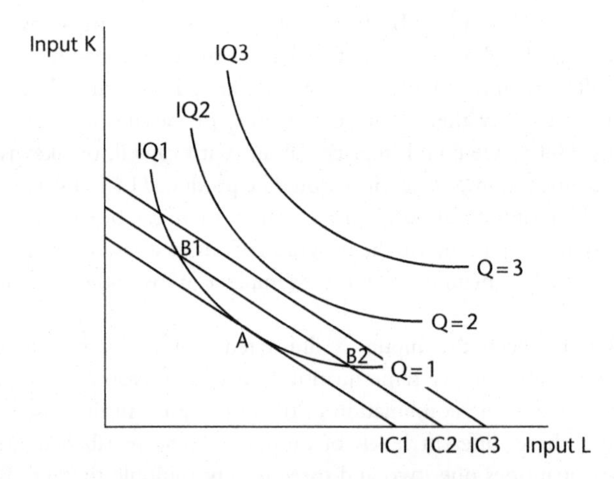

Figure 15.3 Graphical example for identification of cost efficiency

that represents 'the best' combination of the two factors. Put another way, whilst IQ1 connects points of equal production that could be produced with different combinations of labour and capital, it is the cost/prices of the factors of production that will determine which combination of the factor inputs to use.

'Efficiency' as such was described in the introduction to this chapter as occurring where the right combination of the least inputs was used to produce goods/services to be consumed by the right people. In light of the preceding discussion, each of these components can now be formally defined as a measure of efficiency:

Technical Efficiency (the least inputs) – this is the output to input ratio, and occurs where either the maximum output (quantity) is achieved from a given level of the inputs, or a given quantity of the output is produced using the minimum level of the inputs. The very clear implication from Figure 15.2 is that there can be more than one point of technical efficiency.

Cost Efficiency (the right combination) – requires the condition of technical efficiency to be met, and occurs where the maximum output is produced for the minimum cost. Unlike technical efficiency, there is only a single point of cost efficiency (Figure 15.3).

Allocative Efficiency (consumed by the right people) – occurs where we have cost efficiently produced products/services consumed by the 'right' people, normally those willing to pay the market price. Therefore, if the output is specified in terms of a demand measure, cost efficiency will equate to allocative efficiency, which is why sometimes the terms are used interchangeably. Another definition of allocative efficiency commonly found in the literature takes the consumption issue as a given, hence occurs where the product or service is produced using the right mix of inputs/resources. For example, while being technically efficient, a train operator might use too many train cars or too few staff in order to achieve full allocative efficiency. This in turn will result in lower cost efficiency as cost efficiency is defined as the product of technical and allocative efficiency.

While it is technical efficiency that is estimated in most studies, one could argue that it should be cost efficiency that should matter most to both the transportation firm's management and all stakeholders (including regulators). As shown by Tsai et al. (2015) in the urban train-operation context, being fully technically efficient does not mean that full cost efficiency is guaranteed as an operator may suffer from poor allocative efficiency. Furthermore, the concept of scale efficiency is of importance as recent studies confirm that in particular the often regulated transportation sector context provides a good example of deviation from economic theory. While theory suggests scale effects are solely related to firm size and are strictly progressive from increasing to decreasing returns, research shows that there exist cases where, depending on their size, firms can on the one hand benefit from economies of scale but also at the same time suffer from diseconomies of scale (e.g. Merkert and Morrell, 2012).

15.2.2 'X-efficiency'

One final piece of theory to consider is Harvey Leibenstein's 'X-efficiency' (Leibenstein, 1966).[1] In his *American Economic Review* article, Leibenstein argued that micro-economic theory obsession with allocative efficiency was overlooking 'other types of efficiencies' (p. 292) that were of considerably larger scale, and these 'other' efficiencies were then termed 'X-efficiency'. In particular, Leibenstein argued that the gains to be achieved through improvements in allocative efficiency were comparably small and in any case were likely to be quickly made up for in natural growth. To clarify, most of the estimates were based on gains in trade from the reduction of trade barriers and gains from the eradication of monopoly power. 'X-inefficiency' is described as being caused by individuals and firms not working as hard, or searching for information (to lead to improvements in productivity) as effectively as they could. The actual concept is never formally defined, however, a general understanding would be that it results in the average cost curve for the firm being above where it should be.

Major criticisms of x-efficiency came from Stigler (1976) and De Alessi (1983). Stigler argued that such a concept could be explained within the framework of mainstream economic theory, due to the fact that no single individual seeks to maximise a single outcome, but rather seeks to maximise utility, and other outcomes such as leisure and health are part of the utility function. Thus what actually occurs is a trade in outcomes, and as such if an individual/firm should at some point re-evaluate this position and choose to devote more time/resources to production, then this does not represent an 'efficiency' improvement but rather an increase in output. De Alessi on the other hand argued that such firms may in fact be producing 'efficiently', as the transaction costs involved of moving to best practice may outweigh any potential gains from doing so.

As a theory, therefore, x-efficiency has largely been discredited. As an idea/perspective, however, it is still useful and commonly referred to in efficiency analysis (e.g. Greene, 2008), as it suggests that firms do produce at points above an idealised average cost function (for whatever reason), and hence an efficiency assessment would seek to measure that distance.

15.3 General approaches to efficiency assessment and terminology

Efficiency assessment goes beyond the evaluation of simple characteristics of firm size, business models or market shares. A number of methods for efficiency evaluation have been developed in the literature (Oum et al., 1999; Merkert et al., 2010; Karlaftis and Tsamboulas, 2012). While there may be industry characteristics that will demand different inputs, outputs or model specifications (such as assumptions on input/output orientation or cost minimisation), the principal methods of efficiency analysis can be applied across all modes of transport and industries. This is why general books on efficiency and productivity measurement such as Coelli et al. (2005), Fried et al. (2008) and more recently Greene et al. (2016) are useful and applicable to the transportation context. Merkert et al. (2012) provide a good overview of the methods when applied not only to mainstream transport but also to the regional and remote context (where more sophisticated econometric methods can be used too). Yu (2016) provides a literature overview of the main concepts and methods of airline efficiency analysis, again of high relevance to all modes

Table 15.1 Airport rankings depending on PPM versus DEA measures

PPM measure	*Top 3 airports*
Pax/FTE	JFK, ATL, EWR
Moves/FTE	ATL, EWR, JFK
Cargo/FTE	JFK, HKG, EWR (NRT very close)
Moves/runway	LHR, ATL, SZX
Pax/gates	SIN, HKT, HKG
Pax/terminal	HGK, VIE, BCN
DEA measure	Top 3 airports
Technical efficiency (constant returns to scale)	BCN, EWR, VIE
Technical efficiency (variable returns to scale)	SYD, VIE, BCN

Source: Merkert et al., 2012

of transport, as their proposed methods have now been applied to all modes of transport including innovative modes such as BRT systems (Merkert et al., 2015).

In its simplest form, efficiency/productivity can be presented using relatively straightforward Partial Productivity Measures (PPM), also referred to as Partial Factor Productivity analysis, where the impact of single-factor productivities are calculated. These measures will again tend to focus on aspects of labour or capital productivity and Table 15.1 shows examples of typical PPM measures for the airport context.

The advantage of the PPM approach is that the required data are easy to collect, analyse and understand, and are favoured by managers and consultants in the transportation business when developing key performance indicators (KPIs). However, a PPM analysis only takes account of one input against one output. As a result, multiple and often conflicting KPIs are computed without any rationale for the way in which they can be combined to give a conclusive indication of overall performance nor of sensible prognosis for improvement, as illustrated in Table 15.1. Furthermore, the PPM approach overlooks the fact that inputs are highly dependent upon each other, and therefore isolating a single factor could be viewed at the one extreme as completely meaningless and potentially misleading. For example, a large investment in capital will inevitably lead to a significant increase in labour productivity, but may actually reduce 'capital' productivity. Nevertheless, PPM results can be useful in the sense of making commentary on the effectiveness or results from more sophisticated efficiency analysis. It is further useful in the sense that once total performance measures are obtained, it is possible then to establish whether partial measures might be good proxies for overall performance.

The Total Factor Productivity (TFP) methodology overcomes some of the problems of the PPM approach and has been used in a number of transportation efficiency-analysis studies (e.g. Benjamin and Obeng, 1990; Hensher, 1992). A key advantage of the TFP method is that a single index is generated based on the ratio of aggregate output and aggregate input quantities with the input and outputs weighted in some way. Nevertheless, Oum et al. (1999) identify that aggregation problems may occur when producing a single indicator from multiple inputs or outputs (as a result of different dimensions/scales of the variables). An alternative is to create the TFP performance between firms using a bilateral index such as the Malmquist index, based on an estimation of the production function (e.g. Hensher et al., 1995) and this is outlined in the next section. The TFP approach, however, is relatively data hungry and generally requires a balanced panel data set and hence as a consequence can be time/labour intensive, a cost which increases with the number of transportation systems under evaluation.

While TFP approaches can combine multiple inputs, parametric methods such as the Corrected Ordinary Least Squares (COLS) analysis or the Stochastic Frontier Approach (SFA) and non-parametric methods such as Data Envelopment Approach (DEA) have been used more extensively in recent years (e.g. Yu, 2016). Parametric methods are appropriate where there are relatively large samples and when data are available over time. Estimating production functions which relate inputs to outputs formally (Q= f (L,K)) is one approach and Cobb-Douglas ($\ln Q_i = \beta_0 + \beta_1 \ln L_i + \beta_2 \ln K_i + e_i$) production functions (which assume constant returns to scale and fixed-factor substitutability), estimation of similar cost function equivalents or Translog cost functions (variable scale returns and elasticities of substitution) have been more popular in the recent past. Under a COLS estimation, for a technical-efficiency assessment the largest positive residual from the production function estimation is notionally added to the constant term so that the frontier bounds the data from above, and then effectively all of the residual associated with each firm is attributed to inefficiency. Under the SFA approach, efficiency (either technical or cost dependent on the measure of interest) is estimated as a parameter with the residuals being assigned to measuring inefficiency (Coelli et al., 2005). All three approaches are illustrated in Figure 15.4, which also highlights the key advantage of the more sophisticated SFA over COLS as

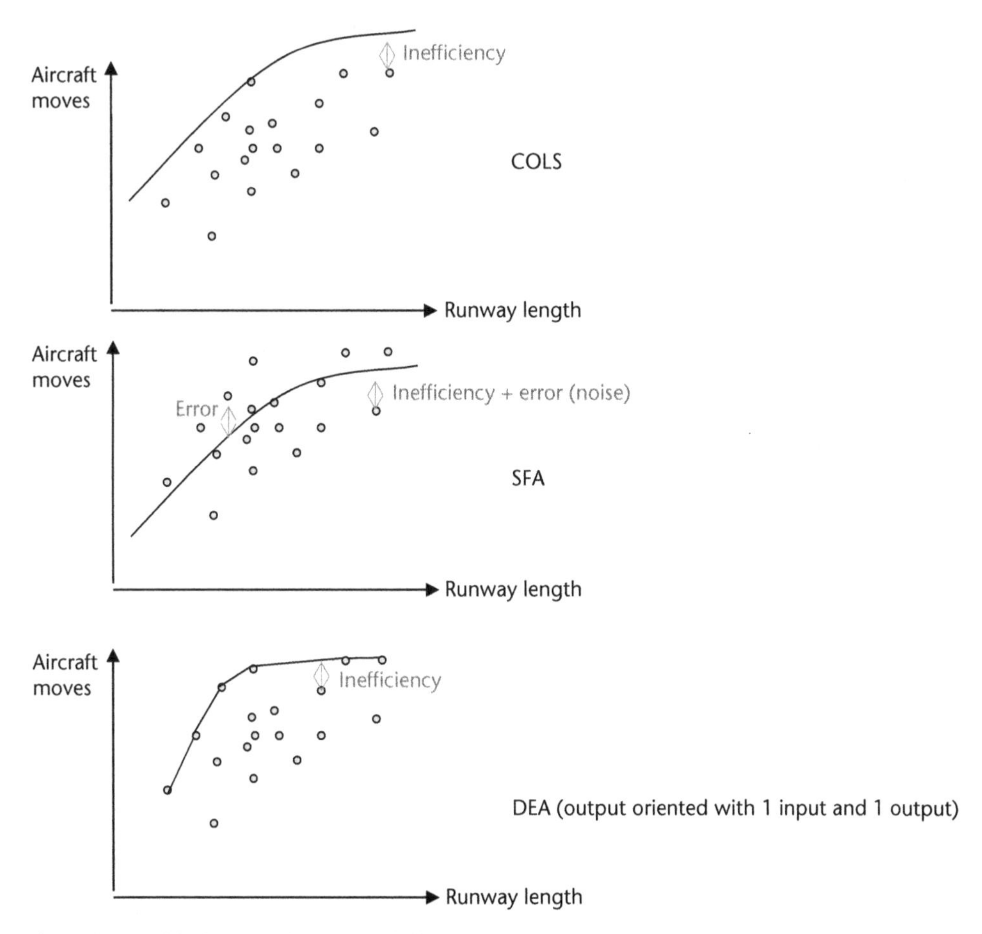

Figure 15.4 COLS versus SFA versus DEA

it possesses the ability to separate the residual effect into two parts – an error component and an inefficiency component.

While the SFA approach is powerful in estimating efficiency scores, it requires strong (and often unrealistic) assumptions to estimate the production frontier and also a large data set to estimate robust results, with ideally panel-based, multiple observations for each operator to control for the unobserved heterogeneity (Karlaftis and Tsamboulas, 2012).

DEA originated and has primarily been developed in the discipline of Operations Research, hence as a technique does not have its foundations in economic theory. It is based upon linear programming methods and its sole focus is on deriving efficiencies. DEA is a non-parametric approach to identifying the linear production (efficient) frontier and inefficiency scores (distance of individual observation from the efficient frontier) for each firm or transport operator in the sample. It has been very popular for estimating technical efficiency, as it does not require any assumptions (for cost efficiency it assumes cost minimisation too but not for technical efficiency) and is flexible, allowing the selection of multiple inputs and outputs. As discussed above technical efficiency (TE) can be expressed as the sum of weighted outputs over the sum of weighted inputs as follows:

$$TE = \frac{Weight_1 \cdot Output_1 + Weight_2 \cdot Output_2 + Weight_3 \cdot Output_3}{Weight_1 \cdot Input_1 + Weight_2 \cdot Input_2 + Weight_3 \cdot Input_3}. \tag{15.1}$$

Outputs and inputs are not simply additive since a unit of each contributes in different ways to overall performance. Hence one uses weights and while the data for all outputs and inputs are available (which makes DEA a deterministic model), the methodological issue is that the weights are unknown. DEA uses linear programming to assign the weights to each of the outputs and inputs and can in its simplest form be expressed as follows (Coelli et al., 2005):

$$\begin{aligned} &\min_{\theta\lambda} \theta, \\ &st \quad -qi + Q\lambda \geq 0 \\ &\qquad \theta xi - X\lambda \geq 0 \\ &\qquad \lambda \geq 0, \end{aligned} \tag{15.2}$$

where λ represents the weights for the inputs and outputs which is a $I \times 1$ vector of constants, X and Q are input and output matrices, and θ measures the distance between the observations x_i and q_i and the frontier (where the frontier represents efficient operation). In other words, the distance (θ) represents the efficiency score. A value of θ =1 indicates that a firm is 100 percent efficient and thus located on the determined frontier. If input prices are known, DEA can also be used to compute allocative and cost-efficiency scores. A key advantage of DEA compared to parametric approaches is that it can be performed with much smaller data samples (although more recent Bayesian SFA models are able to overcome this) and its application has been popular in the transport literature.

While the choice of the appropriate method matters, the literature emphasises that the specification of the model is at least equally important. For example, choosing the right inputs and outputs both in terms of relevance and number of variables is crucial, as the higher the number of variables by definition the higher the average efficiency scores. This is because the addition of each variable increases the dimension(s) under which a firm can improve its estimated efficiency. Non-parametric DEA production frontier model specifications further focus on two important choices: firstly input versus output orientation, and secondly whether constant returns to scale (CRS) or variable returns to scale (VRS) are assumed. In terms of orientation, it is not uncommon to use both input- and output-oriented models, as the intense debate on which of them is appropriate for the transportation sector is ongoing. While the output-oriented model appears beneficial, as it assumes that for example airports have more influence on the outputs (as modifying runways or terminal is difficult at least in the short to medium run), the input-oriented model may still be valid as airport outputs are often heavily impacted by exogenous factors. Output traffic volumes are in many cases substantially influenced by economic factors or pre-determined by long-term slot contract interests. In other transport sectors, often the output level is a contractual requirement, and therefore similarly an exogenous factor. In terms of the returns to scale model specification, most papers use the VRS model (Banker et al., 1984), as the CRS model (Charnes et al., 1978) would require us to assume that all airports in our sample would produce at the optimal size (which is in our view unrealistic given the level of regulation and other constraints). Similarly, in other transport markets with the output contractually specified, the VRS specification is the more appropriate measure of firm-level efficiency. Moreover, when historical data are available, DEA can identify changes in efficiency arising from institutional reform or technical change, thus providing an understanding (for operators and policymakers alike) as to whether the operating strategy has improved efficiency performance (more on that in the next section).

As indicated above, in the recent past, analysts have gone beyond the estimation of efficiency but are nowadays more interested in identifying the determinants of inefficiency and differences in efficiency scores of otherwise similar decision-making units (e.g. transportation firms). In DEA such determinants are revealed by using a two-stage DEA efficiency approach in which, as part of the second stage, efficiency scores estimated in the first-stage DEA models are used as dependent variables in a truncated (censored at 0) second-stage regression model to provide an understanding of the determinants of efficiency. Methodologically, it is important to apply bootstrapping methods (e.g. Simar and Wilson, 2000, 2008) to the first-stage DEA scores in order to minimise bias and unreliable second-stage regression results (the original, by definition non-bootstrapped DEA, overestimates technical efficiency). The advantage of SFA in this regard is not only that it is parametric (produces a separate error component) but also that the determinants of inefficiency are estimated at the same stage as the inefficiency scores. Nevertheless, the DEA method is often more practical as it is not very time consuming to set up and estimate and is intuitively appealing. At this point it is worth stressing that all efficiency-measurement approaches require significant time in collecting good quality data and transport context knowledge.

15.4 Efficiency change over time

Productivity is the measure of the outputs to inputs ratio, and is related to all factor inputs, hence as outlined previously it refers to 'total factor productivity'. Whilst the concept is very often confused with efficiency, and in particular technical efficiency, the difference is that productivity is not time specific. As described, technical efficiency is the extent to which the output to input ratio avoids 'waste', hence is related to best practice at a particular point in time, productivity on the other hand is a standalone concept and is simply the output to inputs ratio, and in practice is normally used to assess change over time. Hence a firm could potentially increase its productivity (increase the output to inputs ratio with reference to itself), but at the same time experience decreasing technical efficiency (the firm's productivity improvement was not as large as best practice). Whilst total factor productivity can be calculated at a specific point in time, as stated it is normally assessed over a time period to examine how it may have changed over that period, and is therefore normally expressed as an index number. Why the time dimension is of interest is because it is through productivity gains above industry best practice that a firm will improve its technical efficiency (or alternatively failure to match best practice gains result in technical efficiency declines). While there are a number of indices available (e.g. Tornqvist productivity index), the most common approach to measuring TFP change over time is by using a Malmquist index.

The Malmquist productivity index breaks down TFP over time into two constituent parts, efficiency change and technical change. To momentarily relate back to efficiency assessment, then one way to measure productivity change would be to simply examine the position of the firm with regard to the efficiency frontier in each comparator year – if it has got closer, then that would result in productivity gain, a movement away from the frontier would represent productivity loss. The problem, however, is that such an approach will not take account of any frontier shift between the two time periods. What was outlined (the change in the relative position to the frontier) refers to the first component, efficiency change; the second, technical change, is measured as the gap between the two frontiers and how this relative difference may have been affected by any change in the firm's production position. Total factor productivity under a Malmquist index is therefore formally measured as a number of relative distances:

$$TFP(x^t, x^s, q^t, q^s) = \left[\frac{d^s(q^t, x^t)d^t(q^t, x^t)}{d^s(q^s, x^s)d^t(q^s, x^s)}\right]^{\frac{1}{2}} \tag{15.3}$$

which for calculation purposes is expressed as:

$$TFP(x^t, x^s, q^t, q^s) = \frac{d^t(q_t x_t)}{d^s(q_s x_s)}\left[\frac{d^s(q_t, x_t)}{d^t(q_t, x_t)} x \frac{d^s(q_s, x_s)}{d^t(q_s, x_s)}\right]^{\frac{1}{2}}. \tag{15.4}$$

It is thus expressed as the ratio of the outputs q to the inputs x over two time periods t (current year) and s (preceding year) and is measured in terms of the relative distances (d) to a theoretical maximum. As stated, under the Malmquist approach TFP consists of two parts, efficiency change and technical change, such that:

$$TFP_{ts} = EC_{ts} \times TC_{ts}. \tag{15.5}$$

The relative measures that need to be calculated in (15.4) are shown graphically in Figure 15.5. What this shows is the combinations of two inputs, capital (X_k) and labour (X_l), required to produce a single unit of the output. As this represents 'the industry', then the lines F_S and F_T are

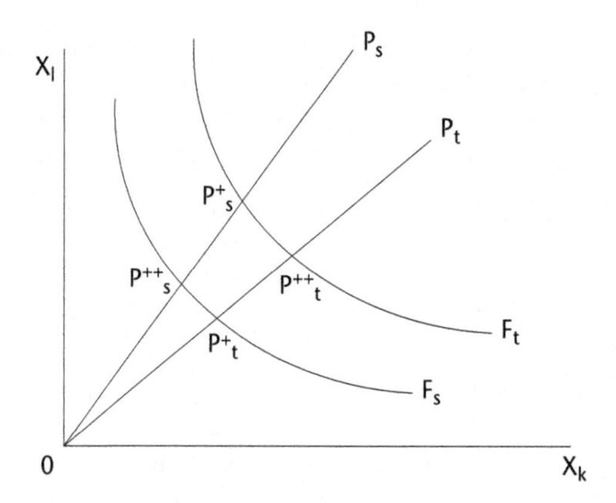

Figure 15.5 Technical and efficiency change

made up of a combination of firms and represent the efficiency frontiers in these two years (as opposed to a single firm isoquant illustrated earlier). The 'problem' to be solved in this example, therefore, is to minimise the inputs required to produce the output. F_S represents the combination of the inputs that minimises this in years, and F_T the frontier in the following year t. P_s and P_t represent the firm's production position in each of these years, hence technical efficiency in each year is given by:

$$TE_s = \frac{0P_s^+}{0P_s} \tag{15.6a}$$

$$TE_t = \frac{0P_t^+}{0P_t}. \tag{15.6b}$$

Therefore, technical efficiency is defined as the ratio of the firm's 'efficient' level of production, in other words, a reference point on the frontier where it should be producing, to the firm's actual production point. In this example, the reference point for year s is defined as $0P_s^+$, with its actual production point, defined again in the case of year s, as $0P_s$. Therefore, if efficiency change is defined as the difference in the relative position of the firm to the efficiency frontier, then it follows:

$$EC_{st} = \frac{TE_t}{TE_s} \tag{15.6c}$$

which is the first part of equation (15.6). Technical change is far more difficult to clearly illustrate. At the general level it represents the shift in the production frontier between the two time periods, or the shift in the technology, either hard or soft, between the two time periods. It can be assessed by either examining the current production position and moving back in time or the previous production position and moving forward in time. Convention is that an average is taken of the two. Hence we examine the firm's production position in year s in comparison to the frontier in year t and the production position in year t in comparison to the frontier in year s. Under a Malmquist measure, an average (the geometric mean) of the two is taken, and this is the second part to (15.6). Following Coelli et al. (2005), in terms of relative distances in Figure 15.4, technical change would be calculated as:

$$TC_{st} = \left[\frac{\left(\frac{0P_t^{++}}{0P_t}\right)}{\left(\frac{0P_t^{+}}{0P_t}\right)} \times \frac{\left(\frac{0P_s^{+}}{0P_s}\right)}{\left(\frac{0P_s^{++}}{0P_s}\right)} \right]^{1/2}. \tag{15.6d}$$

Hence technical change, at the firm level, represents the extent to which the firm's production position has moved in relation to the production frontier. A 100 percent efficient firm across both years experiencing a 3 percent tfp increase will essentially 'capture' all of the technical change, hence technical change would be 1.03 and efficiency change 1.0.

All of these measures could technically be calculated by hand, although software packages are available, with the most commonly used being DEAP (Coelli, 1996). Whilst antiquated (it runs from a DOS[2] prompt and requires an input file), it is relatively easy to learn to use, and once learned quite straightforward. The output can be imported into Excel or other spreadsheet packages for further analysis and graphical presentation. Other software includes Limdep (Econometric Software, 2016), Frontier Efficiency Analysis with *R* (FEAR) and the Excel add-in DEAFrontier (Zhu, 2014), all of which have a modern interface but, unlike DEAP, will only calculate year-on-year productivity change, not across the whole time series.

15.5 Limitations of such approaches

Efficiency analysis is a valuable tool in the assessment of performance within the transport industry, whether that relates to operator, institutional or market performance. Nevertheless, quantitative-based efficiency studies have a number of limitations, of which the main ones can be summarised as:

- highly positivistic;
- ecological validity issues;
- black box problems;
- the need for perfect data; and
- efficiency as a standalone concept.

Beginning with positivism, one of the features of transport, particularly public transport, is that its 'efficiency' as such will in part be determined by the operating environment under which it is provided, with some operators experiencing more conducive conditions than others. The implications are that whilst the assumption under positivism is that all operators 'should' be able to achieve 100 percent efficiency, the reality is very different, and often operators are only able to achieve a fraction of that. This factor is seldom accounted for in such studies. Some of these issues can be captured in particular variables, such as density of population, various local economic indicators, and hence incorporated directly or as outlined in the case of DEA, in a second-stage process. This will provide some form of 'correction', but many other influential factors may remain unmeasurable. Technically what is required, in a pure efficiency assessment, is a secondary qualitative assessment on the extent to which inefficiencies identified in the quantitative assessment could practically be gained, however this has never been done, hence such studies remain purely positivistic.

Ecological validity for those not familiar with the term relates to the extent the findings of the research are applicable to people's daily lives, or more widely to the realities of the situation being studied. As highlighted earlier, with transport studies a major question arises as to what exactly transport does, and in any efficiency study this is a key consideration as it should derive the aim of the producer. Problems occur where we cross somewhere between demand and supply-related measures of output, and involves issues commonly known as the 'fresh air' syndrome. This occurs where companies may be judged to be highly efficient, however one of the very reasons for the high efficiency level is because the transport service, due to low patronage, does not have to stop/slow down to pick up any passengers. As a result, input utilisation is very high. Therefore, taking this logic further, in order to improve 'efficiency', other firms should follow suit and attempt to reduce the number of passengers carried. The real issue here of course is that we are mixing our 'efficiencies', specifically technical/cost with allocative, and whilst the example may be trite, it is nevertheless a very real problem, as ultimately any such measure is secondary (as the primary, profit, is not valid). In this case therefore, would any technical or cost-efficiency measure of a transport service reflect the passenger experience, and that certainly would be questionable, hence it presents a problem of ecological validity.

With regard to black box problems, in practice it is very simple to carry out an efficiency study; all that is required is a set of data that contains an output and two or more inputs, a computer, and that's about it. Enter it all into a programme such as DEAP, and out come the results, 'the answers'. Understanding what the answers mean, and even more importantly, validating the underlying estimation process, is more problematic and often simply overlooked. Black box problems can be overcome through methodical research, hence for example, any two-stage

DEA-based efficiency estimations (with second-stage regressions that explain inefficiencies)should be validated by a parametric estimation and endogeneity tests; note these are not reported, this is purely for the researcher's own assurance that the results produced are valid. Similarly, any parametric estimation can be examined through the three basic principles of econometrics, i.e. are the results consistent with economic theory, are they statistically sound and lastly, are they econometrically sound (i.e. meet the underlying assumptions of the principles being applied). Finally, industry knowledge is important in this respect, hence within broad bounds do the results produced by the efficiency assessment make some kind of general sense.

In some ways, the need for 'perfect' data follows on from the black box issue, and one of the problems with data is that they do not always reflect real life. Efficiency is an assessment of the flow of production, and the efficiency of that flow is measured at different points in time, however, data levels are reported at specific points in time, e.g. capital stock, annual mileage and staff levels, and very often these do not match up. What this can cause is large falls in efficiency followed by large increases, where the reality is that this is a data/data-reporting issue. This can potentially be overcome through data smoothing, hence the data points better meet the underlying principle of a flow. Some early work on Malmquist indices does offer the promise of overcoming some of the large swings that appear in technical and efficiency changes in such evaluations, however these practices are not widespread. The quality of the data in many ways should be considered when the choice of the appropriate estimation method is being considered, with DEA used where data are considered to be of lower quality, and other approaches where better data are obtained. Even with very high-quality data some functions still remain difficult to estimate, particularly the translog cost function, and thus need careful evaluation before being used to generate efficiency estimates.

Efficiency as a stand-alone concept: this is not so much a limitation, but rather has very strong implications on what efficiency studies should actually be used to study. In many respects, efficiency as a stand-alone concept could be argued to be a fairly meaningless measure. What is required in the first instance is a reason to carry out such a study. In most cases, as highlighted in the introduction, this will be to assess the impact of some kind of regulatory reform or some other form of change. Whilst improvements in efficiency mean that there is the avoidance of waste, there is an implication that what this is actually an indicator of is a reduction of management slack. In this sense what is being assessed is something akin to Leibenstein's already mentioned idea of x-inefficiency[3] (Leibenstein, 1966). As such, improvements in efficiency represent far more than simple reductions in costs, but wider improvements in the whole organisational structure under which transport services are provided, which can extend to issues such as the institutional framework, better consumer focus, greater innovation, employment of best practice and so on. A second factor is that efficiency can be used to assess other phenomena, for example improvements in efficiency and more importantly a reduction in the variance of efficiencies would be an indicator of increased competitive pressures, and these are commonly known to produce desirable economic outcomes (Vickers and Yarrow, 1988). Scale effects, i.e. the impact of the size of the organisation, is another related area of study. Nevertheless, there is a danger that individual company efficiency assessment becomes the sole purpose of the exercise, and consequently becomes a fairly meaningless concept and as such could be considered to be naive, as the implication from such studies is that any inefficiency is solely down to poor management. The reality is that it can be down to many different issues, and it is these very issues that should be the subject of the efficiency study, rather than the study of efficiency itself.

None of the issues highlighted in this section should be considered terminal, for example all of the issues surrounding both positivism and ecological validity can be overcome by clearly delimiting the research, and methodically well-defined research the others. What should result is a better understanding of the situation being studied.

15.6 Closing comments

Assessing performance is vital in establishing the success or otherwise of any kind of change. Within the provision of transport services, this 'change' can encompass a large array of issues, ranging from forms of ownership, regulatory change, introduction of competition, supply side reorganisation and so on. A key concept in assessing this performance is efficiency and productivity measurement, hence assessing whether change has led to greater efficiency and higher productivity. As such, this has become a key area of study within transport economics.

The methods and factors to be considered in efficiency assessment are vast and numerous, and draw from concepts and ideas developed in two disciplines, economics and operations research. This chapter has by implication stressed that attention needs to be given to the underlying production processes and that this should be satisfactorily modelled before efficiency and productivity figures are estimated, i.e. derived from economic principles. It needs to be recognised, however, that where efficiency is the only measure of interest, then experience with methods developed in operations research have proved over the years to be robust and consistent. As a consequence, what we have is a very rich toolkit which can be drawn from in order to examine the topic, and should lead to a better understanding of the issues being examined. What actual method or approaches are used will be dependent upon the quality of the data that are available and the purposes of the research. In many cases the prudent analyst will use a combination of discussed efficiency analysis approaches to derive meaningful results that portray the big picture, or at the very least are used to validate insightful results.

Notes

1 Leibenstein subsequently developed his theory of x-efficiency in further articles and three subsequent books, published between 1976 and 1987.
2 For historical information, DOS was the forerunner of Windows, hence was the main computer interface on most PCs pre-1991.
3 Or indeed Stigler's idea of multiple outcomes, in this case less management effort for an 'easier' life and hence a better work/life balance.

Further reading

Coelli, T. J., Rao, P. D. S., O'Donnell, C. J. and Battese, G. E. (2005). *An Introduction to Efficiency and Productivity Analysis*. New York: Springer.

Fried, H.O., Knox Lovell, C.A., Schmidt, S.S. (2008). *The Measurement of Productive Efficiency and Productivity Growth*. Oxford: Oxford University Press.

Greene, W.H., Khalaf, L., Sickles, R., Veall, M., Voia, M.-C. (2016). Productivity and Efficiency Analysis. Cham: Springer.

Merkert, R., Odeck, J., Bråthen, S. and Pagliari, R. (2012). A Review of Different Benchmarking Methods in the Context of Regional Airports. *Transport Reviews*, 32(3), pp. 379–95.

References

Banker, R. D., Charnes, A. and Cooper, W. W. (1984). Some Models for Estimating Technical and Scale Inefficiencies. *Management Science*, 30, pp. 1078–92.

Benjamin, J. and Obeng, K. (1990). The Effect of Policy and Background Variables on Total Factor Productivity for Public Transit. *Transportation Research Part B*, 24(1), pp. 1–14.

Charnes, A., Cooper, W. and Rhodes, E. (1978). Measuring the Efficiency of Decision-Making Units. *European Journal of Operational Research*, 2, pp. 429–44.
Coelli, T. J. (1996). A Guide to DEAP Version 2.1: A Data Envelopment Analysis (Computer) Program. CEPA Working Paper 96/08, www.une.edu.au/econometrics/cepa.htm (accessed 22 November 2016).
Coelli, T. J., Rao, P. D. S. O'Donnell, C. J. and Battese, G. E. (2005). *An Introduction to Efficiency and Productivity Analysis*. New York: Springer.
De Alessi, L. (1983). Property Rights, Transaction Costs, and X-Efficiency: An Essay in Economic Theory. *American Economic Review*, 73(1), pp. 64–81.
Econometric Software (2016). Limdep 11 (Computer Program). Plainview, NY: Econometric Software.
Greene, W. H. (2008). The Econometric Approach to Efficiency Analysis. In Fried, H. O., Knox Lovell, C. A., Schmidt, S. S. (eds), *The Measurement of Productive Efficiency and Productivity Growth*. New York: Oxford University Press.
Greene, W. H., Khalaf, L. C., Sickles, R., Veall, M. and Voia, M.-C. (2016). *Productivity and Efficiency Analysis*. Cham: Springer International Publishing.
Hensher, D. A. (1992). Total Factor Productivity Growth and Endogenous Demand: Establishing a Benchmark Index for the Selection of Operational Performance Measures in Public Bus Firms. *Transportation Research, Special Issue on Performance Measurement*, 26B(5), pp. 435–48.
Hensher, D. A. Daniels, R. D. and De Mellow, I. (1995). A Comparative Assessment of the Productivity of Australia's Railway Systems, 1970/71–1991/92. *Journal of Productivity Analysis*, 6(3), pp. 201–24.
Karlaftis, M. G., and Tsamboulas, D. (2012). Efficiency Measurement in Public Transport: Are Findings Specification Sensitive? *Transportation Research Part A*, 46(2), pp. 392–402.
Leibenstein, H. (1966). Allocative Efficiency vs. 'X-Efficiency'. *American Economic Review*, 56(3), pp. 392–415.
Merkert, R. and Morrell, P. S. (2012). Mergers and Acquisitions in Aviation: Management and Economic Perspectives on the Size of Airlines. *Transportation Research Part E: Logistics and Transportation Review*, 48(4), pp. 853–62.
Merkert, R., Smith, A. S. J. and Nash, C. A. (2010). Benchmarking of Train Operating Firms: A Transaction Cost Efficiency Analysis. *Transportation Planning and Technology*, 33(1), pp. 35–53.
Merkert, R., Odeck, J., Bråthen, S. and Pagliari, R. (2012). A Review of Different Benchmarking Methods in the Context of Regional Airports. *Transport Reviews*, 32(3), pp. 379–95.
Merkert, R., Mulley, C. and Hakim, M. (2015). The Revenue Potential and Performance of BRT Operations as Part of Larger Transport Systems. Proceedings of the 14th Thredbo Conference, Santiago de Chile.
Oum, T. H., Waters, W. G. and Yu, C. (1999). A Survey of Productivity and Efficiency Measurement in Rail Transport. *Journal of Transport, Economics and Policy*, 33(1), pp. 9–42.
Simar, L. and Wilson, P. W. (2000). A General Methodology for Bootstrapping in Non-Parametric Frontier Models. *Journal of Applied Statistics*, 27, pp. 779–802.
Simar, L. and Wilson, P. W. (2008). Statistical Inference in Nonparametric Frontier Models: Recent Developments and Perspectives. In: Fried, H. O., Lovell, C. A. K. and Schmidt, S. S. (eds), *The Measurement of Productive Efficiency and Productivity Change*. New York: Oxford University Press, pp. 421–522.
Stigler, G. J. (1976). The Xistence of X-Efficiency. *American Economic Review*, 66(1), pp. 213–16.
Tsai, C., Mulley, C. and Merkert, R. (2015). Measuring the Cost Efficiency of Urban Rail Systems: An International Comparison Using DEA and Tobit Models. *Journal of Transport Economics and Policy*, 49(1), pp. 17–34.
Vickers, J. and Yarrow, G. (1988). *Privatization: An Economic Analysis*. Cambridge, MA: MIT Press.
Yu, C. (2016). Airline Productivity and Efficiency: Concept, Measurement, and Applications. In Bitzan, J. D, Peoples, J. H. and Wilson, W. W. (eds), *Airline Efficiency (Advances in Airline Economics, Volume 5)*. Bingley: Emerald Group Publishing, pp. 11–53.
Zhu, J. (2014). *Data Envelopment Analysis: Let the Data Speak for Themselves*. Create Space Independent Publishing Platform.

Part IV
Transport and the environment

16
The environment in the provision of transport

Maria Attard

16.1 The natural environment as an economic resource

Considering the natural environment as capital in economic theory dates back at least 200 years, with some of the early work of Ricardo (1817) and Faustmann (1849), and more recently the work of Hotelling (1931). Capital assets store wealth and generate production for future consumption (Hulten, 2006). Similarly, if we use more natural capital to produce economic output today, then we have less for production tomorrow (Barbier, 2014). Over time, many economists developed strong conceptual frameworks for considering the natural environment and its resources as capital, or an economic resource (Weitzman, 1976; Hartwick, 1990; Heal, 1998; Daily et al., 2000; Nordhaus, 2006; Arrow et al., 2012). Despite this, however, efforts to include the natural environment as capital in the decision-making process have been overall weak. This happens in particular where common property or public goods are dismissed and developed.

Barbier (2014) discusses the need to include the depreciation of natural capital in the decision-making process. This depreciation is defined as the value of net losses to natural resources, such as minerals, fossil fuels, forests and similar sources of material and energy inputs into our economy. The idea is that societies squander valuable natural capital that provides important services to the economy such as recreation, flood or sea level rise protection and erosion control without any appreciation of the loss of this important natural capital. In some cases this remains underpriced in markets or unaccounted for in public accounts. In some states, this capital may represent a large share of their wealth. This leads to poor management of resources which in turn reduces future production and can have a significant bearing on sustainability, wellbeing and economic growth.

The Millennium Ecosystem Assessment (MEA) was called for by United Nations Secretary-General Kofi Annan in 2000 to assess the consequences of ecosystem change for human wellbeing and to establish the scientific basis for actions needed to enhance the conservation and sustainable use of ecosystems and their contribution to human wellbeing (MEA, 2005). The conceptual framework for the MEA presents people as an integral part of ecosystems and that a dynamic interaction exists between them and other parts of ecosystems, with the changing human condition driving, both directly and indirectly, changes in ecosystems and thereby causing changes in human wellbeing.

The four main findings of the MEA are represented in Box 16.1. The impact of population growth and development has seen a degradation of many ecosystems services which support wellbeing, vis-à-vis the supply of other services, such as the provision of food. These trade-offs shift the cost of degradation from one group of people to another or defer the costs to future generations which will not benefit from the ecosystems which support food production today. The harmful effects of the degradation of ecosystem services (the persistent decrease in the capacity of an ecosystem to deliver services) are being borne disproportionately by the poor, are contributing to growing inequities and disparities across groups of people, and are sometimes the principal factor causing poverty and social conflict (MEA, 2005).

Box 16.1 Four main findings of the Millennium Ecosystem Assessment

- Over the past 50 years, humans have changed ecosystems more rapidly and extensively than in any comparable period of time in human history, largely to meet rapidly growing demands for food, fresh water, timber, fibre and fuel. This has resulted in a substantial and largely irreversible loss in the diversity of life on Earth.
- The changes that have been made to ecosystems have contributed to substantial net gains in human wellbeing and economic development, but these gains have been achieved at growing costs in the form of the degradation of many ecosystem services, increased risks of non-linear changes and the exacerbation of poverty for some groups of people. These problems, unless addressed, will substantially diminish the benefits that future generations obtain from ecosystems.
- The degradation of ecosystem services could grow significantly worse during the first half of this century and is a barrier to achieving the Millennium Development Goals.
- The challenge of reversing the degradation of ecosystems while meeting increasing demands for their services can be partially met under some scenarios that the MEA has considered, but these involve significant changes in policies, institutions and practices that are not currently under way. Many options exist to conserve or enhance specific ecosystem services in ways that reduce negative trade-offs or that provide positive synergies with other ecosystem services.

(MEA, 2005)

The MEA identified four types of ecosystem services which interact with the constituents of human wellbeing: (i) *provisioning services*: goods obtained from ecosystems, such as a supply of food and fibre; (ii) *regulating services*: benefits obtained from the regulation of ecosystem processes, such as water and climate regulation; (iii) *cultural services*: non-material benefits that people obtain from ecosystems, such as landscapes and recreation; and (iv) *supporting services*: services necessary for the production of all other ecosystem services, such as soil formation and habitats (MEA, 2005).

The discussion can be easily extended to transport infrastructure and impacts that take up land and degrade water resources, contribute to climate change and biodiversity loss amongst other ecosystem services. In a report drawn up for the UK Department for Transport, Atkins and Metroeconomica (2013) assess the application of ecosystem services frameworks to transport-appraisal methodologies. Such a discussion around transport has in fact been primarily guided by articles related to the methods of appraisal adopted in different countries for transport projects, which show an array of methods and impacts on the implemented projects. Comparisons across countries and cities appear evident between the types of infrastructure investment made by governments, with some supporting more environmentally friendly modes of transport and others favouring infrastructure like roads which are primarily seen as adding capacity to a network and therefore reducing (albeit for a short time) travel time.

This chapter will first present the issue surrounding the sustainability of transport and, second, discuss the current methods by which we estimate and take into account the potential impacts of transport operations and proposed transport projects. This is done with a view to highlight the importance of the environment in transport.

16.2 The sustainability (or not) of transport

The European Union (EU) 2001 White Paper introduced the need to integrate transport policy with environmental considerations, emphasising the need for transport growth to be managed in a more sustainable way by encouraging a more balanced use of all transport modes. One of the main messages of the White Paper was that, in addition to facilitating the growing demand for transport, a modern transport system must be sustainable from economic, social and environmental viewpoints. Although it stressed the need to control the growth in air transport and promote the use of non-road transport modes, no specific overall environmental targets were included at the time. Only the need for these to be developed and quantified in the future was highlighted.

The EU State of the Environment Report 2015 analysed the state of, trends in and prospects for Europe's environment and carried messages which encouraged more policies that are working well, but also highlighted the inadequacy of the level of ambition of existing environmental policies to achieve Europe's long-term environmental goals. It identified the need for transitions requiring profound changes in dominant institutions, practices, technologies, policies, lifestyles and thinking as well as a level of commitment, which could put Europe at the frontier of science and technology (European Environment Agency, 2015). In evaluating transport and environment policy integration the European Environment Agency (2015) identified the need for additional ambitious measures to meet the long-term 2050 targets.

Transport systems are critical to all economies and provide substantial benefits to individuals and industry in terms of employment, prices and overall economic growth (European Conference of Ministers of Transport, 2001). In 2013 transport employed around 11 million persons, 5.1 percent of the total workforce in the EU28 and accounted for about 4.9 percent of the gross value added in the EU28 in 2012. These benefits, however, are not without cost. There is well-documented evidence that transport creates substantial externalities through the impacts of congestion, air pollution, noise, accidents and many other factors (Banister, 1998). Indeed, some examples of these are found in other chapters within this book, such as aviation (Chapter 6), private transport (Chapter 13) and road freight (Chapter 21). In addition to these external costs there are other social and distributional costs where the impact on society, such as social exclusion, severance and other equity considerations, is hard to quantify and rarely measured (see Adams, 1999).

The relationship between transport and the environment has always been a complex one. In some cases the environment facilitated transport operations through the provision of excellent waterways and natural harbours. There are examples of some city locations and their development, for example the port of Valletta, Malta (Chapman and Cassar, 2004) and Melbourne, Australia (Wilkinson et al., 2013), which provide ample evidence of the importance of the environment as a resource:

> The role ecosystems play in historic patterns of urban development is clearly recognized. The 1954 Melbourne plan, for example, states 'thus because of the provisions of nature, we find Melbourne the seat of government, the centre of import and export' (MMBW,

> 1954, p. 27). This is a reference to the fact that 'Port Phillip Bay, at the head of which stands Melbourne, [is] the only body of water offering opportunities for large scale harbor development in over 1000 miles of coastline' (MMBW, 1954, p. 27), that extensive timber and pastoral land was present and that a natural freshwater supply existed by virtue of an existing ledge of rock across the Yarra River 'sufficient to prevent tidal water from traveling much further upstream' (Presland, 2009, p. 20). Provisioning services, including 'food' and 'freshwater', are thus recognized as critical.
>
> *(Wilkinson et al., 2013)*

On the other hand, the environment also exerts constraints on the effective mobility of people and goods through elements of physical distance, topographical challenges, hydrological systems, climate and natural hazards or events (Rodrigue et al., 2006). Over time, technological developments overcame many environmental constraints for all modes of transport (Vance, 1990) through the development of road networks, the construction of bridges and tunnels in difficult terrain, innovations in maritime transport and rail, and ultimately developments in air transport and airport infrastructures (e.g. Kansai Airport in Osaka built on an artificial island). There has been continuous work by the EU member states to develop the Trans-European Transport Network (TEN-T) with the construction of mega infrastructures along the Scandinavian–Mediterranean Corridor, such as the Fehmarn Belt Fixed Link between Germany and Denmark and the Brenner Base Tunnel linking Munich (Germany) and Verona (Italy). The Brenner tunnel is set to reduce travel time between Munich and Verona from 5.5 hours to 3 hours and improve the efficiency of rail freight operation by allowing longer and heavier trains due to a significant reduction of the climbing slope (European Commission, 2014a).

In tackling environmental conditions which prevented transport activities, technological developments allowed for the overcoming of obstacles in the physical world. These changes, however, have had an impact on nature and subsequently on the quality of life of people. Environments around transport infrastructures have been modified extensively, to the great loss of natural capital. More importantly are the operations related to the movement of goods and people which have led to major environmental impacts from transport. These fall within three categories (see Rodrigue et al., 2006):

- *Direct impacts*. The immediate consequence of transport activities such as pollution and respiratory diseases. The cause and effect is generally clear and well understood.
- *Indirect impacts*. The second or tertiary effects of transport activities, often with higher consequence than direct impacts but which relationships are often unclear or difficult to establish (e.g. congestion and stress).
- *Cumulative impacts*. These are the additive, multiplicative or synergetic consequences of transport activities. They take into account varied direct and indirect effects on the ecosystem. These are often unpredictable, such as the migration of exotic species.

Table 16.1 summarises the documented impacts of transport on the environment and provides supporting evidence (where available) of the contribution of transport to the degradation of the natural environment (environmental health) and the acceleration of processes such as climate change. It also lists the much underestimated social impacts resulting from transport (adapted from Adams, 1999). And whilst these impacts are a challenge in themselves many are directly related or dependent on the environment, such as the impact on public health and society.

In 1995, the OECD published its estimates for the growth in car and vehicle ownership for 2020 and 2030. It was estimated that by 2030 there would be over 1,000 million cars and 1,600

Table 16.1 Environmental and social impacts of transport

Resource	*Impact*	*Transport's contribution*
Environmental		
Energy	– Energy resources used in transport – Energy resources used in the construction of infrastructure – Energy resources used in manufacturing	– In 2010, the oil import bill of the EU was around €210 billion – Energy demand for transport in 2015 increased to 369,793 ktoe (8.5% increase since 2000) – 31.6% of the EU Final Energy Consumption is attributed to transport
Land and mineral resource	– Land used for infrastructure and mineral resource extraction for construction materials	In 2012 the EU28 had the following transport infrastructures: – 73,236km of motorways (33% increase since 2000) – 339 airports – 215,298km of railway lines – 41,862km of navigable inland waterways – 37,319km of oil pipelines
Water quality	– Surface and groundwater pollution from surface run-off – Changes to natural water systems – Pollution from spillage (oil and heavy metals)	– The number of reported oil spills at sea in the EU totalled 5 in 2014, spilling 4,000 tonnes of oil
Air quality	– Global and local pollutants that affect environmental health	– 23.7% of CO_2 emissions in the EU28 are generated from transport (2012) – 71.8% of CO_2 emissions are generated from road transport alone (2012)
Waste	– Scrapped vehicles – Waste oil, tyres and other materials	– Total number of end-of-life vehicles in the EU27 in 2012 was 6.2 million – 3 million tonnes of waste oil is managed every year in the EU
Soil quality and biodiversity	– Soil erosion and contamination – Destruction of habitats from infrastructure and operations	– An estimated 115 million hectares or 12% of Europe's total land area are subject to water erosion, and 42 million hectares are affected by wind erosion – The number of potentially contaminated sites in EU25 is estimated at approximately 3.5 million

Table 16.1 (Cont.)

Resource	*Impact*	*Transport's contribution*
Noise and vibration	– Noise from roads, rail, port and airport infrastructures	– 125 million Europeans exposed to levels of road traffic noise above legal guidelines
Climate change	– Transport contributions of CO_2, CH_4 and N_4O contributing to greenhouse gases	– Globally 6.9 Gt/year of CO_2 is generated from transport alone – 31% of GHG emissions in the EU28 are generated from the transport sector (2012) – 71.9% of all transport GHG emissions are generated from road transport alone (2012)
Built environment	– Structural damage to infrastructure – Property damage from accidents – Corrosion of cultural heritage from air pollution	
Social		
Health and nutrition	– Deaths and injuries from accidents – Noise disturbance – Premature deaths from air pollution – Obesity and ill health	– 25,938 fatalities from road accidents in EU28 in 2013 – In 2012, 12.6 million deaths globally, representing 23% of all deaths, were attributable to the environment. In children younger than 5 years, up to 26% of all deaths were environment related
Social polarisation	– Societal gaps between those with a car and those without – Societal gaps between those able to afford travel and those that cannot	– In 2012 there were 1.5 million persons at high risk of suffering from 'transport poverty' in England alone – Close to 9% of all Europeans live in severe material deprivation - they do not have the resources to own a washing machine, *a car*, a telephone, to heat their homes or face unexpected expenses
Street life, communities	– Less convivial streets – More anonymous neighbourhoods – Less civic engagement	– 22% of those killed on the world's roads are pedestrians – The cost of road congestion in Europe is estimated at 1% of the GDP, with most congestion occurring in urban areas
Crime and law enforcement	– Crimes related to anonymous neighbourhoods and underutilized infrastructure	
Children	– Hostile environments preventing children from walking and cycling – Obesity amongst children is increasing due to sedentary lifestyles	– In 2014, an estimated 41 million children under 5 years of age were affected by overweight or obesity
Telecommunications	– Widespread increase in travel as telecommunications are easier	

Source: compiled from Adams, 1999; Banister, 2005; Christidis and Ibáñez Rivas, 2012; European Commission, 2006, 2011, 2014b, 2015, 2016a, 2016b; European Environment Agency, 2014; Prüss-Ustün et al., 2016; Rodrigue et al., 2006; Sustrans, 2012; World Health Organization, 2013, 2016

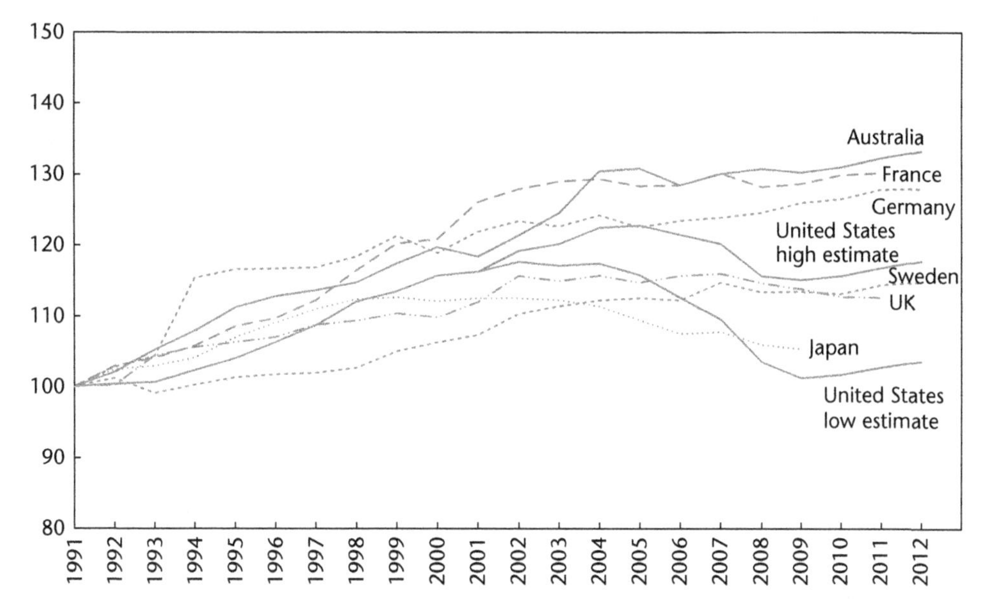

Figure 16.1 Passenger kilometres by private car (1990=100)
Note: the Federal Highway Administration estimate of vehicle occupancy in the US has been revised for 2009 based on the 2009 National Household Travel Survey, resulting in a lower occupancy rate than previously. High estimate applies the vehicle occupancy based on 2001 Survey while low estimate is based on a gradual decline from the 2001 rate to the 2009 rate
Source: International Transport Forum, 2013

million vehicles. Already by 2005 the world's vehicle population reached the 1,000 million mark (Hickman and Banister, 2014). Despite these trends, the International Transport Forum reported a slower growth in passenger vehicle travel volumes (see Figure 16.1) and mixed trends in bus travel across the EU and OECD countries.

The focus on cities is driven by the increasing urbanisation with an increase in the number of mega cities rising to 28 worldwide (compared to ten in 1990). According to the 2014 revision of the *World Urbanization Prospects*, the United Nations estimates 54 percent of the world's population living in urban areas. This percentage is expected to rise to 66 percent by 2050 (United Nations, 2014). Managing cities sustainably is seen as a key challenge for the 21st century, a challenge which is confronted by growing demands for movements of people and goods, urban sprawl and more economic growth.

The impacts identified in Table 16.1 summarise the concerns of many who understand the environmental costs associated with transport. And with the exception of road accidents, with the number of fatalities dropping in years in the developed world, there is little indication of a reduction in the overall impact of the transport sector on the various aspects of the environment, be it natural or man-made. With the signing of the Paris COP21 agreement in 2016 and the decision to limit the global temperature increase to well below 2°C (even limit the increase to 1.5°C), there is renewed hope in decisions that might have significant impact on transport's contribution to climate change and overall environment degradation. Further measures are being taken under the EU Clean Air Policy Package (European Commission, 2013), which aims to reduce the impact of anthropogenic activities, including those related to transport infrastructure and provision.

Operationally, however, there are ongoing debates about the methods used by transport practitioners and decision makers in making the right decisions about sustainable transport projects which serve to reduce the potential externalities and impact on the environment. Many contend that the current methods of appraising transport projects are not comprehensive of environmental and societal needs. The next section discusses these concerns and implications for transport sustainability.

16.3 Transport, environmental cost and appraisal mechanisms

The increasing pressure on governments to tackle the externalities of transport adds fuel to the debate about which projects and measures can address the necessary changes required in the transport sector to reduce amongst others energy use, congestion and emissions. As seen in Table 16.1, transport generates 6.9 Gt/year of CO_2 globally and is a major contributor to climate change. Attempts to curtail this contribution are critical at all levels, especially in urban areas and for road transport. The process of choosing the right and most effective projects is supported by appraisal mechanisms that help decision makers choose the right projects at the right costs. However, many concerns have been raised over the years about the validity of one method over the other, especially when dealing with transport projects.

Projects in the transport sector have wide-ranging impacts such as those on the overall economy, urban form, environmental health, quality of life and many other factors that are difficult to identify, let alone quantify. Despite all this it is common practice to apply cost-benefit analysis (CBA) to support decision making. Proponents of the method, particularly prevalent in the UK, define it as (i) a framework within which impacts are quantified on a consistent basis forcing decision makers to face up to numbers and (ii) a rational, transparent and objective process providing a solid analytical framework for decision making (Worsley and Mackie, 2015).

Over the years there has been discontent with CBA as an overall appraisal method (Ackerman and Heinzerling, 2004) and more specifically in transport (Self, 1970; Adams, 1994; Næss, 2006, 2016; Van Wee, 2012; Dimitriou et al., 2012). The main concerns arise from the difficulty of quantifying the unquantifiable, such as the value of life, the value of natural environments (natural capital) and the impacts on it, and the issues surrounding social equity. It is in reality a concern, as identified in transport projects, that it cannot all be reduced to a monetary value. And this is true for many of the environmental losses suffered over time through the construction of new infrastructures, clean air in cities and overall landscape degradation with the invasion of the car. Self (1970, p.255) goes on to say that:

> many of the judgements relative to the appraisal (and calculation of the likely impacts) of a transport infrastructure project can only be reasonably expressed and argued in fairly broad terms... they belong to the arena of public debate – and not to a world of endlessly hypothecated and quantified sums... ultimately, they can only be taken through a series of policy judgements, which should be as open and explicit as possible, and supported by relevant information which by itself can never be conclusive. Greater rationality in the final decision is not helped, but hindered, by the use of notional monetary figures which either conceal relevant policy judgements or involve unrealistic and artificial degrees of precision. Those who suppose otherwise are heading for a peculiarly dreary version of 1984.

The limitations of the CBA have been tested in a number of projects including the Interreg IVB Project, 'Sintropher', which looked at sustainable transport in north-west Europe's periphery and examples of transport infrastructure projects from the UK (Sintropher, 2015). A list of key problems were identified and included:

- Limits of quantification – confirming earlier statements by Ackerman and Heinzerling (2004) and Næss (2006) that there are certain benefits which cannot be monetised and are therefore a priori left out of the assessment.
- An emphasis on travel time savings – travel time values are disputed (Metz, 2008), especially when compared to travel on public transport (Jain and Lyons, 2008) where time could be productive especially when facilitated by technology.
- Discounting – the practice of discounting does not apply for environmental and social issues.
- Distributional and equity issues – populations are homogenised and poor cohorts suffer the impacts of exclusion and pollution.
- Limited ex-post validation – inaccuracies and number mismatch over time have been found in CBA (Flyvbjerg et al., 2002), thus limiting the effectiveness of the process.

Overall it is evident that CBA favours development, with a particular emphasis on the economic factors that affect development. The use of participatory multicriteria assessment is proposed in the Sintropher project as an alternative to CBA and one which encompasses the use of local policy objectives and weights which reflect the important policy objectives, develop indicators and assess impacts (including the views of different actors) and use public arenas where decisions are debated against the criteria, weightings and impacts identified in the process. This not only increases consensus but incorporates the views of different stakeholders, therefore ensuring ownership.

With increasing awareness of ecosystem services and the value of nature in the decision-making process, however, the UK Department for Transport commissioned a study in 2013 about the application of the ecosystem services framework to transport projects appraisal methods (Atkins and Metroeconomica, 2013). The report discussed current practices in the UK including the guidance provided by the HM Treasury Green Book and Department for Transport's WebTAG guidance for the assessment of transport projects. In analysing the four categories of ecosystem services as identified by the MEA, the report identified 11 ecosystems services that required inclusion in the project-appraisal methodology used in the UK (Table 16.2). The report goes on to compare the ecosystem services identified in Table 16.2 to the WebTAG guidance in place in the UK and offer insights into the valuation of such services.

It is evident from the review by Atkins and Metroeconomica (2013) that a full valuation of the transport impacts (and benefits) cannot be achieved. Difficulties in assigning costs are prevalent in the field and more research is required to develop effective methods for costing particular services (Daily et al., 2009). And in some cases transport projects generate impacts that are beneficial to some ecosystem services, for example cycling lanes that provide users with an improved quality of service. In addition to this there is also the procedure which would require changing, in order to give relative weighting to the different ecosystem services which are degraded or benefitting from such developments.

The discussion has to also be extended to the role that appraisal takes in various countries, especially in relation to transport projects. The developments in the transport sector are fuelled by a desire for economic growth and further mobility, but on the other hand with a wish for less negative impacts. Western democracies have exposed transport projects to a myriad of stakeholder inputs and for the most part seek public consensus prior to decision making. A tool to support this decision-making process was therefore seen as necessary since most transport projects are complex and have significant impacts. Alongside the concerns over the use of CBA (many

Table 16.2 Ecosystem services for transport appraisal

Ecosystem services category	*Ecosystem service*
Provisioning services	Food
	Fuel and fibre
	Fresh water supply
Provisioning/cultural services	Wild species diversity
Cultural services	Recreation
	Aesthetic value
	Cultural heritage
Regulating services	Climate regulation
	Hazard regulation
	Disease and pest regulation
	Pollination
	Noise regulation
	Water quality regulation
	Soil regulation
	Air quality regulation

Source: Atkins and Metroeconomica, 2013

outlined above) there are also institutional and political contexts which affect decision makers (Mackie et al., 2014). These realities of politics and opportunity costs resulting from transport projects make part of the process more institutional rather than analytical.

16.4 Conclusion: the natural environment as an opportunity for sustainable transport

This chapter has discussed the transport impacts and some of the challenges with appraisal methodologies that integrate the value of nature and the environment in transport projects. It is evident that we are still far from the optimum decision-making processes that will ensure there is protection of the environment, alongside economic and social considerations.

The Paris COP21 goal to limit global temperature increase well below 2°C is very ambitious. For transport, the pursuit of sustainable mobility measures will become even more critical as transport contributes significantly to this target. The do-nothing approach will have potentially enormous implications on the environment and public health and will contribute to climate change. The costs of increasing natural disasters, loss of biodiversity, migration and other implications will be too high, as already seen in part in the MEA. This alternate future has been, to a certain extent, mitigated in the Paris Agreement, which requires all parties to report regularly on their emissions and implementation efforts and undergo international review.

The opportunity for the environment is therefore at a high as states agreed to and sign the Paris Agreement in 2016. Governments and transport decision makers have also the opportunity to use these ambitious targets to refocus their transport agendas and rethink transport projects in terms of their environmental gains. So apart from the benefits that nature and the environment provide in facilitating transport and mobility, there is another opportunity to ensure that transport projects are truly sustainable and contribute to the global temperature decrease.

References

Ackerman, F. and Heinzerling, L. (2004). *Priceless: On Knowing the Price of Everything and the Value of Nothing*. New York: New Press.

Adams, J. (1994). *The Role of Cost-Benefit Analysis in Environmental Debates*. London: UCL, http://john-adams.co.uk/wp-content/uploads/2006/The%20role%20of%20cost-benefit%20analysis%20in%20environmental%20debates.pdf

Adams, J. (1999). *The Social Implications of Hypermobility*. Paris: Organisation for Economic Cooperation and Development, www.olis.oecd.org/olis/1999doc.nsf/LinkTo/ENV-EPOC-PPC-T(99)3-FINAL-REV1

Arrow, K. J., Dasgupta, P., Goulder, L. H., Mumford, K. J. and Oleson, K. (2012). Sustainability and the Measurement of Wealth. *Environmental and Development Economics*, 17, pp. 317–53.

Atkins and Metroeconomica (2013). *Applying an Ecosystem Services Framework to Transport Appraisal*. Report for the UK Highway Agency/Department for Transport. Contract ref: PPRO 04/91/16, www.gov.uk/government/uploads/system/uploads/attachment_data/file/193821/esa-report.pdf

Banister, D. (1998). *Transport Policy and the Environment*. London: Routledge.

Banister, D. (2005). *Unsustainable Transport: City Transport in the New Century*. London: Routledge.

Barbier, E. B. (2014). Account for Depreciation of Natural Capital. *Nature*, 515, pp. 32–3.

Chapman, D. and Cassar, G. (2004). Valletta. *Cities*, 21(5), pp. 451–63.

Christidis, P. and Ibáñez Rivas, J. N. (2012). *Measuring Road Congestion*. Joint Research Centre, Institute for Prospective Technological Studies, European Commission.

Daily, G., Soderqvist, T., Aniyar, S., Arrow, K., Dasgupta, P., Ehrlich, P. R., Folke C., Jansson, A., Jansson, B., Kautsky, N., Levin, S., Lubchenco, J., Maler, K. G., Simpson, D., Starrett, D., Tilman, D. and Walker, B. (2000). The Value of Nature and the Nature of Value. *Science*, 289, pp. 395–96.

Daily, G. C., Polasky, S., Goldstein, J., Kareiva, P. M., Mooney, H. A., Pejchar, L., Ricketts, T. H., Salzmann, J. and Shallenberger, R. (2009). Ecosystem Services in Decision Making: Time to Deliver. *Frontiers in Ecology and the Environment*, 7(1), pp. 21–8.

Dimitriou, H., Ward, J. and Wright, P. (2012). *OMEGA Project: Summary Report*. London: OMEGA Centre, UCL.

European Commission (2006). *Thematic Strategy for Soil Protection*. COM(2006)231 final, http://eur-lex.europa.eu/legal-content/EN/TXT/PDF/?uri=CELEX:52006DC0231&from=EN

European Commission (2011). *Roadmap to a Single European Transport Area: Towards a Competitive and Resource Efficient Transport System*. White paper COM (2011) 144 final, http://eur-lex.europa.eu/legal-content/EN/TXT/PDF/?uri=CELEX:52011DC0144&from=EN

European Commission (2013). *The Clean Air Policy Package*. Brussels: European Commission, http://ec.europa.eu/environment/air/clean_air_policy.htm

European Commission (2014a). *Infrastructure: TEN-T–Connecting Europe*. Brussels: European Commission, http://ec.europa.eu/transport/themes/infrastructure/ten-t-guidelines/corridors/scan-med_en.htm

European Commission (2014b). *EU Energy, Transport and GHG Emissions Trends to 2050 Reference Scenario 2013*. Brussels: European Commission, http://ec.europa.eu/transport/media/publications/doc/trends-to-2050-update-2013.pdf

European Commission (2015). *EU Transport in Figures*. Statistics Pocketbook 2015. Luxembourg: Publications Office of the European Union.

European Commission (2016a). *Environment: Waste Oils*. Brussels: European Commission, http://ec.europa.eu/environment/waste/oil_index.htm

European Commission (2016b). *Employment, Social Affairs and Inclusion: Poverty and Social Exclusion*. Brussels: European Commission, http://ec.europa.eu/social/main.jsp?catId=751

European Conference of Ministers of Transport (2001). *Assessing the Benefits of Transport*. Paris: OECD.

European Environment Agency (2014). *Noise in Europe 2014*. Brussels: EEA, www.eea.europa.eu/highlights/a-quarter-of-europe2019s-population

European Environment Agency (2015). *Evaluating 15 Years of Transport and Environmental Policy Integration. TERM2015: Transport Indicators Tracking Progress towards Environmental Targets in Europe*. EEA Report No 7/2015.

Faustmann, M. (1849). Berechnung des Werthes, welchen Waldboden... für die Waldwirtschaft besitzen. *Allgemeine Forst und Jagd-Zeitung*, 25, pp. 441–55. English translation by W. Linnard and M. Gane (ed.) (1968) *Martin Faustmann and the Evolution of Discounted Cash Flow*. Oxford: Commonwealth Forestry Institute.

Flyvbjerg, B., Holm, M. K. S. and Buhl, S. L. (2002). Cost Underestimation in Public Works Projects: Error or Lie? *Journal of the American Planning Association*, 68(3), pp. 279–95.
Hartwick, J. M. (1990). Natural Resources, National Accounting and Economic Depreciation. *Journal of Public Economics*, 43, pp. 291–304.
Heal, G. (1998). Valuing the Future: Economic Theory and Sustainability. In Chichilnisky, G. and Heal, G. (eds), *Economics for a Sustainable Earth*. New York: Columbia University Press.
Hickman, R. and Banister, D. (2014) *Transport, Climate Change and the City*. London: Routledge.
Hotelling, H. (1931). The Economics of Exhaustible Resources. *Journal of Political Economy*, 39(2), pp. 137–75.
Hulten, C. R. (2006). The 'Architecture' of Capital Accounting: Basic Design Principles. In Jorgenson, D. W., Landefeld, J. S. and Nordhaus, W. D. (eds), *A New Architecture for the US National Accounts*. Chicago: University of Chicago Press.
International Transport Forum (2013). *Statistics Brief: Trends in the Transport Sector*. December. Paris: OECD, www.itf-oecd.org/sites/default/files/docs/2013-12-trends-perspective.pdf
Jain, J. and Lyons, G. (2008). The Gift of Travel Time. *Journal of Transport Geography*, 16(2), pp. 81–9.
Mackie, P., Worsley, T. and Eliasson, J. (2014). Transport Appraisal Revisited. *Research in Transportation Economics*, 47, pp. 3–18.
Melbourne Metropolitan Board of Works (MMBW) (1954). Melbourne Metropolitan Planning Scheme 1954: Report. Melbourne: MMBW.
Metz, D. (2008). The Myth of Travel Time Saving. *Transport Reviews*, 28(3), pp. 321–36.
Millennium Ecosystem Assessment (MEA) (2005). *Ecosystems and Human Well-Being*. Washington, DC: Island Press.
Næss, P. (2006). Cost Benefit Analyses of Transportation Investments: Neither Critical Nor Realistic. *Journal of Critical Realism*, 5, pp. 32–60.
Næss, P. (2016). Inaccurate and Biased: Cost-Benefit Analyses of Transport Infrastructure Projects. In Næss, P., Price, L. and Despain, H. (eds), *Crisis System: A Critical Realist and Environmental Critique of Economics and the Economy*. London: Routledge.
Nordhaus, W. D. (2006). Principles of National Accounting for Nonmarket Accounts. In Jorgenson, D. W., Landefeld, J. S. and Nordhaus, W. D. (eds), *A New Architecture for the US National Accounts*. Chicago: University of Chicago Press.
Presland, G. (2009). *The Place for a Village: How Nature Has Shaped the City of Melbourne*. Melbourne: Museum Victoria.
Prüss-Ustün, A., Wolf, J., Corvalán, C., Bos, R. and Neira, M. (2016). *Preventing Disease through Healthy Environments: A Global Assessment of the Burden of Disease from Environmental Risk*. Geneva: World Health Organization, http://apps.who.int/iris/bitstream/10665/204585/1/9789241565196_eng.pdf?ua=1
Ricardo, D. (1817). *Principles of Political Economy and Taxation*. London: John Murray.
Rodrigue, J. P., Comtois, C. and Slack, B. (2006). *Geography of Transport Systems*. New York: Routledge.
Self, P. (1970). Nonsense on Stilts: Cost Benefit Analysis and the Roskill Commission. *Political Quarterly*, 41, pp. 249–60.
Sintropher (2015). *Findings Report October 2015*. Action WP6I12: A New Appraisal Framework and Decision Support Tool. London: University College London, http://sintropher.eu/sites/default/files/images/editors/Findings_Reports/INV12.pdf
Sustrans (2012). *Locked Out: Transport Poverty in England*. Sustrans, www.sustrans.org.uk/sites/default/files/images/files/migrated-pdfs/Transport%20Poverty%20England%20FINAL%20web.pdf
United Nations (2014). *World Urbanization Prospects: The 2014 Revision*. Department of Economic and Social Affairs, Population Division (ST/ESA/SER. A/352), http://esa.un.org/unpd/wup/Publications/Files/WUP2014-Highlights.pdf
Van Wee, B. (2012). How Suitable Is CBA for the Ex-Ante Evaluation of Transport Projects and Policies? A Discussion from the Perspective of Ethics. *Transport Policy*, 19, pp. 1–7.
Vance, J. E. (1990). *Capturing the Horizon*. Baltimore, MD: Johns Hopkins University Press.
Weitzman, M. L. (1976). On the Welfare Significance of National Product in a Dynamic Economy. *Quarterly Journal of Economics*, 91(1), pp. 156–62.
Wilkinson C., Saarne, T., Peterson, G. D. and Colding, J. (2013). Strategic Spatial Planning and the Ecosystem Services Concept: An Historical Exploration. *Ecology and Society*, 18(1), p. 37.

World Health Organization (WHO) (2013). *Pedestrian Safety: A Road Safety Manual for Decision-Makers and Practitioners*. Geneva: WHO, http://apps.who.int/iris/bitstream/10665/79753/1/9789241505352_eng.pdf
World Health Organisation (WHO) (2016). *Report of the Commission on Ending Childhood Obesity*. Geneva: WHO, http://apps.who.int/iris/bitstream/10665/204176/1/9789241510066_eng.pdf?ua=1
Worsley, T. and Mackie, P. (2015). *Transport Policy, Appraisal and Decision-Making*. London: Institute for Transport Studies.

17

The tools available under a green transport policy

Tom Rye

17.1 Introduction

The purpose of this chapter is to review the effectiveness and ease with which the policy tools available to governments (at different levels) can be implemented in order to combat the main natural environmental issues surrounding the provision of transport. The chapter first considers the transport-related environmental problems that governments need to tackle, before summarising the literature that justifies state intervention to reduce environmental impacts. It then looks at the range of policy tools open to governments at different levels to reduce environmental impacts and the theory behind each of these approaches, before describing experience of implementing these policy tools in practice, by the means of case studies. These options range from voluntary agreements, through the imposition of Pigouvian taxes, to direct regulation of transport activities and to emissions trading schemes. This leads to a discussion of the implementation and operational challenges of each type of policy option, including the practicality of turning a theoretical concept such as 'the polluter pays' into a workable system. The chapter concludes with a brief evaluation of the different policy options from the point of view of both their impact on environmental problems and the practicalities of implementation, including reference to the level of cooperation between agencies that is required for them to work.

17.2 Key transport-related environmental problems

Transport causes a wide range of externalities, that is, costs imposed by transport users on other users and non-users for which the user does not pay the full cost. This leads to an economically inefficient overconsumption of transport in locations and at times when the sum of external and internal costs is higher than the cost paid by the user (see Figure 17.1). Externalities cover issues such as congestion, severance and safety as well as environmental impacts, however, due to the available space, this chapter focuses on the environmental impacts. These range from the *relatively* easily quantifiable, such as emissions of particles by international combustion engines or from tyre wear, through to the much less easily quantifiable, such as net loss of biodiversity due to the construction and operation of new transport infrastructure. It becomes even more problematic to monetise some of these impacts once they have been quantified. A non-exhaustive list of the environmental impacts of transport is set out below (based on Litman, 2009 and Department for Transport, 2015):

- Local air pollution such as carbon monoxide or polyaromatic hydrocarbons.
- Global air pollution – primarily carbon dioxide but also other greenhouse gases (GHGs).
- Impacts of the disposal of wastes from transport.
- Visual, townscape and landscape impacts.
- Biodiversity impacts.
- Noise pollution.
- Water pollution and other hydrological impacts.

A number of these impacts have been identified as major threats to human wellbeing and so it is important that they are reduced. For example, the Stern Report (UK Treasury, 2006) stated that a 2-degree Celsius increase in global temperatures by 2100 due to man-made GHG emissions would lead to a 10 percent decrease in global GDP. Over a quarter of GHG emissions in the UK come from transport and this proportion is rising (Committee on Climate Change, 2015). The European Environment Agency state that:

> Around 90% of city dwellers in Europe are exposed to pollutants at concentrations higher than the air quality levels deemed harmful to health. For example, fine particulate matter ($PM_{2.5}$) in air has been estimated to reduce life expectancy in the EU by more than eight months.
>
> *(European Environment Agency, 2016)*

There are very significant healthcare and loss of productivity costs associated with these health impacts.

Where the cost of the environmental impacts of transport is not borne fully by the user, this leads to overconsumption of transport and overproduction of the externality. This is shown in Figure 17.1, where the quantity consumed when externalities are not internalised is Q_M, where the Marginal Private Cost (MC_{PRI}) curve intersects the MB (marginal benefit) curve.

The level of consumption that maximises welfare is at quantity consumed Q_T, where the MB curve intersects the Marginal Social Cost (MC_{PUB}) curve. In order to quasi-internalise external costs, the economist Pigou proposed a tax equivalent to the difference between marginal private and social costs – a so-called Pigouvian tax. However, the environmental externalities of transport are unevenly distributed in time and space and in particular marginal external costs will be at their highest at those times and locations when there are already many other travellers using the

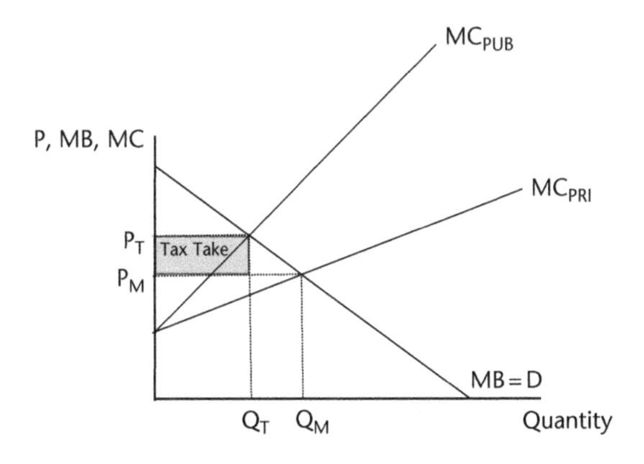

Figure 17.1 The microeconomic theory of a Pigouvian tax (shaded area)

transport system, making it extremely difficult in practice to set a tax that is at the theoretically optimum level shown in Figure 17.1. This should always be borne in mind when assessing the effectiveness of measures designed to deal with these externalities. Increasingly, technology is being developed that will make it possible to assess demand and therefore set prices in real time, but this technology is untested and there remain concerns such as reliability, privacy and fraud prevention that make its practical implementation very challenging (see for example Department for Transport, 2004).

17.3 The role of government in the management of the natural environment

The previous section briefly outlined the environmental impacts of transport. It is clear that these exist and that they can be damaging and costly. For example, the RAC Foundation (2014) estimates the external costs of local air pollution from traffic in the UK to be similar to the external costs of congestion at around £9–10 billion per year. The question must then be asked whether government should have a role in trying to address and reduce these impacts. The answer is affirmative given the economic theory behind these impacts. They are externalities which as previously explained arise because users do not fully internalise the costs of their transport decisions. It is thus a classic example of market failure. More precisely, the market price of transport either does not include or inaccurately values these externalities and so a third party needs to intervene in the market. In mixed-market economies, this role usually falls on the government, and hence it should step in with measures that correct the pricing so that externalities are fully internalised and users then make rational decisions; or governments may select other methods to reduce the scale and impact of the externalities since fully internalising external costs is in practice rather complex, as later sections of the chapter will explain.

Whilst there is a clearly justifiable role for government in general in managing and mitigating the externalities from transport, the term 'government' is a simplification for a complex system whose structure poses significant practical challenges for this activity. This issue is explored at greater length in, for example, Marsden and Rye (2010), who examine *governance* structures in different parts of the UK and their ability and suitability to manage carbon emissions from transport. The essential generic challenge is that government in all states is made up of several levels of formal government organisation (normally some combination of national, regional and/ or local (city/municipal) government, although in some countries such as France, more levels are interposed). On top of this one finds, increasingly, government agencies, business and third-sector organisations which, whilst not possessing (in most cases) formal powers, exercise some influence and so can be seen to be part of the wider system of *governance*. In addition, supranational organisations such as the European Union (EU) exercise formal and informal power over many fields of activity. The entrance of the EU into such areas of activity is argued to be necessary to ensure that all companies in the EU compete on a level playing field with regard to environmental regulation (an issue of the single market) and also to ensure all EU citizens more equal quality of life in terms of their exposure to pollutants. As a large trading bloc, the EU may also possess greater negotiating power with other global trading blocs to ensure that its environmental standards are respected. The other reason for taking an EU-level approach to environmental standards is that pollution knows no geographical boundaries and the effects of pollution generated in one country are felt in another, so an international approach is needed.

Scholars have termed this mixed and not always very clear landscape 'multi-level governance' and it adds great complexity to addressing environmental externalities associated with transport. This is principally because the organisation(s) with the legislative and/or financial competence to deal with the externalities are not necessarily at the same level of government as those at which the externality has its primary impact. For example, pollutants from transport such as nitrogen oxides and particulates have a local impact but in the EU motor vehicle manufacturing standards for air pollutants are regulated at the EU level. Another example might be where local bus services are provided under a long-term concession to a private company (as in some Romanian cities) and the local authority therefore has no control over the emissions standards of the buses, once the concession has been granted. A further example is the introduction of a congestion charge locally or regionally in order to deal with congestion and associated externalities of road traffic. This can only be introduced in the majority of countries if national government passes a law to enable local or regional governments to use this measure. Whilst some local and regional governments may wish to introduce congestion charging, there are wider national political reasons why national governments choose not to pass the relevant enabling legislation. See Chapter 13 for more details of congestion charging. Of course the precise shape of this complex governance system varies from country to country and specific examples cannot be described in detail in a chapter of this length; however, when the case studies of specific types of measure are described in the next section, the governance structure in which they have been implemented will also be explained. The key point is that this structure is not always as conducive as it might be to the introduction of the optimal measure(s) for dealing with transport's externalities.

17.4 Measures and mechanisms open to government to tackle environmental externalities

There is of course a wide range of 'second-best' measures that seek to deal with the environmental externalities of transport – an example is subsidies to public transport, a mode with generally lower externalities than private passenger transport, given adequate vehicle occupancies. However, in this chapter we will consider a more limited range of measures: those that seek to price or regulate the mode of transport that is the source of the externality, rather than to reduce the price or increase the attractiveness of alternative modes. In addition, those measures presented here do not pretend to be an exhaustive list, but rather to highlight the main options available to government, along with a case study of each in practice. Essentially these measures fall into the general categories of regulation, taxation or pricing, with the exception of the first group of measures, that is, voluntary agreements.

17.4.1 Voluntary agreements

As its name suggests, a voluntary agreement is not backed up by any form of regulation, taxation or pricing; it is a non-binding agreement between some level of government and those who are judged to be the source of the externality. An example might be a voluntary agreement between city government and local delivery companies to limit city centre deliveries by truck to a certain time window to minimise noises, space and congestion externalities. An actual example was the agreement made in 1998 between the European Commission and car manufacturers selling vehicles in the EU to limit CO_2 emissions from the average new car to 140g/km by 2008/9. This agreement was signed as an alternative to a mandatory regulation – essentially because the car manufacturers, as rational capitalists, were trying to resist any mandatory measure that would limit their flexibility and potentially impact on their profits. The agreement succeeded in reducing the emissions of new cars sold in the EU by about 1 percent per year, but the target was not achieved (ICCT, 2014). The advantage of the non-binding agreement is that it can be easier to secure than legislation or pricing and will arouse less opposition; concomitantly, because it is non-binding, it is likely to be less effective, as this example shows. It is often used as a precursor to some mandatory measure, as was the case with the EU agreement on CO_2 emissions; the European Commission's line was that it would be implemented first and, if not successful, mandatory emissions targets would be introduced. These came into force in 2009.

Another voluntary approach to reducing externalities is the sharing of best practice and subsidising investments to enable better practice to be implemented. EU programmes such as CIVITAS (www.civitas.eu) aim to do exactly this, by spreading best practice in clean urban transport (such as low-emission vehicles) between cities and providing subsidy for the 'innovative' part of the investment that allows the city to test best practice.

17.4.2 Regulations covering vehicle standards

Governments may seek to reduce the externalities of transport through direct regulation of vehicle standards to improve safety, or reduce exhaust emissions or noise. In the EU, these regulations are the competence (responsibility) of the European Commission – it is not legal for member states of the EU to set stricter or laxer emissions standards for vehicles sold in their territory. The cost of implementing these standards is borne by the vehicle manufacturers and, to the degree that the costs are passed on by manufacturers, to purchasers. The cost is related to the cost of manufacturing the vehicle and is therefore independent of how much, where and when the vehicle will be used. It therefore bears little relationship to the externalities that the use of the vehicle will impose on society – of two identical cars purchased in 2016, one driven 1,000km a year will pollute around ten times less than one driven 10,000km a year, but the price paid for the emissions-reduction measures in the vehicles will be identical in each case. Economically speaking, this is an inefficient non-welfare-maximising use of resources. It is attractive to governments because the concept of a regulation limiting engine emissions is relatively simple to understand (although the interpretation of the regulation may not be, and the technology is not) and also easy to enforce.

An example of such a regulation is the EU emissions standards for all vehicles (different standards apply to different types of vehicle). These so called 'Euro' standards have been in place since 1992 and are now in their sixth iteration, each new one having been more stringent than its predecessor. Figure 17.2 shows the development of Euro standards for buses over time. These apply only to new vehicles and show that over time the limits on what these vehicles' engines are allowed to emit have been reduced significantly for two key pollutants – particles and oxides of nitrogen. It can be seen that the standards are expressed in grams per kWh of engine power, meaning that they can be achieved by increasing engine power, by reducing actual emissions or a combination of the two. This is an example of how a regulation may have unintended impacts (earlier Euro standards led to increases in bus fuel consumption as engine power was increased to meet the standard).

It has been estimated that the cost of complying with the current Euro 6 standard adds €10,000 to €12,000 to the purchase price of a new bus (between 2 and 4 percent), compared to Euro 5. However, it is not reasonable to compare this cost with a 'do-nothing' situation where manufacturers could decide their own emissions standards; a much more probable alternative, were the Euro standards not to exist, would be for each member state to have its own standards. This situation would be more costly and complex for global manufacturers to comply with and would breech a key principle of the single market. In addition, in buses, Euro 6 has been found to produce fuel consumption savings of around 8 percent compared to Euro 5, a saving that helps to offset the additional investment cost to operators, although one that may also lead to something of a rebound effect where operators may allow fuel consumption (and emissions) to rise again

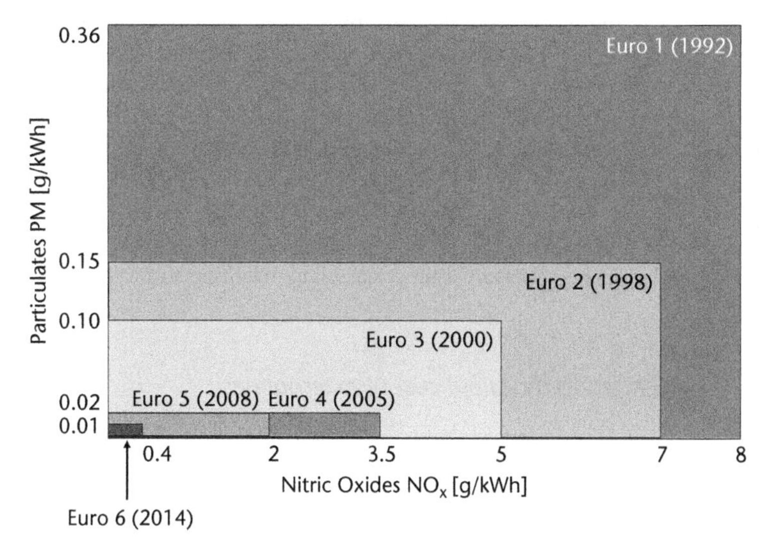

Figure 17.2 Evolution of Euro standards for local buses
Source: redrawn from Transport Resources International, 2014

because the improved technology makes them more relaxed about how much fuel their vehicles consume (Transport Resources International, 2014).

17.4.3 Regulation covering vehicle use in defined areas

Regulation may also be used to seek to manage vehicle use, particularly in areas sensitive to externalities, such as historic city centres, or those vehicles whose externalities are especially great (old polluting vehicles and/or trucks). The use of such regulation is of course predicated on a national legal framework that allows access for (certain types of) vehicles to certain areas to be limited. Since it is limited to certain types of vehicle, time period and location, this type of regulation is more directly targeted at those that impose the highest marginal external costs on other users of the urban area. However, it remains a blunt instrument, economically speaking, as the cost that the regulation passed onto the users of these vehicles is unrelated to the value of the real marginal external cost that they impose, and nor does it allow (directly) users with a higher willingness to pay that cost to do so – the regulation applies equally to all in a given category.

An example of such a permit scheme is the Berlin Low Emission Zone, introduced in 2008 to tackle the very high exceedances of EU emissions limits for nitrogen oxides and particles in many parts of the city. It covers an area of 85km^2 and 1.1 million residents and applies to private cars as well as commercial vehicles. All vehicles wishing to enter the zone must purchase at a small charge a sticker corresponding to their Euro emissions standard; vehicles without a sticker (including foreign vehicles) are prohibited and fined if observed within the zone. In 2008 the minimum was Euro 1 for petrol vehicles and Euro 2 for diesel; this was tightened in 2010, particularly for diesel vehicles. Retrofitting of vehicles (for example by fitting a particulate trap to the exhaust) to improve their environmental performance is permitted. As a result, whilst traffic flows were unaffected, Berlin's vehicle fleet became cleaner more quickly than it would have done with no scheme in place, since it provided an incentive to retrofit existing vehicles or buy new ones at a rate higher than the fleet turnover prevailing before its introduction. Lutz (2009) reports that this led to a 35 percent cut in particulate emissions and 19 percent fall in emissions of oxides of nitrogen in the first year of operation of the scheme. The same author also points out that the scheme, whilst improving the situation, has not led to achievement of the EU emissions limits in the city. This may be because the regulation is not stringent enough (i.e. it allows vehicles that are still too polluting to drive in the zone). For this reason the cost of complying with the regulation is much less than the marginal external cost of the pollution imposed by the most polluting vehicles at the most congested times and locations, and illustrates the issue of the regulation as a relatively 'blunt instrument' to bring about the internalisation of external costs.

17.4.4 Taxes unrelated to marginal cost of externalities

Aside from standard value-added tax applying to all goods, it is relatively common to levy other flat rate sales taxes on transport, principally as a source of revenue. One example is air passenger duty (departure tax) levied at a flat absolute rate on passengers boarding flights from a given country. Clearly, if it is unrelated to precise distance travelled or type or occupancy of the aircraft boarded, it bears no relationship to the externalities imposed by each airline trip. (The UK's air passenger duty is banded by distance and class of travel, but the distance bands are very large.) Another even more common sales tax is duty on fuel, levied at varying percentage rates in a majority of the countries in the world, and in all countries in the EU, where it ranges from a low of 56 percent tax in Estonia to a high of 70 percent in the UK (Directorate General for Climate, 2016). Such taxes normally act as a revenue-raising mechanism, primarily for central government.

Fuel duty bears some limited relationship to the scale of marginal externalities, since vehicles that pollute more tend to consume more fuel, and all vehicles consume more fuel when travelling at congested times/locations. This might be expected to reduce vehicle miles travelled in the short term, and bring about a switch to more fuel-efficient vehicles in the medium to long term. During the 1990s in the UK fuel duty was increased at a rate faster than inflation, but desktop research carried out by this author was unable to find any conclusive studies on the impact of this so-called 'fuel duty escalator' (FDE) on vehicle efficiency, although it is clear that vehicle miles travelled during the period of the FDE grew more slowly than in the preceding period (Potter and Parkhurst, 2005). However, a key review of studies on elasticities of demand for car use with respect to fuel price (amongst other variables) by Goodwin et al. (2004, p. 278) found that a 10 percent real terms rise in fuel price will lead to the following:

(a) Volume of traffic will fall by roundly 1% within about a year, building up to a reduction of about 3% in the longer run (about 5 years or so).
(b) Volume of fuel consumed will fall by about 2.5% within a year, building up to a reduction of over 6% in the longer run.

Fuel consumption will fall faster than traffic levels due to a change to more economical driving patterns and later to more economical vehicles; in this sense, research would suggest that the increase in price does lead to a fall in the external costs of motoring imposed on society, but not necessarily at the times and locations where those externalities are highest. It should also be noted that in the long run some of the reduction in vehicle miles travelled will be lost as people reinvest the fuel savings of more fuel-efficient vehicles in travelling at a lower fuel cost per mile, the so-called 'rebound effect' (see for example Small and van Dender, 2007).

17.4.5 Taxes and charges related to the marginal cost of externalities

A further step towards the optimal Pigouvian tax is to set taxes and charges that vary according to the externalities imposed by a vehicle – so according to its pollutant characteristics, and/or how much it is used. For example, it is increasingly common to set parking charges according to the emissions characteristics of the vehicle parked. In 2015, Madrid introduced emissions-related hourly charging for on- and off-street parking (the latter in city-owned car parks). The charge to park per hour is related to the emissions standards of the vehicle, based on the registration number that the user must enter in order to pay the parking charge. Edinburgh has for several years linked the cost of on-street parking permits for residents within the controlled parking zone to the CO_2 emissions of the vehicle, such that the least polluting vehicle currently costs £72 per year to park, and the most polluting £475 per year. The impacts of these systems have not yet been evaluated, however, and of course they are unrelated to how much the vehicle is used and thus to the externalities imposed. They remain relatively uncommon and have also proven to be politically controversial. In the London borough of Sutton, for example, the introduction of emissions-related residents' parking charges was a key factor in the replacement of a Liberal borough council by Conservatives in local elections in 2010.

A change in taxation whose impacts have been evaluated, is that made to company car taxation in the UK in 2002. Prior to this, employees who were given a company car by their employer had a tax incentive to drive further each year on work's business, and older (and therefore more polluting) cars were treated more favourably in taxation terms. This system was reformed in 2002 and the taxable value of the company car became related to its emissions characteristics, such that the least polluting were taxed at 15 percent of their value and the most at 35 percent of their value; ultra-low emissions vehicles gained further tax discounts and the incentive to drive further each year was abolished. This led to a 0.5 percent reduction in total CO_2 emissions from road transport in the UK in the first year of operation of the new scheme (Potter and Parkhurst, 2005). Of course, this reform still did not operationalise a true Pigouvian tax since the taxation burden paid on a company car is still not directly related to the marginal externalities it imposes – an old polluting car driven primarily in rural areas will impose lower marginal costs than a new less polluting car driven mainly in urban areas, but the taxation burden is the reverse of this. Thus the next section moves on to discuss charges that are much more closely related to vehicle *use* at times and in locations where marginal externalities are at their greatest.

17.4.6 Road user charging and tolling

Road user charging, as distinct from road tolling, is the levying of a charge for all or some vehicles to use an existing road whose use was previously not charged. Such charges have been introduced in a small number of cities in order to reduce congestion and air pollution. Schemes normally apply to a given area only (the most congested/polluted area); charges may vary by time of day, being higher at the times of greatest congestion; larger vehicles are charged more; and there are often exemptions for certain types of vehicle or user, such as buses, or disabled people, or residents. Payment of the charge may be necessary to cross a cordon (boundary) to enter the charged area; or to drive or even to park within the charged area, regardless of whether the cordon is crossed.

A scheme introduced relatively recently, in 2012, is Milan's Area C, whose primary objective was to cut air pollution and secondary objective to reduce congestion. It applies only to a small 8 square kilometre area in a region of 3.7 million people, and it applies to vehicles wishing to enter this zone between 07:30 and 19:30 Monday to Friday. They must pay per entry, to a maximum of €10, with the charge also being dependent on the vehicle emission standard. There are discounts

Table 17.1 Reductions in air pollution within Milan's Area C zone

	Percentage reduction 2014 compared to 2010
Local air pollutants	
PM10 emissions	61%
Nitrogen oxides	30%
Nitrogen dioxide	36%
Volatile organic compounds	31%
Greenhouse gases	
CO_2	33%
Methane	14%
Nitrous oxide	31%

Source: AMAT, 2014

for residents and for frequent users (the latter only for a maximum of 100 entries per year – subsequent entries are charged at the full rate). In addition, certain vehicles with very poor emissions standards are banned completely. The congestion charge replaced an earlier charge that applied only to the most polluting vehicles. The impacts have been impressive, as seen in Table 17.1.

Nonetheless, since the charge is to enter the zone and is the same irrespective of time of day and of how much the vehicle is driven within the zone, it fails to impose a charge equal to the marginal external cost of the pollution and congestion imposed, and in this sense is still not a Pigouvian tax. In addition, it does not apply elsewhere in a very large urban region, although congestion and pollution are present there. A congestion charge that would be 'more Pigouvian' would cover the whole region and would be distance and time based rather than a flat payment for a vehicle to cross a cordon. No such system has been introduced anywhere in the world for private vehicles, although it has been evaluated for the UK and the Netherlands, where modelling showed that it would cut congestion, local air pollution and CO_2 emissions by up to 25 percent (Ubbels et al., 2002). However, problems of implementability and public acceptability ensured that these schemes have not been implemented.

17.4.7 Emissions trading and personal or company travel allowances

The idea of emissions trading is that the total externalities permitted to be generated by a sector, or in total, are capped at some level – hopefully a level that will reduce these externalities at the aggregated level. In order to generate externalities, firms or individual actors must obtain a permit, issued by a regulatory agency. The number of permits should equal the total level of externalities that is sought. Individuals or firms can then trade these permits, such that those for whom it is easy and cheap to reduce their externalities can sell their permits to those for whom it is more difficult to reduce their externalities. The total number of permits should be reduced each year, such that they become scarcer. This scarcity should generate an increase in price, which will make it more economically efficient for increasing numbers of individuals or firms to produce fewer externalities through the adoption of new technology or changed behaviour, as this will become relatively cheaper than buying permits.

The only transport-related sector to be currently subject to such a scheme in practice in Europe is the aviation industry; firms must have sufficient permits in the European Emissions Trading Scheme (ETS) to cover their CO_2 emissions from international flights within the European Economic Area (EEA). When introduced, the scheme covered all international flights departing from EEA airports, irrespective of destination and national origin of the airline, but this is currently (2016) suspended pending the development of an international emissions reduction scheme for civil aviation by the International Civil Aviation Organisation. Of course such a scheme will only have an impact on externalities if the cost of permits is for some actors higher than the marginal cost to them of reducing their externalities; in the case of the ETS this is unclear, as a large number of permits were initially given away, which depressed the price, and there was also the world economic downturn in 2008, which further depressed the demand for and price of permits. In January 2016 the price of carbon on the European markets was only around €7 per tonne. Given that the average flight within Europe generates between 0.15 and 0.5 tonnes of carbon per passenger (depending on how emissions are calculated – see for example www.atmosfair.de), then the cost of ETS permits to cover this is low in comparison to the other operating costs of an airline, particularly considering that 85 percent of permits initially obtained by airlines were allocated to them at zero cost, rather than auctioned at a price (Directorate General for Climate, 2016).

Some transport and environmental economists (see for example Bristow et al., 2010) have also suggested a personal carbon emissions trading scheme, whereby the total amount of carbon emissions, including those from travel, for a given population in a country is capped per person and a system of tradeable permits is introduced. Perhaps unsurprisingly in view of its not inconsiderable problems of implementation and acceptability, no government has yet introduced or even discussed the introduction of such a scheme. Nevertheless, Bristow et al. (2010) argue, based on stated preference research, that such a scheme could be acceptable to a majority of the population where revenues are returned in the form of income or local tax reductions.

17.5 Implementation and operational challenges associated with different policy options

The previous discussion touched on the issue of implementation and acceptability of the different measures. In very general terms, whether or not a measure can be implemented can be seen as a function of a number of factors related to both the overall acceptability of the measure and how implementation is planned and resourced (see Ison and Rye, 2005; McTigue et al., 2016). The order in which the different categories of measures and mechanisms to address transport externalities is listed in the preceding sections reflects in general more challenging implementation issues for the measures later in the list – meaning that voluntary agreements are generally easier to implement than emissions trading schemes. This is for two main reasons. Firstly, regulations may be more acceptable than charges and taxes because they are perceived to apply equally to everyone, and because they require no or little payment. Charges and taxes applied where none have been applied before (for example, the purchase of emissions permits, or congestion charges) encounter significant acceptability problems as a previously free good becomes priced, as can be seen when comparing parking charges with congestion charges (Rye and Ison, 2005). Secondly, the measures later in the list are generally more complex to implement and involve a greater range of implementation agencies; they are also more costly to implement than a regulation or a flat-rate purchase tax. These costs need to be covered by the revenue raised from the measure, and therefore represent a net welfare loss. Such costs can be considerable, as in the case of the London Congestion Charging scheme, where the cost of running the scheme accounts for almost exactly one-third of the revenue raised. In other words, the revenue raised from one in three of the vehicles being charged is simply to cover the cost of the scheme, which therefore only leaves two-thirds of the revenue to be used on measures to negate the impact on those forced off the road, through measures such as improving public transport.

Table 17.2 Evaluation of different measures and mechanisms to reduce environmental externalities of surface transport

	Acceptability	*Implementation complexity*	*Cost*	*Effectiveness*	*How close to Pigouvian?*
Voluntary agreements	7	3	1	1	1
Regulating vehicle specification	5	5	3	4	1
Regulating where vehicles can drive	3	5	3	4	1
Flat-rate taxes	5	4	3	4	2
Taxes related to marginal costs	3	5	4	5	4
Road user charging	1	6	6	6	6
Emissions trading schemes	1	7	5	6	6

17.6 Evaluation of different policy options

From the author's own experience and research in this area, Table 17.2 has been compiled to score the different categories of measure for dealing with the environmental externalities of transport that were listed above. This has been done on an ordinal scale where 1 is low and 7 is high. 'Effectiveness' assesses how well the measure addresses marginal externalities at the scale at which it is implemented. This shows that in general the most effective measures are those that are least acceptable and most complex and costly to implement, echoing the findings of Kocak and Jones (2002) and Schade and Baum (2007).

17.6.1 What needs to change if more and more effective measures and mechanisms are to be implemented?

Table 17.2 shows the generally inverse relationship between acceptability and effectiveness of the different measures considered. Increasing political acceptability is key here. However, political circumstances only rarely conspire to permit the implementation of more controversial measures. Packaging tax changes that tackle environmental externalities as part of wider tax reform to address a broad range of issues can assist in making the former more acceptable. For example, changes to the UK company car tax regime that made it more environmentally friendly, and similar changes to the Dutch personal taxation regime for commuting costs, were packaged with much broader tax changes that brought benefits for many taxpayers. In general, though, for those measures that are more 'Pigouvian', the right set of political circumstances is essential if implementation is to proceed. Milan's Area C is a good example of this, where the election of a new left-wing politician was essential for the previous pollution control scheme to be changed to a congestion charge, but where also various local political events – such as the temporary suspension of Area C after a court case – helped to further build political support for its continued implementation. This coincidence of political power and the right series of events does of course not occur in every case, as has been admirably demonstrated by Noordegraaf et al. (2014) in their analysis of congestion charging plans in the Netherlands.

References

Bristow, A. L., Wardman, M., Zanni, A. M. and Chintakayala, P. K. (2010). Public Acceptability of Personal Carbon Trading and Carbon Tax. *Ecological Economics*, 69(9), pp. 1824–37.

Committee on Climate Change (2015). *Meeting Carbon Budgets: Progress in Reducing the UK's Emissions 2015 Report to Parliament*. London: CCC.
Department for Transport (2004). *Feasibility Study of Road Pricing in the UK: Full Report*. London: DfT, www.london.gov.uk/sites/default/files/gla_migrate_files_destination/DfT%20road%20pricing%20feasibility%20study.pdf (accessed 28 July 2016).
Department for Transport (2015). *TAG UNIT A3 Environmental Impact Appraisal*. London: DfT.
DG Clima, European Commission, https://ec.europa.eu/clima/publications/docs/factsheet_ets_en.pdf (accessed 28 July 2016).
Directorate General for Climate (2016). EU Emissions Trading Scheme Factsheet. Brussels.
European Environment Agency (2016). *Air Pollution*. Copenhagen: EEA, www.eea.europa.eu/themes/air/intro (accessed 3 March 2016).
Goodwin, P., Dargay, J. and Hanly, M. (2004). Elasticities of Road Traffic and Fuel Consumption with Respect to Price and Income: A Review. *Transport Reviews*, 24(3), pp. 275–92.
ICCT, 2014. Briefing Note on CO_2 Emissions from New Passenger Cars in the EU: Car Manufacturers' Performance in 2013, www.theicct.org/sites/default/files/publications/ICCTbriefing_EU-CO2_201406.pdf (accessed 28 July 2016).
Ison, S. G. and Rye, T. (2005). Implementing Road User Charging: The Lessons Learnt from Hong Kong, Cambridge and Central London. *Transport Reviews*, 25(4), pp. 451–65.
Kocak, N. A. and Jones, P. (2002). *Road User Charging: Tools for Option Generation to Increase Acceptability*. Henley-in-Arden: Association for European Transport.
Litman, T. (2009). *Transportation Cost and Benefit Analysis: Techniques, Estimates and Implications*. Victoria, Canada: VTPI.
Lutz, M. (2009). The Low Emission Zone in Berlin: Results of a First Impact Assessment. Unpublished paper to seminar in Birmingham, http://campusmedia.eurist.info/images/4/45/Paper_lez_berlin_en.pdf
Marsden, G. and Rye, T. (2010). The Governance of Transport and Climate Change. *Journal of Transport Geography*, 18(6), pp. 669–78.
McTigue, C., Rye, T. and Monios, J. (2016). The Role of Reporting Mechanisms in Transport Policy Implementation by Local Authorities in England. *Proceedings of the World Conference on Transportation Research*, Shanghai, 10–15 July.
Noordegraaf, D. V., Annema, J. A. and van Wee, B. (2014). Policy Implementation Lessons from Six Road Pricing Cases. *Transportation Research Part A: Policy and Practice*, 59, pp. 172–91.
Potter S. and Parkhurst G. (2005). Transport Policy and Transport Tax Reform. *Public Money and Management*, 25(3), pp. 171–8.
RAC Foundation (2014). *Air Quality and Road Transport*. London: RAC Foundation.
Rye, T. and Ison, S. G. (2005). Overcoming Barriers to the Implementation of Car Parking Charges at UK Workplaces. *Transport Policy*, 12(1), pp. 57–64.
Schade, J. and Baum, M. (2007). Reactance or Acceptance? Reactions towards the Introduction of Road Pricing. *Transportation Research Part A: Policy and Practice*, 41(1), pp. 41–8.
Small, K. A. and van Dender, K. (2007). *Fuel Efficiency and Motor Vehicle Travel: The Declining Rebound Effect*. UC Irvine Economics working paper #05-06-03.
Transport Resources International (2014). European Industry Has Moved to Euro 6. www.dougjack.co.uk/bus-industry-euro-6-emissions-limits.html (accessed 28 July 2016).
Ubbels, B., Rietveld, P. and Peeters, P. (2002). Environmental Effects of a Kilometre Charge in Road Transport: An Investigation for the Netherlands. *Transportation Research Part D: Transport and Environment*, 7(4), pp. 255–64.
UK Treasury (2006). *Stern Report on Climate Change and the Economy*. London: UK Treasury.

18

Options and practicalities of a green transport policy

Rebecca Johnson

18.1 Introduction

As mobility and transport use continue to grow, so do the negative environmental impacts associated with increased transport use. There are a range of solutions available to reduce or mitigate these impacts, and governments have a strategic role to play in encouraging individuals and businesses to adopt these. However, the goal of reducing the environmental impacts of transport is set within a much larger system linking transport to wider economic, social and political factors.

Nevertheless, the environmental impacts of transport are one of the main externalities and are wide ranging and well documented. According to Banister et al. (2000), these include:

- Air-quality reduction as a result of emissions (global pollutants such as carbon dioxide, national and regional pollutants such as nitrous oxides, local pollutants such as particulate matter and secondary pollutants such as volatile organic compounds).
- Water resource contamination associated with demand for petroleum and resultant oil spills and contamination.
- Energy and mineral resource depletion as a result of fuel use and materials for construction.
- Land resources reduction as a result of land for infrastructure and vehicular storage leading to less land availability for agriculture and biodiversity.
- Increased solid waste and transport generated waste that requires recycling, reclamation and disposal.
- Noise and vibration effects (particularly from road, rail and air) that lead to stress, sleep deprivation and decreased social interaction.
- Health impacts as a result of road accidents and pollution.
- Biodiversity impacts as a result of loss of hedgerows and verges, and wildlife severance.
- Damage to the built environment as a result of accidents and corrosive pollutants.
- Other impacts such as community severance and reduced social contact.

At the same time as environmental impacts, however, there are clear benefits emanating as a result of the transport system. These tend to be diffuse and difficult to measure, but can include user benefits, productivity effects and employment benefits. Eddington (2006) posited that a well-maintained and functioning transport system is a facilitator of growth. Further, whilst in developed countries transport in and of itself is unlikely to lead directly to economic growth, in developing countries it can enable increased economic activity (Eddington, 2006; Banister and Berechman, 2001; Crafts and Leunig, 2006; Rosewell, 2012).

Clearly the relationship between the transport system and the economy is complex, with direct and indirect effects on productivity and growth (see Chapter 15). As such, whilst governments are keen to manage or mitigate the environmental impacts of transport and deliver internationally agreed reductions in greenhouse gas emissions to which transport is a major contributor, they are also focused on supporting and enabling economic growth and productivity.

Further, they are acting on behalf of an electorate, and do not want to be perceived to be limiting people's freedom to travel. This means that developing policy options to deliver a greener transport system is fraught with difficulties and requires an approach that maximises impact on the environmental consequences of transport whilst minimising the consequences on other activities.

This chapter explores some of the potential economic policy options available to governments to help achieve this. It does so by considering potential policy options through a political economy lens, thereby focusing on the interaction of political and economic processes within a society and exploring how these affect the potential acceptability and effectiveness of measures. Essentially, political economy is concerned with how 'real-world' policies differ from those that would appear to be the most effective from a theoretical or evidentiary perspective due to consideration of factors beyond the evidence of effectiveness or need.

The chapter begins by considering what measures governments could use to encourage greener transport. Next it provides a detailed discussion of three measures – vehicle scrappage, congestion charging and low-emissions zones (LEZs), before offering a wider discussion of environmental impact and public acceptability. It concludes by considering what this means for governments and policy makers interested in greener transport. Although measures could be implemented affecting various modes, the chapter focuses on road-based transport, and national rather than international policies.

18.2 Potential measures

There are a wide variety of measures that could be implemented by a government in order to encourage more use of greener transport systems. According to Vieira et al. (2007), these fall into one of the following main categories:

Supply side measures that change the quantity or quality of available transport infrastructure, equipment and vehicles. These could include providing more frequent public transport services; providing higher quality public transport services; providing more active travel infrastructure; or reducing parking space availability.

Demand side measures that change the quantity of demand for available transport infrastructure, equipment or vehicles. These could include improved traveller information; land-use planning and flexible working.

Economic instruments that modify agents' behaviour through market-based approaches. These could include differential vehicle acquisition tax; fuel tax; road pricing and public transport subsidisation.

Regulatory instruments which modify agents' behaviour through defining or changing sets of rules (for example to restrict use, set standards or implement controls). These could include emissions requirements and speed limits.

In general these measures are either 'push' measures that are based on implementing disincentives to encourage people to change behaviour (e.g. taxation, vehicle standards or road-use restrictions) or 'pull' measures that incentivise people to change behaviour (e.g. subsidies, improved public transport or better infrastructure). Each potential measure is likely to have different effects in terms of its likely environmental impact, the cost of development and implementation, public acceptability and political will.

The next section explores three of these potential measures: vehicle scrappage which uses a subsidy to provide incentives to consumers to replace a vehicle with a more efficient one sooner than they would otherwise have done; LEZs which force those with the most polluting vehicles to purchase new vehicles or not travel in certain areas at certain times; and congestion charging which charges users to drive in certain locations (sometimes at certain times). For each, it explores what is known about its effectiveness as an environmental tool and its acceptability to individuals, businesses and policy makers.

18.2.1 Vehicle scrappage

Vehicle scrappage refers to policies that provide financial incentives to purchasers to encourage them to upgrade their vehicle for a more modern (and theoretically more efficient) one. They are usually implemented with the aim of acting as a stimulus to encourage purchase of a new vehicle to increase demand within the motor vehicle sector; and sometimes with the twin aim of providing environmental benefits as a result of reduced emissions.

At least 18 countries have implemented short-term (usually for a limited number of years, or until the budget runs out) scrappage schemes latterly since around 2005. In terms of their characteristics, scrappage schemes are voluntary (meaning that the vehicle owner can decide whether or not to participate) and usually offer a financial incentive (funded publicly, or through the motor industry and/or the government) to individuals wishing to 'scrap' their own car and purchase a new one. In most cases, the scrapped car must meet certain criteria in terms of age, fuel economy and length of ownership. For example, the UK Vehicle Scrappage Scheme (2009–10) insisted vehicles were registered in the UK before 29 February 2000, had been registered with the current owner for the past 12 months, had a current tax disc and had a current MOT certificate. The replacement vehicle needed to be brand new and the dealer was required to arrange for the old vehicle to be scrapped (House of Commons, 2009).

The effects of scrappage schemes include environmental effects; effects on travel behaviour (that are linked to environmental effects) and non-environmental effects (including economic effects) (Van Wee et al., 2011). Another potential benefit of scrappage programmes is in the adoption of new technology, especially if the policy is implemented at the early stages of the diffusion of new technologies. For example, Miravete and Moral (2011) found that a programme in Spain seemed to encourage a shift to diesel vehicles. However, the impact of scrappage schemes on the environment and on emissions in particular is unclear and difficult to measure (Dill, 2004).

The Consumer Assistance to Recycle and Save (CARS), commonly known as 'cash for clunkers', from the US in 2009 presents a useful case study here. This programme was marketed as an economic stimulus to the car industry that would also have environmental benefits. It provided purchasers with between $3,500 and $4,500 when purchasing a new vehicle and trading in an old one (for scrapping). One author found that each tonne of CO_2 saved cost the government between $92 and $288, not taking into account the additional costs of scrapping the vehicles and the environmental costs of constructing new vehicles (Li et al., 2013). This is reinforced by Lenski et al. (2010) who undertook a whole-life cycle analysis and found that CARS (taking into account only environmental benefits) was 'an extremely expensive way to mitigate GHGs' (p.7). In addition, 45 percent of people who participated in the scheme would have purchased a new vehicle anyway (Li et al., 2013). The programme was also shown to cause a spike in production during its duration, but this was offset by a fall immediately afterwards meaning the cumulative effect on production after only four months was essentially zero (Copeland and Kahn, 2013). However, the programme is credited with creating 38,000 direct jobs and contributing $4–8 billion to GDP (US Department of Transportation National Highway Traffic Safety Administration, 2009).

Nevertheless, the government deemed the project a success, stating 'The CARS program achieved the objectives set out by Congress to increase automotive sales and aid the environment. In just a few short weeks of sales, nearly 680,000 older vehicles were replaced by new, more fuel-efficient vehicles' (p. 2). However they were rather vague about the environmental benefits: 'The environment will benefit over the longer term because operation of the new vehicles in place of the trade-ins will reduce oil consumption and emissions of carbon dioxide and related greenhouse gases over the next 25 years' (p.2). It is unclear why 25 years was used in the analysis given the majority of vehicles scrapped were 13 years old or younger. Further, the evaluation did not take a life-cycle approach to the environmental benefits meaning they are likely to be overstated. The American Council for an Energy Efficient Economy (2011) suggest that the programme missed an opportunity in terms of maximising the environmental benefits because the criteria on the fuel economy differentials between the cars purchased and those sold were not more stringent. Therefore it is posited that the potential for any scheme to have environmental benefits is dependent on the design of the scheme.

Looking more widely, there is a limited body of evidence to suggest that scrappage schemes lead to any reduction in carbon, with some authors even suggesting they may lead to an increase in carbon on a life-cycle basis (Brand et al., 2013; Van Wee et al., 2011). In addition, there is seemingly little evidence that they are the best, or even a good way of stimulating the economy. This leaves us with a policy that has been widely implemented on the basis of very little evidence that it achieves what the policy makers set out to achieve, at least on the face of it. Van Wee et al. (2011, p. 568) summarise why this may be the case:

> We have the impression that the lobby for such schemes from the car industry was quite strong and successful. Secondly, politicians felt they had to do at least something to reduce the pain of the crisis. And car sales were immediately and strongly affected by the crisis, so they drew the attention of the public, the media, and policy-makers. Thirdly, the reason is derived from Public Choice Theory: policy-makers want to do 'something' visible that attracts the attention of the media and the wider public, to 'score points' in order to be re-elected. A scrapping scheme is a very visible way of doing something for the economy and (at least seemingly) also for the environment.

Despite this apparent lack of evidence in support of either the environmental or the economic benefits of scrappage, in the UK some politicians have been reported as calling for a diesel scrappage scheme to get polluting diesel cars off the road which 'could provide useful incentives for customers to drive vehicles which pollute less' (Environmental Audit Committee, 2015, p.2). This underlines that such schemes are politically popular with the public and business, despite the lack of an evidence base, and therefore politicians feel comfortable suggesting them as policy options.

One of the problems with scrappage schemes is that they have attempted to tackle two policy issues (the environment and the economy) with one policy solution. By having the twin aims of stimulating the vehicle manufacturing industry and helping the environment, policy makers quickly encounter a problem. To maximise the benefit to the sector it is best to widen eligibility of the scheme as far as possible. Conversely, to maximise environmental benefits cost effectively it is necessary to limit eligibility to those with the most inefficient vehicles who wish to purchase much more efficient vehicles. Ideally these people would also be those who would not otherwise have changed their vehicles. Theoretically, such schemes can work (BenDor and Ford, 2006; Lavee and Becker, 2009) and the likely impact on vehicle replacement can be modelled (Lorentziadis and Vournas, 2011) to give some idea of the best eligibility criteria during scheme design. Such schemes are likely to be rather limited in terms of scope and this could reduce their popularity and the scale of any impacts.

In summary, therefore, scrappage schemes have a high level of political, public and business acceptability, but questionable environmental and economic impacts unless the scheme criteria are stringent enough to ensure only the most polluting cars are scrapped and only the least polluting cars are purchased. The schemes can also prove costly to governments that are implementing them.

18.2.2 Congestion charging

Road pricing refers to a set of price measures for road use, including tolls, congestion charges and levies. This section will focus on congestion charging, which aims to reduce congestion and thus have an indirect effect of associated environmental benefits as a result of reduced emissions and reduced levels of noise in the local environment. Congestion charging is covered in much greater detail in Chapter 13.

The economic theory behind road pricing for congestion management is relatively simple – in areas where supply of road space is lower than demand for it, a charge can be made for use of the road space. This charge should be set at a level such that it influences demand for the road space, and theoretically reduces congestion. Therefore it has two main direct positive effects, and two direct negative effects. The positive effects are that certain travellers experience less congestion and revenues can be used to benefit travellers (for example through the provision of better public transport). The negative effects are that travellers have to pay a toll, and that they may be subject to inconveniences if they have to switch to less preferable routes or modes (Johansson and Mattsson, 2012).

Since the literature pertaining to road pricing is so vast, this section will focus on the evidence pertaining to its effectiveness as an environmental measure and public acceptability.

Often the environmental benefits of congestion charging are listed as an indirect benefit after the direct benefit of reduced congestion (in terms of journey times) at the design stage of a scheme. For example, the scheme in London was introduced primarily to reduce congestion, and the potential environmental benefits were not given much consideration during the planning stages (Banister, 2008b). The scheme in Stockholm was marketed as potentially having a positive impact on congestion, accessibility, environment and public transport infrastructure financing. One of the only schemes with the main aim of benefiting the environment (through reducing air pollution) was the Ecopass scheme in Milan which was a 'pollution charge' based on vehicle PM10 emissions (Rotaris et al., 2010). This scheme was replaced by a more conventional congestion charge, 'Area C', in 2012.

The main aim(s) of the schemes can have an impact on the form that charging takes. In Stockholm the charge does not differentiate by vehicle type (below 14 tonnes) but varies by time during weekdays, with peak times costing more (weekends, public holidays and the month of July are free). The charge is levied every time a vehicle passes a control point, but there is a maximum amount per vehicle per day (around £9). In London the charge is £11.50 on weekdays with some discounts available for ultra-low-emissions vehicles. In Milan, when the Ecopass scheme existed, charges varied by vehicle type, with some of the most polluting being banned altogether, and others being charged according to their emissions (Rotaris et al., 2010). However, following a referendum asking whether the charged zone should be extended to all vehicles (Martino, 2013), a new scheme (Area C) was implemented and the charge was changed to a much simpler system comprising a flat rate during weekday daytimes of around £4 (Hensher and Li, 2013; Milano, n.d.).

Evidence in support of environmental benefits linked to congestion charges is mixed. A number of authors suggest that congestion charging can have an impact on the environment through reduced emissions. Tonne et al. (2008) modelled a modest benefit in terms of reduced NO_2 and PM10 as a result of the congestion charging scheme in London. However, in a review of a number of studies pertaining to the impact of the scheme in London on the environment, Givoni (2012) concluded that the scheme only had at best a minor impact on air quality for people living in central London. In Stockholm the charge was found to be lower both in terms of PM10 and NO_2 (Johansson et al., 2009). The Ecopass in Milan was estimated to have a similar impact on NO_x and PM10 to the schemes in Stockholm and London (Rotaris et al., 2010). It was also found to lead to a significant reduction in black carbon (Invernizzi et al., 2011). However, in general research, accurately quantifying the measurable impact on air quality is rare – in part because such changes are difficult to measure and model, and because environmental benefits are perceived as secondary.

Overall, the Ecopass scheme in Milan was measured to have a net economic benefit (Rotaris et al., 2010); the same was found for the scheme in Stockholm which was deemed to generate a significant social surplus (Eliasson, 2009), while the situation relating to the London scheme is unclear.

Congestion charging is a contentious issue amongst the public. Indeed, pre-implementation it can be difficult to achieve public support for such schemes. For example, in Edinburgh residents voted 3:1 against its implementation and consequently the scheme was abandoned (Gaunt et al., 2007).

De Borger and Proost (2012) posit that it appears charging is generally introduced against the will of the voters, but public opinion becomes much more favourable after formal introduction. This is supported by evidence from Norway (Schade and Baum, 2007) and Sweden (Eliasson et al., 2009). In addition, in London an amendment to the scheme to link the charge to vehicle emissions was supported by 66 percent of Londoners (Mori, 2007).

A number of issues seem to influence the public acceptability of congestion charging *ex-ante*. These include uncertainty about the details of any scheme, uncertainty about the benefits, and concerns about the use of the revenues. Nevertheless, Dietz and Atkinson (2005) explored theoretical acceptability of congestion charging in London and found it was relatively acceptable if it considered ability to pay.

The Swedish experience also shed some light on the factors that influence the acceptability of congestion charging amongst the public. In Stockholm, a pilot congestion charge was implemented followed by a referendum on its acceptability as a permanent measure. Public attitudes changed radically after the pilot, possibly because the potential benefits of the scheme were demonstrated to the public.

Research based on the Swedish experience suggests that familiarity with congestion charging has a strong bearing on whether it is deemed acceptable. However, Eliasson and Jonsson (2011) suggest that availability of good transport and low car dependency influence acceptability, but not as much as general environmental benefits and beliefs about the effectiveness of the scheme. For this reason they conclude that in Stockholm the decision to relabel the scheme 'environmental charges' may have helped increase acceptability. Further, in Stockholm acceptance of the congestion charging policy is thought to have increased after the trial compared to before because people experienced the positive impacts of the policy (Schuitema et al., 2010).

A further problem with congestion charging is achieving political acceptability. This is probably linked to the low levels of public acceptability. In New York a road-pricing scheme proposed by Mayor Bloomberg was blocked at state level as a result of opposition based on the individual-level impacts on road users (Schaller, 2010).

Schemes were blocked in Edinburgh and Manchester as a result of local referendums. However, the schemes in London and Stockholm went ahead – in the case of London without any public vote or local legislative approval (though legislation has already been enacted that allowed for such schemes to be implemented), and in Stockholm with public support as a result of a successful pilot.

Overall then, although pricing mechanisms are deemed to be one of the most effective ways of minimising the externalities from transport, implementing them can be hard because it is very difficult to achieve public acceptability, and understandably this can lead to political nervousness. Clearly this can be overcome, or even overridden, as demonstrated by Stockholm and London, but even then the environmental benefits are unclear. Givoni (2012) suggests that perhaps the London scheme has not been as successful as its promoters would suggest and, in a review of the evidence of stated benefits, concludes that there is almost no way of establishing a causal link between them and the scheme (especially because it was introduced as part of a package).

Nevertheless, economic theory would suggest that they have the potential to be an effective measure if the charges are set correctly – but to achieve acceptability, often concessions are made in terms of the level of charge and discounts available (as seen in London, Milan and Stockholm).

18.2.3 Low-emissions zones

LEZs attempt to reduce the concentrations or pollutants that harm human health by banning or restricting the most polluting vehicles from entering certain areas. They are used in areas with high levels of local air pollution and aim to reduce nitrogen dioxide and particulate matter (PM10 and PM2.5) in order to benefit public health. They are chiefly a regulatory measure that restrict behaviour to achieve an environmental benefit but in circumstances where charges rather than a direct ban apply they become more of a market mechanism.

Schemes exist in over 150 cities and in Europe largely came about as a result of clean air legislation focusing on reducing particulate matter (Wolff and Perry, 2010). Schemes vary in organisation, variously applying to all vehicles, freight, buses and/or cars. They range from a total ban on certain vehicles entering a defined (usually urban) area to charges for entering an area with a more polluting vehicle. These policies are also largely designed to benefit human health through minimising the levels of harmful pollutants.

Interestingly, research into LEZs has the opposite focus to that on congestion charging. The majority of the research focuses on the environmental impact, with little to no research on public acceptability. The research into environmental impacts is very focused, looking mainly at localised air pollutants with seemingly little to no research on their wider environmental impacts as a result of behavioural changes including increasing driving distances and early replacement of vehicles.

As noted above, research on acceptability is limited. Dietz and Atkinson (2005) explored theoretical acceptability, and found that whether a policy considered willingness or ability to pay had an impact on perceived fairness. Furthermore, when a policy aimed to tackle air pollution, rather than other issues such as congestion, it was generally much less acceptable if it included cars (though it was judged to be more acceptable if it applied to freight and other large vehicles). This was thought to be because air pollution is less visible to individuals than say congestion, and they were therefore less willing to pay to address it. In addition there is some primary evidence from Germany where LEZs apply to all vehicles in a number of cities. Here the level of public acceptability is low with the majority of people feeling that the schemes are overly bureaucratic and unlikely to have an impact on emissions (Wolff and Perry, 2010).

Some additional research has been undertaken into the likely behavioural changes and economic impacts of LEZs. Economically, the schemes are likely to increase costs to businesses (and individuals if they include private cars) at least in the short term (Anderson et al., 2005). Browne et al. (2005) suggested five likely behavioural modification strategies for freight vehicles that did not meet the requirements of the London LEZ. These were: fit abatement technology, upgrade to compliant vehicles, divert around the area, enter in a non-compliant vehicle risking prosecution, and change to a different vehicle for specific deliveries. Primary research indicated that most companies thought they would try to deal with the LEZ restrictions by retrofitting vehicles so they were compliant, or purchasing new vehicles.

Nevertheless, there will be additional operating costs. Browne et al. (2005) suggested that a greater London LEZ scheme could have a cost to industry of £64–135 million, but didn't state the time period over which this would be realised. The majority of companies would pass these increased costs onto consumers. In Germany, an additional cost is thought to have decreased trade because people are less likely to visit areas within LEZs (Wolff and Perry, 2010).

Reports on the environmental effectiveness of LEZs vary, with some studies citing statistically significant reductions in various pollutants and others having no noticeable impact. Some evidence exists that links LEZs to changes in fleet vehicle composition. In the London LEZ it was reported that 90 percent of freight vehicles and buses complied with the minimum standards by the time the LEZ was introduced, compared to 75 percent of freight and 45 percent of buses nationally. The LEZ appears to have had an effect on fleet composition just prior to its implementation and, despite an increase in heavy vehicles within the LEZ, reductions in PM10 and NOx have been recorded (Ellison et al., 2013). They conclude that the London LEZ has played a part in improving air quality, but the impact has been relatively small. Nevertheless, it does seem to sustainably influence the replacement rate of freight vehicles in a positive way.

Changes to vehicle composition were also recorded in Germany (where all vehicles are often included in the LEZ). There is also some evidence that schemes appear to be more effective the larger they are (Wolff, 2014). The LEZs in Germany overall were found to be cost effective taking into account the monetised benefits to human health versus the cost of vehicle upgrading (Wolff, 2014).

However, in the Netherlands, LEZs focused on reducing heavy freight vehicles did not substantially change levels of traffic-related pollutants. This study concluded that traffic intensity had a role to play in whether LEZs had a measurable impact on pollutants (Boogaard et al., 2012). In Amsterdam though, Panteliadis et al. (2014) found the LEZ led to significant reductions in vehicle-related emissions at a number of roadside monitoring stations. The same was reported in Germany where particulate emissions were reduced by 9 percent (average across a number of cities) (Wolff, 2014).

However, it is noted that LEZs are very difficult to evaluate, and many studies rely on modelled rather than measured impacts (Boogaard et al., 2012; van Erp et al., 2012). It appears that modelled and measured studies may make a difference to results of evaluations with some measured studies showing little impact on emissions compared with modelled studies which showed a greater impact (Boogaard et al., 2012). In addition, Cyrys et al. (2014) suggest that current evaluations (modelled or measured) are likely to underestimate the positive impact of LEZs on PM10 levels and other measures such as black smoke or elemental carbon would be more accurate. They state that 'the benefit of low emission zones on human health is far greater than is presently visible from routine measurements of PM10' (p. 485). This was backed up by Cesaroni et al. (2012) in Rome and Tonne et al. (2008) in London who modelled an extension to life of those living in affected areas. There is seemingly little post-implementation evaluation of the behavioural changes that occurred as a result of the schemes' implementation.

Holman et al. (2015) conducted a review of the evidence in relation to environmental benefits and concluded that outside of Germany (where cars are included in LEZs) there is little evidence that they are effective. In addition, studies generally use overly simplistic approaches that fail to take account of confounding factors. Further, any environmental benefits that do exist are likely to decrease over time as fleets are renewed and vehicle technology advances. Therefore, in order for schemes to be successful on an ongoing basis, they need to be monitored and criteria adjusted as newer technologies become available (Ellison et al., 2013).

Nevertheless, despite the lack of conclusive evidence, as a result of the likelihood of failing to meet European Union air-quality standards in 2020, a number of UK cities are looking to consider the role of access restrictions for certain types of vehicles. Evidence (including some within policy documentation) highlights that a piecemeal 'city-by-city' approach to LEZs could have a negative impact on businesses and be too complicated for easy comprehension (Browne et al., 2005; DEFRA, 2015b; Holman et al., 2015). Somewhat oddly, therefore, whilst DEFRA notes the need for a framework for clean air zones (which could include LEZs as one part of a package of measures) to overcome this issue, their background evidence document notes that decisions would need to be made locally about the design of these (DEFRA, 2015a; DEFRA, 2015b).

In summary, there has been widespread implementation of a range of LEZs in a variety of locations, but despite this evidence of their effectiveness is limited. This could in part be due to the fact that changes in air quality are difficult to measure, and it is also difficult to attribute causality. Alongside this, evidence of public acceptability is minimal, perhaps in part because the schemes are small scale and mainly directly affect commercial operations. Nevertheless, these policies seem to be more politically acceptable than congestion charging and as such we may see increasing numbers of these schemes in the future.

18.3 Acceptability versus effectiveness

There are very few examples of economic transport policies with the main aim of reducing the environmental impact of transport. Often this impact is lauded as being secondary to reducing congestion or generating income. As such, this chapter has explored three very different potential measures that could have primary environmental aims, and has discussed their potential environmental impact and public acceptability.

The first measure was vehicle scrappage, which has predominately been used to stimulate demand in the motor industry in times of economic hardship. This is a 'pull' measure employed to incentivise individuals to switch to more environmentally friendly behaviour in the form of using more efficient (but not necessarily lower emission) vehicles. However, since environmental outcomes have not usually been the predominant aim, qualifying emissions criteria have been relatively wide in most cases, minimising the opportunity for economic gains and according to some, potentially leading to environmental losses if the whole life cycle is assessed. Nevertheless, public and political acceptability do not pose any great barriers to implementation of scrappage policies – perhaps because individuals can see the direct benefits to themselves and do not consider the (often high) public costs of such schemes.

The second measure was congestion charging, which has predominantly been used to improve traffic flow in cities with associated economic and air-quality benefits. This is a push measure which uses pricing to encourage individuals to change behaviour, in this case by travelling at different times or switching modes. It also generates revenues that can be invested in local transport to make alternative modes more appealing. However, the evidence of environmental benefits is mixed, and public and political acceptability are very hard to achieve.

The third measure was LEZs, a measure with clear environmental aims, albeit with highly localised benefits. This is also a push measure which encourages people to change vehicles or adopt different behaviours in order to reduce air pollution in certain areas. There are various arguments regarding whether these schemes actually have environmental benefits in the form of air-quality improvements. There is limited evidence of public acceptability (or lack of) in relation to LEZs. However, in many cases they have been implemented in such a way that they affect businesses directly and the public indirectly meaning that they are more likely to be acceptable to the public.

On the face of it, all three of these measures have the potential to achieve environmental benefits predominantly in the form of air-quality improvements through either changes in the vehicle composition (scrappage and LEZs) or reduced traffic and congestion in certain locations (LEZs and congestion charges). However, as this chapter has demonstrated, evidence of environmental benefits from actual schemes is limited. Research into the environmental benefits has also focused mainly on air quality, perhaps because it is more measurable (in the case of LEZs) or capable of being modelled (in the case of all three measures). Alongside this it is likely that the potential environmental impacts of the measures will have been reduced due to concessions made at the design stage relating to eligible vehicles (scrappage and LEZs) and level of charges (congestion charge). Furthermore it is difficult to build an evidence base to support controversial policies because lessons about the environmental effectiveness of policies are difficult to identify, especially with the absence in many cases of a whole-life-cycle policy evaluation.

It is made even more complex because evidence suggests that policy packages (e.g. congestion charging combined with public transport improvements) are likely to maximise effectiveness (Anas and Lindsey, 2011; Kottenhoff and Brundell Freij, 2009; Stead, 2008). As Vieira et al. (2007) argue, one of the main barriers to the success of policies aimed at reducing the environmental impact of transport is a lack of integration and effective implementation. They posit that a multi-instrument approach is the best way of maximising the benefits of policy instruments, but that this should take the form of one main policy, complemented by others which, at least at the start, sit behind it. However, in such cases, establishing effectiveness and causality is even more complex.

Whilst common sense would dictate that acceptability should at least in part be linked to effectiveness, this does not appear to be the case. In fact it would appear that public judgements on effectiveness are perhaps more a reflection of individual views on personal acceptability than objective effectiveness (Stead, 2008). This means that policy makers need to carefully consider how a policy is marketed to their peers, the public and businesses if they want to achieve acceptability. In reality policies are rarely objectively effective and subjectively acceptable.

Therefore, policy makers need to be aware that acceptability may be underpinned by different factors for different measures. For example, Eriksson et al. (2006) found that positive policies towards public transport were deemed fair and acceptable because they increased freedom; increased fuel duty infringed freedom and was unfair and unacceptable; and an information campaign was a minor infringement of freedom, was to some degree fair and was neither acceptable nor unacceptable. Further Eriksson et al. (2008) found that 'while the pull measures were perceived to be effective, fair, and acceptable, the push measure and the packages were perceived to be rather ineffective, unfair, and unacceptable' (p.1117). As such they concluded that perceived fairness and effectiveness were important for acceptability.

Cherry et al. (2012) also found that pull measures were more acceptable than push, and within push measures, quantity regulation was less supported than taxes. Tillema et al. (2013) agree but note that the cost implications of this are important, for example road pricing (push) generates revenue, while improved public transport (pull) could require revenue support on an ongoing basis. In addition, regulation was better supported if inefficient half measures (watered-down versions of the most efficient policies) were proposed instead of the more efficient models or regulation, although this was less true for taxes and subsidies (Cherry et al., 2012).

However, as de Groot and Schuitema (2012) indicated, push measures need to be presented in the right way (bearing in mind that the language used to describe them can have an influence – as demonstrated in Stockholm) such that either they target low-cost behaviour and/or appear to be supported by the majority. In this way they can become almost as acceptable as pull measures.

The use of any revenue from price-based studies can have an impact on acceptability – with the best approach being to dovetail use of the revenue with the aims of the policy (Schuitema et al., 2010; Thorpe et al., 2000). For example, the likelihood of acceptability could be improved by investing revenues from a congestion charge in public transport improvements. This is reflected by Sælen and Kallbekken (2011), who found a 15 percent increase in the acceptability of a fuel tax policy when the revenues were earmarked for use for environmental purposes. In general, therefore, Pigouvian tax measures, where the tax is aimed at a specific externality, would seem to be more publicly acceptable.

Nevertheless, as Kallbekken and Sælen (2011) state, there is 'no magic formula for increasing public support for environmental taxes' (p. 2966), but support can be influenced by increasing trust in the government use of revenues and educating the public about the effectiveness of policies (Kallbekken and Aasen, 2010; Kallbekken and Sælen, 2011).

Much of the evidence relating to acceptability is associated with congestion charging, or road pricing more widely, with little evidence relating to other specific policy measures. Congestion charging is highly controversial (in part due to its direct individual impact) which perhaps makes research more useful and interesting, nevertheless it would be interesting to have the same degree of research regarding other policy measures to provide a better base for comparison. Furthermore, much of the evidence described above relates to public acceptability of policies and acceptability to businesses is documented to a much lesser degree. This could be because it is harder to research, because the views of the electorate are more important or policy makers don't want to appear to be beholden to the interests of business over those of the public. However, more understanding of the forces and influences in this area would be useful.

Without public acceptability it can be difficult to garner political support whilst taking into account varying policy goals, including economic outcomes, environmental outcomes and equity outcomes. Johansson et al. (2003) found direct conflicts existed between making a policy fair and maximising environmental impacts and economic impacts. It is likely that at each stage of the policy negotiation process concessions have to be made in order to achieve acceptability. A good example of this is the London congestion charge which has a large number of concessions – under 45 percent of vehicles pay the full charge (Banister, 2004). Whilst this may weaken the overall effectiveness of the scheme, perhaps it is a worthwhile compromise to implement what is judged by some to be a successful policy.

Indeed, political support and understanding at the national level is not enough, and national messages need to be passed down to the local level which may not happen without adequate support and financing (Hull, 2008). Further, while support at the national level may lead to legislation that enables controversial policies to be delivered locally, in the era of localism in the UK this still requires a local authority to decide to deliver the policy on the ground. Indeed, two of the defining features of the modern world which have an impact on policy making are its complexity and the speed of change (Tuominen and Himanen, 2007). This means that policy makers working in different fields can have similar aims, but lack the ability to share knowledge and experience, and may encounter conflicts in terms of garnering the support they need to instigate change.

As Banister (2008a) discusses, the policies required to achieve sustainable mobility are well known, however their effective implementation requires the engagement of key stakeholders who can be educated to understand the reasoning behind the policies and thus support their implementation. As Banister (2004) highlights, 'to get any radical transport policy introduced requires extensive negotiation, consultation and public support' (p.450).

18.4 Conclusion

This chapter has explored various economic policy measures that could have environmental benefits and considered their potential environmental impact, and their acceptability to the public. It also explored acceptability in more detail to consider which sort of measure might be more or less effective.

Whilst there is a lack of knowledge relating to the environmental impacts of some measures, this may not be important in terms of helping achieve public acceptability, because evidence clearly demonstrates that this is unlikely to be related to policy effectiveness. More important is the way that the policy is portrayed to the public – including the language used and its perceived 'fairness'. Knowledge of environmental impact is, however, important in terms of being able to design the most effective policy measures and ensure they have criteria that maximise their potential impacts.

It is clear that achieving public acceptability of some of the more controversial policies can be very difficult. Policy officials often try to improve the likelihood of individuals accepting the policy by making compromises . However, this is likely to affect the impact on the environment. This could perhaps be mitigated by setting initial criteria at a higher level than necessary, in order to ensure compromises do not reduce effectiveness. Alongside this, for policies such as congestion charging, where public attitudes tend to shift towards acceptability post implementation, sometimes it is necessary to simply 'bite the bullet' and implement them (for a pilot period if necessary). The timing for policy makers in these situations is key, and avoiding election periods would be important.

Whilst the government clearly has a role to play in facilitating the use of greener transport, policy measures need to be effective to offset issues with public acceptability. Maximising the environmental benefits of policies, even where environmental benefits are secondary, is key, both to ensure the policy is purposeful and to demonstrate that policy makers have the best interests of the electorate and wider sustainability in mind.

References

American Council for an Energy Efficient Economy (2011). *Cash for Clunkers: A Missed Opportunity for Fuel Economy Gains*, http://aceee.org/sites/default/files/publications/researchreports/t112.pdf (accessed April 2016).

Anas, A. and Lindsey, R. (2011). Reducing Urban Road Transportation Externalities: Road Pricing in Theory and in Practice. *Review of Environmental Economics and Policy*, 5(1), pp. 66–88.

Anderson, S., Allen, J. and Browne, M. (2005). Urban Logistics: How Can It Meet Policy Makers' Sustainability Objectives? *Journal of Transport Geography*, 13(1), pp. 71–81.

Banister, D. (2004). Implementing the Possible? *Planning Theory and Practice*, 5(4), pp. 499–501.

Banister, D. (2008a). The Sustainable Mobility Paradigm. *Transport Policy*, 15(2), pp. 73–80.

Banister, D. (2008b). The Big Smoke: Congestion Charging and the Environment. In Richardson, H. and Chang-Hee, C. B. (eds), *Road Congestion Pricing in Europe: Implications for the United States*. Cheltenham: Edward Elgar, pp. 176–97.

Banister, D. and Berechman, Y. (2001). Transport Investment and the Promotion of Economic Growth. *Journal of Transport Geography*, 9(3), pp. 209–18.

Banister, D., Stead, D., Steen, P., Åkerman, J., Dreborg, K., Nijkamp, P. and Scheicher-Tappeser, R. (2000). *European Transport Policy and Sustainable Mobility*. London: E. and F. N. Spon.

BenDor, T. and Ford, A. (2006). Simulating a Combination of Feebates and Scrappage Incentives to Reduce Automobile Emissions. *Energy*, 31(8–9), pp. 1197–214.

Boogaard, H., Janssen, N. A., Fischer, P. H., Kos, G. P., Weijers, E. P., Cassee, F. R., van der Zee, S. C., de Hartog, J. J., Meliefste, K. and Wang, M. (2012). Impact of Low Emission Zones and Local Traffic Policies on Ambient Air Pollution Concentrations. *Science of the Total Environment*, 435, pp. 132–40.

Brand, C., Anable, J. and Tran, M. (2013). Accelerating the Transformation to a Low Carbon Passenger Transport System: The Role of Car Purchase Taxes, Feebates, Road Taxes and Scrappage Incentives in the UK. *Transportation Research Part A: Policy and Practice*, 49, pp. 132–48.

Browne, M., Allen, J. and Anderson, S. (2005). Low Emission Zones: The Likely Effects on the Freight Transport Sector. *International Journal of Logistics Research and Applications*, 8(4), pp. 269–81.

Cesaroni, G., Boogaard, H., Jonkers, S., Porta, D., Badaloni, C., Cattani, G., Forastiere, F. and Hoek, G. (2012). Health Benefits of Traffic-Related Air Pollution Reduction in Different Socioeconomic Groups: The Effect of Low-Emission Zoning in Rome. *Occupational and Environmental Medicine*, 69(2), pp. 133–39.

Cherry, T. L., Kallbekken, S. and Kroll, S. (2012). The Acceptability of Efficiency-Enhancing Environmental Taxes, Subsidies and Regulation: An Experimental Investigation. *Environmental Science and Policy*, 16, pp. 90–6.

Copeland, A. and Kahn, J. (2013). The Production Impact of 'Cash-for-Clunkers': Implications of Stabilization Policy. *Economic Inquiry*, 51(1), pp. 288–303.

Crafts, N. and Leunig, T. (2006). *The Historical Significance of Transport for Economic Growth and Productivity: Research Annex to the Eddington Study*. http://webarchive.nationalarchives.gov.uk/20090104005813/; www.dft.gov.uk/about/strategy/transportstrategy/eddingtonstudy/researchannexes/researchannexes volume1/historicalsignificance (accessed April 2016).

Cyrys, J., Peters, A., Soentgen, J. and Wichmann, H. E. (2014). Low Emission Zones Reduce PM10 Mass Concentrations and Diesel Soot in German Cities. *Journal of the Air and Waste Management Association*, 64(4), 481–7.

De Borger, B. and Proost, S. (2012). A Political Economy Model of Road Pricing. *Journal of Urban Economics*, 71(1), pp. 79–92.

de Groot, J. I. M. and Schuitema, G. (2012). How to Make the Unpopular Popular? Policy Characteristics, Social Norms and the Acceptability of Environmental Policies. *Environmental Science and Policy*, 19–20, pp. 100–7.

DEFRA (2015a). *Draft Evidence Annex: Assessment of the Plans to Improve Air Quality in the UK*, https://consult.defra.gov.uk/airquality/draft-aq-plans/supporting_documents/Draft%20Evidence%20Annex%20%20%20assessment%20of%20plans%20to%20improve%20air%20quality%20in%20the%20UK.%20%20September%202015.pdf (accessed April 2016).

DEFRA (2015b). *Draft Plans to Improve Air Quality in the UK: Tackling Nitrogen Dioxide in Our Towns and Cities, UK Overview Document*, https://consult.defra.gov.uk/airquality/draft-aq-plans/supporting_documents/Draft%20plans%20to%20improve%20air%20quality%20in%20the%20UK%20%20Overview%20document%20September%202015%20final%20version%20folder.pdf (accessed April 2016).

Dietz, S. and Atkinson, G. (2005). Public Perceptions of Equity in Environmental Policy: Traffic Emissions Policy in an English Urban Area. *Local Environment*, 10(4), pp. 445–59.

Dill, J. (2004). Estimating Emissions Reductions from Accelerated Vehicle Retirement Programs. *Transportation Research Part D: Transport and Environment*, 9(2), pp. 87–106.

Eddington, R. (2006). The Eddington Transport Study. Main Report: Transport's Role in Sustaining the UK's Productivity and Competitiveness, http://webarchive.nationalarchives.gov.uk/20090104005813/http:/www.dft.gov.uk/162259/187604/206711/volume1.pdf (accessed February 2016).

Eliasson, J. (2009). A Cost-Benefit Analysis of the Stockholm Congestion Charging System. *Transportation Research Part A: Policy and Practice*, 43(4), pp. 468–80.

Eliasson, J. and Jonsson, L. (2011). The Unexpected 'Yes': Explanatory Factors behind the Positive Attitudes to Congestion Charges in Stockholm. *Transport Policy*, 18(4), pp. 636–47.

Eliasson, J., Hultkrantz, L., Nerhagen, L. and Rosqvist, L. S. (2009). The Stockholm Congestion Charging Trial 2006: Overview of Effects. *Transportation Research Part A: Policy and Practice*, 43(3), pp. 240–50.

Ellison, R. B., Greaves, S. P. and Hensher, D. A. (2013). Five Years of London's Low Emission Zone: Effects on Vehicle Fleet Composition and Air Quality. *Transportation Research Part D: Transport and Environment*, 23, pp. 25–33.

Environmental Audit Committee (2015). Response to Defra Consultation on Air Quality. www.parliament.uk/documents/commons-committees/environmental-audit/Defra-air-quality-consultation-response.pdf (accessed April 2016).

Eriksson, L., Garvill, J. and Nordlund, A. M. (2006). Acceptability of Travel Demand Management Measures: The Importance of Problem Awareness, Personal Norm, Freedom, and Fairness. *Journal of Environmental Psychology*, 26(1), pp. 15–26.

Eriksson, L., Garvill, J. and Nordlund, A. M. (2008). Acceptability of Single and Combined Transport Policy Measures: The Importance of Environmental and Policy Specific Beliefs. *Transportation Research Part A: Policy and Practice*, 42(8), pp. 1117–28.

Gaunt, M., Rye, T. and Allen, S. (2007). Public Acceptability of Road User Charging: The Case of Edinburgh and the 2005 Referendum. *Transport Reviews*, 27(1), pp. 85–102.

Givoni, M. (2012). Re-assessing the Results of the London Congestion Charging Scheme. *Urban Studies*, 49(5), pp. 1089–105.

Hensher, D. A. and Li, Z. (2013). Referendum Voting in Road Pricing Reform: A Review of the Evidence. *Transport Policy*, 25, pp. 186–97.

Holman, C., Harrison, R. and Querol, X. (2015). Review of the Efficacy of Low Emission Zones to Improve Urban Air Quality in European Cities. *Atmospheric Environment*, 111, pp. 161–9.

House of Commons (2009). Vehicle Scrappage Scheme. http://researchbriefings.parliament.uk/ResearchBriefing/Summary/SN05177 (accessed April 2016).

Hull, A. (2008). Policy Integration: What Will It Take to Achieve More Sustainable Transport Solutions in Cities? *Transport Policy*, 15(2), pp. 94–103.

Invernizzi, G., Ruprecht, A., Mazza, R., De Marco, C., Mocnik, G., Sioutas, C. and Westerdahl, D. (2011). Measurement of Black Carbon Concentration as an Indicator of Air Quality Benefits of Traffic Restriction Policies within the Ecopass Zone in Milan, Italy. *Atmospheric Environment*, 45(21), pp. 3522–7.

Johansson, B. and Mattsson, L.-G. (2012). Principles of Road Pricing. In Johansson, B. and Mattsson, L.-G. (eds), *Road Pricing: Theory, Empirical Assessment and Policy*. London: Springer Science and Business Media.

Johansson, C., Burman, L. and Forsberg, B. (2009). The Effects of Congestions Tax on Air Quality and Health. *Atmospheric Environment*, 43(31), pp. 4843–54.

Johansson, L.-O., Gustafsson, M., Falkemark, G., Gärling, T. and Johansson-Stenman, O. (2003). Goal Conflicts in Political Decisionmaking: A Survey of Municipality Politicians' Views of Road Pricing. *Environment and Planning C: Government and Policy*, 21(4), pp. 615–724.

Kallbekken, S. and Aasen, M. (2010). The Demand for Earmarking: Results from a Focus Group Study. *Ecological Economics*, 69(11), pp. 2183–90.

Kallbekken, S. and Sælen, H. (2011). Public Acceptance for Environmental Taxes: Self-Interest, Environmental and Distributional Concerns. *Energy Policy*, 39(5), pp. 2966–73.

Kottenhoff, K. and Brundell Freij, K. (2009). The Role of Public Transport for Feasibility and Acceptability of Congestion Charging: The Case of Stockholm. *Transportation Research Part A: Policy and Practice*, 43(3), pp. 297–305.

Lavee, D. and Becker, N. (2009). Cost-Benefit Analysis of an Accelerated Vehicle-Retirement Programme. *Journal of Environmental Planning and Management*, 52(6), pp. 777–95.

Lenski, S. M., Keoleian, G. A. and Bolon, K. M. (2010). The Impact of 'Cash for Clunkers' on Greenhouse Gas Emissions: A Life Cycle Perspective. *Environmental Research Letters*, 5(4), p. 044003.

Li, S., Linn, J. and Spiller, E. (2013). Evaluating 'Cash-for-Clunkers': Program Effects on Auto Sales and the Environment. *Journal of Environmental Economics and Management*, 65(2), pp. 175–93.

Lorentziadis, P. L. and Vournas, S. G. (2011). A Quantitative Model of Accelerated Vehicle-Retirement Induced by Subsidy. *European Journal of Operational Research*, 211(3), pp. 623–29.

Martino, A. (2013). *Milano: From Pollution Charge to Congestion Charge*. www.trt.it/documenti/Martino%20-%20AreaC%20Milano.pdf (accessed April 2016).

Milano (n.d.). *Area C*. www.comune.milano.it/wps/portal/ist/en/area_c (accessed April 2016).

Miravete, E. J. and Moral, M. J. (2011). *Qualitative Effects of Cash-for-Clunkers Programs*. www.eugeniomiravete.com/papers/EJM-MJM-Clunkers.pdf (accessed April 2016).

Mori, I. (2007). *Emissions Related Congestion Charging*. www.ipsos-mori.com/Assets/Docs/Archive/Polls/tfl-report.pdf (accessed April 2016).

Panteliadis, P., Strak, M., Hoek, G., Weijers, E., van der Zee, S. and Dijkema, M. (2014). Implementation of a Low Emission Zone and Evaluation of Effects on Air Quality by Long-Term Monitoring. *Atmospheric Environment*, 86, pp. 113–19.

Rosewell, B. (2012). Deciding What Transport Is For: Connectivity and the Economy. In Inderwildi, O. and King, D. (eds), *Energy, Transport, and the Environment*. London: Springer, pp. 663–78.

Rotaris, L., Danielis, R., Marcucci, E. and Massiani, J. (2010). The Urban Road Pricing Scheme to Curb Pollution in Milan, Italy: Description, Impacts and Preliminary Cost-Benefit Analysis Assessment. *Transportation Research Part A: Policy and Practice*, 44(5), pp. 359–75.

Sælen, H. and Kallbekken, S. (2011). A Choice Experiment on Fuel Taxation and Earmarking in Norway. *Ecological Economics*, 70(11), pp. 2181–90.

Schade, J. and Baum, M. (2007). Reactance or Acceptance? Reactions towards the Introduction of Road Pricing. *Transportation Research Part A: Policy and Practice*, 41(1), pp. 41–8.

Schaller, B. (2010). New York City's Congestion Pricing Experience and Implications for Road Pricing Acceptance in the United States. *Transport Policy*, 17(4), pp. 266–73.

Schuitema, G., Steg, L. and Forward, S. (2010). Explaining Differences in Acceptability before and Acceptance after the Implementation of a Congestion Charge in Stockholm. *Transportation Research Part A: Policy and Practice*, 44(2), pp. 99–109.

Stead, D. (2008). Effectiveness and Acceptability of Urban Transport Policies in Europe. *International Journal of Sustainable Transportation*, 2(1), pp. 3–18.

Thorpe, N., Hills, P. and Jaensirisak, S. (2000). Public Attitudes to TDM Measures: A Comparative Study. *Transport Policy*, 7(4), pp. 243–57.

Tillema, T., Ben-Elia, E., Ettema, D. and van Delden, J. (2013). Charging versus Rewarding: A Comparison of Road-Pricing and Rewarding Peak Avoidance in the Netherlands. *Transport Policy*, 26, pp. 4–14.

Tonne, C., Beevers, S., Armstrong, B., Kelly, F. and Wilkinson, P. (2008). Air Pollution and Mortality Benefits of the London Congestion Charge: Spatial and Socioeconomic Inequalities. *Occupational and Environmental Medicine*, 65(9), pp. 620–7.

Tuominen, A. and Himanen, V. (2007). Assessing the Interaction between Transport Policy Targets and Policy Implementation: A Finnish Case Study. *Transport Policy*, 14(5), pp. 388–98.

US Department of Transportation National Highway Traffic Safety Administration (2009). *Consumer Assistance to Recycle and Save Act of 2009: Report to the House Committee on Energy and Commerce, the Senate Committee on Commerce, Science, and Transportation, and the House and Senate Committees on Appropriations*. www.nhtsa.gov/CARS-archive/official-information/CARS-Report-to-Congress.pdf (accessed April 2016).

van Erp, A. M., Kelly, F. J., Demerjian, K. L., Pope III, C. A. and Cohen, A. J. (2012). Progress in Research to Assess the Effectiveness of Air Quality Interventions towards Improving Public Health. *Air Quality, Atmosphere and Health*, 5(2), pp. 217–30.

Van Wee, B., De Jong, G. and Nijland, H. (2011). Accelerating Car Scrappage: A Review of Research into the Environmental Impacts. *Transport Reviews*, 31(5), pp. 549–69.

Vieira, J., Moura, F. and Manuel Viegas, J. (2007). Transport Policy and Environmental Impacts: The Importance of Multi-Instrumentality in Policy Integration. *Transport Policy*, 14(5), pp. 421–32.

Wolff, H. (2014). Keep Your Clunker in the Suburb: Low-Emission Zones and Adoption of Green Vehicles. *Economic Journal*, 124(578), pp. F481–F512.

Wolff, H. and Perry, L. (2010). *Trends in Clean Air Legislation in Europe: Particulate Matter and Low Emission Zones*. http://faculty.washington.edu/hgwolff/REEP.pdf (accessed April 2016).

19

Sustainable travel or sustaining growth?

Robin Hickman

19.1 Introduction: frictionless travel and the environmental and social crisis

The planning of new infrastructure, including major infrastructure projects over $1 billion in value and many projects of smaller scale, has become critical to the development of many cities internationally, including London. The ambition has become impressive:

> Among the programmes and projects... are a new four-runway hub airport to the east of London; delivery of up to 36 trains per hour on certain tube lines; Crossrail 2 by 2030; extending the Bakerloo line; new East-London river crossings; four-tracking the West Anglia lines; a South London Metro; an inner orbital road tunnel; improvements to double the number of passengers on London's rail network; and 200km of new cycle highways.
>
> *(Greater London Authority, 2014a, p.3)*

Infrastructure planning is positioned as critical in facilitating economic growth – indeed central to globalisation and capitalism itself – premised on the vision of a highly mobile world. Bill Gates' (1996) notion of 'frictionless capitalism' had a central focus on electronic interaction, but associated with this enhanced level of communication is an increase in physical travel as part of a globally interconnected world. The implication for much of London's planned growth is for the increased mobility of people and goods – aiming for frictionless ease. Infrastructure planning has become synonymous with efforts to promote economic growth across many cities. There are problems, however, with this vision – not least the environmental (e.g. carbon dioxide and local air quality), social (e.g. vehicle-related casualties, severance, poor accessibility for non-car drivers) and associated adverse impacts on the city fabric. The almost universally accepted strategy for sustainable urban mobility is one of high investment in public transport, walking and cycling, alongside compact urban development – yet in many cities this is not being effectively delivered, with too much focus given to highway investment and dispersed development. Infrastructure projects are often developed without sufficient critical assessment. They are marketed as central to sustainable development, yet, in reality, do little more than sustain economic growth, supporting high-income groups in terms of travel and development value uplift.

This chapter considers these issues, drawing on some of the literature from the early radical environmental movement in the 1970s, when there was much scepticism about the desirability of economic growth from an environmental perspective (Ehrlich and Ehrlich, 1968; Meadows et al.,

1972; Daly, 1973). The commentary explores the various definitions of sustainability and how the application of the triple bottom line model has, in practice, led to many problems in project appraisal and implementation. It uses a case study of the London Infrastructure Plan (Greater London Authority, 2014a, 2014b), arguing that a different conception of sustainability – relating back to the ideas of 'limits' and the 'steady state' – would help transport planning to become more sustainable. Yet, the implications of such a refinement in thinking are likely to be fundamental, leading to many changes in transport decision making and project appraisal.

19.2 Sustainability and environmental limits

The concept of sustainable development, it is claimed, was developed as a mainstream reaction to the radical environmental movement of the 1970s, almost as a 'conservative' reaction to the limits-to-growth literature (Pearce and Warford, 1993; Castro, 2004). Sustainability, as a result, was appropriated by the dominant paradigm of growth – and applied at different governmental scales (national and local) and internationally (over the Global North and Global South). There was seemingly broad agreement on sustainability, at least at the conceptual level – including between very disparate groups – but this breaks down on closer examination. There is much confusion in the terminology, definitions and application by different groups. 'Sustainability' is poorly defined – it is a 'fuzzy' concept (Swyngedouw, 2007) – hence people can and do interpret it in different ways to justify their own particular agenda. Questions arise: can we and should we more clearly define sustainability? Would this help in achieving greater sustainability in travel? How might different definitions apply in transport decisionmaking? Or, is all lost in the search for greater sustainability in travel – the fuzzy concept proving meaningless for all?

In definitional terms, sustainability is viewed as incorporating: 'systems and processes that are able to operate and persist on their own over long periods of time' (Robertson, 2014, p.3) – hence there is an important element of being self-sustaining over a period of time. The Oxford English Dictionary (2016) similarly defines the property of being environmentally sustainable as 'the degree to which a process or enterprise is able to be maintained or continued while avoiding the long-term depletion of natural resources'. The most cited definition comes from the Brundtland Report (World Commission on Environment and Development, 1987, p.8): 'meeting the needs of the present generation without compromising the ability of future generations to meet their needs'.

Often these definitions are viewed in terms of the Triple Bottom Line – where projects are assessed against the 3 'Es' of equity, environment and economics (or otherwise known as the 3 'Ps' of people, planet and profit) (Figure 19.1).

There is conceptual simplicity to this model of sustainability (Giddings et al., 2002), where the classification of impacts is put neatly into three convenient categories. Applied to transport, the appraisal process is made straightforward, requiring an assessment of impacts against one or all of the economic, environmental and social criteria. The transport appraisal approach used in the UK is based on this framing, i.e. WebTAG (Web-Based Transport Appraisal Guidance), with its use of Cost-Benefit Assessment (CBA) and Multi-Criteria Analysis (MCA), summarised through the Appraisal Summary Table. Similarly, Environmental Impact Assessment and Sustainability Appraisal are most often structured to assess impacts against a range of criteria.

There are major problems, however, with this mainstream view of sustainability. Many view the internationally accepted interpretation as a political fudge – based on ambiguity of meaning – to ensure widespread acceptability, between countries at the international negotiations and also between different interests (Wackernagel and Rees, 1996; Giddings et al., 2002). Sustainable development is presented as the moment when the three dimensions are brought together – as if there is a point of balance, where all three objectives can be met. This is far from certain, indeed

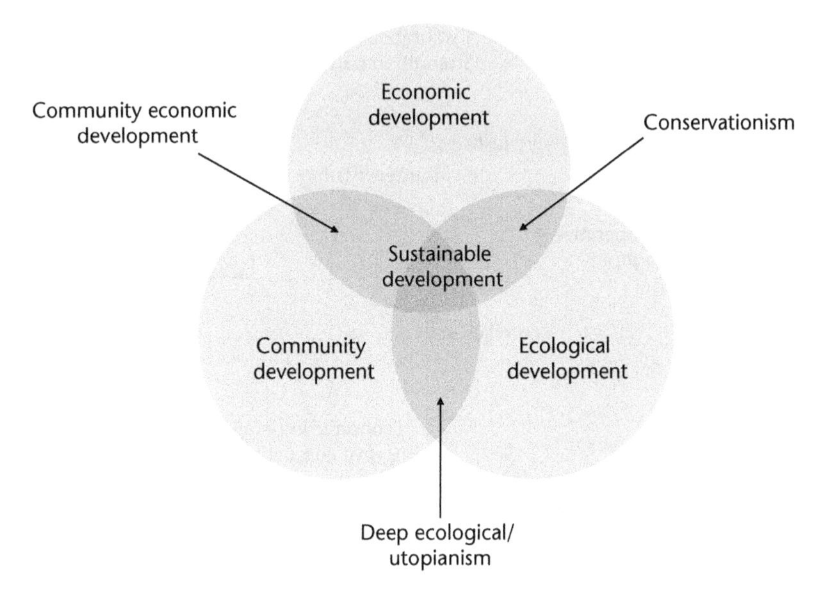

Figure 19.1 The three pillars of sustainability

very unlikely in most major infrastructure projects. Impacts tend to work in opposing directions, and there is usually no investment option that positively addresses all three objectives and multiple criteria within these. The three objectives are given equal sized circles – but, again, there is little reason why this should be the case. In practice, the economic dimension is given much higher priority, but this is not made evident – usually the weighting remains less than transparent. Many of the criteria used to represent overall objectives are poor proxies. For example, in CBA, time savings are used to represent the economic objective, and often account for more than 80 percent of the estimated 'benefits' of a transport project – yet there is little evidence to suggest that time savings result in economic development or growth. In most applications of sustainability, there is an assumption of the separation of each pillar, even of the autonomy of each, and this tends to lead to compartmentalism in practice – where different individuals or even organisations will work on environmental, economic and social appraisal analysis, with little coordination between these. There is, therefore, a large underplaying of the connections and a large assumption made that trade-offs can be made (Giddings et al., 2002).

A different framing of sustainability is to consider the 'prism' of sustainability (Figure 19.2). Here an additional dimension is added, in the form of governance, including participatory mechanisms and the need for strong institutions (Spangenberg, 2002). Yet, this still has its conceptual difficulties. Good governance is perhaps a pre-requisite to sustainability rather than an objective, and the prism still implies there is a position to be found that can satisfy all objectives.

A further framing of sustainability is the nested sustainability concept (Figure 19.3). The viewpoint given here is that the economy is dependent on, or nested within, society and the environment, particularly over the long term (Giddings et al., 2002). For example, our material needs, such as food, shelter, transportation and the consumption of goods, all involve materials and energy. The economy, hence, is viewed as a sub-set of the environmental and social sectors. The implication is that thresholds (or stocks) need to be maintained in environmental, societal and economic terms. For example, an infrastructure project (such as in transport or the

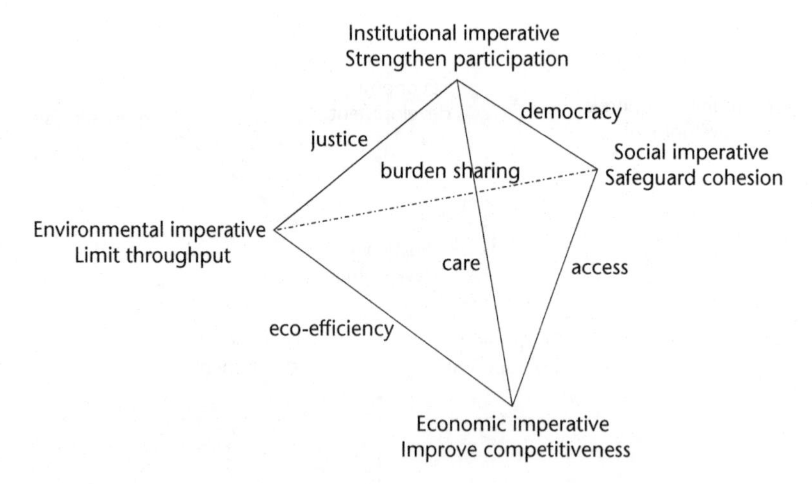

Figure 19.2 The prism of sustainability

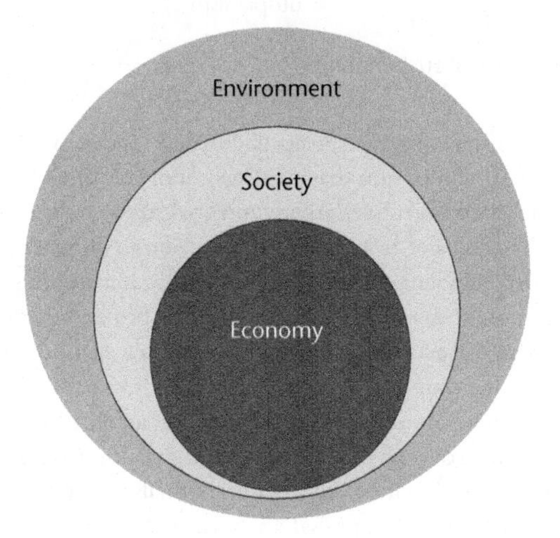

Figure 19.3 Nested sustainability

development of a neighbourhood in a city) needs to contribute positively to all of these dimensions, and not go beyond particular thresholds.

The nested concept draws on the idea of there being limits in consumption (Meadows et al., 1972). There are varied, but independent components that make up the global system that we all live in, including economic, social, environmental and political. If the present growth trends in world population, globalisation, travel, resource depletion and pollution continue unchanged, the 'limits to growth' are very likely to be reached. The use of finite energy sources within transport, such as oil, have to have a time constraint. This leads to the concept of Steady State Economics (Daly, 1973), which warns of the problems of chasing endless economic growth, despite the common parlance in modern capitalist societies:

> The verb 'to grow' has become so overladen with positive value connotations that we have forgotten its first literal dictionary denotation, namely, 'to spring up and develop to

maturity'. Thus the very notion of growth includes some concept of maturity, beyond which point physical accumulation and economic growth gives way to flat-lining maturity; i.e. a steady state. It is important to remember that 'growth' is not necessarily synonymous with 'betterment'.

(Daly, 1973, p.99)

The implication for transport planning is fundamental – supporting continued development growth, particularly where this involves increased (often longer distance) mobility patterns; finite resource use; social equity and gentrification problems; estimating costs against benefits, with benefits including time savings (where the greater usage of a scheme by a larger number of people is seen as positive) are problematic. All of these break down if we view sustainability as the overarching goal for transport planning, and if sustainability is conceived as having limits to be adhered to in environmental and social terms.

19.3 Case study: the London Infrastructure Plan

A case study is used to help explore some of these issues: the London Infrastructure Plan 2050 (LIP) (Greater London Authority, 2014a). The LIP was published as a consultation draft in 2014, including a Transport Supporting Paper (Greater London Authority, 2014b); with an updated version of the LIP published the following year (Greater London Authority, 2015b). The LIP sets out proposals for London's major infrastructure requirements, including transport, parks and open spaces, digital facilities, energy, water and waste, and the estimated costs and potential funding options. The context is that London's population is expected to grow from the current 8.6 million residents (2014) to over 11 million by 2050; jobs in London are to increase from 4.9 million in 2011 to 6.3 million by 2050; and tourist numbers to increase from 15 million international visitors in 2012 to around 21 million by 2022. Though the LIP is focused on enhancing London's competitiveness, it is presumably supposed to be consistent with the London Plan (Greater London Authority, 2015a) and its overarching objective for sustainable development.

The LIP, in style terms, is an uncritical, promotional document, arguing for a high level of infrastructure investment. It is, in effect, a lobbying document, asking for funds from central government – the UK operates a heavily centralised governmental system, where transport infrastructure is largely funded, and prioritised, from Westminster. The LIP claims that 'a clear economic rationale underpins the need for this Infrastructure Plan. Growth in income per head depends on increased productivity, which itself depends on infrastructure' (Greater London Authority, 2014a, p.6). The LIP is clearly put forward as an economic growth-led plan, with direct links made between infrastructure investment, productivity and GDP growth. London is positioned as a 'World City' – 'London has succeeded in placing itself at the heart of a network of World Cities. Being part of this "super network" lifts London to a different level of competition from most other cities' (Greater London Authority, 2014b). There is surprisingly little critical discussion of these ideas, and of the rationale for supporting the Global City concept; it is taken as a given. This is despite critique of the need for continually increased levels of GDP, with this often associated with large distributional inequity, and only certain parts of the population gaining from the GDP uplift. The support given to one industrial sector, i.e. the financial industry, as a focal point of the capitalist system, again, remains largely unquestioned. There are very direct links made between transport investment and the economic growth that will follow – yet there are many other factors involved in supporting growth that remain undiscussed. There are attendant problems of housing affordability, environmental degradation (locally and globally), and many social issues become evident when there is such a narrow focus on GDP growth as a policy objective. There is little empirical evidence behind the need to 'stay ahead' of the competition and the importance of infrastructure in supporting the implied economic growth – the 'evidence' relying on opinion surveys from business leaders (CBI/KPMG infrastructure survey, 2013, cited in the Greater London Authority, 2014a). The close reliance on the consulting industry to provide evidence for strategy making seems self-fulfilling, with the management consultants and engineering practices running and responding to the surveys also likely to be involved in developing the projects that follow. The GLA, with its strong resource base, should develop a much more thorough evidence base for its policy making, and be much less influenced by the consultancy lobby. It can be more critical of positions taken, such as the use of economic growth as a key driver for policy making. There are multiple critiques of these positions – and they should be more thoroughly considered. Without this, the accusations of weak public policy making, with undue influence from the private sector, are difficult to refute.

The major transport projects proposed in the LIP are outlined below (Greater London Authority, 2014a):

- Underground frequency upgrades, including increasing train frequencies from a current maximum of 34 to up to 36 trains per hour across the Jubilee, Piccadilly and Northern Lines by 2035.
- Improved capacity on the National Rail network, including devolution of suburban rail services to Transport for London, and upgrading of frequencies to metro-style services.
- Crossrail 2, running from Wimbledon, across central London from Victoria to Euston, and on to Dalston, Tottenham Hale and Wood Green, by 2030; and increased frequency of Crossrail 1 trains.
- Extending the Bakerloo line south from Elephant and Castle to Southwark, Lewisham and beyond, 'regenerating' areas such as Old Kent Road and Catford.
- Extending the Gospel Oak to Barking line to Barking Riverside, 'opening up' development of a major new quarter with 11,500 new homes.
- Modernised central London stations, including Holborn, Victoria, Waterloo and Euston.
- Redevelopment of Old Oak Common in north-west London, with around 90,000 jobs and 20,000 new homes, with links to High Speed 2, Crossrail and the Overground.
- A comprehensive network of cycle routes, with 200 kilometres of Dutch-style cycle highways (presumably segregated), and at least five new major pedestrian and cycle bridges.
- A series of 'iconic place-changing schemes', such as the Garden Bridge across the Thames; and key locations on the Inner Ring Road, including Vauxhall Cross, Old Street, Euston Road/King's Cross, in the medium term, and the Westway in the longer term.

The LIP is therefore not short on ambition and rhetoric. There are many projects to be supported, including all of the above public transport, cycling, walking and public realm projects. However, some critical commentary can be given. The overall level of spending is not justified, and it is difficult to see whether this scale of funding is required, whether less or more funding is appropriate, whether other schemes are more appropriate (e.g. there seems to be an absence of particular projects, such as trams, in outer London), and whether the investment in London is better than spending the money in other parts of the country. Many of the public transport projects will increase capacity to a significant degree on a crowded network, which is to be supported. The projects will also lead to large development change around stations. Again, in many areas the redevelopment will be a positive feature, improving the local built environment. However, some of this will be associated with gentrification issues – lower-income residents and employees will be forced away from the newly accessible locations, and the property value uplift will be gained by only a certain part of the population – the landowners and higher-income residents that move in. There is evidence from previous public transport projects that the higher-income in-movers gain from the new housing and employment and that the incumbents often fail to take advantage of the new opportunities (Jones, 2015). For example, without strong housing (owner occupied and rental) and employment unit affordability policies, the public investment in the transport infrastructure will lead to high levels of social inequity. Much of the public spending leads to large financial gain by selected cohorts in the population. The political lead at the time of the LIP was mayor Boris Johnson; it is likely that the new mayor, Sadiq Khan (in office since May 2016), will be much more keen on tackling some of these social equity problems.

However, this is not a straightforward problem to tackle within transport planning. Within transport appraisal, the type of development is not considered – all development is considered as a 'benefit' in the CBA, irrespective of the social distribution issues. This is clearly a weakness in the transport-appraisal system, and more generally in transport infrastructure decisionmaking. Transport planning appears to be strangely apolitical, ignoring the strong support for the higher-income groups that it often delivers – both in terms of the higher-income groups using the new transport services and profiting from the development that follows.

Further, some of the cycle schemes and place-changing schemes mentioned in the LIP will be impossible to deliver without a different priority for vehicles on the street network – much space has to be taken away from the private car. Again, there is no critical evaluation of this, and no suggestion that the private car will be deprioritised in such a way. Without this, it is unlikely that effective cycling provision can be delivered – and that the calls to 'Go Dutch' (to invest in segregated cycle infrastructure similar to practice in the Netherlands) are little more than greenwash.

Even more controversial are the suggested 'improvements' to the road network – 'rendering it fit for the future' (Greater London Authority, 2014a, p.35). Included here are some very controversial projects:

- A new inner orbital tolled road tunnel, that aims to reduce congestion in central London; and a series of mini-tunnels and/or decking over roads to overcome severance and transform places across the city.
- A series of new river crossings in east London, including the proposed Silvertown tunnel, Woolwich Ferry replacement, Gallions Reach bridge (a revised version of previous incarnations from the 1970s onwards – the Thames Gateway Bridge and East London River Crossing) and Belvedere Crossing.

Further, there are plans for increasing airport capacity:

- A new 'world class' four-runway hub airport in the Thames Estuary, planned to open by 2029, and 'to make London and the UK the best-connected city and country in the world' (Greater London Authority, 2014a, p.37), incorporating a high-speed link to central London.

These proposals are hugely controversial from an environmental and social perspective, and perhaps even economically in the long term. Road and airport projects seem very difficult to justify under the environmental pillar of sustainability – they can only lead to increased transport CO_2 emissions in a city that has a large latent demand for private car usage and international air travel. It is here that the LIP becomes little more than a long list of projects, with little prioritisation against sustainability objectives. The inner orbital ring road tunnel proposal hails back to the proposals of Abercrombie in the 1940s and is verging on the preposterous – the road-building agenda for London was defeated in the 1970s and this proposal seems an extraordinary backward step. Increasing road capacity in such a congested environment fails to deliver the projected capacity gains due to the induced demand (the new road space is rapidly filled), and the built environment impacts are very severe, with large severance and blight problems along the routes. The cost would also presumably be prohibitive, but, interestingly, is not given in the LIP documentation. The road schemes are also clearly not deliverable in view of likely public protests. There are proposed 'flyunders' and mini-tunnels, as yet unspecified, and perhaps these have more potential. Road severance near attractive urban environments could be reduced if the roads were buried or bridged, with landscaping and parkland covering the road – but highway capacity should not be increased alongside. The cost of these projects is likely to be prohibitive, relative to what else the funding could be used for. But, perhaps these are worth exploring in important locations where there are large environmental gains, such as Euston Road, the inner parts of the A4/M4 and sections of the A406 North and South Circular.

The proposed river crossings in east London have, for years, been put forward on grounds of there being more river crossings in west London, and only one road bridge and two tunnels in east London. Again this seems poor logic. The assumption is that more mobility between the north and south of the river will lead to development and presumably GDP growth – but there is little evidence to support this. It is more likely that roads-based development would not lead to a high-quality urban fabric, and instead only large traffic volumes amidst dispersed, low-quality development – and presumably fairly low GDP growth – at best.

There is a large mismatch between these types of transport projects and urban planning/urban design aspirations, and between the supposed economic objectives and environmental and social objectives of the LIP and London Plan. There is little evidence to suggest that building bridges and roads will lead to economic growth, yet this is perpetuated as almost an unquestionable fact. There is a great opportunity to develop east London around a dense public transport network, perhaps with a spur on the Jubilee line, an upgraded Docklands Light Railway, further orbital public transport links and tram-based or bus rapid transit projects. High-quality development could be orientated around the new interchanges – with high-quality town centres developed. The LIP doesn't discuss these alternative options, instead providing outdated road-based strategies for East London.

The proposed Thames Estuary hub airport is even more poorly thought through. Again this is justified on economic grounds, with environmental and social issues given little weight. The logic is very weak – the case put forward is that there is more demand for international flying, that providing for increased landing slots is critical for maintaining London as a 'World City', in competition with other centres such as Frankfurt, Paris and Amsterdam; and that there is little potential for growth around the existing airports in London. To an extent, this position is correct – extension of Heathrow, and also Gatwick, Luton, Stansted and City Airport, is difficult because of the surrounding residential populations or landscape constraints. The locations of Heathrow and City Airport, in particular, are too close to the dense urban population in London, and it would be much better on noise grounds if the airports could be replaced further from the urban area. Heathrow was opened in 1946, originally located as a military airport, allowing fighter planes to scramble quickly to protect London. It is not an appropriate location for a modern airport in London, let alone an extension, as it is in the midst of the conurbation. The surrounding neighbourhoods in Hounslow are severely affected by noise, and some of the areas further away, on the inbound and outbound flightpaths, such as Chiswick, Kew and Ealing, are also adversely affected. Moving airports away from the city boundary has been the history of recent airport upgrades internationally. For example, in Paris, Le Bourget (13km from the city centre) was replaced by Orly (15km from the centre) in the 1960s. Le Bourget was gradually relegated to a subsidiary role, losing international services in 1977 and regional in 1980. Orly was itself replaced by Charles de Gaulle in 1974 (23km from the centre) (Hall and Hall, 2005). That Heathrow has not been replaced in London is perhaps a result of the failure of regional planning to make and deliver effective long-term strategies for the city on large infrastructure. However, the 'muddling through' approach has perversely helped, as new policy objectives, such as climate change, now mean that it is very difficult to support continued airport growth. The Thames Estuary Airport hub proposal was developed by a consortium of consultancies, led by Foster and Partners and Halcrow (now CH2M), and seems a very odd collection of major infrastructure projects, bundled together more to provide a pipeline of work for the consultancies than a well-thought-through strategy aimed at developing London in a sustainable manner. The need to manage the demand for air traffic is not seriously discussed in the mainstream policy making or politics – yet, if climate change problems are to be tackled, this is the only feasible route to take.

The overall cost of the LIP, covering the total investment in London's infrastructure between 2016 and 2050, is estimated at £1.3 trillion, with a range between £1 trillion and £1.7 trillion according to uncertainties over construction costs, etc. This includes £466 billion for transport projects (Greater London Authority, 2014a; 2014b). The huge cost of the LIP means that additional funding streams are being considered, to supplement the funding requested from central government. These include a number of interesting mechanisms, including a regional income tax, London-only income tax, motoring duty, a hotel bedroom tax, business rate supplement and housing sale stamp duty.

Any rigorous assessment of the sustainability of the LIP seems to be missing, there is no appraisal of the projects against policy objectives, and there are clear inconsistencies with many of the projects proposed and the strategy given in the London Plan and Transport Strategy. Both of these latter documents seem to have a much stronger environmental sustainability theme running throughout. The emphasis on supporting economic growth is problematic on many counts, including the priority that GDP growth is given over environmental and social objectives – and the fallacy that all infrastructure, irrespective of type, will lead to growth. Sen (2001) and many others make an important point that development is much more than increases in GDP or economic indicators, but this seems to be overlooked in transport planning. A stronger understanding of environmental (and social) limits would help in delivering a stronger base for policy making – it is only by developing the public transport network, walking and cycling facilities, supported by a compact, polycentric development form, that travel behaviours will become more sustainable. In addition, use of the private motor car and international flying needs to be constrained, with effective demand-management policies; and the affordability of housing, in central and outer areas of London, much enhanced.

19.4 Conclusions: transport investment and quality of life

It might seem that the working definition of sustainability is an insignificant factor in moving towards greater sustainability in travel behaviours. Yet, as we have seen, the concept is still largely defined to give primacy to the market and economic growth, with environmental and social goals only of subsidiary importance. Use of the three pillars definition is most ubiquitous – but, ultimately, has become problematic in that it assumes there is a solution and a balanced point that serve all objectives equally well. In practice, when this possibility is not found, the economic pillar is given most weight in the decision making on almost all transport infrastructure projects – yet the solutions are presented as being 'sustainable'. The case study of the London Infrastructure

Plan illustrates, perhaps as a polemic example, how transport infrastructure funding can be used to support particular political agendas, in this case the growth of London as a global financial centre – with very little critical discussion of the positions being taken. Much of this seems an odd use of public money, particularly the proposed highway projects and airport investments, ignoring the environmental and social distribution problems that are very likely to follow. Any discussion of alternative approaches that might be followed tends to be brushed aside.

Galbraith (1958), when testifying to the Royal Commission on Canada's Economic Prospects, famously told us that: 'sooner rather than later our concern with the quantity of goods produced – the rate of increase in Gross National Product – would have to give way to the larger question of the quality of life that it provided'. This argument was developed in *The Affluent Society* (Galbraith, 1958), where it was argued that in countries where there have been great rises in economic wellbeing over decades, such as in Europe and North America, promoting prosperity should no longer be the priority. This has continued resonance today, in terms of transport planning in London in general and the LIP in particular – the focus for investment should be on improving environmental, social and built environment goals, and not simply short-term economic aspirations.

There is a need to move beyond this weak understanding of sustainability, and to develop an application of the nested sustainability concept – including limits and thresholds, with sustainability viewed as 'capital' rather than an expendable good. This also means a return to steady state economics, where a simplistic focus on economic growth is no longer used to drive decision making. This, of course, is a long way from the current mainstream policy discussion.

The implications for transport appraisal are also fundamental. For example, the current application of MCA through WebTAG is broadly based on the three pillars definition of sustainability. It suffers from poor coverage of many important environmental and social issues (Hickman, 2016), hence is a very weak application of MCA, and doesn't apply weighting or limits to any of the environmental or social indicators. The CBA element of WebTAG is focused on economic efficiency, i.e. economic issues, and largely time savings, dominate the decision making process. Environmental and social issues are given little priority.

This application of neoclassical economics in transport planning has led to many important environmental and social issues being ignored – and it has become critical to explore different approaches for the framing of transport analysis and decision making. The relationships between transport investment and quality of life issues are often indirect – yet it is these factors that transport infrastructure should seek to address. Concepts from more progressive economic thinking, which incorporate environmental and social dimensions of development, will be important. Ecological economics (see, for example, Shmelev, 2012) may prove useful, whereby environmental (and social) issues can be given much more prominence in strategy development and appraisal. The conventional wisdom must change: to paraphrase Paul and Anne Ehrlich (1968), we must acquire a lifestyle which has maximum happiness for the individual and for society as its goals – and to think through an appropriate role for transport in support of this – not ever increasing levels of mobility and growth in GDP.

References

Castro, C. (2004). Sustainable Development: Mainstream and Critical Perspectives. *Organization and Environment*, 17, pp. 195–225.

Daly, H. (1973). The Steady-State Economy. In Daly, H. (ed.), *Essays toward a Steady-State Economy*. San Francisco: W. H. Freeman.

Ehrlich, P. and Ehrlich, A. (1968). *The Population Bomb*. New York: Buccaneer.

Galbraith, J. K. (1958). *The Affluent Society*. London: Penguin Books.

Gates, B. (1996). *The Road Ahead*. London: Penguin.
Giddings, B., Hopwood, B. and O'Brien, G. (2002). Environment, Economy and Society: Fitting Them Together into Sustainable Development. *Sustainable Development*, 10, pp. 187–96.
Greater London Authority (2014a). *London Infrastructure Plan 2050: A Consultation*. London: GLA.
Greater London Authority (2014b). *London Infrastructure Plan 2050: Transport Supporting Paper*. London: GLA.
Greater London Authority (2015a). *Further Alterations to the London Plan*. London: GLA.
Greater London Authority (2015b). *London Infrastructure Plan 2050: Update*. London: GLA.
Hall, T. and Hall, P. (2005). Heathrow: A Retirement Plan. *Town and Country Planning: Tomorrow Series*.
Hickman, R. (2016). *Incomplete Cost–Incomplete Benefit Analysis in Transport Appraisal*. UTSG Conference, University of the West of England, Bristol.
Jones, P. (2015). Assessing the Wider Impacts of the Jubilee Line Extension in East London. In Hickman, R., Givoni, M., Bonilla, D. and Banister, D. (eds), *Handbook on Transport and Development*. Cheltenham: Edward Elgar.
Meadows, D. H., Meadows, D. L., Randers, J. and Behrens, W. W. (1972). *The Limits to Growth: A Report for the Club of Rome's Project on the Predicament of Mankind*. London: Potomac Associates, Earth Island Ltd.
Oxford English Dictionary (2016). www.oed.com/ (accessed February 2016).
Pearce, D. and Warford, J. (1993). *World Without End: Economics, Environment and Sustainable Development*. New York: Oxford University Press.
Robertson, M. (2014). *Sustainability: Principles and Practice*. London: Routledge.
Sen, A. (2001). *Development as Freedom*. Oxford: Oxford University Press.
Shmelev, S. E. (2012). *Ecological Economics: Sustainability in Practice*. London: Springer.
Spangenberg, J. H. (2002). Environmental Space and the Prism of Sustainability: Frameworks for Indicators Measuring Sustainable Development. *Ecological Indicators*, 2, pp. 295–309.
Swyngedouw, E. (2007). Impossible 'Sustainability'and the Post-Political Condition. In Gibbs, D. and Krueger, R. (eds), *The Sustainable Development Paradox*. New York: Guilford Press.
Wackernagel, M. and Rees, W. (1996). *Our Ecological Footprint*. Gabriola Island, Canada: New Society.
World Commission on Environment and Development (1987). *Our Common Future*. New York: Oxford University Press.

Part V
Freight transport

20
Short sea shipping and ferries

James D. Frost and Mary R. Brooks

20.1 Introduction to short sea shipping

Short sea shipping is usually defined geographically. Transport Canada (2006) defines short sea shipping on a continental basis as 'a multi-modal concept involving the marine transportation of passengers and goods that does not cross oceans and takes place within and among Canada, the United States and Mexico'. The European Commission (1999) defines it within Europe as 'the movement of cargo and passengers by sea between ports situated in geographical Europe or between those ports and ports situated in non-European countries having a coastline on the enclosed seas bordering Europe'. In 2007, it was defined by law in the US (Energy Independence and Security Act of 2007, section 55605) as:

> the carriage by vessel of cargo
>
> (1) that is (A) contained in intermodal cargo containers and loaded by crane on the vessel; or (B) loaded on the vessel by means of wheeled technology; and
> (2) that is (A) loaded at a port in the United States and unloaded either at another port in the United States or at a port in Canada located in the Great Lakes Saint Lawrence Seaway System; or (B) loaded at a port in Canada located in the Great Lakes Saint Lawrence Seaway System and unloaded at a port in the United States.

A study for the US Transportation Research Board (Kruse and Hutson, 2010, p. 1) used a widely accepted definition for short sea shipping in North America, which was defined by the Maritime Economics Panel of the Society of Naval Architects and Marine Engineers:

> Freight service operations carrying either containerized or trailerized cargoes (or empties) via the coastal waters and river systems...and in particular those services where there is a true 'intermodal choice' to be made by the shipper between moving units by water and using one or more land-based alternatives (i.e. highway and/or rail).

For the purposes of this chapter, short sea shipping includes container, roll-on/roll-off (ro-ro), and bulk as well as tug and barge operations, providing interregional, intra-regional and transshipment services. This definition also includes passenger ferries, since commercial cargo is carried on many ferry services worldwide. Ferries tend to operate port to port, and rarely provide door-to-door services. There are different types of ferries, and the differences between them are discussed below under three broad types—pure freight services, pure passenger services and mixed or hybrid options; more information on vessel types can be found in Buzzone (2012). Table 20.1 summarises the vessel types in terms of general characteristics and usual deployment, but it becomes clear that there is some overlap in the abilities of the various vessel types to serve these needs.

Table 20.1 Summary of key vessel types in short sea shipping

Roll-on/roll-off vessels	
Vessel description	Roll-on/roll-off vessels are of two principal types – those used for transporting autos and those which transport truck trailers and other large items. Ro-ro vessels are capable of quick turnarounds. They do not usually carry passengers.
Primary service offering	Routes where high volumes of trailers or autos are shipped and where fast vessel turnaround times are required
Where best used	Routes tend to be 12–36 hours
Examples of routes	Helsinki–Travemumnde, Gothenburg–Immingham, Istanbul–Trieste, and Rotterdam–Killingholme (all Europe and vicinity)
Container	
Vessel description	Fully cellular or geared container vessel, or tug and barge
Primary service offering	Short sea 'feeder' routes or short sea 'door-to-door' services
Where best used	Connecting deep-sea gateway hubs with secondary ports or providing door-to-door service in competition with trucking firms and ro-ro operators
Examples of routes	Hamburg–Gothenburg, Gothenburg–Helsinki and Rotterdam–Dublin (all in Europe), Singapore–Surabaya (South East Asia) and Norfolk–Richmond (US east coast)
Container and roll-on/ roll-off (con-ro)	
Vessel description	Vessels which are capable of carrying containers and roll-on/roll-off cargo
Primary service offering	Short sea routes where a mix of cargoes need to be carried
Where best used	Routes where flexibility is required and where fast vessel turnarounds are not as critical
Examples of routes	Antwerp–Kotka and St Petersburg–Lubeck (Europe), Montréal–St John's (east Canada)
Ro-pax	
Vessel description	A ferry whose primary purpose is to transport trucks and unaccompanied trailers, but which can also accommodate passengers and autos
Primary service offering	Freight service can be more important or as important as the services to passengers
Where best used	May be used on either short or longer routes, but are best deployed on routes of up to eight hours. As the route gets longer, there is a tendency for the percentage of unaccompanied trailers to go up
Examples of routes	Helsinki–Travemunde, Hook of Holland–Harwich and Gothenburg–Kiel (all in Europe), North Sydney–Port-aux-Basques (east Canada)

Table 20.1 Cont.

Cruise ferry	
Vessel description	The cruise ferry offers a cruise/tourism experience on a shorter route, most often less than 24 hours. Therefore on-board facilities are geared towards the expectations of the getaway vacationers with amentities such as restaurants, shops, lounges with(out) entertainment and cabins are provided
Primary service offering	The voyage is the destination with the transport being the secondary service. The service offering reflects the target market – tourists, sometimes with their vehicles. Dependent on the market, the share of passengers who take a car will vary
Where best used	Routes tend to be 8–12 hours, with 24-hour round trip
Examples of routes	Helsinki–Stockholm, Stockholm–Riga, Helsinki–St Petersburg and Oslo–Copenhagen (all in Europe), Yarmouth–Portland (east coast North America)
High speed	
Vessel description	Passenger-only and vehicle plus passenger vessels. Capable of speeds in excess of 25 knots
Primary service offering	Fast transport to destination is the primary service. Amenities on board not extensive
Where best used	Short routes of less than two hours where seas are relatively calm
Examples of routes	Harbour ferries in cities such as Boston, New York, Auckland, Sydney and London Car/passenger ferries to/from Jersey and Guernsey to/from Poole, Portsmouth and St. Malo.

20.2 Pure freight services

Roll-on/roll-off (ro-ro) vessels were first introduced in Scandinavia. There are two principal types – those used for transporting automobiles and those that transport truck trailers and other large items such as farm machinery, paper, lumber and project cargo.[1] They are well suited to the Baltic and North Sea given the need for a quick turnaround. They do not usually carry passengers, although there are some exceptions such as some of the vessels operated by Finnlines Plc, which carry substantial numbers of passengers in the summer months between Finland and Germany when commercial traffic is lighter. As with other types of shipping, the trend in roll-on/roll-off vessels has been towards larger vessels so as to maximise economies of scale.

One alternative to a ro-ro vessel is a small container ship, used in either feeder or door-to-door short sea services (or both). Until recently, the largest of such vessels have been Kiel-max vessels (the maximum size handled by the Kiel Canal) of approximately 1,400 TEUs (a TEU is a 20-foot Equivalent Unit, or container with dimensions of 20 x 8 x 8 foot). Kiel-max vessels have mainly been used in services between Rotterdam/Hamburg/Bremerhaven and the Baltic. Small container ships are chartered by companies such as Unifeeder, Containerships and Team Lines. Unifeeder has a history of providing feeder services although in recent years has begun to offer door-to-door services, sometimes using its customers' own equipment. Since the advent of ultra-large container carriers on the main east–west container trade lanes, a number of mainline carriers have begun to order larger feeder tonnage to secure economies of scale across their networks. Seago, a Maersk Line subsidiary, has ordered seven (with an option for two more) ice-class 3,596 TEU feeders for the Baltic with delivery in 2017, and Evergreen, a Taiwanese global shipping line, has ordered 20 2,800 TEUs feeders, for delivery 2018–19 and expected to be deployed in the intra-Asian market.

Pure freight operations may also be served by tug and barge operations, which were common in North America but most have failed. Kruse and Hutson (2010) provide an excellent summary of this aspect of North American short sea operations, which can only be deployed in locations featuring relatively calm water and so have been considered unsuitable for operations in the coastal North Atlantic, where the sea state is among the most unsettled in the world.

In Europe, most river barges carrying containers are self-propelled. Despite the enormous volume of cargo they carry, river barges in North America do not fit into the US definition of short sea shipping.

20.3 Pure passenger ferry services

Ferries have been in the business of moving passengers for centuries but the vessel typology has changed significantly in the last 25 years or so. In the late 1970s and early 1980s in the Baltic Sea, two companies, Viking Line and Silja Line, invented the cruise ferry concept to expand interest beyond basic transportation from origin to destination. These ferries began to incorporate conference facilities, business and truck driver centres, show lounges and specialised restaurants ranging from Maxim de Paris to McDonald's. The best illustrations of this product are the ships sailing between Stockholm and Helsinki. Total traffic on this route is about 2.2 million passengers, including both Silja Line and its competitor, Viking Line. The newest cruise ferries are operated by Color Line between Oslo, Norway and Kiel, Germany. They were built in 2004 and 2007 and carry 2,750 passengers and 750 autos. The cruise ferry concept is the opposite of derived demand because the ferry *is* the destination; in many cases, passengers do not even disembark once the destination is reached – the journey and its entertainment are the destination. It became (and still is) very 'cool' to sail a 22-hour (round trip) mini-cruise between Helsinki and Stockholm and not even step ashore. Baltic ferry operators created new demand for ferry service by developing a product that appealed to clients looking to enhance their travel experience, as well as travel for travel's sake.

High-speed car/passenger ferries were introduced in Europe as a response to the loss of duty free on intra-European routes as well as the deregulation of air travel, which resulted in the introduction of low-cost airline travel. The first fast ferries were hovercraft, operated by Hoverlloyd and Seaspeed across the English Channel between 1968 and 1981. High-speed vessels offer a faster alternative to conventional ferries, and at the time of their introduction, consumers were willing to pay a premium over fares charged by the slower vessels. In many cases, ferry companies offer both alternatives. In the period from 2005 to 2013, as fuel costs rose dramatically, many fast ferries were withdrawn from service in favour of slower but more stable ro-paxes (discussed below). Many remain in operation, however, as their market niches can support their comparatively higher cost.

20.4 Hybrid services

Ro-pax is a term that was coined in the past ten years to describe a ferry whose primary purpose is to transport trucks and trailers, but which can also accommodate passengers. They started with relatively modest passenger accommodation, in terms of volume and capacity, but demand for passenger accommodation has grown recently, reflecting a desire for greater travelling comfort by passengers. Some vessels have also been built with the ability to expand passenger capacity if demand warrants.

20.5 The economics of short sea shipping

In this section, the economics of short sea shipping are examined. As with many transport sectors, the demand for short sea shipping is dependent upon the characteristics of the market itself and the service on offer. Of particular importance is the part of the market demand that comes from island states; Gouvernal et al. (2010) note that demand for short sea shipping in Europe is overstated by the fact that a significant part of the demand comes from those captive to short sea shipping by virtue of originating in or destined to islands. The success of many short sea operations is directly attributable to their dependence upon an island route and a visible lack of competing services or modes of transport.

Based on research completed in North and South America, Australia and Europe, it is clear that the characteristics of demand are very much specific to the particular route the ship operator serves; the services the operator offers will be tailored to their estimate of demand. As with most freight transport, the cargo owner's requirements will influence, in some measure, the short sea shipping services on offer. Other modes available will feature prominently in the transport mode chosen by a cargo owner, and ferry or short sea offerings may not even be considered as an option since they do not offer the frequency or transit time of other options. For example, as noted in Table 20.2, freight distance will dictate the attractiveness of trucking when compared with rail or short sea services. While the distance itself varies by route, all four key studies examining freight distance in Table 20.2 indicate that if a sea route is too short, the shipper will have a tendency to choose a much faster mode, most notably trucking, which is much more flexible in terms of cargo delivery and more frequent than short sea. Thus freight distance and other modes available are critical and integral to the transport mode choice trade-offs made by those who buy transport services.

While freight distance and mode alternatives are strong factors in determining whether short sea or ferry alternatives are considered by potential users, product characteristics and supply chain requirements are also important determinants of mode choice. Morales-Fusco et al. (2013) detail the supply chain considerations, particularly the product value and inventory-carrying considerations so important to determining whether the slower speed of transport inherent in short sea shipping places the mode into a non-consideration set by the decision maker. The decision-maker's particular supply chain strategy relates directly to the nature of the service offering and perceptions of it (including pre-conceived ideas), thus encouraging or deterring short sea usage. Likewise, García-Menéndez et al. (2004) found that shippers' choice of short sea transport is more sensitive to changes in road transport prices than to changes in sea transport costs, while Brooks et al. (2012) identified the particular trade-offs made in allocating cargo to various transport alternatives on three short sea potential routes in Australia. In the North American case, Kruse and Hutson (2010) specifically noted that the one trade-off between time and cost is critical to US cargo interests and that a short sea offering that is not reliable or seamless would not be acceptable as a result. Morales-Fusco et al. (2013) provide an overview of the factors at play in short sea shipping markets and distinguish that markets serving roll-on/roll-off cargoes have a different demand structure than those serving lift-on/lift-off cargoes.

Finally, the demand situation is heavily influenced by route-specific factors, most notably the perception that road congestion can increase interest in short sea shipping in both Europe and North America. Dense corridors in urban agglomerations and highway bottlenecks often encourage car-driving citizens to press for the availability of non-highway mode alternatives to serve freight movements. As such, the Institute for Global Maritime Studies (2008) proposed that the development of the US marine highways programme focus on corridors where road congestion or ageing road infrastructure had already induced significant delays for the travelling public.

Table 20.2 Relevant demand factors

Demand factor	*Key studies*	*Relevant findings*
Freight distance	Brooks and Trifts (2008) Bendall and Brooks (2011) Brooks et al. (2012) Brooks et al. (2014)	Short freight routes, given vessel loading and unloading times, are not time competitive against trucking. Other characteristics like price need to be superior to attract the cargo, and the critical freight distance is market-specific.
Other modes available in the market	Brooks et al. (2012) MariNova Consulting (2005)	Where there is a competing freight rail market (most particularly in North America and some long-haul Australian routes where the route is not optimised for passengers), cargo shippers will prefer rail over short sea options.
Cargo characteristics	Brooks and Trifts (2008) IGMS (2008) Brooks et al. (2012) Morales-Fusco et al. (2013)	Cargo characteristics like just-in-time and perishability often drive the cargo owner to choose truck and to pay a significant premium for reliable delivery service and reduced probability of delay. Inventory carrying cost can play a significant role here.
Service offering characteristics (e.g. frequency of service, cost, etc.)	Brooks et al. (2012) Kruse and Hutson (2010) García-Menéndez et al. (2004)	Detailed mode choice studies with willingness to pay parameters are required to understand if modal switching to short sea is likely for the particular route being considered.
Perceptions of service offerings	Paixão and Marlow (2002) GAO (2005)	These studies demonstrated that perceptions drive user decisions about the choice of mode, as short sea shipping is perceived to be inferior to truck options.
Route-specific factors	Brooks and Trifts (2008) IGMS (2008) Bendall and Brooks (2011) Brooks et al. (2012)	Perceptions of road congestion drive interest in short sea shipping in both Europe and North America; the most promising demand comes from those corridors/routes with dense urban agglomerations and highway chokepoints.

Table 20.3 presents a number of factors at play in the supply of short sea shipping. Like the factors influencing market demand, supply factors in this segment of the transport sector are complex, made more so by short sea demand often being smaller than demand for trucking, rail and deep-sea services. Shipping companies are unlikely to contemplate providing a short sea service in a market with marginal demand or one-way demand only. There is greater pressure on the operator to consider a market where route characteristics favour short sea development. For example, Brooks and Trifts (2008) identify the congestion in the Hudson River area of New York as so severe that there is an interest on the part of trucking companies to bypass this congested part of the I-95 corridor. Likewise, where tourism is a key factor driving demand, seasonality limits the service demanded to only part of the year, and a year-round operation is simply not wanted (Expert Review Panel, 2012).

Table 20.3 Relevant supply factors

Supply factor	*Key studies*	*Relevant findings*
Route characteristics (including seasonality)	Brooks et al. (2006) Brooks and Trifts (2008) Global Insight and Reeve and Associates (2006) IGMS (2008) Expert Review Panel (2012)	The existence of congestion on the truck route, poor road conditions or bottlenecks may encourage a shipowner to consider the route ready for short sea shipping. Insufficient funds for highway and bridge upgrades may promote short sea shipping usage. Some routes do not have the demand to support year-round service.
Route pricing	García-Menéndez et al. (2004) Brooks et al. (2012)	These studies examined the impacts of pricing of service options and their influence on choice of mode, and hence demand for various service options.
Vessel suitability and availability	Kruse and Hutson (2010) Expert Review Panel (2012)	Channel and port draft (depth) and the existence of locks will limit the type of vessels suitable for use on a service. The market reality is that potential operators may not be able to find a suitable vessel to charter to meet the demand requirements in a timely way as vessel supply from shipyards often lag demand.
Availability of ports interested in serving the short sea shipping market	Brooks et al. (2006) Brooks et al. (2012)	The availability of secondary ports, and the interest of those ports in serving as feeders or short sea hubs, were key factors in the absence of North American east coast short sea shipping. On the other hand, Australian ports were interested in capturing any and all potential business and so were not the barrier to service development.
Market-specific services offered by the carrier	López-Navarro (2013)	To provide an example, López-Navarro discusses the availability of unaccompanied haulage as a feature of a service offering that may attract traffic from road transport.
Citizen support	IGMS (2008) Brooks et al. (2014)	Car drivers facing congested highways apply pressure on public authorities to find alternative routes/modes for freight; as short sea shipping often involves less investment in public infrastructure, taxpayers find a willing partner in governments.
Regulations affecting ship operators	CPCS (2008) Brooks and Frost (2009) Brooks (2012) Brooks et al. (2014)	Regulation can serve to encourage or discourage short sea shipping development and is discussed later in this section.

The price the operator chooses to charge can limit interest in purchasing the service and research has generally found that short sea services for freight must be discounted heavily to attract interest (MariNova Consulting, 2005; Brooks et al., 2012). Only if priced below the end-to-end price for trucking and rail can the service be an attractive alternative; handling charges at two ports coupled with local delivery charges can price short sea freight out of consideration. Ship operators find that willingness-to-pay market research is an invaluable addition to deciding whether they can offer a new short sea service, given discussions with operators in the course of the research conducted by Brooks et al. (2012).

Vessel suitability and availability are critical elements, particularly in new start-ups rather than route extensions. As noted in Table 20.3, a potential operator may not be able to find a suitable vessel for charter in a timely manner; in a start-up it is unlikely that the operator will invest in ordering a new vessel until the new service has proven its worth. This can then become a 'chicken-and-egg' situation as vessel supply from shipyards can lag behind demand by up to two years.

As noted in Table 20.3, Brooks et al. (2006) identified that the fact that many North American ports perceived their role in the marketplace as a 'gateway' port, the idea of being a feeder port was not appealing. No such barrier to development was found in Australia (Brooks et al., 2012).

Carriers may also develop short sea business by being creative in the service offering. Unaccompanied haulage may make the difference between having enough volume for a feasible service or not. López-Navarro (2013) identified such an opportunity in Europe, while MariNova Consulting explored that in eastern Canada on routes to Newfoundland (MariNova Consulting and Geoplan Opus, 2005).

There is also a substantive literature on the promotion of short sea operations as a policy option to address carbon emissions from trucking (e.g. Vanherle and Delhaye, 2010), and governments and citizens may see that suppliers need encouragement to offer short sea services.

Supply and demand are dynamic and interactive, and iterative decision making often results. Cargo owners often examine the value they get from various transport suppliers as a group of options and determine whether inventory carrying costs with a particular supply chain are too high and if they should hold more/less inventory to minimise their costs or optimise their supply chain against production and warehousing costs. The demands on a single carrier's operations are also dynamic, relating to sales to/by new customers/suppliers and the loss of other customers/suppliers.

After examining the specific route and its hinterland (or catchment areas) in the context of these supply and demand factors, more detailed examination of the promise of the specific proposed short sea route can be made. There are a number of relevant studies that demonstrate how the pre-business case may be conducted for a specific route or set of routes. For examples in North America, see MariNova Consulting (2005); Brooks et al. (2006); Global Insight and Reeve and Associates (2006); Brooks and Trifts (2008); and CPCS (2008). For examples, in the UK see Saldanha and Gray (2002) and in Australia, see Bendall and Brooks (2011); Brooks et al. (2012); and Brooks (2012). The focus is then for the potential operator (or policy analyst if the government is considering subsidising a route for public interest reasons) to answer four questions:

(1) Where there is a short sea service already available, are the existing volumes sufficient to sustain an economically profitable service over the decision time horizon?
(2) What is the nature and seasonality of demand? Is the volume of traffic on each leg of the service adequate or are there some legs that must be cross-subsidised by others?
(3) What non-regulatory factors limit the ability of a potential operator to charter vessels internationally and therefore limit ship operator options (like the depth of channels)?

(4) Where the demand volumes are not adequate, do the existing land-based traffic patterns offer promising traffic development opportunities that might support the short sea shipping operations if modal switching is induced through policy changes or subsidies?

20.6 Competition

20.6.1 Direct competition for freight short sea services

The availability of direct competition for freight short sea services is route and mode dependent. For many routes, ferries exist as an extension of the highway network, to cross water where a bridge would be too expensive to build for the volume of traffic or to serve islands that would otherwise be isolated. In these cases, the sole direct competition could be air services. There are instances, however, where short sea services are competitive with road or rail alternatives, where the sea route is less congested or circuitous, or where government policy discourages the use of roads. A good example of this is shipping from Finland or from Sweden to western Europe, where road connections through Russia are very cumbersome, and where truck transport through Germany is discouraged.

For an example of direct competition, there is the St Lawrence–Great Lakes region of Canada to illustrate (see Figure 20.1 for port locations). The idea of operating a short sea shipping service between the Atlantic coast port of Halifax, Nova Scotia and a Great Lakes port like Hamilton, Ontario has been studied numerous times (two of which are publicly available, MariNova Consulting (2005, 2015) and pits short sea services proposed against trucking and/or rail operations in the region. The concept of operating between Montréal and Sept-Îles on the north shore of the St Lawrence River was explored by CPCS (2011).

Ontario is the largest consumer and manufacturing market in Canada, and is viewed as having sufficient critical mass and market demand factors for short sea shipping to provide an alternative to increasingly congested highways through the most populated part of Canada and the perceived high cost of rail service in the region. Besides regulatory hurdles

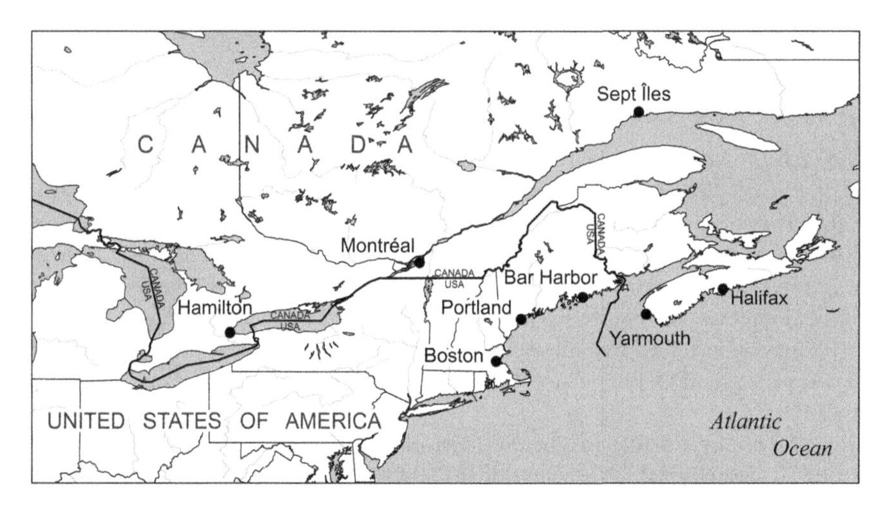

Figure 20.1 Map of ports mentioned in this chapter
Source: created for the authors by James Boxall of the Dalhousie University GIS Centre

relating to Canada's cabotage laws and the cost of marine pilotage in the St Lawrence River, such a service would need to traverse several sections of the St Lawrence Seaway, which is closed for approximately 12 weeks each winter. The need to maintain year-round supply chains also makes it difficult to compete with other modes. While international shippers are prepared to accept weekly service, domestic shippers (often the same companies) require at least daily service to keep store shelves and production lines full. In the North American context, it would be difficult for short sea shipping to compete with truck and rail service even if all regulatory barriers would be removed (MariNova Consulting, 2005, 2015; CPCS, 2011). The most appropriate approach for any operator considering a greenfield short sea freight operation is to look for markets not well served, or impossible to serve by these modes, and congested and dense urban agglomerations that encourage the use of alternate modes.

20.6.2 Indirect competition for freight short sea services

The Canadian province of Newfoundland and Labrador, whose largest population concentration is located on an island in the Gulf of St Lawrence, provides several variations of ferry and short sea shipping. A Canadian government-owned ferry service provides a constitutionally mandated ferry service between the mainland port of North Sydney, NS and Port-aux-Basques, NL with four ro-pax ferries. It also operates a 10-week seasonal service to Argentia, Newfoundland, which is 90km from the capital city of St John's. Marine Atlantic carries a mix of passengers, autos and commercial traffic. Commercial traffic consists of 'straight trucks', 'trailers only' and 'tractor trailers' and amounts to about 100,000 such vehicles per annum (Marine Atlantic, 2013–14). A private company, Oceanex, provides a container/ro-ro service with three ships, operating Montréal–St John's and Halifax–St John's. This service competes with the trucking companies who use the Marine Atlantic service as well as providing an alternative service to those same companies. Both Marine Atlantic and Oceanex have a similar share of Newfoundland's commercial traffic. Perishable cargo and high-priority cargo tends to move via the ferry, while retail goods tend to move with Oceanex, whose shipping terminal is located close to 70 percent of the population and where Newfoundland's major distribution centres are located.

20.6.3 Direct competition for passenger services

As with freight, competition is route dependent, and impacted most by options available on the route. For example, Marine Atlantic, in addition to its freight service, also carries slightly more than 300,000 passengers and their vehicles every year (Marine Atlantic, 2013–14). It was once the principal means of entering and leaving the province, having handled over 500,000 passengers per annum in the last years of the 1990s, but consumers now enjoy considerable choice of both domestic and international flights, from Newfoundland and Labrador to Canadian destinations such as Toronto and Halifax, and international destinations such as Newark, New Jersey, various Florida destinations and Dublin. These services have had an impact on ferry passenger volumes (Table 20.4).

In the case of Nova Scotia (see below), historically the province had three ferry services across the Bay of Fundy, which carried close to 500,000 passengers per annum. They carried a mix of Canadians and Americans travelling in automobiles, recreational vehicles and buses. In the decade after 2001, the market for ferry travel shifted. While American visits declined, those

Table 20.4 Passenger volumes: Marine Atlantic and St John's International Airport

Year	*Ferry passengers (1)*	*Air passengers*
2014	307,256	1,576,130
2013	329,348	1,489,128
2012	354,103	1,448,309
2011	365,398	1,371,417
2010	383,576	1,318,713
2009	397,745	1,166,849
2008	387,642	1,184,655
2007	415,652	n/a
2006	405,336	n/a

Note: 1. For two services: North Sydney–Port-aux-Basques and North Sydney–Argentia.
Source: Shippax (various years); St John's International Airport Authority (2015)

who were travelling took a flight or cruise to the province. It seemed to residents that not as many Americans were visiting their province because not as many foreign licence plates were seen every summer, but visitors were flying to Halifax, renting a car and, in effect, travelling incognito. In the case of cruise passengers, they can board a vessel in New York, unpack their bags and stay in the same cabin for a three, five, seven, 10 or 12-day cruise to Nova Scotia and the Maritime provinces, seeing many of the same sights they would if they drove their own vehicle.

20.6.4 Indirect competition for passenger services

With the advent of low-cost airlines, the world has become a smaller place and the choice of holiday destinations has grown exponentially in the past two decades. Not only that, but the cruise industry has also emerged as a rival and real alternative for both high-end and budget travellers. New and exotic destinations are now within reach and are affordable for consumers in virtually every market. Cruises are no longer limited to traditional Caribbean, Mexico or Alaska routes, but now also include the Baltic, Mediterranean, Oceania, South America, Antarctica, Southeast Asia and the North West Passage. Consumers in New England or northern Europe can fly to destinations such as Thailand, Vietnam, Indonesia, Australia/New Zealand, which may have been out of financial reach before. In North America, the time available for a vacation is more condensed than before, which favours two, three or five-day 'breaks' as opposed to the two or three-week vacation that was prevalent in the 1960s–1980s. These developments have put enormous pressure on traditional tourism offerings including the ferry industry. Indirect competition in the leisure passenger ferry services must now include the many ways that potential ferry passengers can spend their leisure time.

20.7 The role of regulation in short sea economics

Regulation can serve to encourage or discourage short sea shipping development. Brooks et al. (2006) undertook a comparison between Canadian and US jurisdictions, concluding that US legislation deterred the development of anything other than international shuttle services between Canada and the US. This was followed by a later study comparing the Canadian situation with Europe's expanded cabotage market, and Brooks and Frost (2009, p. 242) concluded 'Canada's cabotage restrictions and duties on the purchase of non-Canadian vessels significantly increased feeder and regional short sea start-up costs. These are, literally, sunk costs and thus not recoverable in the event the service is unsuccessful.' In particular, they noted duty of 25 percent on all foreign-built vessels creating a disincentive for vessel replacement, supported by the fact that the average ages in some vessel categories were more than 20 years, and some more than 30 years. The duty was initially imposed to protect Canadian shipbuilding, even though a vessel longer than 129 metres could not be built in a Canadian shipyard. After the publication of this research, the Canadian government removed the duty on all vessels greater than 129 metres in length overall (loa), and replacement purchases ensued.

Turning to Europe, the Brooks and Frost (2009) comparison study noted that the European Commission argued that short sea shipping was a success given the extent of modal shift from road to sea. The Commission's Marco Polo programme provided significant support for short sea operators. Brooks and Frost (2009, p. 242) identified that key factors in EU initial success in developing short sea shipping included:

(1) the cabotage regime plays a large part in the development of short sea services. For example, Europe has a very open cabotage regime, and enjoys a dynamic short sea sector as a result;
(2) most short sea feeder operators charter their vessels rather than own them, to ensure maximum flexibility and ability to respond to market conditions and demand.

The key to understanding the regulatory influence is to do regulatory comparisons for every country involved in a particular route where short sea shipping is being considered. Using the factors identified by Brooks et al. (2014) for their study of six South American countries as a framework, it is instructive to compare not only country regulations but these same factors should be compared between modes where there is significant competition between the modes. Table 20.5 presents the critical regulatory factors and how they may direct specific market factors into being advantageous for the supplier of short sea shipping in one country over an alternate supplier registered in another.

One regulatory factor affecting the transportation industry, for which there is a dearth of research, is the issue of costs of channel maintenance, road provision, air navigation systems and rail trackage (known as way costs). Maritime transport has few such costs that are directly imposed on shippers and so competes fairly with highway where highways are provided as a 'public good'. However, the way costs of rail, if provided by the private sector, as is the case in North America, for example, impose significant infrastructure costs that provide an advantage to short sea shipping. Regulation so as to fully cost all externalities including way provision, safety and emissions alter the operating environment for the carrier and thus impact the cost and services offered in the market and ultimately the playing field on which competition takes place.

In the final analysis, the operator must answer the following questions about the regulatory environment. Do these regulatory factors:

- force the operator to only consider a direct shuttle service when a triangulation or multi-porting strategy would work better?
- limit the size of the potential market for short sea operations?
- add to the costs of supplying a short sea service such that the service is unlikely to be price competitive against other transport options?
- limit the ability of the potential short sea operator to charter vessels internationally and therefore induce the shipbroker to extract a premium price for the domestic charter?

Table 20.5 Regulatory factors and their impacts

Regulatory factor	*How it impacts the development of short sea shipping*
Domestic cabotage	The operator is unable to choose the best route to meet demand if more than one of the ports called is in the cabotage-protected region and the ship is not the required flag of registry/nationality.
Bilateral cabotage agreements	Two countries agree to mutual recognition but the problem in the row above remains.
Shipbuilding requirements	This policy protects domestic shipbuilding and deters the operator from choosing the best ship for the route, or from right-sizing the vessel for service characteristics. It is common for shipbuilders to specialise in particular ship types, which may not be purpose-built for the particular route.
Foreign ownership restrictions on national flag shipping	This may prevent the operator from accessing adequate finance to support the operation, particularly during start-up. Foreign owners may be able to provide capital at a lower cost.
Shipping taxation	If the jurisdiction of the route imposes significant taxation on shipping operations, the operator is at a disadvantage if a foreign flag operator with lower taxation is allowed to compete on the route.
Crewing requirements	A vessel required to use more expensive national crew or a larger crew than found under other flags of registry will then be less able to compete with non-maritime modes of transport.
Carbon pricing for fuels	If the operator uses a fuel with additional carbon taxes in competition with an operator paying the global price for fuel, the first operator is placed at a competitive disadvantage.
Emissions-control areas	If emissions-control areas apply to all operators, then the competition is fair; if, however, a ship's fuel is restricted and that used by other modes is not, the competition rules are not fair.

Source: the first column is adapted from Brooks et al., 2014

The resulting answers impact whether the short sea operator will see a business opportunity in the particular market.

20.8 Case study 1: the private-sector ferry service (Tallink)

The AS Tallink Grupp is an Estonian company that provides ferry services in the Baltic region and has its roots in the break-up of the former Soviet Union in 1989 and the independence of the former Baltic Republics of Estonia, Latvia and Lithuania. Tallink Grupp is a private limited company that was formed in 1989, initially owned by the Estonian government until 1996 when a management buy-out took place. In 2006, it purchased the Swedish-Finnish company, Silja Line (one of the pioneers of the cruise ferry concept in the 1970s) and in the same year it also acquired the Baltic operations of Attica Enterprises of Greece.

The company's rise to prominence in the ferry industry is remarkable. By 2015, Tallink employed almost 7,000 people and had revenues of €945 million, earnings before interest, taxes, depreciation and amortisation of €181 million and net profits of €59 million (Tallink Grupp, 2016b). In this case study, we examine the demand for short sea services in Tallink's market, the company's approach to the supply of shipping and the regulatory environment it operates in, before drawing conclusions about why it is an example of a successful operation.

20.8.1 Demand factors

Overall, the Tallink Grupp carried 9 million passengers in 2014 along with autos and some freight on five routes (Table 20.6).

The northern Baltic region where Tallink operates has a population in the region of 20 million, with half in Sweden, a quarter in Finland and the remainder in the three republics of Estonia, Latvia and Lithuania (see Figure 20.2).

Demand for the company's services does not reflect this population split in that, in 2015, 50% of Tallink's customers were Finnish, and the next largest group were Estonian (20%) then Swedish (12%) (Tallink Grupp, 2015). About 71% of the company's revenue comes from routes

Table 20.6 Tallink Grupp traffic volume, 2014

Route	*Passengers*	*Autos*	*Freight*
Helsinki–Stockholm	1,202,928	47,763	15,872
Turku–Stockholm	1,359,991	89,028	70,355
Helsinki–Tallinn	4,518,013	783,388	167,411
Stockholm–Riga	676,676	77,808	13,537
Tallinn–Stockholm	955,108	71,421	22,013

Source: Shippax, 2015, used with permission

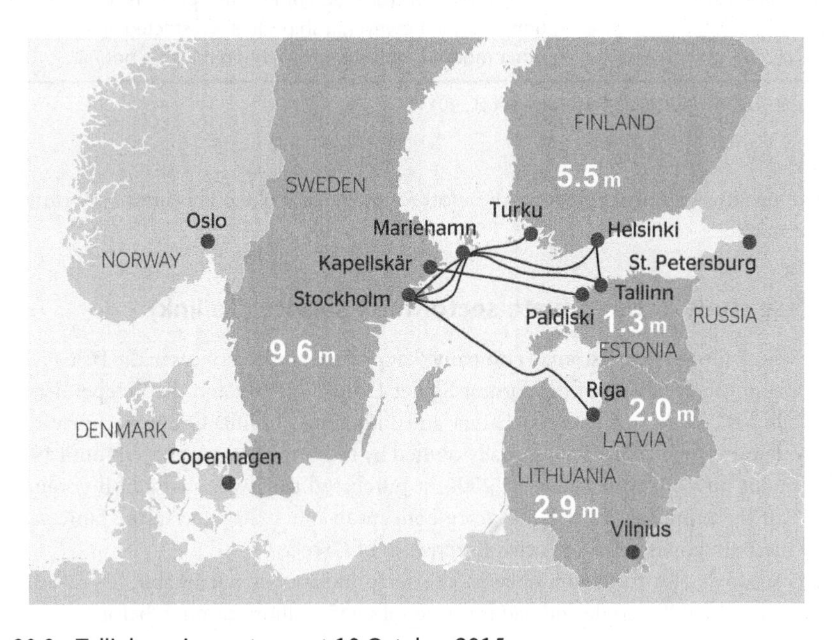

Figure 20.2 Tallink service routes as at 10 October 2015
Source: used with the permission of Tallink

connected to Finland, followed by 15% on routes connected to Sweden and 4% Latvia–Sweden. Tallink's overall market share in the northern Baltic is 46% (Tallink Grupp, 2016a). Realising that its primary markets may be reaching saturation and are experiencing slower growth, Tallink has been targeting consumers in non-Baltic countries and as of 2015, 10% of the company's customers come from outside this region. Bookings through its website are offered in 17 languages (Tallink Grupp, 2016c). It operates 21 sales offices in the Nordic region and has a network of 1,800 travel agents worldwide.

20.8.2 Supply factors

As of writing, all of Tallink's 16 vessels (nine cruise ferries, five ro-paxes and two ro-ros) operate 12 months per year. Cruise ferry pricing is adjusted to attract customers in the off-season, and conference facilities onboard the vessels produce incremental revenue. Restaurant and shop sales are the largest single source of revenue, and Tallink is currently the 11th largest retailer of duty free products in the world, just behind Beijing, Paris and Frankfurt airports (Tallink Grupp, 2016c). Like most northern-hemisphere ferry services, most revenue is earned in the third quarter of the year, followed by the second and then fourth quarters. Annually the company is profitable, but the first quarter is generally loss making; Tallink covers its cost of sales in the quarter but not its administration or financing costs.

As an originator of, and current provider of, cruise ferry operations, Tallink augments its cruise ferry operations by offering full vacation packages, including hotel stays in Tallink-owned hotels in Tallinn (four) and Riga (one). The company charges a wide variety of fares, which change according to the season, the day of the week and the sailing time. It offers packages that include a range of cabin sizes, meal choices and hotel accommodations at each destination. This approach to pricing draws on revenue-management principles used in the airline and hotel industries and is a key factor in the company's profitability. Moreover, Tallink has the youngest fleet in the Baltic, which results in lower operating and maintenance costs; the company has also been able to charter or sell older, less efficient tonnage. It is also progressive in keeping its product current and fresh; in 2014, its two oldest cruise ferries (*Silja Serenade* and *Silja Symphony*) each underwent €15 million upgrades (Tallink Grupp, 2015).

20.8.3 Regulatory factors facing Tallink

Starting in 2002, Tallink embarked on an ambitious new building programme, taking delivery of seven new vessels from 2002 to 2009. Revenues grew tenfold from 1998 to 2012 and the company paid a dividend to its shareholders for the first time in 2013. The biggest regulatory issue facing the company is compliance with the Sulphur Emission Control Area (Tallink Grupp, 2014). To help achieve lower emissions and reduce fuel costs, in June 2015 the company ordered a €230 million LNG-fuelled ro-pax to operate the Helsinki–Tallinn route.

20.8.4 Conclusion: why is Tallink a successful operation?

Tallink is successful because it operates on a purely commercial basis, on a year-round basis and with a diversified product mix in both mature and growing markets. The company also benefits from having strong competition on several routes (Stockholm–Helsinki, Helsinki–Tallinn). The cruise industry has also provided an element of competition, which the ferry industry has been able to withstand by offering products that cater to both leisure and business users. It has been financially successful through sophisticated revenue management and careful attention to onboard product offerings. The company is owned mostly by its management and is also listed on the Nasdaq OMX Baltic stock exchange, which imposes a market discipline. Its performance since the management buy-out in 2006 has been impressive, with revenues increasing from €405 million to €921 million, and passenger levels growing from 3 million to 9 million in 2015 (Tallink Grupp, 2015). It provides an excellent example of sound management practices in the ferry industry.

20.9 Case study 2: the subsidised ferry service – Nova Star Cruises

In this case study, the demand for ferry services in a marginal or fledgling market is examined, seeking to understand the factors described in Tables 20.1 –20.3 and draw conclusions about whether the market has adequate demand for an operation, whether the operator has taken the appropriate approach to supplying the service and examining the regulatory environment for the operation, before drawing conclusions about why a ferry or short sea operation may fail or may require significant government support. The government's role in supplying a subsidised ferry service will be discussed in the conclusions to this chapter.

Ferry service(s) between Nova Scotia, Canada and Maine (US) were operated from the mid-1950s until 2009. The Canadian federal government, through its Crown Corporation Marine Atlantic, operated one service between Yarmouth, NS and Bar Harbor, ME until it was 'commercialised' in 1996 and transferred to Bay Ferries. An unsubsidised service ran between Yarmouth, NS and Portland, ME from 1971 until 2005, offered by a succession of private companies including Prince of Fundy Cruises, which operated an ageing 1,500 passenger cruise ferry *Scotia Prince* (for port locations, see Figure 20.1).

In 1998, a year after Bay Ferries took over the Bar Harbor to Yarmouth service from Marine Atlantic, the company introduced the first of its Incat fast ferries (known as 'The Cat'). These were very popular with the travelling public, particularly as they made day trips possible from Bar Harbor, and as a result traffic levels were very buoyant. In 2004, the rival owners of the *Scotia Prince* withdrew the vessel from service as their passenger numbers had declined and there were environmental issues with the terminal in Portland. Even though the Yarmouth–Bar Harbor route was experiencing robust traffic levels, Bay Ferries responded to the demise of the *Scotia Prince* service by operating their fast ferry on two routes: Yarmouth–Bar Harbor and Yarmouth–Portland. Traffic thereafter began to decline, and the company began to request (and receive) a subsidy from the Nova Scotia provincial government. When this request reached C$9 million in late 2009, the province declined to provide the subsidy, the company withdrew the vessel from service and sold it. Table 20.7 shows the declining passenger numbers from 2001 to 2009 when the Bay Ferries' subsidy was cancelled.

The decline in passenger traffic was attributed by the Expert Review Panel (2012) as being due to the SARS crisis of 2003, the disadvantageous exchange rate between the Canadian and US dollars (the Canadian dollar appreciated from US$0.64 to US$0.94 over the 2002–8 period (Expert Review Panel, 2012, p. 15)), the requirement for passengers to carry passports post 9-11 and the rising price of automotive fuel dampening the American penchant for taking long road trips. Furthermore, international travel to Europe and cruises in the Caribbean had attracted US citizens with passports, while those without one were motivated to travel to places like Las Vegas and other US destinations. Vacations had become shorter in duration and the 'city break' and 'staycation' (vacation at home) had become the new North American tourism patterns. For those looking to visit Atlantic Canada, the cruise industry emerged as a new option, with a large array of products and ships for every budget. It became possible to board a cruise ship in New York or Boston and stay in the same cabin for up to 12 days and enjoy many of the same

Table 20.7 Yarmouth–Maine traffic, 2001–9

Year	*Passengers*	*Passenger-related vehicles*
2000	306,520	69,588
2001	309,583	67,647
2002*	310,000 (est)	65,000
2003	291,498	64,513
2004	242,334	60,752
2005**	149,507	42,100
2006***	120,561	34,738
2007	104,797	30,910
2008	84,518	25,376
2009	75,639	n.a.

Note

* *Scotia Prince* data not available – estimate of total; ** *Scotia Prince* service ceases; *** Bay Ferries commences combined service to Portland and Bar Harbor

Source: CPCS, 2010, figure 4.15, p.64 and table 4.21, p. 66

experiences previously reached by driving; cruise passengers visiting Halifax grew from less than 100,000 in 2000 to about 250,000 in the 2010 and 2011 cruise seasons (Expert Review Panel, 2012: exhibit 3.6, p.18).

The cancellation of the ferry service between Yarmouth and Maine was a blow to the south-western Nova Scotia region as it in fact lost two ferry connections in a period of five years. Had the operator maintained the daily Bar Harbor–Yarmouth service, it might have remained successful, as the ferry type was suitable for that purpose (shorter route and less ocean swell).

After Bay Ferries terminated its service and sold *The Cat* after 2009, there ensued a four-year process to revive the ferry service between Yarmouth and Maine. A group of business people and other stakeholders in the Yarmouth region established the Nova Scotia International Ferry Partnership to urge the government to reinstate the service. A government-appointed advisory panel (Expert Review Panel, 2012) was tasked with examining whether a new service could be financially sustainable, what type of service would be appropriate and what type of financial support would be needed over what time frame. A political decision was made to support a subsidised ferry service to serve the economic development interests of south-west Nova Scotia.

While a Bar Harbor–Yarmouth ferry option was one option considered, the Expert Review Panel (2012) concluded that a cruise ferry service connecting Yarmouth and Portland would be the option most likely to generate the tourism traffic desired by the south-western part of the province. It also concluded that a re-established ferry service could be feasible at around 130,000 passengers per year but that this number of passengers could only be achieved with a significant investment in tourism facilities, restaurants and attractions and a considerable marketing effort to promote use of the service and the province as a destination. It also noted that prices for tourism products had dropped and that aggressive pricing would be needed. As the Expert Review Panel (2012) noted, this was a significant gap given 2009 traffic levels (Table 20.7). Other interested parties also advised the government to decide upfront how much it would be willing to contribute to get a service re-established and to launch a worldwide marketing campaign to find an operator.

After receiving the Expert Panel's report, the Nova Scotia government issued an initial call for proposals in late 2012 which only produced two bids, neither of which was deemed acceptable. In 2013, a delegation attended the Shippax ferry conference and made a presentation, describing the 'opportunity' and outlining the contribution the Nova Scotia government was prepared to make to a new venture (C$3 million a year for seven years, i.e. up to C$21 million to re-establish the service). A new call for proposals elicited three proposals from Quest Navigation (a joint US-Singapore company), the UK-based P&O Ferries (owned by DP World) and one other company.

An evaluation committee consisting of government bureaucrats, two representatives of the International Ferry Partnership and a consultant chose Quest Navigation to operate the service with a new 160 metre length overall (loa), 1,215 passenger ro-pax ferry built by ST Marine in Singapore. Another committee was struck to negotiate a contract between the company and the government of Nova Scotia. Between announcing a tentative deal and concluding the deal, a provincial election was held and the incumbents were defeated. The new government wanted to review the deal and its ratification was delayed until November 2013. The final letter of offer stipulated STM Quest would receive start-up funds of C$13 million, marketing funds of C$2 million and capital upgrades of C$7.2 million. The funds were to be disbursed over seven years, with C$10.5 million in the first year and C$1.5 million every year thereafter.

In the fall of 2013, the province of Nova Scotia signed an agreement with Quest Navigation and ST Marine to re-establish the ferry service between Yarmouth, Nova Scotia and Portland, Maine. The new ferry service would operate under the brand name Nova Star Cruises and was initially contracted to provide daily round-trip service from 15 May to 2 November 2014.

Early bookings were discouraging. There were also significant regulatory impediments like the US Federal Maritime Commission requirement for ticket cancellation insurance. Customs processing and terminal facilities were also not in place as quickly as needed. Bookings picked up over the course of the summer and reached about 59,000 passengers instead of the predicted 95,000 in the first year (Expert Review Panel, 2012). How much of this was due to pricing at levels more than double those proposed in the Panel's report is not clear. The lower than expected passenger volumes probably reflected the late contract signing (November 2013) and a delayed start in marketing the service. It is also not clear how effective those marketing programmes were once they did get under way. Wholesale sales in the tourism market (i.e. to tour companies) have longer lead times than retail sales (i.e. the customer who books his own travel), as bus and tour operators plan their product offerings and conclude contractual arrangements more than a year ahead; that is, marketing a cruise ferry for the summer of 2014 to the tour and bus companies needed to begin even before the fall of 2013.

What was the result? The company used more than the expected C$21 million it was promised over seven years in less than six months of operation and ultimately required C$28.5 million to complete its first season. A US$5 million letter of credit promised by the Governor of Maine never materialised, and the government of Nova Scotia ultimately provided the premium for cancellation insurance required by the Federal Maritime Commission. In spite of low fuel prices and a further 23 percent depreciation in the Canadian–US exchange rates, traffic levels in 2015 were even worse than 2014. The province promised it would continue to support the service; however, by October 2015 they had failed to confirm to the incumbent operator, Nova Star Cruises, that it would have a contract, let alone a subsidy for 2016. It also failed to recognise the impact this would have on marketing the service to wholesale buyers for the 2016 season.

20.9.1 Evaluation of the demand and supply factors

An assessment of demand had been made by the Expert Review Panel in 2012, indicating that it was unlikely that break-even would be reached until at least year 7, and concluding that any decision to re-establish the service would be a political one and 'risky' (Expert Review Panel, 2012, p. ix). Circumstances had changed significantly since the heyday of the early 2000s, and closing the gap between 75,000 passengers in 2009 and the break-even number projected by the

Expert Review Panel would require improving the local tourism experience, the currency remaining devalued, marine fuel and automotive fuel prices remaining low, and Americans increasing the number of passport applications so that Nova Scotia could re-emerge as a favourite destination for the 55 million people living in the US north east.

Vessel availability also became a critical supply issue in the effort to establish the new Portland–Yarmouth cruise ferry service. While the Expert Review Panel did not have a mandate or charge to search for available vessels, it concluded that: 'There are several vessels potentially available on the world market that could be physically accommodated in Yarmouth and rendered suitable for a cruise ferry to Portland' (Expert Review Panel, 2012, p. vi). In parsing this conclusion, there are a number of criteria that were suggested to the Nova Scotia government: (1) not all vessels suitable might be available; (2) the turning basin in Yarmouth would not accommodate many vessels and only a sub-set of ferries would be suitable; and (3) that it was highly likely that a vessel that was available might need to be adapted or refitted to become a cruise ferry. The details of a vessel that would be deemed to be suitable were outlined as: (1) able to carry at least 1,000 passengers; (2) have at least 600 berths; (3) car-carrying capacity of at least 200 cars (assuming some travellers on foot and some via tour bus); (4) a cruising speed of 18–20 knots (to meet schedule requirements); (5) not more than 25 years old; and (6) vessel characteristics that would allow berthing and turning in Yarmouth (draught of 6 metres maximum and a maximum length in the vicinity of 150 metres) (Expert Review Panel, 2012, p. 46). On the last characteristic the Panel was unable to be specific as alterations to the harbour could be effected to address these limitations, but they had been assured that any vessel with its length above 150 metres would have manoeuvring problems.

The Expert Review Panel identified 74 ferry vessels in the world that might be investigated for availability. Of these, the number actually available for charter was not investigated as this was not part of the Panel's mandate and would require the panel to conduct primary research. The Panel concluded that several were 'potentially available'. Of the 74, only four were too old, all but one could meet the cruising speed requirements and car-carrying capacity was an issue. However, only 27, or about one-third, were of an appropriate length and draught. Finding a vessel with the technical ability to service Yarmouth was a significant factor in the Panel's deliberations. Further investigation of that dataset identified that, of those 27, the ability to offer berths and cabins for a 10.5 hour crossing diminished prospects for a feasible service by a cruise ferry; only 13 had more than 125 cabins, e.g. were closer to the concept of a cruise ferry, and only five had more than 200 cabins. The question of vessel availability was left to the province, which would have to undertake a Request for Proposals (RFP) or more thorough investigation to determine whether a suitable vessel could be found.

The ferry that was eventually brought into service, *Nova Star*, had capacity for 1,215 passengers and approximately 300 autos, a length of 161 metres and a cruising speed of 21 knots. With 162 cabins (325 berths), it cost US$180 million when ordered for LD Lines' service between Le Havre and Portsmouth. The vessel was new but not a cruise ferry, as Nova Star Cruises led officials and the travelling public to expect. It was a ro-pax, originally designed to serve a four-hour crossing rather than an 11-hour overnight crossing. While the Expert Review Panel had been approached by the operators of the *Nova Star*, they were of the view that a ro-pax with insufficient berths and cabins for an overnight experience was not the ideal choice of vessel for the Portland–Yarmouth route; this essential point was ignored by the politicians who wanted to announce a service prior to an expected election.

Few details are available regarding *Nova Star*'s financial model, except that the proponents seem to have had little money of their own and were totally reliant upon funding from the province of Nova Scotia. It also appears that the contribution of ST Marine was limited to providing the *MV Nova Star* at (presumably) a favourable charter rate for a new vessel. There was also some attractiveness in starting with a new vessel. Details of the other two proposals have never been made public, but it is likely that the restricted turning basin of 160 metres in Yarmouth Harbor would have limited the number of vessels available, and cruise ferries that are able to sail into and out of Yarmouth would also likely be older tonnage.

In autumn 2015, having lost confidence in Nova Star Cruises, the province issued another, limited request for proposals. In late 2015 it announced that Bay Ferries had been selected to again provide service between Yarmouth and Portland. Surprisingly, given the Expert Panel's previous recommendation to re-establish a cruise ferry service, in March 2016, Bay Ferries revealed that it had chartered a high-speed catamaran from the US Navy, the former Hawaii Superferries' *Alakai*, which it has renamed *The Cat*. The new ten-year contract, most of which has been made public, calls for the province to pay start-up costs of C$4.1 million, C$10.2 million for year 1 operations, C$9.4 in year 2 plus refit costs of C$9 million and an undisclosed management fee. The new contract includes no risk for the operator, with all costs guaranteed by the province. Terms beyond the second year were not disclosed, nor was there discussion regarding any potential impact of a rise in fuel prices, as had taken place during the previous incarnation of high-speed ferry service on this route.

Whether the agreement with Bay Ferries is optimal or not, and there are many critics (New Start Nova Scotia, 2016), it is clear that the province is committed to supporting the service, as it is deemed to be of great importance to the south-western region, particularly its tourism industry. Of Nova Scotia's overall tourist market of 1.9 million visitors, US visitors account for only 9 percent, or about 180,000. Until 2014, however, Nova Scotia was experiencing a long-term decline in US visitation which was exacerbated by the hiatus in ferry service between 2010 and 2014. The resumption of ferry service has had a positive impact. Overall US visitation in 2015 was up 10% from 2014, with New England up 12%. Auto visitation from the US was up 17%, while that from New England and Maine was up 15%. It led to a 41% increase in room nights sold in the Yarmouth and Acadian Shores region between 2013 and 2014 and significant, new property and real-estate investments in the Yarmouth area (Nova Scotia Tourism Agency, 2015). Data for 2015 were not yet available at the time of writing.

Whether ferry traffic will ever reach the levels prior to 2008, particularly in the bus and group tour markets, or whether those markets have simply vanished or found new destinations, remains for future analysis and marketing efforts. As of 31 March 2016, the appreciation of the Canadian dollar by 7.5 percent in the first quarter of 2016 (Bank of Canada, 2016) and the rise in crude oil prices by 41 percent (with knock-on effects on both automotive and marine fuel prices) since hitting a first quarter low on 11 February 2016 (US Energy Information Administration, 2016) are not positive indicators of future adequate growth in US auto visitation.

20.10 Conclusions about the public-sector role in short sea and ferry services

The discussion in this chapter has identified the conditions under which short sea shipping and ferry services may be successful if there is sufficient private-sector interest in supplying the service, demand warrants and government regulation does not deter ship operators from providing the service. To accomplish this, the chapter has provided a typology of vessels used in this industry along with a discussion of how demand factors impact supply of service considerations by operators; relevant regulatory considerations are explored and discussed but both examples operate international services where local cabotage laws are not applicable. However, sometimes the market fails or regulations deter operators from participating in an otherwise attractive situation. The primary question then becomes: what should governments do when the market fails? This section explores the question of government intervention in the provision of short sea and ferry markets, and when that might be appropriate given the above framework and two case studies.

One cause of market failure can be thin routes or service to remote communities not having adequate market demand. Merkert (2012) notes that there must be both political and public will if transportation by ferry or short sea freight services are to be developed to connect remote communities with more populous regions and their cultural, medical, social and other services. Governments then become involved in ensuring that these public services are offered in a citizen-acceptable way that does not drain the public purse yet affords economic development opportunities to be realised. As noted in the case of the *Nova Star*, the province of Nova Scotia had the political will to subsidise the ferry in order to realise tourism opportunities and associated economic development for this otherwise quiet part of Nova Scotia.

As identified by Brooks and Frost (2012) in their study of shipping service to communities in Canada's Arctic, there is a need for governments to understand intimately the circumstances of the particular situation and the role that will be played by both RFP restrictions and public service obligations (PSOs). They note that it is important for government to understand the business model components that will help potential suppliers identify opportunities to grow the business profitably and sustainably. In the case of the Nova Star Cruises, it was clear that the Nova Scotia government failed to understand that with a ro-pax, the business model would never succeed in breaking even, let alone earn a profit, and that a true 'cruise ferry' operation was required to achieve profitability, as the Expert Panel had suggested.

The research by Baird (2012) into the provision of remote services by ferry to the Scottish islands indicates that setting out the contract terms involving the public-service obligations that will accompany any subsidy, the government may miss the opportunity to ensure that the market is served by private-sector operators who require no or less subsidy. As a complement, Cowie (2012) identifies the considerable savings in the subsidies required that may be achieved through competitive tendering. He argues that non-tendered ferry operations tend to perform worse in terms of technical efficiency while tendering results in enhancements on the route. His review presents conflicting evidence as to whether efficiency is enhanced or reduced through the tendering process; he concludes that there must be an adequate level of competition for tendering to ultimately work. Finally, Baird et al. (2010, section 5.3.34) have identified in their examination of 27 tendering processes in the Danish ferry market that there was a change in operator in only two cases; they concluded that the tendering process seeks to improve efficiency with existing operators more than it seeks to identify new suppliers. The absence of competitive and suitable bids can be a telling signal.

In the case of the *Nova Star* presented above, it seems to the authors that the lack of cruise ferry vessels available to meet the requirements for service on the route has resulted in less than satisfactory financial results, among other factors like the timing of wholesale marketing. While politically unacceptable at the time (in the middle of an election), in hindsight calling off the awarding of the ferry contract may have been better for the taxpayers of the province of Nova Scotia who have now invested significant funds (more than C$40 million in the first two years and with more expected annually); these are funds that are not, and will not be available for other government activities. In conclusion, public-service obligations may be defined politically and not necessarily on commercial or economic grounds.

Perhaps most interesting when comparing the European and Canadian cases in this chapter is that the European Cabotage Regulation 3577/92 sets out public-service obligations as well as conditions for public-service contracts and state aid. The European Commission recognises that there is a need to protect ferry services to remote communities; Cabotage Regulation 3577/92 allows member states to intervene by imposing PSOs and by setting out very clearly the terms under which public-service contracts to meet those obligations may be undertaken. In Canada, there are no standard regulated guidelines for public-service contracting (RFP development) and public-service obligations in the development of ferry operations in spite of the country's extensive coastline. Perhaps this is something that the federal government of Canada could do to assist provinces in meeting their public service obligations on routes where short sea freight and ferry operations replace or augment highways.

Note

1 Project cargo is usually defined as large, oversized, heavy, high-value or mission-critical pieces of cargo. Project cargo can include shipments of components that may require disassembly to transport and reassembly after delivery.

References

Baird, A. J. (2012). Comparing the Efficiency of Public and Private Ferry Services on the Pentland Firth between Mainland Scotland and the Orkney Islands. *Research in Transportation Business and Management*, 4, pp. 79–89.

Baird, A., Wilmsmeier, G. and Boglev, Y. (2010). Scottish Ferries Review Final Report Part (a): Methods of Ferry Service Delivery and Operation, Competition, Procurement and Environmental Issues. Edinburgh: Transport Research Institute, Edinburgh Napier University. www.gov.scot/resource/doc/935/0105632.doc (accessed 16 October 2015).

Bank of Canada (2016). *Bank of Canada Banking and Financial Statistics, April 2016*. Ottawa: Bank of Canada, www.bankofcanada.ca/wp-content/uploads/2016/04/bfs_april16.pdf (accessed 9 March 2017).

Bendall, H. B. and Brooks, M. R. (2011). Short Sea Shipping: Lessons for or from Australia. *International Journal of Shipping and Transport Logistics*, 3(4), pp. 384–405.

Brooks, M. R. (2012). Maritime Cabotage: International Market Issues in the Liberalization of Domestic Shipping. In Chircop, A., Letalik, N., McDorman, T. L. and Rolston, S. (eds), *The Regulation of International Shipping: International and Comparative Perspectives: Essays in Honor of Edgar Gold*. Leiden: Martinus Nijhoff, pp. 293–323.

Brooks, M. R. and Frost, J. D. (2009). Short Sea Developments in Europe: Lessons for Canada. *Canadian Transportation Research Forum Proceedings*, 44, pp. 235–49.

Brooks, M. R and Frost, J. D. (2012). Providing Freight Services to Remote Arctic Communities: Are There Lessons for Practitioners from Services to Greenland and Canada's Northeast? *Research in Transportation Business and Management*, 4, pp. 69–78.

Brooks, M. R., and Trifts, V. (2008). Short Sea Shipping in North America: Understanding the Requirements of Atlantic Canadian Shippers. *Maritime Policy and Management*, 35(2), pp. 145–58.

Brooks, M. R., Hodgson, J. R. F. and Frost, J. D. (2006). *Short Sea Shipping on the East Coast of North America: An Analysis of Opportunities and Issues*. Halifax: Dalhousie University.

Brooks, M. R., Puckett, S. M., Hensher, D. A. and Sammons, A. (2012). Understanding Mode Choice Decisions: A Study of Australian Freight Shippers. *Maritime Economics and Logistics*, 14, pp. 274–99.

Brooks, M. R., Sánchez, R. and Wilmsmeier, G. (2014). Developing Short Sea Shipping in South America: Looking beyond Traditional Perspectives. *Ocean Yearbook*, 28, pp. 495–525.

Buzzone, A. (2012). Guidelines for Ferry Transportation Services, TCRP Report 152. Washington, DC: Transportation Research Board.

Cowie, J. (2012). The Cost of Remote Transport Services in the Single European Market: The Case of the Scottish Western Isles Ferries. *Research in Transportation Business and Management*, 4, pp. 90–6.

CPCS (2008). *Study on Potential Hub-and-Spoke Container Transhipment Operations in Eastern Canada for Marine Movements of Freight* (TP14876E). Ottawa: Transport Canada.

CPCS (2010). *South West Nova Scotia Transportation Study*. Ottawa: CPCS Transcom.

CPCS (2011). *Feasibility Study: Marine Cargo Transport to the North Shore, Quebec City*. Ottawa: CPCS Transcom.

Energy Independence and Security Act of 2007, Pub. L. 110–140, title XI, Sec. 1121(a), Dec. 19, 2007, 121 Stat. 1761, section 55605.

European Commission (1999). *The Development of Short Sea Shipping in Europe: A Dynamic Alternative in a Sustainable Transport Chain. Second Two-Yearly Progress Report*. COM (1999) 317 final, 29 June. Brussels: European Commission.

Expert Review Panel for a Yarmouth–US Ferry (2012). *Re-establishing a Yarmouth–US Ferry: An Analysis of the Issues*. Report for the Province of Nova Scotia, Departments of Economic and Rural Development and Tourism and of Priorities and Planning. http://maryrbrooks.ca/?attachment_id=745 (accessed 19 October 2015).

García-Menéndez, L., Martinez-Zarzoso, I. and Pinero De Miguel, D. (2004). Determinants of Mode Choice between Road and Shipping for Freight Transport: Evidence for Four Spanish Exporting Sectors. *Journal of Transport Economics and Policy*, 38(3), pp. 447–66.

Global Insight and Reeve and Associates (2006). *Four Corridor Case Studies of Short-Sea Shipping Services: Short-Sea Shipping Business Case Analysis*. Report for the US Department of Transportation Office of the Secretary, August 15, www.marad.dot.gov/wp-content/uploads/pdf/USDOT_-_Four_Corridors_Case_Study_(15-Aug-06).pdf (accessed 9 August 2015).

Gouvernal, E., Slack, B. and Franc, P. (2010). Short Sea and Deep Sea Shipping Markets in France. *Journal of Transport Geography*, 18(1), pp. 97–103.

Government Accountability Office (2005). *Short Sea Shipping Option Shows Importance of Systematic Approach to Public Investment Decisions* (05-768). Washington, DC: United States Government Accountability Office.

Institute for Global Maritime Studies (2008). *America's Deep Blue Highway: How Coastal Shipping Could Reduce Traffic Congestion, Lower Pollution, and Bolster National Security*. Tufts University, September.

Kruse, C. J. and Hutson, N. (2010). *North American Marine Highways* (NCFRP Report 5). Washington, DC: Transportation Research Board.

López-Navarro, M. Á. (2013). Unaccompanied Transport as a Strategy for International Road Hauliers in Ro-Ro Short Sea Shipping. *Maritime Economics and Logistics*, 15(3), pp. 374–494.

Marine Atlantic (various years). *Annual Report*, 2013–14, 2012–13, 2011–2012. St John's: Marine Atlantic.

MariNova Consulting (2005). *Short Sea Shipping Market Study* (TP14472E). Ottawa: Transportation Development Centre of Transport Canada.

MariNova Consulting (2015). *Short Sea Shipping and Extending the Seaway Season*. Ottawa: Canadian Transportation Act Review Panel.

MariNova Consulting and Geoplan Opus (2005). *The Social and Economic Impact of Marine Atlantic Drop Trailer Service*, Transport Canada.

Merkert, R. (2012). Editorial: Management of Transport in Remote Regions. *Research in Transportation Business and Management*, 4, pp. 1–2.

Morales-Fusco, P., Saurí, S. and De Melo, G. (2013). Short Sea Shipping in Supply Chains: A Strategic Assessment. *Transport Reviews*, 33(4), pp. 476–96.

New Start Nova Scotia (2016). Ferry Tales: Different Operator, Same Blank Cheque. 1 April, http://newstartns.ca/2016/04/ferry-tales-different-operator-same-blank-cheque/

Nova Scotia Tourism Agency (2015). Key Market Profiles. https://tourismns.ca/key-market-profiles (accessed 20 October 2015).

Paixão, A. and Marlow, P. (2002). Strengths and Weaknesses of Short Sea Shipping. *Marine Policy*, 26, pp. 167–78.

Saldanha, J. and Gray, R. (2002). The Potential for British Coastal Shipping in a Multimodal Chain. *Maritime Policy and Management*, 29(1), pp. 77–92.

Shippax (2006–15). *Shippax Market*. Halmstad: Shippax.

St John's International Airport Authority (2015). Personal communication to authors, 27 February.

Tallink Grupp (2014). Company presentation, March, www.tallink.com/presentations (accessed 2 June 2016).

Tallink Grupp (2015). Company presentation, March, www.tallink.com/presentations, p. 18 (accessed 2 June 2016).

Tallink Grupp (2016a). Corporate Fact Sheet, March, www.tallink.com/presentations (accessed 2 June 2016).

Tallink Grupp (2016b). Unaudited consolidated interim financial statements for the twelve months of the 2015 financial year (1 January 2015–31 December 2015), 29 February, www.tallink.com/reports#tabs-content-3 (accessed 13 May 2016).

Tallink Grupp (2016c). Company presentation, March, www.tallink.com/presentations (accessed 2 June 2016).

Transport Canada (2006). *Making Connections* (TP14552). Ottawa: Transport Canada, http://armateurs-du-st-laurent.org/fileadmin/Documents/TMCD/Rapports_et_documents/EN/making-connections.pdf

US Energy Information Administration (2016). West Texas Intermediate Spot Price FOB (Cushing, OK per barrel US dollars), www.eia.gov/dnav/pet/hist/LeafHandler.ashx?n=PET&s=RWTC&f=D (accessed 15 May 2016).

Vanherle, K. and Delhaye, E. (2010). Road versus Short Sea Shipping: Comparing Emissions and External Costs. *Proceedings of the International Association of Maritime Economists*, Lisbon, July.

21

Competition and complementarity in road freight

Key drivers and consequences of a dominant market position

Jonathan Cowie

21.1 Introduction

From whatever economic perspective road freight is viewed, the one characteristic of the mode that stands out above any other is that it is a 'competitive' industry. This chapter will examine the factors that make the sector 'competitive' and then consider what kind of outcomes this leads to. As a consequence, the chapter is largely structured around the idea of competition, what that actually means, how it has been defined, how it works and how this is evidenced in the functioning of the road freight sector. Most of the chapter is based on the UK industry, although examples are drawn from other parts of the world, particularly the US.

The chapter is broken down into five sections, beginning with the general freight market and definitions of road freight haulage. The historical context of the industry, which has a past of strong economic regulation, is then reviewed. The main issue of competition is considered through a mainstream economic approach, hence largely neoclassical, although some consideration is given to other economic perspectives of competition and their applicability to the sector. The outcomes this leads to is then reviewed, and the mode examined as part of the whole supply chain (i.e. a complementary factor input). The chapter ends with an examination of the public economics of road freight, which covers both the environmental aspects and growing research area of road freight and energy use.

21.2 The freight market and definitions of road freight haulage

Figure 21.1 outlines the main divisions and terms often used to describe the different types of operators found within the road freight sector. In many ways the purpose of presenting Figure 21.1 is to illustrate that there is no such thing as a single road freight industry, and furthermore that the multitude of divisions and differing types of operation arise because of the underlying economics of the market. Note also that the terms included in Figure 21.1 are far from exhaustive

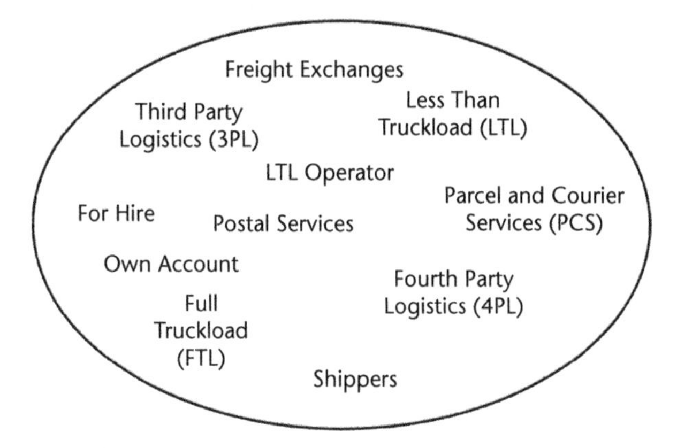

Figure 21.1 The divisions and operators in the road freight industry

and also that many are interrelated. In order to make some sense of the different types of operation and the need for such variety (all of which are mentioned at some point in this chapter), it is easiest to begin at a basic level. If it is assumed that road freight services are demanded on the basis that the consumer is able to provide consignments that will either take up a whole truck or will not (which in general is a valid assumption), then this very neatly divides the market into truckload (FTL) and less than truckload (LTL). In the latter sector, in order to minimise costs, the function of providing full loads is taken up by a third party, which is where some of the other types of operators mentioned in Figure 21.1 can then be introduced, although it should be stressed there is a high degree of cross-over between many of these.

In terms of LTL, consolidation could be undertaken by a parcel and courier service, an LTL operator or an intermediary, such as fourth-party logistics, an online auction or a freight exchange. The last mentioned of these, intermediaries, would have in the past been undertaken by freight forwarders, however, these now relate almost exclusively to shipping and air freight services. 'For hire' services tend to straddle both the FTL and LTL markets, with many operators providing contracted services in both sectors. Within the general LTL market, operations are based around some form of hub-and-spoke system, where large volumes are moved between key points and then broken down into smaller loads to be distributed locally. This usually requires a large investment in bulk break facilities, such as storage and warehousing capacity. PCS services will normally deal with the high-value small-package segment of the market, where all vehicles are owned (and branded) by the company and staff directly employed. The whole PCS model is generally a fixed model with a set maximum capacity and is based on movement through the network and quick delivery times, as this minimises the need for storage capacity. It tends to operate in the very short term, with distribution depots normally found in low-rental areas, as ultimately central locations are not required.

Full truckload generally operates point to point, hence requires considerably less investment in supporting facilities and equipment than LTL. Own account is where the transport function is undertaken in-house, hence operated by a fleet owned by the primary company, thus for example, supermarket chains tend to operate their own distribution channels. For hire is where the transport function is contracted out to a third party, either directly or through a shipper, and is based on truckload shipments. A good example occurs in the quarrying industry, which tends to involve the primary company contracting the transport function of shifting the uncut stone for processing to a number of usually local independent haulage companies. Third-party logistics providers (3PL) in many respects fall between LTL and FTL, in this context (FTL) this would occur where the whole logistical function of a particular company is contracted out to a third party. Transport services are integrated with other elements of the supply chain, hence a 3PL operator will normally also provide warehousing, inventory management, packaging and other related activities.

In terms of business models/modes of operation, both FTL and LTL tend to employ a wide variety of different approaches depending on the market conditions, but generally the key to operation is a high degree of flexibility and contracting/use of intermediaries. Vehicles can be owned or leased, drivers directly employed or contracted, and haulage services contracted or brokered to third parties, usually owner-operators. What this results in is a real mix, which varies from the 'simple' for hire owner-operator driver, to firms with a 'base' level operation of vehicles and drivers directly employed, with additional services that meet fluctuations in demand contracted over and above the base level either through the leasing of vehicles and contracting of drivers to fully sub-contracting the whole service. As such, this is a very flexible mode of operation and hence offers a very high degree of flexibility in the supply side of the market. The classic example is the US LTL operator Landstar System, which employs its own fleet of nearly 5,000 tractor units and drivers, but also acts as intermediary/contractor for around 10,000 independent owner-operators.

21.3 Contemporary historical background: the economic regulation of road haulage

In contemporary times, road haulage has been an industry that throughout the world has been heavily regulated and publicly controlled, with some countries such as the UK even going as far as nationalising large segments (through the Transport Act 1947), albeit that a subsequent change in government led to the 'denationalisation' of those elements that could be sold six years later. In other parts of the world, market entry, company mergers, carriage rates and fleet sizes have all been carefully monitored and controlled at some point in time.

Reasons for regulation in the sector are unclear, although at the time, such measures were evidently high on the political agenda. Ponsonby (1938) for example states that at the time of the passing of the Road and Rail Traffic Act 1933, which introduced qualitative and quantitative licencing into the UK sector, further regulatory measures such as fare regulation were also being seriously considered. In the US, Silverman et al. (1997) highlight that strong lobbying from the incumbent railroads in the 1930s led to the for-hire sector of the US industry coming under the regulatory control of the Interstate Commerce Commission. Pressure to regulate also came from within the industry itself, as many hauliers had suffered during the Great Depression and held strong concerns over the destabilising effect that competition could have in the prevailing economic climate. Rothenberg (1994) however convincingly argues that in reality none of the aforementioned reasons led to the imposition of regulatory controls, but rather measures were solely motivated by politicians' desire to rescue the railroad industry and protect its pricing structure. Accepting the importance of the sector to the wider economy and hence one 'worthy' of protection, the US Congress passed the Motor Carrier Act 1935 that resulted in the imposition of strong controls over market entry and fleet sizes and the establishment of regional price boards to determine both route and freight specific price floors. This had the required effect in terms of industry stabilisation, and in fact led to generous returns to those in the sector (Silverman et al, 1997).

Changing perceptions on the role of regulation and the effect it was having on the industry led to a change in the regulatory environment. In the UK, the Geddes Report in 1965 noted that the regulatory regime that was in place was having little effect on the specific policy objectives (such as improving public safety and reducing road congestion) and in fact was having a detrimental effect by lessening competition. This produced restrictive workings that resulted in the inefficient use of vehicles and lessened the adaptability of the industry, i.e. classic x-inefficiency behaviour. The Geddes recommendations were largely written into the Transport Act 1968, which deregulated the industry, although at the time, this was considered to be a change in the emphasis of regulation rather than deregulatory per se (away from economic, more toward qualitative). In the US during the 1970s major concerns were raised over inflation levels and the impact that regulatory bodies were having in countering the possible effects competition would have on market prices in the regulated sectors. This led to a considerable shift in political ideas over the strong economic regulation of transport industries, with airlines (US Deregulation Act 1978), railroads (Staggers Act 1980), interstate buses (Bus Regulatory Reform Act 1982) and interstate trucking (Motor Carriers Act 1980) all reregulated in terms of removal of control over entry, company size and freight carriage rates. As such this represented a considerable shift towards market principles. With deregulation of the interstate sector, several states followed suit, however the vast majority continued to regulate, with 60 percent of states continuing to impose entry restrictions and 40 percent still continuing to impose strict rate regulations (Allen et al., 1990, cited in Trick and Peoples, 2012). This unsatisfactory situation continued until the passing of the Airport Improvement Act in 1995 which prohibited state and local authorities from the regulation of rates, routes or services within the transportation industries (Trick and Peoples, 2012).

Throughout the European Union (EU), most member states had some form of economic regulation of the sector, with similarities and differences that resulted in a considerable variation in the extent to which the sector was under regulatory control. Regulation of international intra-EU traffic was limited to the for-hire sector and regulated through a combination of bilateral agreements which imposed quotas that limited the number of movements or community permits which allowed a limited number of vehicles free movement within the EU. Lafontaine and Malaguzzi Valeri (2009) highlight that bilateral agreements in many cases also specified price brackets at which transactions could occur, which firstly became 'suggested' in 1984 and were then completely abolished in 1990. Note in this example, regulation has quite a different purpose to that highlighted before, basically, despite the existence of a 'common' market, this was to limit imports. Deregulation of the whole sector began in the 1980s with a substantial annual increase in the number of community permits being issued, and complete deregulation throughout the EU achieved in 1998 when the limit on cabotage[1] authorisations was abolished. The level of cabotage, however, remains relatively low, being less than 1 percent of all tonne kilometres in the majority of member states. Responsibility for qualitative regulation remains the remit of member states, although again driven by the single market this area has also seen a degree of commonality emerging, such as in the requirements to be met in pursuing a profession as a transport manager or driver as well as basic rules for tolls and user charges for heavy goods vehicles.

Since the removal of regulatory controls in most developed countries, what has emerged is a highly competitive industry, hence the next sections examine this aspect and the outcomes that have emerged as a consequence.

21.4 Competitiveness in road freight services

As stated in the introduction, when examining competitiveness in the sector the main perspective taken is from a mainstream economic view. However, where relevant, aspects from other schools of thought are used to give further insight. In what follows, the extent to which the industry meets the requirements of five basic assumptions of perfect competition are examined, with the British road freight industry used as the primary example, although data and research are also considered from elsewhere, particularly the US.

21.4.1 Large number of buyers and sellers

This assumption ensures that all firms in the market are price takers, none are of a size to dominate the market and hence exhibit brand loyalty which may give them a market advantage not based on cost. As regards road freight, in 2009 in the UK (the last year for which statistics are available), there were 30,149 registered enterprises in the road freight sector and 91,000 who held an HGV operator's licence. With a combined fleet size of 397,200 vehicles, this gives an average fleet size of just over 4.36 vehicles, suggesting that most firms in the sector are relatively small. Furthermore, the Freight Transport Association reported in 2008 that three-quarters of the sector operated a fleet size of two vehicles or less, with many of these operated by owner-drivers (FTA, 2008), hence owner-controlled firms. There does exist some larger firms with bigger fleets, with around 10 percent of operators owning half the fleet. Exactly why the industry should be structured in this manner is difficult to ascertain, however one possible reason is that not only is the market segmented between truck load and less than truck load, but also divides into national and local, with the local market serviced by small local firms, but the national market by a combination of smaller and larger operators. Although registrations have fallen considerably in more recent times due to the effects of the 2008 recession, the large number of registrations that remain more than suggests that this criterion is met. Furthermore, within the EU only two countries, Luxembourg and the Netherlands, have an average number of employees for road enterprises of more than ten (AECOM, 2014), further underlining that small-sized firms dominate.

As regards buyers, the situation is far less clear. General perceptions are that buyers do have a market advantage and hence some influence over the price. This advantage arises from two aspects. Firstly, the size of some of these firms is considerable and thus allows them to offer regular business to the HGV operator, which will always put them at a market advantage. The second aspect is the regulatory framework, in which in simple terms buyers (within reason) are unregulated, whilst operators are with regard to vehicle condition, driver qualifications and vehicle weights. These provide a base level which legally should not be breached, however in reality can be. Whilst this aspect of the position of buyers does not detract as a competitive driver for road freight, it may nevertheless breach the conditions of perfect competition, and some of the possible consequences of this will be considered later in the chapter.

21.4.2 Homogeneous good

Due to the derived nature of demand for transport services, it could be perhaps naively argued that all transport services match this criteria, as ultimately all that matters is that individuals and goods are transported from A to B; consequently, how that activity is performed is basically the same. There are, however, considerable differences between various modes of transport, although perhaps less so in freight compared to the passenger sector. Reputation does play an important part in the industry and hence does provide some form of product differentiation. Past research has also shown that shippers rate service quality factors higher than they value shipping rates (McGinnis, 1990), although one may assume that finding is based on the presumption of little variation in rates, hence its importance may be overstated. Countering the importance of reputation is that most firms in the industry operate under contract to large freight-handling firms or big fleet operators (Lacey, 1990), and this facet places very strong downward pressure on prices which tends to ease substitutability between operators.

21.4.3 Perfect information

Perfect information relates to the fact that both suppliers and consumers within an industry should have available to them all of the information required to make a rational economic choice, whether that be with regard to a purchase or a business decision. As regards production, the sheer scale of the number of operators would suggest there are few trade secrets within the industry, hence that would suggest something approaching perfect information. As regards purchase, a simple UK-wide search of 'road haulage' services in yell.com produced 8,399 listings, and even restricting this to 'Edinburgh' still produced 50, albeit that this does include a mix of house moving, liquid and uplifting services. More objectively, the wide availability of professional services in the acquisition of freight transport services in the form of freight forwarders also suggests that a 'true' market price could be obtained by the buyer. McMullen (1987) highlights that one of the arguments against US trucking deregulation in the 1970s was that small firms would be driven from the market due to the difficulties in obtaining information in a market with increased rate-making flexibility. Certainly in the case of the US, this facet was overcome by the massive increase in brokerage firms that followed deregulation, hence the brokering market that emerged largely re-established the symmetry of perfect information. There would therefore appear to be something approaching perfect information within the sector.

21.4.4 Barriers to entry

All industries have barriers to entry, this is one aspect that cannot be avoided – one simple barrier is to have the basic business skills required to operate successfully within a given industry. The most common barriers to entry, however, normally involve an aspect of cost, for example either the size of the initial investment or the risk attached to that investment (i.e. sunk costs), therefore this is the aspect considered here. The basic capital equipment is the vehicle itself. The exact cost of a complete tractor unit and trailer is difficult to determine due to the wide range of models and types available, however, typically these range from around £80,000 to £100,000 for a tractor unit and £30,000 for a trailer. Rigids cost similar prices. There is also a buoyant second-hand market, with three- and four-year-old tractor units going for around £30,000. As such, this does not represent a prohibitive cost to any individual. There are the costs of licencing and driver training, but these again are not prohibitive. The large number of owner-drivers in the industry would also suggest that barriers to entry are not extensive, otherwise over time such operators would ultimately be driven from the market. Few barriers is also underpinned by academic research, with Silverman et al. (1997) finding that the level of new entry significantly increased after the deregulation of US interstate trucking, with the number of small companies (known in the US as Class 3) almost tripling in the ten years following the 1980 Act. This not only suggests few barriers to entry, but also that entry is likely to be quick.

21.4.5 Non-increasing returns to scale

The last aspect considered is the requirement that companies have similar non-increasing returns to scale in production. As such, scale effects can have a significant effect on the extent to which competition is present in the market, and in many respects this is the critical factor with regard to competitive sustainability. Consequently, economies of scale are key to understanding the economics of the mode. Most of what follows is drawn from the research literature on the topic, however, already within this chapter it has been highlighted that a large number of operators exist within the industry. This fact in itself would tend to suggest that, certainly at the general level, scale economies are not significant and certainly not a barrier to competition. If it did, then this would have led to company merger and acquisition. As noted above, the market entry of small operators into the US interstate market following deregulation is also clear evidence of few scale economies. The reality of the situation therefore indicates few scale economies and hence the question would seem to have been answered. Nevertheless, examination of the research literature should give a clearer picture of what the critical factors are in the general case and the extent to which this is widespread or segment specific.

Most of what follows is the research generated by the deregulation of the US industry in 1980. As a consequence, it is over 30 years old and, due to the availability of data, was all focused on the top 100 firms. The terms of reference are only on large and not small companies, which is a major oversight as the latter by far made up (and still make up) the majority of the industry. Taken at face value, this may bias the results towards finding scale economies. Nevertheless, the vast majority of studies have found either slight increasing returns or constant returns, with the former result tending to be 'explained' by the characteristics of the freight that is being shifted. Harmatuck (1981) for example, in a study of TL and LTL operators, found small increasing returns below the average-sized firm and large decreasing returns above that point. For the average-sized firm producing both truckload and LTL services, scale effects summed to unit. By implication, this surprisingly suggests that exclusively truckload firms experience substantial increasing returns. For haul lengths, increasing returns were found, hence longer hauls lead to lower average costs. As larger companies will generally have longer-haul lengths (Bayliss, 1986), these two results could be related and hence (significant) scale effects may only relate to haul length and not firm size. Spady and Friedlaender (1978) reported a large degree of acquisition and merger activity during contemporary times, suggesting large-scale effects. Their results however strongly indicated this may have been driven by qualitative aspects of the freight carried, rather than the amount of freight carried per se. In purely physical output terms, all scale effects were found to be exhausted at an annual output level of 60 million tonne miles, with an average firm size just under 20 million tonnes (note that is the average of the top 100). Based upon current British loading levels and mileages, this equates to around a minimum efficiency scale fleet size of just over 285 trucks, with an average of around 95, but given the different contexts, these figures can be viewed as top-end estimates. These findings the authors described as being due to larger firms having longer hauls, larger loads and smaller proportions of LTL, and thus termed them economies of density and utilisation, and as a consequence most mergers were strategic and not related to (firm size) scale economies. The findings were then incorporated into a hedonic function, which found constant returns, suggesting that equality in loads, haul lengths and LTL traffic would allow smaller operators to compete with larger ones on cost. Given different market sectors, such as local, intrastate and interstate, this would strongly suggest any scale effects that are present are not a barrier to competition, as all operators within a given sector would experience the same returns.

As regards network effects in the LTL market, Wang Chiang and Friedlaender (1984) found that well-defined networks with high concentrations in traffic flows led to substantial cost savings. When these were omitted, scale returns were found to sum close to unity, hence suggesting constant returns to scale. When network variables were added to the underlying function, scale effects were found to be considerable, with potential savings estimated at the upper level of around 70 percent (note that is in relation to the size of the network, not the factor inputs). Given previous findings, larger networks will be associated with longer and heavier loads, hence this tends to confirm the importance of these factors.

All of the above is based on the US industry, with virtually nothing from other parts of the world. One exception is Bayliss (1986), who examined scale effects through a survival analysis. Based on firms in south-east England, what Bayliss found was that there had been a gradual 'drift' over the period to larger-size firms, hence suggesting strong scale effects. Nevertheless, due to the structure of the industry, with many small-sized firms, when this was formally modelled it produced an MES point of only six vehicles. Further work also suggested that economies were only related to vehicle size, and as larger operators tend to have larger vehicles, this 'explains' the results relating to scale, hence as with Wang Chiang and Friedlaender (1984), this suggests economies of density rather than scale. Finally, Flath (2001), based on a sample that included firms of all sizes, examined scale economies in the (loosely) regulated Japanese trucking industry over the period 1970 to 1990. Controlling for differences in average haul weight and distance hauled produced almost uniform constant returns, with the result being applicable to both route firms and area firms.

Even given the age constraints of the research, the above does give some insights into the economics behind road freight, although to some extent what emerges is a chicken and egg argument. Summarising, significant scale effects are only related to the size of shipment and the length of haul, not the size of the firm. In other words, scale effects are associated with the demand side of the market and not the supply side. Based on the US body of research, this was found to be the case for both truckload and perhaps surprisingly LTL traffic, the latter potentially due to the development of an efficient brokering market, although the last paper reviewed did point to some potential network savings. This in some ways is where the age of the research becomes a major factor, as it pre-dates the development of large international courier services (such services at the time were provided by national postal services). The two largest, UPS and FedEx, do not feature in the dataset and hence as an operational model remain unevaluated. A second facet is the development in the US of 'mega' carriers, i.e. 5,000+ fleets. Very few existed in the 1970s and 1980s, and these have emerged as a vibrant business model since that period. Within the current top 100 US trucking firms, 15 would fit into this category. Research in the course of writing this chapter, however, makes it apparent that these have been driven by strategic motivations rather than (scale-induced) cost savings, in other words by market considerations and very much by corporate ambitions.

21.5 Consequences of a competitive road freight sector

In many respects the classical economists may have been correct with their thoughts on competition, in the fact that it was a means to an end rather than an end in itself, and as such not worthy of any great thought. The point being that where the real significance of competition lies is in what it results in, which is considered in this section.

21.5.1 Dominance of the wider freight market: modal comparisons

By far the most notable outcome of the competitiveness of the sector is that it has come to dominate the entire freight market, a position that has been achieved by capturing market segments from other modes and dominating new and emerging ones. This is clearly shown in Figure 21.2, which gives the long-term patterns in modal share for Great Britain for the period 1953 to 2014.

Within Britain the figures are slightly skewed by the modal share of water, which in contemporary times almost exclusively relates to the transportation of North Sea oil, hence constitutes a very distinctive market sector. Examining the chart with regards to the land-based modes, the most distinguishing feature is the rise of road freight. This has followed two distinct phases, pre-1980s and post-1980s. In the former period growth was achieved by a combination of modal shift gains and total market growth, however, in the post-1980s period the vast majority of

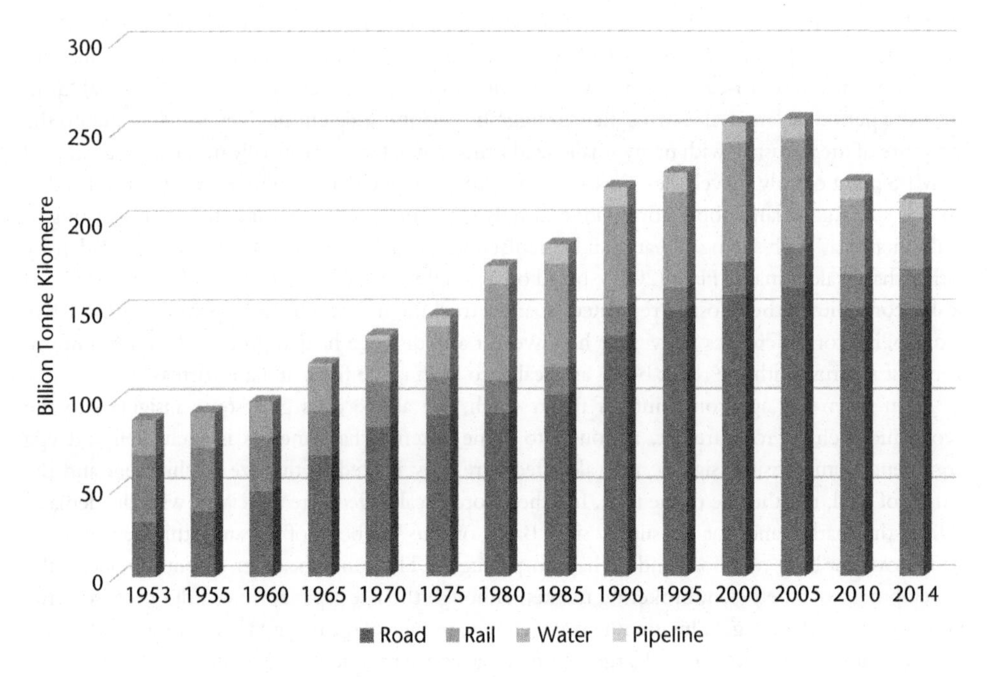

Figure 21.2 Goods transported (tonne kilometre), Great Britain, 1953–2014
Source: drawn from DfT (2015) statistics

gains have come purely from total market growth. In other words, the competitive aspect of the industry has enabled it to gain market share directly from rail in the early part of the period, but once most of these gains were exhausted, further growth has come from adapting to the needs of an expanding market. This is reflected in the fact that since 1985 the increase in road freight tonnage is almost double the increase in the total. In terms of the areas which have seen the strongest growth, Figure 21.3 gives a breakdown by commodity for 1990 and 2010, the latter year the one for which there is the most recent statistics.

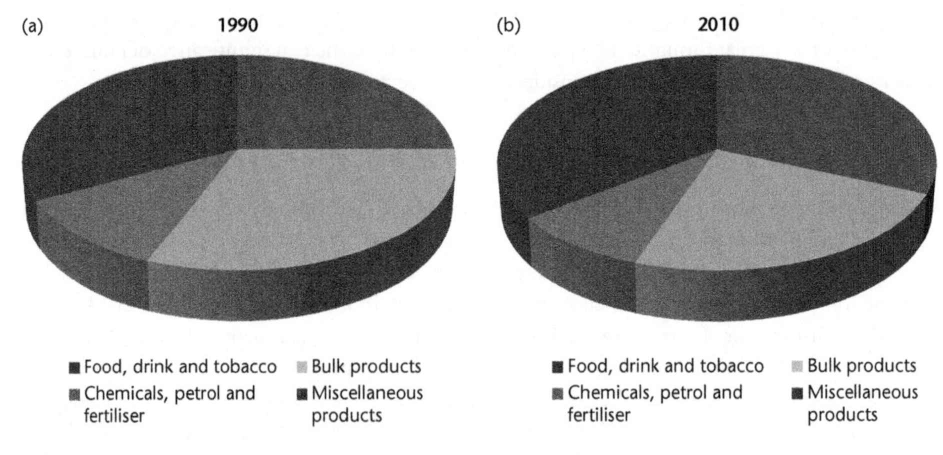

Figure 21.3 Commodity breakdown, road freight, 1990 and 2010, by tonne kilometre
Source: drawn from DfT, 2014

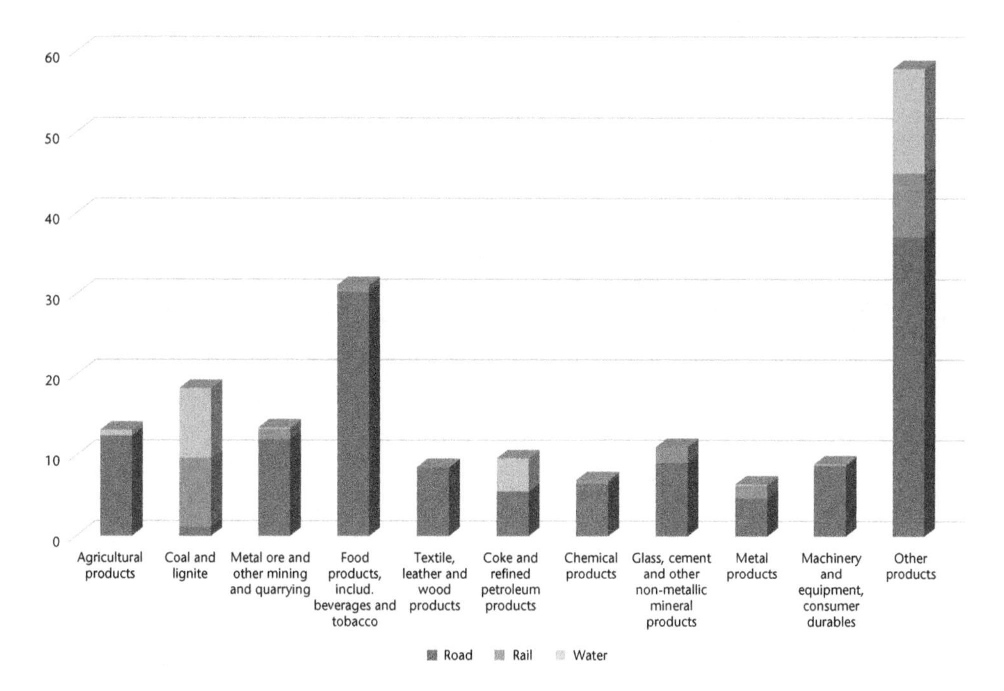

Figure 21.4 Commodity breakdown by mode of transport, 2014, billion tonne kilometre
Source: drawn from DfT, 2015

From Figure 21.3 the most notable expansion has occurred in the proportion of food, drink and tobacco products, which has risen from just over 25 percent in 1990 to just under 32 percent by 2010. In terms of percentage growth of haulage, this represents an absolute increase of almost exactly one-third. Whilst a sweeping and simplified statement, this change would have been strongly driven by wider structural change that occurred in the UK economy over the period, as most of this occurred in the ten years following 1990 (i.e. a wash-over from the 1980s). The largest decrease has been in bulk products, which has seen a 7 percent relative decline, which transmits into a 20 percent absolute decrease, which again reflects broader structural change.

Figure 21.4 shows the commodity breakdown by mode of transport for actual tonnages in 2014. What it underlines is the dominance of road haulage. Of the eleven categories shown, it completely dominates in eight of them, has a large share in two of the remaining three, and only in the coal and lignite sector does it have a small presence. In many respects, the breakdown of the market in this way tends to link in closely to the economics of each mode – rail has a high level of fixed costs, hence requires long hauls with high-volume freight, which basically is the coal market, in all other sectors the economics of road freight would appear to give it a clear advantage. It also strongly indicates that road freight has been able to adapt to the changing structure and needs of the wider market, whilst rail has lost considerable market share over the same period, i.e. has remained stuck in the 1980s, the point at which road freight had maximised its modal shift gains.

The last aspect of this section is to consider how this growth in demand has been supported by the available supply. Figure 21.5 therefore gives the breakdown of the British road fleet over the period 1994 to 2014 by (gross) weight of registered vehicle. Figure 21.5 does not initially appear to show major differences between the start and end years. Closer examination, however, reveals a clear trend towards heavier vehicles. This is partly due to an increase in the maximum gross tonnage weight limit from 41t to 44t in 2001, thus from that point onwards the graph shows increased

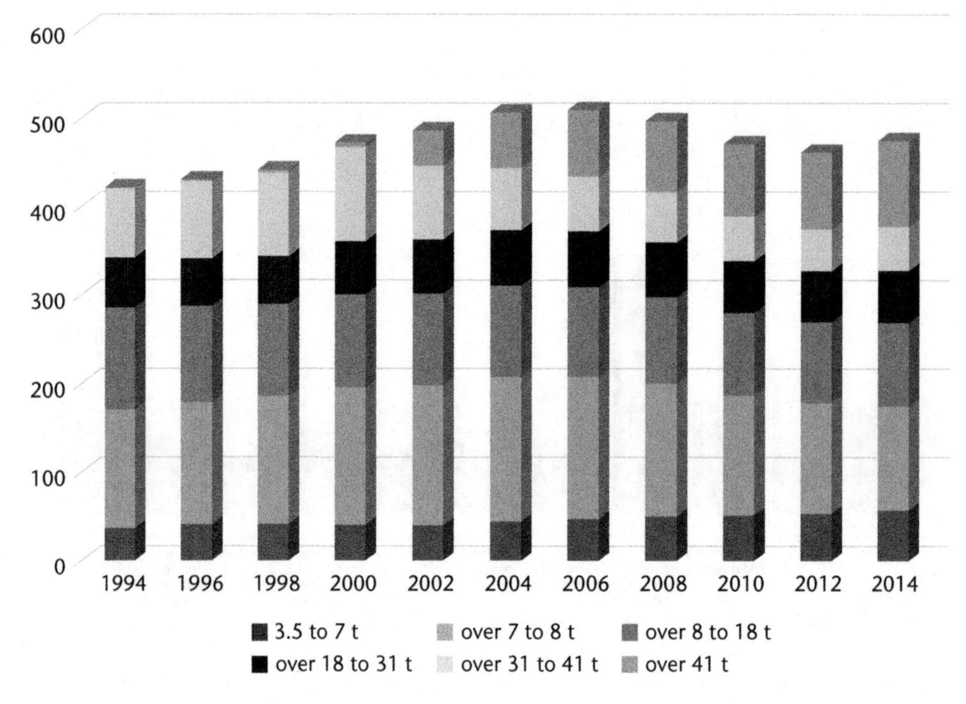

Figure 21.5 British road fleet, gross weight registrations, 1994–2014
Source: drawn from DfT, 2015

weights at the very top end. Most of this increase is in the over 31t range, and hence these vehicles take up a far larger proportion of the total. In terms of total vehicles, there were 421,000 in 1994, and this increased to 474,000 by 2014, a relatively modest increase of around 12½ percent. This tends to mask, however, the clear shift to higher-capacity vehicles. Using the mid-point as an average weight, then the gross vehicle weight has increased from 6.9 million total tonnage in 1994 to 9.5 million total tonnage in 2014, a significant increase of over 41 percent. Whilst that over-estimates the actual capacity figure, as it is based on gross weight, it does nevertheless strongly suggest that for the higher end weights, considerable economies of density exist. Interestingly, for the other categories of vehicle size outside of the now two highest weight categories, in terms of absolute numbers these have generally remained stable, with some small reductions in the 7–8t and 8–18t range, but a significant increase in numbers of vehicles in the smallest category. Figure 21.5 only shows figures relating to HGV vehicles. What it does not show is the dramatic increase that has occurred over the same period with reference to light goods vehicles, which also play a vital link in supply chain management, particularly with reference to delivery over the last mile. These have increased by just over 62 percent, which equates to an annual cumulative increase of over 2.5 percent year on year. When taken all together, what this results in is a wide variety of vehicles with characteristics that are well suited to the particular market segment to be served.

21.5.2 Rule breaking and low profit margins

As any first-year economics student should be able to explain, one of the outcomes of perfect competition is that it results in only normal profits being made, which is generally viewed as an economically desirable outcome as it results in economic welfare being maximised. It does raise the issue, however, as to what is a 'normal' profit and whether this can be better defined than as simply 'a fair return for being in business'. In terms of actual numbers, for the road freight industry research undertaken in the course of writing this chapter would suggest that normal profits are around the 5 percent profit-margin level. Figures from Canada (Transport Canada, 2006) for the Canadian industry in 2005, i.e. pre-crash, gives an average profit margin of 5 percent. Figures compiled for the top 100 US carriers suggest that whilst at the moment profit levels are under 5 percent, the trend appears to be on course to level out at around 5 percent. In the UK, however, profit levels for the top 100 hauliers are reported to be in the order of 3 percent (FTA, 2015), and have been as low as 1 percent in recent years. If normal profit is alternatively viewed as the minimum required to retain the enterprise in the industry, this would suggest a problem and also raises the issue that if competition is perfect, why does there appear to be a barrier to exit? Certainly the level of registrations has fallen in recent years, but this still leaves many firms making less than normal profits. One of the issues identified earlier was that as a barrier to entry, the finance required to be raised was not beyond the means of most individuals. Raising the finance and repaying it, however, are two different things, and once invested it may be very difficult to realise its full financial value in monetary terms, certainly in the short term. The industry is also characterised by a high level of owner-operators, thus in some ways this is a 'full life' investment, as in profession, finance and even in some cases family, and thus the ultimate driver of firm sustainability for many of these concerns is not profitability but rather financial liquidity. In other words, in many cases for owner-operators as long as the firm is financially sustainable, then its presence in the industry will continue irrespective of profitability. The problem with this issue is that whilst in the shorter term this results in (unrealistically) low freight rates, in the longer term it could adversely affect industry development, investment and innovation. Some of these consequences are beginning to clearly emerge in the UK industry, with one example being an increasing shortage of drivers yet a lack of industry-sponsored driver training schemes.

A second consequence considered here is rule breaking. Although economic regulation has been almost completely eradicated in the developed world, qualitative regulation remains. Figures from the UK, however, suggest that the degree to which these are adhered to, certainly in terms of maximum weights, is questionable. The FTA (2015) quote figures that show for random roadside weight checks carried out in 2013 almost 60 percent of HGVs were found to be over the maximum allowed for the class of vehicle, and that this was at a similar level for the three years previous. Importantly, the extent to which these were overweight is not given, and whilst in some respects the figure quoted is difficult to believe, it does nevertheless suggest that rule breaking with respect to loadings is not uncommon and may even be widespread. Where the real concern arises is that some firms may need to break the rules in order to return to any form of profitability and/or to sustain financial liquidity. From a simple general business perspective this is not a particularly healthy business environment in which to be operating, and more specifically is one that again has negative implications for the longer-term development of the industry.

21.5.3 A fluid industry dynamic

In order to examine the fluidity of the industry, data were gathered with regard to the US trucking industry. In this context, lists of the top 100 companies based on annual revenue were accumulated for 2014, 1998 and 1980. Whilst the last year mentioned is too old to use (and is pre-deregulation), the last two provide a basis to consider the extent to which the industry has changed and evolved over time. Whilst the sheer scale and size of the US industry may be regarded as unique, the industry dynamic is certainly not, the only difference being that differences tend to be much bigger in absolute rather than relative terms, but this does mean that the dynamic becomes a lot clearer.

Of the companies appearing in the top 100 of 1998, a surprisingly high number, 74, survived as an independent corporative form through to 2014. Twenty-nine of these, however, had fallen outside of the top 100, with most coming out from the bottom 50. Of the remaining 26, 16 were acquired by rival operators and ten liquidated. In order to calculate a formal statistic with regard to positional change, an estimate was required for the 29 falling outside of the top 100 in 2014, and this was done using annual mileage. Whilst this does not equate with annual revenue, the very high level of correlation between the two ($r = 0.84$ across all 100) means that it may be considered as a good proxy. That said, in terms of positional rankings, the formal statistics probably understate the extent to which changes have occurred. This is because such a statistic can only compare companies that existed in both years, hence only the 74. This completely ignores the remaining 26, hence their relative decline is not taken into account. Furthermore, to a certain extent the performance of the 'improvers' is also understated. Nevertheless, the rank correlation coefficient calculated on adjusted rankings (adjusted to ranks 1 to 74) produces an R value of 0.2832, which has an associated t value of 1.85, which technically is not statistically significant. It is close ($p = .0727$), but as stated this is on an adjusted data set that is known to have a heavily in-built bias towards accepting the null hypothesis (i.e. $r = 0$). Furthermore, the average change in the rankings for each company was over 12 places on the adjusted rankings, which taken across the whole time period would suggest a constantly evolving industry structure.

This is where alternative views of competition emerge, Schumpeter for example viewed competition as a process of change, and argued in criticism of the perfect competition model that it was not that type of competition that mattered, but rather competition from new commodities, new technologies and new types of organisation that was decisive (Demsetz, 1981). This was developed by subsequent writers on the subject who identified as key components of the competitive process issues such as technical progress, innovation, industrial development and business cycles (Hunt, 2000). The Austrian School on the other hand viewed competition as a knowledge-discovery process, one based on a constant state of disequilibrium, where the role of the firm and the entrepreneurial function was key in driving the evolution of the market. Economic value is subjective (i.e. not based on cost), and those firms that succeed in competing are those that satisfy best consumers' needs. This is more generally known as the theorem of consumer sovereignty, first proposed by Ludwig von Mises, the net outcome of which is that in terms of consumers 'they make poor men rich and rich men poor' (von Mises, 1944, p. 21). Again in this respect competition is a process, not an end in itself, the outcome (should be) that through such a mechanism society at large gets what it wants provided by those who are best at providing it.

Both of these types of competition would be evidenced by a fluid industry dynamic, in the first instance where incumbents are replaced by emerging firms with new practices/organisational methods, and in the second by firms that are simply better at using existing technologies and knowledge. In many respects, this bridges the differing views of 'competition' – mainstream economics provides the conditions required for a competitive market, but then how that functions is a different process, with the two listed here, the two examples that perhaps are of most relevance to road freight. What we should end up with are those firms that are best suited to providing the good/service emerging over time, and furthermore, this is something that will continually evolve over time. There are signs, however, that in one particular sector we have now reached a static market position, and that is the parcel courier services sector, where UPS, FedEx and DHL have globally come to dominate, while elsewhere the industry still exhibits a high degree of fluidity. The industry is therefore competitive irrespective of how that concept is defined.

21.6 Road freight as a supply chain factor input

One important aspect, if not key, in understanding the economics of road freight is to consider it as a complementary factor input. In this case, the complementary aspect arises from the need to move a product from a location where it has little economic value to one where its economic value can be maximised. The whole process is known as supply-chain management, part of the wider concept of logistics. Md Zahurul Islam et al. (2013) define logistics as adding 'place utility' to a product and as being concerned with the transportation of goods from one location to another, warehousing and storage in a suitable place, inventory, packaging and other administrative activities such as order processing. In simple terms, therefore, logistics is about all things concerned with taking the raw product (in whatever form that is) and situating it in a location and in a condition ready for private consumption. Hays Russell (2001) gives the classic 7R definition originally conceived by the Council of Logistics Management that logistics should get the right product, to the right customer in the right quantity and right condition, at the right time to the right place at the right cost. To these 7Rs an economist, in pursuit of Pareto optimality, would add an eighth 'to be consumed by the right person'.

What should be clear from the above albeit brief outline is that freight transport is only one part of a whole process that involves the movement of raw material, components and finished goods from source to market, and like factor inputs, all elements are required in the logistics chain. Again like factor inputs, there exists a degree of substitutability between some of the links in the chain. The classic example of this would be storage for transport, the substitutability of which has been developed to such an extent that as a working concept it is more commonly known as 'Just-in-Time' logistics. Thus the whole logistics function is managed so that at all points along the supply chain, materials arrive just at the point or close to the point in time when they are required. This requires an underlying constant flow through the whole chain, which at its most critical point is where the product/material is constantly moved from source, through manufacture, through distribution to the final retail outlet. Whilst in an idealised world a constant flow is required, in a theoretical one the whole chain needs to react to the puller at the end of the chain – in other words, consumer demand. This can fluctuate, hence the system needs to offer a degree of flexibility that allows it to react quickly to these fluctuations.

The transport component in the chain needs to also offer that element of flexibility. It has already been seen that the business model employed by operators in the sector offers a high degree of fluidity and flexibility, but it does nevertheless still raise the question as to what constitutes a flexible mode of (freight) transport. Mode flexibility is determined by two characteristics, the sheer cost of the mode and the way in which these costs accrue. In the first case, a cheaper mode will always win out over a more expensive counterpart, as the opportunity cost of idle time is considerably less. That seems obvious, and too simple, hence needs to be combined with the second, the way in which costs are accrued with respect to fixed verses variable. In the 'real' world this determines when factor costs are actually incurred. Hence a high level of fixed costs means that the costs of the mode are incurred all of the time, even when not in revenue-earning service. A high element of variable costs on the other hand means that costs are only incurred when the mode is in use, and thus whilst idle, it is not actually costing anything. The latter therefore offers a higher degree of flexibility than the former, particularly where these inputs are only contracted when required, as is the case in the road freight industry. These can be constrained by regulatory limits on driver hours and the use of tachographs, hence complete flexibility is not ensured, but

Figure 21.6 Breakdown of road and rail freight costs
Source: compiled from European Commission, 2014 and TAS, 2015

this still leaves considerable scope in this aspect of the operation. Where fixed costs are particularly high, on the other hand, a situation is almost created of constantly decreasing marginal costs, hence average cost can only be minimised where 24/7 working is employed.

In terms of the breakdown of the costs of road freight, the European Commission (2014) identified labour and fuel as the two main cost drivers in the sector, which when taken as an EU average accounted for something around 72 percent of all operating costs. These figures are used in Figure 21.6 to draw a comparison between the structure of road and rail freight costs.

The first thing to note from Figure 21.6 is that the figures shown are not compatible, as these are different modes of transport, therefore the type and structure of such costs are quite different. In the current context, as should become clear, this is unimportant. The three main cost drivers are given for road, which are fuel, staff and other, and similarly the three main cost drivers are for rail freight, staff, rolling stock and other. Whilst these do not equate with fixed and variable, generally staff and fuel costs will be variable, whereas rolling stock and other will be fixed.[2] Note in this context what is also important in many respects is not how costs are incurred, but rather how such costs are accounted for, depreciation being the classic example. To clarify, depreciation is the cost to the firm of using capital equipment, and has two components associated with it, one fixed and one variable. The fixed component arises out of obsolescence, where the value of an asset will fall over time simply because it is becoming dated, to the point that its value may fall to its scrap value. As a working asset, therefore, it would become worthless even though it may never have been used. The second component arises out of use, in which the more it is used the faster it will depreciate, hence the cost (in real terms) will vary with use, and therefore is a variable cost. In practice, however, depreciation relates to a fixed factor, hence is a short-run (fixed) factor and thus a fixed cost. Furthermore, accounting practice, whether by straight line or reducing balance, is to write off a fixed amount irrespective of use, hence again it becomes a fixed cost. Whilst an aside, it nevertheless underlines the importance of the structure of costs when reviewing the economics of a particular transport mode; it is this balance between fixed and variable that can be the success/key to the operation of the transport mode. The classic example of this is the low-cost business model of airline operation, where the success of the operation is in keeping assets associated with fixed costs in revenue-earning service, hence leading to very high utilisation rates and low average costs.

If staff and fuel costs can be considered as variable, and all other costs that are shown as fixed, or certainly a very high element of fixed, then the cost structures of the two modes becomes very clear. Road freight, in terms of the fixed/variable divide, equates to roughly a 30/70 split, whilst rail freight is almost the exact mirror image, with a 70/30 split. Certainly the road freight split equates roughly with earlier research by Shirley (1969), which estimated the level of fixed costs to be 25 percent of total costs, and also Bayliss (1986), who estimated variable costs to be around 65 percent. The implication is that when in use, in order to achieve the same cost levels as road freight, rail freight either needs to be worked all of the time, or alternatively it needs to carry far heavier loads, thereby the fixed element is spread over a larger payload and thus the average cost per tonne reduced. Such operations need to be planned well in advance to ensure that average costs are minimised, hence offer little room for flexibility.

More importantly, what this leads to is a very high break-even point, hence a high level of freight needs to be carried before any profit can be returned. With the very much lower fixed costs associated with road freight, then this almost produces the exact opposite effect and has a low break-even point, which then in turn leads to the contracting of services only when they are required. This not only has direct implications for profitability, but also importantly introduces liquidity issues. Whilst cash flow will always be an issue for any transport company, with the former a far higher level of capital is tied up in the firm, and most of this under a private-sector model will be leased or borrowed. Regular payments are required on these, whereas for the road freight company these are far less of a financial drain.

In simple terms, the outright cost advantage and the nature of cost accumulation in the production of services has led road freight to be the mode that has come to be the transport component in the supply chain. Furthermore, it is the basic economics of the mode that has allowed the business models that are used to be successfully employed.

21.7 The public economics of road freight

The chapter ends with a look at a growing area of research which surrounds the public economics of road freight. In some respects, this is a key area of the economics of road freight and one that in the future is likely to play an increasingly larger role.

With all transport modes, there are four main areas of externalities – time, personal injury/ fatalities, pollution and consumption of potential future resources. Road freight makes a high contribution to all four, but space prevents any further elaboration on the first two mentioned, thus the main focus is on the last two, specifically environmental pollution and energy efficiency. Of the few studies carried out, most have found that road is by far the most polluting in terms of tonnes of freight carried. Short (1995), back in the 1990s, found road to have consistently significantly higher levels of emissions over a range of toxics, while the Freight on Rail (2008) campaign also found road to be more polluting, although relative differences were generally smaller (although still large). As regards carbon dioxide emissions, McKinnon (2008) found that road was around ten times more polluting than the other modes per tonne kilometre.

Within the EU, the main policy tool that has been used in this area is the EU Emissions Standards for new vehicle registrations. These began with Euro 1 in 1993 and have evolved over time with the latest, Euro 6, coming into force in 2015. These have applied increasingly stringent emissions controls on all types of motor vehicles, including obviously LGVs and HGVs. Beyond these standards, how policy has generally tackled the problem has tended not to be through further direct regulation of emissions, but rather by targeting improving energy efficiency, and thus to a certain extent attempting to kill two birds with one stone, i.e. reduce emissions through reduced energy use. As an example, Liimatainen et al. (2012) report on the early outcomes of a voluntary Finnish climate policy programme to reduce emissions by 15 percent from 2005 to 2020. This was done through a series of energy-efficiency initiatives, in which it was found that as a result of the programme around 54 percent of companies within the sample had an 'active' energy-efficiency programme. Significantly, however, all such measures were primarily motivated by cost savings, with the most utilised actions tending to be the inexpensive and simplest ones to employ. The conclusion from this would be that companies were happy to be 'green' just as long as it resulted in cost savings, an understandable position given the nature of the market.

Further evidence is provided by Andrés and Padilla (2015) who examined the main factors that caused change in transport emissions in the Spanish road freight sector. What they found was that over the period studied (1996–2012) whilst energy intensity continually decreased, this followed an irregular path. During years of economic crisis, energy intensity fell due to energy consumption falling faster than road freight activity, i.e. efficiency improvements. During periods of economic expansion, energy intensity reduced because road freight activity grew faster than energy consumption, i.e. operational improvements. When all pulled together, what they found was that the real energy intensity index produced a net overall 3 percent decrease over the period, however this was partially offset by a 1.1 percent increase in the structural index (a partial rebound effect), thus producing a net reduction of 1.9 percent overall. What this tends to underline is that, to date, energy efficiency has been largely driven mainly by economic considerations.

It has been stated that the market on its own will not achieve the required conditions to improve the freight market's environmental sustainability, and hence further government intervention beyond the current emissions controls would be required to bring about a different market outcome (McKinnon quoted in Butcher, 2008). Indeed Piecyk and McKinnon (2010) establish the level of carbon emissions from the road freight sector in 2020 in the absence of any government action on carbon footprint controls – in other words, those driven purely by market actions. The central prediction, termed 'business as usual', predicted a 10 percent reduction in CO_2 emissions, despite a 21 percent increase in road tonne kilometres, but total vehicle kilometres were predicted to be the same in 2020 as in 2006 (the base year). Energy-efficiency improvements would largely be facilitated by wide application of telematics and computerised vehicle routing and scheduling systems, with the level of backloading also suggested to be improved through various collaboration ventures such as online freight exchanges and freight-matching services.

These 'savings' would be well short of the UK government's commitment to achieving an 80 percent reduction (on 1990 levels) of carbon emissions by 2050, hence from a purely isolated viewpoint, this suggests that far stronger and punitive policy measures are required. From a more general and practical viewpoint, however, policy development has been slow in this area for a number of reasons. Perhaps the main one is that politicians have been reluctant to intervene in a market that is seen to be operating along market principles, and thus is one that the behaviour of companies and individuals is regulated by the market such that it produces an efficient market outcome. Furthermore, one way to reduce negative externalities is to encourage modal shift, but due to a reluctance to increase the cost of road transport, this has been almost exclusively pursued through grants to other modes. What we end up with in the road freight sector therefore is almost the classic 'laissez-faire' approach. A final factor is that any intervention becomes problematic – target setting (of emissions) for example is not an easy task to undertake. Road freight is the driver of the whole economy, hence target settings should equate to the opportunity cost of the level of economic wealth that will have to be ceded in pursuit of the proposed target, which in turn needs to be set against similar 'gains'/the opportunity cost of other sectors of the economy and hence down to which ones are the least costly to target. The reality of the current situation means that such a level of analysis is still many years from being required, as there is still sufficient excess in the system to allow naivety to prevail, i.e. 80 percent overall means 80 percent from each sector. Nevertheless, even with such a backdrop, setting appropriate and meaningful reduction targets are still problematic as one of the key issues is that modal shift may not produce the proposed reductions overall. In Finland, for example, Liimatainen and Pöllänen (2010) highlight that if many goods which currently go by rail were to go by road, then they would also be relatively energy efficient compared with average road transport. Why this is the case is that the energy efficiency of the mode is closely associated with the market segments in which they operate. Using rail as the example, as highlighted the economics of the mode means it is best suited to operating in segments that contain large loads and long hauls, hence energy efficiency is ensured (in relative terms).

To summarise what has been an albeit brief discussion, the whole area of the public economics of road freight is a considerably underdeveloped policy area and one in which there remains a very high level of unknowns. To date, most decisions have been left to the market, with only some progress on emission controls. Policy, however, cannot be simply targeted at mode reductions (or indeed better mode balances), as in many cases the externalities of the mode are strongly affected by the characteristics of the freight carried and not just the mode itself. As a result, what policy should actually be doing becomes unclear and given it is perceived as being far from at a critical point, it remains an understated area. This is reinforced by a backdrop of austerity, in which government action in any area becomes problematic due to the cost to public finances, hence to a certain extent how 'green' policy can be is driven by how much the economy can afford it to be. As a result, policy is driven by economic rather than ecological principles. Related to that is the lack of a political champion to drive policy development. Whilst several politicians have made considerable political gain from championing passenger-related causes, there is very little to be gained from taking on the same issue with regards to freight. In many cases, therefore, in this area the market really is king.

21.8 Closing discussion and final thoughts

The chapter began by describing the economics of road freight as only about one thing, namely that it was a competitive industry. Through the chapter this issue has been explored and developed, and what has emerged is an industry broken down into different market segments where various characteristics, such as the quality of service, can be taken as a given and hence all are characterised by strong price competition. Local and regional markets are dominated by what could best be described as the neoclassical model of perfect competition, whilst interregional and international markets, where some scale effects are present, are dominated by large carriers who compete on the basis of price, although the contracting and brokering of smaller operators has a very large part to play. The economics of this has produced a mode that has come to dominate the whole freight market, and one that, due to a combination of competitiveness and the underlying cost structure, is very much in step with current and recent developments in logistics. The only real negative is the public economics of the mode, on which it has a disproportionately larger impact than other modes/road-based transport. Government policy in this area has been considerably underdeveloped due to the importance of the mode to economic welfare and sustainability. In some ways this is the classic economic argument that basically everything has its price.

Irrespective of any further policy development, the economics of the mode will ensure that it will continue to dominate freight markets for the medium and longer terms.

Notes

1 To confirm, cabotage occurs where the operator is not registered in either of the two points between which the transport is occurring.
2 Just to reiterate, this is a very general broad-sweep assumption, for example fuel costs are included in 'other' costs for the railways, but in some respects given these do not have a separate category, this tends to suggest they are a small proportion of rail freight costs, unlike in road freight. This in itself is quite revealing as regards the structure of costs in the two modes.

Acknowledgements

The author would like to express his thanks to Dr Maja Piecyk of the University of Westminster, Dr Jason Monios of Edinburgh Napier University and also Professor Stephen Ison for their valuable comments on an earlier draft of this chapter. The usual caveats apply.

References

AECOM (2014). *Report on the State of the EU Road Haulage Market.* Report for the European Commission.
Allen, B. W., Preechaemetta, A. Shao, G. and Ginger, S. (1990). *The Impact of State Economics Regulation of Motor Carriers on Intrastate and Interstate Commerce.* Washington, DC: US Department of Transportation.
Andrés, L. and Padilla, E. (2015). Energy Intensity in Road Freight Transport of Heavy Goods Vehicles in Spain. *Energy Policy*, 85, pp. 309–21.
Bayliss, B. (1986). The Structure of the Road Haulage Industry in the United Kingdom, and Optimum Scale. *Journal of Transport Economics and Policy*, 20(2), pp. 153–72.
Butcher, L. (2008). The Road Haulage Industry: Costs and Taxes. House of Commons Library Research Paper No 08/68.
Demsetz, H. (1981). Economic, Legal and Political Dimensions of Competition. University of California, Los Angeles, discussion paper no. 209.
DfT (2014). *Transport Statistics Great Britain 2014.* London: HMSO.
DfT (2015). *Transport Statistics Great Britain 2015.* London: HMSO.
European Commission (2014). *Report from the Commission to the European Parliament and the Council on the State of the Union Road Transport Market.* Brussels COM (2014) 222 Final.
Flath, D. (2001). Japanese Regulation of Truck Transport. *Journal of the Japanese and International Economies*, 15, pp. 1–28.
Freight on Rail (2008). DfT Ports Policy Consultation: Rail Freight's Role, Freight on Rail Guidelines for Responses. Press release.
FTA (2008). *Freight as an Employer and Vital Business Sector.* Press release, 27 March.
FTA (2015). *Logistics Report 2015.* Tunbridge Wells: Freight Transport Association.
Harmatuck, D. (1981). A Motor Carrier Joint Cost Function. *Journal of Transport Economics and Policy*, 15(3), pp. 135, 153.
Hays Russell, S. (2001). General Theory of Logistics Practices, the Growing World of Logistics. In Rainey, J., Scott, B., Waller, G. and Ferguson, M. (eds), *Today's Logistics, Selected Readings and Analysis.* Darby, PA: Diane Publishing.
Hunt, S. D. (2000). The Competence-Based, Resource-Advantage, and Neoclassical Theories of Competition: Toward a Synthesis. In Sanchez, R. and Heene, A. (eds), *Competence-Based Strategic Management: Theory and Research.* Greenwich: JAI Press, pp. 177–208.
Lacey, E. (1990). Regulation or Competition in Road Transport. *OECD Observer*, December–January, pp. 27–31.
Lafontaine, F. and Malaguzzi Valeri, L. (2009). The Deregulation of International Trucking in the European Union: Form and Effect. *Journal of Regulatory Economics*, 35, pp. 19–44.

Liimatainen H. and Pöllänen, M. (2010). Trends of Energy Efficiency in Finnish Road Freight Transport 1995–2009 and Forecast to 2016. *Energy Policy*, 38, pp. 7676–86.
Liimatainen H., Stenholm, P., Tapio, P. and McKinnon, A. (2012). Energy Efficiency Practices among Road Freight Hauliers. *Energy Policy*, 50, pp. 833–42.
McGinnis, M. (1990). The Relative Importance of Cost and Service in Freight Transportation Choice: Before and after Deregulation. *Transportation Journal*, 30(1), pp. 12–19.
McKinnon, A. (2008). CO2 Emissions from Freight Transport: An Analysis of UK Data. Briefing paper to the Commission on Integrated Transport report, 'Transport and Climate Change'.
Md Zahurul Islam, D., Meier, J., Aditjandra, P., Zunder, T. and Pace, G. (2013). Logistics and Supply Chain Management. *Research in Transportation Economics*, 41, pp. 3–16.
McMullen, B. S. (1987). The Impact of Regulatory Reform on US Motor Carrier Costs. *Journal of Transport Economics and Policy*, 21(3), pp. 307–19.
Piecyk, M. and McKinnon, A. (2010). Forecasting the Carbon Footprint of Road Freight Transport in 2010. *Journal of International Production Economics*, 128, pp. 31–42.
Ponsonby, G. J. (1938). Freight Charges by Road in Competition. *Economic Journal*, 48, pp. 52–63.
Rothenberg, L. (1994). *Regulation, Organizations and Politics: Motor Freight Policy at the Interstate Commerce Commission*. Ann Arbor: University of Michigan Press.
Shirley, R. (1969). Analysis of Motor Carrier Cost Formula Developed by the Interstate Commerce Commission. *Transportation Journal*, Spring, pp. 22–4.
Short, J. (1995). Freight Transport as an Environmental Problem. *World Transport Policy and Practice*, 1(2), pp. 7–10.
Silverman, B., Nickerson, J. and Freeman, J. (1997). Profitability, Transactional Alignment and Organizational Mortality in the US Trucking Industry. *Strategic Management Journal*, 18, pp. 31–52.
Spady, R. and Friedlaender, A. (1978). Hedonic Cost Functions for the Regulated Trucking Industry. *Bell Journal of Economics*, 9(1), pp. 159–279.
TAS (2015). Rail Industry Monitor, online database, 2009 to 2015, accessed by subscription, www.taspublications.co.uk/content/index.php/reports-about-railways/12-rail-industry-monitor (accessed 9 September 2016).
Transport Canada (2006). *Operating Costs of Trucks in Canada, 2005*. Ottawa: Transport Canada.
Trick, S. and Peoples, J. (2012). Union Compensation Following Intrastate Deregulation: Evidence from the US Trucking Industry. *Transport Policy*, 24, pp. 10–18.
Von Mises, L. (1944). *Bureaucracy*. New Haven, CT: Yale University Press.
Wang Chiang, S. J. and Friedlaender, A. F. (1984). Output Aggregation, Network Effects and the Measurement of Trucking Technology. *Review of Economics and Statistics*, 66(2), pp. 267–376.

22
Rail freight

Allan Woodburn

22.1 Introduction

Rail freight is generally viewed positively in terms of its contribution to society and the environment but is often seen as uneconomic by those requiring the use of freight transport services. While it is often possible to ascertain the cost side of rail freight transport, it is more challenging to identify the pricing policies due to a lack of transparency and commercial confidentiality concerns. As a rule, a higher proportion of rail freight's costs are 'fixed' when compared to road haulage. This leads to the oft-quoted maxim that rail is best suited to high-volume flows over long distances, since lower unit costs can then be reflected in more competitive pricing. Not surprisingly, given the variance in the characteristics of freight transport markets and specific flows, there is a lack of agreement as to the necessary volume or distance for commercial viability. Furthermore, many aspects of the economics of rail freight activity are typically not transparent, so it is a challenging area about which to provide a detailed evidence-based account. That said, this chapter seeks to provide insight into the key characteristics of, and influences on, the economics of rail freight. It focuses mainly on rail freight economics from a European perspective and, in particular, the British situation. Rail freight activity is considered mostly within the context of a mixed traffic railway (i.e. 'shared-user' rail networks catering for both passenger and freight traffic), the dominant form of rail operations across Europe.

The chapter adopts a broad approach to examining the key factors influencing the economics of rail freight activity, starting with a general overview of the nature and structure of the rail freight cost base (Section 22.2), followed by an assessment of the economics of different types of rail freight operation (Section 22.3). Section 22.4 considers the important role of the public sector in influencing the economics of rail freight, with Section 22.5 discussing the attributes of competitive rail freight markets. The role of pricing in influencing companies' mode choice decision making is briefly considered in Section 22.6. A series of short case studies demonstrating rail freight's efficiency and cost competitiveness is then presented (Section 22.7) and a brief summary of the key issues completes the chapter (Section 22.8).

22.2 Overview of the nature and structure of rail freight costs

Fundamentally, rail freight experiences high fixed costs and low variable costs when compared with road haulage, though how this manifests itself is somewhat dependent on the nature of the cost structure applied to the rail industry; the role of the public sector in determining this is

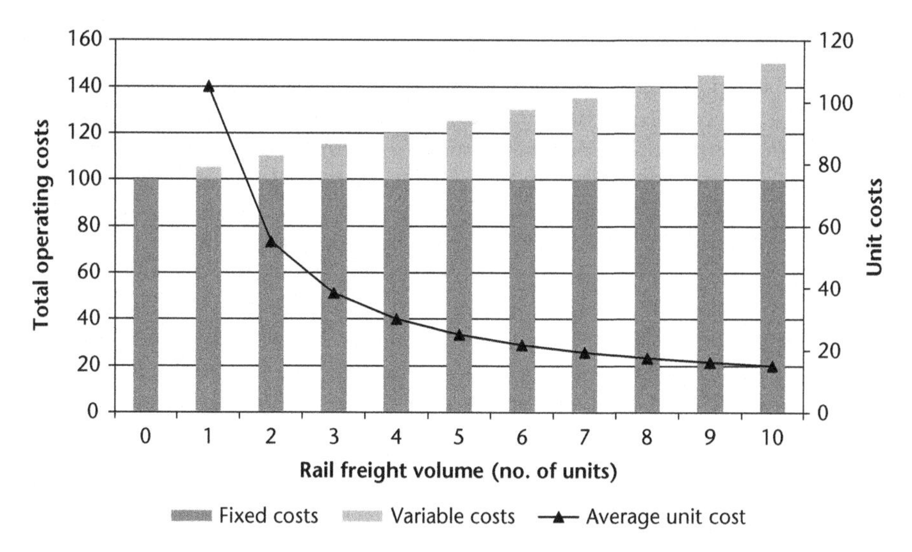

Figure 22.1 Indicative relationship of rail freight costs versus volume carried

assessed later in the chapter but, for now, the basic features of rail freight costs are established. Figure 22.1 presents the indicative relationship between fixed and variable costs. Before any rail freight activity can take place, expensive assets such as track, terminals, locomotives, rolling stock and skilled staff must be in place. A high proportion of the cost of these assets, particularly track and terminals, is fixed with little cost variability resulting from marginal changes in the level of activity.

Another way of considering rail freight costs is in terms of the breakdown between infrastructure costs and train-operating costs, which bears some similarities to the relationship between fixed and variable costs. Sometimes, the infrastructure and operating costs are integrated and considered holistically, particularly where rail infrastructure and train operations are operated by a single entity, typically a nationalised railway organisation or a private rail system dedicated to a particular type of traffic. Where rail infrastructure is provided exclusively for freight activity, all infrastructure and train-operating costs quite clearly are the responsibility of the freight operation. In some cases, particularly for bulk commodity flows (e.g. the Sishen–Saldanha corridor for iron ore exports in South Africa and the rail systems carrying coal for export through the Port of Gladstone in Australia), entire routes or even networks are dedicated to freight activity. The allocation of common network costs to rail freight activity is more challenging on a mixed-traffic railway, prevalent in most European countries, and allocation to specific rail freight flows or customers is more difficult still.

It is increasingly the case across Europe that rail infrastructure is the responsibility of a nationalised infrastructure provider (often referred to as the infrastructure manager) while rail freight services are provided by one or more rail freight operators who may be from either the private sector or the public sector. In these circumstances, the infrastructure and train-operating costs tend to be treated separately. Where the necessary infrastructure is not already in place to commence rail freight operations, the capital costs of providing track, terminals and signalling are high, so a guaranteed rail freight volume over a considerable time period is usually needed in order to present a viable business case. Where this is not possible, public funding may be available to take account of wider economic, environmental and societal benefits (see Section 22.4).

A high-profile European example is the Betuweroute, a dedicated 160km rail freight link from Rotterdam to the German border, opened in 2007 and funded by the public sector.

The actual movement cost by rail (on a tonne kilometre basis) is often cheaper than by road, but the door-to-door comparison between rail and road may be less favourable to rail because of terminal handling costs and feeder road costs. In simple terms, road normally offers a cheaper option than rail for short distance and/or low-volume flows, while rail becomes more competitive as distance and/or volume increases. In particular, the concept of a break-even distance features strongly in the rail freight literature. There is no consensus as to the break-even distance beyond which rail becomes cheaper than road. Harris and McIntosh (2003) argued that rail is unlikely to be cost competitive over distances of less than 100 miles (i.e. 160 kilometres), while recent research for the European Commission found that 200–300km is the typical range at which rail starts to be favoured over road (Directorate General for Internal Policies, 2015). Figure 22.2 conceptualises the relationship between road and rail costs (and prices), identifying a critical distance range within which the two modes tend to compete.

Table 22.1 presents findings from the 2012 Freight Customer Survey (ORR, 2012), where respondents were asked their opinion on the distance at which rail freight becomes competitive.

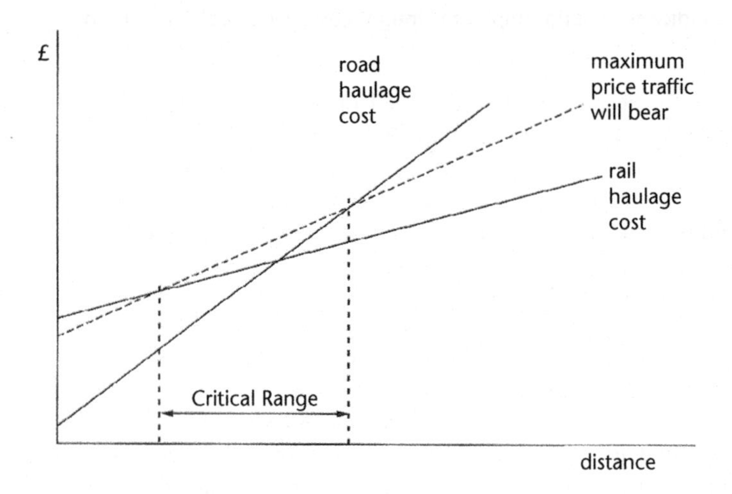

Figure 22.2 Relationship between modal costs and price by distance
Source: Harris and McIntosh, 2003

Table 22.1 Distance at which rail freight becomes competitive

Distance in miles (and km equivalent)	*Percentage of respondents (n = 48)*
0–25 *(0–40)*	2
26–50 *(42–80)*	13
51–100 *(82–161)*	23
101–50 *(163–241)*	29
151–200 *(243–322)*	21
201–50 *(323–402)*	6
> 251 *(> 404)*	6

Source: ORR, 2012

Surprisingly, given the typical break-even distances quoted in the literature, 38 percent of respondents believed rail to be competitive over distances of 100 miles or less and just 12 percent thought distances in excess of 200 miles were needed. As will be seen later in the chapter (Section 22.7), rail freight flows over short distances can be viable given appropriate circumstances.

In reality, the rail haulage cost profile is likely to be more 'lumpy' (i.e. less linear) than that for road as distance or volume increases. As also highlighted in Chapter 24 on intermodal economics, when the maximum train payload is reached, an additional train is needed to cater for any more volume. This will require another locomotive, representing a steep cost increase. It is much easier to keep on adding incremental capacity in road haulage, since each extra lorry marks a small capacity increase compared to the capacity offered by an additional train. Similarly, with respect to distance, costs are likely to be more stepped for rail because of asset requirements and utilisation (e.g. if the round trip time becomes longer then an additional train may be required to offer a specific service frequency). Therefore, even within the critical range, there may be points where the cheaper mode of transport is inverted, with rail being cheaper for specific volumes or distances rather than across a range.

In general, then, rail freight costs are not as predictable and are less transparent than road haulage costs due to the more complex rail cost base and, in a competitive market, concerns over commercial sensitivities (DfT, 2009). In particular, the capital costs of developing new infrastructure such as track and terminals where they do not already exist can be a major obstacle to financial viability. The link between costs and pricing is rarely obvious, in the public domain at least. The standard practice is to charge as much as the market will bear since, for reasons outlined already, much of the cost base is indivisible to a specific commodity flow or customer level, particularly where infrastructure, rolling stock and/or labour is shared. The greater the train payload (in weight and/or volumetric terms) and distance and the simpler the method of operation, the more favourable the economics are for rail movement. However, there are many factors which influence the outcome and the next section considers these within the framework of different types of rail freight operation.

22.3 Economics of different types of rail freight operation

There are various ways in which rail freight activity can be categorised, with the nature of operation having a considerable influence on the economics. The key differences can be summarised using the following categorisation (Woodburn, 2015):

(1) Trainload operation, where the entire train operates from origin to destination in a single block, is typically the most economic form of rail freight activity, particularly where the trainload makes use of rail's heavy-haul capabilities. In most cases, one commodity type (e.g. coal, steel, construction materials) will be carried for a single customer, but there are other types of trainload operation (e.g. of containers) carrying different types of goods for a range of customers.

(2) Wagonload provision, where trunk trains connect hub marshalling yards with each other and feeder trains operate on 'spokes' from the hubs to customers' terminals. Trunk trains usually carry a mix of commodities and/or serve a range of customers, while feeder services typically serve an individual customer or multiple co-located customers. Wagonload operation typically results in a wagon being remarshalled several times on its journey from origin to destination.

(3) Block wagonload, which is basically an intermediate solution between trainload and wagonload. A small number of train portions (or blocks of wagons) are combined for

movement in complete train loads, with portions being exchanged at fewer intermediate marshalling yards than would normally be the case with wagonload operation.

Figure 22.3 shows examples of trainload and wagonload operation. Figure 22.3a is a British example showing an entire train of hopper wagons (for construction materials) running directly between two terminals. Figure 22.3b is a wagonload train in the Czech Republic, with several different wagon types (including boxes, tanks and hoppers) clearly visible. It is likely that the train comprises wagons for a number of customers and with flows from a wide range of origin-destination pairs. Such wagonload operation results in higher operating costs per wagon as a consequence of the additional marshalling of wagons at intermediate locations and the typically poor load utilisation of the feeder services. There are also likely to be indirect cost implications since, for example, the end-to-end journey time is typically much longer for indirect wagonload operation than for direct trainload services, leading to poorer wagon utilisation.

As Table 22.2 reveals, the overwhelming majority of British rail freight activity is trainload. The remainder can justifiably be classified as block wagonload, since there is no true wagonload

Figure 22.3 Examples of trainload operation (a) and wagonload operation (b)
Source: Author's photographs

Table 22.2 Typical types of British rail freight operation, by market (as at January 2016)

Market	*Trainload*	*Block wagonload*
Coal	***	–
Aggregates	***	–
Metals	***	*
Petroleum	***	–
Automotive	**	**
Waste	***	–
Intermodal freight	***	*
Channel Tunnel	**	*
General freight	**	**

Note: *** considerable use; ** moderate use; * limited use; – no (or virtually no) use
Source: based on and updated from DfT, 2010a

rail freight remaining; it is now extremely rare for a freight train to convey portions for more than two or three different flows. The challenging economics for wagonload operation were highlighted in 1990 when British Rail reviewed the 'Speedlink' wagonload network and found it to be hugely unprofitable (Shannon, 2014). In consequence, this network was disbanded in 1991 with traffic lost to road, switched to trainload operation or, in relatively few cases where small volume flows could be combined, retained as block wagonload.

To add to the distance and volume characteristics discussed in Section 22.2, the economics of rail freight are improved when customer requirements are predictable and regular, since this smooths the utilisation of expensive assets. Trainload flows tend only to operate when the customer has sufficient volume to justify this, since the customer will generally be responsible for the train's operating costs. If the flow operates on a fixed day each week, the rail freight operator can potentially share its assets with other flows, whereas if the flow's operating day varies it becomes much more difficult to schedule the assets efficiently. As a result, overall asset utilisation will fall and operating costs per tonne kilometre will most likely increase.

Table 22.3 presents a hypothetical example of a medium-volume flow, identifying pros and cons associated with each of three potential service options. It is assumed that a customer has a flow of 1,000 tonnes of product per week to be moved over a distance of 500km from a single origin to a single destination. This weekly tonnage requires 20 wagon loads. Pros and cons associated with three potential service options are shown in Table 22.3. It is evident that the most cost-effective transport solution will depend on the particular characteristics of the flow and the extent to which it is operated in conjunction with other traffic. For example, the single dedicated trainload per week is likely to be the most cost-effective option in terms of direct rail costs, particularly if the assets can be interworked with other flows. However, this has to be traded off against wider logistics considerations such as likely increased inventory costs associated with receiving an entire week's worth of inventory in a single trainload rather than in smaller, more frequent quantities.

Table 22.3 Comparative positive and negative attributes of different service options

Option	*Positive aspects*	*Negative aspects*
One dedicated 20 wagon trainload per week	Efficient use of rail's bulk haulage capabilities, with low cost per tonne km	Poor asset utilisation unless resources (e.g. wagons, locomotives, labour) are shared with other flows Greater volume of goods to be handled and stored per delivery, with possible time and cost implications
Two dedicated 10 wagon trainloads per week	Smaller number of wagons required than for weekly service if same wagons can do both weekly round trips Shorter terminal time needed to load/unload 10 wagons than 20	Duplicated costs (e.g. fuel, labour) from operating two weekly trains rather than one
Four wagons per day, five days per week on shared-user services	Some or all train-operating costs shared with other flows Possible further improvement in wagon utilisation and reduction in terminal time compared with trainload operation	Additional costs for wagon marshalling and dedicated feeder services if shared-user services do not directly serve same origin and destination

22.4 Public-sector influences on rail freight economics

The role of the public sector in influencing rail freight economics is complex and dynamic, but of considerable importance. This section sets out why rail freight is of wider importance to society and the economy, leading to the economic rationale for government intervention in its economic structure. Examples of interventions made by the British government are then elaborated, followed by a discussion of the broader European context.

22.4.1 The importance of rail freight to society and the economy

Despite having a fairly minor share of the overall British freight market, at around 9 percent in 2013 (ORR, 2015), it is evident that rail freight performs a valuable economic function to society and the national economy. Studies produced by Network Rail (2010, 2013), Oxera (2014) and the Rail Delivery Group (2014) have claimed a range of benefits resulting from the existence of the rail freight industry, including:

- a reduction in road network congestion;
- increased economic output resulting from lower transport costs;
- savings in social and environmental costs.

The Rail Delivery Group (2015) estimated that goods worth more than £30 billion are moved by rail annually in Britain with the rail freight sector cumulatively benefiting the British economy by around £1.5 billion each year, two-thirds of that directly to its customers and the remainder to society as a whole. Given rail freight's economic strengths relative to road haulage, some sectors of the economy rely heavily on rail for their transport requirements and would not efficiently function without it. This is particularly true for raw materials and part-finished goods in the early stages of the supply chain, but rail has increasingly become a crucial element in later supply chain stages moving, for example, imported consumer goods. Some examples of viable rail freight flows of consumer goods are identified in Section 22.7.

As with freight transport in general, rail freight activity is a derived demand, with overall levels of activity linked to the economic cycle. According to the Directorate General for Internal Policies (2015, p. 3), structural changes to the European economy, including 'changes in the industrial production process and the fragmentation of logistics', have had negative impacts on rail freight. Specifically, rail-dominated bulk flows such as coal, construction materials, iron ore and part-finished steel are more susceptible to decline during economic downturns than are many of the road-dominated flows such as essential consumer goods (e.g. food and drink products). With fixed costs making up a high proportion of rail freight's cost base, and thus a very high break-even point, financial viability is more challenging during an economic downturn since the fixed costs are more heavily concentrated on the remaining flows.

22.4.2 Examples of government intervention in British rail freight economics

Government intervention principally relates to the charging regime and to the provision of public funding, and can involve either direct action through the regulatory framework or can result from more general policy direction. Examples of intervention in Britain include the regulatory framework governing network access and charging, grant funding for infrastructure and service provision and broader land-use planning policies relating to issues such as terminal development. It is important for government to provide policy continuity to give confidence to rail freight operators and their customers to invest private capital into rail freight terminals and rolling stock.

Rail operations typically are more heavily regulated than road haulage operations, which can impose a financial burden to the operator but should also provide fairness and transparency within the market. Since the privatisation of British Rail in the mid-1990s, certain cost elements which contribute to the total rail freight economic package fall within the remit of the Office of Rail and Road (ORR, prior to 2015 the Office of Rail Regulation), particularly relating to the regulatory framework. ORR is the independent economic regulator for the British rail network (ORR, 2016), with a remit to ensure that all operators are treated in a non-discriminatory manner so long as network-access licensing requirements are met (see Chapter 8 for more detail on this). Financial fairness and transparency are vital to satisfying this remit. Specific economic functions of ORR include:

- promoting competition in the provision of railway services;
- ensuring value for money and protecting the interests of rail users;
- establishing the level and structure of track access charges;
- conducting investigations into practices which may be anti-competitive;
- regulating Network Rail, the monopoly infrastructure provider, including target setting and monitoring for performance and efficiency.

Rail freight track access charges are determined every five years as part of ORR's funding settlement for Network Rail. This provides certainty for rail freight operators for that time period but creates uncertainty at the time of each review (Network Rail, 2014). The 2008 review led to a 35 percent reduction in track access charges for the 2009–14 period but also introduced a 'freight-only line' charge for power station coal and nuclear waste. After considerable uncertainty, the 2013 review resulted in a phased increase in access charges for traffic considered to be captive to rail (i.e. power station coal, nuclear traffic and iron ore), slight increases in access charges for other bulk commodities and a real-terms reduction for the cost-sensitive intermodal traffic. The effects of track access charges on freight volumes are dependent on modal competition in specific markets. In 2006, track access charges were estimated to represent 17 percent of the total rail freight cost (MDS Transmodal, 2006). It was estimated that a uniform 50 percent increase in track access charges would lead to a 9.2 percent decrease in overall rail freight volumes, but certain markets including intermodal and construction materials would be much more significantly affected.

A specific challenge where rail infrastructure is publicly owned and freight train operations are in private hands is the potential for non-aligned objectives and a lack of synergy between the various industry players. A Freight Alliance has been formed between Network Rail and the main rail freight operators to try to achieve cost savings across the whole industry and to develop a sustainable access charging regime for freight which gives long-term stability (Network Rail, 2014).

While the level at which track access charges are set will influence rail's ability to compete with road haulage on cost grounds, more targeted government funding may be available to support rail freight flows where they are otherwise not commercially viable. Direct rail freight grant funding in Great Britain has mainly taken the form of capital support for assets such as terminal equipment or rolling stock and revenue support for moving freight by rail rather than road. The Mode Shift Revenue Support (MSRS) Scheme is a component of the Sustainable Distribution Fund and has been the main funding source in recent years, with capital support in the form of the Freight Facilities Grant now available only in Scotland and Wales (DfT, 2015). To be eligible for funding, schemes require a benefit-cost ratio of 2:1 or more. Almost £90 million of grant funding was awarded between 2010 and 2015, although a small proportion of this total was awarded to waterborne traffic; a slightly reduced level of funding has been allocated for the 2016–20 period (DfT, 2016).

Infrastructure enhancements to permit heavier trains, such as higher permissible axle loadings, can improve the economics of bulk flows. Of more significance for much of the traffic where rail competes directly with road, particularly lighter-weight consumer goods carried in unit loads, is network capability for longer, higher and wider trains (RFG/RFOA, 2009). Public funding for initiatives aimed at improving the efficiency and competitiveness of rail freight include the Strategic Freight Network (SFN), the Freight Reform Programme and more general funding for network enhancements (Network Rail, 2014). The SFN was initiated in 2007 to coordinate infrastructure enhancements for freight, evolving out of the short-lived Transport Innovation Fund (Productivity) (TIF(P)) which had set out to prioritise network enhancements which would benefit national productivity. Specifically, the SFN aims to 'provide an enhanced core freight trunk network, optimised to freight requirements, and providing greater capability, reliability and availability' (DfT, 2007, p. 81). Around £50 million annually has been allocated to the SFN for the 2009–19 period.

Across the transport sector, changes to the regulatory and policy framework for the different modes of freight transport can influence the competitiveness of rail freight. For example, a detailed study of the likely impacts of allowing longer and/or longer and heavier goods vehicles to operate on the road network found that the economics of key rail freight markets could be undermined by road haulage becoming cheaper (TRL, 2008). Deep-sea container and domestic intermodal markets are particularly vulnerable to increases in the maximum length of lorries, with bulk markets more likely to be affected by increases in weight limits.

Indirectly, other government policies can have an effect on the rail freight market and, as a consequence, its economic performance. For example, policies relating to energy generation can have major impacts on rail freight activity. The 62 percent decline in coal volumes, traditionally rail freight's biggest commodity flow in Britain, between 2014/15 Q2 and 2015/16 Q2 (ORR, 2015) has caused considerable concern about the financial viability of the entire rail freight sector. This dramatic decline in coal traffic has resulted from the introduction of a new tax on coal in the 2015/16 financial year, the closure of power stations as they reach their agreed generating limits and the decision to phase out electricity generation from coal by 2025. All of these factors, which have led to instability in the rail freight market, result from the implementation of public policies designed to limit the effects of climate change.

22.4.3 The European dimension

The British experience fits within the wider regulatory and operational framework governing the economics of rail freight at the European level. Since 1990, the European Commission has been developing its rail policies with the broad aim of improving rail efficiency and competitiveness through liberalisation and harmonisation (see Butcher, 2013 for a concise summary). Progress has been widely regarded as being slow, though there have been some major changes influencing the economics of European rail freight in the intervening 25 years. Key measures include:

- The First Railway Package established the open-access principle for international rail freight.
- The Second Railway Package focused on the subsequent liberalisation of national freight markets together with general interoperability measures to better integrate the European rail system.
- A range of additional agreements to enhance interoperability and improve the performance of European rail freight.

The overall aim is the creation of a Single European Railway Area, with harmonised regulations (e.g. for the approvals processes for new operators or rolling stock) and the legal, financial and operational segregation of infrastructure and service provision so as to engender a more efficient and competitive rail freight market. Particular challenges remain for cross-border freight train operations, especially where infrastructural differences such as track gauge or electrification voltages prevail. Traditionally, this has led to increased cost and transit time as a consequence of having to transship consignments between wagons with different gauges or to change locomotives to match the supplied electrification system. There are two main ways of overcoming such issues, with differing economic implications:

- Standardise the infrastructure across Europe (e.g. with a common track gauge and electrification system): to do this continent-wide, even just for core routes, would require up-front capital investment, most likely publicly funded, but would lead to lower train-operating costs (unless the capital investment was recouped through higher track access charges). Most new strategic rail infrastructure is constructed to a standardised track gauge and with a common electrification system, but there remains the legacy effect of long-established non-standard infrastructure.
- Utilise equipment that can overcome infrastructure differences: technological advances have allowed the introduction of gauge changers which can regauge rolling stock axles where there is a change in track gauge (e.g. on the France–Spain border) and multivoltage locomotives which can draw power from two or more electrification systems. The costs of adopting these technologies are more likely to be borne by rail freight operators themselves and, particularly with multivoltage locomotives, will be an ongoing additional cost in terms of higher leasing or purchase costs because these locomotives are more complex and thus more expensive to provide. However, these additional costs may be outweighed by cost savings resulting from better locomotive utilisation resulting from using the same locomotive over a greater distance and not having to keep locomotives on hand at the location where the electrification system changes. An alternative solution is to use diesel rather than electric traction, but this may not be desirable for economic or environmental reasons.

International Rail Freight Corridors are being implemented to simplify the operation of long-distance freight trains, improving efficiency and reducing costs, with the aim of making rail more competitive.

22.5 Competitive rail freight markets

Given the foregoing discussion concerning the role of the public sector, at both the British and European levels it is evident that rail freight does not operate in an unconstrained free-market environment. However, over the last two decades, intra-rail competition has developed as a consequence of the liberalisation policies already outlined. In this section, the effects of competition and its principal positive and negative influences on rail freight economics are set out. Based on data from the IBM Rail Liberalisation Index, it appears that market liberalisation generally leads to a growth in rail freight market share but does not necessarily guarantee this (CERRE, 2014). Figure 22.4 demonstrates the gradual opening up to competition of the British rail freight market since British Rail was privatised in the mid-1990s. It is evident that English, Welsh and Scottish Railway (EWS) had a near monopoly in the late1990s but its share of the market has been eroded over time. In 1997, EWS and Freightliner had non-overlapping rail freight activities, with EWS monopolising all markets except for the intermodal market which was the preserve of Freightliner. Over time, these two operators have directly competed in each other's traditional

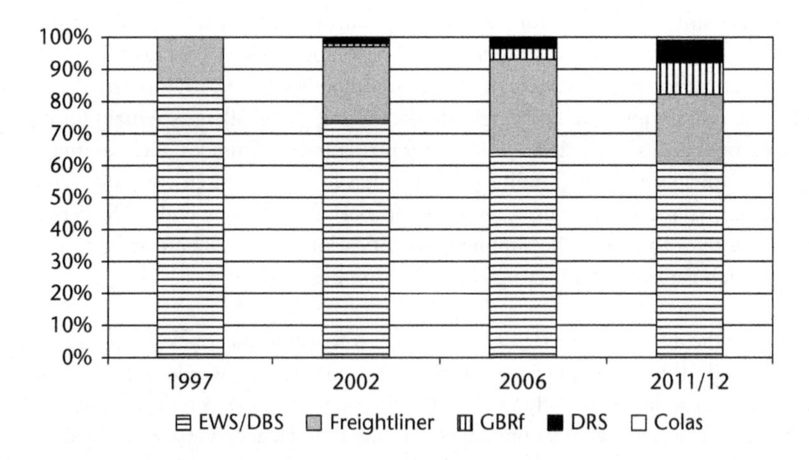

Figure 22.4 Estimated operator market share of British rail freight by revenue, 1997–2011/12
Source: based on Railway Gazette International, 2008 and ORR, 2013

markets and the new operators have made in-roads into certain areas of these markets. Table 22.4 shows the level of competition within the different freight markets by early 2013. There is a clear relationship between operator size and the number of markets in which they are active, with DB Cargo UK (formerly DB Schenker (DBS) and, before that, EWS) and Freightliner having the strongest representation. Even at this level of disaggregation, what appear to be competitive markets may not be so. In the intermodal market in 2013, for example, DB Cargo UK, Freightliner and GB Railfreight were all competing in the port-hinterland containers sub-market, while DBS had a near monopoly of the domestic intermodal sub-market.

It is important to note, though, that there is often competitive tendering to gain contracts, so the absence of multiple operators does not necessarily imply a lack of market competition. There have been examples of contracts changing from one operator to another, and of customers splitting their traffic requirements among two or more operators. Examples include operator changes in the Anglo-Scottish domestic intermodal market (see Section 22.7) as contracts have been retendered and Tarmac awarding new five-year contracts to four of the rail freight operators

Table 22.4 Indicative level of competition in rail freight markets (as at January 2013)

Market	*Rail freight operator*					
	Colas	*DBS*	*DCR*	*DRS*	*FL*	*GBRf*
Coal	○	•	–	–	•	•
Aggregates	–	•	○	–	•	○
Metals	○	•	○	–	○	○
Petroleum	○	•	–	–	–	○
Automotive	–	•	–	–	–	–
Waste	–	•	–	–	•	•
Intermodal	–	•	–	•	•	•
Channel Tunnel	–	•	–	–	–	○
General freight	○	•	–	○	•	–

Note: • highly active; ○ slightly active; – not active

Table 22.5 Average freight train load (2003/4–2014/15)

Year	*Total no. of freight train movements*	*Freight lifted (million tonnes)*	*Average freight train load (tonnes)*
2003/4	416,053	88.9	214
2004/5	381,965	100.9	264
2005/6	455,561	105.3	231
2006/7	364,949	108.2	296
2007/8	332,218	102.4	308
2008/9	316,684	102.7	324
2009/10	278,472	87.2	313
2010/11	265,559	89.9	339
2011/12	273,897	101.7	371
2012/13	275,827	113.1	410
2013/14	288,371	116.6	404
2014/15	282,304	110.5	391
% change 2003/4–2014/15	(32)	24	83

Source: based on ORR, 2015

in early 2016, with each operator taking responsibility for a specific part of the company's requirements (Tarmac, 2016). Given the commercial sensitivities involved, however, the role of pricing relative to other attributes such as service quality and performance (see Section 22.6) in these contract changes tends not to be publicised.

Considering the British rail freight market in its entirety, there is substantial evidence of efficiency improvements in recent years. Comparing official data on tonnes lifted and the number of freight trains operated reveals a large increase in the average freight train payload, though not in a straightforward linear manner. In 2003/4, the average tonnage per train was 214 tonnes; by 2014/15 this had increased by more than 80 percent to 391 tonnes (ORR, 2015; Table 22.5). The specific numbers need to be treated with some caution, since the two variables are not recorded in the same way, but the overall trend towards heavier average payloads is clear.

The rail freight operators have invested more than £2 billion in locomotives, wagons and capital equipment since the mid-1990s (Rail Delivery Group, 2015), with considerable efficiency improvements to be seen. The Rail Value for Money Study (DfT and ORR, 2011) found that staff efficiency had dramatically improved for rail freight but not for passenger rail (see Figure 22.5).

While a competitive market may lead to a focus on cost efficiencies, innovation and investment in order that operators remain (or become) competitive and win contracts, there can be economic downsides. A competitive rail freight market tends to lead to low operating margins and limited options for operators to respond quickly to changing market conditions because of their high fixed cost base. The high fixed costs and the regulatory requirements can also represent a significant barrier to new entrants. In the British market, the economic downturn in 2008/9 generally reduced margins with two of the four largest operators recording losses and two other operators having gone out of business (DfT and ORR, 2011). Similar concerns have been raised more recently in light of the dramatic decline of the coal market (see Section 22.4.2). A more general potential economic downside of a competitive market relates to the potential loss of economies of scale, which may lead to inefficient resource utilisation or the loss of marginal flows. The tendency for competing operators to focus on the more profitable and straightforward trainload flows may jeopardise the continued provision of wagonload services. Furthermore,

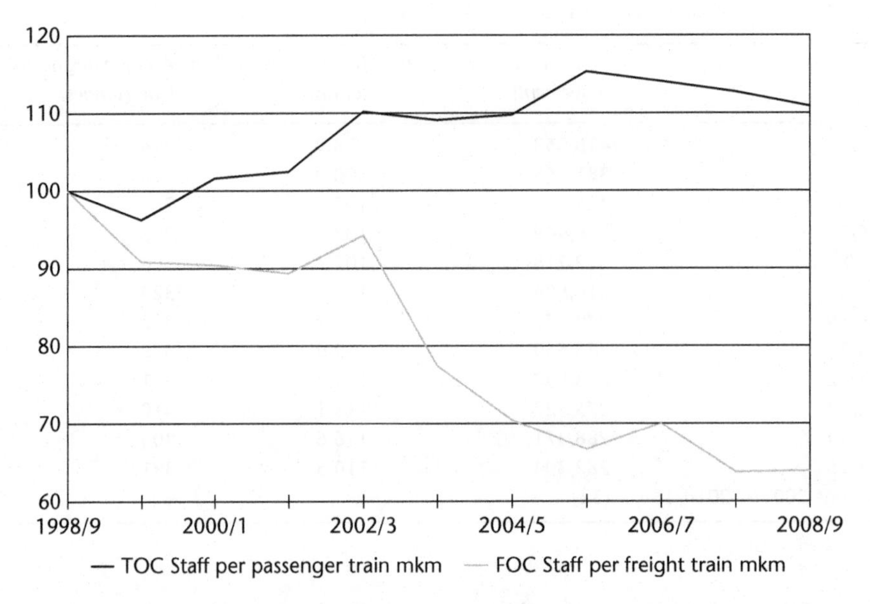

Figure 22.5 Comparison of freight (FOC) and passenger (TOC) staff productivity (per train kilometre)
Source: redrawn from DfT and ORR, 2011

the susceptibility to downturns as part of the economic cycle leads to high risk, which may deter market entrants due to generally insufficient returns.

22.6 Importance of rail freight pricing in mode choice decision making

Based on a survey of British rail freight customers (ORR, 2012), Table 22.6 compares perceptions of the performance and the importance of a range of service attributes. This reveals a major discrepancy between the importance of rail freight cost/price (ranked 1) and its perceived performance (ranked 13).

In some markets, particularly for higher-value commodities such as consumer goods, journey time can have a considerable monetary value. Based on ORR data, the value of journey time to the customer of a deep-sea container train was estimated as £1,069 per hour (DfT and ORR, 2011), meaning that some customers may be willing to pay more for shorter transit times. European research has emphasised that shippers' modal preferences generally include service quality factors (e.g. reliability, capacity) in addition to cost/price (Directorate General for Internal Policies, 2015). Even when rail is well placed to offer a cost-competitive modal option, the greater complexity for rail freight operators compared with road hauliers may place rail at a disadvantage:

> It is common practice to obtain a price and service details within 24 hours from asking for information from a road haulier. This is not as easy in the rail sector as applications have to be made to the network manager and checks made on the availability of train paths and types of wagon required. This tends to delay the process and may even not be provided in time for a potential customer. Even when prices and service details are known there is the possibility there might not be a suitable terminal close enough to the destination.
>
> *(DfT, 2010b, 3)*

Table 22.6 Ranking of perceived importance and performance of rail freight service attributes

Importance rank	*Performance rank*	*Service attribute*	*Mean importance score*	*Mean performance score*
1	13	Cost/price	8.91	5.52
2	4	Service quality – on time/punctual delivery	8.33	6.50
3	9	Access to mainline network	8.11	5.86
4	3	Overall service quality	7.86	6.55
5	8	Access to terminals	7.70	6.04
6	17	Flexible service/recovery strategy	7.66	5.24
7	12	Information/responsiveness to customer needs	7.52	5.55
8	7	Service quality – lead times	7.35	6.04
9	10	Location of logistics hubs	7.18	5.69
10	6	Service quality – journey time	6.84	6.30
11	2	Security of goods in transit	6.73	6.95
12	5	Equipment quality	6.58	6.35
13	1	Environmental considerations	6.35	7.71
14	11	Rail freight experience/past track record	5.73	5.61
15	15	Physical nature of goods	5.56	5.45
16	16	Track and trace	5.18	5.29
-	14	Other	-	5.50

Note: mean scores on a scale of 1 to 10 where 1 is extremely poor and 10 is extremely good
Source: based on ORR, 2012

22.7 Making rail freight more efficient and cost competitive: British case studies

By using a range of practical examples from the published literature and original research, this final section attempts to provide a flavour of how rail freight can become more cost competitive, particularly in the face of competition from road haulage.

22.7.1 Short distance rail freight flows

It is generally challenging to obtain financial information relating to specific flows or customers owing to commercial sensitivities, but a Freight Best Practice Case Study (DfT, 2010b) provided details of a relatively short distance (72 miles/116km) cement flow in Scotland to be commercially viable. Each train conveys the equivalent payload of 37 lorries, with consequent savings in labour and fuel costs making a flow over even this distance commercially viable. The amount of fuel needed for the rail flow is just one-third of that if the flow were to be carried by road. Key to rail's viability is the long-established rail terminal infrastructure at both the cement works and the receiving terminal, keeping capital costs down. Had the terminals not already existed, though, government grant funding may well have been available to help to defray upfront capital costs.

22.7.2 The growth of rail for domestic flows of consumer goods

Since 2000, rail has become considerably more active in carrying consumer goods in unit loads such as containers. In particular, the number of services between the Midlands (especially the

Daventry terminal) and central Scotland has increased to five or six per day in each direction. In a study to emphasise rail's potential, the FTA (2012) summarised the growing use of domestic intermodal rail freight services on this corridor contracted by logistics service providers and carrying loads for key retailers including Tesco, Morrisons, Marks and Spencer, Sainsbury's, Asda and the Co-Operative Group. Tesco is unique in providing trainload volumes, with the other retailers making use of shared-user trains. A number of the retailers have reported cost savings over the road haulage alternative, making rail freight financially viable as well as more sustainable. In many cases, these consumer good flows benefit from the MSRS grant funding discussed in Section 22.4.2. Broader service improvements (e.g. greater service frequency and flexibility, improved responsiveness to customer requirements, additional terminals) are needed to achieve a greater volume shift to rail. The challenge of aggregating sufficient volume from across the customer base to make up sufficient trainload quantities for new routes was also identified as an obstacle to be overcome, reflecting the high fixed costs of freight train operations.

22.7.3 Improved network capability for port-hinterland container traffic

As a result of government funding from sources including TIF(P) and SFN (see Section 22.4.2), many corridors have witnessed improvements in capabilities for train length and weight, benefiting on-train capacity and helping to reduce unit costs. Much of the attention has focused on enhancing infrastructure for port-hinterland container flows, with a gauge-enhancement programme increasing the network coverage for high cube containers to be carried on standard wagons and targeted infrastructure improvements allowing longer container trains to operate. In addition, rail freight operators have invested in new locomotives and wagons that also help to improve efficiency in this key rail freight market. Table 22.7 demonstrates considerable improvements in efficiency between 2007 and 2015, resulting in a 25 percent increase in the typical train load (as measured in 20-foot equivalent units (TEUs)). With one-quarter more containers being moved by broadly the same number of train services per week (578 in 2007 and 579 in 2015), and given the relatively high fixed costs of freight train operation, it is likely that the TEU cost per kilometre will have reduced.

22.7.4 New dedicated rail freight infrastructure

The North Doncaster Chord (in Yorkshire, England) is a 3.2km section of new railway line which was opened in June 2014. It provides a more direct route for imported coal (and now biomass) traffic from the port of Immingham, on Britain's east coast, to the three large power stations in the Aire Valley. Prior to its opening, the majority of these freight trains had to share a 22km section of the East Coast Main Line with express passenger services. The new Chord has helped to segregate the intensive passenger and freight flows, aiming to improve the performance

Table 22.7 Changes in key rail efficiency measures in British port-hinterland container market, 2007–15

Efficiency measure	*2007 survey*	*2015 survey*	*% change*
Mean TEU capacity provided per train	59.99	69.89	16.5
Mean capacity utilisation per train (% of TEU)	72.20	78.14	8.2
Mean TEU load per train	43.76	54.68	25.0

Source: author's surveys

of both and to provide additional network capacity to cater for growth in service provision. A 'before' and 'after' analysis (conducted by the author) of freight train performance revealed reductions in both average journey distance and average scheduled journey time of almost 10 percent and a considerable increase in on-time arrivals at the power stations (up from 83 percent to 89 percent of trains arriving less than 10 minutes late). Improvements in these measures are likely to offer opportunities for cost reduction for rail freight operators through reduced fuel costs and improvements in the utilisation of staff, locomotives and wagons.

22.8 Summary

The link between costs and pricing within the rail freight market is not especially clear, so it is quite challenging to develop a strong understanding of the economic structure. Rail is particularly well suited to handling trainload volumes of bulk goods, but often struggles to achieve commercial viability in smaller volume and/or short distance flows of goods such as consumer products. Increasing intra-modal competition, combined with considerable investment in modern equipment, has resulted in substantial efficiency improvements in the British rail freight market over the last couple of decades and growth in rail's share of non-bulk markets such as port-hinterland container traffic and domestic intermodal flows for major retailers. At the European level, measures are being implemented to try to create a Single European Railway Area in which intra-modal competition is encouraged and barriers to efficient operation are removed.

In some cases, the commercial viability of rail freight is dependent on public funding to develop infrastructure or support service provision, particularly where wider benefits to the economy, environment and society can be achieved by switching flows from road to rail. Overall, the chapter has demonstrated the critical role of the public sector in determining both the economic structure of the rail freight market itself and the ways in which rail is able to compete with other transport modes (especially road haulage). While challenges remain, there are encouraging signs of rail freight becoming more efficient and commercially viable, despite the inherent characteristics which lead to a high fixed cost base in comparison with road haulage.

References

Butcher, L. (2013). *Railways: EU Policy*. SN184, Business and Transport. London: House of Commons Library.

CERRE (2014). *Development of Rail Freight in Europe: What Regulation Can and Cannot Do*. Brussels: Centre on Regulation in Europe.

DfT (2007). *Delivering a Sustainable Railway*. London: Department for Transport.

DfT (2009). *Non-Road Modes Research: Executive Summary*. London: Department for Transport.

DfT (2010a). *Freight Modal Choice Study: Addressable Markets*. Prepared by the University of Westminster. London: Department for Transport.

DfT (2010b). *Short Haul Rail Freight on Track for Profits in Scotland*. London: Department for Transport.

DfT (2015). *Guide to Mode Shift Revenue Support (MSRS) Scheme*. London: Department for Transport.

DfT (2016). *Mode Shift Revenue Support and Waterborne Freight Grants Schemes*. Letter to Freight Grant Stakeholders, 12 January. London: Department for Transport.

DfT and ORR (2011). *Realising the Potential of GB Rail: Final Independent Report of the Rail Value for Money Study*. London: Department for Transport/Office of Rail Regulation.

Directorate General for Internal Policies (2015). *Freight on Road: Why EU Shippers Prefer Truck to Train*. Produced by Steer Davies Gleave at the request of the European Parliament's Committee on Transport and Tourism, IP/B/TRAN/FWC/2010–006/LOT1/C1/SC10. Brussels: European Union.

FTA (2012). *On Track! Retailers Using Rail Freight to Make Cost and Carbon Savings*. Tunbridge Wells: Freight Transport Association.

Harris, N. G. and McIntosh, D. (2003). The Economics of Rail Freight. In Harris, N. G. and Schmid, F. (eds), *Planning Freight Railways*. London: A. and N. Harris.

MDS Transmodal (2006). *Impact of Track Access Charge Increases on Rail Freight Traffic*. Final Report. Chester: MDS Transmodal.

Network Rail (2010). *Value and Importance of Rail Freight*. London: Network Rail.

Network Rail (2013). *Value and Importance of Rail Freight: Summary Report*. London: Network Rail.

Network Rail (2014). *Control Period 4 Freight Review*. London: Network Rail.

ORR (2012). *ORR Freight Customer Survey Report 2012*. Produced on behalf of ORR by AECOM. London: Office of Rail Regulation.

ORR (2013). *GB Rail Industry Financial Information 2011–12*. London: Office of Rail Regulation.

ORR (2015). *Data Portal: Freight Rail Usage*. London: Office of Rail and Road, http://dataportal.orr.gov.uk/browsereports/13

ORR (2016). *What We Do*. London: Office of Rail and Road, http://orr.gov.uk/about-orr/what-we-do

Oxera (2014). *What Is the Contribution of Rail to the UK Economy?* Prepared for the Rail Delivery Group. Oxford: Oxera.

Rail Delivery Group (2014). *Keeping the Lights on and the Traffic Moving: Sustaining the Benefits of Rail Freight for the UK Economy*. London: Rail Delivery Group.

Rail Delivery Group (2015). *Freight Britain: Continuity and Certainty for Rail Freight*. London: Rail Delivery Group.

Railway Gazette International (2008). *Market Reforms Revitalise European Rail Freight*, 6 October. London: Railway Gazette International.

RFG/RFOA (2009). *Paper 4: Unlocking Rail Freight Growth*. London: Rail Freight Group/Rail Freight Operators' Association.

Shannon, P. (2014). *Speedlink*. Shepperton: Ian Allan Publishing.

Tarmac (2016). *Supporting UK Infrastructure Delivery and Cutting Carbon*. Press release, 13 January, www.tarmac.com/news-and-media/

TRL (2008). *Longer and/or Longer and Heavier Goods Vehicles (LHVs): A Study of the Likely Effects if Permitted in the UK: Final Report*. Published Project Report PPR 285, prepared for Department for Transport. Wokingham: TRL.

Woodburn, A. (2015). An Empirical Study of the Variability in the Composition of British Freight Trains. *Journal of Rail Transport Planning and Management*, 5(4), 294–308, doi: 10.1016/j.jrtpm.2015.12.001

23
Air cargo

Thomas Budd and Robert Mayer

23.1 Introduction

The transport of goods by air originated in November 1910, when Philip Orin Parmelee piloted a Wright Model B aircraft a total of 65 miles to transport a consignment of silk from Dayton to Columbus, Ohio. By 1919, the Paris Convention had created the first international regulatory framework concerning the transport of air passengers and cargo, and established for the first time a legal contract between the customer and an airline for the transport of goods by air. Since then the role of the air cargo industry as a facilitator of world trade, employment and economic growth has grown such that in 2015, airlines transported 51.2 million metric tonnes of cargo valued at over US$6 trillion (£4.6 trillion) globally (Air Transport Action Group (ATAG), 2016). This equates to 185 billion freight tonne kilometers (FTKs) per year, where 1 FTK is considered to represent 1 tonne of freight transported 1km. While air cargo represents around 35 percent of world trade by total value, in terms of total volume the contribution of air cargo is considerably smaller, at less than 0.5 percent (ATAG, 2016). This is because while air cargo is generally faster and more reliable than transport by road, rail or sea, these benefits come at a financial cost to the customer. Consequently, goods transported by air are generally restricted to those that are time critical and have a high value-to-weight ratio. Examples of such commodities include high-value consumer electronic products, 'just-in-time' industrial components, perishable goods such as fruit and vegetables, as well as items such as express mail, humanitarian aid or medical supplies. For industries where streamlined global production and reliable on-time delivery of goods and components is key, air transport represents a fundamental component of the global supply chain. The air cargo industry also plays a vital role in terms of employment and growth. This is true both for the direct employment it generates, in roles such as handlers, forwarders and customs officials, but also the myriad of associated indirect and induced jobs it helps support in related industries and business areas. This is particularly significant for regions that rely heavily on exporting goods such as fresh produce or flowers, many of which are located in the developing world. For example, it is estimated that 1.5 million livelihoods in Africa are supported by exports to the UK market alone (ATAG, 2016).

It is estimated that the air cargo market will grow by 4.1 percent per year in terms of freight tonnes carried from 2015 (IATA, 2015). One of the world's major aircraft manufacturers, Boeing, forecast a tripling of revenue tonne kilometres (RTKs, i.e. 1 tonne of revenue generating cargo transported 1km) from 207.8 billion in 2013 to 521.8 billion RTKs by 2033 (Boeing, 2014). This growth is likely to be driven by increasing demand in rapidly developing economies, particularly in Asia, as well as evolving businesses practices, including the increasing decision of firms to operate low 'just-in-time' inventories. This practice seeks to improve efficiency by shipping goods or products only when they are needed, rather than stockpiling large volumes of goods in advance of their use. Yet despite these forecasts, the industry faces significant challenges. The challenging global economic climate combined with factors relating to rising operating costs, fluctuations in the cost of fuel, limited airport capacity and increased competition from land- and sea-based transport modes represent ever present pressures on air cargo yields. These issues collectively make longer-term planning for the sustained growth for air cargo a challenging prospect. This was brought into particular focus by the severe impacts on world trade initiated by the economic recession of 2008/9, which resulted in a 13 percent fall in air cargo traffic (Boeing, 2014). While the sector has recovered to some extent, the 1.7 percent annual growth rate experienced since 2009 is still significantly lower than growth rates experienced before the recession, which were as high as 6 percent during some years in the 1990s and early 2000s (Boeing, 2014).

Given the significant global economic role of air cargo and the critical part it plays in the functioning of modern society, it is notable how comparatively little attention air cargo has received in the academic literature, albeit with some recent notable exceptions (for example, Gardiner et al., 2005; Morrell, 2012; Sales, 2013; Budd and Ison, 2015). What work there is in this area has noted that air cargo is to some extent overlooked in an academic sense compared with the passenger side of the business, which is generally perceived to be more exciting, interesting and glamourous than its cargo counterpart.

The chapter seeks to help address this possible imbalance. Initially, it provides an overview of the air cargo industry. This includes the different types of commodities carried, a description of the air cargo supply chain and a closer examination of three of its vital components; air cargo carriers, aircraft and airports. It then provides an assessment of the air cargo market including its key characteristics and highlights the various challenges it faces. This is followed by an overview of the economics of air cargo, including costs, pricing regimes and yields. The chapter then turns to the importance of security and regulation in securing the air cargo supply chain, before assessing the short- and long-term economic prospects for the air cargo industry, including emerging trends and innovations.

23.2 The air cargo industry

23.2.1 Commodities

A summary of the main categories of air cargo is provided in Figure 23.1. It is important to note that while the terms air cargo and air freight are often used interchangeably, they incorporate two different types of activity. Air cargo is the more encompassing of the two terms as it incorporates both air freight and mail, and is the term that will be used in this chapter.

While the relative costs associated with transporting goods by air has generally been decreasing in recent years,[1] compared with other modes, air cargo is still a relatively expensive mode. For this reason, air cargo is generally employed for carrying specific goods, particularly high-value goods, such as pharmaceutical products or high-end consumer electronics, where the shipping costs (while still relatively high) are marginal in comparison with the total costs of the goods. This is typically equal to around 5 percent of the total value of the product in question. Air cargo is also suitable for transporting goods with a limited life cycle, such as fresh food, flowers, high fashion or livestock, where air transport can provide significant advantages in terms of end-to-end journey time over other modes. Goods may also be transported by air where their delivery is critical to the

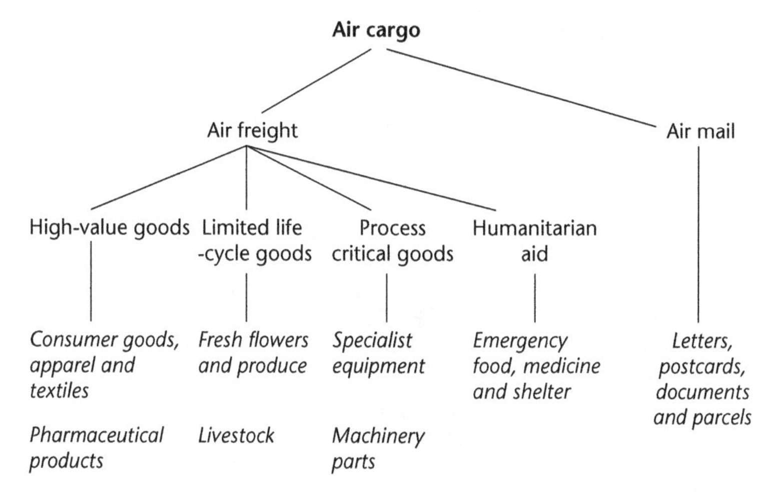

Figure 23.1 Summary of air cargo commodities

smooth running of certain business practices or some other function, even where the goods themselves hold little intrinsic value. Examples of these process-critical goods include delivery of spare machinery parts, particular documents or other very specialist equipment.

Air mail is a major component of air cargo operations. This incorporates carriage of letters, postcards, documents and parcels that are carried according to the national postal regulation in the country in question. Emergency food, medical supplies and other forms of humanitarian aid are another type of air cargo, given the rapid response and wide geographical coverage air transport provides. For example, air transport played a key role in facilitating the movement of medicine, supplies and medical personnel during the Ebola epidemic in West Africa in 2014/15.

Figure 23.2 shows the overall share of commodities imported from North America to Europe, and from Europe to North America in 2013. It can be seen that the type and share of commodities vary. Chemicals, computing and telecommunications equipment, and machinery and electrical equipment, account for nearly half (47 percent) of all air cargo transported from North America to Europe, while metals and documents/express packages account for a further 21 percent of the market (Boeing, 2014). In comparison, transportation equipment and parts account for 9 percent of the imports from Europe to North America, whereas these are absent for trade in the opposite direction.

23.2.2 The supply chain

Many modern supply chains are dependent on fast and efficient transport. While transporting goods by air is usually more expensive than other modes of transport, air cargo can generate competitive advantages and drive down other supply-chain related costs for sellers and/or buyers of goods. Resulting from the faster movement of goods in the air cargo supply chain, lead times (i.e. the order-to-delivery cycle) can be reduced. This means that buyers (e.g. retailers) can decrease their inventories which results in cost savings for the companies. Shorter lead times also compress the forecasting horizon and thus improve forecasting accuracy, and consequently cut stock-outs and forced mark-downs (e.g. due to obsolete stock). Therefore, while air cargo might increase the transport-related component of total supply

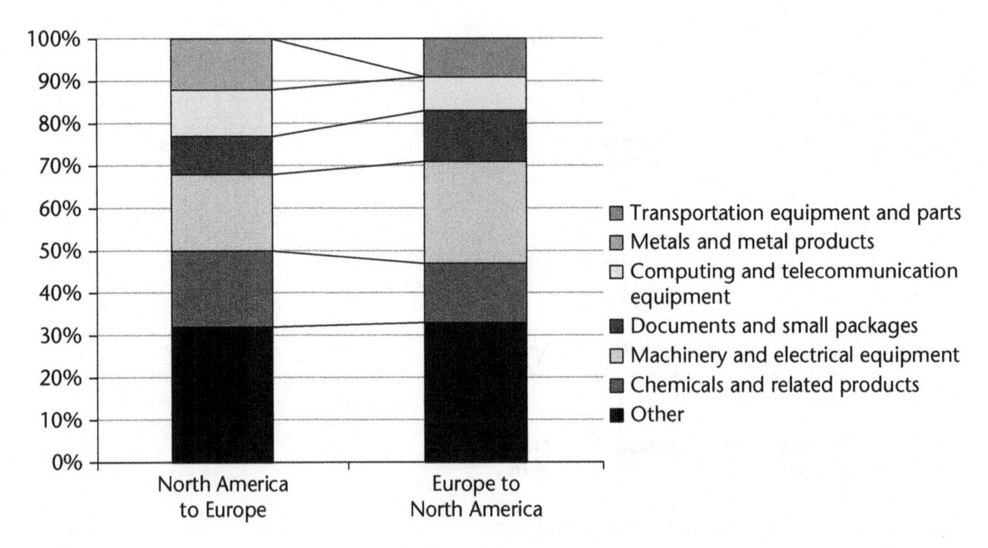

Figure 23.2 Share of cargo commodities to and from North America and Europe, 2013
Source: Boeing, 2014

chain costs, it can have a positive impact on inventory-related costs which, in some cases, can indeed reduce total supply-chain costs.

The air cargo supply chain incorporates a range of different parties, procedures and information exchanges (see Figure 23.3). The chain is initiated by a seller (also referred to as the consignor, exporter or trader) and a buyer, who wish to exchange goods by air. The seller may be the manufacturer of the goods in question and/or responsible for their sale. The seller will often engage a third-party freight forwarder, who is in turn responsible for managing the movement of goods in such a way that they are ready for transport by the aircraft operators. This will generally include dealing with the necessary documentation and meeting the regulatory requirements of customs and border agencies, such as official declaration of goods. Other services performed by the freight forwarders may include consolidation, handling, storage, packing and distribution of goods. These services will typically be located 'landside' at an airport (i.e. not past security), but in some cases freight forwarders may have warehousing or processing facilities located 'airside' at the airport.

In some cases the carriage of goods may involve multi-modes of transport including road, rail and maritime transport. Indeed, air cargo operations are generally heavily dependent on the availability and reliability of road-based feeder services to sustain the supply chain. Freight forwarders will necessarily need to work closely with aircraft operators, from whom they will book space for consignments and arrange contracts (known as air transport service agreements) for the transportation of the goods from their origin to destination.

In some cases the freight forwarder will sub-contract a specialist ground handler. This will generally occur where the freight forwarder and/or aircraft operator do not possess the required facilities or resources at a particular location. Once the goods in question have been 'signed off' by the freight forwarder, the ground handler will then take responsibility for the operational aspects of receiving, storing, preparing, transit, and then loading and unloading of cargo to and from the aircraft. Ground handlers necessarily need to be located airside at the airport.

Air cargo carriers (also referred to as airlines or aircraft operators) are contractually bound to the relevant parties to ensure the safe and secure transport of air cargo from one airport to another.

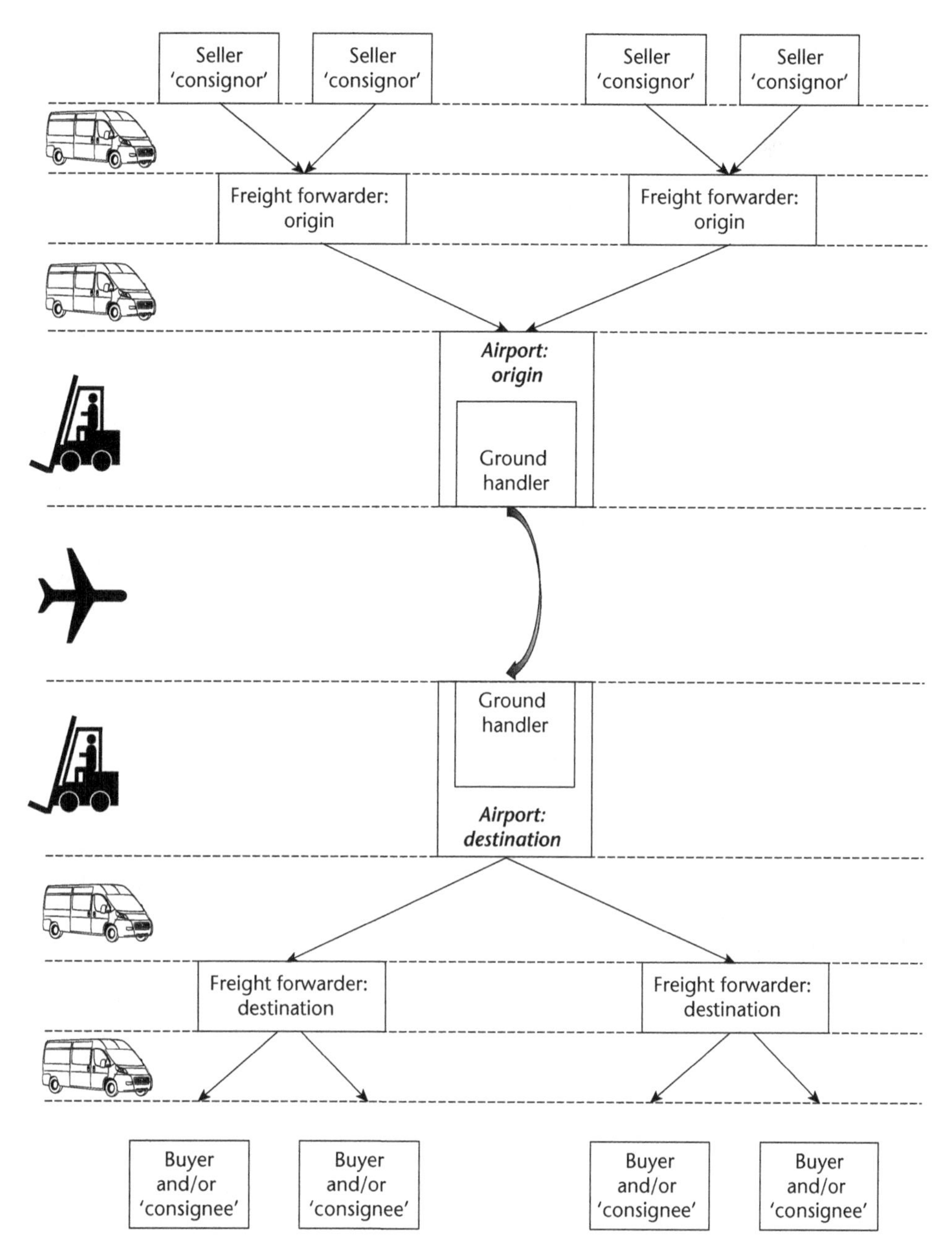

Figure 23.3 The air cargo supply chain

There are different types of air cargo carrier, each providing a differing range of services depending on the demands of the customer. These are discussed in the following section.

The final part of the supply chain involves onward transport from the destination airport by a freight forwarder to the recipient, or consignee. It is important to differentiate between the 'buyer' and 'consignee' here, as while the latter is usually the original purchaser of the goods in question, this is not necessarily always the case.

23.2.3 Air cargo carriers

There are four basic types of air cargo carriers: integrators, all-cargo carriers, combination airlines (i.e. those that carry both passengers and cargo) and ad hoc cargo charter carriers. Integrators manage their own fleet of scheduled aircraft, vans and couriers to offer door-to-door transportation of goods from buyer to seller. This is to say that they combine the responsibilities of the freight forwarder, ground handler and aircraft operator into a single company. This necessarily supports closer integration between different elements of the supply chain, and also allows for the implementation of sophisticated IT-based systems for tracking individual packages or consignments. Three major integrated express operators have come to dominate this market at the global level: UPS, FedEx and DHL. These companies operate extensive 'hub-and-spoke' networks, whereby a number of smaller 'feeder' airports are connected via a single larger hub airport. This allows for significant geographical coverage of their network. Barriers to entry in the global integrator market are generally prohibitively high, given the levels of investment required for funding the lease or purchase of aircraft, ground-based transport logistics and establishing a wide network. In 2013, integrators accounted for 17 percent of the total air cargo market in terms of RTKs, up from 13.4 percent in 2008 (Boeing, 2014). This growth is significantly higher than average annual growth rates compared with air cargo generally, which as noted already are currently around 1.7 percent per year (ATAG, 2016).

All-cargo carriers typically operate scheduled services in wide-body aircraft, including Boeing 747s, but unlike integrators tend to focus on 'point-to-point' services between major long-haul international or transcontinental markets. These services are usually concentrated on large, high-volume market airports, for example New York, London or Tokyo. This inevitably reduces the geographic coverage of their network, and means that they are heavily reliant on the role of freight forwarders for their operations. Generally speaking, the importance and role of all-cargo carriers has been eroded in recent years by growth of integrators and increased competition from other modes of transport.

The third, and largest, type of air cargo carrier in terms of market share are combination carriers, which transport cargo in the lower deck, or 'bellies', of their aircraft. This is especially true for long-haul flights operated by wide-body aircraft, including the Boeing 747 and 777 or Airbus A380 aircraft, which can offer as much as 30 tonnes of cargo capacity (Morrell, 2012). Network carriers including Singapore Airlines, Lufthansa and Emirates use major hub airports to connect a wide range of short- and long-haul destinations, and in some major markets supplement their passenger services with cargo-only flights to increase capacity. Carriage of cargo by low-cost carriers is far less common, given the short- to medium-haul nature of their operations, the smaller narrow-body aircraft they employ for this purpose and the importance of a fast turnaround time to the success of their business model.

Table 23.1 shows the top 10 airlines in terms of total scheduled freight tonnes (both international and domestic) carried in 2014. It can be seen that the two largest domestic carriers are both integrators (FedEx and UPS), whereas Emirates Airlines, who transport cargo as both bellyhold in their passenger aircraft and by their cargo-only subsidiary, Emirates Sky Cargo, are the largest airline on the international market. Economic growth in China is shown by the importance of Chinese cargo in domestic traffic. For both international and domestic cargo, the role of combination carriers is significant.

Table 23.1 Top 10 airlines by scheduled freight tonnes carried, 2014

International			*Domestic*		
Rank	*Airline*	*Tonnage (000)*	*Rank*	*Airline*	*Tonnage (000)*
1	Emirates	2,288	1	FedEx	5,151
2	FedEx	1,977	2	UPS	2,809
3	Cathay Pacific Airways	1,498	3	China Southern	965
4	UPS	1,431	4	Air China	689
5	Korean Air	1,430	5	China Eastern Airlines	571
6	China Airlines	1,296	6	All Nippon Airways	505
7	Qatar Airways	1,158	7	Japan Airlines	336
8	Singapore Airlines	1,078	8	Garuda Indonesia	319
9	Lufthansa	963	9	Hainan Airlines	294
10	Etihad Airways	854	10	Shenzhen Airlines	248

Source: IATA, 2015

Ad hoc cargo charter carriers vary from other types of carrier in that they do not operate regular scheduled services, but instead offer capacity on an 'ad hoc' basis in response to specific demands. Examples where these services may be required include specific construction projects or the need to quickly deliver aid following a humanitarian disaster. In some cases cargo carriers will lease their aircraft (known as 'wet leasing') to other airlines or operators for this purpose. These companies are referred to as 'ACMI' operators, so-called because they provide the aircraft, crew, maintenance and insurance to the lessee.

23.2.4 Aircraft

There are three main types of aircraft that carry cargo: wide-body jets, narrow-body jets and narrow-body turboprop aircraft (also known as 'feeder aircraft'). This classification applies to aircraft that are purely used for carrying cargo and those that are shared with passenger services. It is estimated that there are around 1,600 dedicated cargo aircraft currently in operation globally, compared with just over 25,000 total commercial aircraft in operation worldwide (Airbus, 2014; ATAG, 2016).

The larger, longer-range freighter aircraft, such as the Boeing 747F, 777F or Airbus A330F, are generally used for long-haul international and transcontinental routes, including the major trade routes between North America, Europe and Asia. These aircraft will generally have payloads above 80 tonnes. Narrow-body, single-aisle aircraft are more commonly employed for short- and medium-haul routes in international and some domestic markets, with payloads between 30 and 80 tonnes. It is common for older passenger aircraft to be converted into pure cargo aircraft once they are no longer needed for passenger services, although they are typically less fuel efficient and more expensive to maintain than newer aircraft. Narrow-body turboprop aircraft (i.e. propeller-powered aircraft), such as the Cessna Caravan or ATR 72, act as 'feeders' to and from the main hub airports to smaller outlying airports, as well as operating in niche or remote markets or for high-priority 'overnight' deliveries. Payloads for these aircraft will generally be smaller than 30 tonnes.

The decks of cargo aircraft will be designed to have large doors and 'rollers' built into the floor of the main and/or lower deck in order to allow large containers and pallets to be easily rolled on and off the aircraft. One of the major aircraft manufacturers, Airbus, forecast over 2,300 deliveries

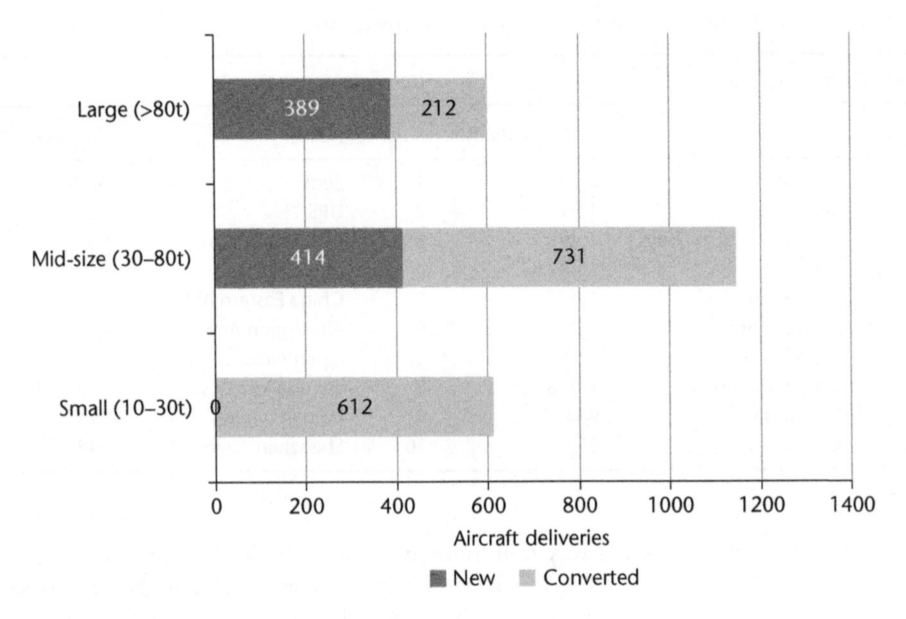

Figure 23.4 Cargo aircraft deliveries, 2014–33
Source: Airbus, 2014

of cargo aircraft (both new and converted) up to 2030, with much of this growth coming from the mid-size narrow-body market in the Middle East and Asia (see Figure 23.4). Airbus, a major aircraft manufacturer, anticipate that cargo fleets in this region will almost triple in size up to 2033 (Airbus, 2014). In contrast, it is expected that the majority of deliveries in the more mature North American and European markets will be for replacing existing fleets (Airbus, 2014).

23.2.5 Airports

Airports represent the vital link in the air cargo supply chain between surface transport and ground-based services and aircraft operations. Airports well suited to handling cargo (and consequently those with a competitive advantage) are able to minimise the amount of time shipments spend on the ground. This requires the provision of extensive and often specialised warehousing facilities, such as in the case of transporting refrigerated goods or livestock (Sales, 2013). This may especially be the case for airports that handle a large share of fresh produce or perishable goods.

Skilled teams of ground handlers will be based at these sites in order to efficiently assemble and disassemble pallets and containers for transport. Competitive airports will also necessarily need to be well connected to surface transport networks, where cargo is often transported during the night to avoid problems of traffic congestion. Indeed, the ability to operate 24 hours a day is a key factor for airports handling cargo. Airports such as Cologne and Hong Kong are examples of sites with 24-hour operations, where they are able to balance their passenger operations during the day with cargo operations at night. However, growing public and political awareness and sensitivity towards noise and environmental issues mean that there is increasing pressure on airports to operate night curfews, which may restrict an airport's capacity to accommodate cargo services (for example, at Frankfurt Airport).

Table 23.2 Top 10 airports by total cargo handled, 2014

Rank	*Airport*	*Cargo handled (tonnes)*
1	Hong Kong	4,415,983
2	Memphis, USA	4,258,531
3	Shanghai, China	3,181,654
4	Incheon, South Korea	2,557,681
5	Anchorage, USA	2,492,754
6	Dubai, UAE	2,367,574
7	Louisville, USA	2,293,231
8	Tokyo, Japan	2,133,542
9	Frankfurt, Germany	2,131,976
10	Taipei, Taiwan	2,088,727

Source: IATA, 2015

Although air cargo operates globally, its spatial distribution is heavily skewed towards the northern hemisphere, and particularly concentrated on key markets to/from and within North America, Western Europe and parts of Asia and the Middle East (Budd and Ison, 2015). Table 23.2 shows the top 10 airports in the world in terms of cargo handled (millions of tonnes) per annum in 2014 (IATA, 2015).

Airports that focus predominantly on passenger services are generally categorised according to the number of passengers they handle and/or their network. However, this is not necessarily the most appropriate way to categorise cargo airports as this may omit key cargo-related criteria. In one of the few attempts to establish a classification system for cargo airports, Mayer (2016) used cluster analysis to statistically group 114 airports based on four key cargo-related variables; total cargo throughput per annum (tonnes), cargo work load units (WLU) as a percentage of total WLUs, freighter aircraft movements as a percentage of all aircraft movements and the share of international cargo as a percentage of total cargo volume. Table 23.3 lists the eight types of airports found in the analysis and average values for each category.

As shown, the importance of and reliance on cargo operations is greatest for the 'cargo-dependent Europeans' and the 'North American primaries', with the vast majority of their WLUs stemming from cargo operations. Leipzig-Halle and Liege are examples of dependent cargo airports in Europe. The major cargo airports in North America have a strong domestic network and are also much larger in terms of volumes of cargo handled than their European counterparts. The 'European dualbases', 'North American cargo secondaries' and 'international primary hubs' are more balanced in terms of the split between the cargo and passenger business. Some of the 'international primary hubs', such as Shanghai, Dubai and Hong Kong, are among the largest cargo airports in the world. This is due largely to the importance of cargo carried as 'bellyhold' freight in passenger aircraft, rather than specialist cargo services. As their names suggest, cargo operations play only a relatively minor role at both the international and domestic 'passenger-dominant airports', such as at Dallas-Fort Worth or Boston Logan.

23.3 Market environment

The air cargo sector is necessarily driven by world and regional growth in GDP and, in particular, the impact this has on levels of world trade. Historically, cargo traffic was thought to grow at twice the rate of global GDP. However, in the last decade this growth has dropped to around 1.5 times GDP as a result of the global economic crisis and changing business practices (Airbus, 2014).

Table 23.3 Classification of cargo-handling airports

Airport category	*Cargo tonnes per annum*	*Cargo WLU share (%)*	*Freighter aircraft movement share (%)*	*Share of international cargo (%)*	*Examples*
Cargo- dependent Europeans	719,592	87.50	73.00	96.50	Leipzig Halle Liege
North American cargo primaries	2,925,008	86.67	50.00	32.00	Anchorage Memphis Louisville
European dual bases	563,049	53.33	27.67	94.00	Cologne East Midlands Luxembourg
North American cargo secondaries	531,445	45.20	19.00	11.20	Indianapolis Oakland
International primary hubs	1,969,389	27.00	6.65	89.12	Shanghai Dubai Hong Kong Amsterdam
International secondary hubs	232,068	12.74	4.05	94.05	Athens Doha Dusseldorf Santiago
Passenger-dominant airports (international)	275,725	8.20	2.20	58.20	Dallas-Fort Worth Toronto
Passenger-dominant airports (domestic)	164,112	7.48	2.40	10.44	Jeju Boston

Source: Mayer, 2016

During times of economic growth, availability of credit from banks, increased investment and spending lead to increased levels of trade. Based on positive forecasts, air cargo carriers may then increase their capacity by purchasing or leasing new aircraft or converting existing aircraft to carry cargo. Currently, the emerging markets in parts of Asia and the Middle East are expected to be the key drivers of growth in air cargo in the next five to ten years, with growing populations and increased consumption in these regions (IATA, 2015). Such growth is often supported and sustained by growth in particular industries such as construction or IT, where demand for air cargo may be highest. However, as easily as they can form, economic 'bubbles' can also burst. Often triggered by a particular event or crisis, such as the sub-prime mortgage crisis in the US in 2008/9, these economic 'downswings' typically lead to cutbacks in consumer spending, reduced lending from banks, and investment plans are reduced in scale or shelved entirely. Where carriers have expanded at the end of an upturn in the economic cycle, and the extra capacity they originally sought is delivered during an economic downturn when demand is much lower, this can lead to significant financial problems for the carrier or even bankruptcy. During, or even preceding, an economic downturn demand for air cargo is often one of the first things to be affected, given its relative cost compared with other modes and the high-value nature of the goods associated with it.

While trade and economic activity are perhaps the main drivers of air cargo demand, there are also a number of other important influential factors. Fluctuations in the price of fuel are a particular (and persistent) challenge for air cargo operators, as is the case with air transport generally. Fuel is typically the largest single cost incurred by an airline, accounting for 29 percent of airline costs in 2014 (IATA, 2015). While oil prices fell considerably in 2015/16 (just over $40 per barrel as of January 2016), as recently as January 2013 this figure was as high as $140 per barrel. This inevitably makes long-term forecasting and strategic planning problematic for carriers.

Competition from other modes also remains a key challenge for the industry. For example, the lower per unit costs offered by containerships (approximately ten times less expensive per unit weight than air cargo) combined with important changes in their business practices, including the introduction of 'track and trace' technology, which was once the sole preserve of air cargo, can offer an attractive prospect for all but the most time critical of cargo. In 2013, containership cargo traffic was estimated at 11.2 trillion RTKs, whereas air cargo represented just over 200 billion RTKs (Boeing, 2014). While containerised cargo traditionally was limited to low-value bulk-commodities, it is increasingly being utilised as a lower-cost alternative for the shipment of goods traditionally associated with air travel. Changes in business, IT and communication practices have also necessitated changes in the market. For example, the increased use of email and internet technologies has reduced the need for shipping of documents and parcels, which once represented a significant part of the air cargo business, especially for the integrators.

23.4 Air cargo costs, pricing and yields

The pricing of air cargo services has traditionally been driven by the prevailing market conditions (i.e. market based), rather than the costs incurred by cargo operators (i.e. cost based). Nevertheless, an understanding of the various costs and cost structures is crucial in terms of long-term profitability and competition in the sector. In comparison with passenger services, there are a number of areas where the costs associated with air cargo services vary (see Table 23.4).

Cargo operations inevitably do not incur costs associated with passenger services, such as the provision and training of cabin crew, providing check-in staff and associated facilities, catering services, airport passenger fees or passenger insurance. Rather, the specific costs for air cargo

Table 23.4 Comparison of passenger-related costs and cargo-related costs

Category	*Passengers*	*Cargo*
Cabin crew	✓	
Check-in, baggage, ramp, lounges	✓	
Catering	✓	
Airport passenger departure fees	✓	
Passenger advertising and publicity	✓	
Sales, ticketing, promotion and commissions	✓	✓
Passenger third-party liability insurance	✓	
Cargo insurance		✓
Loading, unloading, transshipment		✓
Fuel	✓	✓
Aircraft capital (lease, depreciation, interest)	✓	✓
Maintenance	✓	✓
General administration	✓	✓

operations relate predominantly to handling costs for the loading, unloading and transshipment of goods, as well as cargo-specific insurance. While passenger and cargo services both incur fuel and maintenance costs, these are generally higher for cargo operations seeing as cargo aircraft are typically older and less fuel efficient. Cargo and passenger services will also incur costs relating to aircraft capital costs (lease rental payments, depreciation and interest payments), air navigation service charges and airport landing fees.

Where cargo and passengers are carried together, costs that cannot be solely attributed to either cargo or passenger costs will be apportioned accordingly for each product. These costs are known as joint costs, and are calculated either via the share of the volume occupied by each component, the share of the payload available or the share of the revenue generated. For example, costs associated with the provision of cabin crew will only be allocated to passenger-related services, whereas landing fees and flight deck crew fees will be shared between passengers and cargo. For airlines that carry relatively little cargo the situation may be slightly different. These carriers usually generate cargo revenues that exceed their marginal costs, albeit on a small scale, and choose not to allocate joint costs. In this scenario cargo operations will appear to be generating profit. However, if the airline were then to start allocating their joint costs fully, cargo operations would, at best, be likely to only be able to break even.

In terms of pricing of air cargo services, rates were traditionally negotiated through the International Air Transport Association (IATA), the international airline trade body, in much the same way that passenger fares were closely regulated and controlled at this time. This would require the airline to submit their cargo rates to representatives of both the country of origin and destination for approval. However, as with the easing of regulation on passenger fares, increasing liberalisation of the air cargo market has led to a decreasing role for these restrictive measures.

The way in which different cargo carriers sell their capacity varies. Ad hoc charter cargo carriers will negotiate and sell the capacity on an aircraft to a single customer, whereas for carriers operating scheduled services (i.e. integrators, all-cargo carriers, and combination carriers) there will be a standard tariff or system of prices available to different suppliers and agents in the supply chain. These may be negotiated on an individual basis with reduced rates available for regular customers or those shipping large orders. The size and bargaining power of some freight forwarders (for example, Panalpina and Kuehne + Nagel) enable them to negotiate significantly lower rates with airlines than those that are publicly available. Morrell (2013) identifies three broad types of cargo rates:

- Specific commodity rates: these tariffs refer to the carriage of particular products from point of origin to destination. They are often priced in such a way as to encourage the bulk shipment of selected commodities, such as flowers, which otherwise could conceivably be transported by other modes.
- Class rates (also known as commodity classification rates): these are similar to specific commodity rates but apply more to commodities such as live animals, dangerous or hazardous goods, human remains or very valuable products, which may require more specialised handling, processing or screening measures. Additionally, surcharges may also be applied to certain products, such as those that are particularly hazardous, valuable or difficult to handle.
- General cargo rates: these rates refer to all other types of cargo, where the price per kilogram of cargo carried will generally decrease the greater the total shipment.

Aside from the total size of a shipment, other factors such as the available aircraft capacity on a particular route, time, costs, routing and regularity with which the shipment is made may all influence the rates offered by airlines. For example, prices will generally be higher for express cargo, which requires a more direct routing, and during times of peak demand such as the weeks leading up to Christmas. While rates are generally calculated according to a shipment's weight, for low-density products (i.e. high volume to weight ratio) rates may be based on the dimensions of the shipment so that the price better reflects the space used on the aircraft. This method for calculating the price of a shipment based on its dimension is referred to as 'dimensional weight' or 'volumetric weight', and may be calculated differently by different cargo carriers. For example, for calculating dimensional weight (in centimeters and kilograms), DHL (2016) use the following equation:

$$\text{Dimensional Weight} = (\text{Length} \times \text{Width} \times \text{Height})/5,000. \tag{23.1}$$

As with passenger services, revenue management is a key component of the air cargo industry. This involves carefully managing the capacity available and price offered in order to maximise revenue, load factors and profitability. Revenue management of air cargo is typically more complicated than for passengers, seeing as there is far less certainty regarding the size, weight, volume or life cycle of air cargo compared with the relative predictability of carrying passengers. The booking cycle for air cargo is also generally much shorter than for passengers, with many bookings made in the two weeks leading up to departure. Most large freight forwarders negotiate a certain capacity with an airline, which gives the forwarder guaranteed access to available capacity at a particular price. If this capacity is not filled for any reason it is normally up to the airline to try and find ways to fill it, which in some cases may be at very short notice. Balancing when to sell available capacity, and how much to sell at any one time, are key challenges for cargo operators.

Overall, revenues from air cargo account for approximately 8.6 percent of total air traffic revenues (CAPA, 2014a, 2014b). For airlines that operate both passenger and cargo business, the latter can account for as much as 35 percent of their total revenue (Boeing, 2014). However, since the global economic downturn in 2008/9 yields from air cargo have generally been in decline. Boeing (2014) report that from 2003 to 2008 air cargo yields grew at 4.7 percent per year; the economic downturn then saw yields fall by 22.4 percent in 2009. Although this recovered in 2010 to 2012, most recently yields have flattened or declined slightly. This trend reflects a combination of factors including overcapacity (often as a result of increased passenger aircraft with 'bellyhold' capacity), the increased bargaining power of freight forwarders and intense competition from other modes. Yields are also necessarily sensitive to fluctuations in the price of oil, when airlines are forced to increase their surcharges to recover their additional costs. For example, in 2008 increased fuel surcharges in response to the global fuel crisis saw increased yields of 17.2 percent compared to the previous year (Boeing, 2014).

23.5 Securing the supply chain

Air cargo security has been one of the major issues in the sector for the last ten years or so. Air cargo security mainly consists of two parts: guaranteeing the security of air cargo shipments while in the air cargo supply chain and minimising the risks stemming from the transport of goods by air (Figure 23.5).

With regard to the security of shipments, air cargo has a competitive advantage over other modes of transport, as theft is virtually impossible while cargo is on board an aircraft. In contrast, maritime transport has been subject to piracy in recent years, which has had an impact on the reliability of this competing mode of transport. Nevertheless, air cargo is highly dependent on road transport as a form of airport access and egress. Therefore, the surface transport component of the air cargo supply chain is particularly vulnerable to theft and non-accidental damage of air cargo, as well as during the

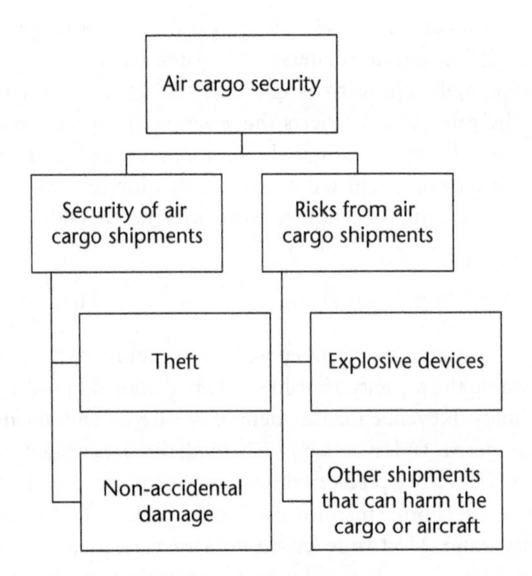

Figure 23.5 Components of air cargo security

storage of airfreighted goods at or near airports. A number of high-profile incidents in recent years have shown that air cargo is not immune to theft and non-accidental damage, for example, the attempted robbery of a Swissport warehouse at London Heathrow in 2004 or the diamond heist at Brussels Airport in 2013, where diamonds were stolen with an estimated value of around US$50 million (£33 million). Consequently, forwarders, airports and airlines have sought to develop security systems and procedures that reduce the likelihood of these events occurring. Examples include the increasing use of CCTV, improved background checks of employees and heightened access restrictions to sensitive areas at airports and warehouses.

While air transport security has been driven predominantly in reaction to different incidents, such as terrorist attacks or criminal activities, until relatively recently the air cargo sector has been slow in enhancing security along the supply chain. The passenger side of the industry has seen major developments such as improved baggage reconciliation (the process of loading bags only if their owners have boarded the aircraft) after the Lockerbie bombing of 1988 or major developments in airport and cabin security after 9/11. Yet the cargo business has generally lagged behind in improving security measures. For example, it was not until 2007 that the United States President signed a law to screen 100 percent of cargo transported on passenger aircraft on routes to, from and within the United States. Although this law was initially to be fully in force by 2010, the target of 100 percent screening had to be delayed to the end of 2012 (US Government Accountability Office, 2012).

The underlying reasons for this relatively slow uptake perhaps lie in the comparatively little attention air cargo has received as a potential source of terrorist activity by regulators, the public or the media. This is possibly because air cargo is seen as less prestigious than passenger services, with fewer potential casualties and possibilities for causing disruption. Cargo routings are also less predictable than passenger services, so it may also be harder to plan and target particular services. Having said that, with security seemingly growing ever tighter for passenger services, air transport regulators must remain cognizant of the potential for terrorists using air cargo to plan attacks on the air transport system, especially given that a large share of air cargo is transported in the bellyhold of passenger aircraft. This has been highlighted by events such as the discovery of two bombs in cargo shipments from Yemen to the United States in 2010 (Elias, 2010). Such events have prompted the European Commission, the United States government and regulators to tighten air cargo security procedures.

As with the air transport industry in general, the economic and commercial realities of the air cargo business combined with heightened safety requirements represent a key nexus in the development of air cargo security. While increasing security is of high importance, such measures may impact the competitive advantage that the air cargo sector can bring to the supply chain due to the added time and cost it entails. The then Director General of the International Air Transport Association highlighted this conflict in 2011:

> We must resist the knee-jerk call for 100% cargo screening. The industry must be secure with effective measures that facilitate the speed needed to support global commerce. Air cargo security must be based on a combination of three measures – supply chain security, scanning technology and better use of e-freight data.
>
> *(Bisignani, 2011)*

However, in some cases new guidance or regulation will necessitate changes to air cargo security operations. IATA publish detailed technical instructions on the safe transportation of goods by air as well as specific regulations regarding how certain dangerous goods should be handled. A recent example of this includes changes to the way lithium metal and lithium ion batteries should be transported (IATA, 2016).

While there is a danger that increased security requirements create bottlenecks at airports, recent developments in different parts of the world enable shippers and freight forwarders to undertake the security inspections of air cargo before the goods arrive at the airport. For example, in the United States, the Transportation Security Administration can certify cargo-screening facilities based away from an airport, provided the screening facility fulfills certain criteria and the shipment is stored and transported securely between the time of screening and loading onto the aircraft. This enables cargo to be screened even before it is delivered to the airport.

Similarly, in the European Union companies can apply for the status of 'Known Consignor' (for shippers) or 'Regulated Agents' (for freight forwarders), which reduce the requirements for screening at the airport. These schemes highlight the need to see air cargo as part of a supply chain, rather than an independent mode of transport. While different regulators have developed their own standards, there is some move towards harmonisation of air cargo security, such as the European Union and the United States formally recognising each other's cargo security regime.

In order to ensure air cargo security, a range of screening methods are available, although not all of these are approved worldwide. Common screening methods include: x-ray screening, physical screening (e.g. by hand), and Remote Explosive Scent Tracing (taking air samples of the cargo shipment and analysing them remotely). With terrorists and criminal activities becoming more sophisticated, air cargo security becomes more timely and costly. Heightened security measures not only result in higher equipment costs but also manpower and management costs. From an economic perspective, herein lies the challenge ahead for a sector that is facing increasing costs on one side and falling prices due to the competition and oversupply in the market on the other side.

23.6 Prospects for air cargo: issues and challenges

As mentioned, air cargo is highly dependent on the economic climate. The 2008/9 global economic downturn had a significant impact on global air cargo demand, with some markets seeing a decline in excess of 20 percent. While overall air cargo demand recovered fairly quickly to pre-recession levels, since 2010 there has been only moderate growth, contrary to the passenger market. One of the major reasons for the stagnation of air cargo demand lies in a modal shift towards maritime transport, which proved to be popular with shippers and freight forwarders during the 2008/9 recession as it offered significantly lower transport costs than by air. The case of the Swedish technology firm Ericsson, an example of a sector that is highly dependent on air cargo, shows that the company managed to increase its surface transport share from 20 percent to 80 percent within ten years, at the expense of the air cargo sector (Airline Cargo Management, 2013). The drop in demand in the first half of the 2010s, exemplified by the case of Ericsson, constitutes a significant challenge for the air cargo sector.

At a time when air cargo faces demand side-related challenges, airlines are also confronted by excess capacity in many markets on the supply side. In particular, wide-body passenger aircraft have a significant bellyhold capacity for cargo. For example, the Boeing 777-300ER can carry up to 18 percent more cargo by volume than the Boeing 747-400 (CAPA, 2014a). With many airlines having modern wide-body aircraft on order, cargo capacity will increase over the next few years, despite many of the aircraft on order being replacements for older aircraft. Besides this increase in total capacity, the air cargo sector is also witnessing a shift from pure freighter capacity to a larger share of bellyhold capacity. The introduction of modern wide-body passenger aircraft on many long-haul routes reduces the necessity for dedicated cargo operations on these routes. Nevertheless, in certain markets and for certain goods (e.g. outsized cargo, certain dangerous goods) the need for pure cargo aircraft will remain. Particularly modern twin-engine freighter aircraft, e.g. the Boeing 777F and Airbus A330F, offer opportunities for cargo operators, be it integrators, cargo airlines or combination airlines. Dependent on oil prices, these aircraft offer good fuel economics, particularly in comparison to older passenger-to-freighter conversions that still have a large share of the global cargo fleet.

These varied challenges both on the supply and demand side have created the economic impacts one might expect; namely, falling yields and declining load factors. Yields have been under significant pressure in a market that is characterised not only by high competition, both from other carriers and competing modes, but also where increased passenger demand has necessitated the introduction of additional aircraft, which in turn has created increased bellyhold capacity in many passenger markets. This creates a situation where goods are, effectively, being offered in joint supply, which typically has a negative impact on yields. Given current aircraft designs, this issue will likely remain for the foreseeable future, with airlines having to balance the revenue potential in passenger markets with the downward pressure on cargo yields. While this is not such a problem for combination airlines, who can focus on maximising passenger revenues, cargo airlines clearly do not have the option to focus on the passenger side of their business. The challenge for these airlines may be to establish profitable niches such as outsize cargo, animal transportation or offering ad hoc charters, which they can serve better than airlines that only offer bellyhold capacity.

At the same time, cargo load factors have remained low, consistently remaining under 50 percent of global air cargo supply, measured in available freight tonne capacity. While this would appear to represent a poor match of supply and demand, to some extent the air cargo market requires a different view in this respect. Low cargo load factors do indeed highlight issues on the supply and demand side, but they do not always give a full picture of the developments in the market. Seeing as cargo load factors are based on weight capacity, it is possible that a flight might show as having a very low weight load factor, while it actually has reached its volume capacity. In practice, it is quite possible that many aircraft 'cube out' (i.e. reach their full capacity by volume) before they 'weigh out' (i.e. reach full capacity by weight) (Holloway, 2008). Therefore, it can be assumed that in reality, volume-based load factors (though hardly reported) are higher and show a far better match between supply and demand. However, it should be borne in mind that freight load factors achieved on passenger aircraft are significantly lower than the freight load factors on pure freighters. Cargo airlines are better at matching cargo supply with demand, as they are driven by the specific needs of the cargo market, rather than by the requirements of passenger markets.

While the current market conditions create significant challenges for the air cargo sector, there are a range of developments under way that have the potential to make the air cargo supply chain more competitive, leaner and efficient in the years to come. At the heart of modernising air cargo is the development of moving from the traditional paper-based cargo processes to 'e-freight'. Driven by the International Air Transport Association, 'e-freight' focuses on the reduction of paper documentation in the air cargo supply chain by substituting them with electronic messages between the different supply chain partners, including government organisations. Traditionally, up to 30 paper documents are required to accompany cargo shipments, which create additional costs in the form of manpower, longer order cycles and customs penalties. Moving to 'e-freight' can significantly reduce these costs (up to US$4.9 billion per annum according to IATA, 2013). Similarly to developments in air cargo security, the implementation of 'e-freight' has been relatively slow, as the sector is characterised by traditional working practices. Nevertheless, there is a steady movement towards 'e-freight', particularly with regards to the introduction of the e-Airway Bill (eAWB). The eAWB represents one of the major documents in the air cargo process, and as such is a benchmark for the implementation of 'e-freight'. Some airlines, airports and freight forwarders that have a very high share of eAWB shipments have reported significant benefits in the form of improved customer service (e.g. the tracking of shipments), improved regulatory compliance, fewer penalties and lower labour costs through reduced document handling and data input. Widespread implementation of e-freight across the air cargo sector may also enhance its competitiveness, particularly against maritime transport, and can help retain its market share.

While the 'e-freight' movement can help the cargo sector to overcome some key issues and challenges, increasing environmental regulation can significantly impede the future developments of air cargo, particularly through operational restrictions and increased costs. These challenges will predominantly affect operators of pure freighters, such as integrators and all-cargo airlines, as these companies rely on 24-hour operations (including night-time operations), especially when operating a hub-and-spoke system, as most integrators do. Besides these operational requirements, freighter aircraft tend to be older (specifically when looking at passenger-to-freighter conversions), which means that they produce more noise and greenhouse gas emissions than more modern passenger aircraft or newer freighter aircraft.

Depending on developments in the oil market, low fuel prices can be an incentive for cargo operators to extend the operational life of older aircraft. In turn, this might result in stricter environmental regulation from governments to curb the environmental impacts of older aircraft. Brussels and Frankfurt airports are examples where operational restrictions have been imposed on airports as a result of increased environmental pressure. These measures have inevitably affected the competitiveness of these airports to some extent. Night-time restrictions at Brussels meant that DHL relocated its hub from Brussels to Leipzig/Halle in the late 2000s, which led to a drop in cargo tonnage at Brussels by nearly 50 percent. In response to the environmental debate, but more importantly because of the negative impact of high oil prices, many companies in the air cargo sector have started to replace their older aircraft with more fuel-efficient equipment. For example, FedEx introduced Boeing 777F freighters to replace McDonnell Douglas MD11F freighters with an environmental and economic benefit of reduced fuel consumption of about 18 percent. As these examples show, while some environmental initiatives also have positive economic impacts (e.g. fuel-efficient aircraft reduce the environmental impacts and operating costs), other measures can lead to increased costs and affect competition.

23.7 Conclusion

The chapter has sought to provide a closer examination of one of the key facilitators of the global economy, yet one that has consistently been underrepresented in an academic context. It has highlighted the various commodities transported by air and the global supply chains that facilitate the movement of these goods. Many of these products, such as overnight parcels or the year-round availability of fruit and fresh produce, we have grown to rely upon in order to sustain our modern lifestyles. However, as the significant impacts of the economic crisis in 2008/9 highlighted, the air cargo industry is generally highly sensitive to fluctuations in the economic climate. Aside from continued intense competition from other, often less expensive modes of transport, air cargo also faces challenges regarding fluctuation in oil prices, overcapacity in some markets, growing environmental pressures and rising costs associated with providing increased screening and security. Yet, as with the air transport industry in general, the air cargo sector has consistently shown itself to be a resilient and durable one. New innovations and trends in air cargo, such as e-freight, as well as forecasted growth in regions such as part of the Asia and the Middle East are testament to this. While air cargo continues to face numerous challenges, and remains an industry where it can be difficult to make substantial financial returns, the continued economic and societal importance of this industry is not in question.

Note

1 Measured in 2013 US dollars, the average price of air cargo in real terms, measured in RTK, has fallen from just under $2 per tonne kilometer in 1990 to around $1 per tonne kilometer in 2014 (ATAG, 2016).

References

Air Transport Action Group. (2016). Aviation: Benefits beyond Borders, http://aviationbenefits.org/media/149668/abbb2016_full_a4_web.pdf (accessed 28 September 2016).

Airbus (2014). *Flying on Demand: Global Market Forecast.* Toulouse: Airbus.

Airline Cargo Management (2013). Shape Up or Ship Out, www.airlinecargomanagement.com/feature/modal-shift-air-versus-sea-freight?session_id=run6i0burn1ed6mvq1j28sv6j7 (accessed 14 January 2016).

Bisignani, G. (2011). Action to Improve Air Cargo Competitiveness. www.iata.org/pressroom/pr/Pages/2011–03-08-01.aspx (accessed 14 January 2016).

Boeing (2014). World Air Cargo Forecast 2014–15. www.boeing.com/resources/boeingdotcom/commercial/about-our-market/cargo-market-detail-wacf/download-report/assets/pdfs/wacf.pdf (accessed 14 January 2016).

Budd, L. and Ison, S. (2015). Air Cargo Mobilities. In Birtchnell, T, Savitsky, S and Urry, J (eds), *Cargomobilities: Moving Materials in a Global Age.* London: Routledge.

CAPA (2014a). Air Cargo: Few Other Industries Would Tolerate Its Structural Overcapacity. http://centreforaviation.com/analysis/air-cargo-few-other-industries-would-tolerate-its-structural-overcapacity-192139 (accessed 14 January 2016).

CAPA (2014b). Asian Air Cargo Overview: Different Profiles for Major Freight Airlines, but United in Weak Outlook, http://centreforaviation.com/analysis/asian-air-cargo-overview-different-profiles-for-major-freight-airlines-but-united-in-weak-outlook-173842 (accessed 14 January 2016).

DHL (2016). Volumetric Weight: DHL Express, www.dhl.co.uk/en/tools/volumetric_weight_express.html (accessed 29 January 2016).

Elias, B. (2010). Screening and Securing Air Cargo: Background and Issues for Congress, Congressional Research Service, 7–5700. https://assets.documentcloud.org/documents/240126/screening-and-securing-air-cargo-background-and.pdf (accessed 28 September 2016).
Gardiner, J., Ison, S., and Humphreys, I. (2005). Factors Influencing Cargo Airlines' Choice of Airport: An International Survey. *Journal of Air Transport Management*, 11(6), pp. 393–9.
Holloway, S. (2008). *Straight and Level: Practical Airline Economics*, Third Edition. Farnham: Ashgate.
IATA (2013). *e-freight Handbook v4.0*. Geneva: International Air Transport Association.
IATA (2015). *IATA World Air Transport Statistics 2015*, 59th Edition. Geneva: International Air Transport Association.
IATA (2016). Lithium Battery Guidance Document, revision to the 57th edition of the IATA Dangerous Goods Regulations, www.iata.org/whatwedo/cargo/dgr/Documents/lithium-battery-guidance-document-2016-en.pdf (accessed 28 September 2016).
Mayer, R. (2016). Airport Classification Based on Cargo Characteristics. *Journal of Transport Geography*, 54, pp. 53–65.
Morrell, P. S. (2012). *Moving Boxes by Air: The Economics of International Air Cargo*. Farnham: Ashgate.
Sales, M. (2013). *The Air Logistics Handbook: Air Freight and the Global Supply Chain*. London: Routledge.
US Government Accountability Office (2012). Aviation Security: Actions Needed to Address Challenges and Potential Vulnerabilities Related to Securing Inbound Air Cargo. www.gao.gov/assets/600/590789.pdf (accessed 14 January 2016).

24

Intermodal freight transport

Jason Monios

24.1 Introduction

While multimodal transport denotes the use of more than one mode in a transport chain (e.g. road and rail), intermodal refers specifically to a transport movement in which the goods remain within the same loading unit. Wooden boxes had been utilised since the early days of rail, but it was not until strong metal containers were developed that true intermodal transport emerged. The efficiencies and hence cost reductions of eliminating excessive handling by keeping the goods within the same unit were apparent from the first trials of a container vessel by Malcom McLean in 1956.[1] The initial container revolution was thus in ports, as the stevedoring industry was transformed in succeeding decades from a labour-intensive operation to an increasingly automated activity. Economies of scale on the sea leg meant that container traffic concentrated in a smaller number of ports, thus hinterlands overlapped and inland regions could be served by a number of ports connected by intermodal transport at a cheaper cost than using the nearest port. In rail terms, intermodal is normally used to distinguish unitised flows from other traffic types such as coal, timber, steel and aggregates, which all have their own specific wagon types. Unitised traffic is frequently made up of flows of containers to and from ports, but also includes non-port traffic which often uses domestic containers, swap bodies and piggyback.

Chapter 22 covers rail freight transport; therefore, while there will be some overlap, this chapter focuses more on the use of intermodal terminals. This chapter provides an overview of the intermodal sector and pays specific attention to the role of the intermodal terminal as the point of interchange between modes. Business models used in intermodal freight transport are introduced and the economic structure of the market is discussed. A brief section on regulation is also included, before a consideration of the key economic drivers behind successful intermodal transport.

24.2 The intermodal sector

Port flows remain the dominant container market segment (see Box 24.1), as a container can be stuffed in an inland region, driven or railed to a port, shipped across the globe, then taken inland by truck, rail or barge to the final destination without the goods ever being handled. Ports are more likely to be served by regular shuttles which can be kept full due to the large loads of containers being picked up and dropped off by the ever increasing size of modern container vessels. Such shuttles have regular timings which aids planning and reliability. They also tend to use the same fixed wagonset which reduces shunting at terminals, and carry a small mix of container types – usually just 20ft and 40ft containers. Thus a rail operator can serve this segment with 60ft or 80ft wagons and keep most wagons full. Using a fixed wagonset also reduces maintenance costs, as they all experience the same level of wear and tear.

Box 24.1 Case study of Freightliner UK

Freightliner was originally the container transport division of the national UK rail operator British Rail. When British Rail was privatised in 1996, its divisions were sold separately and Freightliner was purchased by a management buy-out. As Freightliner was making a loss pre-privatisation, the buy-out was incentivised via a grant of £75 million (Fowkes and Nash, 2004). It has subsequently been bought by a private equity firm. A bulk division was added in 1999: Freightliner Heavy Haul. In the last decade they have also expanded into Poland and Australia, primarily bulk traffic, and in 2013 they purchased European Rail Shuttle B.V., Maersk's intermodal carrier in the Netherlands.

At the time of privatisation, ownership of all British Rail's 12 container terminals passed to Freightliner. Private container terminals connected to the public network already existed at that time, and new ones have been developed since, now operated by a diverse group such as rail operators (e.g. Freightliner, DB Cargo UK, DRS, GB Railfreight), third-party logistics (3PLs, e.g. WH Malcolm, Stobart, JG Russell), port operators (e.g. ABP) and others (Monios, 2015a). Freightliner now serves 14 intermodal terminals in the UK, of which they own and operate nine, four in/near ports and five inland. Their core intermodal business is port–hinterland shuttles, for which they provide the locos and wagons and take bookings directly for the slots. Many of these are purchased by shipping lines as hinterland transport in the UK is dominated by carrier haulage. Freightliner remains the largest intermodal rail freight operator in the UK, carrying more than 80 percent of all the maritime containers that are moved by rail.

The company owns over 75 diesel and electric locomotives and around 3,500 rail wagons. Their trainsets are based for the most part on 60ft flat wagons to handle a mixture of 20ft and 40ft deep-sea containers, but more recently introduced a percentage of 40ft wagons. They run over 100 daily intermodal services, generally around 72 TEU capacity but up to 90 TEU based on 30 wagons.

They do not get involved in logistics, and their business is simply from port terminal to inland terminal. They do a moderate amount of road haulage (they have 300 trucks) but for the most part that is organised by the customer, carrier or freight forwarder.

The business model is based on vertical integration between terminal and rail operations and running their own equipment. This model is facilitated by the carrier haulage trend in the UK, which means that the majority of each service is underwritten by a major deep-sea carrier such as Maersk. Additional containers can then be booked either directly by the shipper or via a freight forwarder or 3PL.

As the terminals were formerly publicly owned, some are now quite old, and there are issues concerning the lack of investment and whether the public sector in the UK should provide some grants for old terminals, as there were until recently grants available for new terminal sites, if they could be shown to be supporting new services facilitating modal shift from road to rail (see Box 24.2).

Imbalance of import and export flows is an issue for many parts of the world that tend to rely on one or the other, e.g. export-dominated China and import-dominated Europe. While this affects all transport modes, it is particularly difficult for intermodal corridors because triangulation is more difficult than for road haulage. This results in the need to 'reposition' empty containers back from the importer to the exporter which induces inefficiencies. For example, in 2014 inbound flows at UK ports amounted to 4.8 million TEU, of which 93 percent were loaded, while outbound movements were 4.7 million TEU, of which only 49 percent were loaded. While total containers handled at world ports have grown throughout the last decade, the percentage of empty containers handled has remained constant at around 21 percent.

ISO containers are the strongest loading unit, as well as being stackable. They are, therefore, the most versatile. The key underpinning of successful intermodal transport was not simply the invention or adoption of these containers but their increasing standardisation. This was a long process (see Levinson (2006) for a detailed history and the role of the ISO), that resulted in a handful of main container types. While there still remain several lengths, heights and widths, 20/40ft long units remain dominant on deep-sea vessels and containers are therefore measured as multiples of 20ft (20-foot equivalent units or TEU). Significant divergence remains, however, particularly domestically. For example, both the UK and the US favour domestic intermodal containers of the same dimensions as articulated road trailers, for obvious reasons (45ft in the UK and 53ft in the US).[2] Standard height is 8ft6 although other heights exist, and 9ft6 (known as high-cube) are increasingly common as they allow extra volume, subject to weight limits. Standard width is 8ft, although again other widths are possible, and in Europe the 8ft2 (known as pallet-wide) is popular because, again, it is closer to the load capacity of a semi-trailer. Refrigerated containers are also wider than regular boxes. Increasing dimensions of maritime containers have caused problems for loading-gauge restrictions in countries like the UK, where bridges need to be raised and tunnels lowered to allow the passage of trains carrying higher and wider containers, in addition to issues of interoperability. In the US, maritime containers are frequently transloaded into domestic containers to get better value per container, but to some extent that forgoes the advantage of intermodal transport which is not to change load unit. This is not common in the UK because the shorter inland distance will not achieve the same saving in cost per unit, therefore it does not warrant the extra handling costs.

Swap bodies can be moved between road and rail vehicles, but are not strong enough to be stacked or to be used on sea transport. They can be fully rigid or curtain-sided for side loading. Finally, semi-trailers are the common sight on today's roads, consisting of a loading unit integrated with the trailer.[3] Again, these can be rigid or curtain-sided or whatever formation is suitable for the cargo. ISO containers, swap bodies and semi-trailers can also carry temperature-controlled goods, with their own integrated refrigerating units (requiring a regular power source). Road vehicles can be carried on rail wagons in their entirety (as in the Channel Tunnel). This is referred to as 'piggyback' and is less common than utilising a container (Lowe, 2005; Woxenius and Bergqvist, 2011).

It was in the United States where true intermodal transport was first established successfully. During the 1980s, carriers operating in the trans-Pacific trade were suffering from excess tonnage and low freight rates. To increase its cargo volumes, American President Lines (APL) formed the first transcontinental double-stack rail services, recognising that intermodal transport provided a ten-day time saving compared to the sea route through the Panama Canal to New York. While the transit time was important, APL also offered more services to the shipper as the customer could receive a single through bill of lading. The growth of discretionary cargoes allowed APL and other shipping lines to expand their capacity in the trans-Pacific sector. By using larger, faster ships, a carrier could offer a fixed, weekly sailing schedule, while the additional capacity reduced per-unit costs. In the US, the geography means they can run long double-stacked trains of around 600 TEU and the vertically integrated model (each operator runs their own track, terminals and trains) reduces transaction costs and produces natural regional oligopolies.

In Europe, intermodal freight transport developed in the 1990s, although the fragmented geographical and operational setting (e.g. national jurisdictions and constraints on interoperability) as well as physical constraints (e.g. limited opportunities for double-stack operation) meant that progress was not as swift nor as successful as in the United States. While intermodal freight transport is developing in other parts of the world such as Africa and South America, in many cases, even though the long distances give rail an advantage, priority for bulk flows, lack of investment and fragmentation of administration constrain its ability to compete with road. Major investment is being made in China to provide capacity for container shuttles, in tandem with a number of double-stack cleared routes and large interchange terminals.

24.3 The role of the terminal in the intermodal network

An intermodal terminal may be as simple as a rail siding (basically just a spur of rail track off the main line) with a small area for a mobile crane or reach stacker to lift the cargo, or it may be a large area with several tracks and large gantry cranes. Some of the key factors in terminal development include market potential, location, funding, entrepreneurship and the planning system, whereas specific factors relating to terminal design include location in relation to the mainline as well as road connections, space for marshalling, slopes in the area and connecting tracks and space for other desired activities within the site such as storage (Monios and Bergqvist, 2016). The number and length of tracks will depend on local demand as well as the maximum train length on the network.

The size of an intermodal terminal will depend on its role and how many functions it provides. Trains coming from the mainline will often need to be marshalled in yards beyond the perimeter of the terminal itself. They may need to be split into sections for different parts of the terminal or simply because many terminals are not long enough to handle a full-length train. This is especially the case in the United States with very long trains reaching over 10,000ft in some cases (meaning that, with double-stacking, US trains can reach capacities of 650 TEU, compared to around 80–90 TEU in Europe). Additional staff and shunting locomotives are required for this purpose, before the wagons are in place for unloading and loading to commence. Then the train sections will be brought into the site and onto the handling tracks.

An intermodal terminal can be operated by a transport provider as part of their transport network or it can be operated by a dedicated terminal operator handling trains from multiple individual rail operators. A terminal requires a small office building, and will often provide some basic services such as container cleaning and maintenance and some space for an empty depot. If the cargo is international, a secure building and land area will be required for customs inspection. In both Europe and the United States, joint customs jurisdictions and a single currency, as well as streamlined systems, electronic paperwork and authorised operator agreements, make customs clearance procedures simpler, faster and cheaper, as fewer organisations are involved and currency conversion expenses are eliminated. In countries where this is not the case, being able to perform administrative duties (including but not limited to customs) inland at a location of their choosing can produce significant cost savings. Therefore, much literature on inland terminals considers their role as inland clearance depots or dry ports.

24.4 Business models and integration

Terminal ownership and operation is an important part of the economics of intermodal transport. Several different models exist, from private sidings for company trains or a single customer with a

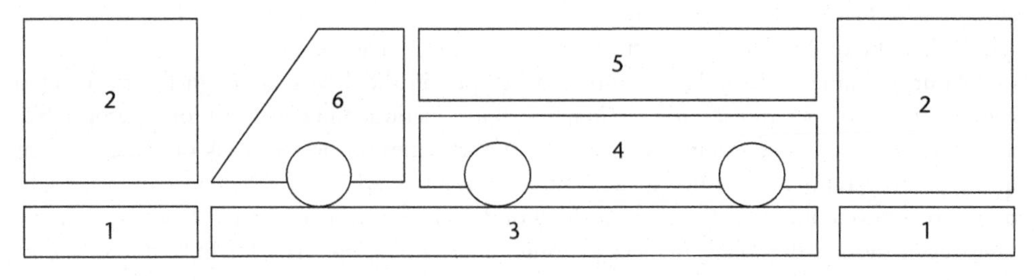

Figure 24.1 Main actors in the rail element of intermodal transport

large flow having its own siding at a warehouse, to open-user third-party intermodal terminals. This searching for economies of scale and scope characterise the modern intermodal sector with very low margins.

As shown in Figure 24.1, there are a number of different elements that make up the operational aspects of the intermodal business model. The discussion that follows is relevant mostly to Europe; in the US, a vertically integrated business model is used, whereby all items in the figure (1–6) are operated by a single rail company, who then sells cargo space (5) either directly to a shipper or to an intermediary, whether a 3PL, freight forwarder or even a shipping line who offers a door-to-door price to the shipper. This is referred to as carrier haulage, as opposed to merchant haulage which is when the shipper organises their own hinterland transport after the container leaves the ship. Figure 24.1 does not show the pre- or post-haul, which may be road haulage or, if one of the rail terminals is inside a port, it will be by container vessel.

It is important to note that Figure 24.1 only shows the operational components. From a business-model perspective, the cargo flows may be managed by an intermodal operator who has their own traction and wagons and sells cargo space directly to the shipper (linking 4, 5 and 6), or they may sell the cargo space to a 3PL or freight forwarder who then sells it to the shipper. The 3PL may indeed book the entire cargo space on a regular train service at a low rate and then take the risk of selling all these slots to their individual clients. Similarly, the intermodal operator may not provide the traction themselves and may sub-contract a rail operator to provide the traction and/or the wagons. The key aspects are who provides the rail operations, who takes the risk of underwriting the cargo space and who keeps the profit. Given the importance of keeping trains full to achieve economic viability in a low-margin business, the ability of intermediaries like 3PLs to consolidate flows from many clients is often crucial. One of the reasons why port shuttles are the most successful intermodal ventures is because shipping lines with large demand can book several full shuttles in advance. It should also be noted that locomotives and wagons are also frequently leased by operators from specialist lessors so that they can be more flexible with their provision and not take on too many fixed costs by purchasing too much equipment. While this enables some flexibility in the market, locomotives and wagons are rather specialist equipment so it is not as flexible as a road haulier where trucks are far more interchangeable. The track itself is in most cases owned by the public sector and the rail operator will purchase track access for the timetabled routes required. Where it gets more complex is the relationship between the business models above and the terminal ownership and/or operation.

Terminal ownership and operational models can be analysed according to four factors (Monios, 2015b). The first question is who are the various possible developers of a terminal:

for example, government (what kind of government body and which scale), real-estate developers, rail operators, 3PLs, port authorities, port terminal operators, shipping lines, independent operators or others. Each actor will have different motivations; for example, obtaining social and economic benefits (government), to sell the site or parts within it for profit (real-estate developer), as part of an existing business (e.g. rail operator or 3PL) or for hinterland capture (e.g. port actors). The second aspect is the relation between the owner and operator: whether the owner operates the site directly, at arm's length, through contracts or via a concession (landlord) or lease. The third question is the main function(s) of the site, in particular whether the site is an independent intermodal terminal or whether it is part of a logistics platform. Part of this question includes the nature of the operator of each site (intermodal terminal and logistics platform) and the relationship between them. This follows on from the development process (related to the original aim) and points the way towards more specific questions about the operational model. The fourth aspect is operational models, drawing on the discussion in the preceding paragraph.

Integration models determine if the terminal operator also runs train services or just handles the trains of other operators, or a mixture. There may be vertical integration between terminal and trains (e.g. Freightliner, UK) or they may be separate (e.g. J. G. Russell using Freightliner terminals). Port authorities and operators also develop or buy terminals (e.g. Coslada, Spain) and even systems of fully closed-loop 'extended gate' style port terminal to inland terminal (e.g. vertically integrated terminal operator ECT operating the Rotterdam port terminal and the Venlo inland terminal and running fixed-loop shuttles between them). This level of integration can go even further to include the shipping line (e.g. Maersk, although they are recently divesting their inland terminals).

Other more subtle differences exist. For example, Freightliner operate their own traction and wagons between their own terminals as well as some other terminals, whereas HUPAC and PCC operate terminals and schedule train services between them, but they only own the wagons and will sub-contract other companies to provide the traction (Monios and Bergqvist, 2015a). One potential explanation could be that the choice to invest in wagons rather than locos has a more integrating dimension with other stakeholders as it heavily influences the efficiency of all operations, including not just the service but the marshalling and loading at the terminals. It may also suggest that the market for sub-contracting traction works well so operators are confident that they can contract this when they need it rather than invest in expensive assets that are difficult to utilise fully.

A particularly interesting case of integration and collaboration involves large DIY shipper Jula in Sweden (see full description in Monios and Bergqvist, 2015b). The shipper set up an open-book arrangement with a 3PL to operate an intermodal service, whereby they jointly sub-contracted traction and Jula purchased the wagons. They are now setting up additional services, therefore the shipper is becoming, to some degree, an intermodal service provider to other shippers and the service revenues can be used to cross-subsidise their own intermodal costs. They even recently put in a bid to buy the intermodal terminal, having realised the potential of securing their flows and using the terminal as an inbound stock buffer. This interesting case raises the question of whose core business is the provision of transport. If the shipper owns the wagons, offers their service to other shippers and then even owns the terminal, who is the rail provider?

24.5 Economic structure of the market for intermodal terminals

If road haulage is considered to be very close to the model of perfect competition between substitutable providers with low barriers to entry and good quality of information (see Chapter 21), the rail market is in some ways the opposite (Chapter 22). However, the intermodal terminal market is rather different to the rest of the sector, due to their fixed locations. Economists generally feel that economies of scale exist in infrastructure but opinion is divided as to whether it exists in operations (Cowie, 2010). Separation of track and operations (see Section 24.7) in Europe was based on the view that economies of scale did not exist in operations, or were limited, and thus the loss of any potential (limited) scale economies would be more than offset by the benefits of competition. Nevertheless, some evidence exists (Cowie, 1999) to suggest that significant scale economies do exist in operations, and a number of regional monopolies may be better. The US model of competition between a limited number of vertically integrated companies continues to perform successfully, while China is based on vertically integrated regional monopolies. Terminals are a combination of infrastructure and services and, as shown in Section 24.4, different business models exist that attempt to blend ownership and operation of terminals with operation of rail services, generally seeking economies of scale and scope through vertical integration. The question then is how to characterise the intermodal terminal market in economic terms.

Mainstream economic theory identifies the key elements that lead to monopoly situations, such as barriers to entry, minimum firm size, brand loyalty, ownership of key inputs and the potential downsides to society, namely under producing and overcharging. Barriers to entry are significant in the intermodal terminal market due to high up-front and sunk costs and a lack of terminal locations. These require a minimum firm size, although it may be difficult to put a figure on that size due to high variability in the market between local operators and global operators with multiple terminals. Fierce competition will be faced from incumbents, whether through brand loyalty or aggressive marketing and pricing tactics. This is partly due to their ownership of key inputs, because operating one terminal is only one part of successful intermodal operation. The terminal must be served by rail services which in turn must connect with other terminals. While all of these four indicators of monopoly are present, it does not seem that overcharging is common in the intermodal sector, although data limitations make it difficult for quantitative analysis. At the least, there is strong competition from road haulage, and indeed it is quite common for intermodal terminal competition to exist within a distance that would become feasible if prices at the incumbent terminal increased. Underproduction is perhaps more of a problem. The many challenges to intermodal transport outlined in this chapter suggest that there is a larger market for intermodal transport to be obtained if these challenges can be overcome.

Baumol (1982) suggested that if the market could be contestable, then even if there is not currently competition the incumbent will act as though in a competitive market. This could be the case in the terminal market which tends towards a natural monopoly but a new operator could conceivably enter the market. Yet the high entry barriers remain, so it is still only likely to be an existing large operator looking for a new market who would do so. Brand loyalty would protect the incumbent up to a point, but if the new entrant were a recognised operator then this would be less of an issue. However, as already mentioned, there is no evidence of super-normal profits in the terminal sector, therefore less need for the threat of competition to encourage the incumbent to lower their profit seeking. Underproduction (or, perhaps more accurately, inability to release latent demand) is the problem that needs to be addressed. It might even be argued that the incumbent monopoly operator is less incentivised to grow their market (i.e. attract more business from road to rail) because that would increase the possibility of (a) the market being able to support two operators or (b) even if the market can only support one operator, a larger market makes it more attractive to be worth the risk of a new operator competing for it, or indeed (c) that the possible returns in terms of profit from doing so are very seldom worth the business risk. Growing the market is in any case more the province of the rail operators, and if they grow the market then they can indeed expect other operators to enter as entry and exit barriers are lower (though not insignificant) due to the ability to lease equipment or move it from another part of an existing business.

If competition does not arise naturally it can be implemented by regulation. Ensuring features of a competitive market in a natural monopoly situation is difficult, and may lead to market distortion through public-sector intervention. The issues here with regard to competition relate to whether the benefits of competition (more produced at lower price than under monopoly conditions) might be outweighed by destructive competition. In cases of natural monopolies (where the Minimum Efficient Scale (MES)is too high to attract a new firm to enter the market), there are different possible responses. The state might intervene and attempt to lower the MES via some form of subsidy (direct or indirect), or facilitate Demsetz competition (competition for the market rather than competition in the market). These responses raise further issues of regulation (see Section 24.7). The question of what kind of intermodal terminal market structure is appropriate to obtain the optimum results for the private sector and for society has not yet been answered. Measuring all of these indicators for a selection of terminals presents practical difficulties, and the MES will vary widely for different terminals or networks. It also depends on the definition of the size of the market, whether one considers a total market of a fixed number of terminals (e.g. the whole network of a country) and calculates how many operators should operate those terminals, or whether one considers each local market of a fixed demand (e.g. a city) and how many terminals should compete for that business without splitting economies of scale from a single large terminal company or restricting the increasing returns to scale available to a single larger terminal with a higher output.

In many markets the provision of intermodal terminals naturally tends to broadly substitutable large firms in an oligopoly market, competing for the most part on price, subject to a minimum service quality. However, as shown in Section 24.8, there are other methods of competition, such as unique service attributes and sources of advantage through long-term collaboration. Thus, as in theory an oligopoly market tends to compete on non-price and this is certainly true in the intermodal market which involves product differentiation through personal tailoring and relationships, the freight transport market is notoriously competitive with high price elasticity of demand, driven to a large degree by the high levels of competition in the road haulage sector and the less perfect market but nonetheless highly competitive maritime sector, therefore the lowest price must be offered by rail and intermodal operators. On one hand, terminals compete on price subject to an assumed unchanged minimum service quality, but they also compete on quality by offering tailored services, while nonetheless must be offered at the same unchanged maximum price that the market will bear. This explains why it is such a difficult market to grow, demonstrating both the low profit of perfect competition with the underproduction of a monopoly. Operators tend to sweat the fixed assets and find it difficult to justify large investments in new assets on such small profit margins. Hence they are sometimes considered worthy of government subsidies (see Section 24.7).

24.6 Costs and pricing in the intermodal sector

For an intermodal terminal to be successful, regular traffic is required, which generally means a large amount of production or consumption nearby with a suitable distance between origin and destination to support regular long-distance trunk hauls where rail or barge is the natural mode. Various break-even distances have been suggested in the literature (usually averaging at around 500km, although much lower if pre- and end-hauls are not needed), but the reality is that it depends on operational considerations as well as differentials in track charges in different countries and other economies that may or may not have been achieved, e.g. through vertical integration.

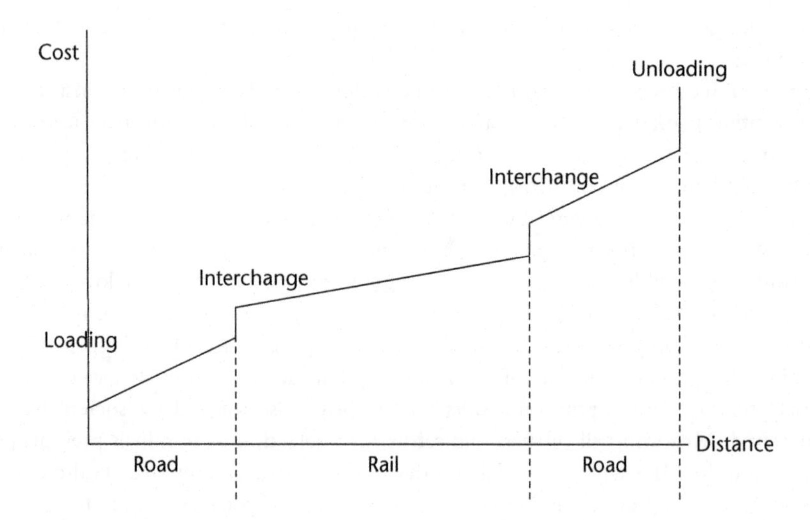

Figure 24.2 Intermodal transport distance and time

The longer the distance, the more likely that the increased handling costs of changing mode from road to rail will be offset by the cheaper per-unit transport cost (Figure 24.2). High-volume short-distance rail is also possible under certain circumstances by running regular full shuttles and getting the most use out of expensive fixed assets, but such situations are relatively unusual in intermodal transport, being more likely to occur in the bulk trade.

As discussed in Chapter 22, rail becomes cheaper than road as distance increases, before sea transport becomes the most cost effective at longer distances. Figure 24.2 illustrates the importance of the handling time and cost to the intermodal cost function. However, this depends on the quality and capacity of the intermodal infrastructure as well as suitably scheduled services at the right departure and arrival times, without unnecessary delays along the route. It also depends on the total quantity of cargo, as such services will not be economic unless they achieve high utilisation in both directions. For these and other reasons, road haulage still retains a large proportion of medium and even long-distance flows. At short distances, road obviously has the advantage in most cases, but it has proven possible to run intermodal services at short distances, if very high volume is achieved, with good timetables allowing quick turnaround and high utilisation of expensive rail assets (Bärthel and Woxenius, 2004). Finally, the administration savings from avoiding port congestion can be another reason to choose an intermodal shuttle, which may offset the higher transport cost. That is why any intermodal scheme (terminal or corridor) must have a clear business model, relating both to transport cost savings (assessing the base transport cost as well as loading and capacity utilisation considerations) and logistics cost savings (including assessment of administration, customs clearance, storage and delays).

In rail services, fixed costs of locos and wagons account for the majority of costs to start with, while the proportion of total costs from variable operating costs grows as the fixed costs are spread over a larger volume of output. The marginal cost of adding another container is low, except for when a new service needs to be put on, requiring a new payment of fixed costs which is what produces a stepped cost function (Figure 24.3).

It is similar for terminals but with longer steps, because the fixed costs (e.g. terminal area, track, cranes) will only need to be increased occasionally, therefore there will be a long period of output growth at marginal cost before another investment step needs to be taken. Once fixed costs have

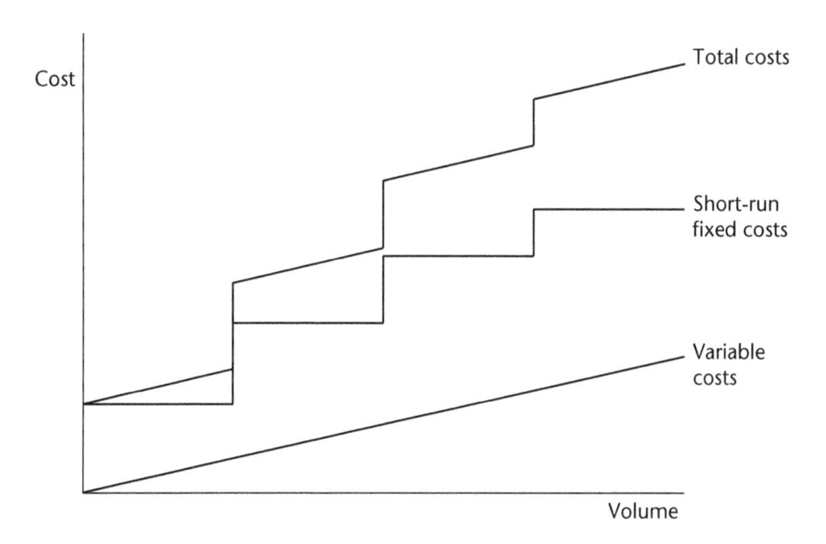

Figure 24.3 Stepped cost function for intermodal transport
Source: based on Harris, 2003

been recouped, keeping variable costs to a minimum is the real challenge for terminals, where unnecessary delays can arise due to disputes over terminal capacity, priority access, maintenance and bad weather events. It is often the case that poorly specified contracts lead to uncertainties and disputes that can produce unforeseen delays and costs (Bergqvist and Monios, 2014).

The difficulty in examining production and pricing lies in defining the intermodal market, in which there is the intermodal sector itself, which tends to be dominated by a few medium to large operators, hence oligopolistic, and the wider freight market, which due to the very strong influence of road haulage is closer to perfect competition. The market for freight transport is one in which the purchaser (usually either the shipper or a freight forwarder) purchases e.g. a container movement from a road haulier or rail operator. The price set by the rail operator will usually be a door-to-door movement including the terminal handling and the last mile by road haulage, so, from the perspective of the purchaser, they are simply selecting a container movement for which they pay a given price for a given level of quality (e.g. the price may be the same but the delivery time for rail may be longer). The rail transport market was addressed in Chapter 22; this chapter looks at the cost profile of the terminal itself and how it sets the quantity and price for the container loading/unloading. Another aspect to consider is the market size. If there is only one terminal in an area then they will have a local monopoly on intermodal transport provision, but not a monopoly on transport provision. So if the price set by a road haulier is below the minimum achievable by rail then the rail operator and hence the terminal cannot enter the market. It is only in cases where the overall rail price becomes competitive with road (usually due to longer distance but also on the intermodal operator's ability to consolidate flows) that they can enter the market, and then at a later stage as the market grows there is likely to be more than one terminal operator, hence the intermodal market becomes oligopolistic in nature.

It is essential at this point to recall the difference between the short-run and long-run AC curves. Figure 24.4 shows how the long-run AC curve envelops several short-run AC curves. An increase in output in the short term will lower the short-run average cost. This is illustrated as production increases from points A through to E. Hence the operator when deciding on terminal size will build in future expansion, thus build a terminal where the short-run average cost is

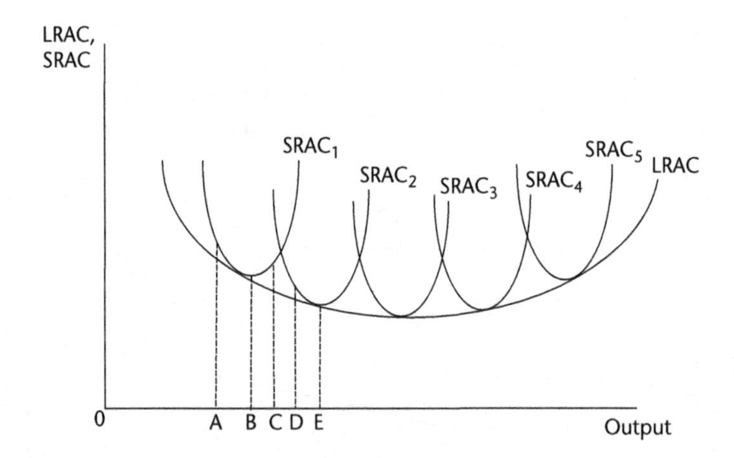

Figure 24.4 Short-run and long-run AC curves

minimised at point B. As production begins to expand from A to B, the operator moves along SRAC1 as short-run increases in production will soak up some of the spare capacity of the fixed factor of capital; in other words, the marginal product (of the variable factor) increases as the spare capacity (of the fixed factor) is utilised. Demand conditions allowing, this will continue until these possibilities are exhausted at point B, which is the optimal terminal size at that level of output. Without increasing the fixed factor, i.e. terminal size, further increases in production face the law of diminishing marginal returns, meaning that continuing along SRAC1 will see average costs rise, say until point C. At this point, further increases in output will encounter considerable increases in average costs, and indeed may not be profitable. In order to increase production, therefore, say to point D, the operator may decide to invest more capital to expand the terminal capacity. This decision would suggest that the transaction costs of purchasing the capital to move to a larger-sized operation are offset by the savings this brings in operational costs. Note again that future expansion is built into these decisions, hence the optimal terminal size occurs once output has risen to point E. Nevertheless, through this investment the operator moves to a new short-run average cost curve (SRAC2) with a lower average cost, and the whole process starts again. Over the longer term, this will gradually move the terminal size towards the long-run MES point.

While some transport service providers (mostly airlines but in some cases rail service operators) utilise marginal cost pricing and market segmentation for purposes of yield management, terminals more commonly set a fixed price. Their supply of terminal services is relatively fixed in the short run and assets are less transferable to other markets, as opposed to a locomotive or container vessel. In order to consider the market in which the terminal sets their price, the way the freight transport market is segmented by distance needs to be understood. At lower distances, road haulage has a clear cost competitive advantage, hence intermodal providers have found it almost impossible to penetrate this market. Over medium distances the rail price drops significantly as the fixed costs are spread over a larger output (in terms of train kilometres) so that they can enter the market, thus both road and rail compete on price, subject to an assumed level of quality (part of which calculation is the price and quality of the terminal handling services). At long distances rail is usually cheaper than road (unless difficulties in balancing imports/exports or consolidating flows reduce the distance advantage), so at that point it tends to be rail competing against rail, which produces a classic oligopoly market (due to barriers to entry, etc.) and a small number of terminals in an area competing for the business of the rail operator.

The lack of visibility of the true cost of rail movements is considered an issue by users. Retailers have complained that the rail quote they are given is simply based on being 'slightly cheaper than road'(Monios, 2015a) rather than being based on the actual costs of providing the service (i.e. the marginal cost (MC)). For a road haulier to carry one more unit, the MC is usually the additional operating costs of an entirely new round trip, whereas it costs relatively little for a rail operator to add one more container onto an existing train or for the terminal operator to load/unload one more container. As a higher proportion of a road haulier's costs are variable, they incur most of their costs when in service, whereas the high proportion of fixed costs in both rail service and intermodal terminal operation have long payback periods that must be spread over a large range of output.

Service purchasers would like increased visibility of the operating cost structure for intermodal terminals. Large shippers with market power frequently contract road hauliers on this basis, known as a cost-plus or 'open-book' arrangement, whereby the purchaser has visibility of the actual costs of the service including an agreed profit margin. This arrangement allows the purchaser to ensure that only a normal profit is being earned. So the user of a terminal service desires to know the MC of one more container handling, but the terminals argue that they cannot price that way because they have to account for their lumpy investment and irregular demand, so they have to calculate the average cost over a certain level of inputs and outputs (i.e. at their current short-run position) and offer a (relatively) fixed price. Some discounts and market segmentation will occur at higher levels of demand but these are less common.

24.7 Regulation

The public sector can play a variety of roles in the intermodal sector, the key economic underpinning of which is how to manage an imperfectly competitive market. Government funders want to achieve modal shift by removing barriers to rail freight such as upfront costs, sunk costs and availability of suitable terminal locations, rail authorities want to provide sufficient capacity and quality of infrastructure for freight operators, rail regulators want to ensure fair competition and open access to infrastructure and terminals. Operators will only enter the market and provide services if they believe they can operate profitably, but government agencies must decide how to incentivise this market entry without granting monopoly power to an operator that would inhibit fair competition with other operators. There is no point exchanging the previous public monopoly with a new private monopoly.

While regulation is a large topic beyond the scope of this chapter (see Chapter 8 for a discussion of aspects of rail regulation), a brief discussion is necessary here as a result of the issues raised in the preceding section. The reason for regulation is mostly to address market failure based on total costs (i.e. when including external costs such as emissions, the market is not producing the ideal distribution of resources, e.g. more modal shift to environmentally friendly modes). From the perspective of transport customers, the market may well be producing an acceptable level of quality and price in terms of meeting the demand for moving their goods.

Another reason for regulation is to provide necessary services where the market is not providing them, although this is more likely the case in passenger transport (e.g. rural bus routes). In terms of freight transport, access to transport services most likely already exists (most locations generating freight demand can be accessed by road), but local and regional bodies may want a terminal to improve trade access to their region (lower transport costs), to grow industries or to reduce emissions (although the latter tends to be a national concern, as the terminal may actually increase local emissions).

Subsidy may be provided either for terminals or for operations. The latter tend to be ongoing, effectively buying emissions savings but not resolving the underlying lack of competitiveness under the current system. Terminal grants may be a one-off grant or an ongoing public-private partnership model, depending on the appetite of the public sector for direct intervention. The UK prefers to leave operations to the private sector and only provide a pot of grant money for modal shift, for which operators can apply (see Box 24.2). Other supportive regulatory changes can also be introduced, such as a change of road regulation to stimulate intermodal flows. While

Box 24.2 Case study of funding for intermodal terminals in the UK

Government grants (FFG for infrastructure and MSRS for operating subsidies) have been used to support the shift of retail (and other) flows from road to rail. While FFG infrastructure grants were introduced in the UK in 1974, rail-operating grants began with the TAG scheme set up in 1993 by the UK Department for Transport, with the Scottish portion transferred to Scotland in 2001. TAG was complemented by CNRS from 2004 to 2007. Both of these were replaced by REPS (2007–10) and then MSRS (since 2010).

Woodburn (2007) reported on previous assessments of the FFG system in the 1990s as well as assessing the grants from 1997 to 2005. He made an interesting comparison with continental European countries, where national rail operators are still subsidised at a general level, suggesting that the liberalisation of this market will invalidate this approach and require a similar system to the flow-based FFG awards in the UK. He concluded that the FFG system had been largely successful, providing on average two-thirds of the required funding for the facilities, meaning that one-third of the cost was paid by the private operators in situations where these facilities may not otherwise have been built. He found that the vast majority of these grants can be considered successful, with the failed projects attributable mainly to 'company or supply chain changes that were not foreseen at the time of the award' (p.325).

Table 24.1 lists FFG funding for intermodal terminals in England and Scotland. This does not include other rail investments such as bulk terminals, rail-connected warehouses or wagons. For example, Stobart received £200,000 in 2006 from the Scottish Government towards the Tesco containers and a further £525,000 in 2008 towards the Grangemouth to Inverness Tesco route.

Table 24.1 shows that many of the main intermodal terminals in the UK have received infrastructure funding through the FFG programme. More money has been spent in Scotland on intermodal terminals, while many grants in England and Wales have gone to other operational requirements, as well as some large intermodal projects in ports. It is also interesting that no awards have been made in four years, suggesting either no need or the funding requirements do not align with industry features. For instance, an operator has to identify a road flow, set up a service to shift it, then apply for the funding and develop the terminal facilities, by which time the flow may have evaporated. It is also difficult for a shared-user terminal because only the 'owner' of the newly shifted flow can get the grant. The lack of applications may also suggest that the level of public money that is available is not sufficient to bridge the commercial gap between road and intermodal.

Economic and operational realities of the freight business can make it difficult to use this funding strategically (e.g. by using the planning system to designate strategic terminals via a top-down process rather than relying on ad hoc funding applications). Another issue is the misalignment of

Table 24.1 List of FFG awards in England and Scotland to intermodal terminals 1997–2015

Company	*Terminal*	*Year*	*Department for Transport*	*Scottish Government*
Freightliner	Trafford Park	1997	£723,000	
JG Russell	Deanside	1997		£3,045,000
TDG Nexus (site now owned by DB Cargo UK)	Grangemouth	1999		£3,233,000
Potter Group	Ely	2000	£373,046	
WH Malcolm	Grangemouth	2000		£246,000
Potter Group	Ely	2001	£101,000	
Freightliner	Leeds	2002	£196,656	
Potter Group	Selby	2002	£1,579,051	
WH Malcolm	Grangemouth	2002	£582,602	
Roadway Container Logistics	Manchester	2002	£328,350	
ABP	Hams Hall	2002	£1,192,965	
PD Stirling	Mossend	2002		£1,878,300
EWS (now DB Cargo UK)	Mossend	2003		£654,000
WH Malcolm	Grangemouth	2003		£882,000
ARR Craib	Aberdeen	2004		£144,546
WH Malcolm	Grangemouth	2004		£137,678
WH Malcolm	Elderslie	2005		£1,647,000
WH Malcolm	Elderslie	2006		£572,000
JG Russell	Coatbridge	2008		£1,842,617
Lafarge	Dunbar	2011		£128,769
Ferguson	Grangemouth	2011		£50,000
Total			£5,076,670	£14,460,910

Source: compiled from data from Department for Transport and Scottish Government

approach between track and terminals. Network Rail has identified a 'strategic freight network' of core and diversionary routes in England and Wales on which to focus investment, with Transport Scotland set to designate a similar route in Scotland by 2016. So there is a strategic plan for the infrastructure network (as this is managed by Network Rail) but not for terminals (as these are privately operated). These are developed through ad hoc funding applications without strategic focus.

It could be more appropriate to look at this problem strategically. One option could be to merge the FFG funding into the strategic Network Rail programme, thus considering terminals as infrastructure, as some authors have suggested (Woxenius and Bärthel, 2008). Some of the budget for the Strategic Freight Network could be made available for terminal upgrades. Network Rail could put out a call for terminal operators to apply, based on their previous flows and business, current usage, upcoming business, etc. This could be supported like a TIGER grant (see Monios and Lambert, 2013) by a public body and even combined in a package with relevant network upgrades into a corridor approach, which would be a suitable role for a regional body such as the Regional Transport Partnerships in Scotland, which are currently underused. This is easier in the United States with vertical integration linking track, terminal and operator, but even if that system cannot be replicated, a strategic system based on invited applications might work better than the current ad hoc system.

in some countries longer heavier vehicles are allowed on roads to improve the economic and environmental efficiency of road haulage, such allowances can be made specifically for feeding terminals, e.g. in Sweden a recent trial allowed operators to use longer heavier vehicles (2x 40ft instead of the normal maximum 20ft + 40ft) to feed terminal services (Bergqvist and Behrends, 2011).

Rail regulation was discussed in Chapter 8, but the vertical separation of track and operations as well as a liberalised market place to incentivise market entry should be mentioned briefly here. The existence of a functioning rail freight market in Europe (as opposed to the heavily subsidised and criticised passenger rail franchise system in the UK) suggests that, even though rail freight can be shown to exhibit economies of scale, competition and rail freight flows have increased in many European countries. The degree to which one has caused the other, however, remains open to question. For instance, Cowie's (2015) study of the production economics of British rail freight since privatisation found few new entrants and a current industry status of apparent stagnation, suggesting that increased productivity is required to grow the intermodal market. In the US, there is much less passenger traffic and rail has priority because they own the track, therefore vertically integrated freight railways work well there. It would be difficult to copy this system in Europe due to high volumes of passenger traffic on the same network.

Terminals are a rather unique element due to the reasons provided in the previous section. As shown in Box 24.1 and Box 24.2, a degree of rationalisation of terminals has taken place in the UK, somewhat analogous to what has occurred in the port sector. The question is now whether intermodal terminals should be regulated. Some problems with lack of open access have been identified, and dangers exist of terminals being bought up by large operators who then introduce anti-competitive practices (Box 24.3). Even worse could be the increasing interest of ports in securing their inland flows (see section above). What would happen if a handful of large ports buy up a network of terminals and do not allow open access as their motivation is to compete with competitor ports rather than serve the local trade? Should such a difficulty be addressed through regulation? What if a publicly subsidised terminal development is sold off to the private sector? How can the public sector maintain and secure the public interest? These difficulties relate to another motive for regulation which is to ensure quality of service. Unfortunately, one of the key drawbacks of regulation is its ineffectiveness. As discussed in Box 24.3, transgressions are difficult to investigate, to prove and to fix.

Box 24.3 Case study of DB Schenker terminals in the UK

At the time of privatisation in the mid-1990s, around 85 percent of UK rail freight was non-unitised general freight (mostly bulk), and the vast majority of freight handling sites were transferred to the national infrastructure owner Railtrack/Network Rail. These sites were then leased to private operators, some on commercial rents but mostly on token or 'peppercorn' rents. The majority of these leases were for 125 years, with few requirements of the operators other than that the sites must remain open access and if they are not being used then they will return to the infrastructure owner. The majority of these sites were leased to the constituent companies that then formed EWS and were since acquired by DB Schenker (renamed in 2016 as DB Cargo UK, but their name at the time will be used throughout this case study). Ninety-two sites remained in the property of Railtrack (now Network Rail), listed on a strategic freight site list that meant they could not be sold on for other use and must remain available for rail use. This list is reviewed regularly and sites may be taken off this list if it is felt that there is no realistic possibility of them being used again, in which case they can be sold for other purposes.

In 2011, the UK regulatory agency Office of the Rail Regulator conducted a study into the current list of leased sites, due to concerns that they were being used as a competitive advantage by the incumbent operators (ORR, 2011). Three key issues were identified:

(1) Membership of the committee to decide on releasing a site from the strategic list was restricted to the largest service providers with 10 percent of the total UK market, thus excluding some small operators.

(2) A site currently leased can only be transferred either voluntarily by the operator, or else forced (what is called 'alienated') by the infrastructure owner. This process can be blocked by the timetabling of 'ghost' trains or tabling spot bids (ORR, 2011). In theory, if a site operator loses all its traffic to another operator, that operator can then take over lease of the site. But this makes it very difficult for a new operator to bid for traffic with the proviso that they have to take over the site; this uncertainty makes the new bid very unreliable and risky for both operator and potential customer. UK rail operators gave examples of both positive and negative transfers through the alienation process, but in the worst cases, claims were made that potential business had been lost because site transfer could not be effected quickly enough to begin handling the new traffic. This issue therefore represents a major barrier to entry in this market.

(3) Open-access provisions are frequently contested and charges of anti-competitive behaviour have been laid, arguing that incumbents will claim a terminal to be full, or charge additional fees, even if a competitor only has to cross some of their track (so-called 'ransom strips').

In 2012, the infrastructure owner Network Rail moved to reacquire around 250 sites in the UK from DB Schenker, in order to facilitate competition and open access. It must also be remembered that these sites are not all terminals but sometimes sidings and depots that are important parts of the network for marshalling trains and storing wagons. The difficulty is that the infrastructure owner does not want to become a terminal operator or even an active terminal owner. They do not have the capacity for regular contractual negotiations and approvals, and do not want to pay maintenance costs, which is why the sites were leased for such long terms in the first place.

One key aspect of regulation and planning of terminals is the importance of anticipating later difficulties as terminals decline (Monios and Bergqvist, 2016). In cases where a public actor has been needed to intervene directly in the market by developing (or supporting the development of) a terminal, is it realistic for them then to step back and be a landlord? Bergqvist and Monios (2014) showed that the public-sector actor will continually be drawn into operational difficulties. How can this be managed through regulation?

24.8 The key economic drivers behind successful intermodal operation

Wiegmans et al. (1999) used Porter's model of five competitive forces to consider the intermodal freight terminal market. They discussed barriers to entry and threats of substitute goods and which actors exercise power in the market. The industry competitors are other terminals operating within the local area, while potential entrants are new terminals that could be developed or perhaps old terminals re-entering the market. This is not normally a very immediate threat due to high entry barriers such as high investment costs, lack of market potential and lack of suitable locations; therefore, the threat of substitutes (i.e. road haulage) is far more serious and this is where the usual difficulty for intermodal transport lies. In terms of negotiating power, there is the negotiating power of suppliers, in this case the owner of the terminal facilities, if different from the operator. This is not a very credible difficulty, as in many cases the operator is the owner or if not then they have a fairly stable relationship or concession with the owner, and both their interests are in alignment. The negotiating power of buyers is far more of an issue, usually rail operators bringing their trains to the terminals or 3PLs managing trains. There is also a second level of buyer power because the ultimate buyer of the transport service is the shipper, who will use road haulage if rail costs are too high or service quality too low, but these concerns are mediated through the rail operator or 3PL through whom the shipper contracts their transport services. If the terminal costs are too high or the service quality too low then the rail operator cannot ultimately provide attractive rail services to the shipper.

Transaction cost economics supports vertical integration when uncertainty, asset specificity and transaction frequency are high, but market transactions when they are low. This explains why a large operator like Freightliner has integrated terminals and services, including locos and wagons. It does not explain why other operators such as HUPAC and PCC do not operate their own traction. Such operators espouse the importance of neutrality with regard to customers (who are transport providers), which is not a particular problem for Freightliner as the majority of their bookings come from shipping lines. The resource-based view (RBV) suggests vertical integration when greater efficiency (and thus competitive advantage) can be obtained through the use of resources such as assets or staff. For HUPAC and PCC, wagon ownership means that they can maintain them in-house and ensure their safety and reliability, as well as marshalling and utilising the most efficient length and composition of wagon sets required for their traffic. RBV proposes that strategically valuable resources should be kept inside the firm. Examples of asset utilisation include not just economies of scale through increased firm size as a result of integration, but economies of scope and density gained by the integration of two firms possessing unique resource configurations that then enable the provision of more than one kind of service as well as increasing asset utilisation by adding additional routes. According to RBV, which seeks ways to exploit asset specificity, resources should be non-substitutable. Intermodal terminals are a fairly interchangeable resource unless they can offer better service or, ideally, more innovative and unique services. Thus Monios and Bergqvist (2015a) showed how moving from the resource-based view to the relational view can produce resource heterogeneity from an interfirm relationship, for example a terminal integrating or collaborating with a rail operator and a shipper.

Ng and Gujar (2009) applied Porter's Competitive Diamond model to terminals, which is an updated version of the Five Forces. They argue that this model is more dynamic, moving beyond improving terminal operations by investment in factor conditions towards innovative strategies through which a terminal can differentiate itself from its competitors and even overcome deficits in factor conditions such as location or capital. As transport decisions and requirements become more integrated with the larger logistics strategy of terminal users, better customer focus and integrated solutions with rail operators can help terminals embed themselves more stably within a customer's supply chain. Cooperation with competitors and intensive marketing can also be applied, therefore using this lens reveals the importance of intermodal terminals taking a proactive stance on marketing strategy, particularly with regard to the demand side of the market, rather than simply focusing on terminal efficiency and competing through price against broadly substitutable competitors.

24.9 Conclusion

Scale is obviously very important in the economics of intermodal transport – market size, distance, train length, capacity, weight. Yet these advantages remain subject to its operational limitations compared to road-only, i.e. lack of flexibility. The diversity of business models in the sector suggest that cost is not the only motive, as business strategy can also intrude, producing incentives for vertical integration and a close involvement of the shipper in planning their own intermodal transport system.

In terms of market structure, an oligopoly can be identified in the intermodal terminal market, as many features of monopoly are present but substitutability of resources allows a certain number of market players to enter the market. There appears to be evidence of underproduction in the intermodal market due to a number of inefficiencies that have not yet been entirely eradicated, despite high competition from road haulage.

What is intriguing is the search for economies of scope through vertical integration, to reduce not just operational but transaction costs. This has been seen in the integration between shipping lines and port terminals, and the integration of rail services with intermodal terminals, and, in some cases, an entirely vertically integrated chain. Most interesting is the role of shippers in this business model through innovative forms of open-book arrangement and profit sharing, leading to them becoming quasi-transport providers themselves.

Therefore, the key issues from a strategic perspective are integration, reducing transaction costs, reducing the need to pay margins to every actor, collaborative planning and how these influence obtaining the available economies of scale and scope. The question is, therefore, despite some evident success through introducing competition, is the European vertically separated model the correct approach? American rail operators would never consider such a concept. Regulators impose a competitive market on what some economists feel would work better as a system of regional monopolies. In the US there is much less passenger traffic, whereas vertically integrated freight railways would be difficult in Europe due to high passenger traffic on the same network. It seems that challenges remain in understanding and applying the best economic model to the intermodal market.

Acknowledgements

Many thanks to Jonathan Cowie for helpful advice that enhanced the whole chapter, particularly Section 24.6.

Notes

1 See *The Box* (Levinson, 2006) for a historical account of the advent of containerisation.
2 Deep-sea container vessels are fitted with cellular holds with twistlocks at regular intervals to hold multiples of 20ft units and are therefore unable to mix these containers with 45ft or 53ft boxes. Specialist intra-European vessels are fitted for 45ft boxes.
3 Trailer is the preferred term in Europe for the wheeled unit on which a container or swap body rests, while chassis is used in the United States.

References

Bärthel, F. and Woxenius, J. (2004). Developing Intermodal Transport for Small Flows over Short Distances. *Journal of Transportation Planning and Technology*, 27(5), pp. 403–24.

Baumol, W. (1982). Contestable Markets: An Uprising in the Theory of Industry Structure. *American Economic Review*, 72(1), pp. 1–15.

Bergqvist, R. and Behrends, S. (2011). Assessing the Effects of Longer Vehicles: The Case of Pre-and Post-Haulage in Intermodal Transport Chains. *Transport Reviews*, 31(5), pp. 591–602.
Bergqvist, R. and Monios, J. (2014). The Role of Contracts in Achieving Effective Governance of Intermodal Terminals. *World Review of Intermodal Transport Research*, 5(1), pp. 18–38.
Cowie, J. (1999). The Technical Efficiency of Public and Private Ownership in the Rail Industry: The Case of Swiss Private Railways. *Journal of Transport Economics and Policy*, 33(3), pp. 241–52.
Cowie, J. (2010). *The Economics of Transport: A Theoretical and Applied Perspective*. London: Routledge.
Cowie, J. (2015). Does Rail Freight Market Liberalisation Lead to Market Entry? A Case Study of the British Privatisation Experience. *Research in Transportation Business and Management*,14, pp. 4–13.
Fowkes, A. S. and Nash, C. A. (2004). Rail Privatisation in Britain: Lessons for the Rail Freight Industry. ECMT Round Table 125. European Integration of Rail Freight Transport.
Levinson, M. (2006). *The Box: How the Shipping Container Made the World Smaller and the World Economy Bigger*. Princeton, NJ: Princeton University Press.
Lowe, D. (2005). *Intermodal Freight Transport*. Oxford: Elsevier Butterworth-Heinemann.
Monios, J. (2015a). Integrating Intermodal Transport with Logistics: A Case Study of the UK Retail Sector. *Transportation Planning and Technology*, 38(3), pp. 1–28.
Monios, J. (2015b). Identifying Governance Relationships between Intermodal Terminals and Logistics Platforms. *Transport Reviews*, 35(6), pp. 767–91.
Monios, J. and Bergqvist, R. (2015a). Vertical Integration in the Rail Sector: Using Wagons as 'Relationship Specific Assets'. *International Journal of Logistics Management*, 27(2).
Monios, J. and Bergqvist, R. (2015b). Using a 'Virtual Joint Venture' to Facilitate the Adoption of Intermodal Transport. *Supply Chain Management: An International Journal*, 20(5), pp. 534–48.
Monios, J. and Bergqvist, R. (2016). *Intermodal Freight Terminals: A Life Cycle Governance Framework*. Farnham: Ashgate.
Monios, J. and Lambert, B. (2013). The Heartland Intermodal Corridor: Public–Private Partnerships and the Transformation of Institutional Settings. *Journal of Transport Geography*, 27(1), pp. 36–45.
Ng, K. Y. A., and Gujar, G. C. (2009). Government Policies, Efficiency and Competitiveness: The Case of Dry Ports in India. *Transport Policy*, 16(5), pp. 232–9.
ORR (2011). *Rail Freight Sites: ORR Market Study*. London: ORR.
Wiegmans, B. W., Masurel, E. and Nijkamp, P. (1999). Intermodal Freight Terminals: An Analysis of the Terminal Market. *Transportation Planning and Technology*, 23(2), pp. 105–28.
Woodburn, A. (2007). Evaluation of Rail Freight Facilities Grants Funding in Britain. *Transport Reviews*, 27(3), pp. 311–26.
Woxenius, J. and Bärthel, F. (2008). Intermodal Road-Rail Transport in the European Union. In Konings, R., Priemus, H. and Nijkamp, P. (eds), *The Future of Intermodal Freight Transport*. Cheltenham: Edward Elgar, pp. 13–33.
Woxenius, J. and Bergqvist, R. (2011). Comparing Maritime Containers and Semi-Trailers in the Context of Hinterland Transport by Rail. *Journal of Transport Geography*, 19(4), pp. 680–8.

Index